D1104341

History of New Testament Research:
From Deism to Tübingen

History of
New Testament Research

VOLUME ONE: FROM DEISM TO TÜBINGEN

William Baird

FORTRESS PRESS   MINNEAPOLIS

HISTORY OF NEW TESTAMENT RESEARCH
Volume One: From Deism to Tübingen

Book Design by Publishers' WorkGroup
Cover Design by Brian Preuss

Library of Congress Cataloging-in-Publication Data

Baird, William, 1924–
    History of New Testament research / William Baird.
       p. cm.
    Includes bibliographical references and indexes.
    Contents: v. 1. From deism to Tübingen.
    ISBN 0-8006-2626-5 (v. 1 : alk. paper)
    1. Bible.   N.T.—Criticism, interpretation, etc.—History.
I. Title.
BS2350.B35   1992
225'.072—dc20

92-22629
CIP

The paper used in this publication meets the minimum requirements of American National Standard for Information Sciences—Permanence of Paper for Printed Library Materials, ANSI Z329.48-1984. ∞™

Manufactured in the U.S.A.   AF 1–2626

96   95   94   93   92   1   2   3   4   5   6   7   8   9   10

To my students
1952–1992

Scholars and preachers
Authors and teachers
Learners and leaders

Contents

Acknowledgments

The study of the history of NT research is an awesome task. Over the years, many friends and colleagues have encouraged my efforts, some expressing their relief that I, and not they, had undertaken the project. Yet, in spite of the magnitude of the undertaking and the extent of my limitations, I have found the endeavor not only significant for current biblical study but fascinating in its own right. Although I have been at work for almost a decade, a large portion of the research and writing was accomplished during a leave of absence in 1989 and 1990. I am grateful to the administrations of Brite Divinity School and Texas Christian University, which have supported me in this, as in all my scholarly efforts over the last twenty-five years. My leave was also sustained by a grant from the Association of Theological Schools and by the hospitality of the Disciples Divinity House at the University of Chicago. The Regenstein Library at Chicago provided a treasury of material, and, without the assistance of the Interlibrary Loan Department of the Mary Couts Burnett Library at TCU, my research could never have been accomplished. Throughout the process—from original prospectus to the penultimate draft—this work has been helpfully reviewed by my friend and colleague, James O. Duke. The book is dedicated to my many students—at Phillips, Lexington, and Brite. Although I cannot name them all, I wish to mention one—Fred Francis, whose untimely death brought an end to a promising career in NT scholarship. Fred was one of the first to urge me to write the history of New Testament research, and his faith is symbolic of the encouragement I have received from the others throughout the years.

Introduction

When the writers of the New Testament put down their pens, they could not have imagined the amount of industry their works would generate. This small collection of twenty-seven short books was to become the object of an incredible effort of research. To the modern observer, the New Testament appears like a tiny treasure buried under a mountain of scholarly debris. The attempt to uncover its riches has enlisted the arduous labor of scores of persons employing a multitude of methods, like a crowd of excavators using everything from trowels to bulldozers.

NEW TESTAMENT RESEARCH BEFORE
THE ENLIGHTENMENT

The history of New Testament research is a long and complex story. In this volume and its companion I intend to focus on one segment of that chronicle: the study of the New Testament from the period of the Enlightenment through the first two-thirds of the twentieth century. This historical segment has an integrity of its own. It encompasses the era of the modern world—the era in which the scientific method of inquiry has been applied to all fields of learning. Intoxicated by the new intellectual spirit, biblical scholars took up the same tools that linguists and historians were using in the study of other ancient documents. This was a time of the secularizing of Scripture, a time when no ground was recognized as holy and when biblical critics, approaching the New Testament, did not stop to take off their shoes.

The modern segment of the history of New Testament research, of course, belongs to a larger story. Before the canon of the NT was complete, scholars had begun to assess its meaning. The writer of 2 Peter says that some things in the letters of Paul are "hard to understand" (3:16), and readers of the epistles—not to mention the Gospels and Acts of the Apostles—have been trying to comprehend them ever since. This larger history need not be rehearsed in detail; surveys of the development and detailed studies of each period are noted in the bibliography.

The Early Church

In the ancient period, the first question was not how to interpret but what to interpret, in other words, the problem of the canon. The authoritative collection of NT books identical with our canon was not universally accepted until the fourth century. The process of selection involved a rudimentary form of historical criticism. According to the tradition, those books recognized as canonical had to command apostolic authority, that is, the NT documents were supposed to have been written by an apostle or a disciple of an apostle. The establishment of the twenty-seven-book canon, therefore, affirmed that every book in the NT was written by the author to whom it had been traditionally attributed. As to methods of interpretation, the early fathers wavered between the literal and the allegorical approach. To oversimplify, the historian can say that the School of Alexandria tended to stress the allegorical or figurative, and the School of Antioch, the literal or historical meaning. Clement of Alexandria, for example, believed that the Scriptures could contain five senses: the historical, the doctrinal, the prophetic, the philosophical, and the mystical. While the historical and doctrinal adhered to the literal meaning of the text, the other three opened the door to allegory. According to Clement, this affirmation of multiple meanings was fully justified. The God of the Bible was the transcendent God who spoke in many and various ways, so that Scripture was laden with meaning. Origen, taking a clue from Paul's anthropology (1 Thess. 5:23), favored a threefold meaning: the body (the literal), the soul (the moral), and the spirit (the allegorical). The Scriptures, according to this master of textual and linguistic techniques, contained the ultimate mystery of divine truth, and its interpretation required methods sensitive to sign and symbol, able to probe the depths of the biblical revelation.

The Alexandrians had been influenced by elaborate Hellenistic methods; the Antiochians, on the other hand, followed the more prosaic steps of the Jewish exegetes. In Antioch, one of the first ancient cities to boast illuminated streets, scholars subjected the Scriptures to the light of literal interpretation. They opposed the allegorical excesses of exegetes like Origen and emphasized the historical meaning of the text. To be sure, the Antiochians did not close their eyes to metaphor and symbol, but they insisted that the deeper meaning had to be grounded in the literal understanding of the text. The most renowned exegete of the School of Antioch was Theodore of Mopsuestia. He not only employed literal interpretation but also engaged in historical criticism. Theodore believed that some biblical books (Job, for instance) were neither inspired nor canonical. He interpreted the Gospels literally, giving attention to grammatical details, and he questioned the authenticity of the Catholic Epistles. John Chrysostom, the golden-mouthed preacher of Constantinople, also favored literal interpretation. He did not totally eschew allegory, however, although he preferred typology. By this method, events of the biblical narrative could be seen as predictive of the future without losing their foundation in history. Jerome, at first fascinated with the allegorical method, moved toward the literal at the same time he migrated to Bethlehem in order to translate the Bible. Informed by his Judean setting and encouraged by his study of the textual and linguistic details, Jerome increasingly emphasized the historical meaning of the text.

In spite of different emphases, the early church reached a hermeneutical consensus: normative interpretation was the prerogative of the apostolic church. Tertullian, who had been trained as a lawyer, argued that Jesus had preached the truth; this truth had been conveyed to the apostles; and the apostles had transmitted this truth to the church. Therefore, the orthodox church, as the custodian of apostolic truth, had the sole right of interpretation. Since the church held this exclusive right, and since leaders of the church employed allegorical interpretation, allegorical exegesis was to be allowed. Tertullian, however, preferred the literal, historical meaning, although he could use allegory on occasion. Sounding a note that would often be repeated in the history of NT research, he insisted that obscure texts ought to be interpreted by texts whose meanings are clear. Augustine, the early church's most able theologian, advocated a twofold authority of interpretation: the authority of Scripture itself and the authority of the tradition of the church. In regard to the former, interpreters needed to master the biblical languages and knowledge of the historical backgrounds and customs of biblical times. They also needed to be able to distinguish literal from figurative meanings. For his own part, Augustine gave priority to the literal, although he could not resist the lure of the allegorical. Actually, he, like Clement and Origen, believed the Bible was to be understood in more than one meaning, thus sowing the seeds of a hermeneutic which was to flourish in the Middle Ages.

The Middle Ages

In the medieval period, Scripture was often interpreted according to four senses: the literal, the allegorical, the moral (or tropological), and the anagogical. For example, in Gal. 4:24-25, "Jerusalem" could properly be interpreted to mean the historical city in Judea (literally), the Christian church (allegorically), the human soul (morally), and the heavenly city (anagogically). Like Clement, Origen, and Augustine, the medieval exegetes were convinced that God's truth was a many-splendored thing and that Scripture reflected a spectrum of meanings. Sensitive to the dangers of confusion and subjectivity, some medieval theologians emphasized the historical meaning. Andrew of St. Victor, a Hebrew scholar who had been influenced by Jewish methods, stressed the literal, historical meaning of the text. Many OT texts which in his view were not prophetic at all had been forced into a prophetic mold. Thomas Aquinas, while not throwing the spiritual meaning overboard, continued to steer an exegetical course with his eye on the literal meaning. According to Aquinas, the three spiritual senses (allegorical, tropological, and anagogical), although appropriate, needed to be rooted in the literal. Nicholas of Lyre, a competent Hebrew scholar, argued that texts should be interpreted messianically only if they met certain criteria: if they were quoted as messianic in the NT; if they were interpreted as messianic by the rabbis; and if they fit the context of the NT better than the OT.

The strong voices of Aquinas and his followers did not silence the advocates of the spiritual sense. In particular, fifteenth-century preachers found the wonders of allegory to be an appealing way to entice the itching ears of their auditors. By this sort of fascinating exegesis, ancient texts, dull and distant, could be made vital and contemporary. Jaime Perez, for example, argued that most of the psalms were messianic, because the very purpose of the psalmist was to prophesy about Christ. Thus, in spite of some strong attacks from the forces of literal interpretation, the many towers of the medieval citadel remained secure. Even those who emphasized historical interpretation continued to defend the right of spiritual exegesis. This debate about method of interpretation was to continue into the Enlightenment, a debate heralded by the voices of the Reformation.

The Reformation

In the Reformation, the study of the Bible dominated the theological discussion. A basic foundation stone of the reformers was the principle of *sola scriptura*. According to this principle, faith was built not on tradition or on the doctrines of the hierarchy; rather, it rested solely and securely on the Bible. Luther, when confronted with a stack of his books at the Diet of Worms, declared that he would stand by what he had written unless convinced of the contrary by Holy Scripture and clear reason. Calvin argued that the authority of the Bible was evident in its divine origin and that the special revelation of Scripture was necessary for the saving knowledge of God. Although rational proofs could be enlisted, the authority of

Scripture must be accepted by faith—a faith confirmed by the Holy Spirit. In the actual study of the Bible, the reformers were the heirs of the Renaissance humanists who had recovered ancient texts and learned to read and analyze them. Erasmus, making use of these textual and linguistic methods, produced a popular Latin translation of the NT based on a small collection of Greek manuscripts. He also published *Annotations* on the NT, a philological commentary that engaged in literary criticism and theological exegesis. The Complutention Polyglot, a multicolumned version of the Scriptures, offered the biblical scholar an edition of the Bible that presented the Greek text in parallel with the hallowed Vulgate. The sixteenth century also saw the publication of harmonies of the Gospels, whereby the texts were published in parallel columns, a significant step in the historical study of the life and teachings of Jesus.

More significant than texts and tools of exegesis was the development of the Reformation hermeneutic. For the reformers, the biblical text had essentially one meaning—the literal. Allegorical interpretation was only allowed where the biblical author intended it. The medieval notion of the four senses was attacked as both wrong and dangerous. According to Luther, heresies had been fostered by the failure to follow the simple, literal meaning of the text. The Bible, as word of God, had a unified message; thus Scripture was to be interpreted by Scripture: *scriptura scripturae interpres.* However, as the complex vagaries of the history of interpretation show, the practice of interpreting Scripture was not as simple as the reformers had imagined. Among the obvious problems, interpreting the Bible required an interpreter, and every interpreter interpreted from a perspective. A subjective element, therefore, was inevitable. Luther's approach, for instance, was christocentric, that is, his hermeneutical key was faith in Christ. On the basis of his understanding of this faith, he was able to decide that Hebrews, James, Jude, and Revelation were of doubtful authenticity. Calvin, who did not adopt a christocentric norm, nevertheless acknowledged an implicit subjectivity in his belief that the external witness of Scripture was confirmed by the internal experience of the Spirit.

In practice, the reformers' quest for the literal meaning encouraged critical study of the Bible. Luther's masterful translation of the Scriptures into German testifies to his grasp of Hebrew and Greek linguistics. In the wake of Luther's work, a flotilla of translations sailed into the public domain. The Olivetan version appeared in France in 1535, while, in England, a long procession of translators was at work: William Tyndale, Miles Coverdale, and, finally, the scholarly committee that produced the venerable Authorized Version. Calvin's biblical research was more scholarly than Luther's. He wrote commentaries on virtually every biblical book except Revelation. Working in the humanist tradition, Calvin's exegetical research reflects competence in classical and patristic scholarship. In the latter part of the sixteenth century, the Reformation produced scholars who turned their attention to the methods of biblical research. Matthaeus Flacius Illyricus published a key to the Scriptures that included an essay on the proper understanding of the Bible. In opposition to the four senses of the medieval church, Flacius advocated a fourfold understanding of the Bible: (1) the understanding of words (which demands knowledge of Greek and Hebrew linguistics); (2) the understanding of sentences (which requires competence in Semitic and Hellenistic grammar); (3) the understanding of the purpose of the biblical writers (which calls for a kind of historical criticism); and (4) the understanding of the message of the Bible as it is applied to the times of the interpreter (which implies the practice of biblical hermeneutics). Adopting this sort of methodology, scholars such as Joachim Camerarius published commentaries that gave primary attention to grammatical and historical interpretation.

The Reformation, therefore, encouraged vigorous searching of the Scriptures. The Bible, as the rule of faith and practice, was of unquestioned authority and utmost theological significance. To understand the Scriptures, the interpreter needed to attend to the literal meaning, that is, what the authors, ultimately, what God, intended to say. To discern the literal meaning, the interpreter needed to employ a grammatical and historical method. The reformers, however, were not fully prepared to follow their methodology to its logical conclusion. Their conviction that the message of the whole Bible was one and the same, that Scripture could not contradict Scripture, that the words of the Bible were infallible kept them captive to the ancient era. As a result, the distinctions within the Bible—the differences of historical setting and purpose, the varieties of perspective and expression—could not be recognized. At the same time, the reformers' conviction that the Bible was to be interpreted from the perspective of faith introduced into biblical research the persistent problem of subjectivism—a subjectivism which could readily subvert the quest for historical objectivity. To be sure, the more sophisticated view that interpretation should be in accord with the agreement of faith (*analogia fidei*) provided a corrective against rampant individualism. Nevertheless, as the reformers had learned from their encounters with ecclesiastical tradition, the questions remained: Which faith? What agreement? Yet, perhaps there was another criterion. Had not Luther said Scripture *and reason*? Could it be that reason, that God-given attribute of all human beings, could provide a norm for discerning biblical truth? A new day was about to dawn in which scholars alive with confidence in the human intellect would suppose that all the secrets of divine reality could be disclosed, that the word of God witnessed in Scripture could be exposed to the searching light of human inquiry so as to be clearly understood—the age of the Enlightenment.

METHODOLOGY OF THIS BOOK

The task of tracing the history of NT research from the Enlightenment into the twentieth century is staggering. The number of laborers in the vineyard of biblical study is legion. G. W. Meyer's comprehensive survey of biblical research from Pietism to the beginning of the nineteenth century fills two large volumes[1] and includes people like Sebastian Mutschelle and Johann Reinhard Hedinger who are not mentioned in the standard histories. Moreover, the major scholars of the period have filled entire libraries with their works; the bibliography of J. S. Semler, for example, lists over 170 items. Thus, a comprehensive survey of all the scholars and all their writings would require several lifetimes with a few generations of purgatory thrown in. The limited work which follows is, at best, the result of a judicious process of selectivity. For the purposes of this volume, I conceive of NT research in broad terms, that is, as the whole field of the study of the NT. Although attention is given to textual criticism and philological research, I place more emphasis on higher criticism—questions of the authorship and historical contexts of the biblical books. I consider the issue of the authority of the Bible—how the NT is understood as word of God or divine revelation—to be prominent. In addition, I assume questions of hermeneutics and methodology to be significant, and I present examples of exegetical practice. I also give attention to the results of exegesis: how the interpretation of the NT results in an understanding of early Christian history or how it offers a theological exposition of biblical doctrine.

Since the intention is to trace the history of NT research, the material is presented more or less chronologically. Biblical scholars usually stand on the shoulders of their predecessors, and new research is made possible by earlier results. Given the magnitude of the topic, this survey will be divided into two volumes. This first volume includes NT research from around 1700 to around 1870. Such a division already illustrates the problem of a pure chronological approach—the reason for the "more or less." American scholarship, which has its roots in the nineteenth century, will be discussed in the second volume. Moreover, the date of 1870 is somewhat fuzzy. Some scholars who have written important works prior to this time, for example, Wescott and Weizsäcker, are left to volume 2, because

---

1. Gottlob Wilhelm Meyer, *Geschichte der Schrifterklärung*, vols. 4 and 5 (Göttingen: J. F. Römer, 1805, 1809).

their major works are related to topics treated there. Thus, chronology will sometimes give way to regional, topical, or thematic developments. The scope of this first volume includes the progress of NT study from deism through the Tübingen School and responses to the latter. During that period, virtually all issues of NT research—almost all the questions in NT criticism and interpretation—were addressed. New methods and solutions, and even some new artifacts, would be discovered, but the fundamental problems had been identified—almost no stone had been left unturned.

Within the two volumes, the research is ordered primarily according to scholars in relation to developing trends. I am convinced that NT research is essentially the work of creative individuals who, although in dialogue with their predecessors, peers, and pupils, spend long hours in the isolation of their studies. They do not remain, however, isolated from the world in which they live. Consequently, I have incorporated biographical data into the text and also note contemporary cultural and theological developments. Sometimes this will appear to provide only features of human interest, but often it offers insight into the character of the scholars and cultural context that shapes their work. As well as being shaped by the historical patterns of their times, scholars such as D. F. Strauss and Bruno Bauer had a dramatic impact on the political and social milieus in which they lived and worked.

In selecting scholars, I have made an effort to consider those scholars whose work is most influential in the ongoing development of NT research. If a scholar is repeatedly followed or refuted by others, that scholar is usually included. Scholars like Karl Bretschneider and Johann Gieseler are not among the giants of biblical research, yet the former's pioneering work on the Fourth Gospel and the latter's seminal study of oral tradition make them worthy of attention. Scholars who swim against the mainstream, for instance, nineteenth-century conservatives like August Neander and J. P. Lange, have all too easily been neglected by historians who seem oblivious to the fact that their works have been extensively translated and avidly read in England and America. Yet sometimes the decision to include or exclude is only a judgment call. Scholars like H. A. Credner and Friedrich Bleek, who produced significant introductions to the NT, are left out in favor of the more representative scholars like W.M.L. de Wette and Adolf Hilgenfeld. Although some representatives of French and Swiss scholarship and one Dutch scholar are included, as well as a few Roman Catholics, the majority of the subjects are British and German Protestants. With the exception of one translator, no woman is mentioned. A case can be made, of course, that the most important action in this period was carried out by Protestant men on British and German soil.

Nevertheless, the limitations of this first volume are apparent, and I will attempt to give serious attention in the second volume to the neglected scholars, including the Dutch and Scandinavians, so that the inclusive, international, and ecumenical character of NT research will be better represented.

In ordering the work of the various scholars, I have intended to consider each scholar in a single locus, although there are exceptions. The work of most scholars has an integrating center—a fundamental concern or commitment which gives meaning to the whole. Thus, J. A. Bengel is not treated separately as a text critic and as an exegete. His passion to point out the exact meaning and authority of the text, so apparent in his *Gnomon*, was the compelling reason for undertaking text criticism and biblical studies in the first place. The placing of an individual scholar in a particular locus has been determined by that scholar's role in the unfolding drama of NT research. Bengel, to take the same example, is discussed in the context of the biblical research of continental Pietism. In investigating the selected scholars, I have attempted to present their main contributions to NT research in terms of their most important works. This, too, has involved subjective judgments, but the major contours of a scholar's work are usually apparent. Although many items have been studied in detail and with care, sometimes only preliminary soundings have been attempted and only representative samples presented. English translations have been used when available, although the originals have sometimes been compared. In the main, the method of investigating these scholars and their sources is descriptive, although critical evaluation in terms of contextual criteria is sometimes employed in the service of more precise understanding.

Translations from Latin, German, and French, unless otherwise noted, are my own. To aid the reader, titles of foreign works are often presented in translation where no English edition exists—a matter that can be clarified by checking the notes and bibliography. Students of the history of NT research are sometimes confused by the variation in the spellings of the names of scholars—a phenomenon which has resulted usually from Latinizing or Anglicizing. My procedure is to follow the practice of the source which is being cited, but to use the standard form of the name (the usage of the scholar in his own historical setting) in my text.

Readers who expect to find what a particular scholar says about a particular verse, or even a particular critical question, are likely to be disappointed. To be sure, many examples of the exegetical and critical results of many scholars are to be found, but the purpose of the work is to recount and assess the larger historical development of NT research. Such a study, of course, has an obvious antiquarian interest, and the sheer

magnitude and boundless energy of NT scholarship is a fascinating phenomenon in its own right. But more than this, the study of the history of
the criticism and interpretation of the Bible is a crucial feature of the
history of Christianity and the development of Western culture. Biblical
scholars neglect this history at their own peril. Failure to know one's
history is a failure to understand one's identity, a failure that destines one
to repeat old mistakes and neglect venerable solutions, to put old wine in
new wineskins without even knowing that it is old. Above all, the study of
the history of NT research will move modern scholars to humility in the
presence of a monumental accomplishment and will encourage them to
continue their work in celebration of a splendid tradition.

Part I

EARLY DEVELOPMENTS IN NEW TESTAMENT RESEARCH

1

Backgrounds and Beginnings

The critical study of the Bible began in the eighteenth century. At a time when all fields of inquiry were undergoing a revolution, so, too, was the investigation of the NT. The old ways, with their authoritarian presuppositions and orthodox conclusions, were being challenged. The new methods of science, devoted to empirical observation and rational deduction, swelled into a tidal wave, engulfing the entire intellectual landscape.

FORMATIVE FACTORS

Biblical research at the beginning of the Enlightenment was the heir to a large legacy from the Reformation and the Renaissance. From the Reformation, the eighteenth century inherited the belief in the importance of the Bible. If the Scriptures were the sole authority in faith and practice, then study of the Bible was of utmost significance. Moreover, the emphasis the reformers had placed on the single meaning—the literal, or historical—gave impetus to the study of the NT as a historical document. The quest for the one meaning encouraged a search for the original meaning, that is, the meaning which the text had had in the historical situation of the original writers and readers. From the Renaissance, the NT scholars of the eighteenth century inherited the spirit and skills of the humanists. The old scholastics with their eyes on the supernatural were replaced by a new breed of persons who focused their concern on mundane affairs. While they eschewed medieval culture as the dark ages, the humanists leapt across the centuries to the clear, bright worlds of Greece and Rome. In the process, they discovered classical texts and developed the linguistic tools to investigate them. Erasmus, a brilliant example of humanistic learning, was also interested in the study of the Bible. In addition to producing a significant Latin translation, he engaged in biblical exegesis that was characterized by philological learning, a christocentric hermeneutic, and a concern for ethical application.[1] Most important, humanists like Erasmus employed the same methods for interpreting the Bible that they used for other ancient texts.[2] The scholars of the eighteenth century, therefore, were heirs to a rich tradition in linguistic and grammatical research.

The heritage of the Renaissance and Reformation came to fruition in the era of the Enlightenment. At that time, the mysterious shadows of the cosmos were exposed to the light of human inquiry. Following the method of Francis Bacon, with its stress on empiricism, researchers made rapid advances in the physical sciences: Edmund Halley and Pierre Simon de Laplace in astronomy, Robert Boyle and Joseph Priestley in chemistry, Carolus Linnaeus in botany. Most important for all these developments was the work of Isaac Newton. In 1687, Newton had published his monumental *Principia mathematica*, which provided a mathematical formula by which the movements of all the heavenly bodies could be explained. Thus the universe was viewed as a grand mechanism whose principles of operation were comprehensible to the human mind. For Newton, who believed the Bible from cover to cover, the ordered cosmos was the work of the Almighty God. God had not only promulgated the laws of gravitation, God continued to maintain the cosmic order. The world, however, was no longer a supernatural mystery but a rational machine—constructed and serviced by God, to be sure, but open to the inspection of humans. During the Enlightenment most intellectuals agreed with Alexander Pope:

> Nature and Nature's laws lay hid in the night:
> God said, *Let Newton be!* and all was light.[3]

The task now was to let that light shine—to focus its penetrating beam on every aspect of human inquiry.

A massive symbol of this quest for human knowledge is Denis Diderot's *Encyclopedia*. Eventually encompassing twenty-eight large folios, the first volume appeared in 1751. Diderot's purpose was to collect all knowledge about everything and to make it available to the reader. For many of its authors—Voltaire, for instance—almost nothing was sacred—all was secular, everything was open to human scrutiny. The kind of self-confident

---

1. For a short summary of Erasmus's contribution to the rise of biblical criticism, see Henning Graf Reventlow, *The Authority of the Bible and the Rise of the Modern World*, trans. John Bowden (Philadelphia: Fortress Press, 1985), 39–48. Reventlow's notes also provide additional bibliographical resources. See also Erika Rummel, *Erasmus' Annotations on the New Testament: From Philologist to Theologian*, Erasmus Studies (Toronto: University of Toronto Press, 1986).

2. See Jerry H. Bentley, *Humanists and Holy Writ: New Testament Scholarship in the Renaissance* (Princeton, NJ: Princeton University Press, 1983).

3. "Epitaph Intended for Sir Isaac Newton" in *The Works of Alexander Pope*, collected by J. W. Crocker, ed. W. Elwin and W. J. Courthope (New York: Gordian Press, 1967), 4.390.

optimism that the project symbolized was typical of the times. The human mind, in this view, could comprehend and explain everything. Given time and industry, all the problems of the world could be solved, all mysteries mastered. Humanity had progressed out of darkness and into a new light, and the glories of the future knew no limits. As well as being secularized, learning was becoming democratic. Literature was written not just for the dons of Oxford and Cambridge but also for common folk who could identify with the characters of Henry Fielding's *Tom Jones* or Samuel Richardson's *Pamela*. While Thomas Gainsborough and Joshua Reynolds were painting the portraits of the aristocracy, William Hogarth was depicting the seamier side of life in works such as his series, *The Rake's Progress*. Opposition to authority, especially ecclesiastical, was widespread, and religious tolerance was on the increase. The hero of G. E. Lessing's *Nathan the Wise*, set in the period of the interfaith conflicts of the crusades, was modeled after his friend, the Jewish philosopher Moses Mendelssohn.

The new biblical criticism that emerged in the eighteenth century reflected the features of the Enlightenment. Classical philologists like J. A. Ernesti applied their linguistic and grammatical skills to the study of Scripture. Ancient manuscripts were discovered, providing sources for critical editions of the text. Buried cities like Pompeii were unearthed, supplying more data for understanding the historical setting of the biblical books. Material of this sort was studied by empirical method and rational analysis. Scholars like J. D. Michaelis approached the critical and exegetical problems with boundless optimism, confident that mastery of the Semitic and classical languages and the amassing of historical data could unlock the Bible's secrets. Thinkers such as J. G. Herder were convinced that humanity had progressed out of its childhood through adolescence and into a time of maturity. Old orthodoxies concerning the inspiration of Scripture and the reliability of tradition came into question, and radical views, once held heretical, were tolerated in the theological discussion. Scholars, accustomed to conversing among themselves, began to forsake Latin in favor of writing in the vernacular, which was available to a larger public. In Goethe's *Sorrows of Young Werther*, the impetuous hero, Werther, bewails the destruction of some beautiful walnut trees. The trees were cut down, he discovers, at the whim of the vicar's wife, who had been upset because boys had thrown rocks at the nuts and "disturbed her profound meditations, when she was weighing the merits of the differing arguments of Kennicot, Semler, and Michaelis."[4]

---

4. Johann Wolfgang von Goethe, *The Sorrows of Young Werther and Novella*, trans. E. Mayer and L. Bogan (New York: Random House, 1971), 109.

PRECURSORS:
GROTIUS, LIGHTFOOT, AND SIMON

Although the beginning of critical research in the NT is usually dated to the eighteenth century, it was anticipated by some significant precursors. Even a hasty perusal of the third volume of Meyer's massive *Geschichte der Schrifterklärung*[5] will disclose a long line of scholars who prepared the way for the developments of the Enlightenment, for example, Georg Pasor (noted for his lexicographical work) and Solomo Glassius (remembered for his grammatical research). Although primarily noted for his importance in the history of philosophy, the Jewish thinker Baruch Spinoza made significant contributions to biblical study.[6] In his *Tractatus theologico-politicus* (1670), Spinoza devoted a chapter to the interpretation of Scripture, in which he argued that the study of the Bible required reason, linguistic knowledge, and historical inquiry. He went on to conclude that the Pentateuch was not written by Moses and that miracles are philosophically impossible. Because God and nature are united, a phenomenon that is against nature—a so-called miracle—is against God. In regard to the NT, Spinoza observed that the apostles contradicted each other, and that their ways of expression in the epistles showed "that these [epistles] originated not from revelation and God's command but from their own natural faculty of judgment."[7] Brief mention can also be made of Jean Le Clerc, or Clericus (1657–1736), a professor at Amsterdam who opposed Spinoza.[8] Le Clerc argued that the Bible was largely reliable and authoritative, but it was not inspired—this latter point indicated by contradictions within Scripture. Actually, the biblical writers did not claim to be inspired, nor did they know all the facts. They were, nevertheless, trustworthy, as their willingness to suffer for their faith indicates. In controversy with Richard Simon, Le Clerc argued that 2 Tim. 3:16 ought to be translated: "all scripture inspired by God is profitable . . . ," with the implication that some Scripture was not inspired. The empirical evidence for miracles, claimed Le Clerc, was strong enough to counter the a priori assumption that miracles cannot happen.

---

5. Gottlob Wilhelm Meyer, *Geschichte der Schrifterklärung,* vol. 3 (Göttingen: J. F. Römer, 1804).

6. See Sylvain Zac, *Spinoza et l'interprétation de l'écriture* (Paris: Presses universitaires de France, 1965); Leo Strauss, *Spinoza's Critique of Religion,* trans. E. M. Sinclair (New York: Schocken, 1965).

7. Baruch Spinoza, *Tractatus theologico-politicus,* trans. Samuel Shirley (Leiden: E. J. Brill, 1989), 199.

8. For a summary of Le Clerc's contribution, particularly in relation to Richard Simon, see Jean Steinmann, *Richard Simon et les origines de l'exégèse biblique* (Paris: Desclée de Brouwer, 1960), 201–7; 229–38; Henri Margival, *Essai sur Richard Simon et la critique biblique au xviiᵉ siècle* (Geneva: Slatkine Reprints, 1970).

From among the various seventeenth-century precursors of eighteenth-century criticism, three of the most important may be selected for fuller discussion: Hugo Grotius, John Lightfoot, and Richard Simon.

Hugo Grotius (1583–1645)

The son of the burgomaster of Delft, Hugo Grotius was a gifted child who wrote Latin elegies at the age of eight. At the University of Leyden his teachers included the renowned Latinist Joseph Scaliger. Later Grotius studied law at Orléans in preparation for his work as a lawyer in The Hague. In 1607, Grotius was appointed attorney general of Holland, and later in his career, he served as Sweden's ambassador to Paris. His sympathy with the Arminians and Remonstrants led to conflict with the Calvinistic government of the Netherlands, a conflict that resulted in his imprisonment in 1618. After three years, Grotius escaped with the aid of his wife, who had been permitted to bring him a large number of books from time to time. On one such occasion, he was smuggled out in the box that supposedly contained books he had finished reading. In religious conviction, Grotius was an Arminian who worked for the unity of the churches, but later in life he became increasingly sympathetic to Roman Catholicism.

Grotius's main contribution to Western culture is in the area of international law. In 1625, his classic *De jure belli ac pacis* was published, in which he made the case that all nations should be governed by laws that are ultimately based on natural law. According to Grotius, "Natural law is so unalterable that God himself cannot change it."[9] He also wrote significant classical studies and from 1600 to 1604 served as the official historiographer of Holland. Grotius was vitally interested in religion[10] and composed two religious dramas: *Adam exul* (Adam in exile) and *Christus patiens,* a dramatic poem on the death of Christ. In this pious drama, Caiaphas argues that the Jews do not have the right of capital punishment, but Pilate accedes to the demands of the Jews, who are ultimately responsible for the execution of Jesus. For NT research, however, Grotius's two most important works are *De veritate religionis christianae* (1627) and *Annotationes in Novum Testamentum,* which was written during his residence in Paris, ca. 1640.[11]

9. Cited in Peter Gay, *The Enlightenment: An Interpretation* (New York: Alfred A. Knopf, 1968), 299.

10. See René Voeltzel, "La Méthode théologique de Hugo Grotius," *Revue d'histoire et de philosophie religieuses* 32 (1952): 126–33.

11. For a brief summary of Grotius's biblical research, see Dean Freiday, *The Bible—Its Criticism, Interpretation and Use—in 16th and 17th Century England,* Catholic and Quaker Studies 4 (Pittsburgh, 1979), 51–58.

The first of these, *The Truth of the Christian Religion,* is an apologetic work that presents a summary of Grotius's theology. Originally written in poetic form, the book offers instruction for sailors who in their worldwide travels encounter people of other faiths. According to Grotius, God is the primal cause, apart from whom nothing can exist. Belief in God is widely attested by multitudes of people in various times and places. Proof of God's existence is seen in creation, and, in particular, in the ordering of the human body. God is wholly good—all wise and all powerful. According to Grotius, Christianity is the best of all religions because its "rewards are more excellent . . . [and its] precepts more perfect."[12] Moreover, Jesus was a unique manifestation of God, as is evidenced by his fulfillment of the ancient prophecies and by his potent miracles. In particular, the resurrection of Christ, attested to by many witnesses, is proof of his divinity. Central to Christianity are the ethical teachings of Jesus. Jesus did not require sacrifice but, rather, advocated a pure worship of God that expressed itself in duties to humanity. Moreover, Jesus did not approve retaliation, for "the law of Christ forbids requiting any injury done us."[13] According to Grotius, Christianity has a view of women that is devoid of lust and higher than that of other religions. All in all, the excellence of these teachings was confirmed by the character of their teacher—Jesus was totally without sin.

Later in the *Veritate,* Grotius turns to the Bible, the primer that contains the principles of Christianity. He believed that most of the books of the NT were written by the authors to whom they have been traditionally attributed, and he argues that those books whose authorship is questionable, for example, Hebrews and Revelation, should be accepted as canonical. Among the biblical writers, some were surely apostles—Matthew, John, and Peter—while James was either an apostle or a relative of Jesus, and Mark wrote under the direction of Peter. Grotius believed that a biblical author, Luke, for example, did not need to be inspired to write reliable history. Elsewhere he says, "For there was no need that the histories should be dictated by the Holy Spirit. It was sufficient that the writer had a good memory concerning the things he had seen or that he was careful in transcribing the ancient records."[14] The credibility of the biblical witnesses is confirmed by the quality of their lives and teachings: people who acted and talked like these did could not be guilty of fraud.

---

12. Hugo Grotius, *The Truth of the Christian Religion,* trans. John Clarke (Cambridge: J. Hall, 1860), 70.

13. Ibid., 80.

14. Cited in William Lane Craig, *The Historical Argument for the Resurrection of Jesus During the Deist Controversy,* Texts and Studies in Religion 23 (Lewiston, N.Y.: Edwin Mellen Press, 1985), 672.

Anticipating a theme of eighteenth-century critics, Grotius argues that no proof has ever been offered that can demonstrate that the truth of Scripture is contrary to reason. On the larger truths, the various writers of the Bible agree. Minor discrepancies only serve to confirm the reliability of the whole, because false witnesses would have attained agreement by fraudulent collusion.

The rest of the *Veritate* supports Grotius's Christian imperialism. He argues that Christianity is superior to the other religions of the Hellenistic age, that Christian monotheism is surely to be preferred to the polytheism and idolatry of the pagans, and that the alleged miracle workers like Apollonius of Tyana were merely skillful magicians. Regarding Judaism, Grotius expresses the hope that the Jews "would not look on us as adversaries,"[15] yet his spirit of tolerance appears to wear thin when he concludes that the chief sin of the Jews is their rejection of the Messiah. Instead, he says, they ought to accept the miracle of Jesus and his fulfillment of their prophecies as proof that the Christ had indeed come. Grotius also argues that Christianity is superior to Islam—that point by point (miracles, ethics, the resurrection) Jesus surpasses Muhammed. In a final section, Grotius admonishes Christians to gird their loins and uphold their superior religion: believe the right doctrine, study the Scriptures, and do the will of God! All of this should be carried out in a spirit of ecumenism. Thus he concludes that since "all Christians were baptized into the same name, therefore there ought to be no sects or divisions among them."[16]

The *Annotationes*[17] is a massive work consisting of eight volumes of notes. In overall plan, the notes are presented on each book of the NT in canonical order. Some of the books are prefaced by an introduction that usually deals with the authorship and historical setting of the particular book. Grotius's view of the relative importance of the various NT writings is suggested by the amount of space he allots to each. Matthew, for example, is assigned two volumes (more than eight hundred pages), while Mark is given only slightly more than one hundred pages. John is covered in a single volume of 288 pages. The four great Pauline letters (Romans, 1 and 2 Corinthians, and Galatians) comprise one volume of more than six hundred pages, while all the rest of Paul's epistles (including the Pastorals and Hebrews) are assigned a volume of a little more than five hundred pages.

---

15. Grotius, *Truth of the Christian Religion*, 143.
16. Ibid., 195.
17. Hugo Grotius, *Annotationes in Novum Testamentum*, 2d rev. ed. (Gronigen: W. Zuidema, 1826).

In the main, Grotius presents a historical interpretation of the NT that is marked by attention to textual, linguistic, and grammatical detail. Commenting on Matt. 6:13, he notes that the phrases beginning "thine is the kingdom" are lacking in the oldest Greek manuscripts, although they are included in the Syriac. His note on Matt. 1:23 discusses the usage of παρθένος in the Septuagint in relation to the Hebrew terms *almah* and *bethulah*. In regard to John 1:9, Grotius concludes that ἐρχόμενον should be taken with φῶς rather than with ἄνθρωπον; that is, it is the *light*, not every *person*, that is said to be coming into the world. As to historical matters, Grotius observes in his introduction to 2 John that two tombs have been found in Ephesus that have been traditionally associated with the name John. Grotius's interpretation of the Apocalypse does not take flight into the distant future but focuses on events of the first century: the beasts of Rev. 13:2 are related to Rome, the leopard symbolizes Claudius, and the lion, Domitian.

On matters of historical criticism, Grotius makes some significant judgments. He believes that Matthew is the oldest Gospel, and that Mark used Matthew and knew the birth stories but left them out because of his special purpose in presenting Jesus to the Romans. In regard to the Fourth Gospel, Grotius thinks that John is writing in opposition to heresy, notably Gnosticism, and that, in the process, John uses gnostic terms in his portrait of Jesus. Galatians is also directed against opponents, although they are not Judaizers but the followers of Cerinthus who believe that Christians ought to keep the Jewish laws in order to maintain the privileges that the Jews enjoyed under Roman rule. Grotius concludes that John 21 was not a part of the original Gospel but was added later by the church at Ephesus. Second Thessalonians, in Grotius's view, was written prior to 1 Thessalonians and was directed to the Jews of the Thessalonian church whose leader was Jason, Paul's host. Paul, in Grotius's opinion, could not have written the Epistle to the Hebrews, as the vocabulary and style make clear; the author was probably Luke. Grotius questions the traditional authorship of both Jude and 2 Peter. The former, he thinks, was written by Jude, the Bishop of Jerusalem at the time of Hadrian. The reference to the "brother of James" (Jude 1) has been added by a scribe who wanted to make the epistle appear apostolic. In regard to 2 Peter, Grotius notes the differences between it and 1 Peter and decides that it was written by Simon or Simeon the Bishop of Jerusalem following James. Like many later conservative critics, Grotius posits two Roman imprisonments for Paul. This makes possible the additional journeys in the East so that Titus was written between the two imprisonments and the writing of 2 Timothy took place in Rome just before Paul's execution.

On theological matters, Grotius's exegesis is not innovative. He finds the primary background for the Logos of John's prologue in the first verse of Genesis: it represents the powerful, creative word of God. Grotius has little difficulty with the miracles, which he takes as literal, historical happenings. As to the reason the other evangelists neglected to record the raising of Lazarus, Grotius adopts the hypothesis—popular with later apologetic exegetes—that Matthew, Mark, and Luke wanted to protect Lazarus and his family from the wrath of the high priests (12:10) and, therefore, kept the story secret. Years later, after their Gospels were written and the danger had passed, John was able safely to recount the miraculous event. In interpreting Rom. 3:25, Grotius believes that the debated term ἱλαστήριον refers to the cover on the ark of the covenant which signified God's presence and favor toward the people; Christ, in the same way, represents God's concern to will good for the human race. Grotius does not stress substitutionary, sacrificial atonement, and his interpretation of Romans minimizes the idea of predestination. In regard to Rom. 11:26, however, Grotius concludes that "all Israel" means the "Israel of God" (Gal. 6:16), that is, the people who embraced Jesus as the Christ.

In sum, Hugo Grotius presents a solid, essentially historical interpretation of the NT. His work is marked by broad philological and historical leaning. On the basis of this research, his conclusions tend to be conservative, largely untainted by his Arminian bias. On the other hand, Grotius is not dominated by orthodox or authoritarian traditions; he thinks for himself and exposes his arguments to the clear light of reason. Knight's conclusion about Grotius is no doubt correct: "As a critic, he is so bold as to treat the Scriptures as if they were no more than a mere literary work. He approaches them as he would any work of classical antiquity."[18] In the history of research, Grotius's *Notes* constitutes a vast treasury of critical and exegetical information from which scholars continued to draw throughout the eighteenth and nineteenth centuries.

John Lightfoot (1602–1675)

John Lightfoot was born near Birmingham, the son of an Anglican clergyman. He was educated at Christ College, Cambridge. After spending two years teaching, he was ordained and held various ecclesiastical positions. Lightfoot sided with Parliament during the civil war and was a member of the Westminster Assembly, where he supported the presbyterian position. In 1650, he was appointed master of Catherine Hall at Cambridge. The university conferred on him a doctor of divinity in 1652. Lightfoot's essential conservatism is disclosed in the title of his thesis: *Post*

---

18. W.S.M. Knight, *The Life and Works of Hugo Grotius* (London: Sweet & Maxwell, 1925), 250.

canonem Scripturae consignatum, non sunt revelationes expectandae (After the establishment of the canon of Scripture, revelations are not to be expected). Lightfoot was a brilliant Semitic scholar. Gibbon is reported to have said of him that he "by reading the rabbis, became almost a rabbi himself."[19]

Lightfoot's primary contribution to NT research is his pioneering use of rabbinic literature to illuminate the historical setting of the biblical texts. He produced a variety of publications on the OT as well as the NT, and he aided Brian Walton in the preparation of the Polyglot Bible of 1657. Among his earlier works, Lightfoot's *Harmony of the Foure Evangelists*[20] appeared in 1644. In studying the Gospels, Lightfoot had observed that each evangelist includes material that the others omit, so, he argued, comprehension of the whole requires an overview of all four Gospels. To this end, his *Harmony* prints the texts of the Gospels (in English translation) in parallel columns, sometimes with footnotes that explain Greek terms and present cross-references to the NT and the LXX. After he has presented the texts of a particular pericope, Lightfoot provides a discussion of the reasons for the order in which the accounts have been placed. He then includes a section entitled "Harmony and Explanation," in which a verse-by-verse exegesis of the parallel texts is presented.

In general, Lightfoot's exegetical work is characterized by attention to syntax and grammar and by a persistent interest in historical details. In a long prolegomena to the *Harmony*, he diligently pursues the question of the date of Jesus' birth, concluding that it occurred Anno Mundi 3928. He readily harmonizes discrepancies in the parallel texts, noting, for example, that the words from heaven announced on the occasion of Jesus' baptism are reported with slight differences in the three Gospel accounts, although he believes they are materially the same. The differences are explained by the fact that Matt. 3:17 records what was spoken *about* Christ, whereas Mark 1:11 and Luke 3:22 (which agree) record what was spoken *to* him. Lightfoot, however, does not gloss over all of the difficulties. He observes, for instance, that Matthew's genealogy of Jesus includes four "women once of notorious infamy," although this simply serves "to shew that Christ came to heal all sores."[21] Using a typological exegesis, Lightfoot explains Luke's variation on the order of the temptations as an effort to present the experience of Jesus in a way parallel to the pattern of Eve's temptation in Genesis: the lust of the flesh (hunger); the lust of the eyes (the glory of the kingdom); the lust of pride (the leap from the temple).

---

19. *Dictionary of National Biography*, s.v. "Lightfoot, John."

20. John Lightfoot, *Harmony of the Foure Evangelists: Among Themselves, and with the Old Testament* (London: A. Crooke, 1644).

21. Ibid., 55.

A year later, Lightfoot published another work which illustrates his concern with biblical interpretation in historical context—his commentary on Acts.[22] Lightfoot presents no introduction but begins with a verse-by-verse exposition that simply assumes that Luke is the author. He makes use of material from the Pauline letters, the works of Philo and Josephus, and, of course, the Talmud. Cross-references and chronological data are sometimes printed in the margins. From time to time, Lightfoot inserts into the commentary summaries of Roman and Jewish history. For example, after he has presented his exegesis of Acts 1–5, Lightfoot presents "The Roman Story," more than ten pages of Roman history focusing on the career of Tiberius. In the course of the commentary, Lightfoot displays some imaginative exegesis: he thinks, for example, that the gift of tongues at Pentecost serves to overcome the confusion of languages which has plagued humanity since the tragedy of Genesis 11.

> Two thousand two hundred and three yeares had now passed, since that sad and fatall curse upon the world, the confusion of languages; and millions of soules had it plunged in Error, Idolatry, and Confusion: And now the Lord in the fulnesse of time is providing, by the gifts of tongues at Sion, to repaire the knowledge of himselfe among those Nations that had lost that Jewell, by the confusion of tongues at Babel.[23]

Unfortunately, Lightfoot fails to explain the phenomenon of tongues here (although he does later, in his major work) but notes that the reference to fire and the occurrence on Pentecost signify a striking parallel between the gift of the law at the beginning of the Jewish nation and the gift of the Spirit at the beginning of the Christian church.

Lightfoot wrote a book that described the priests and practices of the Jewish temple in the time of Jesus,[24] but his major work is *Horae Hebraicae et Talmudicae*. Originally written in Latin and published in sections over twenty years (1658–78), this work eventually appeared in a four-volume English edition.[25] Gustaf Dalman summarizes the three main purposes of the work: (1) to show that Jesus made use of the language of the Talmud; (2) to demonstrate that the Pharisaic opponents of Jesus ought to be understood on their own terms; and (3) to indicate that the geographical,

22. John Lightfoote, *A Commentary upon the Acts of the Apostles: Chronicall and Criticall* (London: A. Crooke, 1645).

23. Ibid., 41.

24. John Lightfoot, *The Temple Service, As it stood in the dayes of our Saviour* (London: A. Crooke, 1649).

25. John Lightfoot, *Horae Hebraicae et Talmudicae: Hebrew and Talmudical Exercitations*, 4 vols., ed. Robert Gandell (Oxford: Oxford University Press, 1859). An earlier, two-volume version, edited by G. Bright and J. Strype, had appeared in 1684.

historical, and ritual references in the Gospels can be explained by the study of rabbinic literature.[26]

In the English edition of 1684, the geographical material that had originally preceded the notes on each Gospel is brought together at the beginning of the first volume. This material, which Lightfoot calls "chorographical," contains information about the geography of Palestine. However, in an age when scholars were beginning to study geography by direct observation, Lightfoot's approach seems bizarre. Rather than traveling to the Near East to observe the sites, he derives a topography from references detected in rabbinic and other Jewish literature. By this method he attempts to solve, for example, the baffling problem of the location of Emmaus. Employing the same literary approach, Lightfoot locates the abode of the Essenes on the west side of the Dead Sea, north of Engedi, a location confirmed by twentieth-century excavations at Qumran. Sometimes, however, Lightfoot's method of doing geography betrays him: he mistakenly thinks the Pool of Bethesda and the Pool of Siloam are one and the same. Likewise, in discussing the disputed location of Tiberias, Lightfoot places it south of the Sea of Galilee, disagreeing with Pliny who correctly locates it on the west side. In addition, in discussing various geographical locations, Lightfoot presents historical information that is not always accurate. Concerning Tiberias, for example, he displays his ignorance of the origin of the Hebrew system of vocalization, that is, the system whereby vowel points were added to the text. "There are some," he says, "who believe the holy Bible was pointed by the wise men of Tiberias. I do not wonder at the impudence of the Jews, who invented the story; but I wonder at the credulity of Christians, who applaud it."[27]

Following the geographical material, the bulk of the *Horae* consists of notes, or, as Lightfoot calls them, "exercitations," on the Gospels and Acts. The notes are presented by chapter and verse on each Gospel individually and in canonical order. After the discussion of Acts, the last volume also includes a short section on Romans and 1 Corinthians. The actual notations are presented by first citing the text in Greek and then adding comments. Some notes are extensive; some notes are brief; and some verses receive no comment at all. Within the longer notes, Lightfoot follows an analytical procedure: he raises a major question, presents an enumerated list of possible solutions, and concludes with his own deliberate opinion.

Some representative samples of Lightfoot's results are worth mention-

---

26. Gustaf Dalman, "In the Footsteps of John Lightfoot," *Expository Times* 35 (1923–24): 71–73.

27. Lightfoot, *Horae* 1.160.

ing. Against ancient tradition, Lightfoot asserts that the Gospel of Matthew was originally written in Greek and later translated into Hebrew. Lightfoot's harmonizing of the genealogies and the virgin birth is more conventional: Matthew traces the ancestry of Jesus through Joseph to demonstrate that Jesus was legally a descendant of David; Luke, on the other hand, presents the genealogy of Jesus through Mary. According to Lightfoot, Matthew's phrase "the kingdom of heaven" refers "to the inward and spiritual kingdom of Christ."[28] Lightfoot admits that Jesus used the word "dogs" in his conversation with the Syrophoenician woman (Matt. 15:26), but he blames the derogatory expression on the Jews rather than on Jesus: "From the common speech of the nation, rather than from his own sense, our Saviour uses this expression,"[29] an exegesis that anticipates the later accommodation theory.[30] Lightfoot also blames the Jews for disguising the prophecy of the virgin birth in Isa. 7:14 by using the word *almah* (young woman) where the LXX correctly reads παρθένος.

Lightfoot harmonizes the conflicts of the Johannine and Synoptic texts. For instance, he identifies the supper of John 13 with the supper in Bethany recorded in Matt. 26:6-13 (Mark 14:3-9) so that this supper takes place prior to the Passover in accord with John 13:1. However, Lightfoot does not identify this Johannine supper with the last supper, which, as the first three Gospels clearly state, was a Passover meal—a meal that Jesus observed according to Jewish practice on the fourteenth day of the month Nisan. The discrepancy created by John 18:28, which says that the Jewish leaders would not enter the praetorium for Pilate's trial of Jesus (the morning after the last supper) for if they did they would be defiled and unable to eat the Passover meal, is only apparent, not real. The meal these leaders were anticipating was actually a later meal of the continuing Passover celebration—the Chagigah, which was observed on the fifteenth of Nisan.

Lightfoot offers some significant comments on the Pauline letters. The schisms of 1 Cor. 1:12, in his judgment, represent only two main factions: the gentile and the Jewish segments of the early church (a view made famous by F. C. Baur almost two hundred years later).[31] Within the gentile faction, the party of Paul includes the original Pauline converts, while those of Apollos are people who prefer a more elegant expression of the Gospel. Within the Jewish faction, the followers of Cephas are Judaizers, while the Christ party may consist of Jewish Christians, baptized with the baptism of John (Acts 19:4). According to Lightfoot, the gift of tongues described in 1 Corinthians 12 is actually the ability to speak Hebrew. This

---

28. Ibid. 2.51.
29. Ibid. 2.230.
30. See pp. 123–24, below.
31. See pp. 258–69, below.

gift, as Lightfoot would be the first to affirm, is of great service in inter-preting the OT, an endeavor essential for expounding the Christian gos-pel. When this gift is exercised at Corinth—just as when the Hebrew Scriptures are read in the Aramaic-speaking synagogues of Palestine—Paul insists that an interpreter is necessary.

More important are interpretations illuminated by Lightfoot's knowl-edge of the Jewish literature. He concludes, for example, that the back-ground to John's baptism is to be found in Jewish proselyte baptism. Anticipating later research, Lightfoot notes that where the Hebrew uses *Abi* for "my Father," the Targums use *Abba*, as, for example, where Isaac speaks directly to Abraham (Gen. 22:7). However, when someone other than a natural father is addressed as "my father"—for example, Naaman by his servants (2 Kings 5:13)—the Hebrew uses *Abi* while the Targums use a term meaning "my lord." Thus, Lightfoot concludes that it is one thing to speak to God as *Abi* (meaning Lord, King, Teacher), as was fre-quent in the Jewish sources, but something vastly different to address God as *Abba,* a term of direct address to a natural father, used by the early Christians.

In regard to the "Hellenists" and "Hebrews" of Acts 6:1, Lightfoot con-cludes that the former are Greek-speaking Jewish Christians who had been reared in areas where Greek was the major language, and the latter are Semitic-speaking Jewish Christians of Palestine, like the people addressed in the Letter to the Hebrews, written, in Lightfoot's opinion, by Paul. Lightfoot is also knowledgeable about text-critical matters, noting, for example, that the story of the woman caught in the act of adultery (John 8:1-11) is not included in some of the ancient manuscripts. Occasionally Lightfoot's interpretations are fanciful. For example, in an effort to iden-tify the resurrection appearance to Cephas (1 Cor. 15:5), he concludes that it occurred on the road to Emmaus (Luke 24:13-35), because the unnamed companion of Cleopas is none other than Simon Peter! And he says that Paul's reference to fighting with the beasts (1 Cor. 15:32) describes an actual happening in Ephesus where "the apostle was really cast to wild beasts in the theatre."[32]

In spite of some fanciful interpretations and occasional preoccupation with trivia, Lightfoot's concern to illuminate the Jewish context has made a monumental contribution to the historical understanding of the NT. His erudition, especially in rabbinics, is impressive, and his insights are often brilliant. To be sure, his penchant for harmonizing has impeded a rigor-ous historical investigation. His method, too, lacks clarity and precision. He acknowledges that the rabbis, on occasion, contradict each other. For

32. Lightfoot, *Horae* 4.272.

example, in discussing John 9:2, Lightfoot observes that some rabbis believed sin comes after birth, while others give examples of a child doing evil (such as kicking in the womb) before it is born. But surely this sort of inconsistency recommends cautious discretion, since one might be able, given the vast amount of rabbinic material, to find parallels for almost anything. Moreover, Lightfoot's indiscriminate way of using Jewish material is magnified by his failure to give adequate attention to the problem of dating his sources. Nevertheless, Lightfoot's work informed generations of biblical scholars and anticipated research which was to be done in the nineteenth and twentieth centuries.

Richard Simon (1638–1712)

If any individual can be named as the founder of modern biblical criticism, that person would have to be Richard Simon.[33] Described as an unattractive little monk with a falsetto voice and weak constitution, Simon was neither an academician nor theologian. He was a historical critic— nothing more, nothing less. During his life, Simon did battle with almost everybody: the Jesuits and the Jansenists, the Protestants and the Roman Catholic hierarchy, members and leaders of his own order. In all these skirmishes, the one thing he could not tolerate was sloppy scholarship.

Born in Dieppe, Simon was the son of a humble blacksmith. He attended the local parish school which was operated by the order of the Oratorians. His intellectual capacity was soon recognized, and he was sent to Rouen to study with the Jesuits. Later, Simon matriculated at the Sorbonne, where he concentrated on Semitic languages and developed his lifelong aversion to scholastic theology. Returning to Dieppe, Simon completed the novitiate and joined the Oratorian order in 1663.

Simon served for a short time as a teacher of philosophy at his order's college in Juilly. He found the study and teaching of philosophy personally unsatisfying, however, and was pleased to move to the order's house at Rue Saint-Honoré, near the Louvre. This Paris chapter was noted for its singing, but Simon could scarcely carry a tune. More in harmony with his talents, Simon was appointed to a duty which for him was the best in the house: to work in the library. After another sojourn in Juilly, Simon was ordained to the priesthood in 1670. In Paris, he made acquaintance with

---

33. For surveys of the life and work of Simon, see Steinmann, *Richard Simon et les origines de l'exégèse biblique;* Henri Margival, *Essai sur Richard Simon et la critique biblique au xviiᵉ siècle;* Paul Auvray, *Richard Simon (1638–1713)* (Paris: Presses universitaires de France, 1974); Henning Graf Reventlow, "Richard Simon und seine Bedeutung für die kritische Erforschung der Bibel," in *Historische Kritik in der Theologie: Beiträge zu ihrer Geschichte,* ed. Georg Schwaiger (Göttingen: Vandenhoeck & Ruprecht, 1980), 11–36; Pierre-Marie Beaude, "L'Accomplissement des prophéties chez Richard Simon," *Revue des sciences philosophiques et théologiques* 60 (1976): 3–35.

Jona Salvador, a Jewish scholar with whom he discussed Scripture and the Talmud. The experience encouraged his continuing sympathy for the Jews and stimulated some of his earliest publications, which dealt with Jewish customs and ceremonies. "Those who wrote the New Testament," said Simon, "were Jews, and it is not possible to understand it except by rapport with Judaism."[34]

Simon turned to the study of the OT and, in 1678, published his monumental *Histoire critique du Vieux Testament*. In this work, Simon's erudition was everywhere apparent, and his linguistic skill in Hebrew, Greek, Syriac, and Arabic was equally stunning. His conclusions, however, were less than pleasing to the larger public. He rejected the Mosaic authorship of the Pentateuch and argued that the meaning of many OT texts was far from certain. The vowel points had been added centuries after the original composition by the Masoretes, who certainly were not inspired. Although his work had been officially approved by the church, Simon was bitterly attacked by Bishop J. B. Bossuet, the florid preacher and favorite at the court of Louis XIV. As a result, the book was condemned and burned, and Simon was expelled from the Oratorians.[35] In 1683, Simon retired to Bolleville, a small town in Normandy, where he served as prior of its little church. Here he continued his writing and engaged in controversy with scholars like Isaac Vossius and Jean Le Clerc. Also in this period he began his voluminous work on the NT, which culminated in his French translation of 1702.[36] Again Bossuet rushed to the ramparts. Simon's NT did not always use the orthodox terms dear to the Bishop's heart. The translation was banned, and clergy who allowed it to be read were threatened with excommunication. Simon remained a controversial figure until his death in 1712, and the controversy did not end with his death. The tragedy of this is ironic: one of the greatest scholars French Catholicism has ever produced was condemned by the church he ardently loved and defended.

Simon did not articulate a clearly defined theological position. In general, his theology is a theology of controversy: Simon's position is found by investigating what he was against. He opposed Augustine, for example, because he was uncomfortable with Augustine's notion that unbaptized

---

34. Cited in Steinmann, *Richard Simon*, 72.

35. See Patrick J. Lambe, "Biblical Criticism and Censorship in Ancient Régime France: The Case of Richard Simon," *Harvard Theological Review* 78 (1985): 149–77; M. Jacques Denis, *Critique et controverse ou Richard Simon et Bossuet* (Caen: F. Le Blanc-Hardel, 1870).

36. Richard Simon, *Nouveau Testament Notre-Seigneur Jesus-Christ* (Trevoux: E. Ganeau, 1702); Eng. trans.: *The New Testament of Our Saviour Jesus Christ: According to the Latin Edition: With Critical Remarks upon the Literal Meaning in Difficult Places*, trans. W. Webster, 2 vols. (London: J. Pemberted and C. Rivington, 1730). See Michel de Certeau, "L'Idée de traduction de la Bible au xviième siècle: Sacy et Simon," *Recherches de science religieuse* 66 (1978): 73–92.

children were to be assigned to eternal punishment. In issues of this type, Simon betrays a sort of rational tolerance, a kind of moderation that is apparent, too, in his aversion to the doctrine of predestination. Simon's antipathy toward Augustine was also abetted by Bossuet, who was fond of Augustine—as was Luther, another of Simon's foes. In his battle with the reformers, Simon sharpened historical criticism into a weapon that could be used in the attack on Protestantism's most fundamental error: the doctrine of *sola scriptura.*

Simon's quarrel with the Protestants had mainly to do with Scripture and tradition. For one thing, he believed they had devalued the Vulgate. "Protestants," he wrote, "do not always act with Reason, when they forsake the ancient Latin Edition, and adhere to the Greek."[37] Simon argued that Paul's advice to the Corinthians—that they needed an interpreter when someone spoke in tongues (which Simon, like Lightfoot, took to mean in Hebrew)—proved that Latin (the Vulgate) could be read in church so long as interpretation was available. Moreover, the Catholic divines who made the rule against the use of the vernacular "did not make their Prohibition until after having found by Experience that Bibles in the Vulgar Tongue being put into the hands of all People, usually brought more detriment than advantage to the affairs of Religion."[38] Protestants, he argued, with their stress on Scripture, had neglected tradition. "Although the Scriptures are a sure Rule on which our Faith is founded," said Simon, "yet this Rule is not altogether sufficient of itself; it is necessary to know, besides this, what are the Apostolical Traditions."[39]

In these controversies, Simon's own position is implicit: an affirmation of the fundamental faith of the NT as interpreted by the early fathers. "In effect," he wrote, "the principles of our faith are founded on the Holy Scripture and on the tradition or unanimous agreement of the Fathers."[40] Simon was repelled by the speculations of the scholastics, the theological squabbles of the Jansenists and the Jesuits, and, above all, the authoritarian dogmatism of an ecclesiastic like Bossuet. For Simon, the Christian faith was built upon facts, and the historical facts could be found by free investigation of the primary sources. Simon believed it was better to be a grammarian than a theologian. In regard to the Bible, he was quick to affirm its importance: "where the Scripture is concerned, every word, every syllable, every letter, every little point has a meaning."[41] Simon,

37. Richard Simon, *A Critical History of the Text of the New Testament* (London: R. Taylor, 1689), part 2, 116.
38. Richard Simon, *The Critical History of the Versions of the New Testament* (London: Newborough & Bennet, 1692), 377.
39. Simon, *Critical History of the Text,* pt. 1, 31.
40. Cited in Steinmann, *Richard Simon,* 23–24.
41. Simon, *New Testament of Our Saviour Jesus Christ* 1.28.

however, rejected the concept of verbal inspiration and the notion that the Scriptures were dictated by the Holy Spirit, although he did describe the biblical writers as "sacred penmen."[42] With Grotius, he agreed that biblical historians did not need special inspiration, since their work was based on the accounts of eyewitnesses. Nevertheless, Simon affirmed a belief in inspiration based on 2 Tim. 3:16, which involved the conviction that the Spirit guided the biblical authors "so as not to fall into error."[43] The avoidance of error, however, did not mean accuracy in the minutiae of detail. According to Simon, the Gospels differ on minor matters but are in agreement in substance. There is nothing false in the Scriptures, but "the expressions therein are frequently accommodated to the Opinions commonly received amongst the People, and they are not always very exact."[44]

In regard to the method of interpreting Scripture, Simon thought that exegesis was a science that made use of scientific procedures. Fundamentally, he favored grammatical interpretation—a method that resulted in a literal, historical understanding of the text. Simon, however, allowed allegorical interpretation, since not everything in the NT was literal. Paul used allegory, and the criticism of the Jews that Christians interpreted messianic texts allegorically is answered by the response that the Christians had learned this method from the Jews themselves. "It is true," Simon acknowledged, "that a Passage of Scripture taken Allegorically, cannot serve for a Proof; but we speak here of such Allegorical Senses as were received, and which were also founded on Traditions that were warranted by Authority."[45] Moreover, "the Miracles of Jesus are evident Proofs of his Mission: And therefore, if it should be supposed with them that the Passages we speak of, are not always justly applied, it cannot be concluded from thence, that the Christian Religion is built on a false Foundation."[46]

In expounding this biblical faith, Richard Simon published three major works on the NT: *Histoire critique du texte du Nouveau Testament* (1689),[47] *Histoire critique des versions du Nouveau Testament* (1690),[48] and *Histoire*

---

42. Ibid. 1.351.
43. Simon, *Critical History of the Text*, part 2, 61.
44. Ibid., part 2, 79.
45. Ibid., part 2, 57.
46. Ibid., part 2, 36.
47. Richard Simon, *Histoire critique du texte du Nouveau Testament, où l'on établit la vérité des actes sur lesquels la Religion chrétienne est fondée*, par Richard Simon, prêtre (Rotterdam: R. Leers, 1689); Eng. trans.: *A Critical History of the Text*, cited above, n. 37.
48. Richard Simon, *Histoire critique des versions du Nouveau Testament, où l'on fait connâitre quel a été l'usage de la lecture des Livres sacrés dans les principales Églises du monde* (Rotterdam: R. Leers, 1690); Eng. trans.: *The Critical History of the Versions of the New Testament*, cited above, n. 38.

critique des principaux commentateurs du Nouveau Testament (1693).[49] The publication of these three massive works within a period of four years is itself an awesome monument to scholarly industry. The title of the first of these works, *Critical History of the Text of the New Testament,* can be misleading. The book is not primarily a study in text criticism, although matters of lower criticism are discussed. For example, Simon notes that the longer ending of Mark is not found in many manuscripts. He observes the same about John 8:1-11 (the story of the woman caught in the act of adultery) but concludes, with Calvin, that the story is in accord with the spirit of Christ and ought to be included. Moreover, it is in the Vulgate, which the Council of Trent has declared authentic. As to the notorious text of 1 John 5:7 (which he also discusses in the *Critical History of the Versions*), Simon believes the reference to the Trinity was not in the original but had been copied into the text from the margin, a conclusion that raised the ire of his critics. According to Simon, only the original autographs—not the imperfect copies—were inspired.[50]

Most of the *Critical History of the Text* is concerned with higher criticism. In regard to the Gospels, Simon observes that they originally had no titles and, thus, were anonymous. Nevertheless, he concludes elsewhere that "we can prove, by constant tradition among Christians, that the four Gospels really belong to those whose name they bear."[51] Simon believes, with the tradition, that the Gospels were written in the order in which they appear in the canon: Matthew was written eight years after the ascension, while Mark, Luke, and John were written ten, fifteen, and thirty years after the ascension respectively. Simon also argues that Matthew was originally composed in Aramaic, or what he calls "Chaldaick" or "Syriack." Against Augustine, Simon insists that Mark is not an abbreviation of Matthew; and against earlier and later scholarship, he concludes that John 21 was written by John the apostle. In regard to the epistles of Paul, Simon notes that they are arranged not in chronological order but in order of importance. He agrees that Paul did not write the Epistle to the Hebrews but believes it was written by one of his scribes or interpreters. Typically loyal to the tradition, Simon supports the apostolic authorship of the Catholic Epistles, including Jude and 2 Peter. On matters of this sort, he says, "I prefer the express Judgment of the Church, before any human Reasons what-

49. Richard Simon, *Histoire critique des principaux commentateurs du Nouveau Testament, depuis le commencement du christianisme jusqu'à nôtre tems, avec une Dissertation critique sur lex principaux actes manuscrits qui ont été cités dans les trois parties de cet ouvrage* (Rotterdam: R. Leers, 1693).

50. See Jacques Le Brun, "Meaning and Scope of the Return to Origins in Richard Simon's Work," *Trinity Journal* 3 (1982): 57–70.

51. Simon, *New Testament of Our Saviour* 1.43.

soever."[52] He goes on to recognize that the church's decision about canonicity is at the same time a decision about authenticity.

The *Critical History of the Versions* is an extensive survey of the history of
translation. In a brilliant display of erudition, Simon analyzes translations
of the NT from the earliest Latin until the most recent French versions.
He gives much attention to the beloved Vulgate—about one hundred
pages. Simon admits that this ancient version of Jerome is not without
error, but he prefers it to vernacular translations. He believes that in the
process of translating the Vulgate, the ancient Greek texts can be of service. Other ancient versions are given attention, notably the Syriac (about
twenty pages), while the Coptic, Ethiopic, Arabic, and Gothic are allowed
less space. Simon gives considerable attention to the more recent Latin
translations, particularly those of Erasmus and Beza. After a lengthy discussion of modern French translations, Simon turns a critical eye toward
Luther's renowned German version. Elsewhere Simon says of Luther that
"being no great Critic in Grammar, he was found guilty, and condemned
of several misinterpretations."[53]

The *Histoire critique des principaux commentateurs* is a comprehensive history of NT interpretation from Clement of Alexandria to Simon's own
time. This massive work is 926 pages long, not counting an additional
dissertation on the sources Simon used in his research. In the course of
the survey, Simon gives attention to more than 160 major scholars. At the
outset, he notes that some early fathers used allegorical interpretation in
their debates with the heretics, while others, notably Irenaeus and Tertullian, employed a more literal method in applying the rule of faith. Clement of Alexandria used gnostic terms to refute Gnosticism. In evaluating
exegetes, Simon prefers Chrysostom (to whom he allots four chapters) to
Augustine. He observes that the latter's treatises on the Gospel of John are
tainted by an excessive use of allegory, although Augustine's work on the
Sermon on the Mount is better. Simon believes that Pelagius deserves to
be studied.

Simon gives more attention to the Protestant than to the scholastic
commentators. The great medieval exegetes—Peter Lombard, Albertus
Magnus, Thomas Aquinas, and Nicolas of Lyre—are covered in a single
chapter. Erasmus, who rates two chapters, appears to be more important.
The Lutherans alone are allotted more than forty pages, and Luther and
Melanchthon are given a chapter of their own. In Simon's opinion,
Luther's exegesis is marked by prejudice, and Luther's preference for

52. Simon, *Critical History of the Text*, part 1, 152.
53. Richard Simon, *Critical Enquiries into the Various Editions of the Bible*, trans. N.S. (London: T. Braddyll, 1684), 229.

books like Galatians rests on Luther's notion that they support his own mistaken views. Melanchthon is better, although Simon finds him to be more a theologian (an almost pejorative term) than an interpreter. Camerarius, on the other hand, is praised for being a grammarian. He argues that a major weakness of the Protestants is their passion for the literal and that, moreover, they should recognize the importance of the patristic sources for the historical understanding of the text. Besides, Simon notes, many of the texts of the NT are not to be taken literally, such as Paul's word about the hardening of Pharaoh's heart. Simon commends Calvin for his concern for brief, clear exposition. He notes that the Geneva reformer wrote commentaries on all the books of the NT except the Apocalypse and observes that "perhaps he is not to be blamed for that."[54] As to the seventeenth-century exegetes, Simon recognizes the erudition of Lightfoot but rates his knowledge of Hebrew and Syriac as mediocre. Grotius is largely praised, although his comments, in Simon's view, sometimes give too much comfort to the anti-trinitarians.

Many of the results of Simon's own criticism are expressed in his French translation and notes on the NT, *Nouveau Testament de Notre-Seigneur Jesus-Christ*, of 1702. In the preface, Simon clarifies the goal of a competent translator: "the chief care of a translator, should be to express the pure word of God with all possible exactness."[55] Rather than striving for elegance, the translator should try to express the meaning of the original. This original meaning is not always appropriately represented by a word-for-word translation, for a version can be too literal. In regard to Simon's notes, a few samples can be observed.

Commenting on Matt. 16:18, Simon detects the difference between πέτρος and πέτρα but concludes that Jesus intends to depict Peter himself as the rock. Simon goes on to say:

> Thus Christ gives St. Peter all power under the new Law of declaring what was sin, and what was not, and of absolving it. The rest of the Apostles had likewise the power of the keys. But St. Peter, as their head, enjoyed it in a more eminent manner.[56]

Simon's note on Matt. 27:45 represents a mixture of natural and supernatural interpretation. He thinks the darkness that occurred on the day of the crucifixion was caused by an eclipse but believes the eclipse "did spread darkness over a great part of the earth." Simon notes the problematic character of John 18:28, which suggests that the Passover supper did not take place until after the trial of Jesus, whereas the other Gospels

---

54. Simon, *Histoire critique des commentateurs*, 749.
55. Simon, *New Testament of Our Saviour* 1.10.
56. Ibid. 1.107.

clearly identify the last supper, which was held the night before, as a Passover meal. Simon, acknowledging the need for an extensive commentary on the problem, concludes in favor of the Johannine tradition: "Jesus Christ must have kept the passover of the Jews before-hand, or not have observed it at all."[57] The discrepancy between Mark 15:25 (which states that the crucifixion took place on the third hour) and John 19:14 (which indicates that it occurred after the sixth hour) is blamed on a scribal error.

Although Simon sometimes seems to offer easy solutions to difficult problems, he is often less than satisfied by the answers of others. For instance, in noting the discrepancies between Stephen's speech (Acts 7:2-53) and the historical references in the OT, Simon says that most of the efforts to solve the problems are more subtle than they are sound. On theological matters, Simon is frequently less than profound. He believes that the words "You are my Son; today I have begotten you" (Acts 13:33) refer to the resurrection and prove the divinity of Jesus, but he seems oblivious to the possibility that his interpretation might be used in support of an adoptionist Christology. Simon finds it difficult to acknowledge that God actually hated Esau (Rom. 9:13) and thinks instead that the word translated "to hate" frequently means "to love less." Similarly, he says that the term "all" in reference to the salvation of Israel (Rom. 11:26) does not really mean "all." "This may be understood," says Simon, "also of a great part of the Jews only: for the word *all*, among the Hebrews signifies often only a great number."[58] Simon admits that 1 Cor. 15:29 (about the baptism for the dead) is a difficult text but concludes that the early Christians appear to have practiced a baptism by proxy. Ordinarily, "to baptize" (as in Romans 6) means "to plunge," that is, "to immerse," as baptism is practiced by the Eastern churches. The notorious thorn in the flesh (2 Cor. 12:7) Simon interprets symbolically: it stands for Paul's experience of constantly being tormented. In regard to the Apocalypse, Simon avoids fanciful interpretation and declares that "most of the commentators have sought for mysteries where there were none."[59]

In the history of NT research, little Richard Simon stands as a towering figure. He was a scholar of enormous erudition, and the scope of his work is staggering. Since Simon was so roundly rejected in his own time, some historians have supposed that his influence prior to Semler was minimal. Woodbridge has shown, however, that Simon cast a long shadow over subsequent biblical study, an influence detected in Diderot's *Encyclopedia*

57. Ibid. 1.160, 1.435.
58. Ibid. 2.604.
59. Ibid. 2.985.

and in the work of the English deists.[60] S. J. Baumgarten, who taught such students as J. D. Michaelis, wrote reviews of Simon's work, and, later, Semler had high praise for Simon's biblical research. To be sure, Simon's work was flawed by certain biases, and at times his combative personality was his own worst enemy. He overvalued the Vulgate and resonated too readily to the voice of tradition. Yet the latter point provided a useful corrective to some Protestant scholarship, and Simon's attack on the *sola scriptura* principle by means of historical criticism was nothing short of prophetic. Bossuet castigated him for writing in French rather than Latin and thus threatening the faith of ordinary believers. Yet, Simon, for all his opposition to vernacular translations of the Bible, believed the results of biblical criticism ought to be available to the intelligent public. In this, he was a herald of NT research in the era of the Enlightenment.

TEXT CRITICISM:
MILL AND BENTLEY

John Mill (1645–1707)

At the beginning of the Enlightenment, a notable advance was made in the study and editing of the Greek text of the NT.[61] In 1707, a critical edition of monumental proportions appeared, the product of the tireless effort of one man: John Mill. The son of a weaver, Mill was a brilliant student who entered Oxford at the age of sixteen. At Oxford, he distinguished himself as a Latinist. Mill was ordained in 1670 and served as master of Queen's College from 1670 to 1682. During that period, he was recognized for his effective preaching and his able work as a tutor. Mill occupied various ecclesiastical posts, including the position of chaplain to King Charles II. From 1685 to 1707 he was principal of Edmund Hall, Oxford.

Mill published sermons and works on the classics and the Bible, but the energy of his life was poured into one great book, his *Novum Testamentum*.[62] He died in 1707, two months after this work was completed. About Mill, J. J. Wettstein, one of the greatest text critics of the eighteenth century, said, "This learned man alone did more, in the labour of thirty years,

---

60. John D. Woodbridge, "German Responses to the Biblical Critic Richard Simon: From Leibnitz to J. S. Semler," in *Historische Kritik und biblischer Kanon in der deutschen Aufklärung,* ed. H. G. Reventlow, W. Sparn, and J. Woodbridge (Wiesbaden: Harrassowitz, 1988), 65–87.

61. See Lyle O. Bristol, "New Testament Textual Criticism in the Eighteenth Century," *Journal of Biblical Literature* 69 (1950): 101–12.

62. John Mill, *Novum Testamentum. Cum lectionibus variantibus MSS. exemplarium, versionum, editionum, SS. Patrum et Scriptorum ecclesiasticorum; et in easdem notis* (Oxford: Sheldonian, 1707).

than all those who had preceded him."[63] Mill's interest in work on the NT text was originally aroused by Edward Bernard, a professor of mathematics at Oxford. He was also encouraged by Bishop John Fell, who had himself published a text of the NT in 1675. Mill's text is beautiful to behold. Published in a large folio volume, it contains a prolegomena, the text itself, an appendix, and twenty-five illustrative engravings. Each NT book is introduced by a collection of relevant sayings from the early fathers, printed in Greek. Romans, for example, is prefaced by quotations about Paul from 2 Peter, 1 Clement, and patristic authors. At the bottom of the pages of the text is the critical apparatus. Mill worked on the apparatus from 1678 to 1686, the appendix from 1691 to 1696, and the prolegomena from 1698 to 1705. The text itself is virtually a reproduction of the third edition of Robert Stephens (1550), although Mill made some minor corrections. His intent was not to produce a totally new text but to present the Received Text with an extensive collection of variants and text-critical comments.

The prolegomena is divided into three parts. In the first, Mill discusses the canonicity and historical setting of the NT books. Here his judgments are consistently traditional. The Gospels were written in the order in which they appear, and written quite early: Matthew in 59, Mark in 63, Luke in 64, and John in 97. Paul is the author of Hebrews, and John is the author of both Revelation (written in 96 from Patmos) and the Fourth Gospel. The Pastoral Epistles were written by Paul, and, to fit them into Paul's itinerary, Mill assumes two Roman imprisonments. Mill thinks the Gospels had virtually achieved canonical status by the end of the first century. More interesting is his discussion of the early Christian apocryphal writings. Mill observes that some of these, for example, the Gospel of the Hebrews and the Gospel of the Egyptians, were written earlier than the canonical Gospels. Attention is also given to apocryphal works like the *Kerygma Petri*, which Mill dates at 69, and the *Shepherd of Hermas*, which he puts in the same year. In spite of his conservative conclusions, Mill does not avoid critical questions. For example, he attends to the problem of the authorship of Jude, although he thinks its authenticity is confirmed by 2 Peter.

The second and longest part of the prolegomena deals with "the state of the text through all the ages of the church."[64] This is in effect a history of the text and of the use of the NT from ancient to modern times. Mill discusses the use of the NT by the heretics, and Marcion's "corruption" of

---

63. Quoted in Samuel Prideaux Tregelles, *An Account of the Printed Text of the Greek New Testament; with Remarks on Its Revision upon Critical Principles* (London: S. Bagster, 1854), 43.
64. John Mill, *Novum Testamentum*, ed. Ludolph Küster (Rotterdam: C. Fritsch and M. Böhm, 1710), 28.

the text. He presents the early citations of NT writings by the orthodox, like Justin, Tatian, and Irenaeus. He traces the history of the text through the Middle Ages to the Renaissance, where attention is given to scholars like Laurentius Valla. In regard to modern editions, Mill discusses the work of Stephens and Beza. He also describes the history and character of some of the most important manuscripts, including Alexandrinus and Claramontanus.

The final section of the prolegomena introduces Mill's own text. He recounts his involvement in the project and notes the materials he has used. He observes that his text essentially follows the third edition of Stephens. Finally, Mill presents the system by which he notes textual variants. In Mill's original edition (1707) much of his discussion of variants was included in the appendix. In later editions of the work, this material has been incorporated into the notes at the bottom of the pages of the text. According to Adam Fox, Mill's prolegomena refers to more than thirty printed editions and gives an account of eighty-seven manuscripts.[65] In regard to principles of text-critical practice, Mill puts considerable weight on the Old Latin texts and especially on the NT quotations from patristic writings. Generally, he makes judgments on the basis of the sheer number of texts supporting a particular reading. Fox, however, detects an early expression of the principle *difficilior lectio potior* (the more difficult reading is better), which was more clearly explicated by Bengel.[66] This principle is implied in Mill's prolegomena, where he says "just as something is more obscure, so it is generally more authentic, and from various readings which occur, those which appear clearer are justly suspected of falsification."[67]

The character of Mill's critical work can be illustrated by one or two examples. In his note on Rom. 16:25-27 (the epistle's doxology), Mill observes that most texts place this pericope at the end of the epistle. Codex Alexandrinus, however, has it both here and at the end of chapter 14. Mill's note on 14:23 points out that some patristic authors also locate the doxology after this verse, including Chrysostom and Theodoret. Mill believes that although the doxology might appear to fit what precedes in 14:23, it seems to interrupt the continuity of Paul's argument in chapters 14 and 15. He concludes, on the basis of this evidence, that Paul originally

65. Adam Fox, *John Mill and Richard Bentley: A Study of the Textual Criticism of the New Testament 1675-1729* (Oxford: Basil Blackwell, 1954), 70.

66. Ibid., 147–48. According to W. G. Kümmel (*The New Testament: The History of the Investigation of Its Problems*, trans. S. M. Gilmour and H. C. Kee [Nashville and New York: Abingdon Press, 1972], 414), the formulation *difficilior lectio potior* was probably derived from various rules proposed by Griesbach. For Bengel's formulation of the principle, see p. 73, below.

67. Mill, *Novum Testamentum*, ed. Küster, 115.

intended to end the epistle at chapter 14 and thus wrote the doxology after 14:23, but that he later resumed his argument and wrote chapters 15 and 16. The final form of the ending was left, as customarily, to Paul's amanuensis, Tertius. Mill gives extensive attention to the hotly contested 1 John 5:7. After more than seven large, two-columned pages of discussion, he concludes that this is indeed a vexing text. "Which side should prevail," he writes, "we leave to the erudite"[68]—although more erudition than Mill has already displayed is hard to imagine. His own opinion—although he wishes he had more time to devote to the issue—is that the arguments in favor of authenticity are so strong that the verse should not be removed from the text.

Mill's magnificent accomplishment had a continuing effect on the development of text criticism. In 1710, a new edition of his text was published in Rotterdam by Ludolf Küster, a professor at the University of Utrecht. Küster made corrections, and improved Mill's system of noting variants. He also included variants from twelve manuscripts Mill had not used. Küster's edition was widely used on the continent and became the basis for further text-critical research in the eighteenth century.

Not everyone, however, was pleased with Mill's results. Daniel Whitby,[69] the distinguished English exegete, believed Mill's collection of variants constituted a threat to faith. While acknowledging that errors may have crept in, Whitby was convinced that the God who established the Scriptures as the only rule of faith would also protect them from any kind of serious corruption. "I GRIEVE therefore, and am vexed," he says, "that I have found so much in Mill's Prolegomena which seems quite plainly to render the standard of faith insecure, or at best to give others too good a handle for doubting; or to add strength and support to the wretched arguments of the Papists and others against this Rule."[70] Whitby, in any event, belonged to the old world which was passing away. What he seemed to presuppose was not only the special inspiration of those who originally wrote the NT but also some sort of supernatural guidance for a succession of copyists. This point of view draws attention to the reverence in which the *textus receptus* (the Received Text) was held.[71] To publish a multitude of variants—as Mill had done—was risky; to revise the text, at this time, out of the question. This bolder move would have to await the work of Griesbach and Lachmann.[72]

68. Ibid., 586.

69. See chap. 2, below.

70. Cited in Fox, *John Mill and Richard Bentley*, 106.

71. In England, the Received Text is usually understood as the text of the third edition of Robert Stephens (1550). On the continent, it is usually identified with the similar Elzevir text of 1633.

72. See pp. 141–43, 321–22, below.

Richard Bentley (1662–1742)

As a matter of fact, a complete revision of the text was proposed by a younger contemporary of Mill, the brilliant classicist Richard Bentley.[73] Bentley had collected and collated manuscripts and had corresponded with Mill and the Swiss text critic, J. J. Wettstein.[74] Bentley actually published a prospectus for a text that was to be based on more manuscripts and better collations, a text that would reproduce the NT used in the fourth century. Although a sample page was advertised and subscriptions sold, the project was never completed. The prodigious Bentley was too busy delivering the Boyle lectures against atheism and proving the Epistles of Phalaris to be a fraud; too occupied in the quarrel between the ancients and the moderns (the "battle of the books"); too involved in ecclesiastical and academic politics to tend to the mundane duties of text criticism. Nevertheless, when a fire broke out one night in the Cottonian library in Cambridge, Bentley, almost seventy years of age at the time, was seen in his dressing gown, carrying the four heavy volumes of the Codex Alexandrinus to safety—no small service to the future of textual criticism.

SUMMARY

A review of the work of these precursors of Enlightenment criticism indicates that a new era in biblical research had arrived. Most important, the books of the NT were being viewed as historical documents, and scholars had exercised—although with some limitations (Bossuet versus Simon)—the freedom of research. New data had been collected, reviewed by empirical observation, and evaluated by rational reflection. Progress had been made in the editing of a reliable, critical text (Mill). Major advances were evident in the area of philology (Grotius and Simon) and in the knowledge of historical backgrounds (Lightfoot). In the exercise of these methods, scholars had addressed problems that would continue to occupy future research: the question of the authorship and integrity of NT books, the relation between the Johannine and the Synoptic Gospels, the exegesis of particular texts. As scholars would come increasingly to see, the answers to critical questions of this sort would have serious implications for related theological issues: canon and authority, revelation and inspiration, Scripture and tradition, miracles and the supernatural.

In regard to the critical issues, the accomplishments of the precursors—although substantial and innovative for their time—were modest:

---

73. For a lively summary of Bentley's extraordinary career, see R. J. White, *Dr. Bentley: A Study in Academic Scarlet* (East Lansing: Michigan State University Press, 1968).

74. See pp. 103–7, below.

text-critical work had been limited to collecting and editing variants; the question of authorship had only been raised in regard to a few books (Hebrews and the Catholic Epistles); the issue of integrity had largely been restricted to the ending of Romans and John 21; and the problem of the interrelation of the Gospels had not been rigorously probed. Moreover, the application of new critical methods had not produced substantial historical reconstruction—no clear delineation of the Jesus of history, no comprehensive description of the beginnings of Christianity, had been advanced. As to the related theological issues, the precursors did not venture far from orthodoxy. Their view of the shape and authority of the canon was traditional, although Grotius and Simon had questioned the idea of verbal inspiration and infallibility. Although Grotius's concern with natural law and Simon's stress on foundational facts suggested larger hermeneutical perspectives, no attempt had been made to integrate critical method and constructive theology into a comprehensive understanding of reality. This issue, in an era when reality was conceived in cosmic dimensions, would become increasingly acute for biblical scholars who believed the history and message of the NT to be of ultimate significance. In sum, the precursors of modern criticism left a legacy of problems that would continue to challenge NT scholars for the next three centuries.

2

The Attack on Revealed Religion: The English Deists

In the hands of the English deists, NT research took a sharp turn to the left. Actually, the deists were not Bible scholars but advocates of a religious philosophy that brought the biblical message into question. Captivated by the cosmology of Newton and the rationalism of the Enlightenment, the deists stressed a religion of nature. For them, God was disclosed not in a mysterious burning bush or in the supernatural light of the Damascus road but in the regular order of the cosmos. Religious truth was not revealed to a particular people on tables of stone or in sacred books but to all human beings—to all who had eyes to see and reason to comprehend. As advocates of this natural, universal religion, the deists opposed the old, orthodox faith, along with the authoritarian establishment that supported it. England supplied the fertile soil for this new religious movement to take root and flourish. There revolution had succeeded, a monarch had been executed, ecclesiastical authorities had been challenged, religious pluralism and toleration had emerged; all those British qualities so admired by Voltaire (himself a deist) provided the climate for the development of deism. In their efforts to demolish the orthodox establishment, the deists had to contend with the Bible, for the Bible was the inspired and authoritative witness to special revelation and supernatural religion, everything the deists were against.

AN ADVOCATE OF REVEALED RELIGION: DANIEL WHITBY (1638–1725)

In order to assess the impact of deism on biblical studies, it might be helpful to review the state of NT research in England at the beginning of the century. Daniel Whitby can serve as an example. Entering Oxford as a commoner, Whitby graduated in 1653 and was elected fellow of Trinity College eleven years later. He held a variety of ecclesiastical posts and engaged in extensive scholarly publication. His early writings were anti-Catholic, and later he wrote works opposing the Calvinists. He also published a book about the religious Dissenters which the high church officials considered too sympathetic; the book was burned at Oxford. Whitby's liberalism was apparent in his Arminianism and in his growing appreciation for Unitarianism. Consequently, his NT research can be assessed according to the standards of the day as moderate or even progressive. His attack on Mill's text, noted in chapter 1, simply serves to show that moderation in Whitby's time was far from radical. His major work in biblical research is *A Commentary on the Gospels and Epistles*, originally published in 1703. The continuing importance of this work can be seen in the fact that it was reprinted as part of a larger series as late as 1848 in America.[1]

In the preface, Whitby sets forth his basic belief about the Bible. He says that the apostles, in writing the NT, were inspired in the same way as the OT prophets, that is, inwardly, by an impression made on their brains. Proof that they were inspired is seen in their miracles and in the fulfillment of their prophecies. Whitby did not believe that everything in the Scriptures had been dictated by the Holy Spirit but was convinced that "in these writings the apostles were assisted and preserved from error by the Spirit of God, and therefore were enabled to deliver to us an unerring rule of faith."[2] According to Whitby, the cornerstone of the Christian faith is belief in Jesus as the Messiah. Jesus fulfills all the expectations of the ancient prophets, and his own prophecies about the future have been fulfilled. The miracles of Jesus prove his Messiahship and his uniqueness—miracles acknowledged even by his opponents. Most important, the resurrection of Jesus, a unique event in history, confirms the truth of Christianity. Here Whitby argues primarily from the empty tomb. He insists that the opponents of Jesus could not have removed the body, because if they had, they would have used it to discredit Christian belief. The disciples, on the other hand, could not have removed it, because if they had, they would scarcely have been able to carry out their ministries, which were accompanied by miraculous deeds and confirmed by their willingness to suffer and die for their belief.

As to the books of the NT, they were not only written by inspired apostles, they were protected from corruption in their transmission. "Who can imagine," asks Whitby, "that that God, who sent his Son out of his

---

1. Daniel Whitby, *A Commentary on the Gospels and Epistles of the New Testament*, A Critical Commentary and Paraphrase on the Old and New Testament and the Apocrypha, by Patrick, Lowth, Arnald, Whitby, and Lowman, 4 vols. (Philadelphia: Carey & Hart, 1848), vol. 4.
    2. Ibid., 8.

bosom to declare this doctrine, and his apostles by the assistance of the Holy Spirit to indite and preach it, and by so many miracles confirmed it to the world, should suffer any wicked person to corrupt and alter any of those terms on which the happiness of mankind depended?"[3] This confidence in the biblical record is confirmed by data throughout Whitby's commentary. Whitby concludes that the original language of the Gospel of Matthew was Greek. If Matthew had been originally written in Hebrew, as some tradition suggests, then it must have been lost, but how could divine providence have allowed an inspired Gospel to be lost? Commenting on Matt. 1:23, Whitby argues that παρθένος is the proper translation of *almah,* which he takes to mean "virgin." To Whitby, it seems obvious that Isa. 7:14 was not talking about an ordinary birth, for how could an ordinary birth be a sign of anything? Thus, the prophet was depicting a miracle and, therefore, predicting the supernatural birth of Jesus. Whitby has a special theory for confirming the inspiration of Luke's Gospel. He believes that Luke had been a member of the seventy, commissioned by Jesus (Luke 10:1) and, hence, with the same authority as the Twelve. Moreover, the seventy were also a part of the 120 who participated in the events of Pentecost, so that Luke received the same Spirit which endowed the other apostles with infallibility. Throughout the commentary, Whitby confirms all the traditional views of authenticity. Paul, of course, wrote the Pastoral Epistles, as well as Hebrews. Even the authenticity of 2 Peter is assured: "That this epistle was written by the apostle Peter, is evident beyond all exception."[4] In sum, Whitby presents a moderate version of the biblical religion the deists set out to destroy.

THE SIGNIFICANCE OF JOHN LOCKE
(1632–1704)

As Whitby represents the structure the deists attacked, so Locke presented the framework upon which they could build. Locke was not himself a deist,[5] but he formulated a philosophy that the deists continued to exploit. Educated at Oxford, John Locke studied classics and was introduced to chemistry by the pioneering Robert Boyle, who encouraged his interest in the empirical method. For a time, Locke taught at Oxford but later studied medicine. He became involved in political activity and was appointed to various government posts. Because of his political associations, Locke was forced to flee to Holland in 1683, but he returned to England after five years abroad. After additional government service, Locke retired to

---

3. Ibid., 28.
4. Ibid., 972.
5. See S. G. Hefelbower, *The Relation of John Locke to English Deism* (Chicago: University of Chicago Press, 1918).

the country and devoted his latter years to religious writings. Important for the deists was Locke's theory of knowledge, a theory which came to expression in "An Essay on Human Understanding" (1690). Locke was opposed to the notion of innate ideas, which had been made famous by Descartes, and, instead, advocated an empirical epistemology. According to Locke, there are two sources of knowledge: external sensation and internal reflection. He depicted the mind as a blank tablet upon which data, received through the senses, can be written. This data, in turn, can be appropriated and arranged by the reflection of the human mind, so that all knowledge comes by observation, and what is observed is ordered by reason.

John Locke was a pious Christian. His basic theological position can be found in *The Reasonableness of Christianity* (1695). In the first part of *Reasonableness*, Locke argues for the necessity of the Christian gospel—a necessity confirmed by the fact that human beings are sinners, and sinners are destined to die. Locke rejects the doctrine of inherited original sin, although he thinks Adam's fall resulted in death for all. However, in spite of this universal predicament, people can be restored to life by the gift of Christ. Acceptance of the gift requires that they observe two laws: the law of works and the law of faith. The latter compensates for those deficiencies whereby frail human beings fall short of full obedience. For Locke, faith primarily means assent to doctrines: that Jesus is Messiah, that he performed miracles, and that he rose from the dead. In later sections of *Reasonableness*, Locke discusses the teachings of the apostles and the ministry of Jesus. The apostles, like John the Baptist, witness to Jesus' Messiahship. Jesus' own ministry confirms this testimony by miracles and statements he makes. In this discussion, Locke displays sensitivity to what later became identified as the "messianic secret." He observes that Jesus did not openly proclaim himself as Messiah because of the threat of the Jews and in accord with his intention to gradually disclose his Messiahship. Although salvation requires faith in Christ, it also demands repentance and works, as the Sermon on the Mount and the Epistle of James show.

In the last sections of the book, Locke takes up objections to his arguments. For example, how could people who lived before Christ have faith in Christ? "Nobody was, or can be required to believe," answers Locke, "what was never proposed to him to believe."[6] What of people who have never heard the divine promises that were fulfilled in Christ? Even they, according to Locke, were provided with an inner light—"the light of reason, revealed to all mankind . . . the spark of divine nature and knowledge

6. John Locke, *The Reasonableness of Christianity*, ed. I. T. Ramsey (Stanford, Calif.: Stanford University Press, 1958), 52–53.

in man."[7] What then is the advantage that is given by Christ? Locke replies that although humans can know God through reason, in practice they do not. Thus, they need the revelation that is given in Christ, a revelation in full harmony with reason. For Locke, truth was communicated by both reason and revelation, and although revelation was superior, it was not contrary to reason. In his later works, he increasingly magnified the importance of revelation, especially the revelation communicated by God through the infallible Scriptures. In a letter of 1697, Locke wrote, "The holy scripture is to me, and always will be, the constant guide of my assent: and I shall always harken to it, as containing infallible truth."[8] The Bible discloses doctrines like the Trinity and immortality, which cannot be perceived by reason alone. Revelation can be confirmed by two proofs: miracles and fulfilled prophecy.

Locke gave special attention to the problem of miracles. In "A Discourse of Miracles" (1702–3), he provided a definition: "A miracle then I take to be a sensible operation, which being above the comprehension of the spectator, and in his opinion contrary to the established course of nature, is taken by him to be divine."[9] Miracles are confirmed as acts of God by their quantity and quality. True miracles are seen, for example, to be bigger and better than the portents of the Egyptian sorcerers who competed with Moses. "So likewise the number, variety and greatness of the miracles, wrought for the confirmation of the doctrine delivered by Jesus Christ, carry with them such strong marks of an extraordinary divine power, that the truth of his mission will stand firm and unquestionable, till any one rising up in opposition to him shall do greater miracles than he and the apostles did."[10]

In addition to discussing issues important in biblical thought, Locke made a significant contribution to NT research. Late in life, he wrote *A Paraphrase and Notes* on the major epistles of Paul, a work which is now available in a superb critical edition.[11] Drafts of the work were composed as early as 1701, but the finished book did not appear until 1705, a year after his death. Locke turned to the study of the epistles because he thought he had neglected them in *Reasonableness,* in which he had emphasized the Gospels. In the main, Locke is more conservative in *Paraphrase and Notes* than in his earlier writings. His view of the Trinity, however, is not fully orthodox, even though he affirms the preexistence of Christ. In

7. Ibid., 55.

8. Cited in Henning Graf Reventlow, *The Authority of the Bible and the Rise of the Modern World,* trans. John Bowden (Philadelphia: Fortress Press, 1985), 263.

9. John Locke, "A Discourse of Miracles," in *The Reasonableness of Christianity,* 79.

10. Ibid., 83.

11. Arthur W. Wainwright, ed., *John Locke: A Paraphrase and Notes on the Epistles of St. Paul to the Galatians, 1 and 2 Corinthians, Romans, Ephesians,* 2 vols. (Oxford: Clarendon Press, 1987).

regard to the doctrine of salvation, Locke declares that humans have no hope apart from Christ, but he rejects the idea of propitiatory, substitutionary atonement. Likewise, Locke abandons predestination, although he recognizes grace to be a gift and human freedom to have limitations.

The work opens with "An Essay for the Understanding of St. Paul's Epistles, by Consulting Paul Himself." As this title suggests, Locke proposes a historical and grammatical interpretation of the Pauline letters. He observes that the individual epistles were addressed to particular situations that were known to the original readers but are not apparent to the modern interpreter. When these situations are known, the epistles can be understood. Paul, according to Locke, wrote his letters in Greek, but his idiom was Hebrew or Syriac. Locke is baffled by the evidence that Paul's speeches in Acts are so clear and consistent while his writing in the epistles is so complex. He says, "It was hard to think that a Man, that could talk with so much Consistency and Clearness of Conviction should not be able to write without Confusion, inextricable Obscurity, and perpetual Rambling."[12] Locke, of course, was unaware of the later critical judgment that the speeches in Acts are largely the composition of its author.

As well as noting the problems of setting and language, Locke notes other detriments to the understanding of the Pauline letters. He gives special attention to the danger of reading Paul's words out of context or interpreting them in accord with one's own opinions. On an earlier occasion, Locke had written to a friend, "I read the word of God without prepossession of bias, and come to it with a resolution to take my sense from it, and not with a design to bring it to the sense of my system."[13] As a corrective to reading words out of context, Locke proposes a procedure whereby one reads the entire epistle straight through again and again to detect Paul's primary purpose and then proceeds to analyze the constituent arguments by which the larger purpose is developed. In spite of the complexity of his rhetoric, Paul's thought is essentially consistent, and what he wrote in one place can be illuminated by his writing on the same subject in another locus. "Thus, indeed, one part of the Sacred Text could not fail to give light unto another."[14] In an earlier essay, Locke had written, "The most certain interpreter of Scripture is Scripture itself, and it alone is infallible."[15]

In the actual structure of *A Paraphrase and Notes*, Locke presents the epistles in the chronological order of their composition. He introduces

12. Ibid. 1.111.

13. Cited in Kathleen M. Squadrito, *John Locke* (Boston: Twayne, 1979), 26.

14. Wainwright, *Paraphrase and Notes* 1.113.

15. John C. Biddle, "John Locke's Essay on Infallibility: Introduction, Text, and Translation," *Journal of Church and State* 19 (1977): 327.

each epistle with a synopsis that includes a discussion of the occasion, purpose, and overview of the epistle. Then, the epistle is divided into sections, and longer sections are divided into subsections (usually five to ten verses). The discussion of these sections and subsections is presented under three rubrics: a summary of the content, the text (in the Authorized Version), and the paraphrase itself. Locke's notes are printed in the footnotes. The paraphrase expands the text, usually to about twice the original length. Its purpose is to present exegetical solutions and clarify the meaning. The notes consist of brief comments on words, phrases, historical details, and textual variants.

In the synopses of the various epistles, Locke presents some significant historical observations. He believes Galatians was written from Ephesus in 57. Paul's first visit to Galatia took place in 51 (Acts 16:2), and a second had occurred in 54 (Acts 18:21-23). Galatians 1:6 suggests that it was written soon after the second visit and thus was composed a year or two later. All of this indicates that Locke, like most eighteenth-century interpreters, adopted what came to be called the "north Galatian hypothesis," that is, the theory that the Epistle to the Galatians was addressed to churches of the original Galatian territory, not the churches of the southern part of the province of Galatia. According to Locke, the opponents of Paul in Galatia and in Corinth were Judaizers. In Corinth, this opposition took the shape of "one Party, under one Leader."[16]

Locke's notes present a variety of exegetical, historical, and theological comments. Dealing with matters of grammar, as he often does, Locke argues that πνευματικῶν in 1 Cor. 12:1 is masculine, that is, Paul is considering "spiritual people" rather than spiritual things (neuter). In commenting on 1 Cor. 7:14 (where Paul says that children of a believer and an unbeliever are holy), Locke observes that the children of proselytes were similarly considered holy by the Jews. Acknowledging his dependence on Lightfoot, Locke concludes that the speaking in tongues in Corinth was speaking Hebrew. The problem, in Locke's opinion, was that Paul's Judaizing opponent was promoting the use of Hebrew in the Corinthian worship services. In discussing the resurrection, Locke argues, as he had done earlier in a controversy with Edward Stillingfleet, that the body that will be raised is not the same corpse that is buried, but a body that will be transformed into a new and different nature. Commenting on Rom 5:12, Locke says that "all have sinned" means "all became mortal," or in other words, what human beings inherit from Adam is not guilt, but mortality. The debated term ἱλαστήριον in Rom. 3:25 means "mercy seat" rather than "propitiation." Commenting on 2 Cor. 5:3 and referring to 1 Thess. 4:15

16. Wainwright, *Paraphrase and Notes* 1.163.

and 5:6, Locke observes that "the apostle looked on the coming of Christ as not far off"[17]—a comment which shows that Locke, for all his support of biblical infallibility, did not consider NT writers to be totally immune to error.

In spite of his intent to interpret Paul according to Paul himself, Locke occasionally reads his own views into the epistles. For example, commenting on how Gentiles who do not have the law can keep the requirements of the law (Rom. 2:14, 26), he says that Paul is referring here to the universal, rational law of God: "the natural and eternal rule of *rectitude* which is made known to men by the light of reason"—the law which "came from god [*sic*], and was made by him the moral rule to all mankind, being laid within the discovery of their reason."[18] The term "revelation" (Eph. 1:17), on the other hand, refers to "Truths which could not have been found out by humane Reason."[19] Some truths that are revealed in Scripture, however, are difficult to understand. Displaying a refreshing candor not always found among exegetes, Locke admits that he does not know all the answers. On 1 Cor. 15:29, he says, "What this baptizeing for the dead was I confess I Know not."[20]

Reactions to Locke's work were mixed. Whiston wrote a favorable review, while the famous hymn writer, Isaac Watts, found Locke's approach too rationalistic:

> Reason could scarce sustain to see
> Th' Almighty One, th' Eternal Three,
>   Or bear the Infant Deity;
> Scarce could her Pride descend to own
> Her Maker stooping from his Throne,
> And dress'd in Glories so unknown.[21]

Nevertheless, the book was widely used in England and in America, and German scholars like S. J. Baumgarten and J. D. Michaelis held it in high regard. In any event, Locke's stress on linguistics and historical reconstruction anticipated the method of the grammatico-historical interpreters of the eighteenth century. Most important for the immediate future, however, was his understanding of revelation and reason. What cannot be known by reason, claims Locke, God reveals by revelation—a revelation that can never be in conflict with reason. Yet, the deists asked, if revelation could never contradict reason, what was the need of supernatural revelation at all? Surely God could be detected in the ordered heavens

17. Ibid. 1.284.
18. Ibid. 2.501.
19. Ibid. 2.623.
20. Ibid. 1.251.
21. Cited in Wainwright, *Paraphrase and Notes* 1.63.

above and in the rational mind within. Besides, the two pillars that supported revelation—fulfilled prophecy and supernatural miracles—seemed to be set on sinking sand. Solid rock would be found in the rational religion of nature. On this rock, the deists would attempt to construct a shrine according to the blueprint of reason—a religion that had no room for revelation.

THE DEISTS:
TOLAND, TINDAL, COLLINS, AND WOOLSTON

The deists were children of the Enlightenment.[22] They breathed the pure air of the new rationalism and inhaled the atmosphere of the new science. Lord Edward Herbert of Cherbury (1583–1648), usually identified as the father of the movement, advocated rationalism, monotheism, and morality. Deism was advanced by Charles Blount (1654–93) who opposed the power of the clergy and expressed skepticism about revelation and the miracles. In general, the deists believed reason to be an innate faculty of all people. Reason, the very image of God in which all humans are created, makes possible knowledge of the will of God. By the exercise of reason, people possess the possibility of adopting a natural religion, that is, a religion grounded in the nature of the universe. At creation, God established this rational order, but although the prime and necessary cause of this order, God had become increasingly remote. The world, nevertheless, continued to function according to the laws that God had established at creation, laws that operate without the need of divine intervention.

Deism's Basic Concepts:
Toland and Tindal

Two works set forth the basic tenets of deism: John Toland's *Christianity Not Mysterious* (1696) and Matthew Tindal's *Christianity as Old as the Creation* (1730).

John Toland (1669–1722)

John Toland was an Irishman who studied at Edinburgh, Glasgow, Leyden, and Oxford. Compared with later deists, Toland's views are moderate. He notes in his preface to *Christianity Not Mysterious* that in his work, "The

---

22. For a concise summary of the work of the major deists, see Leslie Stephen, *History of English Thought in the Eighteenth Century*, 2 vols. (New York: G. P. Putnam's Sons, 1927), 1.74-277. See also E. Royston Pike, *Slayers of Superstition: A Popular Account of Some of the Leading Personalities of the Deist Movement* (Port Washington, N.Y. and London: Kennikat, 1931); John Orr, *English Deism: Its Roots and Its Fruits* (Grand Rapids: Wm. B. Eerdmans, 1934).

divinity of the New Testament is taken for granted."[23] Toland is concerned to show that reason and revelation—indeed, reason and Scripture—are in harmony. His fundamental thesis is that "there is nothing in the gospel contrary to reason, nor above it; and that no Christian doctrine can be properly call'd a mystery."[24] Toland believes that reason is a human faculty by which people can discover certainty about the unknown by comparison with the known. With Locke, Toland agrees that information enters the mind through the senses. When people follow the clear evidence their senses provide, they cannot really err. Moreover, when the doctrine of the Gospels is exposed to the clear light of empirical reason, it is seen to be rational and free from every taint of the arcane. The clergy, to be sure, have conspired to make the NT seem mysterious, but their conspiracy is simply designed to keep the laity in captivity. By way of contrast, the NT itself advocates reasonable service (Rom. 12:1) and calls upon Christians to give a reason for the hope that is within them (1 Pet. 3:15).

In discussing the Bible, Toland does not deny that it contains revelation. Yet, "to believe the divinity of Scripture . . . without rational proofs, and evident consistency, is a blameable credulity."[25] Toland, moreover, is willing to entertain as proofs evidence which later deism would dismiss as supernatural, for instance, the miracles as confirmation of the truth of Christ's Messiahship. In the course of this discussion, Toland articulates a principle that was to become axiomatic in eighteenth- and nineteenth-century biblical criticism: "Nor is there any different rule to be follow'd in the interpretation of Scripture from what is common to all other books."[26] The Scriptures, he maintains, are written in the plain language of Hebrew and Greek, and, by the use of sources like the Talmud, the literature of the NT can be made easily intelligible. Some doctrines implied in the Bible, although not mysterious, cannot be fully fathomed. For example, we cannot know the essence of God, but, then again, we cannot know the essence of many other things either. We cannot, for instance, know the essence of the sun, but we can indeed bask in its benefits. What cannot be known—the essence of things—is not a mystery; it is simply the unknown. Thus, "what infinite goodness has not been pleas'd to reveal to us, we are either sufficiently capable to discover ourselves, or need not understand it at all."[27] The use of the term "mystery" in the NT, therefore, refers not to hidden secrets but to things previously unknown—things like those unknown to the Jews but made known later by the apostles.

23. John Toland, *Christianity Not Mysterious* (Stuttgart-Bad Cannstatt: F. Frommann, 1964), xxvi.
24. Ibid., 6.
25. Ibid., 36.
26. Ibid., 49.
27. Ibid., 89.

Finally, Toland answers objections to his position. Some opponents, for example, argue that texts like Col. 2:8 castigate philosophy, but Toland replies that what the NT opposes is Greek sophistry, not the actual use of reason. To the objection that miracles involve the mysterious, Toland acknowledges that they exceed human power and represent happenings beyond the ordinary operations of nature. Miracles, however, are not truly mysterious, he argues, but are in accord with the laws of nature and are merely accomplished by divine assistance. Most important, in answering Anglican rationalists like Edward Stillingfleet, Toland argues that the Bible primarily presents not mysteries but clear and distinct ideas.[28] Thus Toland, while denying the mysterious, has not opposed revelation, miracle, and even supernatural influence. All these phenomena, however, function in accord with reason. In sum, Toland's aim is to eliminate the mysterious, reduce the unknowable, and make religion fully accessible to rational comprehension.

Matthew Tindal (1657–1733)

Matthew Tindal, the son of a high churchman, was educated at Oxford, where he was elected a fellow of All Souls' College. For a time, Tindal became a Roman Catholic, but he returned to the Anglican fold, although with low church sympathies. Written when he was seventy-three years of age, Tindal's *Christianity as Old as the Creation* (1730) has been called the Bible of deism, a book widely read in England and translated into German in 1741. In essence, Tindal argues that the Christian gospel is only a revised version of the original religion of nature. The true religion was established by God in creation and is available to all people by the exercise of reason. Thus, "Christianity, tho' the Name is of a later Date, must be as old, and as extensive as human Nature; and the Law of Creation, must have been Then implanted in us by God himself."[29]

Although Tindal did not reject revelation, he rendered it superfluous. He held that revealed religion and natural religion were essentially the same. They were grounded in the same God who created the natural order, and their goals were similarly the same—morality and human happiness. "The Good of the People," writes Tindal, "is the supreme law."[30] If revelation is necessary for the good life, then revelation must be universal—available equally to all people in all times. A wise and rational God could scarcely expect people to obey what they did not know, and, conse-

28. See Gerard Reedy, "Socinians, John Toland, and the Anglican Rationalists," *Harvard Theological Review* 70 (1977): 285-304.
29. Matthew Tindal, *Christianity as Old as the Creation*, ed. G. Gawlick (1730; reprint, Stuttgart-Bad Cannstatt: F. Frommann, 1967), 4.
30. Ibid., 46.

quently, God had disclosed the divine will in the natural order, perceptible by universal reason. The divine will consisted of two basic laws: to honor God and to do good to humanity. These laws, according to Tindal, are found in both natural and revealed religion: "Whatever is true by Reason, can never be false by revelation."[31]

Failure to use reason has led to all sorts of superstition and religious malpractice. Toland is especially critical of OT ritualism, which he considered to be largely irrational. He argues that Abraham, for example, learned the ridiculous practice of circumcision from the Egyptians, and the Hebrew priests promoted senseless sacrifices for their own benefit. Many of these errant ceremonial practices, maintained by the OT, he notes, were properly abolished by the New. The OT also condoned practices of questionable morality. God's people, for instance, had been provoked to destroy the Canaanites, and a prophet of God had cursed forty-two mischievous children so that they were devoured by two she-bears (2 Kings 2:24). Inferior concepts of God abound in the Bible, for example, the notion that God's hand covered Moses so that he could not see God's face but only God's back (Exod. 33:20-23). Even in the NT, Jude quotes an apocryphal work of Enoch as authoritative, and writers like Paul are mistaken about the time of the end of the world. In the book of James—noted for its concern with ethics—a prostitute is praised for prevarication (2:25).

Tindal's criticism of the Bible is sharper than Toland's. Pointing to the weakness of the circular argument that is often used in defense of biblical authority, Tindal says that "it is an odd Jumble, to prove the Truth of a Book by the Truth of the Doctrines it contains, and at the same Time conclude those Doctrine to be true, because contain'd in that Book."[32] Tindal also calls attention to the problem of the NT text. Referring to Bentley's proposed edition and the large number of variants collected by Mill, Tindal asks how anyone can be certain about the wording of any particular passage. Moreover, the difficulties of the ancient languages and their obscure terms make every attempt at translation and interpretation problematic. For Tindal, the one valid hermeneutical principle is reason: "If the Scripture was design'd to be understood, it must be within the Reach of human Understanding; and consequently, it can't contain Propositions that are either above, or below human Understanding."[33]

In the interpretation of Scripture, natural theology, perceived by reason, serves as the final arbiter. Tindal, therefore, questions the notion that the Bible is itself the rule by which truth is to be judged.

31. Ibid., 178.
32. Ibid., 186.
33. Ibid., 222–23.

If it be such a Rule, must it not have all the Qualifications necessary to make it so? But if Reason must tell us what those Qualifications are, and whether they are found in Scripture; and if one of those Qualifications is, that Scripture must be agreeable to the Nature of Things; does not That suppose the Nature of Things to be the standing Rule, by which we must judge of the Truth of all those Doctrines contain'd in the Scriptures?[34]

In criticizing the notion that God adapts truth to the limitations of people (the accommodation theory), Tindal points to the important distinction between rectifying human mistakes and confirming them. If God sometimes confirms human mistakes, then how can the reader trust the biblical record in regard to any particular passage? "Or," asks Tindal, "can the God of Truth, stand in need of Error to support his Truth; his eternal Truth?"[35]

For traditional, orthodox believers, Tindal's whole approach was an anomaly: how could Christianity be as old as creation? Jesus Christ, although identified with the eternal Word and prophesied by the OT, was surely the founder of Christianity, and Christianity was a new religion that superseded the old, with a Scripture of its own, a New Testament. For Tindal, however, a religion that had its setting in a single nation, was not founded until the first century, and was the captive of a particular tradition and culture was too recent, too narrow, too exclusive. Indeed, the special significance of Jesus was not the establishment of a new religion but the recovery of the old. He called people back to the religion of creation—the religion of nature, the religion of reason. The special revelation of Jesus affirmed that there was no special revelation at all. The concept of Christian particularity had been swallowed up by natural theology, and the distinctive message of the Bible had been eroded by rationalism. At the same time, Tindal's affirmation of an unchanging, original religion of nature implied a denial of insights dear to the later Enlightenment—the idea of human evolution and the concept of progressive revelation.

Fulfilled Prophecy: Anthony Collins (1676–1729)

Beyond the denial of the supernatural and the elimination of special revelation, the deist attack on revealed religion took a more serious turn when it began to undermine the dual foundation on which Christian apologetics had been built: the proof from miracles and fulfilled prophecy. The deists had been suspicious of the argument from prophecy for some time, but the issue came into the center of the discussion by a devious route. The person who most clearly articulated the criticism was Anthony

34. Ibid., 190.
35. Ibid., 208.

Collins. Educated at Eton and Cambridge, Collins was a friend of John Locke. About Collins, Locke is reported to have said, he has "an estate in the country, a library in town, and friends everywhere."[36] Collins's *Discourse of the Grounds and Reasons of the Christian Religion* was published six years before Tindal's *Christianity as Old as the Creation*. In the second part of this book, Collins exposes the error of a bizarre theory of William Whiston, the noted translator of Josephus. According to Whiston, the prophecies of the OT must be understood literally in order for them to constitute solid proof for Christianity. Study of the proof texts used by the early Christians, however, does not seem to indicate that the prophecies had been literally fulfilled. This discrepancy between the OT texts and the early Christian interpretation of them had resulted, according to Whiston, from a massive effort on the part of the Jews to revise the texts so radically that they would not appear to be fulfilled in Christ and the NT at all. Whiston, making use of such sources as the Septuagint, the Samaritan Pentateuch, and the Aramaic Targums, attempted to reconstruct the original OT text.

Actually, the notion that the Jews had changed their own Scripture in order to confound the Christians was not invented by Whiston. The theory had been concocted by Isaac Vossius and, in turn, demolished by Richard Simon.[37] In any event, Collins did not have great difficulty in displaying the weakness of Whiston's argument. The notion that the Jews would have perverted their own Sacred Scriptures is ridiculous on the surface, and the theory that the early Christians, who had previously known the OT in Hebrew, would have been fooled by such a deception is difficult to believe. To be sure, the OT, like every other ancient text, had been corrupted in the course of its transmission, but not according to some malicious plot on the part of the Jews. Whiston's reconstructed text, argues Collins, is a scholarly fabrication, based on fallible sources. More important, the texts Whiston cites, even in his revised version, do not provide literal proof that Jesus was the Messiah. For instance, Whiston's emendation of Isa. 7:14 to read "virgin" (in harmony with the LXX and Matt. 1:23) instead of "young woman" (Heb. *almah*) does not prove that the prophet was predicting the birth of Jesus. Taken literally, the text referred to a young woman who would bear a son in the time of King Ahaz. According to Collins, "To understand the prophet as having the conception of the virgin Mary and birth of her son Jesus literally and primarily in view, is a very great absurdity, and contrary to the very intent and design of the sign given by

---

36. *Dictionary of National Biography*, s.v. "Collins, Anthony."
37. See Paul Auvray, *Richard Simon (1638-1712): Etude bio-bibliographique avec des textes inédits*, Mouvement des idées au XVII siècle 8 (Paris: Presses universitaires de France, 1974), 76–92.

the prophet."[38] In short, literal interpretation of OT prophecies cannot establish the truth of Christianity.

In the first part of the *Discourse,* Collins observes that Christianity is founded on Judaism, "so that the truth of christianity depends, as it ought, on antient revelations, which are contain'd in the Old Testament."[39] The OT was the canon of the early Christians, and they used it to establish the fundamental article of the Christian faith: "that Jesus of Nazareth was the Messias of the Jews, predicted in the Old Testament."[40] In using the OT to confirm their faith, however, the Christians had resorted to exegetical methods they had learned from the rabbis, including allegory. Indeed, according to rabbinic method, a text could have a variety of meanings, and the interpreter was encouraged to tear a text out of its context to detect a hidden, mysterious meaning. In this way, Matt. 2:15, ignoring the literal sense of Hos. 11:1, could find there a prediction of Jesus: "Out of Egypt I have called my son." Thus, the claims of Christianity had been supported by OT prophecies, interpreted allegorically.

Moreover, the proof from prophecies allegorically interpreted was decisive, because, according to Collins, the correlative argument—the proof from miracles—was fallacious. "In fine," he wrote, "the miracles wrought by Jesus are, according to the gospel-scheme, no absolute proofs of his being the Messias, or of the truth of christianity."[41] Miracles do not constitute proof, because miracles may rest on mistaken testimony. Collins concludes, therefore, that proof from prophecy is the only surviving support for orthodox Christianity. "Proof rests on the fulfillment of the words of the prophets."[42] However, since proof from prophecy requires allegorical exegesis, the argument—subject to the fancy of the imaginative interpreter—can hardly be clear and convincing. As Collins had pointed out, the rabbis could use as many as ten different ways to cite and interpret the OT. Given this exegetical variety, one could prove almost anything from OT prophecy. When the dust had settled, Collins's argument with Whiston had demonstrated that neither literal nor allegorical interpretation of prophecy could support biblical revelation and establish the truth of Christianity.

Miracles: Thomas Woolston (1669–1733)

The frontal attack on miracles was led by Thomas Woolston, who was educated at Cambridge and ordained in the Church of England. Wool-

---

38. Anthony Collins, *A Discourse of the Grounds and Reasons of the Christian Religion* (New York and London: Garland, 1976), 42.

39. Ibid., 25–26.

40. Ibid., 12.

41. Ibid., 37.

42. Ibid.

ston was for a time a fellow at Cambridge, but he moved to London where he worked as a journalist. In this era, popular publishing flourished: Addison and Steele had issued *The Tattler*, which was succeeded by *The Spectator*; and authors like Jonathan Swift were masters of satire. Writing in this genre, Woolston published popular works which, like the political tracts of the time, were widely read. He lampooned the clergy—always a favorite sport—and treated the miracles with heavy-handed satire. Woolston was like a comical bull gone berserk in the orthodox china closet. Although England was more tolerant than most countries, it found Woolston too much to endure; reasoned arguments could be allowed, but ridicule was hard to tolerate.[43] Repeatedly charged with blasphemy, Woolston eventually died in prison.

From 1727 to 1730, Woolston was occupied in publishing his infamous *Six Discourses on the Miracles of Our Saviour*. Each of the discourses is dedicated to a bishop who is sarcastically ridiculed. The third, for example, was dedicated to a bishop who had attacked one of Woolston's earlier discourses in a sermon. Woolston says that the bishop's ignorance proves that he had not actually read the discourse but must have learned of it from "some Ecclesiastical Noodle."[44] In the first discourse, Woolston observes that proof from prophecy has failed and that the attempt to support Jesus' Messiahship by miracles is equally fallacious. Woolston's shocking thesis is that the miracles, taken literally, represent "Improbabilities, and Incredibilities, and grossest Absurdities, very dishonourable to the Name of Christ."[45] The bulk of the *Discourses* is a collection of miracles made laughable by Woolston's satirical interpretation. The most caustic criticisms— for instance, the attack on the resurrection—are put into the mouth of a fictitious dialogue partner, an astute Jewish rabbi.

Examples of Woolston's treatment of the miracles can be given in abundance, but a few samples may be sufficient. The miracle in which Jesus cast demons into swine caused damage to the owner of the swine. According to Woolston, if someone in his own day had cast demons into a flock of sheep with similar consequences, the judges "would have made him swing for it."[46] The miracle of cursing a fig tree for not bearing figs when it was not even the season for figs seems to Woolston to be particularly ludicrous. If, in an analogous way, a farmer in Kent should cut down his trees because they did not bear fruit out of season, he would become a

---

43. See John Redwood, *Reason, Ridicule and Religion: The Age of Enlightenment in England, 1660-1750* (Cambridge: Harvard University Press, 1976).

44. Thomas Woolston, *Six Discourses on the Miracles of Our Saviour and Defences of His Discourses 1727-1730* (New York and London: Garland, 1979), Discourse 3, p. iv.

45. Ibid., Discourse 1, pp. 19–20.

46. Ibid., Discourse 1, p. 35.

laughingstock, and "if the Story got into our publick News, he would be the Jest and ridicule of Mankind."[47] As to the changing of water into wine, Woolston notes that a similar miracle had been attributed to Apollonius of Tyana. Moreover, when taken literally, the story is damaging to Jesus' reputation, since he made "for a company of Sots . . . a large quantity of Wine . . . enough to intoxicate the whole Town of Cana of Galilee."[48]

The miracles of healing and the raisings of the dead fare no better. In regard to the woman with the issue of blood, Woolston notes that the nature of her illness is not explained. He argues that she could not have been very sick, in any case, since she had been able to endure the illness for twelve years. Perhaps, he says, the hemorrhage was actually beneficial to her health, or the cure resulted from her own anticipation of the action of Jesus. Since the healing required human faith, the miracle could not have been an overwhelming demonstration of divine power. The cure of a blind man by clay made from dust and spittle could scarcely be considered a miracle, because Jesus utilized a kind of ointment. "But Jesus's Eye-Salve," says Woolston, "for absurdity, whim and incongruity, was never equall'd, either in jest or in earnest, by any Quack-Doctor."[49] In regard to the raising of the dead, Woolston notes that only three incidents are recorded in the Gospels. About these reports, Woolston raises all sorts of questions: Why did not Jesus resurrect someone important, like John the Baptist? What happened to Lazarus and the others after they were raised? Why is not the raising of Lazarus reported in any Gospel other than John? Moreover, asks Woolston, if miracles like these were intended to prove something, why did Jesus put potential witnesses out of the room when he raised Jairus's daughter?

The bombshell comes in the last discourse, where Woolston attacks the resurrection of Jesus—the supernatural event that confirms the whole Christian story. In Woolston's opinion, the resurrection is essentially a fraud. Jesus, according to the prediction, was supposed to have been raised on the third day. If the crucifixion took place on Friday, Saturday would have been the first day, Sunday the second, and the resurrection should have happened on Monday. However, when the officials arrived to assess the event, they found the tomb empty, because on Sunday the disciples had stolen the body. Woolston also considers the traditional proofs of the resurrection to be unconvincing. Many people, he says, claim to have seen apparitions, and the argument that disciples were ready to suffer for their faith carries little weight, since people throughout history have been willing to die for their mistaken convictions. Moreover, the risen Christ did

47. Ibid., Discourse 3, p. 7.
48. Ibid., Discourse 4, p. 39.
49. Ibid., Discourse 4, p. 11.

not appear to any Jewish official—something he should have done if he had understood the resurrection to be proof of his Messiahship.

Many of his contemporaries thought Woolston deranged, and it is difficult to detect a serious fragment amidst the rubble of his bombardment. Yet Woolston apparently thought he was doing religion a service, for he insisted that he was moved by "the Love of Truth and Advancement of Christianity," and that he had entered into controversy "with a View to Honour Jesus, our spiritual Messiah, to whom be Glory for ever."[50] Throughout the *Discourses,* he argues that the miracles should be interpreted allegorically, that is, by the same method the church fathers had employed. When the allegorical method is adopted, the spiritual truth of the miracle stories can be discovered. In the account of the healing of the woman with the hemorrhage, for example, the woman symbolizes the church from which there is an issue of evil, and the physicians who have tried in vain to heal her represent the ineffectual clergy. If the church were to be cured of its ills, that would be a miracle indeed. As to the three persons raised from the dead, they stand for sinners who have been converted. Spiritual miracles, then, are proper and true; the mistake is the literal interpretation of the miracle stories. "I believe upon the Authority of the Fathers," writes Woolston, "that the Ministry of the Letter of the Old and New Testament is downright Antichristianism."[51]

After all the impious laughter has been stifled, the results of Woolston's work can be assessed. His arguments, for all their excesses, surely show that the proof from miracle is not without problems. Moreover, Woolston's program is much more threatening than Collins's: it is one thing to interpret OT prophecies allegorically; it is something else to deny the veracity of the biblical accounts. According to Woolston, literal miracles simply did not happen. This denial of the historicity of the miracles struck a responsive chord in an era when belief in the supernatural was evaporating, when the universe was believed to be ordered by Newton's law, and when physical phenomena were attributed to natural causes. At the same time, Woolston raised questions about the interpretation of miracles. His conclusion that they should be interpreted allegorically—like Collins's view of prophecy—hardly supplied proof for the truth of Christianity. Moreover, Woolston had uncovered evidence in the NT that suggests that proof was not the primary significance of miracle stories within the biblical record. Is the NT narrative to be reduced to bare facts? or, on the other hand, Do the miracles signify some symbolic or spiritual meaning? Can facts ascertained by human observation exercise judgment about the

50. Ibid., Discourse 6, p. 71.
51. Ibid., Discourse 5, p. 68.

truth of divine revelation? On what basis and in what way, if any, can the message of the NT be validated? In any case, Woolston, for all his tomfoolery, had presented a serious challenge to biblical orthodoxy, and he did not help matters by making believers look ridiculous in the process.

OTHER DEISTS:
ANNET, MORGAN, AND CHUBB

The deist movement continued to flourish in England until the middle of the century. Two or three additional representatives may be mentioned because of their work on the NT. In the aftermath of Woolston, the resurrection continued to be a hotly contested issue. Vigorous battles were fought in defense of the orthodox belief by scholars like Samuel Clarke and William Paley.[52] One of the most dramatic answers to Woolston was presented by Thomas Sherlock (1678–1761), Bishop of Bangor and formerly Master of Catherine Hall, Cambridge. Sherlock, couching his argument in the dramatic form of a courtroom scene, wrote *The Trial of the Witnesses of the Resurrection* (1729), a work of such enduring popularity that it continued in reprint for more than a hundred years.[53] In the mock trial, the counsel "representing" Woolston acts as prosecutor, and the counsel for the apostles as the defense. Two major charges are made against the apostles: the resurrection is a fraud, and the testimony in support of the resurrection is unreliable. The charges are answered, and after the summary of the issues by the judge, the jury renders the verdict: Not guilty!

Peter Annet (1693–1769)

Sherlock was in turn answered by Peter Annet, a schoolmaster who held a minor government post for a time. Late in life, like Woolston, he was sentenced to prison for blasphemy. In an attack on the OT, Annet had charged Moses with being an impostor. Earlier Annet had published *The Resurrection of Jesus Considered; in Answer to the Tryal of the Witnesses.* Annet did not write in his own name, instead attributing the book to a "Moral Philosopher." Although he answers Sherlock, Annet does not fully agree with Woolston. He says the idea that Jesus predicted his resurrection, although it is reported five times in the Gospels, is an invention of the evangelists, a charge proved by evidence he has detected in the resurrection narratives. The women, for instance, come to the tomb to anoint the body of Jesus without the slightest supposition that he will be alive.

52. See William Lane Craig, *The Historical Argument for the Resurrection of Jesus during the Deist Controversy* (Lewiston, N.Y.: Edwin Mellen Press, 1985), 303–17.
53. Bishop Sherlock, *The Trial of the Witnesses of the Resurrection of Christ: In Answer to the Objections of Mr. Woolston and Others* (New York: Lane & Scott, 1849).

Annet gives more careful attention to the biblical records than did either Woolston or Sherlock. In doing so, he notes a host of discrepancies in the Gospel accounts. The appearance to Mary Magdalene, for example, is variously described. In Matthew she is accompanied by the other Mary, while in John she is alone; in Matthew the appearance takes place on the way to the tomb, while in John it occurs at the sepulchre; in Matthew Jesus is touched, while in John he is not to be touched; in Matthew the risen Christ says he is going to Galilee, while in John he is going to the Father. If the risen Christ can walk through closed doors, why was it necessary for the stone to be rolled away? Why were the Emmaus pilgrims unable to recognize Jesus on the road but able to recognize him in the house? "Why did he thus play Hide-and-seek with them?"[54] Annet is particularly critical of Matthew's story of the guard at the tomb. The account is not found in any of the other Gospels, and leads to all sorts of questions. If the disciples did not expect the resurrection of Jesus, how could the priests and Pharisees have expected it? If the latter believed that Jesus predicted he would rise "after three days," what sense would it make to secure the tomb "until the third day" (Matt. 27:63-64)? Surely the Jewish leaders could come up with an explanation better than their story that the soldiers had fallen asleep. And why would these soldiers, if they had actually witnessed the power of God, be willing to be silenced for a handful of coins?

Annet argues in the mode of the deists. "Reason is my only Rule, and displaying Truth my only Aim."[55] God, he asserts, does not expect people to believe what is against evidence or reason. For example, in regard to the resurrection, people are required to believe the most incredible story on the basis of the flimsiest evidence. Addressing broader implications of the issue, Annet denies that faith can or should rest on provable fact. His purpose is "to convince the world that an Historical Faith is no Part of true and pure Religion, which is founded only on Truth and Purity. That it does not consist in Belief of any History, which, whether true or false, makes no Man wiser nor better."[56] What Annet means by "truth and purity" is not explained, but he seems to suggest that faith rests on an ethical understanding of religion, intuitively perceived. In denying that faith can be based on fact, Annet anticipates G. E. Lessing's argument that truths of history cannot establish the truth of faith.[57]

In the last part of his book, Annet gives attention to the question of

54. Peter Annet, *The Resurrection of Jesus Considered; in Answer to the Tryal of the Witnesses, By a Moral Philosopher* (London: Author, n.d.), 56.
55. Ibid., 10.
56. Ibid., 87.
57. See p. 168, below.

miracles in general. There he argues that evidence, no matter how clear or convincing, is unable to contradict the order of nature.

> Positive and presumptive Evidence, is of no Weight against the Reason and Nature of Things. Such Evidence should be rejected, rather than the Nature of Things should be reason'd against to support such Evidence.[58]

Because of the fixed pattern of this natural order, miracles are not possible. The order of nature functions according to the will of God, and since God is wise and reasonable, there is no need for any intervention or change in this order. Miracles, however, constitute a change in the will of God, but God's will, according to Annet, does not, indeed, cannot change. "As the will of God cannot change, neither can the Execution of his Power; which is directed by his Will."[59]

Whereas most of the deists aimed their arrows at the Gospels, Annet launched an attack against Paul. In *The History and Character of St. Paul,* Annet notes the discrepancies between the Pauline letters and the Acts of the Apostles. Acts, according to Annet, is more reliable, because Paul is not trustworthy. Evidence of the apostle's lack of credibility can be seen in his assertion that he could even curse an angel from heaven (Gal. 1:8). Annet thinks Paul is actually guilty of perjury, for the apostle claims that he did not confer with the Jerusalem apostles after his conversion, while the account in Acts 9:26-30 proves that he did. Perhaps, quips Annet, "the buffetings of Satan had beat all truth out of his head."[60] Captive to rationalism, Annet cannot appreciate Paul's penchant for paradox; the exhortation to "work out your own salvation . . . for it is God who is at work in you" (Phil. 2:12-13) is nothing but a flat contradiction. Although more reliable than the Pauline letters, the Acts of the Apostles is not without problems. Annet prints the three accounts of Paul's conversion in parallel columns and points out their inconsistencies. For example, in Acts 9:7 the companions of Paul remain standing, while in 26:14 they fall to the ground. Annet finds the report of Acts 19:12 to be ludicrous. He wonders "how long these aprons or handkerchiefs must have been with the holy Paul, to be thus impregnated with this healing quality," and if, after they had been used, they "resisted sweat, or could stand a lather."[61] Speculating on a question of historical criticism, Annet supposes that the author of the "we-sections" in Acts may have been Silas. He is convinced that Luke could not have been their author, nor could he have been the writer of the

---

58. Annet, *The Resurrection of Jesus Considered,* 92.
59. Ibid., 94.
60. Peter Annet, *The History and Character of St. Paul, examined: In a Letter to Theophilus, a Christian Friend* (London: F. Page, n.d.), 47.
61. Ibid., 88–89.

whole document, because the account at the end of his Gospel clearly contradicts the ascension story of Acts.

Thomas Morgan (d. 1743)

Paul suffered at the hands of Annet, but he was more kindly treated by Thomas Morgan. Morgan grew up in the poverty of a Welsh farmhouse but was provided an education through the generosity of a Dissenting minister. Ordained by the Presbyterians, he was dismissed because of his dangerous views and became a physician. From 1738 to 1740, Morgan published *The Moral Philosopher*, a multivolume work presented in the form of a dialogue between Pilalethes (Lover of Truth), a Christian deist, and Theophanes (Purveyor of Theophanies), a Christian Jew. The denominating of the two partners of the dialogue sets the tone for the whole piece: an argument in which deism prevails over false religion. In the main, Morgan follows deism's party line: opposition to hierarchy and ceremony with their attendant miracles; promotion of natural religion and reason in the service of a universal morality. As to miracles, Morgan says that "false Prophets, the most wicked Seducers, and even the Devil himself may work Miracles. And therefore Miracles alone consider'd can prove nothing at all."[62]

Morgan, however, adds a new theme to the deistic composition: a special, although not clearly articulated, understanding of history. He believes humanity originally followed the rational religion of nature, evidenced, for example, by the faith of Abraham, Noah, and Enoch. With Moses, who had learned senseless rituals from the Egyptians, came the false religion of law which included ceremonial as well as moral precepts. Christ restored the true religion and founded Christianity. "I take Christianity," writes Morgan, "to be that most complete and perfect Scheme of moral Truth and Righteousness, which was first preach'd to the World by Christ and his Apostles, and from them convey'd down to us under its own Evidence of immutable Rectitude, Wisdom and Reason."[63] Christ was the restorer of natural religion; he was not the Jewish Messiah.

This true religion of Christ is correctly interpreted by Paul. Indeed, the apostle is opposed to every vestige of Jewish ceremonialism. According to Morgan, Paul could understand law in three ways: as natural law (the law of wisdom and moral truth), as moral law (which was given by Moses and is holy and good), and as ceremonial law (which was also given by Moses but is hopelessly bad): "St. Paul preached a new doctrine, contrary to

---

62. Thomas Morgan, *The Moral Philosopher*, ed. Günter Gawlick, 3 vols. (Stuttgart-Bad Cannstatt: F. Frommann, 1969), 1.98.
    63. Ibid. 1.96–97.

Moses and the Prophets."[64] Thus, Morgan presents the apostle in the guise of an eighteenth-century deist: "The Truth is that St. Paul was the great Free-thinker of his Age, the bold and brave Defender of Reason against Authority, in Opposition to those who had set up a wretched Scheme of Superstition, Blindness and Slavery, contrary to all Reason and common Sense."[65]

Along with his interpretation of Paul, Morgan offers a rudimentary reconstruction of early Christianity. Just as Paul was against a false Judaism, so he opposed a Judaizing Christianity. At the Jerusalem council, Paul was able temporarily to persuade the leaders, but he could not win the majority of Jewish Christians to true religion. As the conflict in Antioch shows (Gal. 2:11-14), Paul preached a gospel different from that of Peter, a gospel "as opposite and inconsistent as Light and Darkness, Truth and Falsehood."[66] Thus, the history of early Christianity is the story of the conflict between Pauline and Petrine Christianity—a point to be taken up in the nineteenth century by the Tübingen school.[67] For Morgan, this early history presented an analogy for the church of his own day, a church in which the forces of reason and nature were in mortal conflict with the powers of hierarchy, ceremony, and superstition.

In the course of the dialogue, Morgan engages in biblical criticism. He argues that the Scriptures should be interpreted historically: "The Books of the New Testament, therefore, ought to be read critically, with an Allowance for Persons, Circumstances, and the situation of Things at that Time; and not taken in gross, as if every Thing contain'd in them had been at first infallibly inspired from God, and no Corruptions could have ever since happened to them."[68] Morgan, whose condemnation of the OT is reminiscent of Marcion, does not think Moses wrote anything beyond the primitive book of the law. Daniel, in Morgan's opinion, was the first biblical writer to mention the resurrection of the dead. Morgan believes the genealogies of Matthew and Luke contradict the doctrine of the virgin birth. The Apocalypse was written by the apostle John in the time of Nero; it is not only wrong in its predictions, it advocates the mistaken message of the Jewish Christians.

In regard to Hebrews, Morgan, reversing his earlier opinion, believes Paul cannot be the author because of the non-Pauline style. Moreover, Hebrews must have been written after the destruction of Jerusalem, because it assumes that the sacrificial system of the Jews has been abol-

---

64. Ibid. 1.41.
65. Ibid. 1.71.
66. Ibid. 1.377.
67. See pp. 258–69, below.
68. Morgan, *Moral Philosopher* 1.442.

ished. According to Morgan, Paul did not approve the doctrine of the atonement, although he used sacrificial language in a symbolic way because of the limitations of his readers. The whole idea of substitutionary sacrifice is theologically mistaken. How, asks the rationalist, could the sacrifice of an innocent person make satisfaction for the sin of the guilty? And if the idea were true, how could this satisfaction be transferred from one to the other? And why are the Jews blamed for the death of Jesus if it did so much good? The true meaning of the death of Jesus is found in deeper moral truth: Jesus demonstrates by his own martyrdom obedience to the true law of God; he illustrates God's gift of righteousness to all people; he gives an example of obedience for others; he exemplifies the necessity of trust in the God of nature and reason.

Thomas Chubb (1697–1747)

Also important for biblical study is Thomas Chubb, although he knew neither Latin nor Greek. Born near Salisbury, Chubb was a self-educated commoner who supported himself by manual labor—making gloves and candles. One of his early essays attracted the attention of Whiston, who introduced Chubb into the intellectual circles of London. After a time in the city, he returned to Salisbury and in 1731 published *A Discourse Concerning Reason,* a work which shows his allegiance to the deist cause. Chubb's main thesis is that reason is the sufficient guide in matters of religion. This universal human reason has not been impaired by a primal fall of humanity, for how would a rational Creator expect people to do what they could not do? If revelation is needed to overcome human limitations, then this revelation must have been given equally to all, for "every man has the divine law written upon his heart."[69] Although he rejects special revelation, Chubb does not totally oppose the idea of revealed truth. However, any claim to revelation must be attested: in its internal character (as worthy of God), in its external evidence (as coming from God), and in its content (as totally in harmony with reason). Chubb claims that "all obligations arising from revelation, are *originally* founded in reason."[70]

In studying the Bible, Chubb offers a bold venture into historical-critical method.[71] He believes biblical manuscripts need to be collected and used critically; he believes the question of the authorship of the biblical books should be answered on the basis of external and internal evidence; he

69. Thomas Chubb, *A Discourse Concerning Reason* (1731; reprint, New York and London: Garland, 1978), 15.

70. Ibid., 29.

71. See T. L. Bushell, *The Sage of Salisbury: Thomas Chubb 1679-1747* (New York: Philosophical Library, 1967), 109–28.

believes the transmission of documents should be carefully analyzed. Adopting this sort of approach, Chubb turned his attention to the written sources of early Christianity. He noted that all four Gospels were originally anonymous, so that the authorship of each should be recognized as uncertain. Consequently, Chubb was one of the first Enlightenment scholars to question the authenticity of the Gospels, an authenticity that was virtually axiomatic throughout the eighteenth century.

As to his own opinion, Chubb apparently thought that Mark was the oldest Gospel and that the other evangelists used it as a source. The Gospel of Mark, however, rested on oral tradition and made use of information that was second- or third-hand. None of the Gospel writers, in Chubb's opinion, was supernaturally inspired, and they were all deficient as writers of history. Although they did not intend to deceive, the evangelists were heavily biased in favor of Jesus, their hero. In investigating the transmission of the NT documents, Chubb notes that the original writers did not suppose they were writing Scripture. The collection of these documents into a fixed and official canon did not occur until relatively late— the third century. Moreover, the presence of textual variants in the manuscripts proves that the doctrine of biblical infallibility is mistaken.

Anticipating later developments, Chubb insisted that the life of Jesus should be studied historically.[72] The birth of Jesus, in Chubb's opinion, is largely a mystery. Mark says nothing about it, and discrepancies between the accounts of Matthew and Luke indicate that the stories are legendary. The notion of the supernatural birth of Jesus has been borrowed from pagan myths about the origin of the gods, and christological ideas, such as John's presentation of Jesus as the Logos, arose as Christianity ventured into the Hellenistic world. According to Chubb, the humanity of Jesus is to be affirmed without qualification. Jesus, he says, "was born, was nurtured and brought up . . . was subject to the same wants and infirmities, lived and died, like all other men."[73] In Chubb's reconstruction, Jesus was a prophet who grew up in the hill country of Galilee and preached a simple message among the poor. Yet Jesus was gifted with an exceptional power of imagination. "In fact," comments Chubb's interpreter, T. L. Bushell, "so unerring were the imagination and the understanding of Jesus and so faultless the revelatory process of God to him that the gospel may justifiably be deemed a kind of verbal embodiment of the Law of Nature."[74] In effect, Chubb presents Jesus as a sort of first-century Palestinian deist, garbed in the seamless robe of reason and natural religion.

Although Chubb resonated to the teachings of Jesus, he believed many

72. Ibid., 129–46.
73. Cited in ibid., 133.
74. Ibid., 138.

of the early Christian doctrines about Christ to be distracting and that responsibility for the first phase of this deviation must be laid at the feet of Paul. Among other theological aberrations, Chubb found the doctrine of the atonement particularly offensive. The belief "that Christ hath by his sufferings and death made satisfaction to God for the sins of the world, and thereby merited the sinner discharged from condemnation, this doctrine Christ did not preach; and therefore it cannot be any part of his gospel."[75] Similarly, Chubb thinks the doctrine of original sin should be abandoned: "sin is a *moral* and not a natural evil."[76] With typical deist disdain for the ceremonial, Chubb argues that observance of the sacraments is a matter of choice and is of little import in comparison with moral duties.[77] Chubb finds the doctrine of the Trinity to be unintelligible and in danger of objectifying God. The idea of apostolic succession is a sheer fancy of the hierarchy, for "when the Apostles of our Lord died, the Apostolick office died with them."[78]

SUMMARY

The deists made a major impact on the history of NT research,[79] although the assessment of their contribution must be mixed. For one thing, the deists were not bona fide biblical scholars. With the exception of a few insights from Chubb and Morgan—many of which could have been gleaned from the research of scholars like Grotius and Simon—the work of the deists could have been accomplished by any bright skeptic with the aid of a King James Bible. Nevertheless, the deists raised a host of questions important for biblical research: How are the miracles and the supernatural to be understood? If they are to be discredited, what is the result for the reliability and historicity of the biblical record? If the proof from prophecy and miracle is no longer valid, how is the truth of Christianity to be established? What constitutes proof, and is proof of any sort—for example, historical reliability—the proper ground for faith? The deists also raised a variety of historical-critical issues: the relation of NT and OT; the authorship and order of the Gospels, Jesus versus Paul, the history of early Christianity. Questions like these would continue to concern NT scholars for generations to come.

The deists viewed religion and the Bible from the perspective of their larger perception of reality. Following the best intellects of the time, they

75. Thomas Chubb, *The True Gospel of Jesus Christ Asserted* (London: T. Cox, 1738), 36.
76. Quoted in Bushell, *Sage of Salisbury,* 104.
77. Thomas Chubb, *The Comparative Excellence and Obligation of Moral and Positive Duties, 1730* (New York and London: Garland, 1978).
78. Chubb, *True Gospel,* 82.
79. See Reventlow, *Authority of the Bible,* 289–414.

had adopted the view that the universe was ordered by natural law, and that the meaning and truth of this cosmic order could be appropriated by rational empiricism. The resulting natural theology and rationalistic hermeneutic, however, collided with traditional Christianity and, in particular, with the idea of special revelation. This collision was of crucial significance for the study of the Bible, because special revelation belonged to the essence of the biblical religion. The Scriptures affirmed the particularity of God's revelation in the history of Israel and God's unique self-disclosure in Jesus Christ and, above all, in the conviction that the Bible was itself a vehicle of special revelation. To be sure, some of the deists attempted to salvage remnants of biblical religion, for instance, the notion that Jesus was a rational teacher of universal morality, or that Paul was an advocate of natural law. On the basis of concessions of this sort, the study of the NT could survive as a discipline with antiquarian interest. In the main, however, the acceptance of deism meant the death of biblical religion. Biblical theologians, in response, were required to address the problems of revelation and authority, and, at the same time, the larger question of how the biblical faith relates to a comprehensive ontology.

The method of the deists, too, deserves a mixed review. On the one hand, the excessive character of their attack, supported by ridicule and sarcasm, paved the way for more moderate critics. On the other hand, their radicalism encouraged a counterattack that impeded progress in the study of the Scriptures. Actually, the self-confident deists imagined they rode the rising crest of the future, supposing orthodox biblical religion was about to be washed away. Little did they suspect that England would soon be swept by the mighty current of the Wesleyan revival—a movement which would show that the religion of the heart could overwhelm the religion of the head. The deists did not anticipate, either, that their own demise would be tolled by one who seemed to revel in their own method—David Hume, the master of skepticism. Hume, too, found the miracles incredible and orthodox religion bankrupt. But for Hume, the deists—with their confidence in human good, their belief in the rationality of the natural order, their inability to explain why a religion which was thought to be so natural was so scarce—were not skeptical enough. Above all, they had not been adequately skeptical about their most fundamental assumption—the universal validity of human reason for establishing theological truth. Yet deism, which was about to be laid to rest in England, except for a momentary revival in the skepticism of Gibbon and Paine, would be resurrected again in Germany. There, later in the century, it would create a conflict which would make enemies of two of the most creative minds in the history of biblical research—G. E. Lessing and J. S. Semler.

3

Sensitive to the Spirit:
The Pietists

The scene in central Europe in the early eighteenth century was vastly different from the political and religious landscape of England. Germany did not exist as a unified nation. Instead, a variety of small kingdoms and duchies, with loose connection to the vestiges of the old Holy Roman Empire, dotted the map. Ruled by princes and electors, these small states followed the religious principle of the Peace of Augsburg (1555)—*cuius regio, eius religio*. In other words, the religion of the realm was the religion of the ruler. This meant that most of the northern states were Lutheran. Saxony, in the very heart of the Lutheran territory, became a center of Lutheran strength. Brandenburg-Prussia was to emerge later in the century as the most powerful of the German states, under the stern leadership of Frederick William I (1713–40) and Frederick II (Frederick the Great) (1740–86).

In the Lutheran and Reformed countries, religion had been shaped into the system of Protestant orthodoxy. The dynamic of Luther's revolt had crystallized into an immutable pattern. In the face of the Catholic Tridentine doctrine that tradition could stand on equal footing with the Bible, Protestant scholars of the seventeenth century had reaffirmed the principle of *sola scriptura*. Their understanding of Scripture,[1] however, was different from Luther's. For him, the Bible was the word of God; for them, the words of the Bible were the words of God. The very words of the text were given by the dictation of the Holy Spirit and were written down with unfailing accuracy by God's penmen. Every word and every letter, including the tiny vowel points of the Hebrew text, had been accurately put in place by the hand of God. Every part of the Bible—OT and NT, every-

---

1. See Jack B. Rogers and Donald K. McKim, *The Authority and Interpretation of the Bible: An Historical Approach* (San Francisco: Harper & Row, 1979), 147–99.

thing from Genesis to Revelation—was equally expressive of the inspired revelation. The information of the Bible on all subjects, including creation and history, was unquestionably correct. The Scriptures were viewed as a system of divine dogma, authoritative in all areas of thought and practice. Although the Bible recorded history, it was not viewed as a historical document, that is, it was not seen as a collection of writings that reflected the variety and development of human life and culture.

At first glance, then, this biblical scholasticism might seem to have been an impediment to the progress of NT research. The orthodox, to be sure, affirmed a doctrine of verbal inspiration and infallibility, and a view of biblical authority that stood in defiance of the secularism and new science of the Enlightenment. Nevertheless, the scholastic concern with the words of the text—particularly of the Hebrew and Greek originals—encouraged the study of linguistics; and the stress on the inspiration of the original writings gave impetus to text-critical investigation. Moreover, in spite of their aversion to modern skepticism, the Protestant scholastics were influenced by Enlightenment ideas. In their defense of the infallibility of Scripture, for example, they made extensive use of reason, arguing at length that the Bible contained no contradictions. Actually, the scholastics were inclined to favor reason over faith and to understand faith as intellectual assent to revealed doctrines. Like the confident deists, the orthodox assumed that they could know the truth about God, for it had been clearly disclosed in words which they could read and understand. Moreover, this truth was available to the masses, since, in contrast to the decision of the Council of Trent, the Protestants advocated lay reading of the Bible. Above all, the Protestant scholastics, with their high doctrine of biblical authority, considered serious study of the Bible to be the essential duty of the theological enterprise.

BEGINNINGS OF THE PIETIST MOVEMENT:
PHILIP JAKOB SPENER (1635–1705)

The Pietists revolted against the orthodoxy of Protestant scholasticism.[2] In the Pietist view, the orthodox had squeezed all the vitality out of the biblical message.[3] The Bible, with its wonder at the mysterious brooding of the Spirit, its excitement in the pneumatic gifts, its enthusiasm for the

2. The historical relation of Pietism to the Reformation and Protestant orthodoxy is a matter of debate; see Johannes Wallmann, "Pietismus und Orthodoxie: Überlegungen und Fragen zur Pietismusforschung," in *Zur Neueren Pietismusforschung*, ed. Martin Greschat (Darmstadt: Wissenschaftliche Buchgesellschaft, 1977), 53–81. For a history of the relationship, see Friedrich Wilhelm Kantzenbach, *Orthodoxie und Pietismus* (Gütersloh: G. Mohn, 1966).

3. For summaries of the Pietist view of the Bible, see Dale W. Brown, *Understanding Pietism* (Grand Rapids: Wm. B. Eerdmans, 1978), 64–82; Hans Stroh, "Hermeneutik im Pietismus," *Zeitschrift für Theologie und Kirche* 77 (1977): 38–57.

fruits of love, joy, and peace should not be reduced to arid dogma. For the orthodox, the Bible contained a precise system of doctrine; for the Pietists, it presented the way to life and salvation.[4] This practical concern had a compelling appeal to a Europe which had been devastated and demoralized by the ravages of the Thirty Years' War.

The father of German Pietism was Philip Jakob Spener.[5] Born near Strasbourg, Spener was deeply influenced by the personal piety of his godmother. As a youth, he read widely, especially the Bible and devotional works. At sixteen, Spener entered the University of Strasbourg, where he studied history, philosophy, and languages. He later turned to theology and read extensively in the works of Luther. After completing his theological studies, Spener was ordained to the Lutheran ministry. In 1666, he was called to Frankfurt am Main as senior minister. There he made the acquaintance of Leibnitz, with whom he came to share sympathy for the cause of Christian unity. In 1670, Spener began to sponsor meetings in his home for prayer and Bible study; the small devotional conventicles were called *collegia pietatis*. After twenty years in Frankfurt, Spener moved to Dresden where he served as chaplain to the Elector of Saxony. There he met and befriended A. H. Francke. In 1691, Spener left Dresden for Berlin to become a member of the Lutheran consistory. Spener was noted as a popular and effective preacher. Late in life, he served as sponsor at the baptism of Count von Zinzendorf, the founder of the Moravian Brethren.

Spener was not a systematic theologian but a pastor committed to Christianity as a way of life. Instead of the orthodoxy of Protestant scholasticism, he favored the simple piety of the apostles. He accepted the orthodox view of the inspiration of the Scriptures but stressed the content of the biblical message in its historical context. He considered the Lutheran confessions to be witnesses to faith rather than rigid rules of religion. He rejected the Calvinistic belief in predestination but favored the Reformed view of the Eucharist. Lutherans and Reformed Christians, he thought, should overlook their differences in order to cooperate against the common enemy of Rome.

Spener's major work was *Pia Desideria* (1675).[6] Originally designed as an introduction to a new edition of the devotional classic *True Christianity* by John Arndt (1555–1621), Spener's three-part work was published separately. In the first part, Spener bewails the present condition of society and

4. See Martin Greschat, "Orthodoxie und Pietismus: Einleitung," in *Orthodoxie und Pietismus*, ed. Martin Greschat (Stuttgart: W. Kohlhammer, 1982), 7–35.

5. For a comprehensive presentation of the life and work of Spener, see Johannes Wallmann, *Philipp Jakob Spener und die Anfänge des Pietismus* (Tübingen: J.C.B. Mohr, 1970).

6. Philip Jacob Spener, *Pia Desideria*, trans. T. G. Tappert (Philadelphia: Fortress Press, 1964), 46. For a theological analysis of this work, see Martin Schmidt, *Wiedergeburt und neuer Mensch: Gesammelte Studien zur Geschichte des Pietismus* (Witten: Luther-Verlag, 1969), 129–68.

the church. He notes that civil officials, common people, and even the clergy are guilty of sin and corruption. He criticizes preachers who "without the working of the Holy Spirit, have learned something of the letter of the Scriptures, have comprehended and assented to true doctrine, and have even known how to preach it to others, but they are altogether unacquainted with the true, heavenly light and the life of faith." In the second part, Spener, like an inspired prophet, declares that conditions within the church can be improved. He believes the Scriptures promise better things and asserts that the same Spirit that vitalized the early church is "neither less able nor less active today to accomplish the work of sanctification in us."[7]

In the third part of the *Pia Desideria*, Spener makes specific proposals for reform. First and foremost, serious attention must be given to the study of the Bible.

> If there is to be any good in us, it must be brought about by God. To this end the Word of God is the powerful means, since faith must be enkindled through the gospel, and the law provides the rules for good works and many wonderful impulses to attain them. The more at home the Word of God is among us, the more we shall bring about faith and its fruits.[8]

The Bible must be studied at home, studied in special groups, and extensively read in public worship. Spener's other proposals include increased participation in the life of the church by the laity; recognition that Christianity requires practice as well as belief; attention to the education of the clergy; and more stress on preaching. In regard to the education of pastors, Spener argues that they must be trained in universities and schools that should be recognized as "workshops of the Holy Spirit rather than places of worldliness and indeed of the devils of ambition, tippling, carousing, and brawling." In the selection of candidates for the ministry, Spener is convinced that "a young man who fervently loves God, although adorned with limited gifts, will be more useful to the church of God with his meager talent and academic achievement than a vain and worldly fool with double doctor's degrees who is very clever but has not been taught by God."[9]

In spite of this implicit anti-intellectualism, Spener advocated thoughtful interpretation of the Scriptures.[10] His stress on the simplicity of the biblical message encouraged him to seek the original, literal meaning. He also recommended the Reformation principle of interpreting Scripture by Scripture. Spener believed the Bible should be viewed as a whole, but he placed primary emphasis on the message of the NT. In the process of

---

7. Spener, *Pia Desideria*, 46, 85.
8. Ibid., 87.
9. Ibid., 103, 108.
10. See Martin Schmidt, "Philipp Jacob Spener und die Bibel," in *Pietismus und Bibel*, ed. Kurt Aland (Witten: Luther-Verlag, 1970), 9–58.

interpretation, Spener gave attention to the Greek text and made use of the philological and exegetical tools which were available, for example, in the work of Grotius. Historical research was employed in the service of biblical theology, for, as Schmidt says, Spener "combined Reformation dogmatical biblical understanding of the NT with modern historicizing."[11]

In 1697, after having preached some fifty sermons on the subject, Spener published a commentary on the Epistle to the Galatians. Although there he stressed the inspiration of the epistle, for Spener, persons—the biblical authors—are more inspired than words. In the process of exegesis, Spener begins with an explanation of terms, then moves on to doctrine, and finally presents the application of the biblical message to life. Praxis is always more important than doctrine. The Epistle to the Galatians, he argues, must be interpreted in its historical situation. Consequently the exegete must understand that Paul is combatting false teachers who have come into the church demanding observance of the Jewish law. Spener is especially interested in the call of Paul; and for Spener, highlights in the epistle are 5:22 (the fruit of the spirit) and 6:15 (the new creation). He also emphasizes the importance of spiritual unity with Christ. The fact that Paul signed the letter is, for Spener, proof of its authenticity.

In studying the Scriptures, Spener found certain biblical themes to be of major importance. He thought the idea of promise and fulfillment was a key to understanding the message of Scripture. God's promises were fulfilled in history by the response of people. Also significant was the idea of the new birth. This involved a spiritual experience of believers whereby they became "participants of the divine nature" (2 Pet. 1:4). Spener understood this to be a gift of God through Christ, an ongoing process with mystical overtones that could not be fully explained. Yet the new birth, with all its cryptic meaning, was publicly manifest in the practicing life of love. Most important, Spener advocated a dynamic biblical theology in place of scholastic dogmatics. Within that biblical theology, spirit was closely related to the word.

PRINCIPLES OF INTERPRETATION:
AUGUST HERMANN FRANCKE (1663–1727)

More important for NT research was Spener's friend, August Hermann Francke.[12] Born in Lübeck, Francke was educated at Erfurt and Kiel. In

---

11. Ibid., 24.

12. For concise accounts of Francke's life and work, see Ernst Bunke, *August Hermann Francke: Der Mann des Glaubens und der Liebe*, 2d ed. (Giessen and Basel: Brunnen, 1960); Gary R. Sattler, ed., *God's Glory, Neighbor's Good: A Brief Introduction to the Life and Writings of August Hermann Francke* (Chicago: Covenant, 1982); Johannes Wallmann, *Der Pietismus* (Göttingen: Vandenhoeck & Ruprecht, 1990), 59–79.

1684, he entered the University of Leipzig, which at the time was a bastion of Lutheran orthodoxy. There Francke participated in the *collegium philo-biblicum,* a group of faculty and students who met for study of the Bible in the original languages. Although Francke found this experience meaningful, he was generally dissatisfied with his life in Leipzig. Later he reflected,

> Since I had studied theology for about seven years and I knew indeed what our basic principle was, how to uphold it, what the opponents objected against it, and I had read the Scripture through and through again, indeed I was not lacking in the other practical books, but since all this was grasped by me only in my reason and in my memory, and since the word of God was not in my case transformed into life, but I had strangled the living seed of the Word of God and allowed it to be unfruitful, therefore, I had to make as it were a new beginning in order to become a Christian.[13]

Francke's Conversion and Religious Thought

After a lengthy struggle, Francke's hope was finally fulfilled. He left Leipzig for Lüneburg, where he engaged in exegetical studies. While there he was invited to preach and chose as his text John 20:31: "But these are written so that you may come to believe that Jesus is the Messiah, the Son of God, and that through believing you may have life in his name." As he meditated on the text, Francke confessed in despair that he did not himself possess the sort of faith he hoped to elicit from his hearers. On the Saturday evening, before he was to preach, Francke fell to his knees and cried out to God.

> He immediately heard me. My doubt vanished as quickly as one turns one's hand; I was assured in my heart of the grace of God in Christ Jesus and I knew God not only as God but as my Father. All sadness and unrest of my heart was taken away at once, and I was immediately overwhelmed as with a stream of joy so that with full joy I praised and gave honor to God who had shown me such great grace. I arose a completely different person from the one who had knelt down.[14]

This conversion experience was foundational for the rest of Francke's life. Later he was to say, "True faith is a divine work in us, which transforms us and bestows upon us the new birth from God, which kills the old Adam, and fashions us into a new man who is entirely different in heart, soul, mind, and in all his powers."[15] For Francke, conversion was primarily a gift

13. "August Hermann Franckes Lebenslauf," in August Hermann Francke, *Werke in Auswahl,* ed. Erhard Peschke (Berlin: Evangelische Verlagsanstalt, 1969), 24.
14. August Hermann Francke, "From the Autobiography, 1692," in *Pietists: Selected Writings,* ed. Peter C. Erb (New York: Paulist Press, 1983), 105.
15. Cited in F. Ernest Stoeffler, *German Pietism during the Eighteenth Century* (Leiden: E. J. Brill, 1973), 8.

of God, yet the gift had to be received by humans. The process of reception demanded repentance and obedience, and repentance necessitated a soul-rending inner struggle. Moreover, conversion was not merely a matter of righteous living, it was also to become significant for the study of the Bible.

In 1689, Francke returned to Leipzig where he lectured under the auspices of the *collegium*. Although his moving messages drew large crowds, Francke's antipathy to the spirit of the Enlightenment[16] and his Pietist convictions soon brought him under the censure of the university authorities. Francke was dismissed from Leipzig, but with the support of Spener he was granted a post at the University of Halle. In Halle, Francke also served as a pastor of various churches and eventually became the spiritual leader of the entire community. He founded schools for the poor and an orphanage and, in time, became the leader of the educational system of Halle, from the elementary level through the university. The classics and other disciplines were studied, but the Bible was the center of the curriculum, and Pietistic discipline was rigorously enforced.

Francke and the Pietists of Halle believed the whole Bible to be important; the OT and NT were fully inspired by the Holy Spirit.[17] As Emanuel Hirsch has written, "Pietistic theology has placed the Scripture so firmly in the center as the source and origin of all Christian knowledge, all personal piety, and all Christian preaching, that it must always be the main object of theological instruction and the main content of all theological formation."[18] Christ is the center and hermeneutical key to the understanding of the Old Testament as well as the New. Indeed, the purpose of biblical study is to lead to faith in Christ, a faith which effects salvation. The Bible contains two kinds of inspired doctrine: law and gospel. The law presents God's demands and brings people to the consciousness of sin. The gospel is the message of the grace of God which leads people to saving faith in Christ. The two are found in both the OT and NT and are not in conflict. After being saved by response to the gospel, people continue to be shown the way of obedience by the law. The NT, as witness to law and gospel, is clearer than the OT and should be studied first.

As the reformers had urged, every text of the Bible has one meaning—the meaning intended by the Spirit. For Francke and his friends, the

---

16. See Friedrich de Boor, "Erfahrung gegen Vernuft: Das Bekehrungserlebnis A. H. Franckes als Grundlage für den Kampf des Hallischen Pietismus gegen die Aufklärung," in *Der Pietismus in Gestalten und Wirkungen: Martin Schmidt zum 65. Geburtstag*, ed. H. Bornkamm, F. Heyer, and A. Schindler (Bielefeld: Luther-Verlag, 1975), 120–38.

17. For a comprehensive survey of Francke's understanding and use of the Bible, see Erhard Peschke, *Studien zur Theologie August Hermann Franckes*, 2 vols. (Berlin: Evangelische Verlagsanstalt, 1966), 2.13–126.

18. Emanuel Hirsch, *Geschichte der neuern evangelischen Theologie*, 5 vols. (Gütersloh: C. Bertelsmann, 1951), 2.163.

spiritual meaning constitutes not a different sense of Scripture alongside other meanings, but the true sense of Scripture, detected in the words of Scripture. In the search for this true meaning, faith is more important than reason. For example, one can only understand the meaning of the mystery of the cross if one's eyes are opened like those of the blind man of Luke 18:35-43.[19] The true student of the Bible approaches it with childlike simplicity and in a spirit of prayer and devotion. In this way, the practical usefulness of the Scriptures can be discerned. The message of the Bible should be easily available for all to read and understand, and, to this end, Francke published a revision of Luther's German Bible in 1712. In the minds of many, however, Luther's version had attained a sacredness of its own, and Francke's translation was therefore severely criticized. He responded that the Bible needed to be rendered into the speech of contemporary times. Although he believed the Scriptures should be available to the common folk in their own language, Francke's translation was based on scholarly research. He did not, for example, base his translation simply on the Received Text but made use of John Fell's critical edition. With the support of the wealthy C. H. von Canstein, Francke established a biblical institute at Halle (Cansteinischen Bibelanstalt), which by the end of the century had distributed more than two million copies of the Bible.

Francke's Method of Biblical Interpretation

In 1693, Francke published a student handbook on exegetical method, *Manuductio ad lectionem scripturae sacrae.*[20] According to this work, the major goal in interpretation of the Bible is to distinguish between the husk and the kernel, the letter and the spirit. The husk consists of textual matters and historical details; the kernel is the very heart of the biblical message. Actually, Francke's metaphor may be ill chosen, for he does not intend to suggest that the letter is unimportant. Rather, the letter must be understood in order to comprehend the spirit. The first part of Francke's handbook, therefore, presents the methods for finding the meaning of the letter (*sensus litterae*). The interpreter must begin with the grammatical reading (*lectio grammatica*) of the text. Here Francke insists that exegetes must master the biblical languages: Hebrew, Chaldee (Aramaic), and Greek. The writings of the rabbis are helpful in understanding the biblical idiom, although Francke says, "I would caution the reader against filling

19. See Francke's sermon, "The Mystery of the Cross," in Sattler, *God's Glory, Neighbor's Good,* 115–31.

20. Eng. trans.: Augustus Herman Frank, *A Guide to the Reading and Study of the Holy Scriptures,* trans. William Jaques (Philadelphia: D. Hogan, 1823).

his mind with Judaical absurdities."[21] As to learning Greek grammar, Francke proposes a method revolutionary for his time: the student need not start with the classics, nor even with the study of grammar, but with the NT itself. Thus, Francke advocates a sort of inductive method whereby the student learns vocabulary and syntax by an analysis of the Greek NT. At the same time, the interpreter is to make use of the best linguistic and grammatical tools available. A word-for-word translation, however, will not adequately render the biblical idiom.

After attending to the grammatical reading, the interpreter turns next to the historical meaning (*lectio historica*) of the Bible. This approach includes ascertaining the setting and occasion of the various biblical books. As well as recognizing the historical setting, the exegete must also master the content of the biblical books and know where in Scripture particular subjects are addressed. The historical reading, however, is never an end in itself, for "the Letter is examined only for the sake of the Spirit of the Sacred Oracles."[22] After the historical reading, the interpreter should engage in an analytical investigation (*lectio analytica*) of the text. First, one should classify the biblical books according to their literary type (what scholars later were to describe as "genre"), determining whether they are doctrinal, historical, or prophetic. In regard to the analytical reading, Francke is anxious to avoid the impression that the biblical writers followed the ways of worldly wisdom: "This branch of reading is not prescribed, on the supposition that the Sacred Penmen affected to compose and arrange their subjects, according to the rules of Logic, for it were absurd to entertain so unworthy an idea of men divinely inspired."[23]

After the various books of the Bible are classified according to literary type, their content is further analyzed into component parts. For example, the epistles (which are generally classified as doctrinal) are usually structured in four parts: exordium, doctrinal section, hortatory section, and conclusion. To analyze a doctrinal text, Francke suggests some helpful rules, such as (1) determine how the particular passage relates to the argument of the whole book; (2) note how the text is related to the immediate context; and (3) analyze the basic proposition of the argument. Francke notes that doctrinal arguments are frequently expressed in polemical contexts. Therefore, to understand the argument, the interpreter has to reconstruct the opponents' position which the argument is designed to answer. In other words, theological understanding requires historical investigation.

21. Ibid., 42.
22. Ibid., 50.
23. Ibid., 53.

In the second main part of the handbook, Francke presents methods for discerning the spiritual meaning of the Bible. First, the interpreter must engage in an expository reading (*lectio exegetica*) of the text. In this reading, the goal is to find out what the Spirit purports to say—what Francke understands as the literal (*sensus literalis*) of the text. Thus, the literal sense is different from the sense of the letter that Francke discussed in the first part of the handbook. The sense of the letter has to do with details of grammar and history; the literal sense is the one true, spiritual meaning of the text. "It is a universal axiom, that—One Word or Sentence having respect to one and the same subject has but one Literal Sense."[24] In attempting to discover what the Spirit intends to reveal, the interpreter is aided by the Protestant principle of interpreting Scripture by Scripture. Parallel texts shed light on each other, for the Bible is a harmonious unity. Francke follows this method in his own preaching, taking texts from all over the Bible to support his message. In doing exposition, the interpreter needs to be reminded that the Scriptures largely interpret themselves, so that exegetical aids must be chosen with care.

> We must therefore be careful to select such Commentaries as are most agreeable to the object we have in view; and especially such as evidence the illumination of that Spirit who speaks in the Sacred Oracles. This is essential; for if we cannot understand the Scriptures, without the aid of the divine Spirit who dictated them; is it possible to derive assistance from a Commentator who has presumed to judge spiritual things, while he himself is carnal?[25]

After the expository reading, the student must next attend to the doctrinal reading (*lectio dogmatica*) of the text. By this reading the interpreter attempts to apprehend those truths through which a saving knowledge of the nature and will of God is attained. At the heart of the biblical message is Jesus Christ.[26] Francke says:

> Since Jesus is the very *Soul* of Scripture and the Way by which we have access to the Father, he who, in Doctrinal Reading, does not fix his eyes on Him, must read in vain. Truth and Life are attainable only through this *Way*. To know Christ and the doctrines concerning Christ, only in theory, is not the Soul of Scripture; it is faith in Him, and that imitation of Him which flows from faith.[27]

---

24. Ibid., 66.
25. Ibid., 81.
26. Erhard Peschke, "August Hermann Francke und die Bibel: Studien zur Entwicklung seiner Hermeneutik," in *Pietismus und Bibel*, 67: "The goal of doctrinal reading is Christ as the heart of the scriptures and the way of life." See Franke, "Christus der Kern Heiliger Schrift, 1702," in *Werke in Auswahl*, 232–48.
27. Frank, *Guide to the Reading and Study of the Holy Scriptures,* 91.

This kind of understanding requires a spiritual perspective. According to Francke—and in opposition to the main trend of Enlightenment research—one cannot understand Scripture in the way one understands any other book. The Bible should not be read in the same way a scholar reads Aristotle. Related to the doctrinal meaning is the inferential meaning (*lectio porismatica*) of the text. By this, Francke means the quest for meanings that are not immediately apparent to the literal reading of the text but may be inferred. Again, the use of parallel passages by which the further meaning can be deduced is encouraged. Here Francke recommends applying biblical teaching directly to the modern situation without notice of the gap between one world and the other. He supposes, for instance, that Paul's advice to Timothy is immediately applicable to the conduct of the ministry in eighteenth-century Europe.

Finally, Francke recommends the practical reading (*lectio practica*) of the text. The student must seek to discover how the Scripture is applied to matters of faith and life. Normally, the simplest application is the most profitable. One should begin with the clearest books and passages and move on to those which are more complex. This sort of practical exegesis should be practiced throughout life with the help of God's grace, constantly aided by prayer and meditation. In other writings, Francke attends to the spiritual or mystical sense (*sensus spiritualis, sensus mysticus*)—that deeper meaning of Scripture discerned beyond the meaning of the word and through the literal meaning by insight provided through the experience of the Spirit.[28] In any case, this spiritual or mystical sense cannot differ from the one literal meaning of the text.

A sample of Francke's biblical criticism can be seen in his "An Analytical Introduction to St. Paul's Epistle to the Colossians."[29] As to the historical occasion, Francke notes that the Colossians had been converted by Epaphras. Since the founding of the church, Judaizers have invaded the Colossian congregation. Epaphras has brought word of the problem to Paul, who is in prison, and encouraged him to write the letter. The purpose of the epistle is the confirmation of the faith of the Colossians in face of the Judaizing error. The tone of the letter is, therefore, polemical. Paul's approach, like Francke's own, is positive: supporting faith rather than engaging in controversy. Finally, Francke presents the structure of the letter and sums up his exegetical results in a paraphrase of the whole epistle.

At various points in his handbook, Francke emphasizes the importance of the *Affekte* (the emotions or feelings). This important hermeneutical

---

28. See Peschke, *Theologie A. H. Franckes* 2.71–89.
29. Frank, *Guide to the Reading and Study of the Holy Scriptures*, 161–77.

concept is more fully developed in his "Treatise on the Affections."[30] In this treatise, Francke argues that sensitivity to feelings and emotions is essential to proper interpretation, because the feelings and emotions were involved in the writing of Scripture. As he says, "The Holy Spirit kindled sacred Affections in the Writers' Souls."[31] Since there is a close connection between the inner feelings and the outward expression of speech, the experience of the Spirit could be communicated through the particular words of the biblical authors. Francke believes there are four types of feelings or affections: those of animals, those of carnal humans, those of spiritual persons, and those that belong to God. The latter two are closely related, for the Spirit of God gives the spiritual affections to believing Christians. Since the spiritual affections are necessary to understand the spiritual experience of the biblical writers, only those who have the Spirit are able to understand the Scriptures. This is the source of the Pietist belief that only born-again Christians are able to interpret the Bible properly. To make the case, Pietists cite texts like Mark 4:11, in which those on the outside are said to be unable to understand the parables, and 1 Cor. 2:14, in which those who do not have the Spirit are said to be unable to understand the gifts of the Spirit. In spite of this exegetical imperialism, Francke's presentation of the method of interpretation—especially the first part of his manual—made a significant contribution to NT research.

TEXT CRITICISM AND EXEGESIS:
J. A. BENGEL (1687–1752)

Johann Albrecht Bengel was the most important biblical scholar among the Pietists.[32] Compared with some Pietists, Bengel was a moderate. He was not given to spiritual enthusiasm, and his ordered view of religion was reminiscent of Protestant scholasticism. Bengel did not have direct connection with the Pietists of Halle but spent his lifetime in Württemberg, where he remained loyal to the established church. During this period, Württemberg suffered from a variety of misfortunes: invasion by the French and a series of luxury-loving, ineffective dukes. In this setting, Bengel is sometimes described as the father of Swabian Pietism, but, in actuality, the troubled soil of Württemberg had produced Pietists before he appeared on the scene.[33] Born near Stuttgart, Bengel was the son of a

30. Ibid., 123–48.
31. Ibid., 129.
32. For summaries of Bengel's life and work, see Werner Hehl, *Johann Albrecht Bengel: Leben und Werk* (Stuttgart: Quell, 1987); and Gottfried Mälzer, *Johann Albrecht Bengel: Leben und Werk* (Stuttgart: Calwer, 1970).
33. See Stoeffler, *German Pietism*, 88–130.

clergyman. His father died when he was only six, and he was raised by a high school teacher in Stuttgart. After his preparatory studies, Bengel entered the University at Tübingen, where he participated in a student group that met for Bible study and prayer. Bengel was ordained in 1706 and spent a year serving a parish. In 1708 he became a tutor at Tübingen, and, a few years later, he made a trip to Halle where he met Francke. From 1713 to 1741, Bengel served first as instructor and later as leader of the theological preparatory school located in the ancient cloister at Denkendorf. Bengel never held a university professorship, declining invitations from Tübingen and Giessen.

At Denkendorf, the curriculum included a two-year study of the entire NT according to the Greek text. Bengel demanded rigorous scholarship and stern discipline. Writing to a parent who was preparing his son for entrance to the school, Bengel stressed the need for proficiency in Latin and then added, "You must also give him some knowledge of Hebrew, and still more of Greek." To the father of one of his pupils, Bengel wrote, "Whence our young student acquired such a liking for the violin, I know not; for my own part I prefer some musical instrument more suitable for solitary recreation . . . but, as he prefers the violin, I shall see that he continues to make a prudent use of it." Throughout his career, Bengel was noted as an effective teacher and preacher. During his tenure at Denkendorf, he taught more than three hundred students. Among his pupils were scholars like J. C. Storr, the father of G. C. Storr, the founder of the conservative "old Tübingen school" of the early nineteenth century. Bengel's sermons were crammed with scriptural references. Preaching on Acts 2:40, he insisted that "save yourselves" meant "allow yourselves to be saved."[34] Thus, salvation was primarily the gift of God's grace, and the person receiving salvation needed to pray and ask for the influence of the Holy Spirit.

Later in life, Bengel was appointed to posts of ecclesiastical leadership in the Württemberg church. Among his more unpleasant tasks was the duty of passing judgment on the orthodoxy of the Moravian Brethren. This group of Pietists, under the leadership of Count von Zinzendorf, had been seeking an official relationship with the established church of Württemberg. Actually the count had visited Bengel in little Denkendorf in 1733—no doubt a scene of dramatic contrast: the humble pedagogue and the distinguished nobleman.[35] Bengel was favorably impressed. However, when official action had to be taken some twenty years later, Bengel

34. Cited in John Christian Frederick Burk, *A Memoir of the Life and Writings of John Albert Bengel*, trans. R. F. Walker (London: W. Ball, 1837), 50, 111.

35. See Gottfried Mälzer, *Bengel und Zinzendorf: Zur Biographie und Theologie Johann Albrecht Bengels* (Witten: Luther-Verlag, 1968).

pronounced the Moravians to be heretics. He believed their teachings departed from Scripture and Lutheran doctrine. The Brethren, in Bengel's opinion, were confused about the Trinity, and their interpretation of the book of Revelation (Bengel's favorite) was in error. According to Bengel, an authentic Pietism needed to be cultivated within the boundaries of the orthodox church.

Bengel was a prolific writer. In the area of classical philology, he produced editions of Cicero and Chrysostom. In 1736, Bengel published a harmony of the Gospels, a work in which the pericopes from the four Gospels are presented in German translation in parallel columns, followed by extensive notes.[36] In 1740, Bengel's lengthy commentary (over seven hundred pages) on the Apocalypse appeared,[37] a work based on his revised text and disclosing his distinctive apocalyptic eschatology.[38] Bengel's fascination with chronology is expressed in *Ordo temporum*, written in 1741.[39] Printed in a compact format with more than four hundred pages, this book is replete with chronological tables. It traces the history of the world from creation until the end, and presents the precise dates of major events. The Bible, which Bengel sees as an organic unity, presents reliable data that is computed into a comprehensive chronological system. With unwavering confidence, Bengel delineates the periods of time between such distant events as creation and the flood (1,656 years). Jesus was born, Bengel is sure, on December 25, three years before the beginning of the Common Era. Bengel presents a table in which he dates the writing of the Gospels: Matthew in 39, Mark in 41, Luke in 46, and John in 63.[40] Making use of prophecies from Daniel and Revelation, Bengel predicts the future. The entire history of the world, which has been predetermined by the will of God, will consist of 7,777ⅇ⁰ years.

---

36. *Johann Albrecht Bengels Richtige Harmonie der Vier Evangelisten, da Die Geschichten, Wercke und Reden JEsu Christi unsers HErrn, in ihrer geziemend natürlichen Ordnung zur Befestigung der Warheit, wie auch zur Ubung und Erbauung in der Gottseeligkeit vorgestellet werden* (Tübingen: C. H. Berger, 1736).

37. Johann Albrecht Bengel, *Erklärte Offenbarung Johannis oder vielmehr JEsu Christi. Aus dem revidirten Grund-Text übersetzt durch die prophetische Zahlen aufgeschlossen*, ed. Wilhelm Hoffmann (Stuttgart: Brodhag, 1834).

38. See Friedhelm Groth, *Die "Wiederbringung aller Dinge" im württembergischen Pietismus: Theologiegeschichtliche Studien zum eschatologischen Heilsuniversalismus württembergischer Pietisten des 18. Jahrhunderts*, Arbeiten zur Geschichte des Pietisums 21 (Göttingen: Vandenhoeck & Ruprecht, 1984), 61–88.

39. Io. Alberti Bengeli, *Ordo temporum a principio per periodos oeconomiae divinae historicas atque propheticas ad finem usque ita deductus ut tota a series et quarumvis partium analogia sempiternae virtutis ac sapientiae cultoribus ex scriptura V. et N.T. tanquam uno revera documento proponatur* (Stuttgart: C. Erhard, 1741).

40. Ibid., 293.

Bengel's Text-Critical Research

For the history of NT research, two major works deserve serious attention: Bengel's Greek NT and his famous *Gnomon*. While a student at Tübingen, Bengel came across a copy of the Greek NT, recently published by Francke. This was essentially the Oxford edition that had resulted from the work of Bishop Fell. When Bengel discovered the large number of textual variants (someone had estimated a total of around thirty thousand), he was mightily disturbed. If the manuscripts display thousands of differences, how could the reader be sure of the reliability of any particular word?—a question that launched Bengel's career as a textual critic. Although at first disturbed, the more Bengel studied, the more he became convinced of the reliability of the NT text. In 1721, he wrote to his former student J. F. Reuss:

> If the sacred volume, considering the fallibility of its many successive transcribers, had been preserved from every seeming defect whatsoever, this preservation itself would have been so great a miracle, that faith in the written word of God could be no longer faith. I have only to wonder that there is not a much larger number of those readings than there is; and that there are none which in the least affect the foundation of our faith.[41]

Like many conservative scholars who followed in his steps, Bengel believed the variants resulted from errors in the transmission of the text; the original writings were infallible. Thus, text criticism became a holy crusade— the restoration of the word of God to its original purity.

In 1725, Bengel wrote his *Prodromus Novi Testamenti Graeci,* which announced his intention to publish a critical text of the NT. That intention was realized in 1734 when Bengel's *Novum Testamentum Graecum*[42] appeared—a monumental accomplishment. With the exception of the book of Revelation, Bengel does not produce a revised text but merely reprints the Received Text (the Elzevir edition of 1633). The Greek text itself, arranged in paragraphs and printed in double columns, occupies 368 pages. At the bottom of each page, Bengel lists textual variants, and, beneath them, cross-references to the OT and NT. The variants are rated according to a system of notations indicated by Greek letters: variants evaluated by α represent readings that Bengel considers superior to the text; by β, readings that are somewhat better than the text; by γ, readings that are equal to the text; by δ, readings that are somewhat inferior; and

---

41. Cited in Burk, *Memoir of Bengel,* 52.
42. *H KAINH DIAΘHKH Novum Testamentum Graecum ita adornatum ut Textus probatarum editionum medullam. Margo variantium lectionum in suas classes distributarum locorumque parallelorum delectum. Apparatus subiunctus criseos sacrae Millianae praesertim compendium, limam, supplementum ac fructum exhibeat inserviente Io. Alberto Bengelio* (Tübingen: G. Cotta, 1734).

by ε, readings that are clearly inferior. The massive *Apparatus criticus* at the end of the volume consists of more than five hundred pages. It is divided into three parts. First, Bengel presents an introduction which deals with the general character of text criticism, including such things as critical problems, the nature of the manuscripts, and the history of text criticism (pp. 371–449). In the second part, Bengel offers a tractate that discusses a selected list of particular variants, presented in canonical order (pp. 450–860). Finally, Bengel adds an epilogue in which he presents a defense of textual criticism in general as well as the particular features of his own text-critical work (pp. 861–84).

As a text critic, Bengel developed principles that are important in the history of lower criticism. For one thing, he classified manuscripts according to geographical groupings: he identified an Asiatic text and an African text. The latter he subdivided into Greek texts represented by Codex Alexandrinus, and a text type exemplified in the Old Latin manuscripts. Bengel had high regard for the ancient versions, including the Vulgate, and made use of patristic quotations. In solving textual problems, Bengel had a low regard for conjectures. Variants should be evaluated according to clear criteria: the antiquity of the witnesses, the diversity of their origin, the obvious evidence of a corrupt reading, the intrinsic quality of an authentic reading. Bengel believed that the number of manuscripts in support of a variant was not as important as the antiquity of the witnesses. His most famous text-critical principle is *proclivi scriptioni praestat ardua* (to the easier reading the harder is preferred).[43] Behind this principle is the assumption that scribes tend to change (or corrupt) a text in order to make it more readable.

In actual practice, Bengel's text-critical conclusions are conservative. He believed, for example, that the words referring to the heavenly witnesses, "the Father, the Word, and the Holy Spirit" (1 John 5:7-8), were genuine—words omitted by virtually all modern editors. After devoting a lengthy discussion to these verses in his *Apparatus* (pp. 745–71), Bengel concludes that the longer text is correct, although he believes vv. 7 and 8 should be reversed in order. His reasons for accepting the text are largely contextual, betraying theological bias. Later he was to write, "Almost all of December I spent examining the passage of 1 John 5:7, and now believe to have saved its genuineness."[44] In regard to the ending of Mark, Bengel argues in favor of the longer ending.[45] He thinks there is more evidence in support of the text than some critics have recognized and notes that without these verses the story of Jesus ends abruptly. After an extensive

---

43. Ibid., 433.
44. Cited in Stoeffler, *German Pietism*, 101.
45. Bengel, *Novum Testamentum*, 515–16.

discussion of the tradition, Bengel concludes that the notorious story of the adulteress (John 8:1-11) is genuine.[46] Its omission from some manuscripts, he thinks, is the result of a reluctance to read the text in public assembly.

Bengel's Exegetical Contribution

Bengel's *Gnomon Novi Testament* (1742)[47] was a byproduct of his work at the Denkendorf school. It consists of notes used in his two-year trek with his wary students through the Greek NT. Reprinted and translated many times, the work is still in use.[48] The title, *Gnomon*, means "pointer," like a pointer on a sundial. As Bengel says in the preface, his intention is "briefly to point out or indicate, the full force of words and sentences, in the New Testament."[49] In actuality, the *Gnomon* is a multivolume collection of notes on the NT, in the tradition of the *Annotationes* of Grotius[50] and Simon's *Nouveau Testament de notre seigneur Jésus-Christ*.[51] In the *Gnomon*, Bengel affirms a high view of biblical authority and applies the hermeneutical principles that are articulated in his various writings. The Scriptures, he says, "contain the utterances of God" and are "unimpaired by defect."[52] The whole Bible is inspired, although the authors are allowed to employ their individual ways of expression. Thus, "though each of the inspired penmen has his own manner and style of writing, one and the self-same Spirit breathes through all."[53] The Bible contains all the truth humans need for salvation, and not one minute detail is unimportant in the total system of divine disclosure. All parts of the Scriptures are equally inspired, but some parts are more equal than others! "Indeed," writes Bengel, "in the NT, divine inspiration is loftier than in the OT."[54] Like Francke, Bengel affirms that Christ is the center of the biblical revelation.

For Bengel, the most important hermeneutical principle is the Reformation doctrine that Scripture is to be interpreted by Scripture. The Bible is like a bright jewel in which each facet reflects the luminous light of the whole. The meaning of Scripture is essentially clear and is expressed in

46. Ibid., 585–87.
47. J. A. Bengel, *Gnomon Novi Testamenti, in quo ex nativa verborum vi simplicitas, profunditas, concinnitas, salubritas sensuum coelestium indicatur,* 3d ed., ed. M. E. Bengel and J. Steudel, 2 vols. (Tübingen: L. F. Fues, 1850); Eng. trans.: *Gnomon of the New Testament,* trans. J. Bandinel and A. R. Fausset, ed. A. R. Fausset, 5 vols. (Edinburgh: T. & T. Clark, 1866).
48. Bengel's *Gnomon* was issued as *New Testament Commentary,* 2 vols. (Grand Rapids, Mich.: Kregel Reprint Library, 1982).
49. Bengel, *Gnomon of the NT* 1.9.
50. See pp. 9–11, above.
51. See pp. 23–24, above.
52. Cited in Bengel, *Gnomon of the NT* 1.5, 1.6.
53. Burk, *Memoir of Bengel,* 255.
54. Bengel, *Novum Testamentum,* 372.

the literal meaning of the text. Again with Francke, Bengel believes letter and spirit are bound together, so that the unravelling of the letter releases the spirit. Thus "the true commentator on divine revelation will fasten his primary attention upon the letter, (literal meaning,) but never forget that the spirit must equally accompany him."[55] At the same time, Bengel warns against the subjectivity of some Pietistic exegetes: "The expositor who nullifies the *historical* ground-work of Scripture for the sake of finding only spiritual truths everywhere, brings death on all correct interpretation."[56]

In the face of the rising tide of rationalism, Bengel builds a breakwater against the flood of reason. Although it can be used for perceiving truths in the natural realm and employed as an instrument for understanding truths of revelation, reason is inferior to faith.

> When Scripture directly testifies anything in plain words, Reason has nothing to do with arbitrating upon its *possibility*. . . . Therefore we do not rightly handle divine subjects, when, borrowing from Scripture what can be learnt *from Scripture only*, we proceed to show its possibility by our own mere reasonings; for this looks like attempting by natural knowledge to supersede faith in the Divine testimony.[57]

Similarly, Bengel betrays some of the anti-intellectualism that often plagues Pietism. "It is fearful to observe," he says, "how men in our universities 'spoil' themselves 'through philosophy and vain deceit,' upon the most sacred subjects; how they make shipwreck of their faith, either by their own inventions in theology, or by the definitions and systems of others; and how such things lead them away from the Scripture standard of thought."[58]

In the actual practice of exegesis, Bengel generally adheres to a historical method.[59] First, he insists, the text must be established. Then the interpreter must discern the meaning of individual words and how they are used in sentences. In this linguistic work, the exegete should recognize that the Greek of the NT has a Hebraic cast. Attention must be given to the context of the sentence within the individual book and within the entire scope of Scripture. The interpreter should ascertain the purpose of the biblical writer. Throughout the process, the exegete—as Francke had taught—should be sensitive to the *Affekte* (emotions or feelings) of the biblical writers in order to perceive the deeper truth which they have been

---

55. Cited in Burk, *Memoir of Bengel*, 261.
56. Cited by A. R. Fausset, "Sketch of the Life and Writings of J. A. Bengel," in Bengel, *Gnomon of the NT* 5.xvii.
57. Cited in Burk, *Memoir of Bengel*, 257–58.
58. Ibid., 374.
59. See Ernst Ludwig, *Schriftverständnis und Schriftauslegung bei Johann Albrecht Bengel* (Stuttgart: C. Scheufele, 1952), 52–71.

inspired to write. Finally, the results of exegesis ought to be applied to life. The study of Scripture is designed to strengthen the soul and move people to obedience.

Illustrations of these general principles abound in the massive *Gnomon*. In its overall structure, Bengel gives special attention to particular NT books, a point apparent in a simple survey of the English translation: Matthew is assigned over four hundred pages, while Mark is allotted a little less than ninety; Hebrews is assigned 169 pages, slightly less than Romans (198 pages); Revelation is given more space (217 pages) than either Romans or Hebrews. In the first volume of the *Gnomon*, Bengel attends to the problem of the relationship among the Gospels. He notes that Matthew and John are apostles, while Mark and Luke "derived their sure and accurate knowledge of the Gospel from others."[60] Mark, as Augustine had supposed, abbreviates Matthew, and Luke knows Mark's Gospel. John knows all three of the previous Gospels, and his use of Mark and Luke confirms their authority. John, the most important Gospel, provides a supplement to the history that the other evangelists have reported.

Bengel's exegesis frequently focuses on linguistic issues. For instance, he devotes a lengthy discussion to the use and meaning of the Greek article.[61] In regard to the anarthrous use of θεός in John 1:1 (where the modern exegete would apply Colwell's rule that predicate nouns preceding the verb are anarthrous), Bengel says, "The absence of the Greek article, especially in the predicate, does not weaken its signification, as meaning the true God. . . . Moreover, when the predicate is placed before the subject, there is an emphasis on the word."[62] Bengel often analyzes the style of the biblical author according to the figures of classical rhetoric. He also uses classical sources, as well as the Septuagint and patristic and rabbinic writings, to illuminate the meaning of biblical terms. For example, in commenting on the "unknown god" (Acts 17:23), Bengel refers to Diogenes Laertius, Pausanius, Philostratus, Tertullian, and Jerome.

Although Bengel affirms the limits of reason, he sometimes engages in rationalistic interpretation. In commenting on Luke's reference to Lot's wife (17:32), Bengel says that she naturally ran slower and, thus falling behind, was just at the edge of the shower that fell on Sodom, so that her body was partially consumed and turned into a kind of salt. However, literal interpretation usually prevails. Thus when Luke 22:44 says that Jesus' sweat "became like great drops of blood," Bengel asserts that even though the weather was cold (information he derives from John 18:18), Jesus actually sweat "drops, thick and clotted, of real blood." In spite of this

60. Bengel, *Gnomon of the NT* 1.71.
61. Ibid. 1.349–50.
62. Ibid. 2.235.

commitment to literal exegesis, Bengel occasionally lapses into allegory. For example, in commenting on the setting of the Sermon on the Mount, he says, "A mountain, as being a lofty part of the earth, and thereby nearer to heaven, is best suited for the most holy actions." Commenting on the parable of laborers (Matt. 20:1-16), Bengel, always enchanted by the symbolic meaning of numbers, asserts that the division of the day into twelve hours represents not the whole history of the world but merely the period from the call of the disciples to the ascension of Christ! As to the frequent use of the double "Amen" in the Gospel of John, Bengel says that Jesus was speaking both for himself and for God. Commenting on John 13:2, Bengel writes, "Precaution was taken by the washing of feet, that the impurity of Judas should not infect the hearts of the rest."[63]

Bengel's theological observations are sometimes superficial but consistently conservative. His Christology, for instance, is high. Commenting on Phil. 2:6, Bengel says that "the form of God is not the Divine nature, nor is the being on an equality with God the divine nature; but He, who was subsisting in the form of God, and who might have been on an equality with God, is God." Bengel has no difficulty accepting the miracles. In regard to the account of Jesus casting demons into swine, he notes that swine were unclean animals which the Jews were forbidden to own, so that "the Gergesenes were guilty, and deserved to lose the herd." The skeptical objection that whales do not have throats large enough to swallow a human being like Jonah is answered by Bengel's claim that there are many species of whales, and some have throats sufficiently large. Anyway, if that were not the case, God could have provided a special fish for the particular occasion. Commenting on how Philip was caught up by the Spirit with "miraculous velocity" (Acts 8:39), Bengel speculates that "by a like mode of transit one or two apostles *might* (*may*) have reached even America, if no other way was open to them."[64]

Bengel's exegetical work is marked by a variety of insights. He notes, for example, that the title "son of man" is used by no one except Jesus himself. On the basis of Dan. 7:13, Bengel understands this title to be messianic, but, commenting on Mark 8:31, he says that Jesus took for himself a "humble title." Bengel does not sidestep the difficult texts. In regard to the reference to someone being "salted with fire" (Mark 9:49), he interprets the text metaphorically, suggesting that salting with salt describes discipline, while salting with fire means stronger discipline—all with a view to avoiding the eternal fire of hell. A lengthy discussion of the baptism for the dead (1 Cor. 15:29) concludes that the practice does not refer to a practice of baptizing a person above a sepulchre but means to be baptized

63. Ibid. 2.214, 1.160, 2.417.
64. Ibid. 4.131, 1.221, 2.592.

with an eye to the constant threat of death. Bengel believes the "Hellenists" of Acts 6:1 are Jews born outside of Palestine who speak Greek. He thinks that Paul at Rom. 2:1 turns his attention from the Gentiles to the Jews, an interpretation based on the context and Paul's use of pronouns (third-person for Gentiles, second-person for Jews). Bengel, like many before and after him, attributes the Third Gospel to Luke the physician. Thus, commenting on Luke 8:43 where it is reported that the woman with the hemorrhage could be cured by no one, Bengel says, "Luke, being a physician himself, writes candidly."[65] Bengel's pious view of the "gravity of the apostle" impedes a literal interpretation of Gal. 5:12, where Paul, according to Bengel, cannot mean that the circumcisers should "mutilate" (let alone "castrate") themselves. The apostle must have some figurative meaning in mind, probably that the opponents ought to be cut off from the church.

Distinctive features of Bengel's theology are evident in his notes on Hebrews and Revelation. The Letter to the Hebrews, which Bengel accepts as Pauline, presents Bengel's emphasis on the necessity of the blood of Jesus for atonement. In a long note on Heb. 12:24,[66] Bengel claims that at Jesus' death all the blood was drained out of his body. Totally devoid of blood, the body of Jesus was raised and transported to heaven by the ascension. "His body," says Bengel, "was bloodless; yet not lifeless, but alive." The blood, which was totally without corruption, was taken by Jesus himself and offered to God in heaven. "The blood itself, not the shedding of the blood, is the ransom, the price of eternal redemption. That price, paid to God, remains paid, without being restored to the body of the Redeemer." The eternal blood remains in heaven, separate from the body of Jesus but available for the needs of faithful people. By the blood, spiritually sprinkled on believers, they are cleansed from sin and guilt, and in the Lord's Supper they partake of the blood separately from the body. "In short," concludes Bengel, "the precious blood of Christ is applied to us in sprinkling, in washing, in drinking, on account of the personal union in a manner real, yet supernatural, therefore quite incomprehensible."[67]

Bengel was fascinated by the Apocalypse. As well as writing his commentary, he delivered sixty practical addresses on the book of Revelation.[68] The major ideas which he had developed earlier in the commentary and in the *Ordo temporum* are summarized and set forth in the *Gnomon*. In

65. Ibid. 2.80–81.
66. Ibid. 4.474–89.
67. Ibid. 4.476, 479, 488.
68. Johann Albrecht Bengel, *Sechzig erbauliche Reden über die Offenbarung Johannis, oder vielmehr Jesu Christi*, 3d ed., ed. J.C.F. Burk (Stuttgart: Brodhag, 1758). A composite of Bengel's major works on Revelation has been published: see Bengel, *Die Offenbarung des Johannes*, ed. Berthold Burbacher (Metzingen/Württ.: E. Franz, 1975).

regard to the authorship of Revelation, Bengel is convinced that "it is indeed John, the apostle who wrote this book; but the Author is Jesus Christ."[69] John wrote from the Isle of Patmos in 96. The style, which bristles with Hebraisms, was determined by divine dictation. The key to the interpretation of the Apocalypse was given to Bengel by special revelation. In 1724, while he was preparing a sermon, it was disclosed to him that the number of the beast, 666, was a reference to years. Combining Rev. 13:18 with 13:5, Bengel concluded that the 666 years were the equivalent of forty-two months. This meant that a "prophetic" month equaled 15⁵⁄₇ years (666 divided by 42). Bengel also attempted to discern the meaning of "a time, and times, and half a time" (Rev. 12:14), and by a complicated procedure of calculation, he concluded that a "time" (καιρός) was 222²⁄₉ years.

These calculations provided Bengel with a variety of temporal references: ordinary time, prophetic time, biblical καιροί and χρόνοι. Making use of these references, Bengel attempted to construct the chronology of events from the time of the composition of the Apocalypse to the end of the world.[70] For instance, he thought the period of the time, times, and half a time (a total of 777⁷⁄₉ years) had begun in 1058 when the pope achieved independence from the Holy Roman emperor. Adding 777⁷⁄₉ to 1058, he concluded that the return of Christ and the beginning of the millennium would occur on June 18, 1836. Although he was mistaken, Bengel should be credited for deviating from the apocalyptic pattern. The typical prophet of doom, throughout the history of the interpretation of Daniel and Revelation, has thought that the end would come in the immediate future. For Bengel, the eschaton was not expected to arrive until the elapse of a whole century, a moderate view which reflects his confidence in his own "objective" calculations. Nevertheless, in view of Bengel's miscalculation, other aspects of his interpretation of the Apocalypse have only antiquarian interest. He believed the one hundred forty-four thousand of chapter 7 should be taken exactly, although he allowed that the number might refer to fathers and their posterity rather than simply to individuals. Bengel was convinced that the beast out of the sea (Rev. 13:1) represented the papacy of Rome, while the beast out of the earth (13:11) might symbolize the Jesuits or, perhaps, the Freemasons.

In sum, J. A. Bengel is an anomaly: a competent and original text critic,

---

69. Bengel, *Gnomon of the NT* 5.181.

70. See Gerhard Sauter, "Die Zahl als Schlüssel zur Welt: Johann Albrecht Bengels 'prophetische Zeitrechnung' im Zusammenhang seiner Theologie," *Evangelische Theologie* 26 (1966): 1-36; David Brady, *The Contribution of British Writers between 1560 and 1830 to the Interpretation of Revelation 13.16-18 (the Number of the Beast): A Study in the History of Exegesis*, Beiträge zur Geschichte der biblischen Exegese 27 (Tübingen: J.C.B. Mohr, 1983), 218–24.

a careful linguist and historian, a devotee of serious study of the Bible. Although colored by strange concepts, the mass of his work was dedicated to a historical understanding of the NT. His Greek text, together with his text-critical insights, made a significant contribution to the progress of lower criticism. His exegetical work, buttressed by solid grammatical and historical research, continued to point interpreters to the letter of the text. To work through the *Gnomon*, chapter by chapter, verse by verse, is like ploughing through solid rock. Yet now and then the rock yields veins of gold. It was this occasional discovery that led John Wesley to treasure the work of Bengel.

THE EVANGELICAL MOVEMENT AND
NEW TESTAMENT RESEARCH IN ENGLAND:
JOHN WESLEY (1703–1791)

John Wesley was born in Epworth, the son of a priest of the Church of England. His mother was a person of keen intelligence and sincere piety who had a profound influence upon him. At the age of six, young Wesley was saved from a fire in the rectory, an experience which he took to be an omen of a divine destiny. Educated at the Charterhouse School in London, Wesley entered Christ Church College at Oxford in 1720. Trained as a classical humanist, he received the Master of Arts degree in 1727, and was later made a fellow of Lincoln College, Oxford. While in Oxford, John, along with his brother Charles, was a member of the "holy club," a group of students who met for Bible study and prayer, derided by fellow students as "Methodists." Wesley, who was ordained a deacon in 1725 and a priest in 1728, spent two years in America, engaged in a largely unsuccessful mission to the Indians of Georgia.

In 1738, Wesley experienced a spiritual conversion. While attending a meeting of the Moravians in Aldersgate Street, London, as the preface to Luther's commentary on Romans was being read, Wesley felt his heart strangely warmed, and the doubts that had plagued his faith dissolved. Under the sway of the Moravians, Wesley made a pilgrimage to Herrnhut where he met Zinzendorf. He returned to England with a zeal to preach. Since he was excluded from some of the established churches, Wesley followed Whitefield's lead and began to preach in the open. Though small in stature and garbed in his ecclesiastical vestments, Wesley was a popular success with the people. As a result of his preaching, a revival swept over England, and the Methodist movement was begun. Societies were founded and chapels built. The rudiments of the Methodist organization emerged, and, in time and with reluctance, the movement separated from the Church of England. All of this was directed by the ecclesiastical genius of John Wesley. A person of high intelligence and exceptional skills of leadership, Wesley had endless energy. He started his day at 4:00 a.m. and packed it with ceaseless activity. According to informed estimates, he preached over 40,000 times, traveled in excess of 250,000 miles, and produced more than 200 written works.

Wesley's Religious Thought

John Wesley's importance as a theologian has sometimes been overlooked. In the eyes of many, he was a popular revivalist whose preaching provoked emotional outbursts and physical convulsions—a child of his time who believed in the devil and shared the superstitions of his contemporaries.[71] Nevertheless, Wesley was a creative thinker who made a distinct contribution to religious thought. In the best sense of the word he was a "practical" theologian, that is, a theologian who shaped his message to the needs of people. Thus, Albert Outler has described Wesley as a "folk-theologian."[72] Basic to Wesley's thought was his conviction that all theology should be grounded in Scripture. He also believed religion could be informed by reason and natural theology, although with limits. Reason, although useful in theological argument and interpreting Scripture, had been corrupted by human sin. Wesley was also interested in science, but he rejected Newton, and thought his ideas encouraged atheism.[73]

At the heart of Wesley's theology is his soteriology. He is preoccupied by the question of the nature of the Christian life, or, in biblical terms, What must I do to be saved? Wesley's main contribution, as Outler has shown, is his construction of a bridge over a chasm that divided Protestant thought—the split between justification by faith alone and the concern for holy living.[74] On the one hand, Wesley was opposed to a rigid Calvinism with its stress on predestination and irresistible grace; on the other hand, he rejected any notion that humans could earn salvation by their own effort. Instead, Wesley conceived an order of salvation that moved from prevenient grace through repentance, justification, sanctification, and final salvation. He stressed original sin and its consequences in death, yet held that humans were not totally depraved—not unable to receive the

---

71. See Leslie Stephen, *History of English Thought in the Eighteenth Century,* 2 vols. (New York: G. P. Putnam's Sons, 1927; reprint, New York: Harcourt, Brace & World, 1962), 1.409–25.

72. Albert C. Outler, "The Place of Wesley in the Christian Tradition," in *The Place of Wesley in the Christian Tradition: Essays Delivered at Drew University in Celebration of the Commencement of the Publication of the Oxford Edition of the Works of John Wesley,* ed. Kenneth E. Rowe (Metuchen, N.J.: Scarecrow, 1976), 13.

73. See John Dillenberger, *Protestant Thought and Natural Science* (Notre Dame, Ind.: University of Notre Dame Press, 1988), 156–58.

74. Outler, "The Place of Wesley in the Christian Tradition," 11–38.

gift of grace. Justification was God's free gift that was available to all, to be accepted by faith (*sola fide*). The response of faith involved a decision of the will, a decision in which Christ was accepted as Savior. The result was immediate justification, the gift of the Spirit, and regeneration. In the time between justification and final salvation, believers participated in sanctification—a process whereby the Spirit of God moved people toward perfection. Thus, holy living was not in conflict with justification but was a response to God's grace which made possible obedience to the command of love.[75]

Wesley's view of the Bible is basic to his theology.

> I want to know one thing—the way to heaven. . . . God Himself has condescended to teach the way; . . . He hath written it down in a book. O give me that book! At any price, give me the book of God! I have it: here is knowledge enough for me. . . . I sit down alone: only God is here. In His presence I open, I read His book; . . . Is there a doubt concerning the meaning of what I read? . . . I lift up my heart to the Father of Lights: "Lord, is it not Thy Word, 'If any man lack wisdom let him ask of God?' . . . Thou hast said, 'If any be willing to do Thy will, he shall know.' I am willing to do, let me know, Thy will." I then search after and consider parallel passages of Scripture, "comparing spiritual things with spiritual." I meditate thereon with all the attention and earnestness of which my mind is capable. If any doubt still remains, I consult those who are experienced in the things of God.[76]

For Wesley three things are authoritative for life and faith: Scripture, reason, and experience; and the greatest of these is Scripture.[77]

Wesley believed the Bible was divinely inspired and infallible.[78] He accepted the traditional view which the deists had tried to demolish: the inspiration of Scripture is confirmed by miracles and fulfilled prophecy. In a short statement entitled "A Clear and Concise Demonstration of the Divine Inspiration of the Holy Scriptures," Wesley sets forth an argument which he thinks to be unshakable. He asserts that there are only three possible alternatives: either (1) the Bible was written by good men or angels; (2) the Bible was written by bad men or devils; or (3) the Bible was written by God. It could not have been written by good men or angels,

---

75. See Mildred Bangs Wynkoop, *A Theology of Love: The Dynamic of Wesleyanism* (Kansas City, Mo.: Beacon Hill, 1972).

76. Cited in Robert W. Burtner and Robert E. Chiles, *A Compend of Wesley's Theology* (New York and Nashville: Abingdon Press, 1954), 18.

77. See R. Benjamin Garrison, "Vital Interaction: Scripture and Experience. John Wesley's Doctrine of Authority," *Religion in Life* 25 (1956): 563–73; William M. Arnett, "John Wesley and the Bible," *Wesleyan Theology Journal* 3 (1968): 3–9. Scott J. Jones, "John Wesley's Conception and Use of Scripture" (Ph.D. diss., Southern Methodist University), notes that Wesley recognized five authorities: Scripture, reason, experience, antiquity (the faith of the primitive church), and the Church of England; Scripture was the most important.

78. See Larry Shelton, "John Wesley's Approach to Scripture in Historical Perspective," *Wesleyan Theology Journal* 16 (1981): 23–50.

Wesley argues, because it claims to be the word of God, and neither good men nor angels would lie and make blasphemous claims. It could not have been written by bad men or devils because it promotes righteousness and condemns evil, and bad men and devils do not do such things. "Therefore," writes Wesley, "I draw this conclusion, that the Bible must be given by divine inspiration."[79]

In the interpretation of Scripture, Wesley stresses the literal meaning and the principle of interpreting Scripture by Scripture.

> The general rule for interpreting Scripture is this. The literal sense of every text is to be taken, if it be not contrary to some other text; but in that case the obscure text is to be interpreted by those which speak more plainly.[80]

This concern for the literal led Wesley to attend to matters of linguistics, history, and geography. He had been trained in the classics and had a commanding grasp of the patristic sources.[81] According to Mullen, 75 percent of Wesley's sermons contain references to NT Greek.[82] This attention to the literal meaning guards against subjective eisegesis: "You are in danger of enthusiasm every hour, if you depart ever so little from Scripture; yea, or from the plain, literal meaning of any text, taken in connection with the context."[83] Nevertheless, Wesley shared with Francke the conviction that religious experience was essential to valid exegesis—that only those who had the Spirit could understand the things of the Spirit. Wesley also believed that exegesis should make use of the most reliable text and that attention should be given to the literary and historical context.

Basic to Wesley's hermeneutic is his idea of interpreting Scripture by the whole message of Scripture, or, in other words, according to the analogy of faith.[84] In his sermon entitled "Justification by Faith," Wesley observes that many false interpretations of this important doctrine represent "notions absolutely inconsistent with the oracles of God, and with the whole analogy of faith."[85] What he means by the analogy of faith, as Outler

---

79. John Wesley, "A Clear and Concise Demonstration of the Divine Inspiration of the Holy Scriptures," in *The Works of John Wesley*, 14 vols. (Grand Rapids: Zondervan, 1872), 11.484.

80. Cited in Mack B. Stokes, *The Bible in the Wesleyan Heritage* (New York and Nashville: Abingdon Press, 1979), 24.

81. See James T. Clemons, "John Wesley—Biblical Literalist?" *Religion in Life* 46 (1977): 332–42.

82. Wilbur H. Mullen, "John Wesley's Method of Biblical Interpretation," *Religion in Life* 47 (1978): 99–108.

83. Cited in Garrison, "Vital Interaction," 572.

84. This is emphasized and explicated in Jones, "John Wesley's Conception and Use of Scripture." See Timothy L. Smith, "John Wesley and the Wholeness of Scripture," *Interpretation* 39 (1985): 246–62.

85. *The Works of John Wesley: Sermons I*, ed. Albert C. Outler, 4 vols. (Nashville: Abingdon Press, 1984), 1.183.

points out in a footnote, is the total witness of Scripture—the general sense of the Bible as understood by the church throughout its history.[86] In his note on Rom. 12:6, Wesley explains his translation "let us prophecy according to the analogy of faith"[87] by saying that there is in Scripture a "grand scheme of doctrine . . . touching original sin, justification by faith, and present, inward salvation." This summary of doctrine provides a rule whereby all questions should be answered. How the analogy of faith functions in exegesis can be seen in Wesley's sermon titled "Free Grace."[88] In the sermon, Wesley enlists a host of arguments against the doctrine of predestination whereby persons are foreordained to either election or damnation. One of the weightiest arguments, however, is from the *analogia fidei*: the doctrine of predestination tends "to overthrow the whole Christian revelation, by making it contradict itself; by giving such an interpretation of some texts as flatly contradicts all the other texts, and indeed the whole scope and tenor of Scripture—an abundant proof that it is not of God."[89] When, for example, the advocates of predestination take literally a text like Rom. 9:13 ("I have loved Jacob, but I have hated Esau"), they contradict the whole message of Scripture and all the texts that say "God is love."

Wesley's Work on the New Testament

While Wesley's writings are punctuated with scriptural references, two of his publications deal explicitly with the study of the NT: his translation and his *Explanatory Notes*. Wesley's translation of the NT was apparently accomplished during three months in 1754 when he was recovering from an illness,[90] but it did not appear until 1775, when it was published along with the *Notes*. In comparison with the King James Version, Wesley's translation has some twelve hundred points of difference. He says in the preface to *Notes* that he never altered the text simply for the sake of altering, "but only where, first, The sense was made better, stronger, clearer, or more consistent with the context: secondly, Where the sense being equally good, the phrase was better or nearer the original."[91] Changes actually appear to have been made for four reasons: (1) text critical (Wesley made use of Bengel's text); (2) to modernize the English (Wesley used "love" instead of "charity" in 1 Corinthians 13); (3) to better render the Greek (Wesley

86. See also Outler, Introduction, in ibid. 1.57–59.

87. John Wesley, *Explanatory Notes upon the New Testament* (London: Epworth Press, 1976). (Because of the great variety of editions of Wesley's *Notes*, references are to the text by chapter and verse rather than by page numbers.)

88. Wesley, *Works: Sermons* 3.544–63.

89. Ibid. 3.554.

90. For an analysis of Wesley's version of the NT, see Robin Scroggs, "John Wesley as Bible Scholar," *Journal of Bible and Religion* 28 (1960): 415–22.

91. Wesley, *Notes*, preface, par. 5.

translated καταλλαγή in Rom. 5:11 with "reconciliation" rather than "atonement"); and (4) for theological reasons (Wesley made subtle changes to counter the idea of predestination; for example, he changed "shall" to "will" in 1 Cor. 1:8). "The result," in Scroggs's judgment, "is a modern English translation, concise, clear, yet somehow maintaining most of the sonority of the older version."[92]

John Wesley's *Explanatory Notes upon the New Testament* is a readable and highly popular aid to biblical study. The first edition appeared in 1755, and was subsequently revised extensively by Wesley himself.[93] The durable popularity of the work is attested to by the appearance of a handsome, two-volume reprint of the *Notes* in 1983.[94] After a short preface, Wesley presents his translation with notes at the bottom of the page. Each biblical book is introduced with an outline very much like the outlines in Bengel's *Gnomon*. In most cases, a short introductory section, treating such things as setting and purpose, introduces each book. In his preface, Wesley acknowledges that he has been dependent on the work of four major scholars: Bengel, Philip Doddridge, John Guyse, and John Heylyn. However, the lion's share belongs to "the great Bengelius," as Wesley calls him, acknowledging that he himself might have done more for the cause of religion if he had simply translated the *Gnomon*. Instead, he has made abundant use of Bengel, although frequently, to the relief of some of his readers, abbreviating him. In fact, Wesley's dependence on all his sources is considerable. For example, in his notes on Matthew 1, about 90 percent of the material is borrowed from one of the four scholars. Wesley's use of Bengel is sometimes virtually verbatim. Although Wesley was following the Latin text of the *Gnomon*, the verbal parallels can be detected in the English translation:

On Rom. 8:1:

    Bengel: "The apostle comes now to deliverance and liberty."

    Wesley: "Now he comes to deliverance and liberty."

On Rom. 8:15:

    Bengel: "The Holy Spirit was not even in the Old Testament a spiritual bondage."

    Wesley: "The Holy Ghost was not properly a spirit of bondage, even in the time of the Old Testament."

As Wesley says in his preface, "I have endeavored to make the Notes as short as possible."[95] In English translation, Bengel's *Gnomon* fills five sub-

---

92. Scroggs, "John Wesley as Bible Scholar," 417.

93. For an account of the publishing of the *Notes*, see Frank Baker, "John Wesley, Biblical Commentator," *Bulletin of the John Rylands University Library of Manchester* 71 (1989): 109–20.

94. (Grand Rapids: Baker Book House, 1983).

95. Wesley, *Notes*, preface, par. 6.

stantial volumes; Wesley's *Notes*, in some editions, can be fit into a single volume of eight hundred or so pages. Commenting on Matt. 5:17-20, Wesley uses only about ten lines; Bengel takes over three pages.

A few samples from Wesley's *Notes* illustrate his critical and exegetical work. As to historical criticism, Wesley presents data about the cities to which Pauline letters are addressed: Corinth, Philippi, Colossae. In commenting on the Gospels, he provides information about the history and practices of the synagogue. Wesley adopts the "north Galatian" hypothesis,[96] and assumes that the reports in Galatians 2 and Acts 15 refer to the same Jerusalem conference. At the beginning of his discussion of the Pauline letters, Wesley presents a chronology of the epistles that assumes the hypothesis of two Roman imprisonments. Wesley accepts all of the Catholic Epistles as authentic and believes 2 Peter was written prior to Jude. In regard to the Gospels, Wesley follows the conventional view that they were written in canonical order, but he explains their differences in terms of the individual purposes of the evangelists: "each choosing to treat more largely on those things which most suited the time when, and the person to whom he wrote."[97] Wesley's view of Onesimus anticipates later interpretations: "It seems that Philemon not only pardoned, but gave him his liberty: seeing Ignatius makes mention of him as succeeding Timotheous [as bishop] at Ephesus."[98] Wesley gives four reasons Jesus did not want his miracles publicized: (1) to prevent the throng of crowds; (2) to fulfill the prophecy that the Messiah would not be ostentatious; (3) to escape being forced into becoming a king; and (4) to avoid unduly enraging the priests and pharisees. Wesley opts for the Pauline authorship of Hebrews because he believes "St. Paul's method and style are easily observed therein."[99]

The miracles present no problem to Wesley, although he sometimes entertains rationalistic reflection. On Matt. 10:8, he asks whether demon possession may actually refer to a disease like epilepsy, but concludes that even though the symptoms may be the same, the devil could have caused the disease. The raising of Lazarus is accepted without question, but Wesley is concerned with the cloth that wrapped the dead man's face (John 11:44). According to Wesley, the Jews followed Egyptian burial customs, wrapping a napkin only about the forehead and chin, so that Lazarus was perfectly able to see his way to walk out of the tomb. Although Wesley

---

96. The view that the Epistle to the Galatians was addressed to the churches in the original territory of Galatia, not to the churches in the southern part of the Roman province of Galatia.

97. Wesley, *Notes*, preface to Matthew.

98. Ibid., preface to Philemon.

99. Ibid., preface to Hebrews.

generally seeks the plain, literal meaning, he sometimes slips into allegory. In commenting on Mark 8:8 (the feeding of the four thousand), he says, "This miracle was intended to demonstrate that Christ was the true bread which cometh down from heaven; for He who was almighty to create bread without means, to support natural life, could not want power to create bread without means to support spiritual life." Wesley interprets the main sense of the parable of the Prodigal Son (Luke 15) by a single point of comparison: as a father forgives the returning son, so God rejoices and receives the returning sinner. Wesley, however, treats some of the details allegorically: the citizen of the far country is "the devil or one of his children," and the husks that the swine eat are "worldly comforts."

Many of Wesley's notes concern theological issues. For example, he argues that Paul's statement that he thinks he has the Spirit (1 Cor. 7:40) should not be taken to mean he has any real doubts. Similarly, Paul does not need a command of the Lord (1 Cor. 7:25), "for the apostles wrote nothing which was not divinely inspired." Wesley is concerned with Christology. He believes that when Jesus says "The Father and I are one" (John 10:30), his use of the plural "are" confounds Sabellius and his use of "one" confutes Arius. Commenting on Matt. 16:18, Wesley supposes that Jesus may have pointed to himself when he said "on this rock," because the whole witness of Scripture is that Christ is the foundation of the church. The description of Peter as the rock refers to his faith in Jesus. Much attention is given to the problem of sin and salvation. In discussing Rom. 5:12-13, Wesley affirms that sin entered by Adam, and that sin resulted in death for all. "Infants," he adds, "are not excepted, in that all sinned." Christ's sacrifice is clearly a propitiation (Rom. 3:25) designed "to appease an offended God." Final salvation is received only in the future resurrection in which the faithful are clothed with a spiritual body (1 Cor. 15:44); the body, says Wesley, "is raised a more refined contexture, needing none of these animal refreshments, and endued with qualities of a spiritual nature, like the angels of God."

Throughout the *Notes*, Wesley stresses holiness and life in the Spirit. For Wesley, major points in the Sermon on the Mount include an invitation to holiness and a description of holy living. The kingdom of heaven is understood as an "inward kingdom." Like Francke, Wesley emphasizes the religious affections.[100] This, for Wesley, refers primarily to emotions and spiritual experience. Wesley believes that since the biblical writers participated in such experiences, readers of the Scriptures need to share the

---

100. Gregory S. Clapper, *John Wesley on Religious Affections: His View on Experience and Emotion and Their Role in the Christian Life and Theology* (Metuchen, N.J. and London: Scarecrow, 1989).

religious affections in order to understand the basic experience to which
the NT testifies. Commenting on Phil. 1:9 he says, "We must be inwardly
sensible of divine peace, joy, love; otherwise we cannot know what they are."

When all is said and done, Wesley was not an innovative biblical scholar.
He did, however, make important contributions to the history of NT
research. Of particular interest is his use of the analogy of faith as a hermeneutical principle. This principle, which is at least as old as Irenaeus,
has to be evaluated with ambivalence. On the one hand, it represents a
serious effort to reflect thoughtfully about the basic theological message
of Scripture. On the other hand, it encourages the harmonizing of variations within the biblical record and tends to discourage a genuinely historical view of the Bible, a result inconsistent with Wesley's own distinction
between the OT and the NT. More important is Wesley's stress on the
practical application of Scripture. For Wesley, the Bible is the sufficient
revelation of all that is significant for human beings—for justification,
sanctification, and salvation. Wesley's biblical research, therefore, is designed to promote the communication of the biblical revelation to the
people. His intention is to take the best of critically informed and spiritually inspired scholarship and make it readily available for all. As he says, "I
write chiefly for plain, unlettered men, who understand only their mother-
tongue, and yet reverence and love the word of God, and have a desire to
save their souls."[101] The result was a plain, unadorned, and practical biblical scholarship which has characterized much of British research ever since.

SUMMARY

In reviewing the scholars surveyed in this chapter, the observer should be
leery of homogenizing and labeling. Francke's husk-kernel metaphor, Bengel's concern with biblical chronology and apocalypticism, and Wesley's
Arminianism are sufficient examples to display the variations and differences of these individuals. Nevertheless, these theologians share features
that make possible their classification together under the broad rubric of
Pietism, a word used without pejorative intent. First, all three are devoted
to the practical understanding and application of Scripture—all are concerned with educating the clergy and preaching to the laity; all discern at
the heart of the biblical revelation the message of salvation and ethical
living. Second, these three theologians share the conviction that religious
experience is crucial to both the writing and reading of Scripture—all
take note of the religious affections; all stress the role of the Spirit in
inspiration and interpretation.

101. Wesley, *Notes*, preface, par. 3.

These common features influence the way Francke, Bengel, and Wesley pursue biblical research. In their basic view of the Bible, these scholars appear to be one with the orthodox: they accept the authority of the Bible in all things religious and affirm the verbal inspiration and infallibility of the biblical record. Consequently, the Pietist scholars share with the Protestant scholastics the dedication to the serious study of the Bible as the primary theological task. Their emphasis, however, is different: the orthodox see the Bible as a source of accurate information on all topics; the Pietists stress the sufficiency of Scripture for life and salvation. For the latter, the Bible is viewed not as a collection of data and doctrine but as a witness to a normative religious experience. Since this normative experience took place in history—in the lives of the people of the Bible—the historical character of the biblical revelation is affirmed. To reconstruct this history, scholars like Francke, Bengel, and Wesley were dedicated to discerning the plain, literal meaning of the text, the original meaning of the biblical documents in their historical setting. Thus, they dedicated themselves to textual, linguistic, grammatical, and historical interpretation.

This historical understanding of Scripture created a problem for a basic view that the Pietist exegetes shared with the orthodox: the view that the Bible presented a unified, wholly consistent message—that any one part of the Bible (e.g., a verse from the Song of Solomon) had the same revelatory quality as any other (e.g., a verse from the Epistle to the Romans). This concept of a "level" Bible was in tension with the historical view of Scripture that the Pietists had developed out of their concern with religious experience. Moreover, since they tended to stress the Christian experience of the Spirit and to recognize Jesus Christ as the center of the unified message of the Bible, the Pietists were inclined to value the revelation and the authority of the NT as superior to the OT, another step in the direction of a historical understanding of the Bible that disturbed the equilibrium of the level Bible.

Insofar as they viewed the Bible historically, the Pietists moved in the direction of Enlightenment scholarship. Similarly, the Pietist effort to make the message of the Bible available to the masses—seen in translations by Francke and Wesley and in Wesley's *Notes* and Bengel's *Gnomon*—corresponds to the Enlightenment's concern to democratize learning. Even the Pietist stress on experience, which some contemporary intellectuals decried as mindless enthusiasm, participated in the individualism of the Enlightenment. Moreover, this individualism, as Karl Barth has pointed out,[102] involves an implicit emphasis on human authority. After all, if reli-

---

102. Karl Barth, *Protestant Theology in the Nineteenth Century: Its Background and History* (London: SCM Press, 1972), 113–23.

gious experience is the norm and key to interpretation, then the human beings who have these experiences exercise a considerable amount of authority, an authority which qualifies, to some degree, the authority of the divine revelation. This tension between the new world and the old is also seen in the Pietist understanding of reason. Although the Pietists advocate the use of reason in exegesis, Wesley thinks reason has been corrupted by the fall, and both Francke and Bengel betray a suspicious anti-intellectualism. When they conclude, either by implication or explicitly (as in the case of Francke), that the Bible is not to be interpreted like any other book, the Pietists align themselves with the past and not the future.

The major flaw in Pietist biblical research is not difficult to detect; it is the subjectivity implicit in their notion that religious experience is crucial to valid interpretation—that only those who possess the Spirit can understand the Scriptures. This spiritual imperialism, in addition to being in tension with the democratizing of Scripture, was complicated by Pietism's individualism, whereby any born-again believer could claim to present normative exegesis. In theory there was one Spirit, but in practice there were many interpreters and many interpretations. The skeptic might wonder, too, why the Bible was necessary at all, if the faithful could count on direct communication from the Spirit. The Pietists, however, were true to their Protestant heritage: they were people of the book who believed the Spirit spoke through the word, a conviction which moved them to arduous biblical research. Paradoxically, the biblicism of the Pietists protected them from subjectivity, and their subjectivity delivered them from orthodox biblicism.

In the development of NT research, the emerging historical critics were quick to embrace the first part of Francke's manual and to learn from Bengel's painstaking research. But was there not also some elusive truth in the distinctive feature of the Pietistic approach—the concern with religious experience? Was it really adequate to reduce the message of the Bible to vowel points and chronological data? Perhaps, the appreciation of the Scriptures as witness to vital religion was truer *to history* than were the dogmatism of the orthodox and the historicizing of the Enlightenment. In any event, the concern for religious experience would influence the literary interpretation of the Bible by Lessing and Herder,[103] the theology of religious consciousness by Schleiermacher,[104] and nineteenth-century British research which received its inspiration from romanticism.[105]

103. See pp. 165–83, below.
104. See pp. 208–20, below.
105. See pp. 338–60, below.

4

Defining Historical Research: Methods of Interpretation

Despite the Pietist stress on faith and feeling, the European mind was increasingly captivated by the power of reason. Like a luminous cloud, the empiricism and rationalism that had shadowed England moved across the English Channel. In the Netherlands, the air had been cleared by Spinoza's skepticism and Le Clerc's critical research. There the spirit of the Enlightenment had become incarnate in the religion of the Arminians and the Socinians. In France, the deism that had died in Britain was resurrected to a new and vigorous life.[1] The way for this had been prepared by thinkers like Pierre Bayle (1647–1706), who had anticipated Diderot with a dictionary of his own. With Bayle, the traditional proofs for the existence of God came under attack, and history was subjected to rational inquiry. Following in the footsteps of Voltaire, continental intellectuals visited England and became intoxicated by the atmosphere of religious tolerance. French deism, as portrayed in Voltaire's passion to "crush the infamy," became militant in its opposition to every kind of orthodoxy and authoritarianism.

Europe's tastes were set in the Parisian salons. Not only were French manners exported, so also were the ideas of the *philosophes*. The monarchs of Europe became enlightened despots, and rulers like Frederick the Great, who dabbled in music and philosophy, adorned their courts with intellectuals like Voltaire. Thus the Enlightenment, or *Aufklärung*, came to the German states. The writings of the deists had been translated into German, and new universities, like Göttingen, dedicated to the

---

1. For an understanding of the NT in French intellectual thought, see Marie-Helene Cotoni, *L'Exégèse du Nouveau Testament dans la philosophie française du dix-huitième siècle* (Oxford: Voltaire Foundation, 1984).

physical sciences and the *wissenschaftlich* way of studying everything, had been established. Just as Newton's cosmology prepared England for natural theology, so the continent was readied for a rational worldview by the philosophy of Leibnitz (1646–1716). For Leibnitz, the universe was a harmonious whole, made up of individual substances he called "monads." This world, with all its complexities, could be comprehended by logic and mathematics. Humans received knowledge by sense and reason (shades of Locke), so that there were truths of fact, perceived by sense experience, and truths of reason, discerned by analysis and comparison. Leibnitz believed the differences that divided theologians to be insignificant, and he called for the unity of Catholics and Protestants.

The philosophy of Leibnitz was popularized by Christian Wolff (1679–1754). Wolff was a thoroughgoing rationalist who believed the principle of noncontradiction applied to all reality: the world was like a grand machine, functioning by rational principles. Wolff accepted Leibnitz's idea of substances and saw each substance manifesting an essence. The soul, he thought, was a substance within the body, and body and soul, although separate, functioned in harmony. In his youth Wolff had been inclined toward the ministry, and theological issues continued to haunt him. He believed the existence of God could be proved by cosmological argument, and he considered revelation and reason to be parallel, not conflicting, sources of truth. In 1723, Wolff was dismissed from his professorship at Halle and expelled from Prussia, but in 1740, with the cordial invitation of Frederick the Great, he returned as a conquering hero. His description of the event is graphic:

> A great multitude of students rode out of the city to meet me. . . . They were attended by six glittering postillions. All the villagers along the roadside came out of their towns, and anxiously awaited my arrival. When we reached Halle, all the streets and marketplaces were filled with an immense concourse of people, and I celebrated my jubilee amidst a universal jubilee. In the street, opposite the house which I had rented as my place of residence, there was gathered a band of music, which received me and my attendants with joyous strains.[2]

A brass band receiving a philosopher is a rarity, but when the reception is held in Halle—once the bulwark of Pietism—that reception is notorious.

As noted in chapter 1, the deists were amateurs as biblical scholars. In the hands of the Germans, with their persistent industry and penetrating intellect, biblical research became a totally new enterprise. The more radi-

---

2. Cited in John F. Hurst, *History of Rationalism*, 9th rev. ed. (New York: Nelson & Phillips, 1865), 108–9.

cal moves which were to emerge later in the century were anticipated by scholars like S. J. Baumgarten (1706–57),[3] who attempted to combine Wolff's philosophy with the faith of Pietism. Baumgarten published exegetical works that employed grammatical method and sought the historical meaning of the text. However, before this sort of exegetical work could be satisfactorily accomplished, the principles of historical research needed explication. The attempt to delineate the methods of biblical interpretation can be illustrated in the work of two Swiss scholars, J. A. Turretin and J. J. Wettstein, and a German classicist, J. A. Ernesti.

MODERATE RATIONALISM IN SWITZERLAND: TURRETIN AND WETTSTEIN

Jean-Alphonse Turretin (1671–1737)

The move from the old orthodoxy toward the new criticism is poignantly portrayed in the career of Jean-Alphonse Turretin.[4] Born in Geneva, he was the son of François Turretin, who was professor of theology and rock-ribbed defender of scholastic Calvinism. The older Turretin believed that knowledge of God could be received only by divine revelation, a revelation recorded in the inspired and infallible Scriptures of the OT and NT. Indeed, François Turretin had been one of the authors of the Helvetic Consensus (1675), the creedal document that opposed the Calvinistic moderates and affirmed the inspiration of the vowel points of the Hebrew text. The senior Turretin supported the orthodox doctrines of original sin and predestination, and his uncompromising work on the atonement is revered by conservative Calvinists today.[5] He died when Jean-Alphonse was only sixteen and probably was thus spared considerable disappointment.

The career of the younger Turretin is typical of many of the intellectuals of the Enlightenment. He was educated first at Geneva but traveled to Leyden, where he met Le Clerc and Bayle, and studied with Friedrich Spanheim. In 1693, he visited England, where his itinerary included London, Cambridge, and Oxford. In addition to looking at manuscripts in the libraries, which impressed him, Turretin met Newton, had an audience

---

3. A brief account of Baumgarten's work is presented in Karl Barth, *Protestant Theology in the Nineteenth Century: Its Background and History*, trans. John Bowden (London: SCM Press, 1972), 160–61. See also, Hans W. Frei, *The Eclipse of Biblical Narrative: A Study in Eighteenth- and Nineteenth-Century Hermeneutics* (New Haven and London: Yale University Press, 1974), 88–91. For a fuller account, see Emanuel Hirsch, *Geschichte der neuern evangelischen Theologie*, 5 vols. (Gütersloh: C. Bertelsmann, 1951) 2.370–88.

4. Turretin's name is recorded in various spellings (e.g., Turretine, Turrettino, Turrettini), a result of Latinized forms and plural references to the family. His work is cited accordingly.

5. Francis Turretin, *The Atonement of Christ*, trans. James R. Willson (Grand Rapids: Baker, 1978).

with the king, and imbibed the spirit of English rationalism. Upon his return to Geneva, Turretin established a reputation as a popular preacher. In 1697, he began to lecture on church history at the university, and in 1705 he was appointed professor of theology.

Turretin's Theology

Turretin's life was marked by a spirit of moderation and tolerance. A sharp break with his father's position is reflected in his opposition to the Helvetic Consensus. The Consensus had been reaffirmed in 1706, but Turretin's efforts, along with those of Samuel Werenfels and J. F. Osterwald, led to its abolition in 1725. Turretin was a leader of eighteenth-century ecumenism, advocating the unity of Calvinists, Lutherans, and Anglicans,[6] about which he corresponded with Leibnitz, Frederick I of Prussia, and the Archbishop of Canterbury. In 1707, Turretin presented an oration that epitomizes his intellectual spirit to an assembly at the University of Geneva.[7] In it, he begins by expressing his distress at seeing "the coat of Christ so torn to pieces"[8] and goes on to observe that division has plagued the church from the beginning, as seen, for example, in the split between Peter and Paul. A survey of his own time convinces Turretin that there is widespread agreement on the fundamental issues. In spite of differences about the Eucharist, Christology, and predestination, all Protestants recognize the real presence in the last supper and the two natures in Christ, and all acknowledge that God's judgments are unsearchable (Rom. 11:33). Protestants, therefore, can unite without agreeing on all the details—lesser issues which can be left to the resolution of God.

In general, Turretin's theology is stamped with the imprint of the Enlightenment. He was interested in science and affirmed the concept of natural law. As rector of the University of Geneva (1701–11), Turretin advocated a curriculum that integrated philosophy and science into a natural theology that could recognize divine providence and avoid the dangers of atheism and deism.[9] His basic ideas on the relation of revelation and reason are set forth in his treatise on revealed religion.[10] In this

---

6. See Max Geiger, "Die Unionsbestrebungen der schweizerischen reformierten Theologie unter der Führung des helvetischen Triumvirates," *Theologische Zeitschrift* 9 (1953): 117–36. The "triumvirate" includes Werenfels, Ostervald, and Turretin.

7. Joh. Alphonso Turretino, *Oratio de componendis protestantium dissidiis, dicta statis Academiae Genevensis, solemnibus idibus Jun. MDCCVII* (London: W. Taylor, 1709).

8. Ibid., 9.

9. See Michael Heyd, "Un rôle nouveau pour la science: Jean-Alphonse Turrettini et les débuts de la théologie naturelle à Genève," *Revue de théologie et de philosophie* 112 (1980): 25–42.

10. John Alphonso Turretine, *Dissertations on Revealed Religion*, trans. W. Crawford (Belfast: J. Magee, 1778).

work, Turretin first argues for the necessity of divine revelation. He says that although texts like Rom. 1:20 and Acts 17:27-28 confirm that God can be known in creation, natural revelation is not adequate, a claim confirmed by the errors of, among others, the Stoics. Special revelation is necessary for the knowledge of the nature of God and the way of salvation. However, "nothing which contradicts the light of nature can be a revelation of God." Revelation, moreover, must be in harmony with reason: "For God who is the author of revelation, is likewise the author of reason, and he cannot contradict himself."[11]

Turretin believes that the religions of authentic revelation, Judaism and Christianity, are superior to others. The revelation of the OT is confirmed by Christ and the apostles. Christianity, which results from a still higher revelation, surpasses all religions and philosophies. It offers better rewards, for example, the promise of the resurrection. "And, as to the resurrection of the body," says Turretin, "omitting other reasonings which might be advanced on this point, who will deny that to Him, who formed with such exquisite art our bodies and all the parts of universal nature, there can be the smallest difficulty in collecting together and restoring these bodies." In contrast to the deists, Turretin believes the validity of the Christian revelation is proved by miracles and fulfilled prophecy. Turretin defines miracles as works of God that transcend human power and the natural order. "None but a person destitute of reason," he argues, "can ascribe such works to human industry or to any other natural cause." As to proof from prophecy, Turretin cites Jesus' prediction of the destruction of Jerusalem, a prediction spoken and recorded prior to its fulfillment. To make this point, Turretin contends that Matthew, Mark, and Luke were written before 70 C.E. Although this "cannot be mathematically demonstrated . . . the arguments in proof of it are so full, that, if any matter of the kind may be considered as quite certain, this undoubtedly may."[12]

On the major Christian doctrines, Turretin represents a moderate view, sometimes characterized as "supernatural rationalism"[13] or "rational orthodoxy."[14] The doctrine of the Trinity, he says, is beyond, but not against, reason. Christ is divine as well as human, but Turretin stresses the role of Jesus as teacher. In regard to sin, Turretin does not accept Pelagianism, yet he argues that what humans inherit from Adam is merely the tendency toward evil. He rejects rigid predestination and believes salvation to be a possibility for all: everyone who repents and has faith will be accepted by

---

11. Ibid., 60, 61.
12. Ibid., 202, 256, 331.
13. James I. Good, *History of the Swiss Reformed Church since the Reformation* (Philadelphia: Publication and Sunday School Board of the Reformed Church in the U.S., 1913), 175.
14. Geiger, "Unionsbestrebungen der schweizerischen reformierten Theologie," 118.

God. In support of this view, Turretin imagines a prayer which Jesus might have uttered: "If I am dear to you, O Father, if you love me, if the obedience of my life and the pains of my death mean anything to you, forgive, forgive those who believe and who change their lives for the better, and accept in place of sacrifice this my passion, freely undergone for them."[15]

Turretin's Exegetical Method

In terms of NT research, Turretin's major work is his *Concerning the Method of Interpreting Sacred Scripture*, written in 1728.[16] Given the moderate character of Turretin's theology and the conservatism of his critical judgments, this concise statement of exegetical method represents a remarkable achievement. The work is divided into two parts: a discussion of false methods of interpretation and an affirmation of the true methods. Among those which Turretin rejects is the method of the Roman Catholic clergy, who claim that the interpretation of the church is the only correct one. But, responds Turretin, the church does not agree on the exegesis of Scripture, for throughout its history varying interpretations have been advanced. Moreover, some of the allegorical interpretations of the fathers are patently false. And, most important, the authority of the church, rather than being the judge of Scripture, is actually grounded in Scripture.

Also false, he charges, is the method of the enthusiasts, a method which arouses considerable negative enthusiasm in Turretin. In identifying the enthusiasts, Turretin mentions by name only the Quakers of England and Belgium, but some of his criticism could have been directed against Francke and the Pietists, as well. The enthusiasts think that interpretation is possible only by direct inner inspiration. In making this claim, Turretin argues, they cheapen reason, demean linguistic learning (not true of Francke, of course), and assume that anyone, a shoemaker, for example, can become an expositor of the gospel. Although they decry the validity of reason, the enthusiasts attempt to employ it in arguments with their opponents. Their own exegesis is tainted by prejudice and subjectivity; they do not agree among themselves; and some of their results are simply ridiculous.

Turretin also opposes methods which attempt to find too many meanings in Scripture. In particular, he refers to interpreters who seek mystical

---

15. Cited in John Walter Beardslee, *Theological Development at Geneva under Francis and Jean-Alphonse Turretin (1648–1737)* (Ph.D. diss. Yale University, 1956; Ann Arbor, Mich.: University Microfilms, 1965), 518.

16. Joh. Alph. Turrettino, *De Sacrae Scripturae interpretandae methodo, tractatus bipartitus. In quo falsae multorum Interpretum hypotheses refelluntur, Veraque interpretandae Sacrae Scripturae Methodus adstruitur,* in Turretin, *Opera omnia, theologica, philosophica et philologica* (Leovardiae et Franequerae: H. A. de Chalmot et D. Romar, 1775), 2.3–136.

and allegorical interpretations. This approach finds its historical background in the pagan myths and in fanciful Jewish exegesis as represented by Philo and the Cabbalists. Turretin does, however, acknowledge the biblical use of figurative language and is open to the discovery of fuller meanings, such as Paul's use of the unmuzzled ox in support of the ministry (1 Cor. 9:9). But meanings should be enhanced only in harmony with the primary literal sense, and exegetes must not do violence to the text or play games with it. In criticizing the allegorical method, Turretin points out that it provides no criteria whereby the results can be tested. The method is without limitations, and all sorts of fanciful and subjective interpretations can be devised. As a result of this method, the Bible is turned into a book of secrets, closed to the understanding of ordinary people. When Paul says that these things "were written down to instruct us" (1 Cor. 10:11), he does not mean that everything in the Bible is open to some sort of fanciful application; he had in mind specific historical events that applied to particular problems.

Having demolished the false methods, Turretin turns to the true. The importance of proper interpretation, he argues, cannot be exaggerated, for valid theology must be based on correct interpretation of Scripture. He asks, "What is theology except that which is communicated in Scripture."[17] In the process of introducing the true method, Turretin sounds the note that is to become the major theme of NT research in the period of the Enlightenment:

> At the outset, let us observe, in general, that there is no other method for the interpretation of Scripture, than that used for other books; it is necessary to attend to the sense of words and language, according to the purpose of the author, to what precedes and what follows, and to other things of this sort; and this is clearly the way in which all books, indeed all discourses are understood.[18]

In short, Turretin has affirmed with clarity and precision the basic principle of historical criticism. From this principle, he draws a variety of inferences. He notes that words should be understood according to common usage, and that that usage is discovered by research into the linguistic usage of the time of the author and by what comes before and after the appearance of the particular word in the text. In other words, terms and texts must be understood in their historical and literary context. Any interpretation which is against natural theology or reason, however, cannot be the correct interpretation.

---

17. Turretin, *Opera Omnia* 2.80.
18. Ibid., 2.81.

Turretin observes that in all languages people speak in figures, a phenomenon particularly apparent in languages that are not rich in modes of expression (Hebrew, for example) and in cultures in which people speak out of deep emotions. In regard to the interpretation of figurative language, Turretin believes that figures should be interpreted by texts that are literal and plain. The parables present a particular problem because they cannot be taken literally. For instance, the depiction of the coming of the Lord as a thief (Luke 12:39) does not mean that Jesus displays the characteristics of a robber. Parables, according to Turretin, must be interpreted in relation to the aim (*scopus*) of the parable, and the details of the parable should be understood in relation to that basic purpose. For example, the parable of the Prodigal Son makes one main point: every sinner who is moved to repentance will be received by God. Thus Turretin, anticipating later study of the parables, says, "It is proper to argue from the single aim of the parable" (*ex solo parabolae scopo*).[19]

After his discussion of general principles, Turretin turns to special rules of biblical interpretation. These rules are formulated in relation to the four basic types of biblical literature: historical, prophetic, moral, and doctrinal. In investigating the historical books, the interpreter must attend to the major aim of each book. These books, one should recognize, do not present exhaustive historical information but relate only what is necessary for understanding salvation. Moreover, the historical documents are not accurate in all their chronological details. The four Gospels recount many of the same stories but narrate them differently. The interpreter, in any case, must investigate the historical setting, that is, the study of geographical locations and the customs of the times.

The prophetic books bristle with problems. Again, it is essential to view the prophets in their own historical contexts. The interpreter must know both the Jewish history which the prophets address and the history of Israel's neighbors—the Egyptians and the Babylonians—who play a role in the prophetic message. Because the prophets speak of the future, it is also necessary to know the subsequent history. When interpreting prophecies that are to be fulfilled, the exegete must first seek a meaning in the time of the prophet, and only after that effort has been exhausted may one turn to later times. For example, when it is discerned that prophecies are not fulfilled in Jewish history, then it is appropriate to look to the events of early Christianity. At the same time, one should recognize that things that already have had a historical fulfillment may still have a fuller meaning in the future. For example, Joel's prediction of the outpouring of the

19. Ibid. 2.88.

Spirit (2:28) was repeatedly fulfilled in the experience of the OT prophets but was more fully realized in the events of Pentecost.

In dealing with texts relating to morality, Turretin advises flexibility of interpretation. He notes that one should not expect mathematical precision in regard to ethical instructions and warns the interpreter to be wary of taking absolutes absolutely. For example, although Jesus admonishes people not to swear at all, he himself says "Amen," and Paul is not above taking an oath now and then. Biblical ethical requirements are frequently expressed in hyperbole. Thus, Jesus' command to turn the other cheek turns out on some occasions to fly in the face of common sense and should, in Turretin's opinion, be taken with a grain of salt, a conclusion more in harmony with Turretin's spirit of moderation than with the radical character of NT ethics.

In regard to the doctrinal passages, Turretin offers some useful rules. He notes that the teachings of the NT assume the beliefs of the time— that, for instance, the apostles were Jews who accepted the basic teachings of Judaism. Thus, respecting the historical nature of biblical doctrine, exegetes must avoid reading theological notions from their own era back into the text. "An empty mind, if I may say so, ought to be brought to it [Scripture], so that it [the mind] should be like a *tabula rasa* in order that it might perceive the true and genuine sense of Scripture."[20] One should not attempt to find a doctrine—for instance, the divinity of Christ—everywhere in Scripture. Doctrinal books ought to be read not in segments but as a whole, and over and over again. The individual sections need to be interpreted within the context of the whole, and no doctrine can be derived from Scripture that corrupts the whole religion—Turretin's version of the argument from the analogy of faith.

Turretin's application of his method can be assessed by a perusal of his exegetical works. His short commentaries on Romans and 1 Thessalonians were published posthumously.[21] The Thessalonian work was compiled on the basis of students' notes from Turretin's lectures of 1722–24, while the publication of the Romans commentary appropriated his own manuscripts, which were probably also prepared for use in lectures.[22] Romans is especially important, because Turretin believes it presents the authentic summary of the Christian faith. In his commentary on Romans, Turretin begins with a prolegomena which deals with introductory matters such as

20. Ibid. 2.128.
21. *In Pauli Apostoli ad Romanos epistolae capita XI. Praelectiones criticae, theologicae, et concionatoriae*, in Turretin, *Opera omnia* 2.139–435; *Commentarius theoretico-practicus in epistolas Divi Pauli ad Thessalonicenses*, in Turretin, *Opera omnia*, 2.439–45.
22. See E. de Bude, *Vie de J.-A. Turrettini: Theologien Genevois, 1671–1737* (Lausanne: G. Bridel, 1880), 180–201.

the time and place of composition. In regard to the destination, Turretin points out that no mention is made of Peter, who, therefore, had not been in Rome at this time. Various difficulties confront the interpreter of the Pauline letters: a type of Greek in which Hebraisms abound, a unique style marked by abrupt transitions, and a historical situation known to the original readers but not to later interpreters. Moreover, Romans offers problems of its own: difficult terms and pronouns that are used in various ways. For Turretin, the major theological themes are important: the gospel as the full manifestation of justification by grace for all who have faith, and the dignity of Christ as son of God.

In exegetical practice, Turretin attends to textual, grammatical, and historical matters—all in the service of theological meaning. He is also concerned with practical application. Thus his discussion of Paul as slave of Christ shows to ministers the importance of devoting themselves with zeal and obedience to the things of Christ. On most of the larger issues, Turretin employs an analytical approach. Discussing Rom. 1:16, for example, he says there are four things the text affirms about the gospel: its aim is salvation; its condition is faith; its efficacy is the power of God; its benefits are broad. Turretin resonates to texts that confirm his own theological insights, such as the references to natural revelation in Romans 1. "Those who do not have a revealed law," he says, "have the natural law, that is those conceptions of justice and injustice, which are inscribed on the minds of humans from nature."[23]

One or two specific examples can illustrate the character of Turretin's exegetical work. On Rom. 1:17, he argues that "righteousness" refers to God's justification of people, although in 3:26 he understands δικαιοσύνη to refer both to God's fidelity and to God's act of justifying. In regard to the quotation of Hab. 2:4 (1:17), Turretin prefers the translation "the righteous shall live by faith." He also insists that Habakkuk was not uttering a prophecy about Christ and argues that the words of the prophet indicate that faith was the proper response to God then and now; God acts in the same way. On 3:25, Turretin discusses the possible rendering of ἱλαστήριον as "mercy seat," but he rejects that interpretation in favor of "propitiatory sacrifice." He also notes that διὰ πίστεως is lacking in some manuscripts, and he discusses the question of whether this prepositional phrase goes with what precedes or what follows in the text.

In sum, J. A. Turretin represents a transition from the old to the new, and his break with the theology of his father illustrates the dramatic shift that can occur within biblical studies in a single generation. Inspired by the spirit of the Enlightenment, Turretin accepts the new science,

---

23. Turretin, *Opera omnia* 2.149.

embraces reason, and affirms a natural theology. He opposes the deists, however, and retains many features of the traditional faith—but with qualifications. Revealed religion is necessary, although it must be in harmony with nature and reason. The Bible is authoritative as the historical record of special revelation, but it is not exhaustive or completely accurate in its details. The authority of Scripture is confirmed by miracles and fulfilled prophecy, but miracles must be understood in relation to the natural order, and prophecy should be interpreted in its historical setting. Under the influence of his ecumenism, Turretin is impatient with doctrinal precision, and the orthodox understanding of such doctrines as the atonement and predestination is eroded.

Turretin's most important contribution to the history of NT research is his treatise on the method of interpretation. In essence, Turretin calls for a shift from doctrinal to historical exegesis. He is opposed to the imposition of external interpretations upon the Bible—interpretations by the church, interpretations from religious experience, or interpretations based on theological presuppositions. In contrast to medieval exegesis, Turretin rejects the belief that the Bible can have many meanings. To be sure, biblical texts may have figurative or even allegorical meaning, but only if that is the meaning intended by the author. In short, there is one meaning: the historical. In pursuit of the historical meaning, Turretin does not differ widely from the first part of Francke's *Guide to the Reading of the Holy Scripture*,[24] although he is less concerned with linguistic and historical detail. However, Turretin objects to Francke's idea that only those who have the Spirit can properly interpret Scripture. For Turretin, the Bible must be read like any other book, and other books do not require inspired readers. Interpretation, therefore, has been secularized. However, his notion that the interpreter should approach Scripture with a blank mind —without any presuppositions—is betrayed by his own (and every other exegete's) practice. Turretin's interpretation is shaped by his own preconceptions, and these rest on a historical methodology and philosophy of history that had been determined by the rationalism and natural theology of the day—the worldview of the Enlightenment.

Johann Jakob Wettstein (1693–1754)

Although Turretin's novel opinions were largely tolerated, Johann Jakob Wettstein[25] experienced conflict; indeed, he thrived on it. Wettstein was

---

24. See pp. 65–69, above.
25. See C. L. Hulbert-Powell, *John James Wettstein, 1693–1754: An Account of His Life, Work and Some of His Contemporaries* (London: SPCK, 1937). Hulbert-Powell observes that "Wettstein" is the proper spelling; "Wetstein" is derived from the Latin "Wetstenius" (p. 1, n. 2). See J. I. Miller, "Wettstein or Wetstein," *Journal of Theological Studies* 28 (1977): 118–19.

born in Basel, where his father was a local pastor. After receiving bachelor's (1708) and master's degrees (1709) at Basel, the young Wettstein took up the study of theology and in 1713 was accepted into the ministry by the ecclesiastical authorities of Basel. His thesis, as part of the examination, dealt with the variant readings in the text of the NT. Wettstein argued that the variants did not destroy the integrity and authority of the Bible, although they did erode the doctrine of verbal inspiration and infallibility. In 1714 Wettstein traveled to Paris and London to visit scholars and collate manuscripts, including the treasured Codex Alexandrinus. He was appointed chaplain of a detachment of Swiss troops stationed in Britain in 1715, which gave him the opportunity to visit Bentley. After his return to Basel, Wettstein was appointed assistant to his father at St. Leonhard's Church, where his duties included instruction of the youth. Wettstein was a popular preacher and an outspoken opponent of the Helvetic Consensus.

Wettstein's Conflict with Orthodoxy

In 1729 the first shots were fired in Wettstein's long battle with the conservative theologians of Basel. He was summoned before the theological committee to answer questions about his views on the Trinity and Christology. The conservatives were actually troubled by his plans for revising the NT text, and his somewhat flippant responses did little to alleviate their anxiety. Charges were then taken before the town council, where evidence from his students' notes disclosed that, among other things, Wettstein considered demon possession to be a form of illness. The conservatives published a book attacking Wettstein's views, and citing evidence of heresy in his preaching at St. Leonhard's.[26] In self-defense, Wettstein feigned orthodoxy, but his views on the subordination of Christ and the Spirit betrayed the taint of rationalism. In 1730, the council voted to remove him from the diaconate.

Wettstein moved to Amsterdam, where the intellectual climate was freer. The Remonstrants (Dutch Calvinists sympathetic to Arminian theology) offered him a teaching post in their seminary, but the Municipal Council, controlled by the more orthodox Calvinist majority, insisted that the charges made in Basel be resolved before Wettstein could teach in Amsterdam. Returning to his native city, Wettstein spent 1731 to 1733 seeking reinstatement. At first the Basel authorities were sympathetic and took official action to restore Wettstein to ministerial office. The conservatives

---

26. *Acta oder Handlungen, Betreffend die Irrthümer und anstössige Lehren H.J.J.W. gewesenen Diac. Leonh., Enthaltend Die Bedencken E. Ehrwürd. Conventus Theologici, Und seine Hrn. W. selbst eigene Schutz-Schrifften, samt Andern dazu dienlichen Documenten* (Basel: J. H. Decker, 1730).

continued their opposition, however, and Wettstein, who should have been satisfied to leave well enough alone, turned on his critics, accusing them of heresy. The tone of his attack, made in both writing and public address, was so caustic that the town council ordered Wettstein to appear for reprimand. Before the meeting could be held, he returned to Amsterdam. There the Dutch authorities, still harboring suspicions, agreed to allow Wettstein to teach, but only on the conditions that he would not support Socinianism and would not persist in his plan to revise the NT text. The first condition presented little problem, since Wettstein was no Socinian. He largely ignored the second and, along with teaching philosophy, church history, and theology, gave major attention to his work on the text of the NT. Wettstein was largely vindicated when, in 1744, he was offered the chair of Greek at the University of Basel. At first attracted, he decided to spend the rest of his career in Amsterdam where there was greater freedom and a better salary.

Wettstein's Text-Critical Research

Wettstein's major contribution to NT research is in the area of text criticism.[27] In 1730, while the controversy was raging in Basel, a *Prolegomena* to his proposed NT text appeared, published anonymously in Amsterdam.[28] In this work, Wettstein argues that a study of the available editions of the NT makes evident the need for a textual revision. His own proposal was to base a revised text primarily on the Codex Alexandrinus. In text-critical practice, Wettstein favored extensive use of the patristic sources. He held a low view of the Latin versions but planned to rely heavily on the Syriac. Wettstein praised Mill's edition, but he found this British critic guilty of errors in collation. The *Prolegomena* also included a section on "observations and precautions necessary for the consideration of variant readings of the NT."[29] In this section, Wettstein presents nineteen principles for

27. See Lyle O. Bristol, "New Testament Textual Criticism in the Eighteenth Century," *Journal of Biblical Literature* 69 (1950): 105–8.

28. *Prolegomena ad Novi Testamenti Graeci editionem accuratissimam, E Vetustissimis Codd. MSS. denuo procurandam; in Quibus agitur De Codd. MSS. N. Testamenti, Scriptoribus Graecis, qui N. Testamento usi sunt, Versionibus veteribus, Editionibus prioribus & claris Interpretibus; & proponuntur Animadversiones & Cautiones ad Examen Variarum Lectionum N. T. necessariae* (Amsterdam: R. & J. Wettstein and G. Smith, 1730). This work was also reprinted with notes and an appendix by J. S. Semler as *Ioh. Iac. Wetstenii Prolegomena in Novum Testamentum, notas adiecit atque appendicem de vetustioribus latinis recensionibus quae in variis codicibus supersunt Ioh. Sal. Semler cum quibusdam characterum graecorum et latinorum in libris manuscriptis exemplis* (Halle: Rengerian, 1764.)

29. This section of the 1730 *Prolegomena* is reprinted in Wettstein's later edition of the text: *Η ΚΑΙΝΗ ΔΙΑΘΗΚΗ Novum Testamentum Graecum editionis receptae cum lectionibus variantibus codicum MSS., Editionum aliarum, Versionum et Patrum nec non commentario pleniore, Ex Scriptoribus veteribus Hebraeis, Graecis et Latinis, Historiam et vim verborun illustrante opera et studio Joannis Jacobi Wetstenii* (Amsterdam: Dommerian, 1751–52) 2.851–74.

evaluating textual variants. Among the most important is his insistence that no special sanctity should be attributed to the Received Text. Conjectural emendations, he thought, should be neither accepted nor rejected hastily. Some of Wettstein's principles are reminiscent of Bengel's canon of the "harder reading." Thus he says that where there are two readings, the one that is clearer or expressed in better Greek should not be chosen, and fuller readings should be rejected in favor of shorter variants. Readings which agree with the style of the author or with usage elsewhere in the author's writings should be accepted. Wettstein also argues that, all other things being equal, the older manuscripts and the majority of manuscripts present the preferred readings.

Wettstein's text appeared in 1751 and 1752, in two handsome folio volumes of 966 and 896 pages, respectively.[30] Following the advice of the Remonstrants, Wettstein agreed to print the Elzevir edition of 1624 rather than a revised text. In the prolegomena—a revision of the earlier one—Wettstein declares that two things are necessary for understanding Scripture: the establishment of the text and the interpretation of its words. Wettstein also presents his questionable theory that many early Greek manuscripts had been corrupted by a Latinizing influence. He gives a full description of the major textual materials: Greek codices, Latin translations, patristic authors, and other ancient versions. In discussing the modern editions, Wettstein is his typical irascible self. Excerpts from his correspondence with Bentley are included that present the Cambridge scholar in an unfavorable light. Bengel is criticized at length for, among other things, printing a revised text of the Apocalypse. Iselin and Frey, Wettstein's conservative opponents at Basel, are attacked. Included is a letter, dated 1733, from J. A. Turretin in which he encourages Wettstein to abandon Basel for a more peaceful place to pursue his work. This sort of petulant personal material seems quite out of place in the introduction to a critical edition of the NT text.

The text itself is printed at the top of the page (usually only a few lines) followed by the critical apparatus which lists variants. The sources of the variants are identified by a system of abbreviations wherein capital letters stand for uncial manuscripts (e.g., D = Claramontanus) and Arabic numerals represent minuscules, the system refined at the beginning of the twentieth century by C. R. Gregory and still in use today. Wettstein's apparatus increased the number of variants available to the text critic and included material from more than one hundred manuscripts which he himself had collated. One or two samples from

---

30. Wettstein's text, in slightly reduced format, was reprinted in 1962 by Akademische Druck- u. Verlagsanstalt, Graz, Austria.

Wettstein's apparatus can illustrate the character of his textual-critical results. In a long note on 1 Tim. 3:16,[31] Wettstein concludes that the relative pronoun ὅ should be read rather than ὅς (as in the Nestle text) or Θεός (as in the Received Text). Thus the text would be translated "the mystery of our religion: which was manifested in the flesh," rather than "the mystery of our religion: God was manifest in the flesh." Actually, Wettstein had reached this conclusion earlier when he detected in Codex Alexandrinus evidence that the original Greek omicron had been misread as a theta, so that Θεός was mistakenly introduced into the text. In supporting his conclusion, Wettstein reviews the manuscript and patristic evidence, and he asks how Cyril of Alexandria—if Θεός had stood in his text—could have failed to mention this verse in his argument with Julian the Apostate, who claimed that Paul had never referred to Christ as God. Another lengthy note discusses the problematic 1 John 5:7.[32] Wettstein concludes that the three heavenly witnesses of v. 7—the Father, the Logos, and the Spirit—represent a gloss, added for dogmatic purposes in opposition to the Arians. Wettstein surveys the manuscript and patristic evidence and reviews the opinions of the modern editors. He notes that Erasmus omitted the verse from his first two editions. Bengel, who included it, comes in for harsh criticism.

Wettstein's exegetical notes are printed in double columns below the text-critical apparatus, usually occupying about two-thirds of the page. The notes regularly deal with terms, phrases, and historical details, and include an extensive collection of classical and rabbinic references. Weighty theological commentary is largely lacking. The presentation of each biblical book is prefaced by a brief introduction, and the critical judgments therein are, in the main, conservative. For example, on the Gospels, Wettstein supports the traditional authorship and believes they were written in canonical order; Mark presents a short summary of Matthew and adds material he had received from Peter: "For since Mark had the Gospel of Matthew before his eyes, which is evident from a Harmony, and since he knew the order of events was not preserved by Matthew . . . he was able to make use of the same freedom which Matthew had used, and because variation was pleasing to the reader, he did not make the mistake to submit to servile, indeed, tedious imitation."[33] John, the son of Zebedee, is accepted as the author of the Apocalypse, which he composed on Patmos. After returning to Ephesus, he wrote the Fourth Gospel, which supplements the others. Wettstein

31. Wettstein, *Novum Testamentum Graecum* 2.330–35.
32. Ibid. 2.721–27.
33. Ibid. 1.552.

devotes a long discussion to the question of the authorship of Hebrews. He argues that it was originally written in Greek but could not have been composed by Barnabas or Clement of Rome. Grotius's hypothesis of Luke is given serious attention, but Wettstein finally opts for Paul. He explains the difference of style with the theory that authors are able to modify their way of writing. The absence of a Pauline salutation is answered by his claim that Paul is writing to Jewish Christians in Rome who would have been indifferent to the qualifications of the apostle to the Gentiles, qualifications which Paul usually includes in his epistolary introductions.

In discussing exegetical issues, Wettstein is largely traditional, although he presents material his critics found disturbing. In regard to the census of Luke 2, Wettstein acknowledges the problem and rejects easy solutions—for example, emending the text or removing it as a gloss. He concludes that the event at the time of the birth of Jesus was not really a census but some sort of a preliminary enrollment. In discussing the virgin birth, Wettstein includes references to the myths of the pagans which depict unique births. Although he argues that these, in contrast to the birth of Jesus, involved the shameful deeds of the deities, his opponents considered these pagan parallels unmentionable. In his discussion of the miracle at the wedding in Cana, Wettstein's parallel to the fable about Bacchus turning water into wine was similarly offensive.

At the end of the second volume of his text, Wettstein discusses methods of interpretation.[34] He acknowledges that ordinary people can read the Bible in the vernacular and learn all they need for salvation but argues that trained scholars can make the meaning clearer. Like Turretin, Wettstein maintains that one should interpret the Bible as one interprets any other book: "Since with the same eyes we read both sacred books and edicts of a ruler, both ancient and modern books, therefore the same rules should be used in the interpretation of the former, which we use in the understanding of the latter."[35] In following this principle, Wettstein formulates rules that essentially lead to the literal and historical understanding of the text. When interpreting a word or phrase, attention must be given to what comes before and after, in other words, the context. Meanings are to be discerned more from usage than from etymology. Usage is assessed by first investigating the use of the term elsewhere by the same author, then its use by other writers of the NT and the LXX,

---

34. Wettstein, "De interpretatione Novi Testamenti," in idem, *Novum Testamentum Graecum* 2.874–89.
35. Ibid. 2.875.

and finally its use by writers of the same historical situation. Wettstein's seventh rule is especially enlightening:

> There is another rule which is much more useful and easier to understand: if you desire to understand the books of the NT more clearly and fully, assume the personage of those to whom they were first delivered by the apostles for reading; transfer yourself in understanding into that time and place where they first were read: take care, in so far as possible, that you understand the rites, habits, customs, opinions, accepted sentiments, proverbs, parables, and daily expressions of those people, and the ways and means for persuading others and the occasions for establishing faith.[36]

In overview, Wettstein's place in the history of NT research is assured by his text-critical accomplishment. His work encompassed a larger number of manuscripts and variants than did his predecessors', and his system of identifying manuscripts provided a useful tool for future text-critical work. In comparison with a critic like Bengel, Wettstein's textual judgments, freed from orthodox presuppositions, represented an advance in the direction of the modern, critical text. Although his prejudice against the Latin texts was questionable, Wettstein's criticism of the Received Text was prophetic. However, his hope to publish a revised text—impeded by the opposition of his critics—had to await the work of bolder critics like Griesbach[37] and Tischendorf.[38] Actually, this concession to his critics was one of the few situations in which Wettstein was accommodating and, in fact, the one in which his own position was clearly superior to that of his opponents. To be sure, Wettstein, like a trained gamecock, seemed always eager to provoke a fight, and some of his theological views, tainted with rationalism and reflecting a low Christology, were clearly in conflict with Calvinist orthodoxy. Thus, although opposition to Wettstein's exegetical work was predictable, the attack on his text-critical research seems surprising. After all, if more and older texts were being appropriated, that would appear to give promise for a text that more closely approximated the inspired original. In this time of intellectual revolution, however, nothing was feared so much as change. The Received Text represented the old, and many people, like the wine tasters of Jesus' parable, said, "The old is good" (Luke 5:39). However, in spite of growing opposition to the Enlightenment approach to the Bible, the future belonged not to the old, but to the new—the new historical understanding of Scripture which Wettstein so sharply articulated.

---

36. Ibid. 2.878.
37. See pp. 141–43, below.
38. See pp. 322–28, below.

PHILOLOGICAL AND GRAMMATICAL METHOD:
JOHANN AUGUST ERNESTI (1707–1781)

Johann August Ernesti was a noted classical philologist, sometimes called the "German Cicero." The son of a superintendent of clergy in Saxony, Ernesti studied at Wittenberg and Leipzig. In 1734, he was appointed principal of the Thomasschule at Leipzig, an elementary school with seven grades and eight teachers. There Ernesti had the misfortune of having on his staff a genius—J. S. Bach. Bach had been cantor and instructor of music at St. Thomas since 1723, and when young Ernesti (age twenty-seven) assumed leadership, conflict between the two strong personalities was inevitable.[39] Actually, Bach, a devout Lutheran, was suspicious of Ernesti's Enlightenment sympathies, while Ernesti, who was preoccupied with philology, had little appreciation for music. A dispute arose between them in 1736 concerning the authority to appoint and discipline the student musical assistants, an authority each claimed as his. The dispute, which raged for months, was brought before both the town council and the church consistory and was finally decided in Bach's favor by the intervention of the king of Saxony.

No doubt Ernesti found university life more peaceful. In 1742, he was appointed associate professor at the University of Leipzig, and in 1756, he was awarded the important chair in classical rhetoric. In 1759, he moved to the theological faculty. As to theology, Ernesti was a moderate, although Jean Paul Richter, one of his pupils at the Thomasschule, said, "Most of the students were set in the direction of heterodoxy during Ernesti's time."[40] Ernesti's basic view of Scripture was actually orthodox, for he believed the Bible to be authoritative and infallible. "Since the books of Scripture are written by inspired men," he wrote, "it is clear that no real contradiction can exist in them."[41] In his approach to the Bible, Ernesti opposed pietistic subjectivism, on the one hand, and extreme rationalism, on the other. Against the increasingly popular claim of the superiority of truths of reason, Ernesti affirmed the truths of history. The truths of the Bible belonged to the latter category; they were factual. Scripture, which recorded these facts, should be recognized as the norm of doctrine.

---

39. See Paul Minear, "J. S. Bach and J. A. Ernesti: A Case Study in Exegetical and Theological Conflict," in *Our Common History as Christians: Essays in Honor of Albert C. Outler*, ed. J. Deschner, L. T. Howe, and K. Penzel (New York: Oxford University Press, 1975), 131–55; Robert Stevenson, "Bach's Quarrel with the Rector of St. Thomas School," *Anglican Theological Review* 33 (1951): 219–30.

40. Cited in Stevenson, "Bach's Quarrel," 225.

41. J. A. Ernesti, *Principles of Biblical Interpretation*, 2 vols., trans. Charles H. Terrot (Edinburgh: T. Clark, 1832) 1.38.

Ernesti's *Principles of Interpretation*

Although the bulk of his publishing was in the area of classical philology, Ernesti produced a few works on the Bible. For NT research, his most important book is *Institutio interpretis Novi Testamenti* (1761),[42] an introduction to exegetical method in the tradition of Francke's *Guide*[43] and Turretin's *Methodo*. In the prolegomenon, Ernesti asserts that "all sure knowledge, and all effective defence of divine truth, must be derived from a clear understanding and accurate interpretation of the sacred records."[44] For Ernesti, hermeneutics is the science of obtaining clarity. His method is the grammatico-historical, a method that employs philology and grammar to discern the literal meaning of texts in their historical and literary setting. Basic to Ernesti's approach is the principle which has already become familiar to readers of Turretin and Wettstein: "the meaning of sacred books can be discovered by no other means than those which are employed upon other books."[45]

Reminiscent of Francke, the first part of Ernesti's *Principles* is dedicated to discerning the meaning of words. Every word, in Ernesti's judgment, has a meaning, a literal sense. This does not imply that biblical terms can have only one meaning, but it does suggest that interpreters are not free to fancy all sorts of meanings. Ernesti, like Turretin, is opposed to excessive allegorical and typological exegesis. The meaning of words is to be discerned by their linguistic usage in the text. "There is no other sense of words," claims Ernesti, "except the grammatical, and that which the grammarians deliver."[46] By this Ernesti does not intend to deny that the Bible uses figurative language. However, when tropical or metaphorical language is used, it is used with the intent of the author, so that it, too, has a "literal" meaning—the meaning the author intends.

Ernesti proceeds to present rules of interpretation. In interpreting ancient texts, the exegete must search for the meaning the words had at the time they were originally written. Each author must be understood according to that author's particular style and choice of literary genre. The meaning of terms can be discerned by the study of their use in context, what comes before and after, and their relation to the scope of the passage and the aim of the whole document. Ernesti recommends what he calls the analogy of language whereby words of the same class or

---

42. Ioannis Augusti Ernesti, *Institutio interpretis Novi Testamenti*, 4th ed., ed. C. F. Ammon (Leipzig: Weidmann, 1792); Eng. trans.: see n. 41; abbreviated English version: *Elements of Interpretation*, trans. Moses Stuart (Andover, Mass.: Flagg & Gould, 1822).

43. See pp. 65–69, above.

44. Ernesti, *Principles* 1.1.

45. Ibid. 1.30.

46. Ernesti, *Institutio*, 24.

words that treat the same subject are compared. In studying NT language, it is important to recognize that biblical Greek has a Semitic quality; "it imitates the Hebrew, not merely in single words, phrases and figures of speech, but also in the general texture of the style."[47] This means that the NT exegete must have a knowledge of Hebrew, Chaldee, and Syriac as well as Greek. In the comprehension of NT language, the study of the LXX is helpful, because it "must form the basis of all sound knowledge of the Hebrew-Greek idiom."[48] Since Scripture is given by inspiration, new expressions appear in the NT that are to be interpreted by NT parallels, with the help of the fathers of the church. This common NT and patristic norm provides what Ernesti calls the analogy of Scripture, his version of the analogy of faith.

Ernesti devotes a chapter to the interpretation of tropical or metaphorical language. He insists that the exegete must always seek the literal meaning first and only resort to figurative interpretation when the text itself demands it. In interpreting allegories, attention must be given to the scope of the whole allegory and then to the relation of words to that primary meaning. Although Ernesti considers parables to be "nothing more than allegory,"[49] he actually opposes the allegorization of the parables. For example, in regard to the parable of the Prodigal Son, he says that the interpreter should not search for some esoteric meaning in the robe, the calf, or the ring.

Ernesti presents a chapter on reconciling apparent discrepancies. When two texts flatly contradict, the interpreter must conclude that one of the texts has been corrupted—an easy answer to a difficult problem. Apparent doctrinal discrepancies between two texts are explained by "the want of dogmatic accuracy in the one or the other, or by the wide difference that exists between the idioms of the eastern and western languages."[50] Seeming discrepancies in historical texts are due to differences in language and modes of narration rather than to contradiction of facts. In harmonizing apparent discrepancies, the interpreter should use clear texts to explain the obscure.

In the second part of his *Principles*, Ernesti offers advice to scholars preparing translations or commentaries. The aim of translation is to reproduce the exact meaning of the original author "without diminution, addition, or alteration." In writing a commentary, the author should first attend to the text and its variants, then to the meaning of individual

47. Ernesti, *Principles* 1.104.
48. Ibid. 1.116.
49. Ibid. 1.156.
50. Ibid. 1.174.

words, and finally to the larger historical or doctrinal subject matter. In summarizing the research, the opinions of others should be offered first, then those of the commentator together with the supporting reasons. The commentator should strive not to display erudition but to present the results briefly and with clarity. "The excellence of an interpreter," says Ernesti, "consists much in simplicity."[51]

Most of the third part of Ernesti's work is devoted to higher and lower criticism. In general, he believes the NT books to have been written by those authors to whom they have traditionally been ascribed. He thinks attacks on authenticity by heretical critics ought to be repulsed. Ernesti's treatment of the issue of authorship can be illustrated by the prolegomena to his lengthy commentary on Hebrews, published posthumously.[52] After noting that the authorship has long been debated, Ernesti proceeds to dismiss the hypotheses that Barnabas or Clement of Rome could have been the author. He gives special attention to the possibilities of authorship by either Luke or Apollos and rejects them. He then takes up the main arguments against Pauline authorship, such as style and lack of a salutation. After answering these, he presents reasons to support Paul as author, for example, the ending of the letter and historical references which fit Paul. He concludes that Paul is probably the author but says that even if Hebrews had been written by Luke (the next most likely candidate), the inspired, authentic, and canonical character of the epistle would be assured.

As to the text, Ernesti acknowledges that minor errors have crept in, but he believes that divine providence has cared for the transmission of Scripture. By careful study of the extant manuscripts, he thinks "a complete and uncorrupted text may be formed."[53] Ernesti describes the major materials of text criticism: Greek manuscripts, ancient versions, and quotations from the fathers. In evaluating variants, he attends to the age and quality of the manuscripts. The quality of a manuscript is not determined by age alone, however, but by the paucity of faults and variations—although faulty manuscripts sometimes contain correct readings. Ernesti has his own version of the principle of the harder reading: "Readings which are difficult, unusual, and . . . far-fetched, are to be preferred to those which are plain, usual and direct." In reviewing the history of lower criticism, Ernesti notes the work of Mill, Bengel, and Wettstein, saying

51. Ibid. 1.185, 206.
52. Ioannis Augusti Ernesti, *Lectiones academicae in epistolam ad Hebraeos, ab ipso revisae cum eiusdem excursibus theologicis, edidit commentarium in quo multa ad recentissimorum inprimis interpretum sententias pertinentia uberius illustrantur,* ed. Gottlib Immanuel Dindorf (Leipzig: C. Fritsch, 1795), 1–7.
53. Ernesti, *Principles* 2.13.

about Bengel, "He was deficient in the knowledge of Greek." Concerning the future of text criticism, Ernesti concludes, "We must not suppose that the work of Biblical criticism is exhausted, and that nothing remains for us to do."[54]

The final section of Ernesti's *Principles* discusses resources that aid in the task of interpretation. He stresses the importance of the study of the Jewish sources—the rabbinic writings, Philo, and Josephus. After reviewing the history of exegesis from Origen to Wettstein, Ernesti concludes that the interpreter ought to make use of the commentaries of two representatives of the grammatical method, scholars like Grotius. In addition to the study of rhetoric, philosophy—particularly logic—is helpful for clarifying meanings. By studying history, the exegete will be able to understand customs and rites, festivals and sacrificial practices, the nature of the Jewish sects, the religion of the Greeks, the political administration of the Romans, all of which is important information for interpreting the NT in its historical setting. Anticipating a later dispute, Ernesti mentions scholars who "think that in the Epistles of St. Paul, there are allusions to an eastern system of philosophy out of which the Gnostics drew their system," but goes on to conclude, "It is well known, however, that the Gnostics . . . were posterior to the Apostolic age."[55]

Ernesti's Exegetical Practice

Examples of Ernesti's application of his principles can be seen in his *Notes on the Books of the New Testament*, published posthumously but based on lectures given in 1767 and 1768.[56] Ernesti generally adheres to his intent to present a grammatico-historical interpretation. The *Notes*, in regard to higher criticism, offer almost nothing by way of historical introduction to the NT books. In the course of the work, some verses receive extensive notes, while others are totally ignored. Ernesti, however, usually wrestles with problematic texts like Matt. 2:23, where the word of the prophets, "He will be called a Nazorean," cannot be found in any OT book. To his credit, Ernesti avoids an easy solution, discrediting theories which suppose that Matthew is citing some lost prophetic sources.

Ernesti's concern with textual matters and grammar is apparent. He believes that μαρτύριον is to be preferred to μυστήριον in 1 Cor. 2:1, where weighty manuscript evidence is on his side. In regard to John 1:14, he argues that παρὰ πατρός ("from the father"; my trans.) should be construed with δόξαν rather than with μονογενοῦς, so that the text stresses the

54. Ibid. 2.130, 140, 144.
55. Ibid. 2.345.
56. Johann August Ernesti, *Anmerkungen über die Bücher des neuen Testaments* (Leipzig and Quedlinburg: C. A. Reussner, 1786).

glory from the Father rather than the *only son* from the Father. In a lengthy note on δεδωρημένης ("has granted") in 2 Peter 1:3, Ernesti discusses whether the term is active or passive, noting that it could have active meaning even though the form is passive. He also mentions the rule that verbs which lack a passive form in the perfect tense use a middle construction to express passive meaning. Ernesti remarks that he adds this grammatical tidbit for the benefit of young students who are attempting to learn their biblical languages correctly; for the old who have neglected this sort of study, "it is too late."[57] Ernesti also observes that the Gospel of John employs a Hebraic kind of Greek that renders the author's use of tenses imprecise.

Ernesti's concern with historical matters is evident. In regard to Luke 2:1, for example, he observes that some critics believe a census like that described in the text could have taken place only in Rome. Ernesti argues that there were two types of censuses, one for citizens, and one for people of the provinces. In commenting on Luke 5:19 (about the paralytic let down through the roof), Ernesti presents a description of the architecture of Near Eastern houses. In discussing Matt. 14:2, in which Herod thinks Jesus may be John the Baptist raised from the dead, Ernesti argues that this text, along with Matt. 16:14, John 9:2, and Wisd. of Sol. 8:19-20, offers little proof that the Jews or the disciples believed in the transmigration of souls.

As his *Principles* indicates, Ernesti is harsh on allegorical interpretation. In an extensive comment on John 3:14-15, he refutes those who identify the serpent (of Num. 21:9) as a type of Jesus. Serpents, he notes, regularly symbolize evil in the Bible. The type, properly understood, refers not to Jesus but to the act of Moses in lifting up the serpent. "So Jesus himself explains it here," concludes Ernesti, "and he without doubt is the best interpreter of his own examples."[58] Similarly, Jesus is not to be identified with a lamb. The phrase "Here is the Lamb of God" (John 1:29, 36) means that Jesus would die for the sins of humanity in the same way that an innocent lamb would be sacrificed.

Along the way, Ernesti offers some insightful exegetical suggestions. Commenting on 2 Cor. 3:2, he solves a text-critical problem by an exegetical argument from context: the letters of recommendation (*Recommendationsbriefe*)[59] must have been written on "your" (ὑμῶν, not ἡμῶν) hearts in order to be known and read by all people. Ernesti argues that the speaking in tongues described in Acts 2:4 should be understood in relation to

57. Ibid., 262.
58. Ibid., 56.
59. Ibid., 208.

the phenomenon described in 1 Corinthians 12–14. There it is evident that glossolalia is not a miracle of translation that early Christian preachers could use for propagating the gospel in foreign lands. Instead, it is a gift from the Spirit to be used for prayer and praise within the worship of the faithful community.

Ernesti's effort to explain problems in relation to his conservative presuppositions is sometimes apparent. He finds it difficult to understand, for example, how Paul could have supposed the eschaton to be imminent. Thus, according to Ernesti, the assertion "The Lord is near" (Phil. 4:4) must either mean that Paul is reminding his readers of the shortness of life or admonishing them to seek the help of the ever-present Lord in prayer. Ernesti has no trouble in accepting the miracles. Thus he understands the cursing of the fig tree (Mark 11:12-14, 20-22) as a sign of both the divinity and humanity of Jesus. "Through the miracle, Jesus wanted to give proof of his deity (*Gottheit*), as by the fact that he hungered, he proved that he was a true human being." Ernesti is bothered by Jesus' word "the Father is greater than I" (John 14:28), but he seems to suppose that Jesus' entrance into history involved a self-limitation of his power. Thus he concludes that Jesus means "the Father can do more, therefore, than I in my presence among you can do."[60]

Looking back over the work of Ernesti, one cannot avoid marveling at his erudition. Moreover, his main contribution to the history of NT research is apparent: the rigorous use of linguistic and grammatical analysis in the service of historical interpretation. Ernesti's work, nevertheless, is troubled by inner tensions: on the one hand, he employs the new philological method; on the other hand, he holds to traditional views of biblical authority, views that predetermine his historical judgments concerning issues like authenticity. Although he echoes the claim that the Bible should be read like any other book and employs the same rules of grammar he uses in interpreting the classics, Ernesti assigns the Bible a unique place. A book that is recognized as inspired, infallible, and without discrepancies is no ordinary book, and an exegete who approaches it with such presuppositions is not using a secular hermeneutic. In effect, Ernesti's work involves a tension between faith and method, a tension which continues to disturb NT research throughout its ongoing history.

SUMMARY

The three scholars reviewed in this chapter represent a preliminary stage in the development of the historical criticism of the NT. In some ways, all

---

60. Ibid., 30, 85.

three belong to the pre-critical world: Turretin affirms the special revelation of the Bible; Wettstein accepts biblical authority; and Ernesti believes in scriptural infallibility. To be sure, Turretin and Wettstein, who acknowledge discrepancies in the Bible, stand to the left of Ernesti, but all three maintain a worldview that recognizes the supernatural and the reality of miracles. At the same time, these three scholars were profoundly influenced by the Enlightenment: Turretin embraces natural theology; Wettstein probes the ancient sources; and Ernesti practices the science of philology. All three are devoted to the use of reason, and, like their contemporaries in other fields of learning, they all are preoccupied with the problem of methodology. Most important, the methods which they adopt, although varying in details, represent a fundamental shift in the study of the Bible away from a concern with doctrine to a concern with words. The new methodologies not only consider doctrinal presuppositions to be anathema but also believe doctrinal conclusions to be secondary. Of primary importance is the analysis of words in the service of historical reconstruction; doctrine follows and is built upon literal, historical exegesis.

In the pursuit of historical interpretation, these scholars had acquired a variety of skills and amassed a mountain of useful information: materials and procedures of text criticism had been advanced; knowledge of linguistics and grammar had been learned from the classicists; techniques of literary criticism had been employed whereby terms and sentences could be analyzed in their context and in relation to the larger literary genre; historical information had been collected to provide a better understanding of the biblical data in their original setting. Yet, in spite of this erudition, one may wonder whether the passion for the historical, like orthodoxy's pursuit of the dogmatic, did not tend to purge the Scriptures of their vitality. Perhaps Ernesti's opponent at the Thomasschule, J. S. Bach, was more sensitive to the deeper meaning of the Bible than was Ernesti.[61] In any case, Turretin, Wettstein, and Ernesti, with their concern for historicity, appear to have played a preliminary role in the "eclipse of biblical narrative."[62] Yet, whatever the outcome, the future belonged to the historians.

61. See Minear, "J. S. Bach and J. A. Ernesti," 131–55. See also Jaroslav Pelikan, *Bach among the Theologians* (Philadelphia: Fortress Press, 1986).
62. See Frei, *The Eclipse of the Biblical Narrative.*

5

Refining
Historical Research:
Canon and Higher Criticism

As methods continued to be refined in pursuit of the historical under-standing of the NT, attempts were made to resolve the increasing tension between faith and criticism. How could the new discoveries in science, literature, and history be assimilated into the Christian religion? How could the enlightened persons of the eighteenth century continue to be people of faith? What authority could be affirmed for the Bible—this antique book, abounding in the supernatural—in a day when the truths of the universe were being discovered by the rational inquiry of intelli-gent human beings? Questions of this sort were addressed by a group of eighteenth-century progressive thinkers who were labeled "neologians."[1] Among them, popular preachers like J.F.W. Jerusalem (1709–89) attempted to present a sensible understanding of the gospel to the thoughtful people in the pews.[2] The neologians did not deny the validity of divine revelation but assigned priority to reason and natural theology. While faith in God, morality, and immortality were affirmed, older dogmas such as the Trinity, predestination, and the inspiration of Scripture were seriously compromised.

Although J. S. Semler and J. D. Michaelis are sometimes classified as neologians, they were independent historical critics who belonged to no party.[3] The neologians, however, appropriated the results of the historical-critical work of Semler and Michaelis, and the questions the neologians addressed were questions that concerned these biblical scholars. Semler was preoccupied with the problem of truth: How did biblical research

---

1. See Karl Aner, *Die Theologie der Lessingzeit* (Hildesheim: G. Olms, 1964).
2. See Wolfgang Erich Müller, *Johann Friedrich Wilhelm Jerusalem: Eine Untersuchung zur Theologie der "Betrachtungen über die Vornehmsten Wahrheiten der Religion,"* Theologische Bib-liothek Töpelmann 43 (Berlin and New York: de Gruyter, 1984).
3. See Aner, *Theologie,* 98–99.

relate to a comprehensive understanding of reality? What was the nature and authority of the biblical canon? Michaelis, less sensitive to theological issues than Semler, used the tools of historical criticism to build support for biblical authority and, in the process, made a monumental contribution to the science of NT introduction. Their two most famous students, J. J. Griesbach and J. G. Eichhorn,[4] carried on the tradition of their teachers. For Griesbach, an accomplished text critic and pioneer in Gospel research, the truth of Christianity was historical. With Eichhorn, a master of higher criticism, the truth of the Bible was interpreted by a hermeneutic of myth.

THE PROBLEM OF CANON:
JOHANN SALOMO SEMLER (1725–1791)

Born in Saalfeld (southwest of Leipzig), Johann Salomo Semler was a child of two spirits of his time: the older pietistic mysticism and the new empirical rationalism. He was interested in alchemy; he wrote an important treatise on entomology. The son of an ecclesiastical official, Semler was reared in the atmosphere of Pietism.[5] His father came increasingly under the sway of pietistic religion, and his mother, a deeply religious person, made an indelible mark on his life. Semler, with considerable despair, was never able to experience the new birth which Pietists thought essential to authentic faith, a point of increasing tension with his father. Nevertheless, Semler maintained throughout his life a serious religious concern, exemplified in a spirit of personal piety.[6] At an early age, he displayed exceptional intellectual gifts. He frequented his father's library, collected books of his own, and read Latin, Greek, and Hebrew fluently. In 1743, he entered the University of Halle, where he came under the spell of S. J. Baumgarten.[7] Semler later said that in the presence of the eminent professor he felt like "a poor midget."[8] For Baumgarten, a disciple of the philosophy of Wolff, both supernatural revelation (recorded in the Bible) and natural theology (discerned by empiricism and reason) were essential. In spite of his efforts at synthesis, a tension between faith and understanding remained in Baumgarten's thought.

4. Aner classifies both Griesbach and Eichhorn as neologians (Ibid., 138–39).

5. For a discussion of Semler's treatment of pietistic thought in his early writings, see Gottfried Hornig, "Semlers Lehre von der Heilsordnung: Eine Studie zur Rezeption und Kritik des halleschen Pietismus," *Pietismus und Neuzeit: Ein Jahrbuch zur Geschichte des neueren Protestantismus* 10 (1984): 152–89.

6. For an account of Semler's personal piety, including his reaction to the death of his daughter, see John F. Hurst, *History of Rationalism*, 9th ed. (New York: Nelson & Phillips, 1865), 133–36.

7. See p. 93, above.

8. Cited in Fritz Huber, *Johann Salomo Semler: Seine Bedeutung für die Theologie, sein Streit mit Gotthold Ephraim Lessing* (Berlin: R. Trenkel, 1906), 16.

Semler's master's thesis dealt with the text-critical problems of 1 Tim. 3:16 and 1 John 5:7. In response to Whiston's use of these texts to support an Arian Christology, Semler argued for the authenticity of the reading "God" in the first passage, and the heavenly witnesses in the second—positions which he was later to abandon. Semler also wrote reviews of the works of the English deists for the periodical *Nachrichten von einer Halle-schen Bibliothek*, edited by Baumgarten. After completing his studies, Semler was for a time a teacher at a high school in Coburg. In 1751, he was appointed professor of history and classics at Altdorf. The next year, at the instigation of Baumgarten, he accepted a professorship at Halle. A prolific writer, Semler's bibliography lists over 170 items. Wading through a small portion of these is like crossing a tangled swamp wearing heavy boots. According to Emanuel Hirsch, Semler's German is "certainly the worst which any German intellectual has ever written."[9] Semler's personality, from all reports, was apparently as dull as his prose. During his honeymoon, he spent an extra day in Erlangen in order to visit the library in search of papers of Melanchthon and Camerarius. Nevertheless, Semler enjoyed a happy domestic life, and was devoted to his wife and children.

Semler's Theological Perspective

In theological method, Semler owed much to Baumgarten, for, like the latter, he attempted to harmonize revelation and reason. Semler believed there were two sources of truth: supernatural, or immediate, revelation and natural revelation. The Bible was a record of divine revelation, but it was in harmony with the truths of nature and reason. Semler attempted to navigate a distinct course, avoiding the shoals of orthodoxy, Pietism, and extreme rationalism. He opposed the biblicism of the orthodox, rejecting the traditional inspiration doctrine and the reduction of the message of the Bible to dogma. He opposed the enthusiasm and subjectivity of the Pietists, advocating a scientific and historical theology. He opposed the rejection of revelation by the rationalistic deists,[10] supporting instead a concept of the divine disclosure of truth, perceived in the depth of human experience. In harmony with the optimistic spirit of the Enlightenment, Semler adopted a view of progressive revelation whereby the Christianity of the early church was seen not as normative but as only a preliminary expression of truth which would evolve toward perfection.[11]

9. Emanuel Hirsch, *Geschichte der neuern evangelischen Theologie*, 5 vols. (Gütersloh: C. Bertelsmann, 1952) 4.50.

10. J. S. Semler, *Antwort auf das Bahrdtische Glabensbekenntnis* (Halle: C. H. Hemmerde, 1779). See also pp. 174–77, below.

11. See Gottfried Hornig, "Der Perfektibilitätsgedanke bei J. S. Semler," *Zeitschrift für Theologie und Kirche* 72 (1975): 381–97.

A principle feature of Semler's theology is his distinction between religion and theology, a distinction rooted in his own religious life and responsive to the individualism of the Enlightenment.[12] Religion, according to Semler, is the private, personal appropriation of divinely revealed truth; theology is the conceptual formulation and public explication of that truth. Religion, therefore, is not a system of dogma but a flexible, dynamic experience. Religion has to do with the knowledge of faith—the appropriating of the fundamental truths of salvation. Above all, religion is concerned with those universal, moral truths affirmed by an inner, intuitive certainty. Theology, on the other hand, is intellectual reflection about the truths of religion. Theology employs reason and enlists a host of supporting disciplines: linguistics, hermeneutics, textual criticism. Theology is academic; theology is science (*Wissenschaft*).

Related to the fundamental difference between religion and theology are other significant distinctions. Semler notes, for instance, the difference between subjectivity and objectivity. The former has to do with the inner experience of faith, while the latter concerns the external expression of faith in history, the biblical record, and theological formulation. Semler also distinguished two kinds of theology for two sorts of people: (1) an elementary formulation of belief for the laity—a theology of the church; and (2) a more complex expression for the scholars—an academic theology. In the spirit of the Reformation, Semler distinguished between law and gospel: law was expressed in the OT and was superseded by the gospel. Although the law shows humans to be sinners in need of reconciliation, it is not needed to ensure good works, for they are the fruit of faith in Christ. Indeed, Christians are under the spiritual law, which is the same as the gospel—the law of love.

These distinctions provided Semler with a method for investigating Christianity. Since religion belonged to those inner truths of personal experience, it remained untouched by the sharp tools of criticism. Theology, on the other hand, was concerned with the external data of the faith and its objective expression. Thus, criticism was the appropriate instrument for investigating the historical ground and conceptual formulation of theology. In short, Semler had provided the rationale for the unrestricted use of criticism. Faith, since it was a matter of religion, could not be harmed by criticism; theology, which was a matter of objective expression, required the ruthless application of critical research. Thus, the persistent problem of the tension between faith and criticism was resolved by a drastic measure—a separation terminating in divorce.

12. See Gottfried Hornig, "Die Freiheit der christlichen Privatreligion. Semlers Begründung des religiösen Individualismus in der protestantischen Aufklärungstheologie," *Neue Zeitschrift für systematische Theologie und Religionsphilosophie* 21 (1979): 198–211.

Also related to the basic distinction between religion and theology is Semler's understanding of the essence of Christianity. Since matters like essence belong in the area of religion, with its personal and dynamic character, no clear and definitive statement is possible. However, Semler on occasion and in his convoluted style could approach a formulation that affirms "the doctrines of one God, who exists in three persons; of the redemption of Jesus, the son of God, in human nature, through whom Judaism is superseded and heathenism nullified; of the results of this redemption, through the moral transformation of the otherwise natural frame of mind of humans, which transformation has especially the Holy Spirit as author."[13] In a word, the essence of Christianity is expressed in a confessional form that affirms an economic Trinity and stresses the experience of redemption through Christ.

According to Semler, this understanding of the essence of Christianity is based on the Bible. Indeed, the Bible is the record of the historical disclosure of God and divine redemption. Revelation unfolds progressively and reaches its apex in Jesus Christ. About Christianity, Semler says, "This religion is the most perfect; it is also universal and promotes the true bliss of all its adherents."[14] Consequently, the NT is more important than the OT, and, even within the NT, the essence of Christianity is more clearly comprehended by Paul (especially in Romans) and by the author of the Gospel of John. Since Christ is the focal point of revelation, the NT must be interpreted christocentrically. Most important, because divine revelation has occurred in history, the revelation of God has an objective character. Thus, historical criticism, the refined method for investigating objective and historical phenomena, is essential to the understanding of the Bible. Historical criticism is able to distinguish between the essentials of religion and the details of historical and theological expression, a distinction implicit in the Bible itself.

Semler's Critique of the Canon

Semler's most important work for the history of NT research is his *Abhandlung von freier Untersuchung des Canon*. This work, a jumble of confusing disorder, was published in four parts, from 1771 to 1775.[15] The original part, published in 1771 and revised by Semler in 1776, has been edited

---

13. Cited in Hartmut H. R. Schulz, *Johann Salomo Semlers Wesensbestimmung des Christentums: Ein Beitrag zur Erforschung der Theologie Semlers* (Würtzburg: Königshausen & Neumann, 1988), 68a.

14. Cited in Trutz Rendtorff, *Church and Theology: The Systematic Function of the Church Concept in Modern Theology*, trans. R. H. Fuller (Philadelphia: Westminster Press, 1976), 56.

15. *D. Joh. Salomo Semlers Abhandlung von freier Untersuchung des Canon.* 4 vols. (Halle: C. H. Hemmerde, 1771–75). Volumes 2, 3, and 4 develop further the themes of vol. 1 and include Semler's responses to his critics.

and reprinted in a more accessible and readable format.[16] According to Heinz Scheible, the editor of the revised edition, Semler "dealt the doctrine of verbal inspiration a fatal wound and blazed the trail for the critical investigation of the Bible."[17] Semler's main thesis is that the canon is a historical problem that can be solved by the free use of the critical method. The effect of Semler's work is the dissolution of the classical, orthodox understanding of the canon.[18]

In expounding his thesis, Semler gives attention to the historical development of the canon. He notes that in different times and places different books were recognized as canonical. Some segments of the church have accepted the Apocrypha, while others have rejected it. The Reformers used a canon different from that of the Roman Catholics. The actual process of canonization was gradual, extending over a long period of time, and decisions as to what was to be included were made by bishops and councils of the church and were based on external, historically conditioned circumstances. "The witness of the so-called church," writes Semler, "can like every historical witness affirm or deny something only from an external occurrence; but the question, whether one or more books have a divine origin or an author inspired (from God), has to do with no external occurrence; there can be for this matter therefore no external or historical witness."[19] In short, Semler questions the traditional criteria for determining canonicity.

The content of the canon which has evolved historically displays remarkable variety. In Semler's opinion, much of it is not relevant for Christians, since "not all parts of these writings are useful or necessary for our attention."[20] Books like Ruth and Esther have meaning for Jews, but they are of little significance for Christians. In order to embrace the Song of Solomon as canonical, Christians have had to resort to fanciful interpretations. Even within the NT, the message is dressed in a coat of many colors. Matthew writes for Palestinian Jews, while John addresses a different audience for different purposes. Is it necessary, asks Semler, for all Christians to know what is in the Gospel of Matthew? Nowhere, he points

---

16. Heinz Scheible, ed., *Johann Salomo Semler, Abhandlung von freier Untersuchung des Canon*, Texte zur Kirchen- und Theologiegeschichte 5 (Gütersloh: G. Mohn, 1967).

17. Ibid., 6.

18. See Herbert Donner, "Gesichtspunkte zur Auflösung des klassischen Kanonbegriffes bei Johann Salomo Semler," in *Fides et communicatio: Festschrift für Martin Doerne zum 70. Geburtstag*, ed. D. Rössler, G. Voigt, and F. Wintzer (Göttingen: Vandenhoeck & Ruprecht, 1970), 56–68; Hermann Strathmann, "Die Krisis des Kanons der Kirche: Joh. Gerhards und Joh. Sal. Semlers Erbe," in *Das Neue Testament als Kanon: Dokumentation und kritische Analyse zur gegenwärtigen Diskussion*, ed. Ernst Käsemann (Göttingen: Vandenhoeck & Ruprecht, 1970), 41–61.

19. Scheible, *Semler, Abhandlung*, 31.

20. Ibid., 45.

out, does Paul claim that the acceptance of a twenty-seven book canon is essential for salvation. Within the NT there are various types of material: historical, doctrinal, parenetic. This varied material is applicable to Christians in different ways, and some of it, not at all. Paul, for example, gives advice concerning the clothing women should wear in public, advice which has little use for eighteenth-century Christians. Much of the content of the NT required no special inspiration. Mark, for example, did not need divine guidance to write his Gospel, because he simply used a copy of Matthew. The Epistle of Jude, oblivious to the rules of canonicity, quotes from an apocryphal work which, according to traditional views of the canon, is not recognized as inspired.

Semler's judgment about canonicity can be illustrated from notes he published for a commentary on the book of Revelation written by an anonymous scholar.[21] In these notes, Semler asserts that material in the OT and NT that does not conform to the teaching of Jesus is not authoritative for Christian believers. The Apocalypse, in particular, includes much that is sheer Jewish speculation, parallel to concepts found in apocryphal books like 2 Esdras. Semler concludes, therefore, that "the book is also not written out of the inspiration of the Holy Spirit."[22] Semler also finds it strange that Christians are expected to accept as divine revelation what they cannot even understand. "Of Christ and the fundamental teachings of Christianity there is indeed in this book almost nothing at all."[23] In sum, Semler has destroyed orthodoxy's view of a "level" Bible, that is, the notion that any verse from Genesis to Revelation is equal in inspiration and authority to any other.

What, then, is the criterion for canonicity? If the level Bible has been replaced by the crags and canyons of Semler's terrain, how can the high points be distinguished from the low? According to Semler, there is one primary test of canonicity: does the document convey universal, moral truth? "The only proof that completely satisfies an upright reader," says Semler, "is the inner conviction brought about by the truths that confront him in this Holy Scripture (but not in all parts and individual books)."[24] Thus, one cannot claim that all of the Bible is inspired or that everything written in Scripture has its origin in God. This means that some books and some parts of books are not to be taken as inspired and authoritative. As

21. *Christliche freye Untersuchung über die so genannte Offenbarung Johannis, aus nachgelassenen Handschrift eines fränkischen Gelehrten herausgegeben.* Annotated by J. S. Semler (Halle: J. C. Hendel, 1769).

22. Ibid., 173.

23. Ibid., 199.

24. Cited in Werner Georg Kümmel, *The New Testament: A History of the Investigation of Its Problems,* trans. S. M. Gilmour and H. C. Kee (Nashville and New York: Abingdon Press, 1972), 64.

Semler says, "I have taught a distinction of the books of the Bible according to the distinction of their content."[25] Semler, therefore, erects a wall of separation between the Bible and the word of God. "Holy Scripture and the Word of God are clearly to be distinguished, for we know the difference."[26]

Although Semler distinguished between the word of God and Scripture, he believed the Bible contained the word of God. Semler, in many ways, represents a return to the Reformation. For him, as for Luther, the word of God was embodied in Christ. God had acted decisively in the Logos in history. Since revelation has occurred in history, historical criticism is necessary for recovering revelation. Truth, therefore, is detected in history studied scientifically. Semler was not concerned with metaphysics; he was not a systematic theologian; he was a biblical theologian who practiced historical exegesis. For Semler, the principle of *sola scriptura* meant that Scripture, studied historically, was the norm. However, the word of God which is detected by historical research is not subject to human criticism because it transcends it. "The word of God," says Semler, "is outside and beyond criticism."[27] The word of God in the Bible that is identified by historical research can only be understood by the inner experience of the truth of Scripture, confirmed by the witness of the Spirit. Semler believed that the human writers of the books of the NT were the authors of Scripture, but he was convinced that God was the author of the biblical message.

A significant feature of Semler's exegesis is his use of the theory of "accommodation." Semler, to be sure, did not invent the theory, for it is at least as old as Origen, and it was refined by Calvin.[28] According to this theory, the truths of revelation had been accommodated to the capacity of people to appropriate them. Semler developed his version of the theory as a result of his reflection about demonology. In the town of Kemberg, a woman had been accused of being possessed by a demon. This incident provoked Semler to write a series of works about demons in which he applied historical-critical method to the study of Hellenistic, biblical, and rabbinic sources. In discussing the relation of Jesus to demons, Semler constructed his accommodation doctrine. Jesus, according to this view,

25. Cited in Gottfried Hornig, *Die Anfänge der historisch-kritischen Theologie: Johann Salomo Semlers Schriftverständnis und seine Stellung zu Luther* (Göttingen: Vandenhoeck & Ruprecht, 1961), 199.

26. Cited in Kümmel, *The New Testament*, 63.

27. Cited in Gottfried Hornig, "Hermeneutik und Bibelkritik bei Johann Salomo Semler," in *Historische Kritik und biblischer Kanon in der deutschen Aufklärung*, ed. H. G. Reventlow, W. Sparn, and J. Woodbridge (Wiesbaden: Harrassowitz, 1988), 228.

28. See Jack B. Rogers and Donald K. McKim, *The Authority and the Interpretation of the Bible: An Historical Approach* (San Francisco: Harper & Row, 1979), 9–11; 98–100.

did not himself believe in the existence of demons, but he trimmed his teaching to fit the unenlightened minds of his hearers. "The yielding, the condescension in the face of such weak and incapable people," said Semler, "must be distinguished from authentic instruction."[29]

The accommodation concept, however, was not simply a matter of enlightened pedagogy; it was grounded in Semler's understanding of historical revelation. God, in disclosing divine truth, had to accommodate the message to the limited perspective of humans. Jesus and the apostles, in witnessing to God's revelation, had to accommodate their teaching to the capacity of their auditors. Thus Semler concluded, "That teachers, after the undeniable example of Jesus and the apostles, condescended to their listeners' mode of thought, or accommodated themselves to their own circumstances, is historically certain."[30] Above all, the accommodation theory stresses Semler's fundamental belief in the historical character of Christianity—his conviction that all truths are revealed and appropriated historically. The idea of accommodation also serves to clarify the distinction between the word of God and words of the Bible. The gospel, the word of God, was not itself accommodated, but it was expressed through accommodating words. Thus, the biblical writers were free to use their own vocabulary and style to employ contemporary myths and metaphors to give expression to the gospel. Since the gospel is always expressed in accommodating words, it is never to be equated with the words of Scripture. The gospel is not objective truth but universal moral truth, intuitively perceived and practically and individually appropriated.

Semler's New Testament Research

The application of these concepts can be illustrated by a few examples from Semler's other writings. His hermeneutical principles are set out in a four-volume work on theological hermeneutics, published from 1760 to 1769.[31] Much of the work is devoted to the text criticism of the OT and the NT and illustrates Semler's concern for the details of exegesis. The first volume, however, includes a discussion of hermeneutical theory. In the preface, Semler states the rationale for historical exegesis: it is needed to refute the bad interpretation frequently heard in the pulpit; it is useful in overcoming the errors of allegorical interpretation and the subjectivity of pietistic exegesis. In contrast to the Pietists, Semler denies that only born-again Christians are able to interpret the Bible and says instead,

---

29. J. S. Semler, *Versuch einer biblischen Dämonologie, oder Untersuchung der Lehre der heil. Schrift vom Teufel und seiner Macht* (Halle: C. H. Hemmerde, 1776), 341.

30. Cited in Rendtorff, *Church and Theology,* 47–48.

31. J. S. Semler, *Vorbereitung zur theologischen Hermeneutik,* vols. 1 and 2 (Halle: C. H. Hemmerde, 1760–61); *Hermeneutische Vorbereitung,* vols. 3 and 4 (Halle: C. H. Hemmerde, 1765–69).

"The illumination and new birth is accomplished in us by God through the known content of scripture."[32]

In the first section of his hermeneutics, Semler proceeds to broaden his appeal for historical-critical interpretation. He notes that throughout the history of exegesis, various parties have attempted to ground their views in Scripture. Thus, the danger of eisegesis is omnipresent. "The interpreter," insists Semler, "should carry nothing into a text . . . out of his own thoughts."[33] Historical method is needed to ascertain what the Bible actually said in its own time and setting. Christians need to know what Jesus said and taught, and this requires critical analysis of the historical reports. In a theological discussion, one must not resort to esoteric or allegorical methods; one must use the same method "whereby all the books in the world are interpreted."[34] The exegete must recognize that only one interpretation is true—the historical. To find the correct interpretation, the scholar must master text criticism, philology, grammar, and rhetoric.

Scattered throughout his works are Semler's judgments on a host of critical issues. Many of these are found in several paraphrases which Semler wrote on various books of the NT: Romans (1769), 1 Corinthians (1770), John (1771), 2 Corinthians (1776), Galatians (1779), Hebrews (1779), James (1781), 1 Peter (1783), 2 Peter (1784), 1 John (1792). His paraphrase on Romans can serve as an example of these exegetical handbooks.[35] Published in a small format, the actual paraphrase totals 210 pages and is divided into sections and subsections. The paraphrase consists of a loose Latin translation interspersed with parenthetical expressions which further explicate the meaning of the text. Semler's notes, which deal with Greek terms and include biblical and patristic references, are printed at the bottom of the page. After the paraphrase, Semler presents the Vulgate translation of Romans with text-critical footnotes (pp. 211–76). The final part of the book (pp. 277–311) presents a dissertation on chapters 15 and 16 which Semler takes to be a double appendix added later to the epistle. In this dissertation, Semler employs arguments which have since become commonplace: the different locations of the doxology in the various manuscripts; the question of the provenance of the people named in Romans 16; the problem of the polemic section (16:17-20) in a letter addressed to the Romans. Semler's sensitivity to the question of canon made him aware of issues related to the collection of the Pauline letters. Consequently, he was one of the first scholars to give serious atten-

---

32. Semler, *Hermeneutik* 1, foreword.
33. Ibid. 1.7.
34. Ibid. 1.129.
35. Io. Sal. Semleri, *Paraphrasis Epistolae ad Romanos, cum notis, translatione vetusta, et dissertatione de appendice Cap. XV, XVI* (Halle: C. H. Hemmerde, 1769).

tion to the issue of the integrity of the NT writings. Just as he disputed the unity of Romans 1–16, so Semler also considered 2 Corinthians to be a composite of epistolary fragments.[36]

Semler's critical work also resulted in a reconstruction of early Christianity. Anticipating the work of F. C. Baur,[37] he believed the early church to have been made up of two parties: a Jewish faction represented by Peter, and a Hellenistic group under the leadership of Paul—two parties which, at the end of the second century, were merged into the catholic church. On questions of authorship, Semler was much less traditional than Turretin, Wettstein, and Ernesti. He rejected the Pauline authorship of Hebrews and assigned the composition of 2 Peter to the second century. Above all, Semler's major contribution to higher criticism is found in his thesis about the canon. If one accepts his challenge of a free investigation of the canon, this means that the authenticity of every book in the NT is open to question.

Semler's significance for the subsequent study of the NT is difficult to overestimate. Probably the most important biblical scholar of the eighteenth century, Semler's greatness is to be seen in his ability to incorporate the various features of his thought into a comprehensive theological synthesis. Indeed, Semler, although he formulated no system,[38] reflects more profoundly about the theological aspects of biblical research than did any of his predecessors. Into his synthesis, he incorporates the major elements of Enlightenment thought: natural theology, the use of reason, individualism, and progressive revelation—all enlisted in the service of the historical interpretation of Scripture. In the pursuit of historical interpretation, Semler develops an effective methodology which makes possible a free, unrestricted biblical criticism. This methodology rests on a fundamental theological observation: the distinction between religion and theology. Armed with this distinction, Semler is able to direct his critical method to the basic issue of biblical research: the question of canon. The results of Semler's criticism are the destruction of the orthodox view of biblical authority and a modern restatement of the Reformation distinction between the word of God and the words of Scripture.

At the same time, Semler's distinction between religion and theology makes possible the incorporation of traditional Christian elements into

36. See Hans Dieter Betz, *2 Corinthians 8 and 9*, Hermeneia (Philadelphia: Fortress Press, 1985), 3–10; Victor Paul Furnish, *II Corinthians*, Anchor Bible (Garden City, N.Y.: Doubleday, 1984), 32. Semler's original arguments are found in his *Paraphrasis II. Epistolae ad Corinthios. Accessit Latina vetus translatio et lectionum varietas* (Halle: C. H. Hemmerde, 1776), preface, and note on 9:1, pp. 238–39.

37. See pp. 258–70, below.

38. Rendtorff, *Church and Theology,* 52: "The only program then which we can discover in Semler is this: to guard against any program whatever."

the theological synthesis. Semler can affirm the authority of the Bible as the primary witness to God's decisive revelation in history in Jesus Christ. Indeed, by restricting the function of criticism to the historical data and the theological formulation, Semler is able to shield the faith from the cold blasts of destructive criticism. Moreover, this faith, which has an affinity with pietist religious experience, transcends the limitations of its historical expression and has a universal, moral, and, therefore, practical significance. This faith—this intuitive perception of universal moral truths—becomes the criterion of canonicity, the norm by which religious truth is evaluated. Combined with the accommodation hermeneutic—another feature of Semler's historical method—the universal truth is found to be the essential message of the Bible so that, in turn, the authority of the Bible is affirmed anew.

Although this synthesis of theology and historical method represents an impressive accomplishment, it is not without problems. Most obvious, the question can be raised, How does Semler's norm for determining canonicity by the intuitive perception of universal truth escape the subjectivism which he found so objectionable in the Pietists? Semler's solution to the problem of the relation between faith and criticism—which anticipates Lessing's "ugly ditch"[39]—is also not without difficulty. While one may agree that faith differs from the expressions of faith, the two must somehow be correlated, particularly since the content of faith is revealed in history. Moreover, the critical methodology which Semler employs presupposes the worldview of the Enlightenment, whereas the biblical faith which Semler wants to universalize and appropriate represents a different understanding of reality. Questions of this sort defy easy answers, and Semler must be applauded for raising them. In any event, Semler was to be forced to decide between the priority of faith and the freedom of research when he was confronted with the radical criticism of the Wolfenbüttel *Fragments*.[40]

THE SCIENCE OF INTRODUCTION:
JOHANN DAVID MICHAELIS (1717–1791)

Another wunderkind of the Aufklärung was Johann David Michaelis.[41] Actually, Michaelis was an older contemporary of Semler, and the first

39. See p. 168, below.
40. See pp. 174–77, below.
41. For a concise, thoughtful summary of Michaelis's life and biblical research, see J. C. O'Neill, *The Bible's Authority: A Portrait Gallery of Thinkers from Lessing to Bultmann* (Edinburgh: T. & T. Clark, 1991), 28–38. See also Anna-Ruth Löwenbrück, "Johann David Michaelis et les débuts de la critique biblique," in *Le siècle des lumières et la Bible*, ed. Yvon Belaval and Dominique Bourel, Bible des tous les temps 7 (Paris: Beauchesne, 1986), 113–28.

edition of his famous *Introduction* (1750) antedated Semler's major work.[42] The vastly expanded fourth edition of Michaelis's magnum opus, however, did not appear until 1788. Reared in an academic atmosphere, Michaelis was the son of the renowned Semitic scholar C. B. Michaelis of the University of Halle. The younger Michaelis was educated at Halle, where, like Semler, he was influenced by Baumgarten who introduced him to the philosophy of Wolff. Michaelis wrote a dissertation on the vowel points of the Hebrew text in which he defended their authenticity, a position he was later to abandon. In 1741 and 1742, Michaelis traveled to England where he acquired fluency in English and became acquainted with the thought of the deists. At Oxford, he heard lectures by the prominent OT scholar Robert Lowth. Michaelis was well received in the old university city and was invited to preach in the German church. Later he wrote, "In a certain way, the time of my stay in Oxford was the happiest of my life."[43]

Returning to Halle, Michaelis lectured at the university; among his auditors was J. S. Semler. In 1745, Michaelis moved to the recently founded University of Göttingen, where he was appointed professor in the faculty of philosophy. He taught philosophy, history, geography, and archeology, along with his special interest, the Semitic languages. Michaelis, whose views were thought to be tainted by rationalism, was never awarded a chair in the theological faculty. According to Eichhorn, Michaelis was a teacher "toward whom the eyes of half the world were directed."[44] Michaelis's style was flamboyant. His students reported that he would stride into the lecture hall with fiery eyes, his Bible under his arm, wearing colorful clothing, his sword at his side, his boots equipped with spurs. His lectures on Psalms 126 and 137 were said to bring tears to the eye. Auditors, Catholic as well as Protestant, and including representatives of the nobility, came from all over Europe to hear him. Although most of his audiences were enthralled, the erudite Alexander von Humboldt found Michaelis's "delivery repulsive . . . and full of obscenities."[45]

Like Semler, Michaelis was a prolific writer. He published lexicographical and grammatical studies in Hebrew, Syriac, Aramaic, and Arabic. He made an important contribution to the study of Hebrew poetry, and his

42. Eng. trans. of Michaelis's early work on the introduction to the New Testament: *Introductory Lectures to the Sacred Books of the New Testament* (London: W. Dawson, 1780).

43. Johann David Michaelis, *Lebensbeschreibung von ihm selbst abgefasst, mit Anmerkungen von Hassencamp* (Leipzig: J. A. Barth, 1793), 29.

44. J. G. Eichhorn, "Eichhorns Bemerkungen über J. D. Michaelis Litterarischen Character," in Michaelis, *Lebensbeschreibung*, 156.

45. Cited in Rudolf Smend, "Johann David Michaelis und Johann Gottfried Eichhorn— zwei Orientalisten am Rande der Theologie," in *Theologie in Göttingen: Eine Vorlesungsreihe*, ed. Bernd Moeller (Göttingen: Vandenhoeck & Ruprecht, 1987), 62.

massive work on the laws of Moses was translated into English.[46] He composed a prize-winning essay on the relation of language and opinions which has recently been reissued in an English-language series.[47] For twenty years, Michaelis was the editor and main contributor to a periodical which first appeared as *Orientalische und exegetische Bibliothek* (1771) and later continued as *Neue orientalische und exegetische Bibliothek*.

Michaelis's Theological Position

Michaelis was more conservative than Semler, which can be seen in his lengthy review of Semler's work on the canon.[48] At the outset, Michaelis observes that it is hard to disagree with Semler because he is difficult to understand and is prepared to call anyone who disagrees with him a blockhead (*Tölpel*). While agreeing with Semler's call for a free investigation, Michaelis rejects many of Semler's results. He argues, for example, that the canonicity of the Jewish Scriptures is confirmed by Jesus and Paul. Material from the historical books of the OT, which Semler finds irrelevant, Michaelis believes to be instructive for Christians. Most important, Michaelis thinks Semler's criterion of canonicity to be subjective. In deciding against the authority of biblical books, Michaelis argues, one must not simply reject "what does not please him, or is not edifying enough for him."[49] Instead, the authenticity of biblical books should be decided by historical research. Although Semler appears to affirm biblical authority by his claim that the source for edifying moral truth is found in Scripture, the way he subjects the canon to rationalistic natural theology undermines, in Michaelis's view, the authority of the Bible.

In some ways, the theology of Michaelis has affinity with the thought of the neologians, because he attempts to harmonize orthodoxy with reason. His pervasive orthodoxy can be seen in his book on dogmatics.[50] In this work Michaelis argues that revelation is essential to the knowledge of God; the two sources of divine truth are the Bible and reason. Actually, Michaelis affirms virtually all the traditional doctrines: the omnipotence and omniscience of God, the sovereignty and righteousness of God, the unity and Trinity of the Godhead, the personality of the Holy Spirit, the two natures in the one person of Christ. Michaelis also discusses the good and the

46. John David Michaelis, *Commentaries on the Laws of Moses*, trans. Alexander Smith, 4 vols. (London: F. C. and J. Rivington, 1814).

47. Johann David Michaelis, *A Dissertation on the Influence of Opinions on Language, and of Language on Opinions* (New York: AMS Press, 1973).

48. Johann David Michaelis, "D. Joh. Sal. Semlers Abhandlung von freyer Untersuchung des Canon," *Orientalische und exegetische Bibliothek* 3 (1772): 26–96.

49. Ibid. 3.56.

50. Johann David Michaelis, *Dogmatik*, 2d rev. ed. (Tübingen: C. G. Frank and W. Schramm, 1785).

fallen angels, and he stresses the importance of the resurrection of the body and the last judgment. Nevertheless, for all these orthodox doctrines a case is made by reason. Humans, Michaelis argues, are created in the image of God, and this means that people, in contrast to animals, are bestowed with reason. Although the doctrine of satisfaction for sin through the sacrifice of Christ cannot be rationally proved, it is, nevertheless, not opposed to reason. This idea is more fully developed in Michaelis's *Thoughts Concerning the Doctrine of the Holy Scriptures about Sin and Satisfaction, as a Doctrine in Agreement with Reason.*[51] In all these works, Michaelis goes to great length to be understood by the masses. The second edition of his *Dogmatik*, in contrast to the first, was intentionally written in German instead of Latin. The same effort to communicate is seen in his German translation of the NT, published with "notes for the uneducated."[52]

Agreeing with the older orthodoxy, Michaelis believes the truth of revelation is confirmed by fulfilled prophecy and miracles. The resurrection of Christ, for instance, is the "corner-stone of Christianity."[53] In response to the furor created by the Wolfenbüttel *Fragments*,[54] Michaelis delivered lectures on the resurrection (1782). Although he acknowledges that the writers of the Gospels were not infallible, he believes they produced reliable accounts. Minor discrepancies serve to confirm their reliability, because total agreement would suggest collusion. John, who had read the reports of the others, was an eyewitness to the resurrection events, and proof of the honesty of the apostles is demonstrated by their willingness to shed blood for their belief. The bulk of Michaelis's work on the resurrection is a historical and exegetical investigation of the gospel narratives. He answers objections to the historicity of the resurrection, for instance, the argument that Christians should have insisted on an investigation to prove that the tomb was empty and the body not stolen. His answer: the lowly Christians had no power to instigate such a procedure. Along the way, Michaelis engages in considerable harmonizing. The variation in the number of angels at the tomb (one or two) results from reports of different incidents. The charge to stay in Jerusalem (Luke 24:49; Acts 1:4) does not contradict the order to go to Galilee (Mark 16:7), since the disciples were to go to Galilee first and then return to stay in the holy city. In sum, Michaelis finds the testimony of the witnesses reliable, and what he says

---

51. Johann David Michaelis, *Gedanken über die Lehre der heiligen Schrift von Sünde und Genugthuung, als eine der Vernunft gemässen Lehre*, rev. ed. (Göttingen and Bremen: J. H. Cramer, 1779).

52. Johann David Michaelis, *Anmerkungen für Ungelehrte, zu seiner Uebersetzung des Neuen Testaments*, 4 vols. (Göttingen: Vandenhoek & Ruprecht, 1790–92).

53. John David Michaelis, *The Burial and Resurrection of Jesus Christ: According to the Four Evangelists* (London: H. Hatchard, 1827), 2.

54. See pp. 170–74, below.

about the doubting Thomas is true for all: "The belief which arises from direct evidence of our senses, cannot fail of being complete, and is certainly true belief."[55]

Michaelis's Introduction to the New Testament

For the history of NT research, Michaelis's most important work is his monumental *Introduction to the New Testament*.[56] Prior to Michaelis, details of historical introduction to the NT books were presented in notes and paraphrases by, for example, Grotius, Bengel, and Wettstein. In particular, Richard Simon's *Critical History of the Text of the New Testament* (1689)[57] was a pioneering work in higher criticism which encouraged study of NT introduction as a distinct scholarly discipline. In 1704, Johann Georg Pritz, or Pritius (1662–1732), a professor of theology at Frankfurt an der Oder, published a formal introduction,[58] printed in a small but lengthy format (726 pages, plus index). In the early chapters, Pritius takes up problematic books. He begins with Hebrews and, after a discussion of the issues, opts for Pauline authorship. He is aware of the problems in regard to the authenticity of the Catholic Epistles but decides in favor of apostolic authorship in all cases. He thinks the Gospels were written in canonical order, the later ones supplementing the accounts of the earlier. However, the bulk of Pritius's *Introduction* is devoted to tradition about the apostles, the language and text of the NT, and material concerning the historical setting. A final section on principles of interpretation encourages the search for the literal meaning and the use of the *analogia fidei*.

With Michaelis, the treatment of NT introduction as a distinct historical science takes on new significance. A major concern of Michaelis is to answer the question of canonicity posed by Semler: to investigate the authenticity of the books of the NT by historical research. Michaelis believes that authorship is established by the same procedures used for the classical sources. From external evidence, it can be seen that both the orthodox fathers and the heretics accepted the NT books as authentic. From internal evidence, it can be shown that the authors of the NT write in a Hebraic Greek, that an author like Paul has an inimitable style, and that contemporary events confirm the NT accounts. In the course of the discussion, Michaelis draws an important distinction between inspired and

---

55. Michaelis, *Burial and Resurrection*, 274.
56. Johann David Michaelis, *Einleitung in die göttlichen Schriften des Neuen Bundes*, 4th rev. ed., 2 vols. (Göttingen: Vandenhoek & Ruprecht, 1788); Eng. trans.: *Introduction to the New Testament*, trans. Herbert Marsh, 2d ed., 4 vols. (London: F. and C. Rivington, 1802).
57. See pp. 20–22, above.
58. Io. Georgii Pritii, *Introductio in lectionem Novi Testamenti in qua, quae ad rem criticam, historiam, chronologiam et geographiam pertinent, breviter et perspicue exponuntur* (Leipzig: Gleditsch, 1704).

reliable documents. For a document to be inspired, it must have been written by one of the apostles who were promised the assistance of the Spirit. Historical works, however, may be genuine (*ächt*) or reliable (*glaubwürdig*), without necessarily being inspired. Luke, for example, was not an inspired apostle, but his work rests on reliable reports.

> The question, whether the books of the New Testament are inspired by God is not so important as the question whether they are genuine (*ächt*); the Christian religion does not absolutely stand or fall with the former. In fact, had God inspired none of the books of the New Testament, but left Matthew, Mark, Luke, John, and Paul purely to themselves to write what they knew, the books would have been old, genuine (*ächt*), and reliable (*glaubwürdig*), so that the Christian religion would have remained true.[59]

This distinction provides Michaelis with a useful hermeneutical device for assessing the relative merits of the various NT books. The Gospels of Matthew and John are apostolic and inspired; the other two are not. Consequently, contradictions between Matthew and Mark or between John and Luke are of no moment. Apparent discrepancies between John and Matthew, on the other hand, would appear to constitute a problem. However, the ingenious Michaelis has a solution: the extant Gospel of Matthew is not the original but a fallible translation, so that minor discrepancies are not unexpected.

Early sections (volume 1 of the English edition) of Michaelis's *Introduction* also give attention to the language of the NT. The language spoken in Palestine at the time of Jesus, he observes, was Aramean; in Jerusalem, East-Aramean or Chaldee; in Galilee, West-Aramean or Syriac. The writers of the NT occasionally made grammatical errors, but neither these nor their failure to write classical Greek speaks against their inspiration or reliability. Michaelis gives attention to the use of the OT by the authors of the NT. In his opinion, the inspiration of the NT is called into question if it is not faithful to the original meaning of the OT text, "unless we at once allow that the Christian revelation is incapable of being tried by rules as severe as those which are universally applied to other writings."[60] On the basis of such rules, Michaelis finds the use of Isa. 7:14 in Matt. 1:22-23 to be questionable, because he believes Isaiah was referring not to the Messiah but to a child who was to be born in Isaiah's own time. This difficulty, however, affects only the inspiration of the first two chapters of Matthew and not the whole Gospel.

The balance of the first part of Michaelis's *Introduction* (volume 2 of the English edition) deals with text criticism. He devotes much attention to

---

59. Michaelis, *Einleitung* 1.75–76 (my trans.).
60. Michaelis, *Introduction* 1.210.

the ancient versions: Syriac, Coptic, Arabic, Ethiopic, Armenian, Persian, Latin, Gothic, and Slavic. In regard to the Armenian, he apologetically acknowledges that he is not himself fluent in the language and has had to rely on secondary sources. In regard to the Greek manuscripts, Michaelis believes they should be classified according to four early recensions: Western, Alexandrine, Edessene, and Byzantine. Michaelis also presents a history of lower criticism from Laurentius Valla to Semler, and he discusses the major editions from the Complutention Polyglot to Griesbach. Finally he points to the need for a new critical edition. The herculean task of collecting, collating, and publishing is too large for an individual scholar, however, and should become a project of national scope: "Germany is divided into too many petty states, to be able to form an union sufficient for the purpose; and I know of no country, except England, which possesses the will and the means to execute the task."[61]

Part 2 (volumes 3 and 4 of the English edition) of Michaelis's *Introduction* takes up the typical issues of higher criticism: such things as authorship, date, and place of writing. In regard to the four Gospels, Michaelis applies his distinction between inspiration and reliability: "I have my doubts whether two of them, namely St. Mark and St. Luke were divinely inspired."[62] Yet even inspiration does not mean omniscience, so that one writer may supply what the others have left out. Narratives which appear to be contradictory may be separate accounts of two similar but actually different events. In regard to what became known as the "synoptic problem," that is, the question of the literary relationship between the first three Gospels, Michaelis betrays a lack of clarity. In his first edition (1750), he accepted the view that the Gospels were written in canonical order and believed Mark used Matthew. Later, influenced by the work of Nathaniel Lardner,[63] Michaelis rejected this view. By the time of the fourth edition, he was almost convinced that none of the first three Gospels used any of the others as primary sources and that their agreements resulted from the use of common sources. Thus, he argues at some length that Mark did not use Matthew or Luke, and that Luke did not use either of the others. Michaelis believes, nevertheless, that Luke was probably composed prior to Mark, so that the possibility that Mark had known Luke's Gospel remains open. However, if Mark had known Luke, he used only that part of the Lucan material that was confirmed by the testimony of Peter.

Michaelis proceeds to give separate treatment to each Gospel. He believes that the Gospel of Matthew was written by Matthew the tax collector whose call is recorded in 9:9. It was originally written in Hebrew (that

---

61. Ibid. 2.505.
62. Ibid. 3.2.
63. See pp. 160–65, below.

is, Aramaic) about 41 C.E., and the Greek translation was made some
twenty years later. "If the Greek Gospel of St. Matthew is not the original
. . . we cannot ascribe to it a verbal inspiration, and it is moreover not
impossible that the translator in some few instances mistook the sense of
his author."[64] Michaelis believes Mark was written by John Mark, the son of
Mary of Jerusalem, and Luke by Luke, the travel companion of Paul. That
Luke was a physician is confirmed by his recognition of the "high fever" of
Simon's mother-in-law (4:38) and other expressions which were thought
to represent medical language. According to Michaelis, Luke was neither
an apostle nor an eyewitness, and "instead of losers we should be real
gainers, if we considered St. Luke as a mere human historian."[65]

The Fourth Gospel was written by John the Apostle and son of Zebedee. John was not only an eyewitness, he had welcomed the mother of
Jesus into his home, and she was able to supply him with extensive information. "No writer whatsoever therefore was better enabled to give a cir-
cumstantial and authentic history of Christ."[66] John's purpose in writing
his Gospel was to refute the errors of Cerinthus, a Gnostic, and the
Sabians, a sect who revered John the Baptist as their leader. Michaelis
thinks the apostle John had read all three of the other Gospels and that
he omitted things which the others had reported and included things
which emphasized or supplemented their accounts. "If it be true that
there are passages in St. John's Gospel, which are at variance with the
accounts given by the other Evangelists, we cannot hesitate to give the
preference to St. John, who, of the sacred historians, wrote last, who was
eyewitness to almost all the facts which he has recorded, who appears to
have had an excellent memory, and paid attention to the most minute
circumstances."[67]

Michaelis's work on the Acts of the Apostles and the Pauline letters
offers few surprises.[68] He thinks Acts was written at the end of Paul's first
imprisonment at Rome, that is, 65 C.E. Luke, in Michaelis's opinion, wrote
better Greek than most of the other NT authors, evidenced especially in
the speeches, some of which were originally delivered in Chaldee
(Aramaic). The Pauline letters are arranged according to their importance, but Michaelis discusses them in their chronological order. Galatians

64. Michaelis, *Introduction* 3.154.
65. Ibid. 3.231.
66. Ibid. 3.273.
67. Ibid. 3.315.
68. Michaelis also gave attention to the shorter letters of Paul in his *Paraphrasis und
Anmerkungen über die Briefe Pauli an die Galater, Epheser, Philipper, Colosser, Thessalonicher, den
Timotheus, Titus und Philemon*, 2d rev. ed. (Bremen and Göttingen: G. L. Förster, 1769). This
work presents a German paraphrase of these epistles with extensive notes. In regard to
Ephesians, Michaelis notes his use of Locke's *Paraphrase and Notes* (see pp. 35–38, above).

was written first and addressed to the descendants of the original Gauls, in other words, the residents of the territory of north Galatia. Paul's opponents there were "Jews of the New Pharisaic sect."[69] Michaelis's discussion of the Corinthian correspondence provides insight into his understanding of the Pauline churches. The factions in the church represent only one party of opposition whose leader was a Jewish Christian. In his first edition, Michaelis had identified this leader as Crispus, but in the fourth edition, on the basis of material from 2 Corinthians, he believes the troublemaker had invaded Corinth from the outside. In any event, Michaelis views the church to be disrupted by a schism between the Jewish and gentile members. First Corinthians is an answer to a letter the Corinthians had written to Paul. Michaelis attempts to reconstruct their letter and believes it included such questions as, Is it good to marry? and Is is necessary to separate from an unbelieving spouse? Glossolalia, in Michaelis's opinion, refers to the Corinthian practice of speaking publicly "in foreign languages," a gift which they thought "proved the divine origin of the Christian religion."[70]

In regard to the Pastoral Epistles, Michaelis has no problems with Pauline authorship, although he has revised his views on the time and place of writing. Titus, according to the first edition, was written after the first Roman imprisonment. In his second edition Michaelis wavered, but in the fourth he is convinced that Titus was written after 2 Thessalonians and before 1 Corinthians. This means that the journey to Crete implied in Titus 1:5 took place during Paul's year-and-a-half ministry in Corinth. First Timothy was written after Paul had left Ephesus and traveled to Macedonia (1 Tim. 1:3; Acts 20:1), probably shortly before he wrote 2 Corinthians. To account for the journeys implied in 2 Timothy, Michaelis resorts to the increasingly popular hypothesis of a second Roman imprisonment and dates this letter in 66 C.E. During the first imprisonment (63–65 C.E.), Paul wrote Philemon, Colossians, and Ephesians, all at about the same time. After considerable attention to the letter to the Laodiceans (Col. 4:16), Michaelis concludes that it is to be identified with Ephesians, a circular letter which was sent to various churches of Asia, including Ephesus and Laodicea. The opponents of Paul in Colossae were Essenes or, possibly, Gnostics. Philippians was composed during the last part of the first Roman imprisonment, and the opponents in Philippi were similar to those who had troubled the Galatian churches. In a special section on the apostle's character and lifestyle, Michaelis asserts that Paul was not a visionary enthusiast but a rational, moral teacher.

---

69. Michaelis, *Introduction* 4.17.
70. Ibid. 4.56.

Michaelis allots much attention to the Epistle to the Hebrews. In his 1750 edition he had given it scant consideration, but in the meantime, he had published his two-volume commentary on Hebrews which includes an extensive discussion of the critical problems.[71] In the fourth edition of the *Introduction*, these issues have been articulated in a series of questions: Was Hebrews actually an epistle? Answer: yes, as use of the second-person pronoun indicates. To whom was it written? Answer: to Hebrew (Aramaic)-speaking Jews. What was the original language? Answer: Chaldee (Aramaic), the language of the Jewish Christians of Jerusalem. However, about the big question, Who wrote Hebrews? Michaelis provides no certain answer. The Greek style, of course, is not Paul's, but since the epistle is a translation, Pauline authorship cannot be ruled out. Nonetheless, Michaelis finds it difficult to believe that Paul's name would have been removed from the beginning. He concludes:

> If then the Epistle to the Hebrews was written by the Apostle St. Paul, it is canonical. But if it was not written by an Apostle, it is not canonical; for, however excellent its contents may be, they alone will not oblige us to receive it, as a work inspired by the Deity.[72]

The Catholic Epistles present problems of authorship. Michaelis is undecided about James, but he is reluctant to excise it from the canon. Because its contents are more moral than doctrinal, Luther called James an epistle of straw, but Michaelis asserts this epithet "might as well be applied to the sermon on the mount."[73] In regard to 1 Peter, Michaelis has no quarrel with traditional apostolic authorship. However, he argues that the mention of Babylon (5:13) is a reference not to Rome but to the ancient city on the Euphrates where Peter had gone on mission. Michaelis does not ignore the problem of the authenticity of 2 Peter but decides in favor of Petrine authorship. Jude, on the other hand, was written not by an apostle but by the brother of James, the leader of the Jerusalem church, a half-brother of Jesus.

In discussing the Johannine literature, Michaelis accepts all three epistles as apostolic. First John, however, he argues, was not actually a letter, but a treatise, written not to a single congregation, but to Christians in general. A long discussion of the notorious text of 1 John 5:7 concludes that the words about the three heavenly witnesses are not genuine. Michaelis considers the Apocalypse to be "the most difficult and the most doubtful book in the whole New Testament."[74] After discussing the external

71. Johann David Michaelis, *Erklärung des Briefes an die Hebräer,* 2d rev. ed. (Frankfurt and Leipzig: J. G. Garbe, 1780) 1.1–86.
72. Michaelis, *Introduction* 4.264.
73. Ibid. 4.313.
74. Ibid. 4.457.

evidence, he says that "the authenticity of the Apocalypse appears to me very doubtful, and I cannot avoid entertaining a suspicion, that it is a spurious production, introduced probably into the world after the death of St. John."[75] Efforts to support authenticity by argument from fulfilled prophecy falter, because the meaning of the prophecies cannot be ascertained. After considerable effort, Michaelis simply throws up his hands: "Even the immortal Newton, the greatest genius of modern ages, who with powers almost divine discovered the eternal laws which the Almighty had prescribed to his creation, has afforded in his attempt on the Apocalypse, in which he was not more successful than his predecessors, a mortifying proof of the weakness of human nature."[76]

One cannot take the tiring trek through Michaelis's *Introduction* without marvelling at his extensive learning. Michaelis has mastered the skills of Enlightenment scholarship: text criticism, linguistics, philology, command of historical information. Above all, he has established at a high level the science of introduction as a distinct discipline which will continue to be imitated, although often with less competence, by a succession of NT scholars. Although the *Introduction* now appears to be conservative, an early nineteenth-century British reviewer found Michaelis's work "to lower the credit of the sacred writings, and consequently to weaken the foundation of our faith, by raising doubts and magnifying little difficulties."[77] Actually the purpose was the opposite: Michaelis intended to use the new historical-critical method to support authenticity. Thus Michaelis, who was orthodox on the major theological doctrines, was concerned to defend the apostolic authorship and canonicity of most of the NT books. More conservative than Semler, he gave priority to the Gospel of John and found only a few of the NT documents to be questionable—primarily Jude and Revelation, with minor questions about James and Hebrews.

Moreover, Michaelis's distinction between inspiration and reliability was designed to support the fundamental historicity and authority of the biblical record. In actuality, however, this distinction, along with Michaelis's acknowledgment of errors and inconsistencies, called into question the belief that the whole Bible was equally inspired and infallible. The attempt to harmonize revelation and reason, faith and history—typical of Michaelis and the neologians—ran the risk of compromising both sides of the equation: divine revelation was subjected to human judgment, and dynamic faith was reduced to historical facticity. Although Michaelis had written

75. Ibid. 4.487.
76. Ibid. 4.503.
77. John Randolf, *Remarks on "Michaelis's Introduction to the New Testament, Vols. III. IV. Translated by the Rev. Herbert Marsh, and Augmented with Notes," By way of caution to students in Divinity, second Edition, with Preface and Notes, In Reply to Mr. Marsh* (London: T. Bensley, 1802).

impressive works on dogmatics and reflected profoundly about the meaning of language, his weakness was a failure to think theologically about his historical criticism. His notion that the promise of supernatural assistance was awarded exclusively to the apostles is arbitrary and rests on a superficial reading of the sources. In the course of his work, he advances no thoughtful analysis of the meaning of inspiration, no serious investigation of the concept of revelation. To be sure, Michaelis might reply that historical method is intentionally neutral, but careful analysis of his work indicates that his use of the method rests on presuppositions. These presuppositions include, on the one hand, the natural theology of the Enlightenment, and, on the other hand, the traditional theology of the orthodox—presuppositions which cannot easily be resolved. What is needed is not just a method but a methodology, a hermeneutic that can understand biblical research in relation to the larger questions of reality.

THE STUDENTS OF SEMLER AND MICHAELIS:
GRIESBACH AND EICHHORN

Johann Jakob Griesbach (1745–1812)

Johann Jakob Griesbach was born in the little town of Butzbach but grew up in Frankfurt, where he made the acquaintance of Goethe. Griesbach's father, a pastor, had been influenced by Pietism, and his mother read both Latin and Greek. The young Griesbach was educated at Tübingen, Halle, and Leipzig. At Halle, he studied with Semler, who encouraged him to pursue text-critical research. Like many of the young Enlightenment scholars, Griesbach toured Paris, the Netherlands, and London. In 1771, he wrote a treatise on the importance of the Greek fathers for text criticism and was appointed an instructor at Halle. He was promoted to a professorship in 1773 but in 1775 was called to Jena where he taught church history and dogmatics, as well as introduction to and exegesis of the NT. Griesbach was a person of commanding presence: "Of large, powerful physical build, Griesbach's outward appearance, even at first sight, announced his serious, discreet, upright and reliable character."[78] Griesbach was also noted for his irenic spirit; H.E.G. Paulus observed that "no matter how ardently he argued for his own view in a learned or a practical dispute, if the opposite view won the day he dropped all partisan spirit and worked wholeheartedly for the success of what had been agreed, as though he had

---

78. F. A. Koethe, in a memorial speech of 1812, cited in Gerhard Delling, "Johann Jakob Griesbach: His Life, Work and Times," in *J. J. Griesbach: Synoptic and Text Critical Studies 1776–1976*, ed. B. Orchard and T.R.W. Longstaff (Cambridge: Cambridge University Press, 1978), 13.

never held a contrary view."[79] Paulus knew whereof he spoke, for although Griesbach disagreed with his theology, he supported Paulus's appointment to the faculty at Jena.

Theologically Griesbach was close to Michaelis and the neologians. While opposing the orthodox doctrine of verbal inspiration, Griesbach maintained that the apostles had been given the Spirit on the day of Pentecost, a Spirit which continued to be effective in their lives. Consequently, the gifts which they received "surpassed the powers of nature" and made it possible for them to "both understand and transmit doctrine without danger of error."[80] Nevertheless, Griesbach confirmed the truth of Scripture in terms of the current rationalism and interpreted the Bible by a hermeneutic of accommodation like Semler's. Basic to Griesbach's theology was his doctrine of revelation in history, a history for which the NT provided a reliable record. The crucifixion, resurrection, and ascension constitute the facts of theology. "God," says Griesbach, "has caused to happen something extraordinary, which is beyond human power to do, thus confirming his revelation."[81]

Griesbach's Hermeneutic

Griesbach's basic approach to the Bible can be seen in his *Lectures on the Hermeneutics of the New Testament*, preserved in the meticulous notes of his students and published posthumously.[82] Actually, this work is a presentation of principles of interpretation in the tradition of Turretin and Ernesti, although it is often more thoughtful. In essence, Griesbach affirms grammatico-historical exegesis in opposition to dogmatic interpretation. The purpose of exegesis is to find the meaning of the NT text in its historical setting. When the NT is interpreted correctly, that is, historically, the truth of Christianity comes into clear focus: "Christian religion is nothing other than what Christ and his apostles have taught." Theology, therefore, must be based on the results of sound historical research. "First the philologian and exegete must speak; after the completion of his work, then the theologian and philosopher comes." Like his predecessors, Griesbach argues that the Bible should be interpreted by the same methods used for other documents: "The N.T. must be explained as every ancient book is explained."[83] Yet, although the same method must be used, the Bible is a unique book that requires a special hermeneutic: it is a book of excep-

---

79. Cited in Delling, "Griesbach: His Life, Work and Times," 13–14.
80. Ibid., 11.
81. Ibid., 15.
82. Johann Jakob Griesbach, *Vorlesungen über die Hermeneutik des Neues Testament*, ed. J.C.S. Steiner (Nürnberg: Zeh, 1815). Cited hereafter as *Hermeneutik*.
83. Ibid., 49, 47, 53.

tional importance; its content is more difficult to comprehend than other books; its language is distinctive. By these qualifications, Griesbach does not intend to compromise the essential principles of grammatico-historical exegesis; he wants rather to identify the particularity of biblical literature.

The first section of Griesbach's *Hermeneutics* is concerned with finding the meaning of written texts in general. In this section, stress is placed on the importance of biblical linguistics. Fundamentally, every word, sentence, and passage has, in Griesbach's opinion, one meaning: the literal, historical sense. Theological baggage should not be smuggled in, and the meaning must be found within the historical and literary context. Attention should be directed to the time, place, and purpose of the author, and to the setting of the text in the context of the total biblical book. Anticipating subtleties of twentieth-century hermeneutics, Griesbach says, "One and the same expression (*Rede*) in different circumstances can have a totally different meaning (*Sinn*)."[84] In the next section, Griesbach presents rules for interpreting special words and expressions. He gives attention, therefore, to metaphorical and figurative language, emphatic usage, *hapax legomena*, and biblical words like χάρις and πίστις. While insisting on the literal meaning, Griesbach does not object to interpreting figurative expressions as figurative, for that is what historical criticism demands. The trick, however, is to know a metaphor when one sees one. To distinguish a figurative from a literal text, the exegete must attend to the usual style of the author and the rhetoric of the particular passage.

In the third section, Griesbach turns to the interpretation of the content of the NT books (*Sacherklärung*). All of this has become familiar to the readers of eighteenth-century hermeneutics: the need of informed historical knowledge about the Jews, Greeks, and Romans, making use of geography, archeology, topography, and chronology. In interpreting historical narratives, the exegete must not suppose that every detail is exact. "The accuracy, especially of the NT writers, often errs." Moreover, the people of the ancient Near East were limited by their worldview and ascribed to divine intervention what was the result of natural causes. "The truth of the Christian religion," says Griesbach, "rests not on miracles, but partly on its excellence, partly on its history." In regard to the interpretation of NT content, Griesbach also draws a distinction between dogmatic and biblical theology. Dogmatic theology makes use of philosophical analysis, while biblical theology deals exclusively with the content of the Bible. The Bible, however, contains both essential and nonessential doctrine. Much of the NT—the temporally conditioned data, the limited perspec-

84. Ibid., 100.

tive of the original readers—belongs simply to the garment in which the universal truth is clothed. The interpreter must not become preoccupied with the nonessential clothing in which the word of God is clad. The Bible itself is not to be identified as the word of God; "it is merely the history of revelation, the presentation of the revealed truth."[85]

Illustration of Griesbach's exegetical application of his hermeneutical principles can be seen in his "Explanation of the Passion and Resurrection Narrative of Christ,"[86] a collection of notes taken from an edition of his Gospel synopsis. True to his own principles, Griesbach gives attention to major historical and exegetical problems of the passion and resurrection narratives. He considers the question, Did the Jews in the time of Jesus have the right of capital punishment? He answers that they did, but that sentencing by the Roman governor was required. Griesbach also investigates the meaning of the phrase "son of man" and concludes that Jesus took the title from Daniel and used it to portray his role as the humble and exalted Messiah. In discussing Jesus' response to the question of the high priest (Matt. 26:63-64), Griesbach notes, "This is the first time where Jesus clearly and in plain words declares himself to be the Messiah."[87] In general, Griesbach's exegesis is a mixture of orthodoxy, creative insight, and fanciful rationalism. He believes that John's Gospel presents the most accurate account of the passion narrative. In regard to Luke 22:43 (a reference to the ministering angel in Gethsemane, omitted by many modern editors), Griesbach says that the disciples could not have seen the angel because they were asleep. Luke, however, may be using a symbol, for "it belongs generally to the character of Luke to have everything important take place through an angel."[88] The Emmaus pilgrims did not recognize the risen Christ because his appearance had been altered by the physical punishment he had suffered, and, moreover, he was dressed in an unfamiliar garb, probably the clothes of the gardener. Of course, as he broke bread at the table, the disciples readily recognized the nail prints in his hands.

Griesbach's Greek Text

Although Griesbach's hermeneutical and exegetical studies have largely been forgotten, he is remembered for his work on text criticism and the synoptic problem. Griesbach's contribution to lower criticism was dramatic:

85. Ibid., 139, 144, 164.
86. J. J. Griesbach, "Erklärung der Leidens- und Auferstehungs-Geschichte Christi, nach Griesbach's *Synopsis Evangeliorum*, 3. verb. u. verm. Ausg. Halle, 1809," in idem, *Hermeneutik*, 202–319.
87. Ibid., 239.
88. Ibid., 228.

he was the first of the Enlightenment scholars to present an actual revision of the hallowed Received Text.[89] In 1774, he published the Greek text of the Gospels, making use of readings from the editions of Mill and Wettstein together with his own additional collations. This text printed the accounts from Matthew, Mark, and Luke in parallel columns, a work which came to be called a *Synopsis*.[90] Later he worked on the text of John and Acts, and in 1775, he published the text of the epistles and the Apocalypse as the second volume of his *Novum Testamentum*. In 1777, the first volume appeared, composed of the Gospels (not in synoptic form) and the Acts of the Apostles. Actually, Griesbach's revision is not radical. He largely followed the Received Text and made cautious changes where extensive evidence from the Greek manuscripts, the ancient versions, and the church fathers supported them. He classified the material according to three main recensions: the Alexandrine (witnessed by the oldest uncial manuscripts and Origen), the Western (attested by Codex Beza, Codex Claramontanus, and the Old Latin), and the Byzantine (seen in the bulk of the later manuscripts). For revising the text, the Byzantine was of tertiary importance, and Griesbach preferred the Alexandrine to the Western text.

Griesbach's text-critical achievement is consummated in his two-volume second edition of *Novum Testamentum* (1796, 1806).[91] Although the publishers were in London and Halle, the actual printing was done in Jena under Griesbach's personal supervision. Volume 1 contains a lengthy prolegomena of 130 pages and the text of the Gospels and Acts. In the prolegomena, Griesbach discusses the origin of the Received Text and the question of its reliability. He then presents the plan and method of this new edition. A section is also devoted to his principles of text criticism which includes fifteen canons for evaluating textual variants. The first canon, for example, states that the shorter reading is normally to be preferred, although there are exceptions (e.g., when the shorter text results from homoioteleuton[92]). The second canon is Griesbach's version of the principle of the harder reading: "The more difficult and obscure reading should be preferred to that in which all things are plain and

---

89. See p. 28 n. 71, above.

90. J. J. Griesbach, *Synopsis evangeliorum Matthaei Marci et Lucae una cum iis Joannis pericopis quae omnino cum caeterorum evangelistarum narrationibus conferendae sunt. Textum recensuit et selectam lectionis varietatem adjecit D. Jo. Jac. Griesbach*, 3d rev. ed. (Halle: L. Curtian, 1809). Griesbach began to include the material from the passion narrative of the Gospel of John in his second edition of 1797.

91. *Novum Testamentum Graece. Textum ad fidem codicum versionum et patrum recensuit et lectionis varietatem*, 2d ed., 2 vols. (Vol. 1: London: P. Elmsly; and Halle: J.J.C. Haeredes 1796; Vol. 2: London: Payne & Mackinlay; and Halle: J.J.C. Haeredes, 1806).

92. Homoioteleuton occurs when two words with the same ending are confused, with the result that the intervening words are omitted.

clear."[93] The prolegomena also includes a catalog of the manuscripts which Griesbach uses and the abbreviations which identify them, a system similar to Wettstein's.[94]

The text itself is presented in two columns. Immediately beneath the text is a band across the page in which the variants are printed, accompanied by symbols which indicate Griesbach's evaluation of them. For example, in regard to 1 Cor. 2:1, the text reads μαρτύριον, and this term is preceded in the text by a symbol which is repeated in the note with the variant μυστήριον; the symbol in this instance indicates that the variant is equally good or even preferable to the Received Text. Below this band of evaluated variants are Griesbach's extensive critical notes that give the evidence supporting the variant reading. In the case of 1 Cor. 2:1, μυστήριον is supported by such texts as Alexandrinus, Claramontanus, the Syriac, the Coptic, and Ambrosiaster.

The second volume contains the text of Acts, the epistles, and the Apocalypse. A preface explains the delay in publication and includes a list of the manuscripts which are to be used in this volume. At the end, an appendix has been added that includes a twenty-five page treatise or "diatribe" in which Griesbach discusses the disputed text of 1 John 5:7-8. The treatise presents Griesbach's rationale for eliminating the words of v. 7 that refer to the three heavenly witnesses. In volume 1, Griesbach had been less radical in his treatment of John 7:53—8:11 (the story of the adulteress) which he prints in the text but marks with the symbol that indicates that the passage is probably not genuine.

Griesbach's Synoptic Hypothesis

Griesbach gave serious attention to the synoptic problem. The publishing of his synopsis—a term he apparently coined—aroused Griesbach's interest in the problem of the interrelation of the first three Gospels. Recognition of the problem was not new. As early as the fifth century, Augustine had argued that Mark was an abbreviation of Matthew, and Griesbach's position had been anticipated by Henry Owen. In 1764, Owen, an English clergyman, had written *Observations on the Four Gospels.*[95] Owen begins by affirming the traditional view that the Gospels were written by those to whom they had been attributed. He also assumes that once a Gospel had been written it was used by the writers of subsequent Gospels. Matthew, the first Gospel, was directed to the Jews of the holy land and was written around 38 C.E. When Gentiles joined the church in large numbers, they

93. Griesbach, *Novum Testamentum* 1.lxi.
94. See p. 104, above.
95. Henry Owen, *Observations on the Four Gospels; tending chiefly, To ascertain the Times of their Publication; and To illustrate the Form and Manner of their Composition* (London: T. Payne, 1764).

needed an account of the life and teaching of Jesus—a need supplied by Luke.

Owen presents material from Matthew and Luke in parallel columns to show how the latter used the former. Thus, to Matt. 3:3, Luke adds "all flesh shall see the salvation of God" (3:6) in order to show that Gentiles are included. "The use I would make of these Collations at present," says Owen, "is only to shew, that St. Luke, quoting thus largely from St. Matthew, must necessarily have written after him."[96] Owen fancies that "the brother who is famous . . . for his proclaiming the good news" (2 Cor. 8:18) is none other than Luke, and that Paul quotes from the Gospel of Luke in his account of the Lord's Supper (1 Cor. 11:23-25). Consequently, Luke must have been written prior to 1 Corinthians, that is, in Owen's judgment, about 53 C.E. After the controversies between the Jewish and gentile Christians had been resolved, a short, simple Gospel was needed. This need was supplied by Mark, who wrote at the request of the Christians at Rome. "In compiling the narrative, he had but little more to do, it seems, than to abridge the Gospels which lay before him."[97] According to Owen, Mark worked with copies of Matthew and Luke at hand, sometimes following one, sometimes the other. As to the place of writing, Owen argues from tradition and content that Mark was composed in Rome. He also observes, on the basis of Philemon 23, that Mark and Luke were together with Paul in Rome. There Mark learned of the Gospel of Luke and used it in writing his own Gospel around the year 63.

In addition to Owen's hypothesis, other theories about the order and relationship of the first three Gospels were current at the time of Griesbach. These can be arranged under four main rubrics: (1) the theory that the Gospels depend on tradition that had been handed down orally; (2) the theory that the Synoptics make use of a primitive gospel which was either oral or written; (3) the theory that the Gospels use a variety of fragments, written or oral; (4) various theories which assume an interrelationship among the first three Gospels: that Matthew is the source of Mark, and Matthew and Mark are the sources of Luke (Grotius); that Matthew is the source of Luke, and that Matthew and Luke are the sources of Mark (Owen); that Mark is used independently by Matthew and Luke (G. C. Storr).

In the course of refuting these alternatives and defending his own, Griesbach published two essays on the synoptic problem. The earlier of these was presented in 1783 as a lecture during the Easter celebration at the University of Jena and was entitled "Inquiry into the sources from

96. Ibid., 43.
97. Ibid., 51.

which the Evangelists drew their narratives of the resurrection of the Lord."[98] Whereas Griesbach's major thesis is that Mark used Matthew and Luke as sources, this paper attempts to demonstrate a secondary hypothesis: that Luke used Matthew. The hypothesis is supported by Griesbach's complex analysis of the resurrection narratives, especially the accounts of the women at the tomb. On the basis of several fanciful conjectures, Griesbach attempts to show that Luke's narrative is dependent on Matthew's written account. Along with this analysis of the resurrection stories, Griesbach presents a selection of common Matthean and Lucan passages which he thinks show Luke's dependence on Matthew to be virtually self-evident. In reaction to the arguments of this lecture, even the most ardent supporters of the main Griesbach hypothesis are highly critical.[99]

More convincing is Griesbach's later essay, "Treatise by which it is demonstrated that the entire Gospel of Mark was extracted from the records of Matthew and Luke" (1789).[100] "This," says Griesbach, "is a summary of the opinion we are defending: That Mark when writing his book had in front of his eyes not only Matthew but Luke as well, and that he extracted from them whatever he committed to writing of the deeds, speeches and sayings of the Saviour."[101] In general, Griesbach maintains that Mark set out to write a shorter Gospel, primarily following Matthew, but sometimes using Luke instead. With his own readers in view, Mark omitted material he considered irrelevant and, at the same time, added details of interest which he believed would better explain the narrative.

Griesbach develops his hypothesis through major lines of argument. In regard to order, he argues that whenever Mark departs from the order of Matthew he follows Luke but later returns again to the order of Matthew. This zigzag manner of following his sources can always be explained, according to Griesbach, by Mark's purpose. For example, in 1:40—3:6, Mark has been following Luke 5:12—6:11, but at 3:7 he abandons Luke (because Luke introduces the Sermon on the Plain, which Mark intends

98. A summary and analysis of this address is presented by Hans-Herbert Stoldt, *Geschichte und Kritik der Markushypothese*, 2d ed. (Giessen and Basel: Brunnen, 1986), 239–64. The original, *Paschatos solemnia pie celebranda civibus indicit academia Jenensis. Inquiritur in fontes, unde Evangelistae suas de resurrectione Domini narrationes hauserint. Jenae. MDCCLXXXIII*, was reprinted in Griesbach's *Opuscula academica*, ed. Io. Philippus Gabler, 2 vols. (Jena: F. Frommann, 1825) 2.241–56.

99. See Stoldt, *Markushypothese*, 264.

100. A copy of the original, together with an English translation, is found in Orchard and Longstaff, *J. J. Griesbach: Synoptic and Text Critical Studies*, 74–135. The original, *Io. Iac. Griesbachii Theol. D. et Prof Primar in academia Jenensi commentatio qua Marci Evangelium totum e Matthaei et Lucae commentariis decerptum esse monstratur, scripta nomine Academiae Jenensis, (1789. 1790.) jam recognita multisque augmentis locupletata*, is reprinted in Griesbach, *Opuscula academica* 2.358–423.

101. Orchard and Longstaff, *J. J. Griesbach*, 106.

to omit) and returns to Matt. 12:14 which is parallel to Mark 3:6. In regard to content, Griesbach notes that, except for twenty-four verses, there is nothing in Mark that is not found in Matthew. This dearth of original material seems incredible when one recalls that Mark's mother owned a house in Jerusalem where the early Christians met, so that all sorts of information would have been available to him. The evidence that he does not include such independent information serves to demonstrate, in Griesbach's view, the extent of his dependence on Matthew.

Griesbach turns to possible objections to his hypothesis. For example, he notes that the tradition, going back to Papias, that Mark received his material from Peter would seem to conflict with the theory that Mark's source was the Gospel of Matthew. Griesbach counters this argument by asserting that the tradition is shaky and that the content of Mark's Gospel does not represent what Peter would actually have preached. Griesbach also takes up a variety of objections related to the character and intention of Mark's Gospel, for example, the argument that Mark's account would have been unnecessary, or never would have achieved the status of a Gospel, if it had not been written prior to Matthew, an objection which assumes that the shorter Gospel is surely earlier. Griesbach replies that Mark wrote a Gospel intended to meet the needs of his readers, and that we cannot know the attitude or practice of the early churches in receiving Gospels. Whether an author chose to write a longer, more complete Gospel or a shorter, abbreviated Gospel is a matter of that author's own discretion and tells us nothing about the relative date of the Gospels.

Griesbach gives considerable attention to the objection that the priority of Mark would offer a better explanation for the interrelationship of the Synoptic Gospels, the view which was to become dominant at the end of the nineteenth century. He assumes the traditional authorship of all the gospels[102] and replies that it would be inconceivable that Matthew, an apostle and eyewitness, would copy from the records of a writer who had not even been present during the events. Griesbach also thinks that Mark was sometimes more accurate than Matthew and asks why Matthew would not then have followed Mark in these details, since he appears (according to the theory of Marcan priority) to follow him verbatim in other places. Moreover, continues Griesbach, Mark includes details and even a few accounts which are not included in Matthew and Luke, but why (if they were using Mark as a source) would Matthew and Luke omit these if their intention is to expand information? Matthew arranged his material in topical rather than chronological order, and this, according to Griesbach, is more likely if he is earlier than if he is following the order of Mark.

---

102. "Very far from the truth is the opinion of some who think that the Evangelists are not the true authors of the books that are circulated under their names" (ibid., 134).

Griesbach also gives attention to the objections raised in view of Mark's omissions and discrepancies. How, asks the objector, could Mark have omitted material from Matthew and Luke which is of such obvious importance? Griesbach replies that Mark's omissions are readily explained in terms of his own purposes. Mark omits the account of the temptation, for instance, because it contains Jewish expressions and OT references which are irrelevant for his audience. In some places, Mark's account conflicts with those of Matthew and Luke, but if he were using them as sources (so runs the objection), he could have avoided these discrepancies. Griesbach replies that Mark did not expect his Gospel to be scrutinized. Moreover, when he deviates from Matthew, he sometimes follows Luke, and when he deviates from both, he sometimes supplies more accurate information of his own (e.g., Mark 10:46-52). In general, however, Griesbach's estimation of the Gospel of Mark is disparaging: "Those who argue that Mark wrote under the influence of divine inspiration must surely regard it as being a pretty meagre one!"[103]

In sum, Griesbach made a distinctive mark on the study of the NT. Like Semler and Michaelis, he attempted to accommodate traditional Christianity to the mind of the Enlightenment, and he thus was plagued by the same tension between faith and criticism which troubled his predecessors. The qualifications Griesbach placed on the thesis that the Bible should be interpreted as any other book simply serve to illustrate that tension. Nevertheless, Griesbach tried to ground his hermeneutic theologically in the conviction that God had acted in history, so that historical-critical method was essential to understanding the divine revelation that was recorded in Scripture. On the basis of this conviction, Griesbach engaged in critical research with serious commitment and scholarly competence. His devoted work on the Greek text, especially his bold departure from the Received Text and his attention to the early recensions, advanced the progress of lower criticism. Griesbach's solution to the synoptic problem, particularly his affirmation of the priority of Matthew, continued to influence research on the Gospels. Although his hypothesis was restricted by his traditional view of the authorship of the Gospels, Griesbach presented a plausible explanation for the origin and composition of Mark. Of particular importance is the implication of Griesbach's work for theories about the development of the gospel tradition, especially his argument that the use of sources and the length of a Gospel depend on the purpose of the author. In any case, Griesbach's hypothesis was embraced by a significant group of nineteenth-century scholars including Paulus, de Wette, F. C. Baur, and the controversial D. F. Strauss. Although it seemed to have been laid to

103. Ibid., 135.

rest by the advocates of the increasingly popular two-document theory, the Griesbach, or "two-Gospel," hypothesis has been resurrected in the twentieth century.

Johann Gottfried Eichhorn (1752–1827)

Johann Gottfried Eichhorn, like many eighteenth-century scholars, was the son of a pastor. He studied at Göttingen under Michaelis and C. G. Heyne. Compared with Michaelis, Eichhorn was more sympathetic to Enlightenment ideas and more skeptical about such things as miracles and the resurrection.[104] In 1775, he was appointed professor of Oriental (Semitic) languages at Jena, where he was admired by Goethe who lived in nearby Weimar. In 1788, Eichhorn moved to Göttingen, where he lectured, among other things, on the history of the world from its beginning to the eighteenth century. To master this incredible amount of material, Eichhorn adopted an arduous study schedule in which he worked from 5:00 a.m. till 9:00 p.m., with half-hour breaks for meals.[105] On top of this, he usually lectured twenty hours a week.[106] Alexander von Humboldt, who had been critical of Michaelis, praised Eichhorn's lecturing: "he speaks clearly and coherently, almost without notes, but he has the singular weakness of a sing-song monotony."[107]

The product of this untiring industry was a mountain of publications. Eichhorn produced the six-volume history of the world, a six-volume history of the last three centuries, and a six-volume *History of Literature from the Beginning to the Most Recent Times*.[108] The first volume of this latter series begins with the work of Moses (dated 1483 B.C.E. by Eichhorn), and the final volume concludes with a survey of theological literature from the beginning of the eighteenth century until Eichhorn's time. Eichhorn also published in the area of Semitic languages and edited two journals over a period of more than twenty years. His biblical work included a widely used introduction to the OT which first appeared, in 1780 to 1783, as three volumes, but by the time of the fourth edition (1823–26), had swelled to five weighty tomes. In 1795, Eichhorn published a pioneering historical-critical introduction to the books of the OT Apocrypha.[109]

104. See O'Neill, *Bible's Authority*, 78–94. O'Neill argues that Eichhorn's basic philosophy was Stoicism.

105. This routine staggered two young Bostonians, George Ticknor and Edward Everett, who had left Harvard to study at Göttingen; see Van Wyck Brooks, *The Flowering of New England: 1815–1865* (New York: Modern Library, 1936), 83.

106. See T. Witton Davies, *Heinrich Ewald: Orientalist and Theologian, 1803–1903: A Century of Appreciation* (London: T. F. Unwin, 1903), 4–5.

107. Cited in Smend, "Johann David Michaelis and Johann Gottfried Eichhorn," 73.

108. Johann Gottfried Eichhorn, *Geschichte der Litteratur von ihrem Anfang bis auf die neuesten Zeiten*, 6 vols. (Göttingen: Vandenhoek & Ruprecht, 1805–11).

109. Johann Gottfried Eichhorn, *Einleitung in die apokryphischen Schriften des Alten Testaments* (Leipzig: Weidmann, 1795).

Eichhorn's Hermeneutic of Myth

Eichhorn makes two significant contributions to NT research: his use of the category of myth in exegesis and his work on critical introduction. Following the lead of his teacher, Christian Gottlob Heyne (1729–1812), Eichhorn believed myth represented the way in which primitive people conceived and expressed their experience of reality. Heyne, who taught classical philology at Göttingen, devoted a lifetime to the study of Greek and Roman myths.[110] He believed that myth was the mode of expression used by people in the childhood era of the human race. Myths were necessary and indispensable because of the inadequacies of primitive people, who were limited in knowledge and in their ways of expression. Unable to express their ideas in the abstract, ancient people communicated their concepts in sensual, concrete form. As a result, natural forces were personified, and powerful events were attributed to divine intervention. Heyne identified two main types of myths: historical myths, whereby myth was used to describe the founding of a city or the deeds of a great person; and philosophical myths, whereby ancient people explained the origin of things or speculated about the meaning of reality.

Eichhorn borrowed Heyne's understanding of myth and applied it to the study of the Bible. The result was a new hermeneutical approach which has been called the "mythical method of interpretation" (*mythische Erklärungsart*).[111] In 1779, Eichhorn wrote an essay on primitive history which applied the new method to the study of Genesis 1–3.[112] In this study, the book of Genesis was primarily interpreted as a philosophical myth that explained the origin of the world. As a result, the biblical account of creation was shown to be the mythical expression of primitive people—an account that was neither historical nor verbally inspired. Later, in an article on angel appearances in the Acts of the Apostles, Eichhorn applied the mythical method to the interpretation of the NT.[113] Along with other texts, Eichhorn discusses the appearance of an angel in connection with Peter's escape from prison (Acts 12:3-13). Peter, according to Eichhorn, did not know how his deliverance had been accomplished. Only as he stood on the street and reflected on his sudden and surprising release did

---

110. See Christian Hartlich and Walter Sachs, *Der Ursprung des Mythosbegriffes in der Modernen Bibelwissenschaft* (Tübingen: J.C.B. Mohr, 1952), 11–19.

111. Ibid., 21.

112. "Urgemeinde: Ein Versuch" was published anonymously in Eichhorn's periodical, *Repertorium für Biblische und Morgenländische Litteratur* 4 (1779): 129–256. It was later published in a new edition: *Johann Gottfried Eichhorns Urgeschichte*, 2 vols. (Altdorf and Nürnberg: Monath & Kustler, 1792). See Hans-Joachim Kraus, *Geschichte der historisch-kritischen Erforschung des Alten Testaments*, 2d rev. ed., Neukirchen-Vluyn: Neukirchener, 1969), 147–51.

113. Johann Gottfried Eichhorn, "Versuch über die Engels-Erscheinungen in der Apostelgeschichte," *Allgemeine Bibliothek der biblischen Litteratur* 3 (1790): 381–408.

Peter come to the conviction that it had been accomplished by divine intervention.

> The visible hand of providence had set him free: this Peter was compelled to conclude on the basis of the whole incident. Jewish theology, which always provides Providence with a host of angels to perform its purposes, could express this in no other way than that an angel of the Lord had delivered him from the prison. Once this expression was chosen, everything that had happened—the shaking, the speaking, the leading—an angel of the Lord must have done.[114]

In short, miracle had been swallowed up by myth.[115] This mythical way of interpreting the NT would be further exploited by J. P. Gabler and G. L. Bauer.[116]

Eichhorn's Introduction to the New Testament

In relation to the pioneering work of Michaelis, Eichhorn's massive *Introduction to the New Testament* has two distinctive features: a complex theory about the synoptic problem and a more critical evaluation of authenticity. The first volume appeared in 1804, a second in 1810, and a third in 1812. In 1820, a second, improved edition of volume 1 was published, and in 1827, volumes 4 and 5 were added.[117] In his preface, Eichhorn observes that much work has been done in lower criticism, while higher criticism has been neglected. His effort to remedy the situation is evidenced by an overview of his work: the revised volume 1 on the Synoptic Gospels totals 736 pages; volume 2 on Acts and the Johannine literature totals 512; volume 3 on the epistles totals 656; volume 4 on canonicity, authenticity, and language totals 504; and volume 5 on text and translations totals 324.

Basic to Eichhorn's work on the Gospels is his sharp distinction between the Synoptics and the Gospel of John. "Indeed," he writes, "one must through this research separate the Gospel of John from the first three Gospels."[118] The Fourth Gospel has a different purpose and a different quality and spirit. Also distinctive is Eichhorn's belief that the canonical Gospels were not accepted and widely used until late in the second century. The apostolic fathers, in Eichhorn's view, did not know Matthew, Mark, Luke, or John. According to Eichhorn, these Gospels all depend on a written *Urgospel* which had been lost. Thus, he takes up a theory which

---

114. Ibid., 398.
115. Eichhorn's interest in myth is also seen in his work on Revelation: Jo. Godofr. Eichhorn, *Commentarius in Apocalypsin Johannis*, 2 vols. (Göttingen: J. C. Dieterich, 1791).
116. See pp. 183–94, below.
117. Johann Gottfried Eichhorn, *Einleitung in das Neue Testament*, 2d rev. ed., 5 vols. (Leipzig: Weidmann, 1820–27).
118. Ibid. 1.160.

Lessing had proposed[119] and develops it into a hypothesis of baffling complexity. In developing this theory, Eichhorn begins with an analysis of the oldest gospels. He believes the first reports about Jesus were oral accounts by Jewish Christians, confirming Jesus as the Messiah. The essentials of the life of Jesus were then incorporated into the missionary preaching of the early Christians. In time, written gospels appeared, like the Gospel of the Hebrews and the Memoirs of the Apostles (used by Justin), but these accounts rested on earlier formulations which in turn depended on an ancient life of Jesus, a primitive gospel. Eichhorn believes that through research into the Synoptics, it is possible "after so many centuries to separate the earlier life of Jesus from all later additions, and out of that to establish a life of Jesus free for all later tradition."[120]

Turning directly to the Synoptics, Eichhorn detects three kinds of material: material that appears in all three Gospels, material that appears in two, and material that appears in one. The material that stands in all three makes it evident that the Gospel writers have either made use of each others' Gospels or are all dependent on a common source. By citing parallels (and by making assumptions as to how copyists work), Eichhorn argues that the evidence indicates that none of the Synoptics used either of the others. Thus, he affirms his own hypothesis that the Gospels used a common source—the lost *Urgospel*. In Eichhorn's view, this gospel was not written by an apostle, but by an unknown, well-informed disciple of the apostles. It contained a life of Jesus and was originally written in Aramaic. It was then taken up and reworked by other hands, and eventually translated into Greek. By use of the synoptic parallels, Eichhorn attempts to reconstruct the *Urgospel*, which he prints in Syriac script. Material in which all three Gospels agree verbatim clearly belongs to the primitive gospel.

On the basis of the material that two Gospels have in common and material found exclusively in one Gospel, Eichhorn proceeds to unfold his complex solution to the synoptic problem. Mark, for example, makes use of the *Urgospel*, as his agreements with Matthew show. The *Urgospel*, however, was used by these two evangelists in two different versions: a short translation used by Matthew and a free translation used by Mark. The material that Matthew and Luke have in common also gives evidence that the authors have independently used a common source. In the case of these Gospels, however, that source represents various combinations of three different editions of the *Urgospel*. Material that is unique to each Gospel indicates that other sources were employed; Matthew, for example, made use of information about Jewish thought and practice. In regard to

---

119. See pp. 168–69, below.
120. Eichhorn, *Einleitung* 1.160.

the Gospels individually, Eichhorn argues that Matthew is post-apostolic, since passages like the birth stories, which come from a later time, could not have been composed by an apostle. The Gospel of Mark was written by John Mark, but it does not represent the preaching of Peter. Luke, in Eichhorn's opinion, was written by the travel companion of Paul. Of course, affirming the traditional authorship of the second and third Gospels did little to support the apostolic origin of the Gospels, and, with the fall of Matthew, apostolic authority had crumbled. True apostolic authority, however, finds its locus in the lost, primitive gospel. "Only the sections of the *Urgospel* which the three first Gospels have in common have in themselves the sure authority of the apostles."[121]

This newly discovered ground of authority provides, in Eichhorn's judgment, a foundation for an enlightened reconstruction of the NT message. In the *Urgospel*, amazing events which have been attributed to divine intervention can be explained by natural causes. Similarly, the hearers of the earliest gospel were not required to believe in such supernatural happenings as the virgin birth of Jesus. "In the *Urgospel* which served as the foundation for the first instruction in Christianity, there was nothing about the miraculous conception: in it Jesus is everywhere a son of Joseph and Mary."[122] In Eichhorn's opinion, the new approach to the Gospels presents a significant advance: "Through this separation between the apostolic and the unapostolic, which the higher critic . . . with weightiest grounds commends, is found the means which can establish unshakably the inner reliability and truth of the gospel history."[123]

The rest of Eichhorn's *Introduction* is more conventional. For example, he argues that all five documents attributed to John, including Revelation, are probably authentic. In the Fourth Gospel, John used the *Urgospel* as a source, but the latter part of his narrative is highly reliable, because he was himself an eyewitness to most of the events. Eichhorn accepts Ephesians as Pauline and, against Semler, defends the integrity of 2 Corinthians. However, he believes that Romans 16 was a separate letter of recommendation for Phoebe which was later attached to the epistle. Eichhorn is more critical in his evaluation of the Pastoral Epistles, Hebrews, and the Catholic Epistles. The Pastorals are different in style and thought from the authentic letters of Paul, and the fabrication of a second Roman imprisonment to salvage their authenticity is faulty. Hebrews was not written by Paul, Luke, Barnabas, or Clement of Rome, but by an educated Alexandrian, possibly Apollos. The authorship of both James and 1 Peter is problematic. The latter appears to have been composed by a disciple of Peter, perhaps John Mark. Second Peter is certainly not from the pen of an apostle; it uses Jude as a source, an epistle which was probably written just before 70, since it makes no mention of the destruction of Jerusalem.

Although Eichhorn stands in the tradition of Michaelis, his work displays important distinctions. For one thing, his conclusions on higher critical matters, for example, the authorship of the Pastoral and Catholic Epistles, are less conservative. His work on the Gospels, however, makes a major contribution to the history of NT research. To be sure, his hypothesis of a lost primitive gospel presents only one of many alternatives to Griesbach, but Eichhorn's conviction that recognition of the Synoptics is relatively late and that none of these Gospels is apostolic constitutes a radical break with the tradition. At the same time, Eichhorn's reconstruction of the primitive gospel as apostolic has significant implications for the future study of the NT. For one thing, it gives impetus to the investigation of the oral tradition prior to the writing of the Gospels, but it also provides Eichhorn a device whereby he can eliminate as nonapostolic those elements of the tradition (e.g., the birth stories) which he finds incompatible with Enlightenment ideas—a procedure which escapes evaluation, since the primitive gospel that embodies the true tradition has been lost. Eichhorn's hermeneutic of myth functions in a similar fashion: it frees Jesus and his gospel from the primitive limitations of the written Gospels and makes possible a historical reconstruction on which the abiding truths of Christianity can be built. However, all of this is confused by Eichhorn's assessment of the Gospel of John. On the one hand, his conclusion that the Fourth Gospel must be distinguished from the Synoptics anticipates later scholarship, which has a low estimate of the historical value of the Johannine narrative. On the other hand, Eichhorn's acceptance of its authenticity implies that the Fourth Gospel is a reliable witness to the apostolic gospel, a gospel which can be harmonized with Eichhorn's vision of Christianity only by a radical application of his hermeneutic of myth.

SUMMARY

With the work of Semler and Michaelis and their students, the historical-critical approach to the NT has come of age. Perhaps, the most obvious accomplishment has been in the area of lower criticism, where the sanctity of the Received Text has been broken and progress has been made toward the establishment of a critical text. With Semler's call for a free investigation of the canon, the way has been opened for the unrestricted use of higher criticism, a result realized in the discipline of NT introduction, masterfully developed by Michaelis and Eichhorn. Taken together, this energetic attention to lower and higher criticism confirms the shift in biblical studies undertaken by the earlier Enlightenment scholars: the shift from doctrinal to historical exegesis. As a result of this shift, the authority of the Bible—indeed, the whole idea of special revelation—has come into question. While the orthodox view of the canon and biblical inspiration has been abandoned, efforts have been made to salvage the Bible's significance. Theologically, this attempt has involved an affirmation of divine revelation in history and the accompanying conviction that the Bible, especially the NT, is a witness to that historical revelation. The result was a distinction between revelation and the Bible—a distinction between the word of God and the words of Scripture. On the basis of this distinction, historical research could be rigorous in its assessment of Scripture while devoted in its concern to reconstruct historical revelation.

At the same time, new methods were developed that could contribute to this important goal. By the theory of accommodation (Semler) and the hermeneutic of myth (Eichhorn), the scholar could account for the primitive form of the biblical expression without denying the authenticity of the biblical message. Since that essential message of Scripture was related to the fundamental revelation of God in Jesus Christ, attention was turned to the historical reconstruction of the gospel tradition. Michaelis's confusion about the issue, together with the conflicting theories of Griesbach and Eichhorn, indicate the unresolved character of the problem, a problem further complicated by the question of the authenticity of the Gospel of John. Yet, although all the problems have not been solved, and critical voices will be raised in protest, the approach of Semler and Michaelis will continue to dominate biblical studies for the next two centuries. What is surprising in all this is that the primary source will continue to survive the critical onslaught—like every other book, but somehow different, as Eichhorn himself affirmed:

> No book in the world can in its influence be compared with the New Testament. None has served so widely for instruction; none has contributed so much to the cultivation and enlightenment of the human spirit; none so powerfully and essentially promoted the ethical formation of the heart; none has through its content produced so many happy human beings.[124]

124. Ibid. 4.3.

6

New Testament Research and Theological Meaning

Although the new historical criticism had captured the intellectual citadel of biblical scholarship, much of the surrounding territory remained in hostile hands. The sort of theology Semler and Eichhorn had advanced was embraced in only a few academic centers. Even in progressive Göttingen, Michaelis had not been welcomed to the theological faculty. Elsewhere, especially in the pulpit and pew, the older orthodoxy, sometimes enlivened by Pietism, continued to prevail. This state of affairs is illustrated in Friedrich Nicolai's novel *The Life and Opinions of Sebaldus Nothanker*, a three-volume work, published from 1773 to 1776. Sebaldus, the hero of this complicated romance, is a preacher of neological views, who advocates religious tolerance and believes in universal salvation. Because of such convictions, he is dismissed from the ministry and thrown out of his manse. His wife and younger daughter are forced to live in a peasant's cottage, where they become ill and die. The bereaved Sebaldus engages in a series of adventures in which he travels to such places as Leipzig, Berlin, and Amsterdam. Throughout his many misfortunes, he is lectured to by Pietists and condemned by Lutherans and Calvinists—but seldom helped. Although there is a moderately happy ending, the moral of the story is clear: those who accept the new theology are in for trouble!

The eighteenth century also saw events which contributed to the counter-enlightenment. In 1755 a devastating earthquake shattered Lisbon, a tragedy in which some five thousand persons were killed in about five minutes. As a result, many people began to question the order and rationality of the cosmos and to wonder if theirs really was the "best of all possible worlds," a slogan derived from an oversimplification of Leibnitz's thought and satirized in Voltaire's *Candide*. In the face of such senseless disasters, the older, more stable beliefs seemed more reliable. Similarly, the French Revolution, with its early promise of liberty, equality, and fraternity, soon turned into the Reign of Terror. In response, many people rushed to the conclusion that this sort of chaos had been the outcome of the liberal movements of the Enlightenment.

Related to the revolution was a rising cultural tide called romanticism. A prophet of the new faith was Jean Jacques Rousseau, a malcontent who wandered around Europe in search of meaning. Bothered by a sense of sin, he unburdened his troubled soul in his frank and intimate autobiography, the *Confessions.* Rousseau protested against civilization and against the French intellectuals of the Enlightenment. For him, truth was to be found in nature and was best expressed by the emotions. In Germany, society was shaken by the parallel "storm and stress" (Sturm und Drang) movement. Goethe's hero in *The Sorrows of the Young Werther* was overpowered by the forces of nature and moved by every kind of emotion. So captivated was he by the passion for his beloved, but unattainable, Lotte that he performed the ultimate act of irrationality: he committed suicide.

Suffice it to say that NT scholarship during the eighteenth century was influenced by a variety of forces. The purpose of this chapter is to present some alternatives to the main line of historical-critical research. First, we will give attention to two conservatives: a French Roman Catholic and a British Dissenting Protestant. Then, we will trace early currents in the romantic stream as evidenced in Lessing and Herder, two creative minds who insisted on reading the Bible as literature. Finally, returning to the main line, we will assess attempts to formulate the meaning of historical-critical work in terms of biblical theology.

CONSERVATIVE ALTERNATIVES:
CALMET AND LARDNER

In the chronicle of NT research, the conservatives rate few headlines. Their number was legion, however, and their influence extensive. The term "conservative," in this context, is used loosely to designate scholars who stand closer to orthodoxy and who resist the secular and rationalistic tendency of the historical-critical movement. From the long list of possibilities, Augustin Calmet and Nathaniel Lardner seem to provide likely examples. Calmet, as a French Catholic, illustrates the character of biblical research among the heirs of Richard Simon.[1] Lardner, as a Dissenting Protestant, displays the prevailing conservatism of English thought in the eighteenth and early nineteenth centuries. One of the ironies of the history of biblical study is that the critical method which flowered in Ger-

---

1. See pp. 17–25, above.

many had its roots in France with Simon and in England with the deists. After these innovative beginnings, however, biblical study in France and England became cautious and apologetic.

Augustin Calmet (1672–1757)

Augustin (or Antoine) Calmet is usually recognized as the greatest Roman Catholic biblical scholar of the eighteenth century. He studied at the priory in Breuil and learned Hebrew from a Protestant minister. After further education at the University of Pont-à-Mousson, Calmet entered the Benedictine order at the Abbey of Saint-Mansuy in Toul in 1689. He also studied at Saint-Evre (philosophy) in Toul and at Münster (theology), and was ordained in 1696. Calmet taught theology and philosophy at the abbey at Moyen-Moutier and in 1706 was appointed a professor in Paris. In 1718, he was made abbot of Sainte-Leopold in Nancy, and in 1728 he was moved to the same position in Senones.

Calmet's biblical research is encyclopedic in character and quantity. He was dedicated to historical interpretation but loyal to the principles of the Council of Trent. Consequently, Calmet revered the Vulgate and considered tradition to be crucial in the exegesis of Scripture. Calmet produced two major works of importance for the history of NT research: an extensive commentary series and a comprehensive dictionary of the Bible. Published from 1707 to 1716, Calmet's *Commentary on All the Books of the Old and New Testament* originally appeared in twenty-three volumes. The standard third edition (1724–26) consisted of eight folio volumes, the last two devoted to the NT.[2] Each biblical book is introduced by a preface and various dissertations or excurses on biblical topics; the text is printed in parallel French and Latin translations; the commentary, actually a collection of notes on the text, usually fills the bottom half of the page. Much of this material was reprinted in *La Sainte Bible,*[3] a new edition of Calmet's commentary, published in fourteen volumes in 1750.

In volumes 10 through 14 of the *Sainte Bible,* Calmet considers matters of NT criticism: he presents prefaces to each NT book, provides notes to the text, and writes dissertations on topics of historical and exegetical interest. The divine authority of Scripture and tradition is everywhere presupposed, discrepancies are uniformly harmonized, and conservative conclusions are persistently affirmed. For example, in research on the

---

2. Augustin Calmet, *Commentaire litteral sur tous les livres de l'Ancien et du Nouveau Testament,* 8 vols. (Paris: Emery, Saugrain, P. Martin, 1724–26).

3. Augustin Calmet, *La Sainte Bible en Latin et en François; avec des notes litterales, critiques et historiques, des prefaces et des dissertations tirées du Commentaire de Augustin Calmet, Abbé de Senones, de M. l'Abbé de Vence, & des Auteurs les plus célèbres; pour faciliter l'intelligence de l'Écriture Sainte,* 14 vols. (Paris: G. Martin, et al., 1750).

Gospels, Calmet explains the difference between Matthew's genealogy and Luke's according to the timeworn solution: Matthew traces the lineage of Jesus through Joseph; Luke traces it through Mary. The problem of the delay of the parousia—that is, the fact that Jesus did not return as soon as he seemed to have predicted—is solved by the notion that Jesus had prophesied two separate events: the destruction of Jerusalem and the second (*dernier*) coming. Moreover, he says, the delay is not really significant, "because the day of our death is for each of us the day of the coming of Jesus Christ."[4]

Calmet has no hesitation about embracing supernaturalism while remaining loyal to his ecclesiastical tradition. The demons, in his view, were real demons, and the exorcisms were real miracles. Calmet discusses the various theories about the cause of the darkness that accompanied the crucifixion, and he rejects rational hypotheses, such as the occurrence of an eclipse or the interference of a thick cloud, in favor of a cosmic miracle. He thinks the unpardonable sin is the heresy of attributing to a demon the miracles of Jesus. Calmet points out that the difference between πέτρος and πέτρα in Matt. 16:18 would not have pertained in the original situation, because in Syriac there would have been no distinction in gender. Thus, Jesus clearly intended to address Peter as the rock on which the church was to be built. Calmet believes the church at Rome was founded by Peter and that, in spite of criticism to the contrary, his early mission there was "certain and indubitable."[5]

On critical matters Calmet is usually conservative. He believes the longer ending of Mark to be original. About the debated 1 John 5:7, Calmet opts for authenticity and claims that the omission of the three heavenly witnesses in some manuscripts was due to errors by the copyists. In a long discussion on the authorship of Hebrews, he concludes that Paul was the writer and the original language was Greek. Like other conservatives, Calmet advocates two Roman imprisonments for Paul: Philippians, Philemon, Colossians, Ephesians, and Hebrews were written from the first, 1 Timothy and Titus during the interim, and 2 Timothy from the second imprisonment. Sometimes Calmet's criticism shows more imagination. In regard to the problem of dating the last supper, for example, he argues that Jesus actually celebrated the Passover a day early: the supper was on Thursday the thirteenth of Nisan, and Jesus was executed on the day of the sacrifice of the paschal lamb. Calmet also gives serious attention to Grotius's contention that John 21 was a later addition, but he concludes

4. Ibid. 11.64.
5. Ibid. 13.466.

that this chapter was originally written by John. The baptism of the dead is interpreted as a sort of proxy practice whereby persons who had been unable to receive baptism prior to their deaths were represented by a friend or relative.

Calmet's *Dictionnaire historique, critique, chronologique, géographique et littérale de la Bible* also appeared in a variety of editions and formats. The original edition (1720–21) was published in two volumes, and the fourth edition of 1730 had expanded to four. As early as 1732, a version appeared in English containing three volumes; the popular edition of 1847 included five:[6] the dictionary proper is contained in two large folios, and the fragments fill volumes 3 and 4; a final volume includes tables and maps (material largely added by later editors). Calmet's original work is found primarily in the main part of the dictionary. In scope, the dictionary covers everything from *Aaron* to *Zuzim* and is a monument to the comprehensiveness of Calmet's scholarship. The articles attend to matters of history, geography, biblical criticism, chronology, biblical terms, customs, festivals, coins, measures—a vast treasury of significant information.

An example or two can illustrate the nature of Calmet's work. A long article on Jesus Christ faithfully follows the biblical record. It harmonizes the varying birth narratives of Matthew and Luke. Jesus' ministry is chronologically ordered according to four Passovers, an arrangement which displays unfailing confidence in the Johannine narrative. A similar article on Paul harmonizes the accounts of Acts with those of the epistles, so that Calmet reports the "famine" visit of Acts 11:30 without mention of the conflicting account in Gal. 1:18—2:1. Calmet also is confident that Paul actually carried the apostolic decree (Acts 15:23-29) to Antioch, and he takes no notice of Acts 21:25 (where Paul seems to be informed of the decree for the first time) or Paul's implicit opposition to the decree by his discussion of meat offered to idols in 1 Corinthians 8 and 10.

Somewhat surprising is Calmet's conclusion that the author of the Gospel of Mark is not John Mark. Instead, he identifies the writer as a convert of Peter, possibly a member of the seventy (Luke 10:1), who may have accompanied Peter to Rome in 44. Also of interest is Calmet's article on Onesimus. According to Calmet, the runaway slave visited Paul in Rome in 61, was baptized, and returned to Philemon. Philemon manumitted him and sent him back to Paul. According to tradition, Onesimus not only served Paul but was appointed to ecclesiastical office. Calmet notes the tradition that Paul made Onesimus bishop of Berea, but he seems more

6. Augustin Calmet, *Calmet's Dictionary of the Holy Bible; with the Biblical Fragments*, ed. Charles Tayler, 9th ed., 5 vols. (London: H. G. Bohn, 1847).

sympathetic to the tradition that Onesimus succeeded Timothy as bishop of Ephesus and is the bishop mentioned by Ignatius, a tradition which Calmet acknowledges "has no solid proof."[7]

All in all, Calmet's research is somewhat disappointing in view of the creative beginning which had been made by Simon.[8] How exciting it might have been if, on the one hand, Calmet had advanced Simon's attack on Protestant orthodoxy's doctrine of *sola scriptura* and, on the other hand, joined hands with the Protestant historical critics of the Enlightenment. Instead, he displayed more confidence in the reliability of the words of Scripture than did the innovative Protestants, and, in spite of his loyalty to ecclesiastical tradition, he held a higher view of biblical authority than scholars like Semler and Eichhorn. Nevertheless, Calmet's dedication to the serious study of the Bible is significant within his own tradition, and his concern for literal interpretation is especially notable in view of French Catholicism's penchant for the mystical meaning, under the continuing influence of Simon's great nemesis, J. B. Bossuet. In any event, Calmet did not ignore the critical questions, and his collection of useful information contributed to the cause of historical research.

Nathaniel Lardner (1684–1768)

Largely ignored by the historians of biblical research, Nathaniel Lardner was frequently cited by J. D. Michaelis. Born in Hawkhurst in Kent, Lardner was the son of a Dissenting minister. He studied at the Dissenting academy in London and at age sixteen was sent to Utrecht and Leiden for further education. Lardner sought a pulpit but without success, due apparently to the dullness of his homiletical delivery. In 1729 he was appointed assistant minister of a Presbyterian chapel in London where he remained until 1751, when total deafness forced him to resign his duties.

Most of Lardner's scholarly efforts were poured into one major project, *The Credibility of the Gospel History.* The first part, consisting of two volumes, appeared in 1727, and the final supplementary section was not completed until 1757, for a total of seventeen volumes. "The design of this work, from the beginning, and all along," writes Lardner, "has been, to show the truth of the evangelical history, and thereby the truth of the christian religion; for if the facts related in the gospels, and confirmed by the epistles of the New Testament, may be relied upon, the christian religion is from Heaven."[9] The work is arranged in three parts: the first argues that the facts of the NT are confirmed by contemporary ancient authors; the

---

7. Ibid. 2.263.
8. See pp. 17–25, above.
9. Nathaniel Lardner, *The Credibility of the Gospel History*, in idem, *The Works of Nathaniel Lardner, D.D., with a Life by Dr. Kippis*, 10 vols. (London: Holdsworth & Ball, 1831) 5.174.

second demonstrates that the reliability of the NT is supported by sources from the patristic period through the twelfth century; the third includes supplementary essays which deal with historical and critical issues in NT study. The whole of the *Credibility* and the supplements have been reprinted in the first six volumes of Lardner's collected works.[10]

The character of Lardner's research can be illustrated by a selection from the first part of the *Credibility*. In the second book, he presents a lengthy chapter entitled "Three Objections against Luke, Chap. II. Ver. 1,2."[11] The objections, of course, represent questions which have been raised about the historicity of Luke's account of a census at the time of Jesus' birth. The first objection is that there is no record of an empire-wide enrollment during the reign of Augustus, an objection which Lardner acknowledges. He argues, however, that Luke was referring not to an enrollment of the whole world but only of Judea. Lardner tries to establish this point by his claim that the term οἰκουμένη can refer to a particular country. Thus he translates the text "And it came to pass in those days, that there went forth a decree from Caesar Augustus, that all the *land* should be taxed."[12] The second objection involves a variety of problems in connection with the census. Since Herod is the ruler of Judea, and it is not an imperial province at this time, Augustus would be unlikely to require an enrollment there. Lardner, in answer, argues that Herod is a subordinate ruler and Augustus might have had good reason to order a census. The objector also asks why Joseph would have had to go all the way from Nazareth to Bethlehem and why Mary would have needed to accompany him. Lardner answers that enrollment by families and tribes was important for the Jews; Mary did not have to go, but there is no reason (Lardner does not mention her pregnancy) they should not have chosen for her to accompany Joseph. The third objection is that Quirinius (more properly "Cyrenius," according to Lardner) was not governor of Syria until some ten or twelve years after the birth of Jesus. In response, Lardner argues that there were two censuses: this one and a later one of which Luke was fully aware. Thus, Quirinius administered a census on behalf of the Romans prior to his appointment as governor, and a second after he became governor. Lardner thinks that the problem dissolves when Luke 2:2 is read as a parenthetical remark: "(This was the first assessment of Cyrenius the governor of Syria)."[13]

The apologetic shape of Lardner's scholarship is also seen in his treatise "A Vindication of Three of Our Blessed Saviour's Miracles, viz. the

10. Ibid.
11. Ibid. 1.260–345.
12. Ibid. 1.267–68.
13. Ibid. 1.336.

Raising of Jairus's Daughter, the Widow of Nain's Son, and Lazarus. In Answer to the Objections of Mr. Woolston's Fifth Discourse on the Miracles of Our Saviour."[14] In the preface, Lardner decries civil prosecution of Woolston and calls for freedom of inquiry. The first chapter of the essay attempts to answer Woolston's objections to the historicity of these three miracles. Most important, Woolston claims that the three miracles are of varying significance, that the raising of Lazarus is the most significant, and that the latter miracle is related only in the Gospel which is farthest removed from the events (John). Lardner replies that any act of resurrection is significant and represents a momentous miracle. The fact that the raising of Lazarus appears only in the Gospel of John does not discredit its historicity. Lardner argues that there were no doubt many more raisings about which the evangelists had information, but because of their concern for brevity, they selected only one (two in the case of Luke). If the selection had been left to Lardner, he says that he would have preferred the story about Jairus's daughter to the raising of Lazarus, since she was the daughter of a ruler of the synagogue and thus representative of persons usually averse to Jesus, while Lazarus was a friend. In Lardner's opinion, the raising of an opponent is apparently more significant than the raising of a friend. Finally, the narratives of the first three Gospels do not recount the journey during which the raising of Lazarus occurred, so that the omission of the miracle should not be surprising.

Lardner is more convincing in his answers to other objections of Woolston. For example, Woolston's argument that Jesus should have raised people of more importance is answered by Lardner's response that Jesus' mission was not selective but, rather, was directed toward people in need, regardless of their station in life. To the objection that Jesus, in the case of Jairus's daughter, should not have put people out of the room but should have assembled a large number of witnesses, Lardner responds that to have brought in more people would have resulted in crowded confusion, and, moreover, the parents and the three apostles constituted a group of five credible witnesses—more than enough! In the final section of this essay, Lardner argues that the accounts of all three miracles are fully credible. The times, the places, the names of the participants are presented, and the miracles are public events, not fictitious concoctions. However, in all of this Lardner fails to offer a defense against Woolston's most powerful weapon: ridicule. For example, when Woolston asks why Jesus, instead of raising an insignificant boy (the widow's son) and a mere girl (Jairus's daughter), did not raise someone of more importance, such as

14. Lardner, *Works* 10.1–72.

John the Baptist, he is hoping for a laugh. Lardner, although he says it is a "silly"[15] question, proceeds to answer with prosaic seriousness: the Baptist had finished his work, and his resurrection might have detracted from his witness to Jesus.

Lardner's views on the historical (higher) criticism of the NT are found in his "A History of the Apostles and Evangelists, Writers of the New Testament."[16] Written in 1756 and 1757, this lengthy essay was published as part of the supplementary volumes of the *Credibility*. In regard to the Gospels, Lardner argues that all, including John, were written prior to the destruction of Jerusalem. He thinks that none of the first three used any of the others, since each is a full, unique, independent Gospel. For one evangelist to abridge the work of another would have been beneath his character, and if one had been copying another, he would not have omitted important things the other included. John, however, knew Matthew, Mark, and Luke, and intentionally supplemented their information. Lardner thinks that Matthew originally wrote in Greek, and that the Gospel of Mark was written by John Mark who presents the substance of Peter's preaching. The longer ending of Mark, in Lardner's opinion, is genuine.

In regard to the Pauline letters, the traditional fourteen are all accepted as authentic. Hebrews was written in Greek by Paul from Rome or Italy. Lardner believes the thought of this letter to be Paul's, and he observes "some instances of agreement in the style, or phrases of the epistle to the Hebrews, and the acknowledged epistles of St. Paul."[17] He supports the notion of two Roman imprisonments, but he places the writing of 2 Timothy in the first imprisonment. First Timothy and Titus were both written earlier, and he dates them at 56, between the writing of 1 and 2 Corinthians. A lengthy discussion is directed to the question of the destination of Ephesians, but Lardner concludes that Ephesians was, indeed, written to the Ephesians. Contrary to most opinion, he believes that Paul was himself the founder of the churches at Colossae and Laodicea. Lardner accepts all of the Catholic Epistles as authentic. He takes the Epistle of James to be apostolic, for its author is James the son of Alpheus, whom Lardner also identifies as James, the leader of the Jerusalem church.

Despite his basic conservatism, Lardner was not immune to the influence of the Enlightenment. In 1758, he published four discourses on the

---

15. Ibid. 10.33.

16. Lardner, *Works* 5.255–536, 6.3–361. Examples of Lardner's exegesis of the NT can be seen in his "Remarks upon the Late Dr. Ward's Dissertations upon Several Passages of the Sacred Scriptures," in *Works* 10.265–351, and his "Observations upon Dr. Macknight's Harmony of the Four Gospels: As Far as Relates to the History of Our Saviour's Resurrection," in *Works* 10.351–92.

17. Ibid. 6.95.

story of the Gerasene demoniac.[18] In these discourses, Lardner sets the text in its context and makes use of the parallels. He notes that Matthew's account has two demoniacs and concludes that Mark and Luke mention only one of the two because that one—the one possessed by a legion of demons—is the more important. In interpreting the text, Lardner observes that people of Jesus' day believed that maladies were often caused by demon possession: "And those persons, and their friends, attributing these disorders to Satan, and demons under him, our Saviour often adapts his expressions to that opinion, without countenancing or approving it."[19] Thus, Lardner anticipates Semler's accommodation doctrine and goes beyond him to assert that the apostles also shared the ignorance of their contemporaries. Most important, Lardner declares that the notion of demon possession is contrary to reason: "Possession by evil spirits is a thing absurd and impossible, at the least, unreasonable, and improbable, and not supposed, unless there be clear and full proof of it. Which, I think, there is not."[20] Lardner was even accused of Socinianism because of a letter in which he opposed the idea that the Logos took the place of the soul in the body of Jesus.[21] According to Lardner, Jesus was fully human in body and soul. "From all that has been said, it appears that Jesus is a man, appointed, anointed, beloved, honoured, and exalted by God above all beings."[22]

In summary, Lardner's work is essentially an exercise in biblical apologetics. He engages in historical research to prove the factual reliability of the biblical record, an endeavor of ultimate significance because, for Lardner, the truth of Christianity rests on historical facts. Since the biblical accounts are reliable, Lardner has no difficulty in accepting the historicity of supernatural happenings like the miracles and the resurrection. In developing his apologetic, Lardner makes use of the Enlightenment method of historical research, the same method refined by Semler, Michaelis, and their students. Lardner, too, has mastered the skills of text criticism, philology, linguistics, grammar, and historical research. He, too, makes use of empiricism and reason, and even adopts the hermeneutic of accommodation. In method, then, there is no essential distinction between the "liberal" and the "conservative" biblical scholars: the former use the method to question biblical history, the latter to support it. More impor-

---

18. Nathaniel Lardner, *The Case of the Demoniacs Mentioned in the New Testament: Four Discourses upon Mark v.19* (London: C. Henderson, 1758); reprinted in *Works* 1.449–519.

19. Lardner, *Demoniacs*, 69; *Works* 1.480.

20. Lardner, *Demoniacs*, 76; *Works* 1.483.

21. Nathaniel Lardner, "A Letter Written in the Year 1730, Concerning the Question, Whether the Logos Supplied the Place of the Human Soul in the Person of Jesus Christ," in *Works* 10.73–185.

22. Ibid. 10.97.

tant, by embracing this method, both the liberal and the conservative critics have reduced the message of the NT to sheer history. In effect, therefore, the Enlightenment view of the Bible has been adopted by the very scholars who claim to oppose it. The weakness of this conservative surrender to the Enlightenment viewpoint is especially apparent in the effort to defend the inspiration and infallibility of the Bible by use of the new, secular method. The result is a strange anomaly: arguments are advanced in which the attempt is made to establish the authority of the Bible by rational, historical reasoning—as if the transcendent truths of divine revelation could be confirmed by the paltry proofs of humans. In short, the conservatives tried to interpret as any other book a book they believed to be totally different.

THE NEW TESTAMENT AS LITERATURE: LESSING, REIMARUS, AND HERDER

A totally different alternative is provided by two of the most creative minds of the eighteenth century, G. E. Lessing and J. G. Herder. Although they recognized the historical character of the biblical documents and accepted the historical-critical method, Lessing and Herder refused to allow the NT to be reduced to factual history. Instead of the historicizing of the biblical message, they advocated an aesthetic approach which interpreted the NT as a literary expression of religious truth. Lessing, although primarily a literary critic and dramatist, became embroiled in theological controversy as a result of his role in publishing the Wolfenbüttel *Fragments*. Herder, although noted for his extensive work in philosophy and literary criticism, was primarily a theologian and churchman.

Gotthold Ephraim Lessing (1729–1781)

Lessing's Religious Thought

Gotthold Ephraim Lessing was born in Saxony, the son of an orthodox Lutheran pastor.[23] In 1746, he began theological studies in Leipzig but was more interested in literature and drama. For a time he studied medicine, but he moved to Berlin in 1748 to pursue a literary career. In response to his parents' plea that he return to the university and to a more orthodox faith, Lessing wrote to his father:

---

23. For a succinct summary of Lessing's life and thought, see J. C. O'Neill, *The Bible's Authority: A Portrait Gallery of Thinkers from Lessing to Bultmann* (Edinburgh: T. & T. Clark, 1991), 13–27.

Time will tell, whether he is a better Christian, who has the fundamentals of Christian doctrine in his memory, and often, though without understanding them, in his mouth, goes to church and takes part in all the rites, since they are habitual; or he who has once prudently doubted, and through the way of investigation come to a conviction, or at least strives to attain it. The Christian religion is not an enterprise which one should accept on the truth and faith of one's parents. Most people, indeed, inherit it from them as they do their property, but they show through their behavior what sort of Christians they really are. So long as I fail to see that one of the primary commands of Christianity, to love one's enemy, is better observed, so long will I doubt whether they are Christians who declare themselves as such.[24]

In Berlin, Lessing made the acquaintance of leading intellectuals like Friedrich Nicolai and the Jewish philosopher Moses Mendelssohn, the grandfather of the composer, Felix Mendelssohn-Bartholdy. In 1760, Lessing secured a position in Breslau as secretary to a military official, which provided him financial security and the opportunity to study and write. From 1767 to 1769, he worked as a dramatic consultant and literary critic in Hamburg. In 1770, he accepted a position as librarian of the great ducal collection at Wolfenbüttel. Among Lessing's most popular works was *Nathan the Wise*, a drama set in twelfth-century Jerusalem that made a powerful statement on behalf of religious toleration.[25]

Lessing's theology is difficult to characterize. He has no system. Influenced by Spinoza, he stresses the immanence of God in nature and history. He believes ultimate truth to be beyond the grasp of humans.

If God held all truth in his right hand and in his left the everlasting striving after truth, so that I should always and everlastingly be mistaken, and said to me, "Choose," with humility I would pick on the left hand and say, "Father, grant me that. Absolute truth is for thee alone."[26]

Lessing found himself in disagreement with the major theological trends of the day: orthodoxy, deism, and neology. He opposed the biblicism of the orthodox and may have been the first to characterize devotion to the letter of Scripture as "bibliolatry."[27] Although Lessing agreed with the deists that revelation could not be proved by fulfilled prophecy or miracles, he did not reject the concept of revelation out of hand. He opposed the theology of the neologians as a muddling compromise between the older orthodoxy and the new Enlightenment thought. The orthodox, he

24. Gotthold Ephraim Lessing, *Gesammelte Werke*, ed. Paul Rilla, 10 vols. (Berlin: Aufbau-Verlag, 1957) 9.22.
25. See Ronald F. Thiemann, "Gotthold Ephraim Lessing: An Enlightened View of Judaism," *Journal of Ecumenical Studies* 18 (1981): 401–22.
26. Cited in Henry Chadwick, ed., *Lessing's Theological Writings: Selections in Translation with an Introductory Essay* (Stanford: Stanford University Press, 1957), 43.
27. Lessing wrote an essay, "Bibliolatrie," in *Gesammelte Werke* 8.482–89.

exclaimed, were at least clear! In a letter to his brother, Lessing characterized neology as a "real patchwork of bunglers and half philosophers."[28]

Lessing's view of revelation is expressed in one of his last works, "The
Education of the Human Race."[29] Here he presents a concept of progressive revelation. "What education is to the individual man," he says, "revelation is to the whole human race."[30] Thus, revelation is the continuing
process through which truth is disclosed by God and perceived by people—a process which is still going on. This progressive revelation is in
harmony with reason, for "revelation gives nothing to the human race
which human reason could not arrive at on its own."[31] In another place,
Lessing declares that revelation is harmonious with natural theology: "The
best revealed or positive religion is that which contains the fewest conventional additions to natural religion, and least hinders the good effects of
natural religion."[32]

In their earliest history, humans had the idea of one God, but elabora-
tion of this simple idea led to polytheism and idolatry. After God had
revealed divine truth to individuals, God granted revelation to a special
people—the Hebrews. Their understanding of God was limited by their
capacity, for they were like children accepting the idea of divine punish-
ments and rewards. Nevertheless, they became the teachers of others and
produced the first primer of religion, the OT. Later, under the influence
of the Chaldeans and Persians, the Jews recognized the doctrine of immortality and came to a clear perception of the reality of the One God. Still
later in history, "A better instructor must come and tear the exhausted
primer from the child's hands—Christ came."[33] "And so Christ," continues
Lessing, "was the first *reliable, practical* teacher of the immortality of the
soul."[34] Christ was also the first, according to Lessing, to teach "an inward
purity of heart in reference to another life."[35] Because they contain the
teachings of Jesus, the Scriptures of the NT constitute the second great
primer of the human race: "For seventeen hundred years past they have
occupied human reason more than all other books, and enlightened it
more, were it even only through the light which human reason itself put
into them."[36] Revelation, however, is not finished, and human beings

---

28. Cited in Henry E. Allison, *Lessing and the Enlightenment: His Philosophy of Religion and
Its Relation to Eighteenth-Century Thought* (Ann Arbor: University of Michigan Press, 1966), 84.
29. In Chadwick, *Lessing's Theological Writings*, 82–98.
30. Ibid., 82.
31. Ibid., 83.
32. "On the Origin of Revealed Religion," in ibid., 105.
33. Ibid., 91.
34. Ibid., 92.
35. Ibid.
36. Ibid., 93.

should look forward to the time of their perfection: "It will assuredly come! the time of a new eternal gospel, which is promised us in the primers of the New Covenant itself."[37]

Although revelation comes through history, truth cannot be established by proofs from historical facts. This idea is developed in Lessing's essay "On the Proof of the Spirit and of Power."[38] In this essay, Lessing's notorious "ugly ditch"—the chasm between faith and history—comes into view. On the surface, the ditch appears to be merely a temporal gap. Thus, Lessing says that if he had lived at the time of Jesus and could have seen fulfilled prophecies and miracles, he could have believed, but since he lives centuries later, he is dependent on the fallible witness of others. "The problem is," he says, "that this proof of the spirit and of power no longer has any spirit or power, but has sunk to the level of human testimonies of spirit and power."[39] However, as Gordon Michalson has shown, the ditch which Lessing cannot leap across turns out to be a metaphysical chasm.[40] Lessing asserts that even if he could be certain about the miracles and the resurrection, that certainty could not provide the ground for faith: "If on historical grounds I have no objection to the statement that this Christ himself rose from the dead, must I therefore accept it as true that this risen Christ was the Son of God?"[41] Thus, Lessing concludes that "accidental truths of history can never become the proof of necessary truths of reason."[42] The ugly ditch is a division between two different kinds of truth: the truths of history and the truths of faith. Consequently, Lessing asserts that he is not bound to historical facts; he is bound instead to the Christian teachings themselves, to those universal moral truths intuitively perceived as self-authenticating.

In addition to his role in the Reimarus controversy, Lessing made significant contributions to the study of the NT. In his "A New Hypothesis Concerning the Evangelists Regarded as Merely Human Historians,"[43] Lessing articulates the theory that all the canonical Gospels rest ultimately on a lost *Urgospel*, the theory later developed by Eichhorn.[44] According to Lessing, soon after the death of Christ, the followers of Jesus "had a written collection of narratives concerning Christ's life and teaching, which

---

37. Ibid., 96.
38. Ibid., 51–56.
39. Ibid., 52.
40. Gordon E. Michalson, Jr., *Lessing's "Ugly Ditch": A Study of Theology and History* (University Park: Pennsylvania State University Press, 1985).
41. Chadwick, *Lessing's Theological Writings*, 54.
42. Ibid., 53.
43. Ibid., 65–81.
44. See pp. 150–52, above.

arose out of orally transmitted stories of the apostles and all the people who had lived in association with Christ."[45] Evidence for the existence of this primitive written gospel is seen in the "Gospel of the Nazarenes" to which Jerome refers, a later exemplar of the primitive Chaldaic-Syriac gospel. Our Gospel of Matthew, composed some thirty years after the death of Jesus, is Matthew's Greek translation based on this original gospel. Although Matthew, the first of the canonical evangelists, translated an earlier gospel, the religious significance of his Gospel is not diminished.

> If he made this selection in a better known language with all the diligence, with all the caution, of which such an enterprise is worthy, then indeed to speak only humanly, a good spirit assisted him. And no one can object if one calls this good spirit the Holy Spirit.[46]

Later, Luke and Mark made use of this same early Semitic gospel, although Mark had a less complete copy. John, who knew the other three Gospels, also "read the Hebrew document, and used it in his Gospel." He did not, however, write a Gospel to supplement the information of the three earlier Gospels; his Gospel "belongs to a class all of its own."[47]

In regard to the meaning of the Gospels, Lessing stresses the spirit rather than the letter. His essay "The Testament of John"[48] elucidates his hope, expressed at the end of "On the Proof of the Spirit and of Power," that people "who are divided by the Gospel of John may be reunited by the Testament of John."[49] In contrast to the complex doctrine of the Gospel of John, the apocryphal Testament offers a simple admonition: "Little children, love one another." The practice of Christian love, according to Lessing, is more difficult and more important than the confession of dogma. Many Christians, however, are preoccupied with doctrines about Christ. By way of contrast, the earliest gospel was written by people who knew Jesus to be a fully human being. For Lessing, the distinction between the religion *of* Christ and the religion *about* Christ is crucial: "The religion of Christ, is that religion which as a man he himself recognized and practised," while "the Christian religion, is that religion which accepts it as true that he was more than a man, and makes Christ himself, as such, the object of its worship."[50]

45. Chadwick, *Lessing's Theological Writings*, 66.
46. Ibid., 73.
47. Ibid., 79.
48. Ibid., 57–61.
49. Ibid., 56.
50. "The Religion of Christ, 1780," in ibid., 106.

Lessing, Reimarus, and the
Wolfenbüttel Fragments

While living in Hamburg, Lessing made the acquaintance of Hermann Samuel Reimarus (1694–1768). Reimarus, a professor of Semitic languages at the academic gymnasium in Hamburg, had been influenced by the rationalism of Wolff and the writings of the English deists. In 1754, he published *The Principle Truths of Natural Religion,* in which he rejected the miracles and abandoned supernatural revelation.[51] He also wrote the lengthy *Apology for the Rational Worshippers of God,*[52] but fearing the consequences which might befall his family, he did not publish it. After his death, his daughter Elise gave the manuscript to Lessing to publish at his own discretion. In 1774, Lessing began the publication of *Fragments of an Unknown,* pretending to have found the fragments in the Wolfenbüttel library without knowledge of their origin.[53] From 1774 to 1778, Lessing continued to publish the fragments in installments. The first, "On the Toleration of Deists," makes a case for natural theology and rational religion, a case carried on in the second fragment, "On the Decrying of Reason in the Pulpit." The third fragment, "The Impossibility of a Revelation which All Men Can Believe on Rational Grounds," argues that if revelation requires proofs which can convince humans, then it is not divine revelation at all. In the fourth fragment, "The Passage of the Israelites through the Red Sea," Reimarus, in the spirit and style of the English deists, points out the absurdities in the Exodus narrative. The fifth fragment, "That the Books of the Old Testament Were Not Written to Reveal a Religion," argues that interpretation demands understanding of the original intent of the biblical authors. In the sixth fragment, "On the Resurrection Narrative," Reimarus notes discrepancies in the Gospel accounts of the resurrection of Jesus and asks how the faith of the world is supposed to depend on four remote witnesses who contradict each other.

The seventh fragment, "On the Intention of Jesus and His Disciples," is the most important. In essence, Reimarus claims that the intention of

---

51. The 3d edition of 1766 has been reissued: Hermann Samuel Reimarus, *Die vornehmsten Wahrheiten der natürlichen Religion,* ed. Günter Gawlick, 2 vols. (Göttingen: Vandenhoeck & Ruprecht, 1985).

52. Hermann Samuel Reimarus, *Apologie oder Schutzschrift für die vernünftigen Verehrer Gottes,* ed. Gerhard Alexander, 2 vols. (Frankfurt am Main: Insel, 1972). This edition makes use of manuscripts and previous publications and includes more material than Lessing published in the *Fragments.* For a review of this critical edition, see Harald Schultze, "Religionskritik in der Aufklärung: Das Hauptwerk des Reimarus im 200. Jahre des Fragmentenstreites," *Theologische Literaturzeitung* 103 (1978): 705–13.

53. The *Fragments* Lessing published are reprinted in his *Gesammelte Werke,* vols. 7 and 8. See J. K. Riches, "Lessing as Editor of Reimarus' *Apologie,*" in *Studia Biblica 1978: II. Papers on The Gospels,* Sixth International Congress on Biblical Studies, Oxford, 3–7 April 1978, ed. E. A. Livingstone (Sheffield: *Journal for the Study of the New Testament,* Suppl. Series 2 [1980]: 247–54).

Jesus and the intention of the disciples are totally at odds. Thus he writes, "I find great cause to separate completely what the apostles say in their own writings from that which Jesus himself actually said and taught, for the apostles were themselves teachers and consequently present their own views."[54] According to Reimarus, Jesus did not teach a new religion but simply took up the moral message of the OT. "Thus the goal of Jesus' sermons and teachings was a proper, active character, a changing of mind, a sincere love of God and one's neighbor, humility, gentleness, denial of the self, and the suppression of all evil desires."[55] Basic to the teaching of Jesus was his idea of the kingdom of God. The kingdom, as in Jewish expectation, was the rule of God on earth—a kingdom to be inaugurated by the promised Messiah. Jesus viewed himself as the earthly Messiah and called himself "son of man" to depict his humility. According to Reimarus, "When Jesus calls himself God's Son he means to imply only that he is the Christ or Messiah particularly loved by God, and thus he does not introduce to the Jews any new doctrine or mystery."[56] The rite of baptism, if practiced by Jesus at all, was taken over from the Jews, and the observance of the Lord's Supper represented not the founding of a new religion, but merely Jesus' observance of the Passover.

In contrast to Jesus' simple Jewish piety, the disciples created a new religion by means of deception and fraud. The turning point was the crucifixion of Jesus. There it became clear to his followers that Jesus had been mistaken about the imminence of the earthly kingdom, because Jesus had died and the kingdom had not come. Faced with this devastating calamity, the disciples concocted a theology out of their own deceptive imagination. The simple fact of Jesus' death was transformed into "the doctrine of a spiritual suffering savior of all mankind."[57] "Their system then," says Reimarus, "consisted briefly in this: that Christ or the Messiah was bound to die in order to obtain forgiveness for mankind, and consequently to achieve his own glory; that upon the strength of this he arose alive from death out of his tomb upon the third day as he had prophesied and ascended into heaven."[58] The ground on which this whole theological superstructure was built is the story of the resurrection, and the resurrection is nothing more than the fraudulent claim of the disciples who created the empty tomb by stealing the body. The accounts of the resurrection bristle with contradictions: the number of angels, conflicting reports

---

54. H. S. Reimarus, "Concerning the Intention of Jesus and His Teaching," in *Reimarus: Fragments*, ed. Charles H. Talbert, trans. Ralph S. Fraser (Philadelphia: Fortress Press, 1970), 64.
55. Ibid., 69.
56. Ibid., 88.
57. Ibid., 129.
58. Ibid., 151–52.

about the anointing of the body, inconsistent narratives about appearances to Mary Magdalene. The story of the guard at the tomb, found exclusively in Matthew, is full of incongruities, and the attempt to prove the resurrection from the prophecies of the OT entails distortion of the biblical texts.

In time, the earliest version of this fraudulent system ran into difficulties of its own. The new interpretation of the Messiah, borrowed from Jewish apocalyptic, had expected the triumphant return of Jesus on the clouds. When this spectacular event failed to occur as soon as it had been predicted, the disciples had to go back to the theological drawing board. Eventually, new solutions were devised. The author of 2 Peter, for example, was able to erase the problem of the delay of the parousia with one bold stroke of his pen: if one day is as a thousand years, a delay of a day or so should not matter! Reimarus considered this and other props the Christians frantically erected to support their flimsy religion to be equally weak. "In short," he wrote, "I may affirm that one cannot refer to a single quoted prophecy that is not false." Similarly, "a thousand asserted miracles cannot clear up and set straight one single evident contradiction in the accounts of the resurrection now before my eyes."[59]

Why did the disciples perpetrate this gigantic fraud which has held Christendom under its spell for seventeen centuries? Reimarus replies that they were lured by economic and political aspirations. During the time of their association with Jesus, these lower-class disciples and common fisherfolk had been cared for out of the benevolence of others. Naturally, they wanted this to continue, and, freed from the ethical restraints of Jesus, they entertained grandiose dreams of wealth and worldly advantage. To gain the material support of their auditors, the disciples promised abundant rewards in the future kingdom. In all of this, Reimarus sounds like a noisy echo of the English deists. However, there is a distinctive difference: Reimarus did not simply ridicule the supernatural details; he incorporated the elements of criticism into a system that is a total reconstruction of the history of early Christianity.

Albert Schweitzer, reflecting on Reimarus's work, declared, "This essay is not only one of the greatest events in the history of criticism, it is also a masterpiece of general literature."[60] Many of Lessing's contemporaries would not have concurred. Indeed, Lessing himself did not agree with many of Reimarus's opinions, as he notes in his "Counterclaims of the Editor," published along with the *Fragments*.[61] To be sure, Lessing found

59. Ibid., 237, 239.

60. Albert Schweitzer, *The Quest of the Historical Jesus: A Critical Study of Its Progress from Reimarus to Wrede*, trans. W. Montgomery (New York: Macmillan, 1957), 15.

61. G. E. Lessing, "Gegensätze des Herausgebers," in idem, *Gesammelte Werke* 7.812–53.

Reimarus's attacks on the biblical record to be useful in his own intention to show that faith could not rest on historical facts. From this perspective, Lessing thought Christians had nothing to fear in the inquiry. However, in regard to the idea of revelation, Lessing did not think that divine disclosure to a particular people was against reason, although supernatural revelation in the orthodox sense was contrary to the teaching of Jesus and the truth of Christianity. In regard to miracles, Lessing did not believe they were intrinsically impossible.

The earliest critics aimed their blows at the unknown author of the *Fragments,* whose identity was not disclosed until 1814. J. H. Ress, superintendent of the church in Wolfenbüttel, asserts that the *Fragments* fabricate contradictions where there are no contradictions at all. In *A Rejoinder,*[62] Lessing answers that the contradictions are real but that disagreements of witnesses do not necessarily discredit the historicity of an event. Ress's more serious error, in Lessing's opinion, is his attempt to base faith on supernatural proofs. To make his point, Lessing pictures the distinction between the scaffolding (the miracles) and the building (the truth of Christianity); the scaffolding can be torn down and the building still stand. "When will they stop wanting to hang nothing less than all eternity on a spider's thread!—No; scholastic dogmatics never inflicted such deep wounds on Christianity as historical exegesis now inflicts on it every day."[63]

Johann Melchior Goeze's attack was directed not only against the *Fragments* but also against their editor, G. E. Lessing. Goeze, senior pastor of St. Catherine Church of Hamburg, wrote a newspaper article and then a series of essays which were published together in a book, *Something Preliminary against Herr Hofrat Lessing's Direct and Indirect Malevolent Attacks on Our Most Holy Religion, and Its Single Foundation, the Bible.* About the writer of the *Fragments,* Goeze wrote, "How black and at the same time, unconcerned, the soul of the author was, can only be seen in the fourth fragment in which he pursues his main purpose of slandering the disciples of Jesus as the most malicious scoundrels."[64] Goeze defends biblical orthodoxy. He argues that letter and spirit are one and the same, and that denial of the infallibility of one part of the Bible is denial of all.

Lessing responds with a series of counterattacks. In "A Parable," he tells the story of a beautiful palace, intricately designed with many small doors

---

62. G. E. Lessing, "Eine Duplik," in idem, *Gesammelte Werke* 8.24–107.
63. Ibid. 8.37.
64. Cited in G. W. Buchanan, "Introduction," in Hermann Samuel Reimarus, *The Goal of Jesus and His Disciples: Introduction and Translation,* ed. George Wesley Buchanan (Leiden: E. J. Brill, 1970), 11.

and windows, radiantly filled with light.[65] Experts in architecture debated about the structure of the building, each claiming to possess the authentic blueprint. One night the watchman cried, "Fire!" The architectural connoisseurs began to argue about little matters—where were the entrances? what would burn first?—more concerned to save their blueprints than the building. As it turned out, the watchman's cry was a false alarm, but if there had been a fire and if the emergency had been left to experts, the palace would have burned to the ground. The meaning is clear: theologians like Goeze are preoccupied with trivia, concerned with the letter rather than the spirit. Lessing appeals to Luther: "You have freed us from the yoke of tradition: who will free us from the unbearable yoke of the letter!"[66]

In "Axioms," Lessing disputes Goeze's attempt to identify Christianity and the Bible.[67] According to Lessing, Christianity existed prior to the writing and canonizing of the biblical books, and even if the Bible were lost, the truth of Christianity would endure: "The religion is not true because the evangelists and apostles taught it: but they taught it because it is true."[68] In "Necessary Answer to a Very Unnecessary Question of Herr Haupt-Pastor Goeze in Hamburg," Lessing responds to his opponent's challenge to declare openly what he believes the truth of Christianity to be: Christianity, says Lessing, is the faith which is expressed in the creeds of the first four centuries of the church.[69] These confessions witness to the living tradition, the *regula fidei*, which precedes and succeeds the writing of the Bible. "By the undoubtedly proved authenticity of the *regula fidei* its divine nature can be proved with far greater certainty than the inspiration of the New Testament writings can be proved."[70]

J. S. Semler and the
Wolfenbüttel Fragments

The controversy concerning the *Fragments* becomes exciting for the history of NT research when J. S. Semler enters the fray. For many reasons, one might have supposed that Semler would have supported Lessing. Semler had called for the free investigation of the canon and, like Lessing, recognized the distinction between facts and faith. Actually, the differ-

---

65. G. E. Lessing, "Eine Parabel: Nebst einer kleinen Bitte, und einem eventualen Absagungsschreiben an den Herrn Pastor Goeze, in Hamburg," in idem, *Gesammelte Werke* 8.151–63.

66. Ibid. 8.161.

67. G. E. Lessing, "Axiomata, wenn es deren in dergleichen Dingen gibt: Wider den Herrn Pastor Goeze, in Hamburg," in idem, *Gesammelte Werke* 8.164–200.

68. Cited in Chadwick, *Lessing's Theological Writings*, 18.

69. Ibid., 62–64.

70. Ibid., 63.

ences between Lessing and Semler were in part a matter of temperament. Lessing was a creative author who enjoyed controversy and reveled in sarcasm and irony; Semler was a philologist and historian who worked with plodding seriousness.[71] Although both had rejected the faith of their youth, Semler was never fully free from his pietistic legacy. Lessing's distinction between faith and history was not as sharply drawn by Semler, who believed faith always took historical shape. But most of all, Semler thought the *Fragments* to be an impious assault on Christianity. He criticized Lessing for publishing them and found the effect of the controversy to be destructive: "The result is that a new bone of contention has been thrown among the theologians which has given the enemies of Christianity a wonderful opportunity for malicious remarks."[72]

Semler's formal response to the *Fragments* is a case of theological overkill. In 1778, he published *Reply to the Fragments of an Unknown*, a book of more than four hundred pages, plus a lengthy appendix.[73] Never moderate in his treatment of opponents, Semler says, "I confess repeatedly that I can in no way recognize the Unknown to be worthy of respect as an investigator of truth."[74] In developing his reply, Semler takes up the arguments of the seventh fragment, "On the Intention of Jesus and his Disciples," point by point. He disagrees with Reimarus on the two fundamental issues: (1) the intention of Jesus, arguing that he did not simply appropriate the Jewish expectation of an earthly Messiah; and (2) the intention of the disciples, arguing that they did not commit intentional fraud.

In discussing the teaching of Jesus, Semler argues that Jesus did indeed found a new religion. Jesus presented a revelation higher than that of Judaism. His idea of the kingdom was not political, but ethical. If Jesus had taught nothing but Judaism, asks Semler, why was he attacked by the Jews? Into the midst of his discussion, Semler introduces, perhaps a bit immodestly, an imaginary dialogue between himself and Jesus. Jesus, in the course of the dialogue, presents himself as a teacher of universal moral religion who announces the coming of a spiritual kingdom. Thus, says "Jesus," "This invisible great eternal kingdom of God whereby he rules in the souls of people and continually reveals himself unites thus all people through the unity and community of such unworldly purposes."[75] If Semler had not carefully labeled each statement of the dialogue with "Ich"

---

71. See Lothar Steiger, "Die 'gymnastische' Wahrheitsfrage: Lessing und Goeze," *Evangelische Theologie* 43 (1983): 430–45.

72. Cited in Fritz Huber, *Johann Salomo Semler: Seine Bedeutung fur Theologie, sein Streit mit Gotthold Ephraim Lessing* (Berlin: R. Trenkel, 1906), 72–73.

73. Joh. Salomo Semler, *Beantwortung der Fragmente eines Ungenanten, insbesondere vom Zweck Jesu und seiner Jünger*, rev. ed. (Halle: Erziehungsinstitut, 1780).

74. Ibid., foreword.

75. Ibid., 254.

or "Jesus," the reader would have difficulty in determining who was speaking! As to the intention of the disciples, Semler considers laughable the notion that they could have changed Jesus' whole system of doctrine in a few days. The charge that the early Christians committed fraud in order to attain earthly power and glory is refuted by their willingness to endure persecution for their faith. All the available historical evidence shows that the disciples truly believed the message they proclaimed. As to the proofs from prophecy and miracle, Semler, employing his accommodation hermeneutic, believed they had credibility in their own time. The interpretation of OT prophecies, therefore, was designed to convince the first-century Jews, not everyone in all times, of the truth of Christianity.

Semler finds mistaken the notion of the author of the *Fragments* that he could discredit Christianity by disproving the historicity of the resurrection. Semler acknowledges that the details of the gospel narratives cannot be harmonized, but he, with Lessing, argues that faith in the resurrection does not depend on historical data. The resurrection was no "natural event, subject to the laws of motion and the senses."[76] The resurrection was a supernatural event, received by faith. The significance of the resurrection is found in the inner experience of the truth of Jesus' moral teaching.

> Therefore, I contradict the Unknown, when he maintains that all of Christianity, including ourselves today, depends on this narrative of the resurrection of Jesus. . . . Christianity arises out of the teaching of Jesus . . . not solely out of the story that he was raised, apart from the teaching.[77]

Indeed, the truth of Christianity cannot be damaged by the demonstration of the flaws in its presentation, since it is truth of another sort—an inner, moral truth that is self-evident.

Contemporary historical critics like Eichhorn thought Semler, tossed by the waves of controversy, had jettisoned his own critical accomplishment. Lessing, remembering how Semler had characterized him, says he is honored to have been relegated to the lunatic asylum by so important a person, but he expresses surprise that Semler did not agree with the author of the *Fragments*.[78] If he does not agree, says Lessing, Semler must answer questions concerning the content of the universal Christian religion and its call to authentic moral life. In other words, Lessing believes Semler's attempt to answer would force him to acknowledge the essential truth beneath the details of the argument. Semler, of course, is distracted

76. Cited in Colin Brown, *Jesus in European Protestant Thought, 1778–1860* (Grand Rapids: Baker, 1985), 14.

77. Semler, *Beantwortung*, 250.

78. See G. E. Lessing, "Gegen Johann Salomo Semler," in idem, *Gesammelte Werke* 8.477.

by the details, demonstrating that his idea of the free investigation of the canon had its limits. Nevertheless, it was the spirit more than the letter of the *Fragments* that disturbed Semler. For him, the *Fragments* represents a malicious attack on the Christian faith. Consequently, when in 1788 the Prussian government under the conservative minister of education, J. C. Wöllner, pronounced an edict requiring all preachers and teachers to conform to the orthodox creeds, Semler declared his support.[79] Although Semler could scarcely have subscribed to the orthodoxy the edict was designed to defend, he believed it would be useful in promoting public religion. The true religion was inward, a private concern of the individual's free conscience in relation to God. Thus Semler, conforming to the pattern of the times, practiced an accommodation doctrine of his own.

Johann Gottfried Herder (1744–1803)

Johann Gottfried Herder, son of a pietistic father of the working class, began the study of medicine at Königsburg in 1762. Later he switched to theology and came under the influence of Immanuel Kant and J. G. Hamann. In 1764, Herder moved to Riga, where he was a teacher in the cathedral school. During this period, his interests turned to language and literary criticism. In 1771, Herder was appointed court preacher in Bücke-burg, where he fell under the spell of the Sturm und Drang movement with its opposition to rationalism and its stress on feeling and the inner life. While doing research at Göttingen, Herder made a lasting friendship with C. G. Heyne, the noted classicist.[80] Heyne attempted to secure a chair in theology for Herder at the university, but George III of England and Hanover (where Göttingen was located) opposed the appointment, questioning Herder's orthodoxy. In 1776, Herder moved to Weimar as superintendent of the clergy and court preacher. There he spent the balance of his career, sharing the cultural climate with intellectuals like Goethe and Schiller.

Herder was a prolific writer. His collected works fill more than thirty volumes and cover a wide variety of topics in philosophy, literature, and theology. His most famous work, *Ideen zur Philosophie der Geschichte der Menscheit*, was published in four volumes from 1784 to 1791 but was never completed. In this massive opus, Herder presents an interpretation of the evolutionary development of humanity, reminiscent of Lessing. The scope of the work is vast, including discussions about cosmology and nature (in which Herder verges on panentheism), the ancient Chinese (about whom

---

79. See Klaus Epstein, *The Genesis of German Conservatism* (Princeton: Princeton University Press, 1975), 142–53.
80. See p. 149, above.

Herder's knowledge is limited), the ancient Hebrews (whose major achievement was monotheism), and the ancient Greeks (whom Herder prefers to the Romans). Humanity, according to Herder, evolves from the primitive being who stands upright (developing a brain and the ability to speak) to the truly religious human being of enlightened culture. This progress in human development was advanced by Jesus, who had revolted against Judaism and founded a higher religion. He fulfilled the expectations of the best elements of the OT faith and proclaimed "a heavenly kingdom, in which only chosen men could participate, and for the obtaining of which he proposed no external duties and ceremonies, but pure mental and spiritual virtues."[81]

This philosophy of history provides the key for unlocking Herder's theology. For Herder, all truth is historical: it is manifest in history and it is perceived in history, indeed, in the particularities of history. Like Lessing, Herder believes absolute truth is beyond human comprehension. God, the source and ground of truth, is known only in the historical, for God is immanent in the particular events of history, and history is the disclosure of God's unfolding plan.

> If God does not exist *in* the world, *everywhere* in the world, and indeed everywhere immeasurably, wholly and indivisible, then He doesn't exist anywhere. . . . He is the highest, most alive, most active One—not *in* all things, as if they were something outside Him, but *through* all things; that appear to us only as sense-perceptive representations for sense-perceptive creatures.[82]

Herder's picture of revelation is painted with a broad brush: he sees the world as a whole and all individual phenomena within it as manifestations of the divine. The universe encompasses a variety of forces held together by laws; it is a harmonious order in which God is at work. The purpose of revelation is the education (*Bildung*) of humanity.[83]

The Bible plays an important role in revelation, since it is the record of God's unfolding plan in history. In the Bible, God is seen as the living, active, powerful being who is revealed in all the actualities of history—in people and in events. Herder believes the Bible is the word of God because God speaks in it. Nevertheless, the Bible is a wholly human book:

---

81. Johann Gottfried v. Herder, *Outlines of a Philosophy of the History of Man*, trans. T. Churchill (New York: Bergman, 1800), 491.

82. Cited in Robert T. Clark, Jr., *Herder: His Life and Thought* (Berkeley and Los Angeles: University of California Press, 1955), 340.

83. Marcia Bunge ("The Restless Reader: Johann Gottfried Herder's Interpretations of the New Testament" [Ph.D. diss., University of Chicago, 1986]) argues that the concept of *Bildung* is central to Herder's hermeneutic.

The Bible must be read in a human way: for it is a book written through humans for human beings; the language is human; the external means with which it was written and preserved were human; and finally, the meaning with which it can be grasped, and every aid which explains it, as well the whole purpose and use to which it should be applied are human.[84]

With this stress on the human character of the Bible, Herder had abandoned the orthodox view of inspiration. At the same time, he embraced the methods of historical criticism. He advocated the study of linguistics, geography, and history, and the use of scholarly commentaries like those of Semler and Eichhorn. In 1775, Herder published "Elucidations to the New Testament from a Recently Published Eastern Source," in which, anticipating the history of religions approach, he recommended the study of Persian religion as a background for the interpretation of the NT.[85] Advising the young theologian, Herder wrote, "In short, my friend, despise nothing of the accessories of theology and its framework; but do not forget that the accessories are not the thing itself, and the framework is not the building."[86] The details of critical method are to be used as tools to probe the meaning of the text. Each book of the Bible must be interpreted according to its literary genre. In discussing Genesis, Herder insists that it is essentially an expression of Near Eastern poetry.

Although God speaks in the OT, especially in the poets and prophets, God's voice is muted there. The NT is a higher expression of the divine word which is declared most clearly in the Gospels and the story of Jesus. Jesus, in Herder's view, was our brother who shared our humanity, yet he was conceived by the power of God. As son of God, Jesus had a unique relation to the Father; as son of man, he was identified with humanity. The deeds of Jesus embody the working of God's potent love, and the miracles are divine acts whereby the power of evil is overcome. To be sure, Jesus' contemporaries erroneously understood diseases to be caused by demon possession. The exorcism of demons, however, is the authentic work of the Spirit, which restores persons to health. Jesus proclaimed a kingdom that was ethical and spiritual. Open to all human beings, this kingdom embodies the love of God. Jesus' ethical teaching is summarized in the Sermon on the Mount. According to Herder, the death of Jesus was not a sacrificial atonement for sin, but the final expression of his work of love in obedience to God: "He died neither as hero, nor prophet, nor martyr, but as

---

84. J. G. Herder, "Briefe, das Studium der Theologie betreffend," in idem, *Sämmtliche Werke*, 33 vols. (Hildesheim: G. Olms), 10.7.
85. J. G. Herder, "Erläuterungen zum Neuen Testament: aus einer neueröfneten Morgenländischen Quelle," in idem, *Sämmtliche Werke* 7.337–470.
86. Herder, "Briefe, das Studium der Theologie betreffend," 10.11.

the redeemer of humanity in the deepest silence and humility."[87] Herder accepts the historicity of the resurrection but tends to spiritualize it. Following Paul, he claims that the idea of "the Christian resurrection of the dead has actually destroyed the Jewish physical resurrection."[88] Herder, at the same time, rejects the idea of the immortality of the soul and understands resurrection as a transformation in which the human spirit is absorbed into the divine process.[89]

Herder gives attention to the problem of hermeneutics. He found much of the exegesis of his own time reprehensible. "Since his crucifixion," says Herder, "Jesus, on the one hand, has never received more false scepters and purple robes, and on the other, more drinks of gall and crowns of thorns than from the learned exegetes and interpreters of the Bible."[90] Although one must use the critical method for understanding the text in its historical setting, the Bible should not be read scientifically but should be heard as the word of God: "As a child hears the voice of his father, as the beloved the voice of his betrothed, so you should hear the voice of God in scripture and perceive the sound of eternity which echoes in it."[91] Modern interpreters ought to put themselves in the place of the original readers: "Read the letters of the apostles as letters; forget chapters, verses, customary epistles, and read as if you were a Christian of the first century and had received a letter from the hands of the apostle himself."[92] An example of Herder's "historical-aesthetic method"[93] can be seen in his interpretation of the Pentecost events of Acts 2.[94] At the outset, Herder asks why a gift of speech was needed, because all of the audience could have understood Greek. This leads him to surmise that the meaning of the account is not to be found in a miracle of linguistics. In search of the deeper meaning, Herder observes that the festival of Pentecost was historically a commemoration of the giving of the law at Sinai. There, according to Jewish tradition, the divine commands were originally presented in seventy different tongues, that is, in all the languages of the world. Thus, concludes Herder, the Christian Pentecost depicted by Luke is a festival of the giving of the new law—a universal spiritual message proclaimed to all people.

87. Herder, "Erläuterungen zum Neuen Testament," 7.436.
88. J. G. Herder, "Von der Auferstehung als Glauben, Geschichte und Lehre," in idem, Sämmtliche Werke 19.110.
89. See O'Neill, Bible's Authority, 75–77.
90. Herder, "Erläuterungen zum Neuen Testament," 7.350.
91. J. G. Herder, "Briefe an Theophron," in idem, Sämmtliche Werke 11.165–66.
92. Herder, "Briefe, das Studium der Theologie betreffend," 10.258.
93. Klaus Scholder, "Herder und die Anfänge der historischen Theologie," Evangelische Theologie 22 (1962): 432.
94. J. G. Herder, "Von der Gabe der Sprachen am ersten christlichen Pfingstfest," in idem, Sämmtliche Werke 19.4–59.

Herder developed a theory about the origin of the Gospels. Anticipating form criticism, he believed the earliest gospel was oral, consisting of the teachings of Jesus and the preaching of the apostles. Eventually the gospel was reduced to written form. This primitive gospel was a sketch of the life of Jesus which included the baptism, transfiguration, and resurrection; and within this outline, it recorded the miracles and parables of Jesus. Herder thought this *Urgospel* was the written source for the canonical Gospels, but he acknowledged that when we attempt to solve the synoptic problem, "It seems to me we are giving ourselves unnecessary trouble."[95] As to the order of the Gospels, Herder changed his views. In his letters on the study of theology (1780),[96] he argued that Matthew was the earliest Gospel; that Mark had a copy of Matthew's Gospel before him and added material he had learned from Peter; and that Luke studied the accounts of others and used eyewitness reports. In 1797, however, Herder added a section to his essay on the son of God entitled "The Principle of the Agreement of Our Gospels on the Basis of their Origin and Order."[97] According to this revised version, Mark was the earliest of the canonical Gospels. "Mark," says Herder, "is an independent Gospel; not a selection from Matthew, not a compilation from Matthew and Luke."[98] Luke wrote later, and the Greek Gospel of Matthew was composed after Luke. John, a totally different sort of Gospel, did not appear until the end of the first century.

Given Herder's special bent for the spiritual, his fascination with the Fourth Gospel is not surprising.

> Oh John! How often I have learned to admire and love you! How purely and beautifully you presented your master, and remained true to him, as you still would lay on his breast and listen to the words of his heart![99]

Herder believes John portrays Jesus against the backdrop of Persian religion, seen, for example, in the light-darkness symbolism, a background which also explains John's use of gnostic motifs. In contrast to the Palestinian-bound Synoptic Gospels, the Gospel of John addresses the larger Hellenistic audience and presents Jesus as the savior of the world. John is concerned not with the historical Jesus but with the spiritual Christ. "Therefore," says Herder, "it is precisely this *unveiling of Christ*, the *pure glorification of him*, that is most precious to John."[100]

---

95. J. G. Herder, "Von Erlöser der Menschen. Nach unsern drei ersten Evangelien," in idem, *Sämmtliche Werke* 19.206.

96. Herder, "Briefe, das Studium der Theologie betreffend," 10.157–65.

97. J. G. Herder, "Regel der Zusammenstimung unser Evangelien, aus ihrer Enstehung und Ordnung," in idem, *Sämmtliche Werke* 19.380–424.

98. Ibid. 19.420.

99. J. G. Herder, "Aus der Schrift 'Johannes,' 1774," in idem, *Sämmtliche Werke* 7.318.

100. Cited in Brown, *Jesus in European Protestant Thought*, 72.

Distinctive among Herder's biblical essays is his "Letters of Two Brothers of Jesus in Our Canon."[101] The brothers are James and Jude, and, for Herder, they are real brothers because characteristic of the humanity of Jesus is his life among brothers and sisters. The author of the Epistles of James is James the brother of Jesus, who later became the leader of the church in Jerusalem; he may have been an Essene. Although Luther considered James to be an epistle of straw, Herder believes this epistle contains much nourishing food. Moreover, James is not in conflict with Paul: "In no article of faith does he contradict Paul—if one gives attention to the word itself."[102] Paul's seeming opposition to works is shaped by his debate with Pharisees, but actually he agrees with James that faith is demonstrated by ethical behavior. According to Herder, the Epistle of Jude was written by Jude the brother of James and Jesus, and was used by Peter in the writing of his second epistle. The cryptic reference to Michael the archangel disputing with the devil over the body of Moses (Jude 9) is read by Herder as a sign that Jude was addressed to people steeped in "Chaldean" legends—the people of Parthia and Mesopotamia. In conclusion, Herder opts for canonicity, since both epistles confess Jesus as Lord, and Peter puts his imprimatur on the work of Jude.

Herder wrote two works on Revelation. The earlier one, "The Revelation of John: A Holy Vision," is more original and interesting.[103] Herder thinks that the Apocalypse is the "most divine" and also the "deepest and most closed book" of the NT.[104] It deserves a place in the canon because it witnesses to Jesus. According to Herder, it was written by John, the author of the Fourth Gospel, but at a different time and for different purposes. Revelation was written from Patmos during the reign of Diocletian. The symbolism of the book finds its source in Daniel, Ezekiel, and Zechariah, but ultimately in what Herder calls "Chaldean" motifs. Herder believes the Apocalypse should be understood not mystically but historically. Even the cryptic 666 is no mystery, but is, rather, a simple cipher built on the numerical value of the letters LATINUS, signifying Rome. Much of the apparent prophetic material actually describes events of the past with an eye toward the future. The destruction of Jerusalem, for example, is a historical prototype of future events. In his MARAN ATHA (1779),[105] Herder's interpretation is changed: Revelation was written six or seven

101. J. G. Herder, "Briefe zweener Brüder Jesu in unserm Kanon," in idem, *Sämmtliche Werke* 7.471–560.
102. Ibid. 7.503.
103. J. G. Herder, "Johannes Offenbarung: Ein heiliges Gesicht," in idem, *Sämmtliche Werke* 9.1–100.
104. Ibid. 9.3.
105. J. G. Herder, "MAPAN. AΘA.: Das Buch von de Zukunft des Herrn, des Neuen Testaments Siegel," in idem, *Sämmtliche Werke* 9.101–288.

years before the destruction of Jerusalem; the seven heads of the beast refer to the Sanhedrin; the prostitute symbolizes Jerusalem. All of this simply illustrates the flexibility of Herder's imagination.

Herder and Lessing represent a deviation in the course of the development of historical research. To be sure, they accept the grammatico-historical method and make significant contributions to the discussion of the origins of the gospel tradition and the higher criticism and exegesis of NT books. Nevertheless, Herder and Lessing are sharply critical of many of the contemporary practitioners of Enlightenment criticism. Like the orthodox, these historical critics are thought to err in focusing on the letter, that is, on the details of exegesis and historical fact. History, of course, is of utmost importance for Herder and Lessing, since they see in it the disclosure of God's progressive revelation for evolving humanity. History, however, is not a collection of chronological data, but a story with meaning, a meaning which has to do with inward matters, with the human spirit, with feelings, with morality. At a high point in this historical unfolding of divine truth and human development, a special revelation has appeared in Jesus, the teacher of a spiritual, ethical religion. Moreover, it is the religion of Jesus—this realization of the divine-human ideal—that must be emulated, not the religion about Jesus—the concern for external, dogmatic formulation. The Bible, which records this historical disclosure of truth, is fully human, written in the rhetoric of human imagination, in literature and poetry. Consequently, Scripture must be read with imagination, sensitive to the human spirit, responsive to the revelation of God. Although Herder and Lessing move against the stream, their influence surfaces in nineteenth-century theologians like Schleiermacher who were concerned with religious consciousness,[106] and in the disciples of Coleridge who were influenced by romanticism.[107] At the same time, the distinction Lessing draws between truths of history and truths of faith has brought into sharper focus the continuing problem of the relation of historical criticism and faith, a problem made acute by the correlative conviction that faith is revealed in history.

BEGINNINGS IN NEW TESTAMENT THEOLOGY: GABLER AND G. L. BAUER

In the orthodoxy of Protestant scholasticism, biblical theology and dogmatic theology were largely identified. The Bible, although it recorded

106. See pp. 208–20, below.
107. See pp. 338–60, below.

accurate history, was not viewed primarily as the witness to God's acts in history or as the religious experience of the people of God, but, rather, as a compendium of divine doctrine. Every part of Scripture from Genesis to Revelation was a potential source of doctrinal texts, and texts from all over the Bible could be used to support the statements of the church's creeds. Once detected, the texts were often uprooted from their historical and literary contexts and confirmed as independent, infallible expressions of dogma. With Gabler, however, biblical theology moved in a different direction. To be sure, Gabler had his forerunners.[108] The Pietists had opposed the hermeneutic of orthodoxy, and Carl Haymann's *Biblische The-ologie* (1708) offered a pioneering exemplar of the new discipline. In 1758, A. F. Büsching published *Gedanken von Beschaffenheit und dem Vorzug der biblisch-dogmatischen Theologie vor der scholastischen (Thoughts on the Nature and Advantage of Biblical-Dogmatic Theology over the Old and New Scholasticism)* and, later, G. T. Zachariä produced a four-volume work, *Biblische Theologie oder Untersuchung des biblischen Grundes der vornehmsten theologischen Lehren (Biblical Theology, or the Investigation of the Biblical Ground of the Principal Theological Doctrines* [1771–75]), which distinguished biblical theology from systematic theology, and interpreted the biblical books in their historical setting.

Johann Philipp Gabler (1753–1826)

Johann Philipp Gabler was born in Frankfurt am Main.[109] He studied at the University of Jena where his teachers included Griesbach and Eichhorn (1772–1778). After a short time as an instructor at Göttingen, he was called to the faculty at Altdorf (1785), but moved to Jena in 1804, where he eventually succeeded Griesbach. Gabler published works in the areas of NT criticism, church history, and history of doctrine. Among his more important works was his two-volume edition of Eichhorn's *Urgeschichte*, to which he added a long introduction and extensive notes.[110]

Gabler's Proposal

For the development of NT theology, Gabler's most important work is his inaugural address at Altdorf, "Discourse on the Proper Distinction between

---

108. For the history of biblical theology prior to Gabler, see Otto Merk, *Biblische Theologie des Neuen Testaments in ihrer Anfangszeit: Ihre methodischen Probleme bei Johann Philipp Gabler und Georg Lorenz Bauer und deren Nachwirkungen* (Marburg: N. G. Elwert, 1972), 13–28; John H. Hayes and Frederick C. Prussner, *Old Testament Theology: Its History and Development* (Atlanta: John Knox Press, 1985), 53–62.

109. For a summary of Gabler's life and work, see Magne Saebo, "Johann Philipp Gablers Bedeutung für Biblische Theologie: Zum 200-jährigen Jubiläum seiner Antrittsrede vom 30. März 1787," *Zeitschrift für die alttestamentliche Wissenschaft* 99 (1987): 1–16.

110. See pp. 149–50, above.

Biblical and Dogmatic Theology, and the Right Determination of the Aims of Each" (1787).[111] As the title suggests, Gabler draws a sharp line between biblical and systematic theology:

> There is truly a biblical theology, of historical origin, conveying what the holy writers felt about divine matters; on the other hand there is a dogmatic theology of didactic origin, teaching what each theologian philosophises rationally about divine things, according to the measure of his ability or of the times, age, place, sect, school, and other similar factors. Biblical theology, as is proper to historical argument, is always in accord with itself when considered by itself. . . . But dogmatic theology is subject to a multiplicity of change along with the rest of the humane disciplines.[112]

Biblical theology, then, because it deals with historical expressions of religion, remains the same; systematic theology, because it applies doctrine to various times, is constantly undergoing modification. The task of biblical theology is to discern those unchanging, universal truths revealed in the Bible so that systematic theology can incorporate them into a Christian philosophy that addresses the present. As Hendrikus Boers writes, Gabler's "main objective had been to insure that the Bible was reestablished as the basis of all theology, with a biblically based dogmatic theology as its crown and final achievement."[113]

Gabler begins by assuming the authority of biblical revelation. Theologians agree, he says, that "the sacred books, especially of the New Testament, are the one clear source from which all true knowledge of the Christian religion is drawn."[114] They disagree, however, on the interpretation of the Bible, and much of this disagreement is caused by the confusion of biblical and systematic theology. The remedy is a strong dose of historical exegesis. "Theology (Dogmatik) must depend on exegesis, and not the other way around, exegesis on theology."[115] Dogmatic presuppositions and attempts to read doctrines into the text must be abandoned. Historical exegesis, by way of contrast, requires the skills developed by the

---

111. J. P. Gabler, *Oratio de iusto discrimine theologiae biblicae et dogmaticae regundisque recte utriusque finibus.* A German translation is found in the appendix of Merk, *Biblische Theologie,* 273–84. For an English translation, see John Sandys-Wunsch and Laurence Eldredge, "J. P. Gabler and the Distinction between Biblical and Dogmatic Theology: Translation, Commentary, and Discussion of His Originality," *Scottish Journal of Theology* 33 (1980): 133–58. The original is reprinted in Gabler, *Kleinere theologische Schriften,* ed. T. A. Gabler and J. G. Gabler, 2 vols. (Ulm: Stettin, 1831), 2.179–98.

112. Sandys-Wunsch and Eldredge, "J. P. Gabler and the Distinction between Biblical and Dogmatic Theology," 137.

113. Hendrikus Boers, *What Is New Testament Theology? The Rise of Criticism and the Problem of a Theology of the New Testament* (Philadelphia: Fortress Press, 1979), 24.

114. Sandys-Wunsch and Eldredge, "J. P. Gabler and the Distinction between Biblical and Dogmatic Theology," 134.

115. Cited in Merk, *Biblische Theologie,* 52.

earlier practitioners of the grammatico-historical method: the linguistic and grammatical study of words, the analysis of texts within their literary genre, the study of religious ideas in their historical context. On the basis of this critical research, the biblical theologian must proceed to compare and correlate the ideas of one biblical writer with the others and, finally, to discern the underlying unity of the biblical message.[116]

Recent biblical research offered three legacies that enriched Gabler's program: Heyne's understanding of myth (which Gabler had learned from Eichhorn), whereby a distinction was made between the content and the form of religious expression; Semler's accommodation hermeneutic, whereby doctrinal instruction was adapted to the limitation of the hearers; and the distinction between religion and theology (also from Semler), whereby the line between truth and statements about truth was drawn. These three hermeneutical perspectives are incorporated into Gabler's theological method. Agreeing with Heyne, Gabler believed myth was the way in which primitive people expressed their perception of reality.

> Myths are generally legends of the ancient world expressed in the sensual way of thinking and speaking of that time. In these myths, one should not expect an event to be explained as it actually happened; but only as it had to be presented in that age according to its sensual way of thinking and judging, and in pictorial, visual, and dramatic speech and expression in which an event could be represented in that time.[117]

Thus, the hermeneutic of myth provided Gabler with a methodological device whereby he could distinguish primitive expressions of truth from the universal truths of biblical theology.

Similarly, Semler's accommodation theory provided a tool with which Gabler could detect the difference between the essence of the teaching of Jesus and the time-bound expressions of that teaching according to the limited capacity of the original auditors. In the same way, the distinction between theology and religion made possible a separation of the mythical expressions of truth from the truth itself: "The truth itself is eternal and unchangeable: but the form of the truth, like fashion, is subject to continual change and variation."[118] Appropriating all three of these approaches, Gabler concludes that the biblical exegete discerns two types of biblical theology: true biblical theology, that is, a historically accurate representation of what the biblical authors said; and pure biblical theology, that is, a presentation of universal truths expressed by the biblical authors and valid for all times.

---

116. See Robert Morgan, "Gabler's Bicentenary," *Expository Times* 98 (1987): 164–68.

117. Johann Philipp Gabler, "Introduction," in *Johann Gottfried Eichhorns Urgeschichte*, ed. Johann Philipp Gabler, 2 vols. (Altdorf and Nürnberg: Monath & Kussler, 1792), 1.2:482.

118. Ibid. 2.2:63 n.26.

In the course of developing this procedure, Gabler also distinguishes between exegesis (*Auslegung*) and exposition (*Erklärung*). Exegesis is the accurate, literal, historical interpretation of what the biblical writers said; exposition is the explication of what those expressions mean for pure biblical theology. "The true exegete combines both: exegesis is his point of departure; exposition is his goal."[119] This methodological distinction can be seen in Gabler's interpretation of the temptation of Jesus.[120] In actuality, the temptation was an inner experience of Jesus—perhaps induced by a vision—in which he struggles with human temptation and overcomes it by reason. The evangelists, heirs of a Judaism influenced by Persian religion, clothe the event in a mythological garment and personify temptation in the form of Satan. Jesus' triumph over temptation by rational religion represents a universal truth, a truth of pure biblical theology.

In sum, the exegetes play the leading role in the theological drama. For one thing, their script, the NT, is the primary authority in revelation. Moreover, the biblical theology which they discern—both true biblical theology and pure biblical theology—is unchanging. The systematic theologians, then, are dependent on the prior work of the biblical theologians who manage the source of truth and verify its universal validity. The work of the systematic theologians is never done, for their duty is to take what the biblical theologians hand them and reshape it in each new situation. Gabler, to be sure, has not explained how time-conditioned biblical theologians are able to articulate universal truths which (by his own theory) transcend time limitations. His assumption seems to be that the basic idea of salvation—the unifying theme of Scripture—is the heart of pure biblical theology, valid for all people in all times. In any event, the implication is clear: the biblical theologian is superior to the systematic theologian. In the old orthodoxy, dogmatics dominates biblical interpretation; in the new biblical theology, historical interpretation takes precedence over systematic theology.

Georg Lorenz Bauer (1755–1806)

Gabler's program for biblical theology was appropriated by Georg Lorenz Bauer. Born at Hiltpolstein near Nürnberg, Bauer studied at Altdorf (1772–75) and served for a time as a pastor. In 1788, he was appointed a professor at Altdorf, where he met Gabler. In 1805, just a year before his

---

119. J. P. Gabler, "Ueber den Unterschied zwischen Auslegung und Erklärung erläutert durch die verschiedene Behandlungsart der Versuchungsgeschichte Jesu," in idem, *Theologische Schriften* 1.214.
120. Ibid. 1.201–14.

death, Bauer was called to the faculty at Heidelberg. At the time of this appointment, the ruler of the region, Prince Karl Friedrich von Baden, asked Bauer if he was a rationalist. Alhough Bauer denied the charge, his work was more rationalistic than Gabler's. On other matters, Bauer largely agreed with Gabler. He accepted the distinction between biblical and systematic theology, and he interpreted biblical texts according to Heyne's understanding of myth. However, in contrast to Gabler's idea of two kinds of biblical theology, Bauer insisted that there was only one: the pure biblical theology that was discovered by rigorous historical research, a theology that presented universal truths. As well as his work on the NT, Bauer published an introduction to the OT (1794) and a theology of the OT (1796).

Bauer's Theology of the New Testament

Bauer's early NT research attended to exegetical problems. In 1782, he published *Collection and Interpretation of the Parabolic Stories of our Lord*.[121] In the introduction, Bauer defines the parable as essentially a comparison: a story about an earthly event by which an important truth is taught. Anticipating later research on the parables, he insisted that the parables should be interpreted not as allegories but as simple stories with one main point of application. "Every parable," he said, "should designate one certain truth. This is the purpose of the parable."[122] In a book on the hermeneutics of the OT and NT (1799), Bauer insisted on a rationalistic application of the historical-critical method.[123] The goal of exegesis is to reconstruct exactly what the author intended to communicate to the original reader. By use of the principle of accommodation, it is possible to identify what in this historical reconstruction is merely local and temporal in significance.

Like Gabler, Bauer employs the hermeneutic of myth. As to criteria for identifying myth, Bauer names such things as stories explaining the origin of the world and events that are attributed to divine intervention. The basic criterion is nonverifiability, so that all supernatural events are relegated to the category of myth. In 1802, Bauer published a two-volume work, *Hebrew Mythology of the Old and New Testaments, with Parallels from the Mythology of Other Peoples, Principally the Greeks and Romans*.[124] Here Bauer, starting with Genesis and moving through the historical books of the OT,

---

121. Georg Lorenz Bauer, *Sammlung und Erklärung der parabolischen Erzählungen unsers Herrn* (Leipzig: C. G. Hilscher, 1782).

122. Ibid., 30.

123. Georg Lorenz Bauer, *Entwurf einer Hermeneutik des Alten und Neuen Testaments* (Leipzig: Weygand, 1799).

124. Georg Lorenz Bauer, *Hebraische Mythologie des alten und neuen Testaments, mit Parallelen aus der Mythologie anderer Völker, vornemlich der Griechen und Römer*, 2 vols. (Leipzig: Weygand, 1802).

interprets the biblical myths in relation to parallel myths in other cultures. Most significant, Bauer raises the question as to the presence of myths in the NT, a critical question because Heyne's original theory applied only to people of a preliterary culture. Bauer's affirmative response is based on his observation that the earliest Christian expressions were formulated during a period of oral communication. Consequently, Bauer finds a number of myths in the NT: the supernatural conception of Jesus, angel appearances, the descent of the Spirit in the form of a dove, the story of the transfiguration.[125] Indeed, the very concept of the inspiration of Scripture, because it involves divine intervention, is itself a myth.

Bauer's major work for the beginning of NT theology is his four-volume *Biblical Theology of the New Testament*.[126] In the preface, Bauer observes that his work addresses a pressing need: the Christian religion, threatened by supernaturalism, on the one hand, and rationalism, on the other, is facing a crisis. The question is "whether Christianity is a reasonable and divine religion."[127] The answer can be found, claims Bauer, by searching the Scriptures. The search must be conducted without prejudice, and its aim should be to identify what is crucial, separating the kernel from the shell. In Bauer's opinion, the energetic efforts of biblical research in the preceding thirty years had failed to produce a pure biblical theology that answered the decisive question, "What have Jesus and the apostles taught as essential truths of religion valid for all people and times?"[128] According to Bauer, the essential is the highest good of humanity, the establishment of the kingdom of Christ on earth.

Since the essential truths are taught by Jesus and the apostles, Bauer intentionally writes a biblical theology *of the NT*, a theology that supersedes that of the OT. The way in which Bauer structures the material betrays his presuppositions and priorities. He gives major attention to Jesus and the Gospels. The first volume, over 380 pages in length, deals with the Christology of the first three evangelists. The second (390 pages) discusses the theology and anthropology of the Synoptic Gospels and the Christian idea of religion in the Johannine literature. The third volume (310 pages) is devoted to the Christian idea of religion according to the Apocalypse and the Petrine literature. The fourth presents the doctrine of Paul. In each section, Bauer arranges the material under the categories of Christology, theology, and anthropology. Thus, rather than discerning an intrinsic principle of analysis which belongs to the historical expression itself, Bauer, in

---

125. Ibid. 2.216–77.
126. Georg Lorenz Bauer, *Biblische Theologie des Neuen Testaments*, 4 vols. (Leipzig: Weygand, 1800–1802).
127. Ibid. 1.iv.
128. Ibid. 1.vi.

spite of his passion for historical reconstruction, imposes a structure on the NT that results in a systematic theology of the Bible.

In discussing the Christology of the first three evangelists, Bauer first gives attention to the purpose (*Zweck*) of Jesus. Jesus, in Bauer's opinion, thought himself to be the Messiah. This can be seen in his use of the title son of man, a messianic term taken from Daniel 7. As Messiah, Jesus proclaimed the kingdom of God—a moral order already present in the time of Jesus. The account of the triumphal entry to Jerusalem, however, has been distorted by some interpreters (notably the author of the Wolfen-büttel *Fragments*) to imply an earthly kingdom. According to Bauer, Jesus was not a political revolutionary but a "reformer of ethics."[129] "His kingdom should not be of this world, but of the future, for which a person must be made worthy by true virtue and piety."[130] In interpreting the prophecies, the exegete must distinguish between texts which Jesus applied to himself and those which were used by others. Some of the latter were not messianic at all, and even Jesus, following contemporary Jewish hermeneutic, gives texts a meaning different from their original intent. In discussing the miracles, Bauer's work is marked by rationalism. Thus he argues that some of the Gospel accounts do not actually describe miraculous events. When the interpreters of Matt. 14:26 properly understand the use of the preposition ἐπί, they will discover that Jesus was not really walking *on*, but only *by*, the sea. Events which result simply from natural causes are ascribed to supernatural intervention because of the mythological mindset of the Palestinians. In attributing illness to evil spirits, Jesus is accommodating his teaching to the primitive views of his contemporaries, while his cures are performed by psychological power or a superior knowledge of medicine.

Next Bauer turns to the person of Jesus as presented in the first three Gospels. He insists that Jesus is a fully human being who was a descendant of David, and the son of Mary and Joseph. The notion of the supernatural birth is a mythological legend with many pagan parallels, a legend supported by a misreading of Isa. 7:14. When he referred to God as his father, Jesus did not intend to present himself as the preexistent bearer of the divine essence, but as a person with special moral affinity to the divine. Jesus' unswerving obedience to his teaching of the higher moral order eventuated in his execution. The account of the crucifixion is embellished with mythological legends that challenge the imagination of the rationalist. The darkening of the sun cannot be explained by an eclipse (it is the wrong time of the month), but the earthquake (a common occurrence in

129. Ibid. 1.71.
130. Ibid. 1.47–48.

the region) would have stirred up the dust which shut out the light. Bauer is content to leave the resurrection as a mystery, and although the accounts are colored by myth, the divine event is confirmed by reliable witnesses.

In discussing the theology and anthropology of the Synoptic Gospels, Bauer begins with a discussion of Jesus' use of the OT. This discussion illustrates Bauer's application of the idea of progressive stages of revelation. From this perspective, the religion of the OT is incomplete. Jesus, as a reformer of Judaism, took the best of the OT ethic and refined it into a higher religion—a new covenant. Jesus' understanding of God as father is an expression of an intimacy between God and people that is not found in Judaism. In regard to anthropology, Jesus recognizes the moral corruption of humanity but does not formulate a doctrine of original sin. Sin comes from the human heart and is a condition for which humans are responsible. Sin is not only in the deed but, according to Jesus, in the intention. Although Jesus accommodates his description of life after death to the notions of his hearers, using terms like Hades and paradise, he advocates a doctrine of immortality, which is more in harmony with Paul's idea of the spiritual resurrection than with the Pharisaic concept of the resurrection of the body.

Bauer's treatment of the theology of the first three evangelists as separate from the theology of John is significant but undeveloped. As the previous discussion indicates, Bauer does not deal primarily with the theology of the evangelists, but, rather, with the theology of Jesus. This failure to distinguish between the teachings of Jesus and the theology of the evangelists is even more problematic in Bauer's discussion of the Gospel of John. In this discussion, texts from John are used to show that Jesus thought of himself as Messiah and that he viewed the kingdom as otherworldly. To be sure, Bauer's interpretation of the λόγος deals with the theology of the writer, but even here the Fourth Gospel is used to confirm Bauer's understanding of the uniqueness of Jesus: "The power and activity, wisdom and holiness of God worked in a special way in the soul of Jesus, as it had worked on no other human being, thus God or his Logos was in Christ."[131] Bauer does acknowledge that Jesus' method of teaching in the Synoptics is dramatically different from that presented in John, but believes the difference results from different perspectives and intentions of the authors. Although he recognizes the differences in form, Bauer tends to harmonize the theology of all four Gospels.

Bauer has considerable interest in the Apocalypse because of his concern with myth. In essence, he understands the book to be a composition

---

131. Ibid. 2.260–61.

of prophetic rhetoric that uses symbol and allegory to describe the future triumph of Christianity—an expression in the form of poetic myth. In an appendix,[132] Bauer argues that the writer of Revelation cannot possibly be the author of the Gospel of John. Some of the doctrine of the Apocalypse is not in harmony with the teaching of Jesus and is, in fact, immoral. The author, according to Bauer, is an unknown Christian who is acquainted with cabbala and steeped in the symbols of the Apocrypha, not an untutored fisherman from Galilee.

Bauer's final volume deals with the theology of Paul. Again, Bauer follows the threefold pattern of Christology, theology, and anthropology. He fills in this outline with texts from the Pauline letters (including Ephesians and the Pastoral Epistles) and even with the speeches recorded in Acts. In regard to the person of Jesus, Bauer argues that Paul stressed his true humanity. Jesus, a sort of superperson, was endowed with higher gifts and wisdom but was subordinate to God. Bauer gives careful attention to the meaning of the crucifixion of Jesus. He acknowledges that Paul taught the doctrine of the sacrificial death of Jesus, but he asks what this can mean. Resorting to the accommodation hermeneutic, Bauer concludes that the apostle adapted his teaching to the primitive notion of redemption by blood sacrifice, a condescension to meet the spiritual needs of people in that time. Beneath this accommodated doctrine is a universal truth: the death of Christ as a symbol of God's judgment on evil and a sign of God's righteousness and love. In regard to anthropology, Bauer is convinced that Paul did not teach the doctrine of original sin. Although the fall introduced sin, people did not inherit sin and guilt from Adam but sinned by following his example. Paul's expectation of the parousia is a symbolic expression of the ultimate triumph of Christ.

In 1804 and 1805, Bauer's work in NT theology took a decisive new step: he published a two-volume work on NT ethics, probably the first of its kind.[133] Here Bauer shows how morality is at the heart of his understanding of Christianity and how seriously he takes the task of applying biblical teaching to practical living. Again, Bauer's penchant for order leads him to force the NT material into a predetermined mold. The first volume, for example, discusses the ethical teaching of Jesus according to the Gospels. This volume begins with a survey of Hebrew morality prior to Jesus, turns next to the ethic of Jesus as recorded in the Synoptics, and then to the ethics of Jesus according to the Gospel of John. Each section, with minor variations, presents a discussion of moral corruption (sins

132. Ibid. 3.174–81.
133. Georg Lorenz Bauer, *Biblische Moral des Neuen Testaments*, 2 vols. (Leipzig: Weygand, 1804–5).

against God, self, and others), moral laws (duties to God, self, and others), and finally (with some deviation) various issues concerning the ground and motivation of ethics.

In content, Bauer's work on biblical morality expands the ethical teaching he presented in his NT theology. According to Bauer, the ethic of the OT is inadequate and sometimes downright mistaken, as illustrated by its support of religious wars and its tolerance of rape and assassination. To be sure, the Hebrews have progressed from a fragmentary morality to fuller morality in Moses and a higher ethic in the prophets. A still loftier ethic is found in the teaching of Jesus, who stresses tolerance and humility. The parable of the Prodigal Son reveals the necessity of repentance and the importance of receiving God's forgiving grace. Jesus' word about the sick in need of a physician shows that he was concerned with the moral betterment of humanity.

In regard to ethical requirements—he actually calls them moral laws (*Moralgesetze*)—Bauer argues that Jesus stresses the moral law rather than the ceremonial. Thus, there are two main duties toward others: the love of people (expressed in alms giving and helping persons in need), and righteousness or justice (respecting the rights and property of others and following the golden rule). Bauer has difficulty recognizing the radical character of Jesus' ethic and tends to rationalize: the command to love one's enemy, for example, does not mean that we must have affection for our foes, but merely that we should not fail to treat them as persons. The admonition to sell everything and give the proceeds to the poor was addressed to a particular rich young man and should not be generalized. In effect, Bauer has accommodated the ethic of Jesus to the cultural morality of the Enlightenment.

At the end of his discussion of the moral teaching of Jesus in the first three Gospels, Bauer raises a crucial question: What is the highest ethical principle of the teachings of Jesus? In the process of answering, Bauer evaluates the current attempt to find Immanuel Kant's categorical imperative in the teaching of Jesus. Bauer argues that Kant, and those biblical exegetes who follow him, read modern philosophical ideas into the text instead of following the "grammatisch-historische Interpretation."[134] According to Bauer, the highest expression of the moral law is Jesus' call to obey the law of God unconditionally. Jesus' reference to future reward indicates that morality is a life of aspiration toward an ethical ideal that can never be fully realized.

On the whole, Bauer's work on NT theology and ethics represents a groundbreaking achievement. He presents an NT theology separate and

134. Ibid. 1.223.

supposedly superior to the theology of the OT and based on nondogmatic historical reconstruction—a theology which Bauer believes to be authoritative. To be sure, Bauer's imposition of an external order upon the biblical material compromises his historical approach and shows that systematic theology continued to cast its shadow over NT research. Nevertheless, the details of the outline prove Bauer to be a skilled practitioner of the grammatico-historical method, although his analysis of the Gospels betrays a neglect of source criticism. Bauer's use of the accommodation principle and the hermeneutic of myth, together with his emphasis on progressive revelation, rationalism, and universal ethical truths, show him to be a child of the Enlightenment. Like a skilled weaver, Bauer has taken up the threads of the previous historical-critical research and woven them into a pattern that attempts to express the meaning of biblical revelation.

SUMMARY

The scholars surveyed in this chapter represent the variety that will continue to characterize the history of NT research. The conservatives, Calmet and Lardner, demonstrate that a scholar can be a historical critic without abandoning belief in traditional doctrines like the authority of the Bible and the reality of miracles. Indeed, the method of historical criticism can be used in support of the authenticity and reliability of the biblical record. Along with the historical critics, these conservative scholars agree that the Bible is essentially a book of history. However, in adopting the Enlightenment method of historical research, the conservatives appear to assume a secular, rationalistic, natural worldview which is in conflict with the sacred history—fraught with the supernatural—they intend to affirm.

The aesthetic critics, Herder and Lessing, acknowledge the importance of history but look upon history as a lens which brings deeper meaning into focus. This meaning has unfolded in history as humanity has evolved from childlike to mature concepts, and this history is at the same time the story of revelation—the progressive disclosure of divine truth. The truths that are disclosed are not historical facts or arid doctrines that can be proved; they are matters of religious experience, of ethics and the spirit. The Bible which records this revelation is a poetic expression that can be understood only by imagination and sensitivity. Between history and meaning there is a chasm that cannot be bridged by the prosaic application of historical-critical method.

The biblical theologians, Gabler and Bauer, are also concerned with the meaning of biblical history, that is, with the theology of the NT. In their view, the meaning has been obscured by the dogmatic captivity of the Bible, an approach whereby doctrinal considerations have been imposed on Scripture. The new biblical theologians are also interested in biblical doctrines, but they purport to be concerned with the doctrines of the biblical writers themselves. Thus, in tune with the modern outlook, the biblical theologians employ the critical method in reconstruction of the historical doctrines of the Bible. By means of the hermeneutic of myth and the method of accommodation, they are able to show that the literal meaning of the biblical texts does not represent pure biblical theology, that is, the theology which is of universal meaning and application. In the process, traditional doctrines once supported by biblical texts are now shown not to be biblical—doctrines like original sin, predestination, substitutionary atonement, and the deity of Christ. Yet, how the biblical theologians can move from the time-bound teachings of the Bible to the universal truths of Christianity is not clearly explained.

For all these scholars the revelation of God in history comes to focus in the life, teachings, and significance of Jesus. The conservatives view Jesus as the unique son of God and are perfectly content to be concerned with the religion *about* Jesus. The aesthetic critics and the biblical theologians, however, are concerned instead with the religion *of* Jesus. Indeed, with Reimarus, the religion about Jesus is positively false, a fraudulent fabrication of the disciples. While Lessing, Herder, and Bauer are less critical of the development of early Christianity, they nevertheless share the view that Jesus embodies a high manifestation of divine truth which has somehow been distorted in the history of Christian doctrine. Just how they arrive at this conviction is not entirely clear, since the primary sources they use to understand Jesus are those guilty of the alleged distortion. In any event, these considerations give impetus to issues which will occupy NT research in the future: the historical investigation of the sources of the gospel tradition, the use of the Gospel of John in the understanding of Jesus, the development of the life and faith of the early church.

Part II

NEW TESTAMENT RESEARCH IN AN ERA OF PHILOSOPHICAL FERMENT

7

The Rise
of Liberalism

Europe at the beginning of the nineteenth century was like a ship seeking safe haven in a storm. Driven by the strong winds of the French Revolution and the rising tide of the Napoleonic empire, the countries of Europe sought stability and security. The optimism of the Enlightenment, with its bold confidence in the order of the world and the progress of humanity, had been shaken by the Reign of Terror and the threat of tyranny. In the face of these dangers, the Congress of Vienna (1815) attempted to restore the old order. The pre-revolutionary boundaries were retraced, and the ancient monarchies were reestablished. Nations that had suffered during the Napoleonic Wars affirmed their autonomy and encouraged their citizens with a sense of national identity. At the same time, the philosophical forces that had inspired the eighteenth century's self-confidence were weakening. Rationalism, which had ruled the intellectual realm alone, was forced to share dominion with romanticism. Nature, once viewed as the stable ground of universal order, was now seen as a realm comprising mysterious forces. As well as peaceful landscapes, the world displayed cataracts and storms. In place of the arrogant skepticism of the early Enlightenment, anxious people were seeking faith. As Madame de Staël wrote:

> I do not know *what* we must believe, but I believe *that* we must believe! The eighteenth century did nothing but deny. The human spirit lives by its beliefs. Acquire faith through Christianity, or through German philosophy, or merely through enthusiasm, but believe in something![1]

The European ship of state, however, did not dock long in the quiet

1. Cited in Joseph R. Strayer and Hans Gatzke, *The Mainstream of Civilization: Since 1500*, 3d ed. (New York: Harcourt Brace Jovanovich, 1979), 550.

harbor, but soon sailed into the open seas to dominate the world. This domination was encouraged by the Industrial Revolution, a radical change in the manufacture of goods which sought materials and markets around the globe. Supported by new scientific and technological discoveries, this new social and economic movement was accompanied by growth in the population and the creation of a large urban working class. The middle-class merchants who profited from industrialization and the laborers who operated their factories became increasingly disillusioned with the restoration of the old order. Seeking a share of the power that rested in the hands of the nobility, the common people encouraged the revolutions that occurred in the 1820s, 1830s, and, notably, in 1848. The unsuccessful Frankfurt Constitution (1849), which called for a unified Germany and universal male suffrage, was enthusiastically supported by university students, professors, and other intellectuals.

In the midst of this turmoil, theologians were still pursued by the question that had hounded them since the beginning of the Enlightenment: How could the Christian faith survive and address the demands of modern culture? For some, considerable help was supplied by Immanuel Kant (1724–1804). Kant provided a means whereby the vast problems of theology could be managed: he made possible the reduction of theology's concern with metaphysics to a focus on practical morality. According to Kant, human knowledge is restricted to what humans can know from experience. One can not know the essence of a thing in itself, let alone the truth about the transcendent God. Knowledge, however, he argued, is not simply the passive collection of sense experiences; the mind is active, shaping experience according to a priori principles of thinking. Basic to these universal "givens" is an ethical order—a universal moral law that is perceived by faith, a sense of duty that is basic to humanity. This universal law, in turn, points to the *summum bonum* that is grounded in the Supreme Being. Thus, Kant abandoned metaphysical proofs for God's existence but argued from universal morality to the necessity of God.

These cultural and intellectual movements made their mark on NT research. With H.E.G. Paulus, the rationalism of the earlier era reached its final and fatal limits. With Schleiermacher and his school, theology turned inward. Influenced by romanticism, a pietist heritage, and Kant's concern with the self, Schleiermacher made religious consciousness the center of theological concern. This theological perspective was reflected in the work of the two major biblical scholars among Schleiermacher's associates: W.M.L. de Wette and Friedrich Lücke. As an alternative to Schleiermacher's Protestant liberalism, mediating and conservative theologians emerged. Neander, a deeply religious colleague of Schleiermacher, interpreted the history of the church as the manifestation of the divine life of Christ.

EXTREME RATIONALISM:
HEINRICH EBERHARD GOTTLOB PAULUS (1761–1851)

One of the greatest ironies in the history of NT research is seen in Paulus's assertion, "My primary desire is that my views concerning the miracle stories may not be taken as the main point."[2] Yet, from D. F. Strauss until today, Heinrich Eberhard Gottlob Paulus's work is assailed as the extreme attempt to rationalize the miracles. Paulus was born in Leonberg near Stuttgart. His father, a Protestant pastor, tried to mix rationalism and mysticism, but when he claimed the ability to communicate with the dead, he was deposed from his ministerial office. The younger Paulus was educated at the famous theological institute (*Stift*) at Tübingen (1779–84). He began his teaching career at Jena in 1789, and in 1811 he was called to Heidelberg, where he remained until his death in 1851 at the age of ninety. His last words were reported to be: "There is another world."[3] An advocate of academic freedom, Paulus defended his colleague Fichte, who had been charged with atheism. When his own views were attacked, Paulus was supported by Herder; also among his friends were Goethe and Schiller. Paulus edited a journal, *Neues Repertorium für biblische und morgenländishe Litteratur*, and published books on Psalms and Isaiah. In a commentary on the Johannine Epistles, Paulus expressed the opinion that these letters had been written in opposition to a heretical Gnosticism.[4] He also employed his distinctive "philologisch-notiologische Methode," a method which went beyond the details of criticism to find the religious meaning of the text within the context of the author's theology.

Most important for the history of NT research is Paulus's work on the Gospels, which eventuated in his rationalistic *Life of Jesus*. Early in his career, Paulus published a three-volume *Philological-Critical and Historical Commentary on the New Testament*.[5] The title is misleading, because attention is focused exclusively on the Synoptic Gospels. Paulus's purpose—basic for all his work—is an investigation of the sources to establish the historical ground of the Christian faith. After an introduction in which he deals with the origin, purpose, authenticity, and chronology of the Gospels, Paulus presents the Greek text in parallel columns. The material is divided into sections, each with an introduction. Scholia or notes are directed toward a

---

2. Heinrich Ebehr. Gottlob Paulus, *Das Leben Jesu, als Grundlage einer reinen Geschichte des Urchristentums*, 4 vols. (Heidelberg, C. F. Winter, 1828), viii.

3. Cited in Albert Schweitzer, *The Quest of the Historical Jesus: A Critical Study of Its Progress from Reimarus to Wrede*, trans. W. Montgomery (New York: Macmillan, 1957), 49.

4. Heinrich Eberhard Gottlob Paulus, *Die drey Lehrbriefe von Johannes: Wortgetreu mit erläuternden Zwischensätzen übersetzt, und nach philogisch-notiologischer Methode erklärt* (Heidelberg: C. F. Winter, 1829).

5. Heinrich Eberhard Gottlob Paulus, *Philologisch-kritischer und historischer Commentar über das neue Testament*, 2d rev. ed., 3 vols. (Lübeck: J. F. Bohn, 1804–5).

historical understanding of the text. Fundamental to Paulus's research is his assumption that the Gospel accounts do not consistently represent accurate history. "Who can fail to recognize," he says, "that between the narratives and the events a great distinction is made."[6] This presupposition provides Paulus with a license to criticize the biblical accounts and to offer a historical reconstruction of his own. In the process of reconstruction, Paulus evaluates sources according to the Griesbach hypothesis; that is, he accepts Matthew as the earliest and most reliable of the Synoptics and considers Mark to be an abbreviated Gospel, based on Matthew and Luke. Paulus's concern for historical interpretation can be seen in his comment on Matt. 1:23, where he concludes that the promised child of Isa. 7:14 was a child of Isaiah's own time. Paulus's notorious rationalism also appears in his notes on Luke 24:13-43. There, like Griesbach, he concludes that the Emmaus pilgrims failed to recognize the risen Jesus because he was wearing strange clothing and had been disfigured by the rigors of the crucifixion.

These critical and exegetical seeds eventually came to flower in 1828 in Paulus's *Life of Jesus, as Foundation of a Pure History of Early Christianity*.[7] In the preface, Paulus repeats his conviction that the essence of Christianity is historical: "The foundation of early Christianity is its history."[8] Basic to that history is the life of Jesus, for Christianity is nothing more and nothing less than faith in the Jesus of scientific historical reconstruction. Although the Gospel miracles wither away under the burning light of critical inquiry, one incredible wonder remains—the Jesus of history. "The miraculous thing about Jesus," says Paulus, "is he himself."[9] In presenting his reconstruction, Paulus continues to work exegetically. After an introduction, part 1 (vols. 1 and 2) is dedicated to an analysis of the Gospel material by sections. Part 2 (vols. 3 and 4) presents an overview of the life of Jesus, followed by a German translation of the Gospel pericopes, printed in parallel columns.

The clue to Paulus's interpretation of Jesus is disclosed in the introduction, where Paulus presents a unique understanding of the historical development of the messianic idea. He notes that the royal descendants of David were described as sons of God. In times of trouble, the prophets, inspired by the glories of the past, looked forward to a restoration in the future—the time of a messiah like David. During the Maccabean period, the throne no longer belonged to a Davidic descendant. This encouraged

6. Ibid. 1.xiv.
7. Paulus, *Leben Jesu*. Published in two parts, each with two sections, the 1828 edition appeared in four volumes. See n. 2, above.
8. Ibid. 1.ix.
9. Ibid. 1.xi.

the development of the concept of a heavenly or spiritual Messiah or, in Daniel's terms, a son of man. When the the Maccabean rulers failed to establish the messianic kingdom, the Jews reverted to the expectation of a son of David. Jesus, who by his natural descent fulfilled this hope, increasingly conceived of Messiahship in spiritual terms. According to Paulus, "It is the Spirit which makes him to be the true Messiah."[10] Jesus, consequently, adopted the title "son of man," a title which represented the spiritual and rational aspects of a universal humanity.

Before he begins his historical reconstruction, Paulus swallows a healthy dose of skepticism. "A truly complete and comprehensive life of Jesus is not possible,"[11] he admits. But then, with unwavering confidence, he proceeds to present the life of Jesus from birth to ascension according to a clearly ordered chronology. This chronology is based on the accounts of the Jewish festivals as presented in the Gospel of John, a Gospel whose authenticity and reliability are beyond question. "Its historicity in the presentation of particular circumstances is often so clear in regard to details that one can scarcely doubt that it is the report of the reminiscences of an eyewitness."[12] This historical reliability, however, does not detract from the character of John as the "Gospel of the Spirit"[13] that presents Jesus as the spiritual Messiah. For Paulus, the historical Jesus *is* the spiritual Christ.

In examining the birth stories, Paulus finds a historical core. Mary sensed that her son was to be the promised spiritual Messiah, and the birth of Jesus involved a special manifestation of divine power—all this in contrast with Paulus's typical rationalism. Also, in spite of problems with the census of Luke 2, Paulus accepts the journey from Nazareth and the subsequent birth in Bethlehem as historical. In accord with many conservatives, Paulus concludes that the genealogy of Luke 3 traces the ancestry of Jesus through Mary. Paulus attends to the developing messianic consciousness during Jesus' youth, and he considers the possibility that he may have been influenced by the Essenes, an influence more clearly reflected in John the Baptist.

Following the Fourth Gospel, Paulus believes the ministry of Jesus begins in Judea. He reads the narratives of Jesus' encounters with Nicodemus and the Samaritan woman as literal history. When the dialogue with Nicodemus switches from singular to plural, Paulus provides a rational explanation: the "we" of 3:11 refers to Jesus and John the Baptist, and the "you" (plural) of 3:12 describes Nicodemus and the Pharisees. Concern-

10. Ibid. 1.55.
11. Ibid. 1.65.
12. Ibid. 1.149.
13. Ibid. 1.183.

ing the Samaritan woman, Paulus abandons cold rationalism in favor of flowery eloquence:

> Oh the fortunate woman! She had the truly partisan-free person before her. With what a voice of inspiration, with what a note of all inclusive God-consciousness did Jesus desire to have the following words expressed: "Receive from me the conviction, good woman, that a time is coming in which neither on this mountain nor in Jerusalem will you worship the universal, true Father."[14]

Paulus's discussion of the Galilean ministry provides examples of his rationalistic interpretation of the miracles. In regard to the exorcism in the synagogue of Capernaum (Luke 4:31-37; Mark 1:21-28), Paulus observes that what Jesus' contemporaries considered demon possession was actually a mental disorder (*Nervenkrankheit*). Jesus' rebuke was potent and shattering, resulting in a convulsion and cure. Paulus argues that the question of demon possession—the notion that an evil spirit can enter and dominate a human body—is a matter to be decided by modern science. From that perspective, demon possession is impossible. A lengthy note on the Gerasene demoniac states that the exegete must distinguish between the fact of the healing and the opinion about the nature of the malady and its cure. That the healing took place is certain; the opinion about demon possession and exorcism is mistaken. The stilling of the storm was not a miracle but a coincidence. When the boat, buffeted by strong winds, sailed beneath the protective barrier of a coastal mountain, it drifted into quiet water. Since Jesus had spoken, the disciples (who had apparently forgotten all their nautical knowledge) assumed that his word had caused the calm.

Nor was the raising of the dead really miraculous. As a matter of fact, Jesus, with his typical compassion, saved persons from premature burial. According to Jewish custom, burial was to take place within three hours of death, and, as a consequence, people were frequently buried alive. In the case of Jairus's daughter, she was only asleep, as Jesus himself had said. Moreover, Jesus was acquainted with the family, because the girl's father was the ruler of a synagogue, and he knew that she was a healthy young woman who was suffering a temporary paralysis caused by the trauma of her first menstrual period. Similar explanations are offered for the raising of the widow's son and Lazarus. In regard to the former, "Jesus had learned the circumstance of the illness, and that it was not fatal, but that he [the young man] only reposed in sleep."[15] Jesus also said that Lazarus's illness was not to death and that he was merely sleeping (John 11:4, 11), but

---

14. Ibid. 1.187–88.
15. Ibid. 1.282.

Paulus seems to ignore v. 14, where Jesus says plainly that Lazarus is dead. The proof that Jesus expected no miracle is seen in his weeping, and the fact that Lazarus was able to respond to Jesus' command proves that he was not dead in the first place.

In interpreting the feeding of the five thousand, Paulus is at his imaginative best (or worst!). He says that the lonely place where the multitude had gathered to hear the teaching of Jesus was located near a caravan route. Jewish pilgrims who had journeyed to Jerusalem to celebrate Pentecost were passing by—the rich with well-stocked stores of provisions. When Jesus, acting like an Oriental host, blessed a little lunch and began to share it with others, the wealthy pilgrims were inspired to dole out food from their own abundant supplies. In Paulus's opinion, nothing in the text suggests a miraculous multiplication of food.

Paulus detects two types of miracles in the gospel narratives. First, there are historical miracles, usually healings, in which Jesus is depicted as doing good. Since the people could not explain the means of his cures, they attributed them to supernatural causes. For example, when Jesus anointed a blind man's eyes with a clay made from spittle and dust (John 9:6), some sort of mysterious medication had been applied. "But," comments Paulus, "how strange would be the conclusion: since the means of healing is so inadequately described, that it must have been supernatural!"[16] Second, there are events, like the stilling of the storm, which are taken to be miraculous but are not miracles at all. For example, when Jesus instructs Peter to catch a fish with a coin in its mouth (Matt. 17:24-27), no miracle has actually transpired. Jesus is teaching Peter to rely on nature: start fishing and in a short time you will have earned enough to pay the temple tax.

In spite of his apparent preoccupation with miracles, Paulus is primarily concerned with Jesus' ethical teaching. He gives extensive consideration to the Sermon on the Mount and believes that Matthew, whose version of the sermon is more complete than Luke's, heard the original sermon and wrote it down very early. According to Paulus, the ethic of Jesus is primarily concerned with inner motivation and intention. The command to love one's enemy is grounded in a concept of universal humanity, for "to will the good of the enemy is the duty of those who with Jesus view the whole human race as one family of God."[17] The perfection of the will (*Willensvolkommenheit*) of God is the highest principle of religion, and in Paulus's judgment, this sort of perfection can be attained by humans.

16. Ibid. 1.424.
17. Ibid. 1.264.

In discussing the pericope on the purpose of the parables (Matt. 13:10-15; Mark 4:10-12; Luke 8:9-10), Paulus asserts that Jesus shaped his teachings in pictorial form to make them clear enough so that even the uneducated could understand and remember them. Paulus denies the authenticity of the story of the woman caught in adultery (John 7:53—8:11), but on contextual more than on text-critical grounds. Moreover, he says, the account does not conform to the most important rules of proof: agreement with the character of the participants and conformity to reality. In contrast to the usual character of Jesus, he is here depicted as writing rather than speaking, and the Pharisees are described as more sensitive about their behavior than they actually would have been. The account of the confession at Caesarea Philippi is, according to Paulus, most faithfully presented in Matt. 16:13-28. The text affirms the Messiahship of Jesus, and the revelation from God has disclosed to Peter that Jesus is a spiritual Messiah. Thus, what is to be built on Peter's confession is a spiritual temple, and the text does not confer special authority on an ecclesiastical leader. At this time, Jesus may have anticipated his own suffering, but, in Paulus's opinion, he did not predict his resurrection. Similarly, the idea of the future physical return of the Messiah is contrary to the teachings of Jesus.

Paulus's reconstruction of the passion narrative relies heavily on the Fourth Gospel. "For the transition to the last hours of the life of Jesus, his history must be taken primarily from John . . . for there only can correctly be arranged what the three earlier traditions preserve in a purely fragmentary way."[18] In discussing the Gethsemane events, Paulus presents a lengthy note on Jesus' solitary spiritual struggle (*Einsamer Geisteskampf*).[19] Like Socrates, Jesus is willing to die for a higher cause. He makes his decision in response to his understanding of the will of God, for to have fled would have been to deny his messianic call and message. After an analysis of the accounts of the death of Jesus, Paulus attaches a poem that presents a vivid portrayal of the way of the cross, the details of the crucifixion, and the martyrdom of Jesus. The poem begins:

> We tread the way of the crucified. The depths hold us in terror.
> We view the one devoted to God. Oh, the bleeding martyr!
> Death already on his face; his eyes no longer bright.[20]

18. Ibid. 2.153.
19. Ibid. 2.193–210.
20. Ibid. 2.245.

In the end, Jesus lowers his head and appears to die:

Yet, to the divine Father
He was and remains not dead.[21]

According to Paulus, Jesus did not really die, but only fell into a death-like trance. Indeed, the soldier who pierced his side with a spear was performing not a mortal thrust but merely a superficial prick to see if Jesus would show signs of life. In the cool temperature of the tomb and under the pharmaceutical effect of the burial spices, Jesus was resuscitated. Paulus believes Jesus' survival of death and bodily restoration (*körperliche Wiedererleben*) to be factual. He says that "the fact of the resuscitation (*Wiederbelebung*) is historically certain"[22] and that proof of this fact is provided by the accounts of the appearances where, for example in Luke 24:36-43, Jesus is seen not as a spirit but as a body with flesh and bones and the capacity to eat a piece of fish. All of this indicates that the resuscitated body was identical with the crucified body, and not at all like the spiritual body of 1 Cor. 15:44-50.

The crucial issue about the resurrection, therefore, is not the fact of the resuscitation of the body of Jesus, but the question of how it was accomplished. According to Paulus, the resuscitation was effected by the power of God who works through nature. The meaning of the resurrection is clear: God did not permit Jesus and his cause to be defeated, or, as the Scriptures say, the Lord did not allow the Holy One to see corruption (Acts 2:27). To those who object that Paulus has eroded the resurrection faith, he responds that there are two kinds of faith: a faith that attempts to believe the unbelievable, and a faith in what is intrinsically probable. For Paulus, "the true faith is only that which is most tenable."[23] The bodily ascension of Jesus, of course, cannot be accepted as historical. The story is found exclusively in Acts 1, and the rest of the tradition, by way of contrast, claims that Christ as spiritual Messiah was exalted to the right hand of God. Paulus's explanation of the events is fully rational: After forty days, Jesus, whose physical strength had been seriously impaired by the crucifixion, perceived that the end was near. When he was taking leave of his disciples, he became by chance enveloped in a cloud. The disciples, who were kneeling and looking upward, supposed that Jesus had been carried by the cloud into heaven. They never knew where and when he actually perished.

21. Ibid. 2.252.
22. Ibid. 2.264.
23. Ibid. 2.258.

Paulus's work on the Gospels, begun in his *Commentary* and developed in his *Life of Jesus,* was continued in his three-volume *Exegetical Handbook of the First Three Gospels* (1830–33).[24] Again, Paulus affirms the reliability and facticity of the Gospel accounts and betrays his penchant for rationalistic interpretation. Looking back to the beginning of his work, he writes, "The aim of my life, as I could conceive it then in relation to scientific matters, was, in accord with the preparation and resources which I believed I brought to it, directed toward the presentation of a biblical and rationally grounded and harmonious totality of religious certainties."[25]

Although Paulus is frequently maligned by historians, his influence in the nineteenth century was considerable. Schleiermacher, for example, not only agreed with Paulus's evaluation of the Gospel of John but also even sympathized with his explanation of the resurrection. Moreover, Paulus's reconstruction of the history of the messianic idea in Judaism contributed to the ongoing discussion of the self-consciousness of Jesus. Like most of the Enlightenment interpreters, Paulus tended to reduce the biblical message to historical facticity, and, most important, he believed the critically reconstructed historical Jesus to be the ground of faith. In spite of criticism to the contrary, Paulus's rationalistic exegesis had an apologetic purpose. Recognizing that miracles were a problem to the modern mind, Paulus insisted that one should not seek miracles where none exist. Thus, the reduction of the miraculous was a service to faith and, at the same time, a means to reclaim the credibility of the biblical text. Although the biblical writers may have mistakenly attributed happenings to supernatural causes, they were, contrary to Reimarus's view, fundamentally honest and reliable. As to his own faith, Paulus was primarily concerned with the meaning of the texts, in particular with the universal ethical teachings of Jesus, the spiritual Messiah. At times, Paulus's rhetorical expressions betray him: his hand is moved by reason, but his heart by the spirit. His conviction, of course, is that spiritual truth is manifest in history. What Paulus failed to see was that his attempt to clothe the Gospels in rationalizing and historicizing garments resulted in an NT the original readers would never have recognized.

FRIEDRICH SCHLEIERMACHER (1768–1834) AND RELIGIOUS CONSCIOUSNESS

Schleiermacher is widely recognized as the most important theologian of the nineteenth century, although his contribution to NT research is often

---

24. Heinr. Eb. Gottlob Paulus, *Exegetisches Handbuch über die drei ersten Evangelien,* 3 vols. (Heidelberg: C. F. Winter, 1830–33).
25. Ibid. 1.vi.

overlooked. Born in Breslau, Friedrich Daniel Ernst Schleiermacher was the son of a Prussian army chaplain of Reformed faith and pietist sympathies. He attended the Moravian boarding school at Niesky and their seminary in Barby. About this experience, Schleiermacher was later to write to his sister, "There is not throughout Christendom, in our day, a form of public worship which expresses more worthily, and awakens more thoroughly the spirit of true Christian piety, than does that of the Herrnhut brotherhood!"[26] Nevertheless, the young Schleiermacher eventually became dissatisfied with pietist theology and transferred to the University of Halle (1787), where he came under the influence of Kant's philosophy. In 1790, Schleiermacher took his first theological examination in Berlin and qualified as a Reformed minister. After a second examination in 1794, he served as an assistant pastor in Landsberg in Brandenburg. Schleiermacher returned to Berlin in 1796 as the Reformed preacher at the Hospital of the Charité. In Berlin, he participated in the salons and circles of intellectuals, and among his friends were the poet Friedrich Schlegel and Henriette Herz, the hostess of a prominent Berlin salon, with whom he continued to correspond through much of his life. Schleiermacher believed women had a special sensitivity for religious experience. At the suggestion of Schlegel, Schleiermacher wrote his popular *On Religion: Speeches to Its Cultured Despisers* (1799),[27] in which he argues that modern intellectuals who reject religion do so out of misunderstanding. In actuality, religion is concerned with inner experience and is essential to human existence.

In 1804, Schleiermacher became university preacher and associate professor at Halle. When Napoleon's troops invaded in 1806, Schleiermacher's house was plundered, and the university closed down. In 1807, Schleiermacher returned to Berlin as preacher at the Reformed Trinity Church, and in 1810 he also participated in the founding of the new University of Berlin, where he was appointed professor and head of the theological faculty. About Schleiermacher's teaching, D. F. Strauss wrote:

> Here we find the pure method of reasoning, not as in his writings, where everything is held together in a scientific form, but free, running hither and thither through the material, seizing at one moment on this side, at the next moment on the other side. . . . Thus now his lectures have not only attracted

26. Friedrich Schleiermacher, *The Life of Schleiermacher, as Unfolded in His Autobiography and Letters*, trans. Frederica Rowan, 2 vols. (London: Smith, Elder & Co., 1860), 2.23.

27. Friedrich Schleiermacher, *Über die Religion: Reden an die gebildeten unter ihren Verächtern* (Berlin: J. F. Unger, 1799). The work is available in various English-language editions, e.g., Friedrich Schleiermacher, *On Religion: Addresses in Response to Its Cultured Critics*, trans. Terrence N. Tice (Richmond, Va.: John Knox Press, 1969).

me, but I have also learnt something essential from him about the method of presenting academic lectures.[28]

As to Schleiermacher's preaching, Friedrich Lücke, who attended Trinity Church faithfully for several years, noted that Schleiermacher did not write out his sermons. His method was "to let the words arise, fresh and new, from the energy and fulness of the soul at the very moment."[29] Although intellectually stimulating, the sermons could be understood by the unlettered. Schleiermacher was effective, too, in teaching confirmation classes for the young, among whom was Prussia's future chancellor, Otto von Bismarck. When Schleiermacher died of pneumonia at the age of sixty-five, thousands lined the streets of Berlin to view his funeral procession.

Schleiermacher's Religious Thought

Schleiermacher's scholarly production was immense. His books, lectures, sermons, and letters comprise over thirty volumes. A summary of his theology can be found in his *Brief Outline of the Study of Theology,* originally published in 1810.[30] His major work, *The Christian Faith,* first appeared in 1821 and 1822.[31] Written to articulate the beliefs of the new Union Church, composed of Lutheran and Reformed Christians, this book is probably the most important Protestant systematic theology since Calvin's *Institutes.* For Schleiermacher, theology is primarily concerned with religious consciousness. He draws a distinction between religion and theology: religion is a phenomenon of feeling and experience; theology is intellectual reflection about religion. As Schleiermacher was later to confess, his pietistic origins had continued to shape his thinking. "I may say," he wrote to a friend, "that after all I have passed through, I have become a Herrnhuter again, only of a higher order."[32] The pietist legacy is apparent in Schleiermacher's deep sensitivity to religious feeling; the higher order is visible in his perceptive intellectual power.

In essence, he believed that religion is the sense of absolute depen-

---

28. Cited in Horton Harris, *David Friedrich Strauss and His Theology* (Cambridge: Cambridge University Press, 1973), 31.

29. Friedrich Lücke, "Reminiscences of Schleiermacher," in Friedrich Schleiermacher, *Brief Outline of the Study of Theology, Drawn up to Serve as the Basis of Introductory Lectures,* trans. William Farrer (Edinburgh: T. & T. Clark, 1850), 57.

30. Friedrich Schleiermacher, *Kurze Darstellung des theologischen Studiums;* Eng. trans.: see *Brief Outline of the Study of Theology* (see n. 29, above).

31. Friedrich Schleiermacher, *Der Christliche Glaube nach den Grundsätzen der evangelischen Kirche im Zusammenhang dargestellt* (Berlin: G. Reimer, 1821–22); Eng. trans.: *The Christian Faith,* trans. H. R. Mackintosh and J. S. Stewart (Philadelphia: Fortress Press, 1976).

32. Rowan, *Life of Schleiermacher* 1.284.

dence on God. God cannot be an object of speculation but can be known only in relation to humans—in profound religious experience. Christianity represents the highest form of religious expression: "Christianity is a monotheistic faith, belonging to the teleological type of religion, and is essentially distinguished from other such faiths by the fact that in it everything is related to the redemption accomplished by Jesus of Nazareth."[33] Theological reflection about the Christian religion is arranged in three parts: philosophical theology (which includes apologetics), historical theology (which includes exegesis), and practical theology (which applies Christian teaching to the life of the church). As Schleiermacher's definition indicates, Christian theology is always historically conditioned and christocentric.

According to Schleiermacher, sin is the lack of God-consciousness and awareness of the need of redemption. Redemption is accomplished through Christ, the founder of Christianity and the archetype of God-consciousness. Christ is the perfect expression of absolute dependence on God and is, therefore, sinless, although totally human. Faith is dependent on the historical event of Christ, and Scripture derives its authority from its witness to him. Since the Bible is supported by no external doctrine of inspiration, it is fully open to historical investigation. As Lücke was to say about Schleiermacher, "He had but two foes against which, as such, he continually renewed the conflict, even to the last man; the servitude of the letter, which denies the liberty of the Gospel, and the frivolous superficiality which denies its everlasting truth."[34]

Influenced by Spinoza, Schleiermacher believed that God is at work in the world. God works through nature, and the notion of an absolute miracle—an event contrary to nature—is inconceivable.

> Now some have represented miracle in this sense as essential to the perfect manifestation of the divine omnipotence. But it is difficult to conceive, on the one side, how omnipotence is shown to be greater in the suspension of the interdependence of nature than in its original immutable course which was no less divinely ordered. For, indeed, the capacity to make a change in what has been ordained is only a merit in the ordainer, if a change is necessary, which again can only be the result of some imperfection in him or in his work.[35]

Moreover, faith does not rest on miracles: "Scripture itself bears witness that faith has been produced without miracles, and also that miracles have failed to produce it."[36]

33. Schleiermacher, *Christian Faith*, 52.
34. Schleiermacher, *Brief Outline of the Study of Theology*, 19.
35. Schleiermacher, *Christian Faith*, 179.
36. Ibid., 71.

Schleiermacher's Hermeneutical and
Critical Research

Nowhere is Schleiermacher's rare combination of critical skill and theological sensitivity more apparent than in his work on the NT. His publications in this area can be classified into three types: hermeneutical theory, critical research, and exegetical and theological synthesis. To the first group belongs Schleiermacher's remarkable *Hermeneutics*.[37] Readers of earlier works on biblical interpretation (e.g., Turretin, Ernesti, Semler, and Griesbach),[38] will find themselves in a strange new world. To be sure, Schleiermacher, too, is concerned with historical interpretation and the importance of linguistic details. Schleiermacher, however, reflects on the fundamental question of the meaning of understanding. For him, hermeneutics is an art more than a science. It has to do with communication between persons and is, therefore, analogous to conversation. Like his predecessors, Schleiermacher believes the NT should be interpreted like any other book. The NT, however, requires a special hermeneutic, one in harmony with the general principles of interpretation but sensitive to the particularity of the biblical message. The interpretation of Scripture must be historical, for "only historical interpretation can do justice to the rootedness of the New Testament authors in their time and place."[39] History, however, has to do with persons, and thus interpretation must be concerned with psychological and subjective meaning. Schleiermacher rejects the Enlightenment canon that Scripture can have only one sense, the grammatical, since allusions can communicate another meaning. However, the interpreter must not seek allusions where none exists or turn literal expressions into allegory.

According to Schleiermacher there are two kinds of interpretation: the grammatical and the technical-psychological. In regard to the grammatical, Schleiermacher supports the methods of the earlier hermeneuts: attention to language and style, comparison with the Septuagint, recognition of the importance of the context. Concerning the technical-psychological, Schleiermacher intends to show that interpretation involves a technique or art, and that it requires the understanding of the author as person. Thus, interpretation must deal with the life of the author and the forces which moved the author to communicate.

> Both technical and grammatical interpretation begin with a general overview of a text designed to grasp its unity and the major features of its

---

37. Friedrich Schleiermacher, *Hermeneutics: The Handwritten Manuscripts*, ed. H. Kimmerle, trans. J. Duke and J. Forstman (Missoula, Mont.: Scholars Press, 1977).
38. See pp. 96–101, 109–12, 124–25, 139–41, above.
39. Schleiermacher, *Hermeneutics*, 104.

composition. But in technical interpretation the unity of the work, its theme, is viewed as the dynamic principle impelling the author, and the basic features of the composition are viewed as his distinctive nature, revealing itself in that movement.[40]

In the area of critical research on the NT, Schleiermacher had in 1807 already displayed his incisive skill in an essay "Concerning the So-Called First Letter of Paul to Timothy,"[41] in which he disputed the authenticity of this epistle. A summary of Schleiermacher's critical positions can be seen in his *Introduction to the New Testament*, an extensive work based on notes taken from his lectures of 1829–32.[42] Compared to earlier introductions, like those of Michaelis and Eichhorn,[43] Schleiermacher's work is marked by theological reflection about the critical issues. For instance, he observes that the problem of canonicity is not simply a question of authorship.

> The question, whether individual books belong to the authors to whom they were attached, must be distinguished from the other, whether they belong in the canon on the same or dissimilar terms. The canonical nature of the writing remains the same regardless of whether it is proved that it is not from the author to whom it has been ascribed.[44]

The purpose of critical introduction is historical—to put the interpreter in the place of the original reader.

In the first part of his *Introduction*, Schleiermacher presents a general introduction to the books of the NT. Here he reviews the history of the development of the canon and considers issues of lower criticism. In these areas, Schleiermacher displays his command of patristic sources and his competence in text-critical research. He also notes that the presence of textual variants confounds the dogma of verbal inspiration. The second part of the *Introduction* treats the individual sections of the NT. Following chronological order, he begins with the Pauline letters. He surveys the chronology of Paul and notes problems that arise when information from Acts is compared with data from the epistles. For instance, Gal. 2:1 reports an interval of fourteen years for what Acts takes to be a relatively short time. Schleiermacher considers 1 Thessalonians to have been the earliest epistle, and he notes the difficulty of dating Galatians. He defends the integrity of 2 Corinthians (against Semler), and he supports the Pauline

---

40. Ibid., 147.
41. Friedrich Schleiermacher, "Ueber den sogenannten ersten Brief des Paulos an den Timotheos. Ein kritisches Sendschreiben an J. C. Gass," in *Friedrich Schleiermacher's sämmtliche Werke*, pt. 1 (Berlin: G. Reimer, 1836), 2.221–320.
42. Friedrich Schleiermacher, *Einleitung ins neue Testament*, ed. G. Wolde, in *Friedrich Schleiermacher's sämmtliche Werke*, pt. 1, vol. 8 (Berlin: G. Reimer, 1845).
43. See pp. 131–38, 150–53, above.
44. Schleiermacher, *Einleitung*, 30.

authorship of Ephesians while rejecting Ephesus as the place of destination. Typical of Schleiermacher's hermeneutical sensitivity is his observation that "the epistle is a substitute (*Stellvertreter*) for oral speech."[45]

Schleiermacher's work on the Gospels tends to reduce the significance
of the Synoptic Gospels and enhance the authority of John.[46] Schleiermacher believes that the earliest Christians would not have been concerned to record the deeds and words of Jesus in writing. The Gospels, in
his opinion, were not written until after the Jewish war, at the end of the
apostolic age. In regard to the synoptic problem, Schleiermacher rejects
Eichhorn's theory of an *Urgospel*, as well as any hypothesis which affirms
that the Gospels used each other. The first tradition about Jesus was oral,
and then written in small parts—a variety of fragments which were used
independently by the Gospel writers. Although the canonical Matthew was
the earliest of the Synoptics, it was not written by an eyewitness. Schleiermacher is also suspicious of the tradition that Mark recorded the recollections of Peter. He believes John may have been written prior to the
Synoptics and is convinced that it is more reliable. In discussing the failure
of Matthew, Mark, and Luke to report the raising of Lazarus, Schleiermacher says:

> That the three Gospels know nothing about it is so notable that I believe
> there can be no third possibility: either one must take John for a later
> concoction, or one must be convinced that the other three are not of direct
> apostolic origin. I cannot myself waver for a moment to decide for the latter,
> since the Gospel of John bears such undeniable signs of authenticity, and so
> reveals on every page the eyewitness and personal participant, that one must
> be prejudiced and diverted from the natural course so as to doubt its
> authenticity.[47]

In the same vein, Schleiermacher attempts to refute the arguments of
Bretschneider against the authenticity of the Fourth Gospel.[48]

The balance of Schleiermacher's *Introduction* follows the advancing
trends of historical-critical research. In regard to Acts, he believes the
"we-sections" represent sources used by the author, rather than evidence
of the author's own participation in the events. Schleiermacher's judgments about the Catholic Epistles are uninhibited. Although he accepts 1
John and 1 Peter as authentic, he believes all the rest are open to question. Second and 3 John, 2 Peter, and Jude are not apostolic, and James

---

45. Ibid., 133.
46. Schleiermacher's preference for the Gospel of John is already apparent in his *On
Religion*; see Giovanni Moretto, "Angezogen und belehrt von Gott: Der Johannismus in
Schleiermachers 'Reden über die Religion,'" *Theologische Zeitschrift* 37 (1981): 267–91.
47. Schleiermacher, *Einleitung*, 283.
48. See pp. 312–14, below.

was written by a later author who recorded reminiscences of the apostle James. As to the Catholic Epistles generally, Schleiermacher concludes "that it should not be maintained that it would be a great loss if this whole section were lacking from our canon."[49] Hebrews, he argues, was not written by Paul, and Revelation cannot have been composed by John, the author of the Fourth Gospel.

In a final section, Schleiermacher reflects thoughtfully about the historical origin of Christianity. He observes that it arose out of a Jewish background and was transformed by Paul's Jewish speculation and the Hellenistic ideas of John. However, the decisive event in Christian beginnings is the uniqueness of Jesus Christ:

> If Christianity had not had the ground of its unique essence in the person of Christ, and had not emerged from his own presentation of himself, but if it had arisen, as many have wanted to view it, through reflection, study or natural refinement, which other conceptions underwent, when they pass through a purer individual; then it would have been nothing more than a modified Judaism.[50]

Schleiermacher's essay on Luke provides a fuller expression of his critical views on the Gospels.[51] Originally written in 1817, this work is a brilliant display of Schleiermacher's ability to analyze the form and content of a text. Rather than beginning with some hypothesis about the Gospel, Schleiermacher begins with the text itself and, observing details that most readers miss, constructs a theory about its origin and nature. At the outset, he observes that the author of Luke was not an eyewitness but one who collects and reports the witness of others. "And thus the authority of our writer appears to me at least to gain, instead of losing, when his work is referred to earlier works of original and inspired witnesses to the facts."[52] In the introduction, Schleiermacher presents a succinct description of the fragments and collections of material which serve as sources for the Synoptics:

> Many such collections then might have been in existence, greater and smaller, some simple, some composed of several others, not only before any one of them acquired public authority, that is, before it was made even in particular congregations the basis of public discourses as Holy Writ, but even before one of them assumed the character of a regular book with a beginning and conclusion.[53]

49. Schleiermacher, *Einleitung*, 431.
50. Ibid., 481.
51. Friedrich Schleiermacher, "Ueber die Schriften des Lukas, ein kritischer Versuch," in idem, *Sämmtliche Werke* (1836), pt. 1, 2.xi–220; Eng. trans.: *A Critical Essay on the Gospel of St. Luke*, trans. Connop Thrilwall (London: J. Taylor, 1825).
52. Schleiermacher, "Preface by the author," in *Essay on Luke*, vi.
53. Ibid., 15.

Critically, the force of Schleiermacher's essay is to support his fragment theory and refute the two major hypotheses of the day: (1) that the Gospels rest on a lost written gospel; and (2) that Luke used either Matthew or Mark.

In developing these arguments, Schleiermacher arranges the Lucan material into four sections and presents a host of literary and historical observations. The first section includes events which precede the public ministry of Jesus (Luke 1 and 2). Schleiermacher views this material as a mixture of history and tradition. The census, for example, he feels, is historically doubtful, but the account of the shepherds goes back to their own reports. The story of the annunciation is poetry, not history, yet it must be respected because "the traditional foundation of our poetical account of the annunciation repels all the presumptuous interpretations with which vulgar hands would soil the sacred veil which they cannot lift."[54] In the second section, Schleiermacher discusses the actions and discourses of Jesus in Luke 3:1—9:49. Luke's Sermon on the Plain is based on an earlier collection of teaching material, and the account of the raising of the widow's son, found only in Luke, indicates that the Gospels do not rest on a single source.

The third section treats Luke's special presentation of the journey to Jerusalem (9:51—19:49). Here Schleiermacher believes Luke has incorporated into his Gospel an earlier travel narrative whose ultimate source was a companion of Jesus. In regard to the cleansing of the temple, Schleiermacher thinks that Mark's account is preferable to Matthew's, because it is unlikely that the triumphal entry and the attack on the temple would have occurred on the same day. The final section deals with Luke's narrative of the last days of Jesus (20:1—24:53). Schleiermacher believes Luke's account of the last supper is the most original, for only he names Peter and John as the arrangers of the celebration. The tradition about the crucifixion goes back to an eyewitness, but details like the rending of the temple veil are poetic rather than historical. About Luke, Schleiermacher finally concludes:

> He is from beginning to end no more than the compiler and arranger of documents which he found in existence, and which he allows to pass unaltered through his hands. His merit in this capacity is twofold: first, that of the arrangement. . . . But the far greater merit is this, that he has admitted scarcely any pieces but what are peculiarly genuine and good; for this was certainly not the effect of accident, but the fruit of a judiciously instituted investigation, and a well weighed choice.[55]

54. Ibid., 49–50.
55. Ibid., 313–14.

Schleiermacher's *Life of Jesus*

Schleiermacher's NT research culminates in his *Life of Jesus*, a synthesis of exegetical and theological reflection. In all probability, Schleiermacher was the first academician to offer a course of lectures on Jesus' life. He first presented the series in 1819 and repeated it four more times. Based on the lectures of 1832, and recovered from students' notes and Schleiermacher's own outlines, the published work did not appear until 1864.[56] In the introduction, Schleiermacher insists that although Jesus must be seen in his historical setting, the meaning of his inner life transcends historical limitations. Major sources for the historical reconstruction are two: the Synoptic Gospels and the Gospel of John. These cannot be harmonized, but John, an eyewitness of the events, must be given priority. A full and accurate biography is not possible, for "it is undeniable that we cannot achieve a connected presentation of the life of Jesus."[57]

Schleiermacher orders the career of Jesus according to three periods. The first deals with events prior to the public ministry. In regard to the birth stories, Schleiermacher concludes that Matthew is more historical, Luke more poetic. He notes the problem of the place of Jesus' birth but concludes, "For our faith it is in itself of no consequence whether Christ was born in Bethlehem or in Nazareth (or add: elsewhere), whether his parents lived in the one place or the other, whether one of the two accounts is literally correct or neither of them."[58] The idea of the supernatural conception of Jesus rests on the notion of hereditary sin; it is not essential to Christian belief, nor is it a prerequisite to the sinlessness of Jesus. Schleiermacher accepts the account of the boy Jesus in the Jerusalem temple (Luke 2:41-52) as historical, and he believes Mary herself to be the source of the tradition. Throughout this section, Schleiermacher is concerned with the development of God-consciousness in Jesus. He argues that the sense of dependence on God developed gradually and in accord with Jesus' full humanity. Although Jesus could have attended the scribal schools, he would not have accepted their teaching, because he was free from intellectual as well as moral error. Jesus was probably self-taught. He applied the OT prophecies to himself.

> To the extent that his special self-consciousness developed in him, to that extent there developed also the conviction that he was the goal of the entire institution of Judaism, and therefore also the one to whom all these presen-

---

56. Friedrich Schleiermacher, *Das Leben Jesu. Vorlesungen an der Universität Berlin im Jahr 1832*, ed. K. A. Rutenik (Berlin: G. Reimer, 1864); Eng. trans.: *The Life of Jesus*, ed. J. C. Verheyden, trans. S. M. Gilmour (Philadelphia: Fortress Press, 1975).

57. Schleiermacher, *Life of Jesus*, 43.

58. Ibid., 55.

timents and sayings point which were to identify the fulfillment of this divine decree with the Jewish people.[59]

According to his own christological assumptions, Schleiermacher considers the temptation narrative not to be historical. The act of casting himself from the temple pinnacle "would have been wholly unworthy of Christ"[60] and thus constituted no real temptation.

In presenting the second period, that is, the public life of Jesus until his arrest, Schleiermacher distinguishes external from internal events. Among the externals are the miracles. In Schleiermacher's opinion, the miracles were probably not as numerous as the Gospels imply, since inexplicable events were often attributed to supernatural causes. Jesus, nevertheless, possessed the power to perform cures and always employed his power for doing good. The power, however, was in harmony with nature: "I only wish to maintain," says Schleiermacher, "that we do not need to assume anything supernatural, anything that is at the same time contrary to nature, but only a potential ascendancy on Christ's part, which was a constituent of his peculiar nature and disposition."[61] According to Schleiermacher, the miracles did not occupy a central place in Jesus' career: "We conclude, then, that Christ's performance of healing miracles was incidental and occasional."[62]

Under "internal events," Schleiermacher discusses the teaching of Jesus. He is primarily interested in Jesus' instruction about himself, material which is drawn mainly from the Gospel of John. Jesus presents himself as the one sent from God to reveal a unique God-consciousness. His mission is to bring people into community—the kingdom of God, which is not political but a spiritual union of believers. The kingdom will continue to develop in history and eventuate in unity with the presence of Christ. Hence, the idea of the return of Christ does not mean that Jesus will personally come back to the earth: "Rather, what I find is only a general consciousness of a continuation, not only in the interest of a constant spiritual activity of his personality, but also for his union with believers in fellowship with God."[63]

As the ministry progressed, opposition to Jesus continued to grow. To avoid a misunderstanding of his mission, Jesus sometimes prescribed silence concerning his Messiahship. This silence, described by later scholarship as the "messianic secret," creates a problem for Schleiermacher,

59. Ibid., 133.
60. Ibid., 148.
61. Ibid., 209.
62. Ibid., 197.
63. Ibid., 335.

because it is explicit in the Synoptics but lacking in John. Schleiermacher's resolution of the issue is less than convincing:

> The fact that Christ forbade his disciples to say that he was the Messiah cannot be regarded as an actual rule. He must have meant it to apply only to certain situations. He naturally knew that they would only come in contact with people who had only political ideas of the Messiah, and therefore this warning could have been a natural one. However, in the course of his teaching, especially his teaching in Jerusalem, we find that he always designates himself both directly and indirectly as Messiah.[64]

The third period includes events from the arrest to the ascension of Jesus. In discussing these events, Schleiermacher is often confusing. In regard to the death of Jesus, he notes that although death is always accompanied by decomposition, there is no evidence of this in the case of Jesus. Nevertheless, Jesus actually died a "spiritual" death,[65] and the question of the death of the body is only secondary. Schleiermacher also points out that the body of Jesus after the resurrection is the same body he had before. "So then, after the resurrection Christ returned to a truly human life."[66] Although Schleiermacher can refer to this life as a "state of revivification,"[67] he rejects the hypothesis of an appearance of death, a mere trance or coma, from which Jesus was revived.[68] In regard to the resurrection and ascension, Schleiermacher steers an unsteady course between natural and supernatural, arguing that Jesus' departure from the Emmaus pilgrims, for instance, involved nothing miraculous.

> If we hold fast to what Christ himself said, admitting that not all historical statements are clear because they do not consist of properly arranged elements, we see that nothing incomprehensible remains, except Christ's resurrection itself. However, the same thing is true of Christ's whole appearance upon the earth. His coming was a miraculous act, but all that followed it was wholly natural.[69]

Similarly, the ascension involves the removal and exaltation of Jesus, but how could Jesus, whose second life—the life after the resurrection—was human and historical, participate in such an event?

> I regard this whole second life appearance of Christ just as I do every individual miracle. There is something in it that is wholly factual, but the genesis

---

64. Ibid., 386.
65. Ibid., 415.
66. Ibid., 469.
67. Ibid., 464.
68. Schweitzer (*Quest of the Historical Jesus*, 64) thinks Schleiermacher, like Paulus, adopted a theory that Jesus only appeared to die, but Schleiermacher explicitly denies this on p. 455 of the *Life of Jesus*.
69. Schleiermacher, *Life of Jesus*, 445.

of it is incomprehensible to us . . . because it is connected with something that in its way is unique and for which there is no analogy. . . . The facts are genuine facts, but how that second life began and how it ended are matters which we cannot conceive factually.[70]

In evaluating Schleiermacher's contribution to NT research, one is tempted to say that he would have been a great biblical scholar if he had not been preoccupied with theology! Schleiermacher, in any case, did make important contributions to higher criticism and the discussion of the origins of the Gospels. In these matters he reflects the spirit of the Enlightenment—rejection of the orthodox doctrine of inspiration and suspicion of the supernatural. Nevertheless, it is Schleiermacher's theological insight which makes his critical and exegetical work exciting. His *Hermeneutics* is a case in point. Not content to rehearse the mechanics of exegesis, Schleiermacher moves on to the question of understanding and the importance of psychological meaning. His *Introduction*, too, does not stop with a consideration of authorship but proceeds to the issue of the meaning of canonicity. In all of this, Schleiermacher—preacher to the people and instructor of youth—was concerned to express a biblical scholarship that was relevant for the faith and life of the church.

In the wake of Reimarus and the rationalism of Paulus, Schleiermacher's *Life of Jesus* is of significance. This presentation of Jesus, to be sure, suffers from his christological presuppositions. For Schleiermacher, Jesus' willingness to die is important, and the triumph of his consciousness of God is important, but his death and resurrection, so crucial to the Christian gospel, are only secondary. The Christology, too, is partly responsible for Schleiermacher's preference for John as a historical source, although his detractors should understand that most scholars in the early nineteenth century accepted the authenticity of John. Most important is Schleiermacher's attempt to present a history of Jesus that gives expression to his Christology. For Schleiermacher, the Jesus of history and the Christ of faith are one and the same. However, as D. F. Strauss was later to observe, this harmonious resolution was problematic at two points: (1) the questionable character of the historical sources used to sustain it; and (2) the Christology which claims that a totally sinless and absolutely unique manifestation of God-consciousness can exist in a fully human, historical being.[71] Concern with these two problems continued to dominate much of the future of NT research.

70. Ibid., 479–80.
71. See pp. 249–50, below.

FOLLOWERS OF SCHLEIERMACHER:
DE WETTE AND LÜCKE

Wilhelm Martin Leberecht de Wette (1780–1849)

Wilhelm Martin Leberecht de Wette has been called a scholarly Nathaniel, that is, a theologian in whom there is no guile. Born in a neighboring village, de Wette studied at the gymnasium in Weimar, where he came under the spell of J. G. Herder. Later at Jena his professors included Griesbach and Paulus. In 1805, de Wette became an instructor at Jena, and from 1807 to 1810 he was on the faculty at Heidelberg. When called to the new University of Berlin, de Wette wrote to Schleiermacher, noting that in Heidelberg he had taught both OT and NT, which resulted in a lecture schedule of fifteen to eighteen hours a week.[72] At Berlin, de Wette enjoyed association with Schleiermacher who dedicated his essay on Luke to him. Friedrich Lücke, who was a student at the time, held fond memories of Saturday walks with de Wette.[73] In 1816, de Wette wrote a letter in opposition to the call of Hegel to the faculty at Berlin, because he believed Hegel's philosophy constituted a threat to Christianity.[74] In 1819, de Wette was dismissed from Berlin because he had written a letter of condolence to the mother of Karl Sand, a student activist who had assassinated the prominent literary figure, August von Kotzebue. In this time of political unrest, de Wette wrote that Sand "considered it right to do what he did, and so he had done what was right,"[75] an ethic which seemed too permissive to the Prussian authorities. After a three-year period of study and writing at Weimar, de Wette was called to a professorship at Basel, where he spent the balance of his career (1822–49). Alhough noted for his rationalism, de Wette's sober personal life displayed an authentic piety.

De Wette's Theological Perspective

Like Schleiermacher, de Wette published in a variety of theological areas. His work on the OT—perhaps more significant than that on the NT[76] — included a commentary on the Psalms (1811), a textbook on Hebrew-Jewish archeology (1814), and a historical-critical introduction to the OT

---

72. Ernst Staehelin, *Dewettiana: Forschungen und Texte zu Wilhelm Martin Leberecht de Wettes Leben und Werk* (Basel: Helbing & Lichtenhahn, 1956), 68.

73. Friedrich Lücke, *D.W.M.L. de Wette: Zur freundschaftlichen Erinnerung* (Hamburg: R. Perthes, 1850). See also K. R. Hagenbach, *Wilhelm Martin Leberecht de Wette: Eine akademische Gedächtnisrede* (Leipzig: Wiedmann, 1850).

74. Staehelin, *Dewettiana*, 75–76.

75. Ibid., 86.

76. See Rudolf Smend, *Wilhelm Martin Leberecht de Wettes Arbeit am Alten und am Neuen Testament* (Basel: Helbing & Lichtenhahn, 1958), 133–38.

(1817)[77] which went through seven editions during his lifetime. He also produced a translation of the Bible into German and, with Lücke, a synopsis of the Gospels (1818). His work in dogmatics included a two-volume textbook on Christian theology (1813–16), a work entitled *Über Religion und Theologie* (1815), a three-volume work on Christian ethics, a two-volume collection of lectures on ethics (1823–24),[78] a book on the essence, forms, and influence of religion (1827),[79] and, late in his life, a work on the essence of the Christian faith (1846).[80]

Of special interest is de Wette's novel *Theodore, or the Skeptic's Conversion*,[81] written during the Weimar period. In the introduction, de Wette declares that his purpose is to present an alternative to the conflicting views of rationalism, supernaturalism, and orthodoxy—"to interest those who are still capable of free intellectual progress and excitement in favor of a theology truly scientific, and, at the same time, adapted to warm and inspire the soul."[82] In his preface to the American edition (1841), de Wette characterizes his own theological position: "I remain by myself, without any companions, in my critical-aesthetic system, which the present age has either not sufficient courage, or not enough insight, to receive."[83] As these preliminary remarks suggest, the novel employs obtrusive moralizing and is, in effect, a fictional presentation of de Wette's own theology. The plot relates the story of Theodore, an attractive young man raised in a pious home, who loses his faith at the university. After various exploits involving travel, romance, comments on music and the arts, not to mention tedious theological discussions, Theodore eventually returns to the faith, receives ordination, and lives happily ever after as a country parson.

The theology of de Wette has its philosophical basis in the work of J. F. Fries, who stressed the importance of feeling and religious experience.[84] As de Wette says in the preface to his novel, the philosophy of Fries

---

77. W.M.L. de Wette, *Lehrbuch der historisch-kritischen Einleitung in die kanonischen und apokryphischen Bücher des Alten Testaments*, Lehrbuch de historisch-kritischen Einleitung in die Bibel Alten und Neuen Testaments, vol. 1, 7th rev. ed. (Berlin: G. Reimer, 1852).

78. W.M.L. de Wette, *Vorlesungen über die Sittenlehre*, 2 vols. (Berlin: G. Reimer, 1823–24).

79. W.M.L. de Wette, *Ueber die Religion, ihr Wesen, ihre Erscheinungsformen und ihren Einfluss auf das Leben: Vorlesungen* (Berlin: G. Reimer, 1827).

80. W.M.L. de Wette, *Das Wesen des christlichen Glaubens vom Standpunkte des Glaubens dargestellt* (Basel: Schweighauser, 1846).

81. W.M.L. de Wette, *Theodor, oder des Zweiflers Weihe*; Eng. trans.: *Theodore; or the Skeptic's Conversion: History of the Culture of a Protestant Clergyman*, trans. James F. Clarke, 2 vols. (Boston: Hilliard, Gray, & Co., 1841).

82. De Wette, *Theodore* 1. xxviii.

83. Ibid. 1.xxxvi

84. See Karl Barth, *Protestant Theology in the Nineteenth Century: Its Background & History*, trans. John Bowden (London: SCM Press, 1972), 482–89; Rudolf Smend, "De Wette und das Verhältnis zwischen historischer Bibelkritik und philosophischem System im 19. Jahrhundert," *Theologische Zeitschrift* 14 (1958): 107–19.

"taught me how to reconcile understanding and faith in the principle of religious feeling."[85]

> The essence of religion is feeling. In moral actions, this feeling is expressed only in a limited degree, and imperfectly. Still less can it be contained and expressed by doctrines and opinions. There remain then, only poetry and art, as suitable means of expressing the religious sentiment.[86]

According to de Wette, religious feeling makes possible the apprehension of the transcendent, and, therefore, the appropriation of revelation. Revelation is experienced in history, and Christianity is a particular expression of divine revelation.

> In Christianity he [Theodore] saw the perfect moral culture of the human soul, the victory of the spiritual over the natural—over the common, rude, and narrow features of life. Faith in the God-man exalts the soul to a pure self-reliance and self-consciousness.[87]

Jesus Christ is the supreme manifestation of historical revelation. "The true and the good are joined with the beautiful in inseparable connection, and are embodied in the eternal Word made flesh, in the glorified humanity of Christ."[88] Assessing the work of Christ, Theodore, like de Wette, is neither rationalist nor supernaturalist: "I believe that I occupy a middle ground between the two. I believe in miracles, but I will accept as such no particular fact, until I have critically examined it."[89] In speaking about the crucifixion, Theodore declares, "His death, which was a death of triumph, gives to us the confidence of victory; a confidence that human nature, though weak and sinful, is capable both of victory and glory."[90] Christ is the norm for the expression of religious feeling, and Scripture has its authority as witness of Christ. As Theodore says, "It is not a revelation, but it contains the oldest and truest accounts concerning it. Revelation itself came to pass in the incarnation of Christ, and in what he did and suffered on earth."[91] Biblical critics, however, frequently miss the point: "'O, how mistaken are they!' cried Theodore; 'those theologians, who apply their acuteness of mind to explain away the miracles and labor to make plain by their criticisms of the Bible history, and forget, while doing so, the high importance which this history has for the pious feelings.'"[92]

85. De Wette, *Theodore* 1. xxxi.
86. Ibid. 1.230–31.
87. Ibid. 2.217.
88. Ibid. 1.244.
89. Ibid. 1.173.
90. Ibid. 2.358–59.
91. Ibid. 2.23.
92. Ibid. 1.204.

De Wette's New Testament Research

As early as 1813, de Wette published a monograph on the death of Jesus,[93] and throughout his career he continued to produce historical-critical, exegetical, and theological works on the NT. His theory of criticism is set forth at the end of his commentary on the Gospel of John.[94] He contends that gospel criticism must rest on two basic presuppositions: (1) it must be based on solid historical facts; and (2) it must follow clearly defined general and special principles. According to general principles, the historical investigation must recognize that Jesus is subject to the limits of finitude; according to special principles, it must view the particular data as related to the whole understanding of Jesus as originator and redeemer. When this method is applied, some features of the gospel story will come into clear focus: the relation of Jesus to John the Baptist, a ministry in Jerusalem prior to the last Passover, the probability of some miracles, the historicity of the last supper. Complete knowledge of the life and teaching of Jesus is neither possible nor necessary. "Many of the first Christians may have known scarcely a tenth of what our catechumens learn, and probably they were more enthusiastic and faithful than we."[95] Enough can be known for Christians to be able to have faith in Christ and be filled with the spirit of truth and love.

De Wette's historical-critical judgments can be seen in his *Introduction to the NT.*[96] In the preface, de Wette discloses his commitment to higher criticism:

> I would gladly have arrived at results more definite and more in harmony with the views generally received in the Church; but the Truth can alone decide. That is no genuine love of Truth which is not ready to sacrifice its inordinate curiosity where certainty is unattainable, as well as its pious prejudices. The value of criticism I place chiefly in the activity to which it excites the spirit of inquiry; but this spirit of inquiry can never harm a genuine Christian piety.[97]

In general, de Wette's *Introduction* is clear and concise; the main views are

---

93. Guilelmus Martinus Leberecht de Wette, *De morte Jesu Christi expiatoria commentatio* (Berlin: Libraria scholae realis, 1813).

94. W.M.L. de Wette, *Kurze Erklärung des Evangeliums und der Briefe Johannis,* Kurzgefasstes exegetisches Handbuch zum Neuen Testament, 3d ed., vol. 1, pt. 3 (Leipzig: Weidmann, 1846), 224–32.

95. Ibid., 231.

96. W.M.L. de Wette, *Lehrbuch der historisch-kritischen Einleitung in die kanonischen Bücher des Neuen Testaments,* Lehrbuch der historisch-kritischen Einleitung in die Bibel Alten und Neuen Testaments 2, 5th rev. ed. (Berlin: G. Reimer, 1848); Eng. trans.: *An Historico-Critical Introduction to the Canonical Books of the New Testament,* trans. Frederick Frothingham (Boston: Crosby, Nichols, & Co., 1858). Cited hereafter as *Introduction.*

97. De Wette, *Introduction,* v.

briefly presented, and the details are relegated to extensive notes. If research does not warrant a definite conclusion, de Wette is reluctant to draw one.

The first division of the *Introduction* deals with matters of language and text criticism. De Wette displays competence in both areas and affirms such established principles as the preference for the variant which requires the harder reading. The second division considers the individual sections of the NT. Concerning the Gospels, de Wette says, "In regard to their contents, the Gospels may certainly be called *historic* writings; but the history always has more or less the object of establishing *the faith*, and to this the selection and treatment of the historic matter correspond."[98] De Wette reviews the current solutions to the synoptic problem and rejects both the theory that one of the gospels used the others (e.g., Griesbach) and the theory that all of the Synoptic Gospels used a common written source (e.g., Eichhorn). His own hypothesis is that the Gospels rest on an oral tradition (Herder), which was written in a variety of fragments (Schleiermacher), which were used by the author of Matthew, which was used by Luke; finally, Mark used both Matthew and Luke (Griesbach).

As to the Gospels individually, de Wette believes Matthew was composed originally in Greek and written before the destruction of Jerusalem. The author was neither an apostle nor an eyewitness. Luke, in de Wette's opinion, did not write under the direction of Paul, and Mark does not report the reminiscences of Peter. John knew the gospel tradition and could have used Matthew. John, however, is primarily interested not in history but in the presentation of the messianic and divine dignity of Christ. After extensive discussion and in full cognizance of the problems, de Wette supports apostolic authorship of the Fourth Gospel. John probably wrote prior to the composition of Luke and Mark. "The oldest, although indirect, witnesses in favor of the great age of our Gospel [John], are Luke and Mark, who have referred to it."[99]

Acts, de Wette argues, was not written by a companion of Paul, because its narratives are not always consistent with data from the Pauline epistles. One of the author's sources—indicated by the use of the first-person plural "we"—was a participant in some of the events. De Wette rejects the traditional dating of Acts at the end of Paul's two-year imprisonment in Rome and puts it later than the Gospel of Luke, which was written after the destruction of Jerusalem. Paul's imprisonment letters were probably written from Rome, although Caesarea is possible; the hypothesis of a second Roman imprisonment is doubtful. Paul's earliest letter was 1 Thes-

98. Ibid., 84.
99. Ibid., 201.

salonians, and 2 Thessalonians is probably genuine in spite of various problems. Galatians was written during Paul's Ephesian ministry and addressed to Galatians in the north (the territorial hypothesis). Both 2 Corinthians and Romans (including Romans 15 and 16) constitute a unity. Colossians is authentic; it refutes opponents who have combined Jewish asceticism with mystical philosophy. Ephesians is spurious. The Pastoral Epistles are not by Paul; they do not fit the historical situation, and they are written in a different style.

Hebrews was not written by Paul, nor by any of the other hypothetical authors, such as Clement, Barnabas, Luke, or Apollos. It was composed in Greek prior to the destruction of Jerusalem by an unknown Jewish Christian. De Wette believes the Catholic Epistles present problems. First Peter does not represent Petrine Christianity but shows dependence on Pauline thought. Second Peter is dependent on Jude and is not authentic. First John is by the same author as the Fourth Gospel. The Apocalypse, on the other hand, shows a radically different style and Christology: "From all this it follows, (and no conclusion of modern criticism stands more firmly than this,) that if the Apostle John wrote the fourth Gospel and the Johannic Epistles, he did not write the Apocalypse."[100]

De Wette's exegetical work can be seen in his popular commentary series, *Concise Exegetical Handbook to the NT.*[101] The commentary on Romans first appeared in 1835, followed in the next year by commentaries on Matthew, Luke, and Mark. The section on the Gospel of John and the Johannine epistles was published in 1837, and the whole series was eventually completed with the appearance of Revelation in 1848, a year of political unrest. The sections of the series went through different editions and were published in various formats. The commentary on each book is prefaced by a short historical-critical introduction, and the comments, ordered by pericopes, are concise and packed with critical data and scholarly references. A few examples can illustrate the character of de Wette's work.

De Wette's *Commentary on John*[102] is dedicated to Lücke and remembers their time together with "the unforgettable Schleiermacher in our midst."[103] In the introduction, de Wette argues that John did not use the Synoptics but knew the Gospel tradition: "It can scarcely be denied that

---

100. Ibid., 378.

101. W.M.L. de Wette, *Kurzgefasstes exegetisches Handbuch zum Neuen Testament,* 4 vols. (Leipzig: Weidmann, 1845–48).

102. De Wette, *Kurze Erklärung des Evangeliums und der Briefe Johannis,* Handbuch, vol. 1, pt. 3.

103. Ibid., preface.

the author did not use the synoptic gospels, but knew the fundamental oral tradition, and presupposed it as known by his readers."[104] John wrote not a supplementary Gospel but a Hellenistic gospel which presents Christ as the son of God. The discourses of the Fourth Gospel were written by the author, as the similarities to the prologue indicate, although much of the doctrine goes back to Jesus himself. De Wette believes λόγος should be translated "word" rather than "reason." The term has its background in Genesis, where it stands for the word God spoke. Under Hellenistic influence, the λόγος is personified; it represents the essence of God, present in human consciousness.

De Wette's preference for the Fourth Gospel is evidenced throughout the commentary. He takes the story of the changing of water to wine as historical and believes the mother of Jesus expected a miracle. The conflict between John and the Synoptics regarding the time of the cleansing of the temple is resolved in John's favor. In regard to the raising of Lazarus, de Wette reviews the various theories designed to explain the silence of the Synoptics. He refuses to accept easy answers (e.g., that the Synoptics suppressed the story to protect Lazarus and his family), but he concludes that "something historical must be beneath"[105] the account. De Wette notes the conflict between the Synoptics and John concerning the last supper and concludes with John that it took place prior to the Passover meal. Despite this concern with historical reliability, de Wette is sensitive to literary and theological problems. He believes that the account of the dialogue with Nicodemus displays a lack of realism which betrays the hand of the author. In an extensive discussion of the resurrection, de Wette notes the tension between the physical and the spiritual in the accounts of the appearances. He rejects both the rationalist view that Jesus only appeared to die and the liberal notion that the appearances were merely visionary.

> It is best in the spirit of the modern historical-scientific theology to accept the fact that the apostles and first believers believed in the resurrection of Jesus, and indeed to recognize the historical uncertainty of the Gospel reports in view of the individual circumstances as grounded in the nature of the thing; but thus not to deny the fact itself, but rather to recognize the incomprehensibility of it, to reject a theoretical ordering of it in our usual historical and physical knowledge, and thus not to reject it because of its impossibility, but rather (as with many other matters) to leave the view open to a higher nature of things.[106]

104. Ibid., 4.
105. Ibid., 146.
106. Ibid., 216.

De Wette's theological reflection about the NT is displayed in his *Biblical Dogmatics*.[107] A preliminary discussion argues that the thought of the Bible must be understood in relation to the human spirit. The first part presents the religion of the OT and Judaism. The second part, on the religion of the NT, begins with a short historical survey of early Christianity. This survey stresses the importance of Jesus as spiritual Messiah and the significance of the resurrection faith. De Wette believes three types of religion are manifest in the NT: (1) a Jewish Christianity (seen in the Synoptics, Acts, the Petrine letters, James, Jude, and Revelation); (2) an Alexandrian or Hellenistic Christianity (seen in the Johannine literature and Hebrews); and (3) the Christianity of Paul (expressed in the Pauline epistles). According to de Wette, the most important aspect of NT theology is found in the teachings of Jesus as presented by the Gospel of John.

In analyzing this material, de Wette, like G. L. Bauer,[108] imposes the pattern of systematic theology upon the sources; that is, he orders the material according to such topics as "revelation," "God," and "salvation." The central feature of the teaching of Jesus is his idea of the kingdom as God's spiritual rule and presence. As revelation, Jesus has been sent from God to show the way to God. According to Jesus, God is the Creator who wills salvation—a reconciliation with the divine Spirit which encompasses all people: "The story of Jesus is not only an ethical mirror from Christians, but also a symbol and model for the pious feeling in contemplation, just as in art and poetry."[109] In the teaching of the apostles, Christ is understood as the revelation of God—as mediator (Hebrews), as λόγος (John). God is acknowledged as Creator who has foreknowledge of the course of history. Human beings, in spite of their shortcomings, can be changed into the likeness of God. Salvation is accomplished through Christ whose humanity is stressed, for instance, by Paul.

In spite of his claim to stand in theological isolation, de Wette's critical-aesthetic position is not far removed from Schleiermacher's. Both stress the significance of religious consciousness and the importance of communicating the Christian faith to the intelligent layperson. With Schleiermacher, de Wette accepts the authenticity of John, although with qualifications. His *Introduction*, written in the tradition of Michaelis and Eichhorn, displays objectivity and an admirable brevity without sacrifice of scholarly detail. De Wette's judgments concerning Ephesians, Hebrews, Revelation, the Pastoral Epistles, and the Catholic Epistles was largely to be confirmed

---

107. W.M.L. de Wette, *Biblische Dogmatik Alten und Neuen Testaments, oder kritische Darstellung der Religionslehre des Hebraismus, des Judenthums und Urchristenthums: Zum Gebrauch akademischer Vorlesungen*, 3d rev. ed. (Berlin: G. Reimer, 1831).

108. See pp. 188–95, above.

109. De Wette, *Biblische Dogmatik*, 225.

by subsequent scholarship. Nevertheless, de Wette seems to have officiated at an unhappy marriage between rationalism and the supernatural. His concern to go beyond historical reconstruction to the spirit of the NT is suggestive, and so, too, is his perception of theology and exegesis as art. However, his concept of religious feeling does not provide an adequate ontological ground for overcoming the tension between objective history and spiritual reality and, finally, moves in the direction of subjectivity.

Friedrich Lücke (1791–1855)

A moderate in a time of conflict, Gottfried Christian Friedrich Lücke was born in Egeln near Magdeburg. He began his university studies at Halle in 1810, and after two years, he transferred to Göttingen. In 1816, Lücke moved to Berlin where he studied with de Wette and Neander, and made an enduring friendship with Schleiermacher. Lücke was called to the faculty at Bonn in 1818. During this period, he was active in publishing theological journals. In 1827, Lücke returned to the faculty at Göttingen, where he labored for the rest of his career. He was noted for his warm personal faith and was a favorite among the students. During the political crisis in which the "Göttingen Seven" were dismissed from the faculty,[110] Lücke sympathized with the protesters but took no action. He was appointed to positions of leadership in the church and in 1843 was made abbot of Bursfeld.

Lücke's Hermeneutic

Lücke's theology represents a mediating position between the rationalists and the supernaturalists. Influenced by Schleiermacher, his thought was christocentric and always directed toward the life of the church.

> The Christian revelation is primarily not doctrine, but history, that is, the sacred history of the Saviour Jesus Christ, through whom the true redemption of humanity has become a reality for faith. It is only essential to the fullness of this revelation, that Christ himself witnesses and interprets the grace and truth of God which appears in him. . . . This is the meaning of the teaching of Jesus Christ . . . without which there is no certain knowledge of Christian revelation in the church.[111]

According to Lücke, theology has three main tasks: to establish historical knowledge by critical research; to understand the ground and inner meaning of the Christian faith by philosophical reflection; and to combine

---

110. See p. 287, below.
111. Cited in Dietz Lange, "Der theologische Vermittler Friedrich Lücke," in *Theologie in Göttingen: Eine Vorlesungsreihe*, ed. Bernd Moeller (Göttingen: Vandenhoeck & Ruprecht, 1987), 149.

historical and philosophical understanding in order to express a vital message for the life of the church.

Friedrich Lücke's major contribution to NT research is in the area of exegesis. However, his exegetical work is based on thoughtful reflection about the problem of hermeneutics, reflection which came to expression in his *Outline of New Testament Hermeneutics and Its History*.[112] In the preface, Lücke notes the need for hermeneutical understanding in his time: theology is plagued by a dogmatics that has not been based on exegesis, and by an exegesis that ignores theology. Properly understood, exegesis has two aspects: historical and philosophical. Hermeneutics is the philosophical prolegomenon to historical exegesis. For Lücke, systematic theology must be based on historical theology, and "historical theology rests according to its content and its form on the correct interpretation of the historical monuments of Christianity." [113]

The first part of Lücke's *Hermeneutics* deals with the search for a basic hermeneutical principle. He traces the history of interpretation from the early church to his own time, and concludes that eighteenth-century scholarship created a chasm between the church and exegesis. The grammatico-historical method became increasingly rational, and the orthodox reaction moved more and more toward the supernatural. On the basis of his historical survey, Lücke presents a list of hermeneutical principles that he considers unsatisfactory, such as, the mystical, the dogmatic, and the ecclesiastical. He also concludes that the grammatical method, used exclusively, is inadequate: "Since through the literal meaning only individual terms and relations of terms, and never the whole of a speech or writing, still less religious ideas and feelings, can be directly and fully expressed; so is the grammatical principle of interpretation not adequate for the complete probing and exposition of the content of the New Testament documents."[114] Historical interpretation, narrowly conceived, fares no better: "Since in the N. T. as well as external historical beginnings also the inner conceptual origin of Christianity is expressed, so must the historical exegesis which has only the former as its object be recognized as inadequate."[115]

Lücke's own hermeneutical principle rests on his idea of the basic unity of the human spirit, that is, a common ground of understanding that is essential to humanity. To understand a text, one must know the language and historical setting, and, most of all, be united in a spiritual relationship

112. Friedrich Lücke, *Grundriss der neutestamentlichen Hermeneutik und ihrer Geschichte: Zum Gebrauch für academische Vorlesungen* (Göttingen: Vandenhoeck & Ruprecht, 1816).
113. Ibid., 21.
114. Ibid., 80–81.
115. Ibid., 81–82.

(*Seelenverwandtschaft*) with the NT author. On the basis of this principle, Lücke proceeds to develop the details of his methodology. In the second part of his hermeneutic, he attends to the form and content of the NT message. The form must be analyzed according to language, rhetoric, and symbol. The content consists of historical and doctrinal material. The interpretation of historical material requires consideration of the objective and the subjective aspects of the narrative. Miracles must be investigated historically with attention to the laws of historical possibility, and synthesis between the rational and the supernatural should be achieved. In the doctrinal material, the special Christian understanding of religious consciousness is disclosed. Interpretation of this material requires theological analysis and synthesis, and comes to expression in an NT theology grounded in the idea of historical revelation. This harmony of analysis and synthesis—a unity of historical-critical and theological interpretation—Lücke calls "Christian philology." In considering the communication of the exegetical results (part 3), Lücke discusses two forms of expression: scholarly (e.g., in technical commentaries) and popular (e.g., in translations and sermons). Finally, Lücke expresses his hope "in the ever greater increase of the Christian faith, in the ever deeper probing of theological science, in the ever purer marriage of both in individuals who recognize the idea of Christian philology ever more clearly."[116]

Lücke's Johannine Research

From 1820 to 1832, Lücke was engaged in publishing a series of works on the Johannine literature. The last of these, a lengthy work on Revelation,[117] appeared in 1832. Here Lücke attends to the history and character of apocalyptic literature, the history of the interpretation of the Apocalypse, and the major historical-critical issues. He concludes, on the basis of language, style, and thought, that Revelation cannot have been written by the author of the Fourth Gospel. His commentary on the Johannine epistles, however, argues for the authenticity of all three letters.[118] In regard to 1 John, he concludes that the date and place of writing are not certain, although this epistle was written after the Gospel of John, and probably from Asia Minor. In discussing 1 John 1:5—2:2, Lücke observes the symbolic character of the Johannine rhetoric: "But light and darkness, in the language of St. John, are symbols of ethical notions, and more specially of

---

116. Ibid., 216.
117. Friedrich Lücke, *Versuch einer vollständigen Einleitung in die Offenbarung des Johannes oder Allgemeine Untersuchung über die apokalyptische Litteratur überhaupt und die Apokalypse des Johannes insbesondere*, 2d rev. ed., 2 vols. (Bonn: E. Weber, 1852).
118. Friedrich Lücke, *A Commentary on the Epistles of St. John*, trans. T. G. Repp (Edinburgh: T. Clark, 1837).

that primary ethical antithesis of good, in which alone there is life, and evil in which death is."[119] Commenting on 1 John 2:18-28, Lücke concludes that "the last hour" refers to the parousia of the Lord. This reference has its background in the Jewish idea of the coming of the Messiah to usher in the new age, an idea transformed by the Christians so as to refer to the return of Christ. According to Lücke, this futuristic eschatology is increasingly spiritualized, especially by John. In regard to 1 John 5:6-12, Lücke presents a lengthy discussion of the meaning of "water" and "blood," concluding that water represents the baptism which Jesus ordained as a symbol of repentance, and blood refers to his purifying and redemptive death. Lücke rejects the reference to the three heavenly witnesses in 5:7 and concludes, "No result of modern criticism is more certain, than that this passage is spurious."[120]

Lücke's major work is his massive *Commentary on the Gospel of John*,[121] a brilliant execution of his own hermeneutical theory. Throughout the total of almost fifteen hundred pages, Lücke displays the power of his method of Christian philology, a method which combines historical research with theological reflection in the service of the Christian faith. In the introduction, Lücke traces the tradition concerning John the apostle and defends the authenticity of the Fourth Gospel. Apostolic authorship was universally affirmed by the end of the second century, and evidence for use of the Gospel can be detected in the works of Ignatius and Justin. The data of this Gospel fit all that is known about John: the language shows Semitic influence, and the geographical details are accurate. Although John does not name himself as author, the vividness of the narrative indicates the work of an eyewitness. Agreements between the Synoptics and John are greater than the differences, and although the modes of expression differ, the basic historical foundation is the same. To be sure, the teachings of Jesus are presented by John in a form different from that of the Synoptics, because John records instruction to the disciples; the Synoptics, to the public. John is concerned with dogmatics; the Synoptics, with ethics. On matters like the length of the Judean ministry and the time of the cleansing of the temple, John's account is more reliable than the Synoptic Gospels.

Lücke emphasizes the canonical importance of the Gospel of John. As everyone agrees, the Gospels of Mark and Luke are not apostolic, and the authenticity of Matthew has been increasingly questioned. Thus, John remains as *the* authentic, apostolic Gospel, a Gospel that combines history

119. Ibid., 110.
120. Ibid., 267.
121. Friedrich Lücke, *Commentar über das Evangelium des Johannes*, 3d rev. ed., 2 vols. (Bonn: E. Weber, 1840).

and meaning and displays unique spiritual sensitivity. The tradition about the place and time of writing vary, but the Gospel was probably written from Ephesus after the deaths of Peter and Paul. The original language was Greek, not Aramaic, although a Semitic influence is apparent. The nature of the composition is impressive:

> The Gospel gives the impression of an ordered whole, an historical portrait of broad conception, full of vital unity and coherence. The holy expression of light which it presents fascinates first and foremost. But no one can fail to look with pleasure at the author whose heart and spirit, purpose and goal, emerge everywhere in the presentation.[122]

The purpose of the Fourth Gospel is to strengthen the faith of Christians who are disturbed by Gnosticism and is accomplished through a presentation of the historic appearance of Christ in whom they have faith and life. In the course of his argument, John uses gnostic terms to refute the Gnostics. Although he knows the gospel tradition, John's main source is his own memory of events in which he participated. He writes freely and not under the compulsion of verbal inspiration. "We understand the inspiration of John in this broader and higher sense, not as the single isolated moment in the act of writing, but in the continuing holy life of his spirit dedicated to Christ, through which in the course of his apostolic activity, his Gospel arose as a work of truth and faithful remembrance."[123] Study of this reliable historical record is basic to the Christian faith.

> The true theological concern is inseparable from the historical and the critical. Christianity rests according to all conceptual content on the factual, the true, the indubitable. These are to be investigated in the Holy Scriptures with the same critical stringency and fearlessness which is the rule in other areas of history.[124]

In the commentary proper, Lücke organizes the material by sections and subsections, and presents exegesis on virtually every verse. Excursuses on important topics appear at the end of some of the sections. Lücke's exposition of the prologue provides an excellent example of his combination of critical analysis and theological reflection. Concerning the phrase καὶ θεὸς ἦν ὁ λόγος (1:1), Lücke asks whether λόγος or θεός is the subject. He argues that the absence of the article before θεός, because of exceptions to the rule, does not prove that it is the predicate.[125] He decides, on the basis of the context, that λόγος is the subject. But what,

122. Ibid. 1.177.
123. Ibid. 1.239.
124. Ibid. 1.243.
125. Predicate nouns as a rule are anarthrous. Lücke, of course, was unaware of Colwell's rule (1933) that predicate nouns preceding the verb do not take the article.

he asks, is the meaning of the phrase "the Word was God"? He concludes that the phrase primarily describes a relationship: the λόγος is so close to God that it can be called θεός. Lücke thinks the concept is similar to Paul's idea of the image of God, and that although it implies subordination, it affirms the unity of the divine essence.

In an excursus, "The Essential Dogmatic Content of the Prologue," Lücke takes up the crucial theological question: How is the preexistent Logos one with the historical Jesus? The answer involves two other questions: How was this relationship understood at the time of John? and How should it be understood today? In regard to the historical question, Lücke believes John's readers could have understood the relationship on the basis of the platonic idea of the preexistent soul which becomes a human being. In regard to the contemporary issue, he notes, on the one hand, the need to maintain monotheism and on the other, the threat of Arianism. Thus he concludes that the text does not describe the objective content of revelation, but is a way of speaking about a relationship: "Since in the context of Christian thought, we cannot accept it as a presentation of an actual absolute divine Logos-person, so this presentation can only be evaluated as a thought-form of the time, as a temporally conditioned symbolic expression of an essential Christian truth."[126]

Lücke's interpretation of the miracles illustrates his concern to harmonize the rational and the supernatural. He believes that the changing of the water to wine is not to be taken as a parable or mere symbol, but as a real happening. Although the process is not explained, the Gospel is basically reliable, and the miracle has spiritual meaning. In regard to John 6:19, Lücke shows by grammatical investigation that Jesus is depicted as walking "on the sea." Thus, rationalistic arguments that he was walking "by the sea" or swimming in it are rejected. John, therefore, reports a miracle, although in Lücke's opinion, he makes very little of it. Concerning the raising of Lazarus, Lücke observes, "The boundary between the divine and the human in Jesus is nowhere drawn with more difficulty and danger than in this narrative in which both appear in such beautiful reciprocal penetration."[127] Lücke raises and answers the difficult exegetical questions: Why did Jesus weep? Answer: He was human, and therefore, troubled. How could Lazarus walk out of the tomb if his body was bound? Answer: The binding was not that tight! Lücke refuses to resort to easy answers to explain the omission of the miracle from the Synoptic Gospel accounts. His solution is that the Synoptics do not present a complete

126. Ibid. 1.373.
127. Ibid. 2.444.

narrative and, from a large tradition of miracle stories, had to select some and omit others. For Lücke, the crucial issue in the interpretation of miracles is the problem of presuppositions. If one begins with the assumption that miracles are impossible, the individual miracle accounts will, of course, be rejected. Lücke believes this presupposition to be unwarranted, and he advocates a rigorous historical investigation of each account.

In the preface to his second volume, Lücke evaluates his work in relation to the present state of Johannine studies: "The critical research concerning the Gospel of John is not yet completed, and I have enough self-criticism not to presume to have solved all the riddles."[128] But although he may not have answered every question satisfactorily, Lücke has raised virtually all of the issues: no problem is ignored, no exegetical stone left unturned. Lücke displays mastery of all the critical disciplines: lower criticism, linguistic and grammatical analysis, historical understanding. Moreover, as his *Hermeneutics* shows, Lücke is philosophically sensitive and concerned with the theological significance of his exegetical results. Although many succeeding scholars would disagree with his view of the authorship and historical reliability of the Gospel of John, Lücke's commentary remains exciting reading today—one of the monumental achievements in the history of Johannine research.

A MEDIATING ALTERNATIVE:
AUGUST NEANDER (1789–1850)

Johann August Wilhelm Neander was a church historian whose contribution to the history of NT research has attracted little notice. Nevertheless, his biblical work was embraced by the conservative English-speaking theologians, translated, and immediately published. Born to a Jewish family of Göttingen and named David Mendel, he was converted to Christianity after reading Schleiermacher's discourses *On Religion*. Baptized in 1806 at the age of seventeen, he took the name Neander (New-man). He began his university studies at Halle, where Schleiermacher became his mentor. When Napoleon's invasion shut down the university, Neander moved to Göttingen. He began his teaching career in Heidelberg but was called to Berlin in 1813, where he was closely associated with Schleiermacher and de Wette. Neander had a likeable personality but an unattractive appearance. Philip Schaff, who was personally acquainted with Neander, described him as "a man of middle size, slender frame, homely . . . [with] black hair flowing in uncombed profusion over the forehead, an old fashioned coat, a white cravat carelessly tied, as often behind or on one side of

128. Ibid. 2.xi.

the neck, as in front."[129] Despite his appearance and distracting teaching style, students were attracted to Neander. He regularly invited them to his house for dinner and was especially benevolent to the poor.

Neander's church historical writings reflect a biographical interest. By 1812 he had published a monograph on Julian the Apostate. This was followed by books on St. Bernard (1813), Chrysostom (1822), Tertullian (1824), and Pascal (1847). Neander was interested in the early church and published books on Gnosticism and the apostolic age. His major work, the mammoth *General History of the Christian Religion and Church*, began to appear in 1825, and continued to be published until after his death, eventually filling six large volumes.[130] In the introduction, Neander affirms his understanding of the nature of the Christian church:

> Now Christianity we regard not as a power that has sprung up out of the hidden depths of man's nature, but as one which descended from above, because heaven opened itself for the rescue of revolted humanity; a power which, as it is exalted above all that human nature can create out of its own resources, must impart to that nature a new life, and change it from its inmost centre. The great source of this power is the person whose life its appearance exhibits to us—Jesus of Nazareth—the Redeemer of mankind when alienated from God by sin. In the submission of faith to him, and the appropriation of the truth which he revealed, consists the essence of Christianity, and of that fellowship of this divine life resulting from it, which we designate under the name of the church.[131]

Church history is the story of this divine power, moving and developing in history.

Neander had planned to publish practical commentaries on the major books of the NT but was able to complete only three: Philippians, James, and 1 John. These were short, nontechnical expositions of the text. The commentary on Philippians, for example, is largely a meditation on the life and thought of Paul.[132] Neander believes this letter was written during Paul's Roman imprisonment, and he identifies the opponents in Philippi as the Judaizers who had plagued Paul's mission everywhere. The commentary on 1 John is a bit more detailed and presents the exposition

---

129. Philip Schaff, *Germany: Its Universities, Theology, and Religion* (Philadelphia: Lindsay & Blakiston, 1857), 269.

130. August Neander, *Allegemeine Geschichte der christlichen Religion und Kirche* (1825–52); Eng. trans.: *General History of the Christian Religion and Church*, trans. Joseph Torrey, 5th ed., 5 vols. (Boston: Crocker & Brewster, 1852).

131. Neander, *General History* 1.1–2.

132. August Neander, *The Epistle of Paul to the Philippians, Practically Explained*, trans. H. C. Conant (New York: L. Colby, 1851).

by chapters.[133] In regard to 5:7-8, Neander argues that the reference to the three heavenly witnesses should be omitted because it does not fit the context.

More important is Neander's *Life of Jesus*.[134] Published in 1837, this work was considered a potent counterattack to Strauss's revolutionary *Life of Jesus*, which had appeared two years earlier.[135] In the preface to his third edition (1838), Neander wrote, "I cannot, therefore, but rejoice to find that my treatment of the subject, with that of others engaged in the same controversy, has induced Dr. Strauss to soften down his mythical theory of the life of Christ in various points, and to acknowledge the truth of several results arrived at by my historical inquiries."[136] (Actually Strauss's more moderate third edition reflects the influence of Neander and de Wette.) According to Neander, the writer of a life of Jesus must begin with the basic presupposition "that Jesus Christ is the Son of God in a sense which cannot be predicated of any human being,—the perfect image of the person of God in the form of that humanity that was estranged from him."[137] The balance of Neander's book is designed to provide historical support for this fundamental presupposition.

Neander accepts the accounts of the birth and early life of Jesus as factual. Since the incarnation represents a monumental imposition of the divine upon human history, the occurrence of lesser wonders is not surprising: the strange happenings which accompany the miraculous conception, the coming of the magi, the slaughter of the infants. Like Schleiermacher, Neander traces the growth of God-consciousness in Jesus. By the time he launches his public ministry, Jesus is certain of his messianic calling. Thus, "Jesus knew and testified to his Messiahship from the beginning . . . although he did not always proclaim it with equal openness, especially when there was risk of popular commotions from false and temporal conceptions of the Messiah on the part of the people."[138] To designate his Messiahship, Jesus borrowed the less popular title from Daniel and gave it his own meaning: "He called himself the 'Son of Man' because he had appeared as a man . . . because he had done such great

---

133. Augustus Neander, *The First Epistle of John, Practically Explained*, trans. H. C. Conant (New York: Sheldon, Blakeman & Co., 1856).

134. August Neander, *Das Leben Jesu Christi in seinem geschichtlichen Zusammenhang* (1837); Eng. trans.: *The Life of Jesus Christ: In Its Historical Connexion and Historical Developement*, trans. J. M'Clintock and C. E. Blumenthal, 3d ed. (New York: Harper & Brothers, 1850).

135. See pp. 250–55, below.

136. Neander, *Life of Jesus*, xxix.

137. Ibid., 3.

138. Ibid., 81.

things even for *human* nature . . . because he was to glorify that nature; because he was himself the realized ideal of humanity."[139]

Neander recognizes that the proclamation of the kingdom of God is the central theme of Jesus' teaching. Although the kingdom is essentially the spiritual communion of believers who share the consciousness of God, it is also a power working in the world which will eventually be fully realized in history. Jesus taught in two different localities (Galilee and Jerusalem) and by two different methods (parables and discourses). Although the Sermon on the Mount presents a collection of teachings, they were shaped into a unified whole. The original sermon included the material common to Matthew and Luke. For this material, Matthew's account is more original, but the editor of the Greek version of Matthew has added additional details.

Neander reflects thoughtfully on the miracles. Grounded in the omnipotence of God, the miracles transcend the laws of nature but do not contradict them. The miracles are the means by which the suprahistorical comes into history. Human evil has distorted the relationship of people to nature; the miracles restore it. The healing miracles, for example, overcome evil and return persons to health. What the simple Galileans called demon possession was in reality a psychological disorder. The cures, however, are real, and accomplished by Jesus' spiritual power. Neander refutes the notion that Jairus's daughter was only in a sleeplike trance, and he accepts the raising of Lazarus as factual. The Synoptics fail to report the latter miracle because it fits nowhere in their narrative. At Cana, Jesus has simply enhanced the power of natural forces: "He brought out of water, by his creative energy, a substance (wine), which is naturally the joint product of the growth of the vine, and of human labor, water being only one of the co-operating factors; thus substituted his creative power for the various natural and artificial processes."[140]

Throughout his reconstruction, Neander is heavily dependent on the Gospel of John. Just as he prefers John's chronology for the cleansing of the temple, so Neander follows John's implication that the last supper took place on the evening prior to the Passover. In regard to the Gethsemane events, Neander harmonizes. He thinks that Jesus, facing the coming tragedy, had vacillating moods: sometimes he engaged in agonizing struggle (as in the Synoptics); sometimes he displayed courageous confidence (as in John). Just as his birth was accompanied by heavenly portents, so the death of Jesus provoked strange happenings: an earthquake, darkness, the rending of the temple veil. Jesus had foreknowledge of his resurrec-

139. Ibid., 95.
140. Ibid., 167.

tion but did not clearly predict it to his disciples. The facticity of the resurrection is proved by the change in the behavior of Jesus' followers. The ascension must be accepted as historical, since it is the necessary means whereby the earthly existence of Jesus was transformed into the higher, spiritual realm.

> Thus the end of Christ's appearance on earth corresponds to its beginning. No link in its chain of supernatural facts can be lost without taking away its significance as a whole. Christianity rests upon these facts; stands or falls with them.[141]

Also important for NT research is Neander's reconstruction of the history of early Christianity. This is best seen in his *History of the Planting and Training of the Christian Church*.[142] For the investigation of this history, two types of sources are available: the epistles, and the Acts of the Apostles, the latter, probably written by a companion of Paul. The beginning of the church is another momentous event in which the power of God is imposed upon human history: "Next to the appearance of the Son of God himself on earth, this event most distinctly marked the commencement of that new divine life, which, proceeding from Him to all mankind, has since spread and operated through successive ages, and will continue to operate until its final object is attained, and the whole race is transformed into the image of Christ."[143] Little wonder, then, that supernatural manifestations accompanied the event of Pentecost: an earthquake, whirlwind, and flaming lights—external objectifications of what was essentially inward. The gift of speaking in tongues did not convey the power to translate the gospel into foreign languages; it was a phenomenon of ecstatic speech that gave expression to the experience of the Spirit.

Most important, Christianity was built on solid rock: Jesus was the Messiah, a fact proved by his resurrection. Along with the factual events at the church's beginning, history displays accompanying suprahistorical manifestations. Peter was able to cure a lame man, for he recognized that he had "a divine power that could go far beyond the common powers of man and of nature."[144] Affirming the special power that had been bestowed on Stephen, Neander observes, "Although what we say is disputed by persons occupying two opposite stand-points—those who in a rude and lifeless manner advocate the supernatural in Christianity, and those who deny

---

141. Ibid., 438.
142. August Neander, *Die Geschichte der Pflanzung und Leitung der christlichen Kirche durch die Apostel*, 2 vols. (Hamburg: F. Perthes, 1832–33); Eng. trans.: *History of the Planting and Training of the Christian Church by the Apostles*, trans. J. E. Ryland; rev. by E. G. Robinson (New York: Sheldon, 1865).
143. Neander, *History of the Planting*, 7.
144. Ibid., 39.

everything supernatural,—yet we cannot give up an idea which is of importance in relation to the development of Christianity from the beginning, namely, that the supernatural and the natural, the Divine and the human, always work together in harmony."[145]

Following the Acts account with unwavering credulity, Neander views Peter as an instigator of the gentile mission. He believes that in effecting the conversion of Cornelius, Peter was prompted by divine communication, although he is less than clear as to how this came about:

> The appearance of the angel may be considered as an objective event. . . . The Holy Scriptures teach us that occasional communications from a higher spiritual world to individuals used to occur in the history of mankind. . . . We need not, however, suppose any sensible appearance, for we do not know but that a higher spirit may communicate itself to men living in a world of sense, by an operation of the inward sense, so that this communication may appear under the form of a sensuous perception.[146]

In any case, Neander imagines that Peter's vision explains his original decision to eat with gentile converts in Antioch (Gal. 2:12). How Peter so quickly forgot the vision when he withdrew table fellowship from these same Gentiles is explained on the basis of Peter's pre-resurrection character—the rock turned again into sand!

Neander, of course, recognizes Paul as the main actor in the drama of the Christian expansion. In discussing Paul's conversion, Neander again combines the supernatural and historical: the event was inward, but it included external, objective manifestations. Neander's attempt to reconstruct Paul's first visit to Jerusalem after his conversion, like the effort to mix oil and water, is a confusing compromise: the visit was in private (Gal. 1:18-19) because of the Jews, but it also involved public communication with the Hellenistic Jews (Acts 9:29). In tracing the missionary activity of Paul, Neander follows the chronology of Acts. Conflicts with the data from the epistles, for example, the discrepancy in regard to the activity of Timothy (Acts 17:14; 18:5 versus 1 Thess. 3:2, 6), are hastily harmonized. As to the Corinthian factions, Neander believes there were four, although the Apollos party was similar to Paul's. The main trouble came from the Cephas group—the Judaizers—while the Christ party represented a contingent of Greek Christians, loyal directly to Christ. Neander believed baptism in the early church was practiced by immersion and administered to adult believers. Like conservatives before and after, Neander posited a second Roman imprisonment as necessary to explain the Pauline authorship of the Pastoral Epistles.

145. Ibid., 47.
146. Ibid., 72.

After a discussion of the missionary activity of Peter, James (the brother of the Lord), and John, Neander turns to the doctrine of the apostles. He believes the theology of the early Christians was flexible, not dogmatic, and that it took three forms: Pauline, Jacobean, and Johannine. Of these three, Pauline doctrine is the most important. The basic idea of Paul is righteousness—formerly conceived as external, now as internal. Neander sees humanity as alienated from God, but he rejects a rigid doctrine of original sin; rather, sin is the result of a free decision. Redemption comes through Christ, the representative of humanity who fully identified with humans in their suffering. Reconciliation results from God's activity.

> Therefore Paul never says, that God being hostile to men, became reconciled to them through Christ, but that men who were enemies of God became reconciled to him. . . . The obstacle exists on the side of men, and owing to this they do not receive the revelation of the love of God into their self-consciousness; and since by the redeeming work of Christ this obstacle is taken away, it is said of him that he has reconciled man to God, and made him an object of divine love.[147]

Human beings receive redemption by faith—by dying to the old and rising to the new life.

In Neander's opinion, Paul and James have different ways of presenting justification but are in fundamental agreement: "The great difference in their respective positions is, that while Paul fixes his attention principally on the objectively Divine, the ground of God's election, on which the confidence of man must rest: James, assuming the fact of this divine ground, concerns himself with the subjectively human, with what man must do on his part."[148] In discussing the theology of John, Neander is sensitive to the Johannine realized eschatology: "As, according to John's ideas, the future is already apprehended by faith as present, so the divine life in the present is viewed as the commencing point and germ of a creation that embraces eternity."[149] Indeed, Neander understands Johannine thought to be the culmination of early Christianity: "As, accordingly, James and Peter mark the gradual transition from spiritualized Judaism to the independent development of Christianity, as Paul represents the independent development of Christianity in opposition to Jewish conceptions, so the reconciling contemplative element of John forms the closing-point in the training of the apostolic church."[150]

Neander acknowledged that his was a *theologia pectoris*—a theology of

147. Ibid., 412.
148. Ibid., 502.
149. Ibid., 523.
150. Ibid., 530–31.

the heart. He made a valiant effort, too, to make it a theology of the head. His mastery of a huge amount of historical material is proof of his intellectual prowess. Also, in contrast to much of the static historiography of the day, Neander understood historical development as a dynamic process. Moreover, he interpreted that historical development according to a conscious theology of history that affirmed God's redemptive action in history, a *Heilsgeschichte*. Neander also attempted to overcome the conflict between the natural and the supernatural: miracles were not against nature but in harmony with it. But what is the character of that harmony? Had the identity of natural and supernatural in particular events erased the dialectic between God and the world? How, after all, does God work in history? Questions like these, crucial for Schleiermacher and his school, opened the discussion to answers drawn from Hegelian idealism.

SUMMARY

With Schleiermacher and his followers, NT research becomes more sophisticated. The old rationalism and historicism reach their limits in Paulus, and even Paulus is interested in things of the spirit. The concern with historical reconstruction and the methods that attain it continue, of course, and the critical results, such as doubts concerning the authorship of the Pastoral and Catholic Epistles, are mere variations on an older theme. De Wette and Neander simply represent the deviations to the left and right which are possible within the boundaries of the historical-critical method. More important is the question concerning the place of historical reconstruction as the foundation for faith, a question acutely articulated in relation to the study of Jesus. Lives of Jesus presented by the scholars of this chapter (Paulus, Schleiermacher, Neander), although distinctly different, all take Jesus to be in some sense a revelation of God and the ground of faith. Yet, in spite of the growing sophistication in historical methodology, a consensus regarding the sources for the reconstruction of the historical Jesus is lacking. Disagreement continues concerning the synoptic problem, and broad acceptance of the authenticity of John (ably defended by de Wette and Lücke) has not answered the question of the origin and reliability of the gospel tradition.

The complexity of these issues is further confounded by recognition of the depth of the hermeneutical problem by Schleiermacher and, to a lesser degree, by Lücke. From the new perspective, interpretation is not simply a matter of linguistics and grammar, but has to do with the nature of understanding; and historical research is not merely a matter of chronological reconstruction, but has to do with the psychological and religious experience of the writer and reader. At the same time, the call for a correlation between exegesis and theology (especially by Lücke) and the attempt to combine natural and supernatural—important for the continuing effort to understand the miracles and the resurrection—require a consideration of philosophical questions of magnitude. As the boy from Nazareth dialogued with the scribes in the temple, so Jesus would be questioned by the philosophers of nineteenth-century Europe.

8

The Influence of
Philosophical Idealism

In the early nineteenth century, theologians responded to challenges that the Enlightenment had addressed to Christianity. Among these challenges, the ideas of a mechanically ordered world and a rationally mediated religion had questioned belief in divine revelation and the vitality of personal faith. In answer, the neologians of the previous generation had attempted to combine the new and the old—the worldview of the Enlightenment and the biblical faith of the Reformation. But these thinkers offered no ontological ground to hold the conflicting ideologies together and, like the Israelites of Elijah's day, went limping between two opinions. Schleiermacher and his followers, especially de Wette, had turned inward, holding religious experience as the ontological key for understanding reality. For them, revelation and reason, faith and history, were united. Similarly, mediating theologians like Lücke and Neander had tried to harmonize the supernatural and the natural, subject and object, spirit and body—but with limited success. They did not command the intellectual imagination to weave the various conceptual strands into a unified pattern. That task was undertaken by one of the greatest minds of the nineteenth century, Georg Wilhelm Friedrich Hegel (1770–1831).

Influenced by Kant's concern with reason and the mind, Hegel saw the human spirit as a manifestation of the transcendent Absolute Spirit. This Absolute he could call Idea, Mind, Subject, or, to speak in theological language, God. According to Hegel, the Absolute Spirit is manifest in nature and is constantly unfolding itself in history. As it manifests itself, the Absolute is always encountering oppositions: the infinite against the finite, truth against error. Thus, the unfolding of the Absolute involves a dialectical process: the subject encounters the object and is reconciled into a new subject. From his earliest writings, Hegel had been preoccupied with religion. Religion was concerned with the relation of human spirits to the Divine Spirit. In Hegel's opinion, the absolute religion was Christianity, for Christianity affirmed the ongoing process of the Divine Spirit realizing itself in history. Moreover, the unity of divine and human, Spirit and body, infinite and finite, was realized in the idea of the God-man, a concept actualized in the historical Jesus. From this beginning point in Jesus, the unity of the Absolute Spirit and the human spirit continues in the life of the church.

Many theologians hailed Hegel as the new Moses who would lead them out of the Egypt of the old ways of thinking into a new intellectual promised land. Here was a philosopher who believed in God, Jesus Christ, and the superiority of Christianity—a prophet who could bring bread from heaven and water from the rock! Within Hegel's philosophy of religion, orthodox terms were articulated—Trinity, incarnation, and atonement— even though they were given obscure interpretations. Most important, Hegel's philosophy was comprehensive: it encompassed nature and history, reason and feeling, science and art. Just as eighteenth-century theologians had assumed the universal truth of a rational natural theology, the beneficiaries of Hegel's system could do their work under the benevolent shadow of a comprehensive metaphysical structure. Although some of the orthodox noted that Hegel's Absolute seemed different from Israel's Yahweh, and some suspected that the philosopher had pantheism up his sleeve, others believed they could enlist Hegel in support of their causes. If Jesus were the actualization of the God-man, surely that proved that he was fully divine and fully human. And if the Divine Spirit had actually entered into history, surely that confirmed the belief in the supernatural conception of Jesus and the miracles that accompanied his ministry. And surely the spiritual was actualized in the church, and surely the Spirit inspired the records of the church's life—all of this assuming an identification of the Spirit and its realization.

The scholars most fully influenced by Hegel, however, were anything but orthodox. D. F. Strauss, who classified himself as a left-wing Hegelian,[1] accepted Hegel's basic system but rejected the notion that the Absolute could be realized in one historical individual. Thus, he considered right-wing Hegelian Christology to be incompatible with the truth of Hegel's

---

1. Strauss divided the interpreters of Hegel into three classes: the right wing, which used Hegelianism to support orthodox religion and political conservatism; the left wing, which revolted against orthodoxy; and a middle-road, moderate group. The left wing has also been called the "young Hegelians" and has included such thinkers as Ludwig Feuerbach and Karl Marx. See David Friedrich Strauss, *In Defense of* My Life of Jesus *against the Hegelians*, trans. Marilyn Chapin Massey (Hamden, Conn.: Archon Books, 1983); and Lawrence S. Stepelevich, ed., *The Young Hegelians: An Anthology* (Cambridge: Cambridge University Press, 1983).

philosophy. Strauss's teacher, F. C. Baur, applied Hegel's thought to a reconstruction of the history of early Christianity. The life of the church, for Baur, displayed not a pristine realization of the Divine Spirit but a story of opposition and conflict—of the Spirit dialectically at work. Baur, a captivating teacher, inspired a group of disciples, the so-called Tübingen school, which included such brilliant minds as Eduard Zeller, Adolf Hilgenfeld, and the notorious Bruno Bauer. In response to the radical criticism of Strauss, Baur, and their friends, a host of scholars enlisted in the defense of traditional Christianity: Hengstenberg called for a return to orthodoxy; Tholuck exemplified a fervent neo-pietism; and Ewald advocated a mediating historicism. In some ways, the conflicts created by the Hegelians could be said to have set biblical studies back a half-century, but in any event, the impact of German idealism produced one of the most dramatic eras in the history of NT research.

DAVID FRIEDRICH STRAUSS (1808–1874) AND THE LIFE OF JESUS

Strauss's Life and Thought

Strauss's *Life of Jesus* was a theological bombshell. Created by a twenty-seven-year-old genius, this book was the most revolutionary religious document written since Luther's Ninety-Five Theses. Strauss himself, never noted for his modesty, considered it an "inspired book."[2] David Friedrich Strauss was born in Ludwigsburg, the summer residence of the Württemberg royalty. His father was a reluctant merchant who would rather have been a scholar. At the age of thirteen, young Fritz passed examinations in Latin, Greek, and Hebrew and entered the theological preparatory school at Blaubeuren, where his teachers included another rising genius, Ferdinand Christian Baur.[3] As fellow-students remembered him, Strauss was "a slender, fair youth with blond hair, delicate rather sharply cut features and clear blue eyes. . . . He was quiet and shy except with his close acquaintances, and very serious about his studies."[4]

From 1825 to 1829, Strauss studied at Tübingen. Among his professors

---

2. Cited in Edwina G. Lawler, *David Friedrich Strauss and His Critics: The Life of Jesus Debate in Early Nineteenth-Century German Journals* (New York, Berne, Frankfurt am Main: P. Lang, 1986), 18.

3. See Gotthold Müller, "Ferdinand Christian Baur und David Friedrich Strauss in Blaubeuren (1821–1825)," in *Glaube Geist Geschichte: Festschrift für Ernst Benz*, ed. G. Müller and W. Zeller (Leiden: E. J. Brill, 1967), 217–30.

4. Richard S. Cromwell, *David Friedrich Strauss and His Place in Modern Thought* (Fair Lawn, N.J.: R. E. Burdick, 1974), 21.

was J. C. Steudel, a hangover from the old Tübingen school.[5] Strauss said if Jesus Christ had studied with Steudel, he would have abandoned Christianity before he ever started it! On the other hand, Baur had moved to Tübingen, and Strauss was excited by his lectures on church history, the history of dogma, Acts, and 1 Corinthians. By reading Schleiermacher, Strauss was delivered from a temporary flight into mysticism. Later he participated in a study group which was devoted to the reading of Hegel. Strauss passed his examinations in 1830 at the head of his class. For some months he served as a pastor in Kleiningersheim near Ludwigsburg, where he sensed the difficulty of presenting new theological concepts to untutored believers. In 1831, Strauss became an instructor at the theological school at Maulbronn. He taught Hebrew, Latin, and history, and among his students was the brilliant Eduard Zeller.

Strauss had increasingly come under the spell of Hegel's philosophy and later in 1831 moved to Berlin to study with the master. Upon arrival, he had a cordial visit with Hegel and heard him lecture twice. Shortly thereafter, Strauss was talking with Schleiermacher, who remarked that Hegel had died suddenly the night before. Strauss, in a state of shock, exclaimed that Hegel had been the reason for his coming to Berlin. Schleiermacher was offended by the outburst and remained cool toward Strauss who, nevertheless, decided to stay in Berlin and even to attend Schleiermacher's lectures. More important, Strauss secured copies of Schleiermacher's lectures on the life of Jesus. Years later he wrote, "The truth is I found myself repelled by almost every aspect of these lectures."[6] Although repelled, Strauss was also inspired to undertake the study of the life of Jesus on his own.

In 1832, Strauss returned to Tübingen as an instructor at the theological *Stift*. After three semesters of lecturing, primarily on Hegel's philosophy, he devoted full time to writing his *Life of Jesus*, which appeared in 1835. The reaction was swift and drastic. The conservative members of the faculty were incensed that a theologian of this persuasion was aspiring to teach prospective ministers. Strauss was abruptly dismissed. He had been a popular lecturer, and the students threatened demonstrations, but Strauss dissuaded them. Expelled from the university, Strauss found employment as a teacher of classics in the gymnasium at Ludwigsburg. In 1839, the liberals in Zurich attempted to secure a chair for him at their university. Strauss, who had published the more moderate third edition of his *Life of*

---

5. Not to be confused with the Tübingen school of F. C. Baur, the old Tübingen school was founded by G. C. Storr (1746–1805) and was noted for its biblical supernaturalism and opposition to philosophical theologizing. See *New Schaff-Herzog Encyclopedia of Religious Knowledge*, s. v. "Tübingen School, the Older."

6. Strauss, *In Defense*, 6.

Jesus in 1838, was called by a close vote of Zurich's educational committee and confirmed by the town council. However, when word of the appointment became public, protest meetings and petitions were organized. With 156 congregations voting, 39,225 church members were against, and only 1,048 in favor of, Strauss's call. The embarrassed council withdrew the invitation and paid Strauss an annual stipend of one thousand francs for the rest of his life.

For much of the 1840s and 1850s Strauss withdrew from theological activity. He engaged in journalism, freelance writing, and the publishing of biographies. In 1842, he married Agnese Schebest, a temperamental opera singer. Strauss, who loved music, was even more temperamental, and the marriage was chaotic. Although two children were born, contention intensified, resulting in an inevitable separation. In 1848, Strauss became involved in politics. Actually, the revolutionaries of the time considered Strauss an ally: his radical interpretation of Jesus was used as ammunition against the political and ecclesiastical establishment.[7] Strauss favored the unification of the German states under Prussian hegemony, but he was defeated in his bid to represent Württemberg at the Frankfurt parliament. Later he was elected Ludwigsburg's representative to the Württemberg legislature, where he disappointed the liberals by moving resolutely to the right. Disillusioned with politics, Strauss resigned his position. In the 1860s, Strauss returned to theology. He published a favorable essay on Reimarus (1861),[8] his *Life of Jesus for the German People* (1864), and his *The Old Faith and the New* (1872). In these works, in contrast to his increasing social and political conservatism, Strauss moved further and further to the theological left. His attack on the miracles and the church was relentless, and his Hegelianism had turned into pantheism unashamed. Strauss died in 1873. His directions requested a simple service, without benefit of church or clergy.

Although Strauss's theological thought continued to evolve, his position at the time he wrote his *Life of Jesus* is disclosed in his two-volume *Glaubenslehre* (1840–41).[9] Written shortly after the Zurich fiasco, this massive work (almost fifteen hundred pages) expresses Strauss's left-wing reading of Hegel. An introduction deals with the relation of philosophy and theology, and the first section, labeled "Apologetik," discusses revelation

---

7. See Marilyn Chapin Massey, *Christ Unmasked: The Meaning of* The Life of Jesus *in German Politics* (Chapel Hill: University of North Carolina Press, 1983).

8. David Friedrich Strauss, "Hermann Samuel Reimarus and His Apology," in *Reimarus: Fragments*, ed. Charles H. Talbert, trans. R. S. Fraser (Philadelphia: Fortress Press, 1970), 44–57.

9. David Friedrich Strauss, *Die christliche Glaubenslehre in ihrer geschichtlichen Entwicklung und im Kampfe mit der modernen Wissenschaft dargestellt,* 2 vols. in 1 (Frankfurt am Main: Minerva, 1984).

and Scripture. There Strauss concludes that knowledgeable people do not need the traditional notion of revelation. "Therefore," he writes, "let the believer allow the intellectual to go his own way, and likewise the latter the former; we leave them their faith; they leave us our philosophy; and if the super-pious should succeed in shutting us out of their church, we will regard that as a gain."[10] In the second section, "Dogmatik," Strauss turns to the doctrine of God and, after abandoning traditional theism, embraces Hegel.

> [God] is the eternal movement of the Universal which continually makes itself subject, which first comes to objectivity and the true reality in the subject, and thereby absolves the subject into its being-in-itself. Since God in himself is the eternal personality itself, he has eternally allowed his Other, nature, to proceed out of himself, so as to return eternally to him as self-conscious Spirit.[11]

Also in this section, the historical Jesus is rejected as the realization of the Absolute, but the Christ of faith is affirmed as a symbol of the oneness of the divine and the human. All the rest of the traditional doctrines—original sin, sacrificial atonement, redemption—are jettisoned as so much excess cargo. For Strauss, the last enemy is eternal life: "For the other-worldly, in its form as the future, is above all the final enemy against which speculative criticism must battle, and where possible, overcome."[12]

As noted above, the study of Schleiermacher's lectures on the life of Jesus provided an impetus for Strauss's work. Strauss, of course, had to rely on student notebooks, since Schleiermacher's lectures were not published until 1864. At that time, Strauss responded with a caustic critique: *The Christ of Faith and the Jesus of History* (1865).[13] According to Strauss, the crucial question is clear: can Schleiermacher's identification of the Christ of faith as one with the historical Jesus survive critical scrutiny? A negative answer is already prompted, in Strauss's judgment, by Schleiermacher's faulty method, which had attempted to combine supernaturalism and rationalism.

> And if previous theologians were like the companions of Ulysses who stopped their ears against the Sirens of criticism, then Schleiermacher indeed kept his ears open, but had himself tied with cables to the mast of the Christian faith in order to sail past the dangerous island unharmed. His conduct is only half-free, and therefore also only half-scientific.[14]

---

10. Ibid. 1.356.
11. Ibid. 1.523–24.
12. Ibid. 2.739.
13. David Friedrich Strauss, *Der Christus des Glaubens und der Jesus der Geschichte: Eine Kritik des Schleiermacher'schen Lebens Jesu*, ed. Hans-Jürgen Geischer (Gütersloh: G. Mohn, 1971); Eng. trans.: *The Christ of Faith and the Jesus of History: A Critique of Schleiermacher's* Life of Jesus, trans. and ed. Leander E. Keck (Philadelphia: Fortress Press, 1977).
14. Strauss, *Christ of Faith*, 36–37.

The bulk of Strauss's critique proceeds to demonstrate that Schleiermacher's picture of Jesus as the sinless and infallible embodiment of religious consciousness is a theological fabrication. Schleiermacher, he argues, was aided in creating this fiction by his selection of the unreliable Fourth Gospel as his primary source. In perfect harmony with his Christology, Schleiermacher prefered the heroic Christ of John 12:27 to the agonizing Jesus of the Garden of Gethsemane. Schleiermacher was tempted by the rationalistic theory that Jesus' death was only apparent, and he accepted the ascension as a necessary means to explain Christ's transformation from natural to spiritual reality, involving, according to Strauss, "a pure disappearance, an act of becoming invisible."[15] In sum, Strauss believes that Schleiermacher's Christ, like the Jesus of the Fourth Gospel, is neither historical nor human. "Jesus," says Strauss, "is to be regarded as a person, as a great—and as far as I am concerned, the greatest—personality in the series of religious geniuses, but still only a man like others, and the Gospels are to be regarded as the oldest collections of the myths which were attached around the core of this personality."[16]

The Life of Jesus

Almost thirty years earlier, the publication of Strauss's own *Life of Jesus*[17] had provoked an immediate sensation. The book, like a two-edged sword, had a negative and positive thrust: negatively, it assailed rationalistic and supernatural interpretation; positively, it promoted Strauss's mythological method. F. C. Baur wondered why the book had caused such a fuss, since it did not seem to offer much that was new.[18] What Baur missed, however, was the ruthless way in which Strauss pursued his purpose—the clarity of his argument and the power of his rhetoric, lively with irony and ridicule. All of this is available to the English reader through the work of George Eliot (Mary Anne Evans) who at age twenty-three undertook the task of translation and went on to become one of the greatest novelists of her

---

15. Ibid., 157.

16. Ibid., 161.

17. David Friedrich Strauss, *Das Leben Jesu, kritisch bearbeitet,* 2 vols. (Tübingen: C. F. Osiander, 1835).

18. In a letter to his friend L. F. Heyd, dated 2 October 1836, Baur wrote, "In a certain sense, one can rightly say that the work actually contains nothing new; it simply pursues a path long ago struck out and followed to its natural end, draws the conclusions from premises set up long ago and collects together what had hitherto appeared only in an isolated way and lacking most of all the consistency of thinking which is the strength of the book" (cited in Horton Harris, *David Friedrich Strauss and His Theology* [Cambridge: Cambridge University Press, 1973], 87).

day.[19] Later, after visiting with his translator, Strauss wrote to a friend, "She is in her 30s, not pretty, but with an almost transparent face, full of expression, with even more feeling than spirit. Between a man and a lady who is his translator there always exists a mystical marriage."[20]

In the introduction, Strauss presents his understanding of myth. According to his definition, myth is "a narrative relating directly or indirectly to Jesus, which may be considered not as the expression of a fact, but as the product of an idea of his earliest followers."[21] Strauss identifies two kinds of myth: pure myths and historical myths. Pure myths are created by the use of messianic descriptions from the OT, and in response to the impressions made by the personal character and action of Jesus. Historical myths are legendary creations, informed by ancient stories, which have a basis in actual historical events. In general, Strauss tends to apply the term "myth" to supernatural happenings, so that myth is virtually identified as the unhistorical, as the fictitious. Whereas earlier scholars like Eichhorn and G. L. Bauer detected myths in isolated sections of the NT[22]—stories about visions and angels—Strauss applies the category to the whole gospel record: "In consistency with these opinions, this writer applies the notion of the mythus to the entire history of the life of Jesus; recognizes mythi or mythical embellishments in every portion, and ranges under the category of mythus not merely the miraculous occurrences during the infancy of Jesus, but those also of his public life; not merely the miracles operated on Jesus, but those wrought by him."[23] The criteria for identifying myth are negative and positive: negatively, myths include data that are irreconcilable with universal laws and reports that are contradictory; positively, myths can be recognized by their form (e.g., poetic expression) and content (e.g., stories about childless parents).

Strauss organizes the life of Jesus into three main periods: (1) birth and childhood, (2) public life, and (3) passion, death, and resurrection. In discussing the material from each section, Strauss repeatedly presents his main line of interpretation: the accounts describe supernatural events and

---

19. David Friedrich Strauss, *The Life of Jesus Critically Examined*, ed. Peter C. Hodgson, trans. George Eliot (Philadelphia: Fortress Press, 1972). The Eliot translation is based on the 4th edition of 1839–40. After the more moderate 3rd edition (1838) in which Strauss, for example, conceded more credibility to the Fourth Gospel (under the influence of the work of de Wette and Neander), the 4th edition returned essentially to the radical position of the 1st edition.

20. Cited in Harris, *Strauss and His Theology*, 233.

21. Strauss, *Life of Jesus*, 86.

22. See pp. 149–50, 188–89, above.

23. Strauss, *Life of Jesus*, 65.

thus are not historical; attempts to explain them by rationalistic methods are mistaken, even ridiculous; therefore, mythological interpretation is the only viable alternative. In regard to the birth narratives, Strauss's results are not surprising. The stories of the annunciation, the guiding star, and the massacre of the children are unhistorical. The idea of conception without male participation is clearly mythical, reflecting both the ancient notion that great men have supernatural births and the OT belief that the Messiah would be the son of God.

In regard to the public life of Jesus, Strauss discovers much that must be classified as myth. The story of the temptation, for example, is a mythic creation that makes use of the symbolic numbers 40 and 3 and is based on the OT belief in Satan as the tempter. In presenting the transfiguration narrative as myth, Strauss makes a case for the superiority of his method:

> This example may serve to show with peculiar clearness, how the natural system of interpretation, while it seeks to preserve the historical certainty of the narratives, loses their ideal truth—sacrifices the essence to the form: whereas the mythical interpretation, by renouncing the historical body of such narratives, rescues and preserves the idea which resides in them, and which alone constitutes their vitality and spirit.[24]

According to Strauss's interpretation, the myth of the transfiguration has its source in the radiant face of Moses and the Jewish expectation of Elijah; it expresses its meaning in the picture of Jesus conversing with his forerunners and fulfilling the hope for the glorious Messiah.

The mythical is most obvious in the miracle stories. Strauss concedes that some healings might have been facilitated by natural forces.

> Thus in the nature of things there is nothing to prevent the admission, that Jesus cured many persons who suffered from supposed demoniacal insanity or nervous disorder, in a psychical manner, by the ascendancy of his manner and words. . . . But while granting the possibility of many cures, it is evident that in this field the legend has not been idle, but has confounded the easier cases, which alone could be cured psychologically, with the most difficult and complicated, to which such a treatment was totally inapplicable.[25]

According to Strauss, the ongoing myth-making tradition tends to heighten the miraculous:

> We have hitherto been ascending a ladder of miracles; first, cures of mental disorders, then, of all kinds of bodily maladies, in which, however, the organization of the sufferer was not so injured as to cause the cessation of consciousness and life; and now, the revivification of bodies, from which life

24. Ibid., 546.
25. Ibid., 436.

has actually departed. This progression in the marvelous is, at the same time, a gradation in inconceivability.[26]

The myth and miracle reach a high point in the story of the raising of Lazarus. "We . . . distinctly declare that we regard the history of the resurrection of Lazarus, not only as in the highest degree improbable in itself, but also destitute of external evidence; and this whole chapter [John 11], in connection with those previously examined, as an indication of the unauthenticity of the fourth gospel."[27] Strauss's use of ridicule to refute the miraculous is apparent in his description of the feeding of the five thousand according to the notion that the miracle occurred in the act of distribution: "Loaves, which in the hands of the distributors expand like wetted sponges,—broiled fish, in which the severed parts are replaced instantaneously, as in the living crab gradually,—plainly belong to quite another domain than that of reality."[28]

In regard to the passion, death, and resurrection, Strauss finds the narratives crammed with myth. For instance, the belief that Jesus predicted his resurrection is a model of the myth-making process.

Thus the foreknowledge, as well as the prediction of the resurrection, was attributed to Jesus only after the issue; and in fact, it was an easy matter . . . for the disciples and the authors of the New Testament to discover in the Old, types and prophecies of the resurrection. Not that they did this with the crafty design . . . but as he who has looked at the sun, long sees its image wherever he may turn his gaze; so they, blinded by their enthusiasm for the new Messiah, saw him on every page of the only book they read, the Old Testament, and in the conviction that Jesus was the Messiah, founded in the genuine feeling that he had satisfied their deepest need . . . they laid hold on supports which have long been broken, and which can no longer be made tenable by the most zealous efforts of an exegesis which is behind the age.[29]

The actual accounts of the resurrection are filled with supernatural happenings and irreconcilable contradictions. The variation in the number and behavior of angels, for example, inspires Strauss to ridicule reminiscent of the deists:

What a strange playing of hide and seek must there have been on the part of the angels, according to the harmonistic combination of these narratives! First only one shows himself to one group of women, to another group two show themselves; both forthwith conceal themselves from the disciples; but after their departure both again become visible.[30]

26. Ibid., 486.
27. Ibid., 494.
28. Ibid., 513.
29. Ibid., 582.
30. Ibid., 712.

In his concluding dissertation, Strauss is aware of the destructive impact of his work. "The results of the inquiry which we have now brought to a close, have apparently annihilated the greatest and most valuable part of that which the Christian has been wont to believe concerning his Saviour Jesus."[31] As to the historical figure who emerges from the debris of Strauss's bombardment, "Jesus can have been nothing more than a person, highly distinguished indeed, but subject to the limitations inevitable to all that is mortal."[32] Such an individual person cannot be a unique and perfect expression of Absolute, but only a symbolic reflection of the larger divine-human unity.

> In an individual, a God-man, the properties and functions which the church ascribes to Christ contradict themselves; in the race, they perfectly agree. Humanity is the union of the two natures—God become man, the infinite manifesting itself in the finite, and the finite spirit remembering its infinitude; it is the child of the visible Mother and the invisible Father, Nature and Spirit; it is the worker of miracles, in so far as in the course of human history the spirit more and more completely subjugates nature; . . . it is the sinless existence, for the course of its development is a blameless one. . . . It is Humanity that dies, rises and ascends to heaven, for from the negation of its phenomenal life there ever proceeds a higher spiritual life; from the suppression of its mortality as a personal, national, and terrestrial spirit, arises its union with the infinite spirit of the heavens.[33]

Remembering his days in the parish, Strauss suggests that pastors have four possible responses: (1) they can confront the church with the new understanding; (2) they can accede to the old views of the church; (3) they can leave the ministry and perhaps become theological professors; or (4) they can gradually lead their parishioners from the literal and supernatural meaning to the higher, spiritual understanding. Many people thought there was another alternative: denounce D. F. Strauss! One Pietist, giving numerical value to letters, discerned that the name "Strauss" equaled 666—the mark of the beast.[34]

After Strauss's dismissal from Tübingen, other theologians joined the faculty conservatives in opposing him. One of the most judicious responses came from Strauss's teacher, F. C. Baur, the only faculty member who did not vote against him. On the one hand, Baur could hardly oppose Strauss,

---

31. Ibid., 757.
32. Ibid., 773.
33. Ibid., 780. Strauss believed this was the implication of Hegel's position, but actually Hegel maintained both the concrete actualization of the divine in Jesus and the idea of the larger divine-human unity. See Peter C. Hodgson, "Hegel's Christology: Shifting Nuances in the Berlin Lectures," *Journal of the American Academy of Religion* 53 (1985): 23–40.
34. See Harris, *Strauss and His Theology,* 67.

because he had been his teacher and agreed with much that he said. On the other hand, Baur could not openly defend Strauss without endangering his own position, and throughout his career Baur continued to suffer from guilt by association. Fundamentally, Baur supported the right and freedom of criticism. He believed, however, that Strauss's treatment of Jesus was harsh, and his criticism excessively negative: "In addition to the repeatedly offending coldness, especially toward the Person of Jesus, what I most of all object to in the book is the far too negative criticism."[35] For all his own skepticism, Baur believed the gospel accounts contained more history than Strauss was willing to acknowledge. In particular, Baur believed it difficult to explain the rise of the resurrection faith apart from the impact of the historical Jesus. "If Jesus in his whole appearance was not more than results from this [Strauss's] investigation, then it remains all the more puzzling how the conviction of the disciples, that he *must* have risen from the dead, could have developed."[36] Most important for NT research, Baur argued that Strauss had not engaged in an extensive analysis of the gospel sources. Although Strauss was stung by Baur's criticism, he continued to revere his teacher. Shortly before Baur's death, Strauss wrote to him, "While you in your writings and in your scientific school have established a mighty fortress, the flat land of theology has sunk into a condition of incredible degeneration."[37] Compared with other theologians, "You appear as a watchman among the dreamers, as a sober man among the drunken, as a man among boys, a giant among dwarfs."[38]

Although devoted to Baur, Strauss did not take the criticisms from his opponents lying down. In 1836 and 1837, he published a three-part *Defense of My Life of Jesus.*[39] In the first two parts, Strauss counters the attacks of conservatives like Steudel, who had referred to Strauss as the anti-Christ, and Eschenmayer, who had likened Strauss to Judas Iscariot. The third part includes a response to the Hegelians, especially those on the right, who saw in Jesus the unique realization of the Absolute.[40] "Whether this unification of the divine and the human nature actually took place in Christ," says Strauss, "can be decided only by historians, not philosophers."[41]

35. Cited in ibid., 87.
36. Ibid., 87–88.
37. Ibid., 108.
38. Ibid., 109.
39. David Friedrich Strauss, *Streitschriften zur Vertheidigung meiner Schrift über das Leben Jesu und zur Charakteristik der gegenwärtigen Theologie* (Tübingen: C. F. Osiander, 1841); Eng. trans.: *In Defense of My* Life of Jesus *against the Hegelians* (see p. 245 n. 1, above).
40. Strauss, *In Defense.*
41. Ibid., 18.

Strauss's Later Theological Writings

After a lengthy absence from the theological arena, Strauss reentered the fray with the publication of his *The Life of Jesus for the People* (1864).[42] What he hoped to do was to write "a book as suitable for Germany as Renan's is for France."[43] The fundamental question had not changed: "What we especially want to know is this: is the Gospel history true and reliable as a whole and in its details, or is it not?"[44] Strauss presumes the answer in his introduction: "So long as the Gospels are accepted as strictly historical, no historical view of the Life of Jesus is really possible."[45] Prodded by Baur's criticism, Strauss attends to the problem of the sources. He concludes, with Baur, that Matthew is the earliest Gospel, Mark is a combination of Matthew and Luke, and John is a second-century composition of little historical worth. "In the presence of this Gospel [John], it was incumbent upon criticism either to break in pieces all her weapons, and lay them at the feet of her antagonist, or force it to disavow all claim to historical validity."[46] For Strauss, however, the question of sources is not as important as the question of miracle, and on the latter issue, Strauss has simply solidified his earlier stance. He asserts that "there are no instances of events demonstrably contradicting the laws of Nature,"[47] and sets out to demonstrate "that in the person and acts of Jesus no supernaturalism shall be suffered to remain."[48] After all the mythological Christology has been stripped away from the gospel story, only a shadow of the historical Jesus remains, and "it becomes a very doubtful question whether, if Jesus had returned about the time of the destruction of Jerusalem, he would have recognized himself again in the Christ who was at that time being preached in the Churches."[49] When all the dust has settled, Strauss looks back on his forty years of labor on the life of Jesus with a sense of accomplishment.

> Therefore the critic is convinced that he is committing no offence against what is sacred, nay rather that he is doing a good and necessary work, when he sweeps away all that makes Jesus a supernatural Being, as well meant and perhaps even at first sight beneficial, but in the long run mischievous and now absolutely destructive, restores, as well as may be, the image of the historical Jesus in its simply human features, but refers mankind for salvation to the ideal Christ, to that moral pattern in which the historical Jesus

42. David Friedrich Strauss, *The Life of Jesus for the People*, 2d ed., 2 vols. (London: Williams & Norgate, 1879).
43. Ibid. 1.xviii.
44. Ibid. 1.xi.
45. Ibid. 1.47.
46. Ibid. 1.141.
47. Ibid. 1.200.
48. Ibid. 1.xii.
49. Ibid. 2.434.

did indeed first bring to light many principal features, but which as an elementary principle as much belongs to the general endowment of our kind, as its improvement and perfection can only be the problem and the work of mankind in general.[50]

A year before his death, Strauss produced a sort of theological last will and testament under the title *The Old Faith and the New*[51] As a sign of Strauss's lingering popularity, the book went through six printings within the first six months. The task of the book is twofold: "first, to expound our position towards the old creed, and then the fundamental principles of that new Cosmic conception which we acknowledge as ours."[52] In performance of this task, Strauss raises and answers four questions. (1) Are we still Christians? Answer: No, because our knowledge of Jesus is fragmentary, and "what we do know of him indicates a person of fantastic fanaticism."[53] (2) Have we still a religion? Answer: It depends on definition; we no longer have faith in a personal God, but we believe in the cosmic Absolute—"the impersonal but person-shaping All."[54] (3) What is our understanding of the universe? Answer: We hold the latest conceptions of modern science, including Darwin's theory of evolution. (4) How should we order our life? Answer: We acknowledge the moral ideas which have evolved in the history of humanity. In two appendices, Strauss offers high praise to poets and composers—artists like Schiller and Mozart, whose perception of truth transcends the insight of philosophers and theologians.

In many ways Strauss appears as a tragic figure: a genius who suffered bitter hostility, domestic disappointment, and exile from his beloved country—the academic world. Yet, Strauss's struggle called attention to the cause of academic and theological freedom, and his own negative criticism encouraged a critical response on the part of others. To be sure, some scholars exploited the assumption that anything Strauss opposed had to be good, but others were driven to a vigorous study of the Christian tradition and its earliest sources. The synoptic problem took on a new seriousness, and the Gospel of John became the focus of rigorous research. Strauss's mythological method fostered a concern for hermeneutics and exegesis, even though his understanding of myth betrayed a confusion between content and form[55] and his perception of myth as a literary

---

50. Ibid. 2.439.
51. David Friedrich Strauss, *Der alte und der neue Glaube: Ein Bekenntniss* (Leipzig: S. Hirzel, 1872); Eng. trans.: *The Old Faith and the New: A Confession*, trans. Mathilde Blind (New York: Henry Holt & Co, 1874).
52. Strauss, *The Old Faith*, 11.
53. Ibid., xxvi.
54. Ibid., 169.
55. See Hans W. Frei, *The Eclipse of Biblical Narrative: A Study in Eighteenth- and Nineteenth-Century Hermeneutics* (New Haven and London: Yale University Press, 1974), 267–81.

expression was not fully developed. In Strauss's program, historical criticism and constructive theology worked hand in hand: radical criticism demolished the old, and Hegelian philosophy provided the blueprint for the new. The resulting schism between the Jesus of history and the Christ of faith would continue to disturb Christianity, a religion that affirmed that historical revelation belonged to its essence.

THE RECONSTRUCTION
OF EARLY CHRISTIAN HISTORY:
FERDINAND CHRISTIAN BAUR (1792–1860)

Honored as the greatest church historian of the nineteenth century, Ferdinand Christian Baur was also the most important NT scholar of his time. Baur was born in Schmiden, near Stuttgart, the son of a clergyman who taught him Greek, Hebrew, and Latin. He studied at the seminary in Blaubeuren, where he only ranked forty-sixth in his class. Although he made marks of "very good" in Latin and rhetoric, his grade in history was merely "good." After two more years of study at Maulbronn, Baur entered the University of Tübingen, where the theological faculty was dominated by conservatives. Upon his graduation, he served for two years as a small-town pastor.

Baur began his teaching career at Blaubeuren. In 1826, he was called to the faculty at Tübingen over the protest of the orthodox but with the support of 124 students who had signed a petition on his behalf. At Tübingen, Baur taught NT exegesis, Christian ethics, church history, and history of dogma. He was not a dynamic teacher but was respected for his mastery of the material. Later in his career, Baur was proposed for faculty positions at Berlin (where he was opposed by Hengstenberg) and Halle (where he was opposed by Tholuck). In regard to the opposition at Halle, Baur registered a protest with Tholuck:

> How can it escape your notice, how one-sided, how subjective, how self-complacent it is to separate all theologians into constructive and destructive categories? . . . If one cannot build without clearing away all the rubble from the ground on which alone one can build, then those who demolish and cart away the rubble also belong to the builders.[56]

In any event, Baur stayed at Tübingen, where he survived the attacks of his more conservative colleagues. Their cause was enhanced by the arrival

---

56. Cited in Horton Harris, *The Tübingen School* (Oxford: Clarendon, 1975), 34; reprinted as *The Tübingen School: A Historical and Theological Investigation of the School of F. C. Baur* (Grand Rapids: Baker, 1990).

of Heinrich Ewald (1848), who had recently been dismissed from Göttingen.[57] Ewald, who thrived on controversy, had joined the Tübingen faculty but not the Tübingen school. "Could one imagine," he wrote, "anything worse than this Tübingen School, which has been hatched out during the last fifteen to twenty years, with Dr. Baur at its head, anything more pernicious than the overturning and destruction of all intellectual and moral life?"[58]

Baur was an unrepentant academician. His brother-in-law wrote, "Of all the men I ever met Baur was the least wordly-wise, the least experienced or even capable of judgement in the practical issues of daily living, a true child in everyday life."[59] On scholarly matters, however, Baur was a tireless worker. His son-in-law, Eduard Zeller, described Baur's daily routine: "Summer and winter he arose at 4 a.m. and in winter he usually worked for a few hours in the unheated room out of consideration for the servants, even though—as often happened—on especially cold nights the ink froze; and thereafter the regular midday or evening walk was generally the single long interruption in the day's academic work."[60] Baur, however, was not confined to the study or the classroom; he preached regularly at the university church. As he said, "I am not merely a teacher of theology, but also a preacher."[61] Baur died in 1860 of a heart attack, recognized, in the words of Adolf Hilgenfeld, as "a grand and noble man of theological science."[62]

Baur's Theological Work

Above all, Baur was a theologian. Peter Hodgson has written, "Baur's greatness consisted in his unequivocal recognition of the radically historical nature of the Christian Church and Christian faith."[63] With Baur, theology is absorbed into history; theology is *historical* theology. History is the account of God's dealing with humanity, the self-expression of God as Absolute Spirit in the unfolding process of history. God lives in history, and history is the life of God. Thus, Baur understands history from the perspective of German idealism. He also insists that history must be understood by means of historical criticism. Historical criticism can estab-

---

57. See below, p. 287.
58. Cited in Harris, *Tübingen School*, 45.
59. Ibid., 15.
60. Ibid., 51.
61. Cited in Peter C. Hodgson, *The Formation of Historical Theology: A Study of Ferdinand Christian Baur* (New York: Harper & Row, 1966), 19.
62. Cited in Harris, *Tübingen School*, 53.
63. Hodgson, *Formation of Historical Theology*, 1.

lish the credibility of Christianity and explicate Christian truth. In the spirit of Hegel, Baur declares that the reconciliation of the divine and human takes place in history—in the particular manifestation of the God-man in Jesus of Nazareth.[64]

Christology, therefore, is crucial to Baur's theology, and, for Baur, Christology begins with the historical Jesus: "Whether the person of Jesus of Nazareth really possesses the attributes which belong to the established concept of the Redeemer is in fact a purely historical question, which can be answered only through an historical investigation of the literary sources of the Gospel stories."[65] Baur attempts to bridge the chasm between the Christ of faith and the Jesus of history by asserting that God acts in Jesus and that faith is a response to the historical Jesus. The historical revelation in Jesus makes the response of faith possible, and the union of the divine and human in him is a historical manifestation which escapes the threat of dualism and docetism. According to Hodgson, Baur "agrees with Strauss that Jesus of Nazareth cannot be demonstrated *speculatively* to be the God-man of faith, but at the same time he argues historically-critically that Jesus is in fact the original and authoritative exemplification of God-manhood."[66]

In methodology, Baur correlates a philosophy of history and an objective study of the data; fact and interpretation must work together in a continuous dialectical relationship. On the one hand, Baur rejects a supernaturalism in which God is thought to intervene—a divine interruption which precludes the understanding of history as process. On the other hand, he opposes a pure rationalism in which history is secularized, a view which focuses on isolated events and ignores the ongoing movement of God's manifestation in history. For the understanding of this divine process in history, the empirical data are important—but always in relation to the whole process. Although miracle as a supernatural event that interrupts the natural order is not possible, the Divine Spirit does work through the natural processes, and the history of Jesus has a miraculous character. In analyzing the documentary sources of that history, Baur employs his famous "tendency criticism," a method that views each literary composition in the light of its theological intention.

Given Baur's work schedule, it is not surprising that he sired a multitude of publications.[67] Some of his earliest writings are in the area of

---

64. See Hodgson, "Hegel's Christology," 23–40.
65. Cited in Hodgson, *Formation of Historical Theology*, 50.
66. Ibid., 73.
67. Some of Baur's major works are available in a new edition: *Ausgewählte Werke in Einzelausgaben*, ed. Klaus Scholder, 5 vols. (Stuttgart-Bad Cannstatt: F. Frommann, 1963–75).

philosophy of religion. For instance, his *Symbolik und Mythologie* (1824–25) shows the influence of Schleiermacher, Schelling, and Fichte—but not Hegel. Hegel's influence is apparent later in, for example, *Die christliche Gnosis* (1835). In the area of history of doctrine, Baur wrote historical investigations of the doctrine of reconciliation and the doctrine of the Trinity. He produced a handbook on the history of doctrine, and his lectures on the history of Christian dogmatics appeared after his death. In 1852, Baur published *Die Epochen der kirchlichen Geschichtschreibung*,[68] and his monumental five-volume *Geschichte der christlichen Kirche* (1853–62)[69] covered the history of the church from its beginning until the nineteenth century.

In the area of NT research, Baur's earliest works are prophetic of his later writings. His discussion of "The Christ-Party in the Corinthian Church" (1831)[70] presents his programmatic understanding of the conflict between Pauline and Petrine Christianity in the early church. According to Baur, there were not four factions in Corinth but only two: the Pauline group (the followers of Paul and Apollos) and the Judaizers (the parties of Cephas and Christ). In *The So-Called Pastoral Epistles of Paul* (1835),[71] Baur rejects Pauline authorship and locates 1 and 2 Timothy and Titus in mid-second century. These epistles originate in Rome, oppose a Marcionite Gnosticism, and betray a hierarchical tendency. Baur's major NT work is his *Paul the Apostle of Jesus Christ* (1845).[72] Also important is his *Critical Investigations of the Canonical Gospels* (1847),[73] which was followed in 1851 by his book on the Gospel of Mark.[74] After his death, Baur's lectures on NT theology were published.[75]

---

68. Eng. trans.: F. C. Baur, *On the Writing of Church History*, ed. and trans. Peter C. Hodgson (New York: Oxford University Press, 1968).

69. Volume 1 appeared in Eng. trans.: *The Church History of the First Three Centuries*, trans. Allan Menzies, 3d ed., 2 vols. (London: Williams & Norgate, 1878).

70. Ferdinand Christian Baur, "Die Christuspartei in der korinthischen Gemeinde, der Gegensatz des petrinischen und paulinischen Christenthums in der alten Kirche, der Apostel Petrus in Rome," in idem, *Ausgewählte Werke* 1.1-146.

71. Ferdinand Christian Baur, *Die sogenannten Pastoralbriefe des Apostels Paulus aufs neue kritisch untersucht* (Stuttgart and Tübingen, J. G. Cotta, 1835).

72. Ferdinand Christian Baur, *Paulus, der Apostel Jesu Christi. Sein Leben und Wirken, seine Briefe und seine Lehre: Ein Beitrag zu einer kritischen Geschichte des Urchristenthums*, 2d ed., ed. Eduard Zeller, 2 vols. (Leipzig: Fues, 1866); Eng. trans.: *Paul the Apostle of Jesus Christ, His Life and Work, His Epistles and His Doctrine: A Contribution to a Critical History of Primitive Christianity*, trans. A. Menzies, 2d ed., 2 vols. (London: Williams & Norgate, 1876). For a thoughtful summary and analysis, see Robert Morgan, "Biblical Classics: II. F. C. Baur: Paul," *Expository Times* 90 (1978): 4–10.

73. Ferdinand Christian Baur, *Kritische Untersuchungen über die kanonischen Evangelien, ihr Verhältniss zu einander, ihren Charakter und Ursprung* (Tübingen, L. F. Fues, 1847).

74. Ferdinand Christian Baur, *Das Markusevangelium nach seinem Ursprung und Charakter. Nebst einem Anhang über das Evangelium Marcion's* (Tübingen: L. F. Fues, 1851).

75. Ferdinand Christian Baur, *Vorlesungen über neutestamentliche Theologie*, ed. F. F. Baur (Leipzig: Fues, 1864). For a summary and evaluation, see Robert Morgan, "F. C. Baur's Lectures on New Testament Theology," *Expository Times* 88 (1977): 202–6.

Early Christianity:
Jesus and Christian Origins

Baur's analysis of NT literature is related to his reconstruction of the history of early Christianity. Indeed, his argument tends to be circular: NT documents are used to reconstruct early Christian history; the reconstruction of early Christian history provides the framework for the assessment of NT documents. This hermeneutical circle functions in correlation with Baur's tendency criticism: the individual NT documents reveal the decisive tendencies that determine the developing history; the developing history provides the occasion for the expression of the various tendencies. In any case, an appropriate way to survey Baur's contribution to the history of research is to present his NT studies within the framework of his reconstruction of early Christianity as seen in the first volume of his history of the church, *The Church History of the First Three Centuries.*

The first section of Baur's early church history focuses on Christian origins and Jesus. According to Baur, Christianity is the absolute religion, superior to all others because of its spirituality. The point of departure for understanding Christianity is Jesus, "the founder of a new religion."[76]

> Is it possible to speak in any real sense of the essence and contents of Christianity without making the person of its founder the main object of our consideration? Must we not recognize the peculiar character of Christianity as consisting in this, that whatever it is, it is simply an account of the person of its founder?[77]

The teachings of Jesus emphasize righteousness as the condition for entry into the kingdom of God—a spiritual reality realized on earth. As son of man, Jesus shares the common humanity of all people. As son of God, he enjoys a unique ethical relation to God as father. Jesus' oneness with God is expressed in his understanding of Messiahship. At his death, all the particularity of Jewish messianism is destroyed, and with the resurrection the spirit of Jesus becomes available to all humanity. The resurrection itself eludes the grasp of the historian, but the resurrection faith is the foundation of the church.

> The question as to the nature and the reality of the resurrection lies outside the sphere of historical inquiry. History must be content with the simple fact, that in the faith of the disciples the resurrection of Jesus came to be regarded as a solid and unquestionable fact. It was in this faith that Christianity acquired a firm basis for its historical development. What history

---

76. Baur, *Neutestamentliche Theologie,* 45.
77. Baur, *Church History of the First Three Centuries* 1.23.

requires as the necessary antecedent of all that is to follow, is not so much the fact of the resurrection of Jesus, as the belief that it was a fact.[78]

Early Christianity:
Paul versus Jewish Christianity

Baur orders the history of the church according to three chronological periods. The first deals with the conflict between Paul and Judaism and comprises the events from the beginning to 70 C.E. The major sources for investigating this era are the authentic letters of Paul and the book of Revelation. In the introduction to his masterful work on Paul, Baur remarks that he intends to present a historical-critical investigation of Paul just as Strauss had done for the life of Jesus. As to sources, Baur insists that the epistles are primary, although his presentation of the career of the apostle follows the narrative of Acts, albeit with a very critical eye. Prior to Paul, the most important events reported in Acts pertain to the activity of Stephen. In the narrative about Stephen, the split within the church between the Hellenists and the Hebrews is recounted, a split which forebodes the larger conflict between Paul and the Judaizers.

According to Baur, Paul's conversion is an inward, spiritual experience: "The strange brightness, surpassing that of the sun at mid-day, that suddenly shone round the Apostle and his companions, is accordingly nothing but the symbolical and mythical expression of the certainty of the real and immediate presence of the glorified and transfigured Jesus."[79] Almost as if Paul had been reading Hegel, "The principle which takes possession of his consciousness is now the immanent principle of his own self-consciousness; he knows himself free from everything by which he was formerly constrained; he is conscious of his own independence and autonomy."[80] On the basis of this experience, Paul becomes the missioner of a universal faith. Baur's presentation of the first missionary journey notes the tendency of Acts to present Peter and Paul in parallel. The story of the healing of the lame man at Lystra (Acts 14:8-10) encourages Baur to discuss the question of miracles. Like Schleiermacher, he prefers to see the work of God in the natural order rather than in the disruption of that order, but he concludes that each miraculous incident requires a critical investigation.

The accounts of the Jerusalem conference are of decisive importance for Baur. He believes Acts 15 and Galatians 2 describe the same meeting,

---

78. Ibid. 1.42.
79. Baur, *Paul the Apostle of Jesus Christ* 1.70.
80. Ibid. 2.271–72.

but he notes that the two accounts are drastically different. According to Galatians, the dispute is between Paul and the Jerusalem apostles. According to Acts, the opponents of Paul are a third party: converts from the Pharisees, introduced by the author of Acts in order to conceal the real Pauline-Petrine conflict. Historically, the meeting resulted in two gospels, two spheres of mission, and a continuing battle between Jewish particularity and Pauline universalism. After the account of the Jerusalem meeting, the narrative of Acts includes considerable unhistorical material: the legendary escape from prison at Philippi; incredible miracles at Ephesus in which Paul parallels the earlier deeds of Peter; and the farewell speech at Miletus which includes prophecy after the events.

According to Baur, the traditions about the end of Paul's career undergo remarkable development. The author of Acts, in presenting Paul's arrest in Jerusalem, is caught in a tension of his own devising. On the one hand, he has presented Paul as a loyal Jew—attending the Jewish festivals, circumcising Timothy, taking a Nazarite vow. On the other hand, Paul is constantly facing opposition from the Jews, and he is finally captured and imprisoned by them. The author of Acts, of course, is engaged in his tendency of harmonizing, while, in actuality, Paul was opposed by Jewish Christians as well as by Jews. Apart from Acts, an anti-Pauline tradition has been developing in which Paul is opposed as a Gentile who attacks the law and eventually is identified with the arch-heretic, Simon Magus. The harmonizing tradition, on the other hand, presents Paul and Peter in opposition to Simon and eventually depicts the two apostles meeting in Corinth to travel together to Rome to share a common martyrdom. Finally, Peter is presented as the founder of the church of Rome—a leader of universal Christianity, superior to Paul. Baur's concluding comment on myth and history is instructive:

> So considered, and taken for what they really are, these legends possess, notwithstanding the unhistorical nature of their contents, a true historical value. They are living pictures of the age, its motives and its aims. They certainly show, in a striking manner, how seriously history is changed, when not only is legend treated as history, but when, in order to eke out the connection between legends which refuse to fit into each other, new facts are invented and added to the unhistorical facts already rashly received.[81]

The second part of Baur's *Paul* analyzes the Pauline epistles. Most important, Baur believes that only four of the letters attributed to Paul truly represent the historical situation of the apostolic period and the authentic position of the apostle: Galatians, 1 and 2 Corinthians, and Romans. These letters reflect the battle between Paul and his Judaizing

81. Ibid. 1.241.

opponents, although the conflict undergoes development. Galatians is provoked by the arrival of opponents from outside, and, in the argument, Paul opposes not only Judaizing Christians but Judaism. In the Corinthian correspondence the dispute has moved beyond the concern with the law and circumcision to the question of apostolic authority; the dispute becomes bitter with the writing of 2 Corinthians. Romans presents the complete system of Pauline thought wherein Christian universalism overwhelms the particularism of Judaism. "The Apostle aims at refuting Jewish particularism so thoroughly and radically," says Baur, "that it shall appear to the age to have been plucked up by the very roots."[82] From this perspective, Romans 9–11 constitutes the heart of the epistle's argument, rather than a secondary theme or appendix. Baur, like Semler before him, believes Romans 15 and 16 do not belong to the original letter. Added by a later Paulinist, these chapters, according to Baur, attempt to mollify Paul's anti-Judaism for the sake of reconciliation between Pauline and Jewish Christianity. Romans 15, for example, presents Paul as looking beyond Rome to a mission to Spain, so that Rome can remain in the sphere of Petrine influence. Romans 16, on the other hand, lists close associates of Paul who played an important role in the original Roman church, so that Pauline Christianity can also be affirmed at Rome.

The third section of Baur's *Paul* investigates the apostle's doctrinal system, a subject further explicated in the second section of the *Lectures on New Testament Theology.* Actually the two works display slightly different emphases. In *Paul,* for example, the phrase δικαιοσύνη θεοῦ is construed as objective (the righteousness that belongs to the nature of God), while in the *Lectures,* it is taken as subjective (the righteousness that God expresses toward people). Just as the resurrection faith was crucial for the founding of the church, so it is of fundamental significance for the theology of Paul. According to Baur, the resurrection did not take place at the garden tomb, but in the experience of the believer. "It can therefore be said, that since Christ was not raised bodily, he must have arisen spiritually in the faith of the disciples."[83]

The central feature of Paul's theology is his doctrine of justification by faith. For Baur, justification is essentially an inward, spiritual occurrence whereby human consciousness is identified with the person of Christ. In this justification, the believer is united with the Divine Spirit so as to become a new creation: justification is union with God. God is the primary actor in reconciliation, but the condition for receiving justification is faith in Christ. "Faith," says Baur, "is subjectively what grace is objectively (the

---

82. Ibid. 1.341.
83. Baur, *Neutestamentliche Theologie,* 127.

object of faith is indeed just the grace of God which has appeared in Christ), and thus grace is the objective principle of the Pauline doctrine of justification."[84] Those who share the response of faith constitute a community in which the Spirit of God is present—a oneness symbolized by the metaphor of the body of Christ. This concept of justification—so basic to the being of God and the nature of humanity—implies an essential universalism, and this, indeed, is the meaning of Paul's doctrine of predestination: "The apostle's main idea is the universality of the grace of God; no man can be excluded from it, it must extend at last to all, both Jews and Gentiles, in order to achieve the end it has in view."[85]

In addition to the four authentic Pauline epistles, another source that belongs to this first period of Christian history is the Apocalypse. According to Baur, this book was written by the apostle John who came to Ephesus in order to combat Pauline Christianity. The Nicolaitans who follow the teaching of Balaam and threaten the churches of Asia Minor (Rev. 2:14-20) are none other than the Pauline Christians who eat meat sacrificed to idols. John, in Baur's opinion, did his work well, because after the Apocalypse (written before the destruction of Jerusalem) the churches of Asia Minor became largely anti-Pauline.

Early Christianity:
Reconciliation and Accommodation

Baur characterizes the second period of the church's history (from the post-apostolic age to the early decades of the second century) as the era of reconciliation. The documents that record the harmony that develops between Jewish and Pauline Christianity include Hebrews, James, 1 Peter, the Synoptic Gospels, Acts, and the pseudo-Pauline letters (except for the Pastoral Epistles). According to Baur, the reconciliation takes place from both sides. On the one hand, the Jewish Christians replace circumcision with baptism and depict Peter as a promoter of the gentile mission. On the other hand, the Pauline Christians maintain universalism but erode the doctrine of justification by faith with the notion that Paul affirmed the importance of works. The author of Hebrews behaves as Paul does but is actually a Jewish Christian. He sees Christianity as the fulfillment of Judaism and praises Melchizedek as a type of universal priesthood. Colossians and Ephesians make use of gnostic concepts to present Christ as the cosmic reconciler who removes the wall of separation between Jews and Gentiles. Philippians, too, employs gnostic argument and mentions the praetorium and Caesar's household to show that Pauline Christianity is

---

84. Baur, *Paul the Apostle of Jesus Christ* 2.157.
85. Ibid. 2.262.

recognized in Rome. James overtly opposes Paulinism yet presupposes an idea of inward freedom, reminiscent of Paul, in the author's doctrine of works. Written in the name of Peter, 1 Peter in fact echoes the Paulinism of Romans and Ephesians. For Baur, the great reconciler is the author of the Acts of the Apostles.

> The Acts is thus the attempt at conciliation, the overture of peace, of a member of the Pauline party, who desired to purchase the recognition of Gentile Christianity on the part of the Jewish Christians by concessions made to Judaism by his side, and sought to influence both parties in this direction. It thus gives us a very clear idea of the efforts made at that time with a view to a catholic Christianity.[86]

The third period in the history of the early church is the era of final accommodation. This accommodation, which comes to expression in mid-second century, is evidenced in the Pastoral Epistles, 2 Peter, and the Gospel of John. Speaking of Johannine Christianity, Baur says:

> At this stage the development of the Christian principle has reached its definite goal within the sphere which we are at present considering. Christianity is established as a universal principle of salvation; all those antitheses which threatened to detain it within the narrow limits of Jewish particularism are merged in the universalism of Christianity.[87]

As a matter of fact, the Gospel of John provides Baur with the point of departure for his analysis of the entire gospel tradition, an analysis presented in detail in his *Critical Investigations of the Canonical Gospels*.[88] Working like an archeologist, Baur begins with the highest stratum of the tradition, the Fourth Gospel, and digs down through the levels of the three Synoptic Gospels. His work employs the tools of literary and historical criticism, but his primary method is tendency criticism, a method which is more concerned with the intention of the author than with the author's identity.

With the Gospel of John, Christianity's break with Judaism is complete. The Jews become the representatives of unbelief. The principle of love, grounded in the relation of the Father to the Son, is understood as universal: "Love is therefore the highest concept from which the Johannine point of view proceeds."[89] The concept of the Logos provides a cosmic basis for the unity of the divine and the human. In support of these lofty ideas, the gospel tradition is pressed into service, and the author's presentation of the material is frequently unhistorical. The account of the raising

86. Baur, *Church History of the First Three Centuries* 1.135.
87. Ibid. 1.180.
88. See n. 73, above.
89. Baur, *Neutestamentliche Theologie*, 400.

of Lazarus, for example, is designed to show the power and glory of Christ in relation to death and resurrection. The Johannine discourses represent not words of Jesus but utterances of the eternal Logos. In the Gospel of John, the inner consciousness comes to historical expression, the future becomes present experience.

In the next lower stratum, within the period of reconciliation, Baur detects the Gospel of Mark. Written around the middle of the second century, Mark made use of both Matthew and Luke. Baur, to support this case, presents texts (e.g., the temptation narrative) in which he believes the shorter account (Mark) presupposes the longer (Matthew): "According to the result of the foregoing research, the origin of the Gospel of Mark can be fully explained by the presupposition that the author had the two other Gospels of Matthew and Luke before him, and used them for his presentation."[90] Mark, however, was not merely an epitomizer, because he sometimes added material for his own purposes. Mark's tendency is clear: to neutralize the Jewish-Pauline controversy by combining the Jewish gospel (Matthew) with the Pauline (Luke).

In the next stratum below Mark is the Gospel of Luke. Sometime before 139 C.E., a proto-Luke was composed, following Matthew as a major source. This proto-Luke was used by Marcion in the composition of his own gospel. Canonical Luke was written in about mid-second century to combat the Gnosticism of Marcion. Luke's tendency is to revise Matthew in terms of Paul's universalism, a universalism evident, for example, in Luke's narrative of the mission of the seventy. Matthew, the earliest of the Gospels, made use of the earlier Gospel of the Hebrews, a primitive, Semitic gospel, probably written by the apostle Matthew himself. The canonical Matthew, composed around 130 C.E., used as its major source a Greek translation of this Hebrew gospel. Although essentially a Jewish Christian document, the canonical Matthew was not without universalistic sympathies (e.g., Matt. 28:19-20). In any event, Matthew is the earliest and most reliable source for the gospel tradition: "If there is therefore in the circle of our canonical Gospels one Gospel in which we have before us the substantial content of the gospel story in an original, genuine historical source, then it can only be the Gospel of Matthew."[91]

In assessing Baur's contribution to NT research, one wonders how a scholar of such importance could have committed so many historical errors. His dating of the literature of the NT, in which virtually everything except the four authentic Pauline letters and the Apocalypse is relegated to the second century, is clearly mistaken. Similarly, his radical view of

---

90. Baur, *Markusevangelium,* 110.
91. Baur, *Evangelien,* 571.

authenticity in which almost nothing survives beyond Romans, 1 and 2 Corinthians, Galatians, and Revelation is equally erroneous. Moreover, Baur's reconstruction of early Christian history is a vast oversimplification. The reduction of what appear to be three or four Corinthian factions to only two is merely a symbol of Baur's failure to recognize the complexity of the early Christian conflict. To be sure, the charge that Baur's reconstruction was flawed by his arbitrary adoption of the Hegelian dialectic has largely been diffused by Peter Hodgson.[92] Had Baur been an uncritical devotee of Hegel, he would have affirmed the synthesis of the Jewish thesis and the Pauline antithesis in the accommodation of the second century. In actuality, Baur's own theological sympathies are solidly on the side of Paul.

Baur's greatness is to be explained by the creative power of his comprehensive conception. A person of profound insight and a master of critical detail, Baur applied his enormous erudition to the formulation of a hypothesis that offered a compelling explanation of the total development of early Christianity. Baur's approach employed a comprehensive intellectual synthesis composed of three elements: (1) a philosophy (Hegelian idealism) which provided an ontological ground for his understanding of history; (2) historical criticism which provided the method for theological deconstruction and reconstruction; and (3) the Christian tradition which affirmed the essential truth of historical revelation. The three worked in harmony: the tradition provided the content, historical criticism assessed its historicity, and philosophy interpreted its meaning for humanity in relation to ultimate reality. The result was a monumental achievement which, for all its mistakes, has continued to influence NT research.

THE TÜBINGEN SCHOOL:
ZELLER AND HILGENFELD

Baur's vision inspired a host of students and disciples—the devotees of the Tübingen school.[93] Following the lead of Baur, the members of the school were primarily historians. Whereas earlier students of the NT, de Wette, for instance, had been Bible scholars who worked in both OT and NT, Baur and his followers were church historians whose concern with early Christianity aroused their interest in the NT sources. In the course of their

92. See Hodgson's argument throughout his *Formation of Historical Theology*, and his introduction to Baur, *On the Writing of Church History*.

93. Harris (*Tübingen School*, 247) identifies two qualifications for membership in the Tübingen School: "acceptance of the principle of a purely historical interpretation of Christianity and the New Testament"; making an "essential contribution to the historical development of the School." More precisely, the members of the school are theologians who have been influenced by philosophical idealism and who, above all, employ Baur's *Tendenzkritik*.

work, scholars of the Tübingen school made significant contributions to NT research. Albert Schwegler, for example, wrote a two-volume book on the post-apostolic age. Karl Reinhold Köstlin published a work on the origin of the Synoptic Gospels in which he broke with Baur and advocated the priority of Mark. Albrecht Ritschl, whose early writings concentrated on church history, increasingly distanced himself from Baur, turned more and more toward systematic theology, and finally founded a theological school of his own. Gustav Volkmar, a religious and political revolutionary, wrote a life of Jesus reminiscent of the radicalism of Strauss. Without denying the variety and importance of others, the contribution of the Tübingen school can be illustrated by two of its most able scholars: Eduard Zeller and Adolf Hilgenfeld.

Eduard Zeller (1814–1908)

Eduard Zeller was the most honored member of the Tübingen school. Along with historians like Theodor Mommsen and Leopold von Ranke, he was hailed as one of the great humanist scholars of nineteenth-century Germany. Born in Kleinbottwar on the Neckar, Zeller was the son of a minor government official. Since preparation for Christian ministry provided educational opportunity for the less affluent, young Zeller was sent to the seminary at Maulbronn. He was hopelessly bored with the instruction until Strauss arrived in 1831, and when Strauss moved to Tübingen, Zeller was not far behind. He wrote to his father concerning his studies in the philosophical faculty: "My favorite lectures are those given by Strauss. Never have I found such a clarity and dialectical dexterity combined with such ardor and warm conviction as in this man."[94] In 1833, Zeller moved to the theological faculty, where he was captivated by Baur.

> Of all the theological professors of that time, the only one whose pupil in the full sense I could consider myself to be, and have through my life considered myself to be, was Baur. We encountered in him not only the model of a scientific mind in exemplary strength and purity, but while we were still students, we experienced also under his guidance a part of the most important transformations which theology has passed through since Schleiermacher and Hegel.[95]

In 1839, Zeller became an instructor at Tübingen. He married Baur's oldest daughter in 1847, and, in the same year, he was called to the faculty at Bern. His appointment was opposed by the majority of the university senate, but the liberal party in the town council prevailed. After two years at Bern, Zeller moved to the philosophical faculty at Marburg, where he

---

94. Cited in Harris, *Tübingen School*, 61.
95. Ibid., 62–63.

remained until 1862. In 1862, he was called to Heidelberg, and, ten years later, to Berlin. In the latter three posts, Zeller primarily taught philosophy. Indeed, his reputation as a scholar rests largely on his definitive works on the history of Greek philosophy: the massive *Die Philosophie der Griechen in ihrer geschichtliche Entwicklung* (1844–55)[96] and *Grundriss der Geschichte der griechischen Philosophie* (1883).[97]

Although Zeller wrote essays on such topics as NT Christology, the Fourth Gospel, and the Apocalypse,[98] his major contribution to NT research is found in his impressive investigation of the Acts of the Apostles: *Die Apostelgeschichte nach ihrem Inhalt und Ursprung kritisch untersucht.*[99] In effect, Zeller's work confirms Baur's reconstruction of early Christianity and his assessment of Acts as a tendency document. In method, Zeller works inductively, beginning with an appraisal of the external evidence, turning to an analysis of the content, and concluding with a thesis concerning the origin of Acts. As to external witnesses, Zeller argues that evidence for the use of Acts prior to 170 C.E. is largely lacking. He concludes, however, against Baur, that Marcion used the canonical Luke as a source for his own gospel.

The second part of Zeller's book surveys the contents of the Acts of the Apostles. Assuming an approach reminiscent of Strauss, Zeller argues that the author of Acts purports to communicate a literal, historical narrative. The narrative, however, is saturated with the supernatural, so that the literal meaning must be assessed as unhistorical. In judging the historicity of an account, two questions must be raised: How crucial is a particular feature of a narrative to the design of the whole? and Can the origin of this feature be attributed to unhistorical causes? The report of the speaking in tongues at Pentecost, for example, is an essential element of the total narrative, and the function of the report in support of Pauline universalism indicates that it arose out of theological, not historical, considerations. In sum, the Pentecost account, together with the miracle of speaking in tongues, is an unhistorical creation of the author of Acts.

Most of the other reports of the early Jerusalem events—the community of goods, the death of Ananias and Saphira—suffer the same criticism.

---

96. Written in three parts, this work has been reprinted in 6 vols. (Hildesheim: G. Olms, 1963).

97. The popularity of this book is attested by its many editions in German and in Eng. trans.: *Outlines of the History of Greek Philosophy*, 13th rev. ed., ed. W. Nestle, trans. L. R. Palmer (New York: Meridian Books, 1957).

98. Zeller was also the editor of Baur's *Paul* (see n. 72), and the author of a monograph on Strauss, *David Friedrich Strauss in seinem Leben und seinen Schriften* (Bonn: E. Strauss, 1874).

99. (Stuttgart: C. Mäcken, 1854); Eng. trans.: *The Contents and Origin of the Acts of the Apostles, Critically Investigated*, trans. Joseph Dare, 2 vols. (London: Williams & Norgate, 1875–76).

Zeller is not above sarcasm in his attack on the miracles of Peter. He ridicules the notion that wonder-working power operated through the shadow of the apostle "to pour itself, like an electric fluid, indiscriminately on all the needy!"[100] With the death of Stephen, however, the author of Acts turns to sober history. The details of the narrative and the content of the martyr's speech are, to be sure, compositions of the author, but the account of Stephen's opposition to the law is fully reliable. The story of Peter's conversion of Cornelius, on the other hand, is without historical basis. His later behavior at Antioch, as reported by Paul in Gal. 2:11-21, proves that Peter's vision of Acts 10:9-16 is a Lucan fabrication: "After all these discussions, we cannot avoid pronouncing the statement unhistorical that Peter baptized a Gentile previously to the council of Apostles and the missionary journeys of Paul."[101]

The hero of Acts—and of Zeller—is Paul of Tarsus. The author's portrait, however, is blemished by a variety of distortions. In regard to the conversion, the three different accounts in Acts cannot be harmonized. At the same time, they differ from Paul's own reports on the most decisive feature: according to Paul, he had seen the Christ; according to Acts, he had only seen a light. Acts, moreover, presents Paul's conversion as objective happening, while it was surely a subjective, visionary experience—a conclusion confirmed by evidence that Paul was sometimes given to excitement and ecstasy. According to Zeller, this experience was based on "his religious need: the vision which he certainly considered as objective was merely a consequence of this need; not the *foundation*, but the *effect* of his faith."[102]

For Zeller, the Jerusalem council was of crucial importance for the history of the early church. He argues that Acts 15 and Galatians 2 report the same event. The famine visit of Acts 11:29-30 is a doublet on the offering visit of Acts 21, a hypothesis confirmed by the appearance of the prophet Agabus in the context of both accounts. In any case, the report of the council in Acts misses the essential historical point: the sharp conflict between the Jewish and Pauline Christians. The author of Acts conceals this conflict by blunting the weapons of the combatants: Peter is portrayed as the instigator of gentile mission, and Paul is presented as acceding to the apostolic decrees. As a result, the Acts account is a fiction:

> The official mission of Paul by the community of Antioch; the position which he assumes in the Acts with regard to the original Apostles; the discussion of his affairs in the formal assembly of the church; the speeches which

100. Zeller, *Acts of the Apostles* 1.211.
101. Ibid. 1.283.
102. Ibid. 1.293.

are attributed on this occasion to Peter and to James, to Paul and to Barnabas; the resolutions of the assembly and their promulgation by an apostolic missive; the course which Paul is said to have pursued in consequence concerning Timothy,—all these features can only be pronounced unhistorical.[103]

As to the overview of Paul in Acts, Zeller concludes that the author has misrepresented the apostle's doctrine, conduct, and mission.

The final section of Zeller's work draws conclusions concerning the origin of Acts. Above all, he asserts that Acts is a tendency document, for the material is selected and arranged to fulfill the author's purpose. An analysis of the author's tendency (or bias) indicates that he is a Paulinist who accommodates Paul by making concessions to Jewish Christianity. Although the author uses the first-person pronoun "we" to pose as a travel companion of Paul, the evidence indicates that he was not. Indication of a relatively late date of composition can be seen in the legendary features of the narrative and the advanced state of ecclesiastical development. The date cannot be too late, however, since sharp conflict with Gnosticism has not yet become overt. "Hence we regard our book," says Zeller, "as the work of a Paulinist of the Roman church, most probably composed between the years 110 and 125, or perhaps 130, after Christ."[104] As to sources, Zeller believes the author used a variety of written material including the Pauline letters, but he concludes that much of the narrative is the author's free composition.

Adolf Hilgenfeld (1823–1907)

In regard to NT criticism, the brightest star in the Tübingen galaxy was Adolf Bernhard Christoph Christian Hilgenfeld. Born in the small north German town of Stappenbeck, Hilgenfeld was the son of an orthodox pastor who had been moved by Pietism. In 1841, young Adolf was sent to the University of Berlin where his father hoped he would fall under the spell of Hengstenberg and Neander. But, as fate would have it, Hilgenfeld was primarily influenced by Philipp Marheineke, a devotee of Hegel, and Strauss's friend, Wilhelm Vatke. Hilgenfeld moved to Halle in 1843, where he gained proficiency in Persian and the Semitic languages. After reading Baur, Hilgenfeld fell into step with the Tübingen school, although he never set foot in Tübingen and was not always content to bear their banner.

In 1847, Hilgenfeld began lecturing at Jena, but his teaching was so bad that he often attracted only one or two students—sometimes none. In 1850, he was made an associate professor without salary and was forced to

---

103. Ibid. 2.41.
104. Ibid. 2.291.

write reviews to gain income. "The man is almost just too productive," wrote Zeller; "certainly he has to write in order to live and so it is not surprising that he seems almost to live just in order to write"[105]—a literal incidence of "publish or perish"! In an effort to secure a preaching position, Hilgenfeld in 1856 applied for ordination. His statement to the consistory was about as close to orthodoxy as Hilgenfeld ever came:

> I have constantly held fast to the belief in the oneness of truth with what is genuinely Christian—a oneness which must open itself up more and more to the deeper scientific investigations; and this faith of mine rests on the certainty that what is essentially grounded in human nature—such as the interest in religion and in truth—cannot stand in any irreconcilable contradiction. . . . And as I believe in the living God before whom everything past and future is eternally present, so that he does not first require the human spirit for the realization of his own consciousness, so also I acknowledge in the historical Christ as the pioneer and perfecter of our faith his highest archetypal revelation.[106]

The ecclesiastical officials were unimpressed, and when Hilgenfeld's publications were judged to be riddled with heresy, the nomination was denied. Not until 1890 was Hilgenfeld promoted to full professor at Jena, a post he held until his death in 1907 at the age of 84.

Adolf Hilgenfeld published widely in the area of NT research—works on the Johannine literature, glossolalia in the early church, the Gospel of Mark, and Galatians. He had a special interest in Jewish backgrounds, and his book on the historical development of apocalyptic literature has recently been reprinted.[107] Hilgenfeld, like all the members of the Tübingen school, was interested in early church history. He wrote a monograph on the history of the canon,[108] and his work on Judaism and Jewish Christianity was reissued in 1966.[109] However, the results of Hilgenfeld's critical work on the NT are summarized in his weighty (over 800 pages) *Historical-Critical Introduction to the New Testament* (1875).[110] In general, Hilgenfeld presents a thoroughly modern *Introduction*. Virtually every question of historical criticism is addressed, and the analysis is supported by massive, well-documented research. In method, Hilgenfeld—trying to distance himself from Baur—adopts what he calls a "pure literary-historical interpreta-

---

105. Cited in Harris, *Tübingen School*, 118.

106. Ibid., 121–22.

107. Adolf Hilgenfeld, *Die jüdische Apokalyptic in ihrer geschichtlichen Entwickelung: Ein Beitrag zur Vorgeschichte des Christenthums* (Amsterdam: RODOPI, 1966).

108. Adolf Hilgenfeld, *Der Kanon und die Kritik des Neuen Testaments in ihrer geschichtlichen Ausbildung und Gestaltung* (Halle: C.E.M. Pfeffer, 1863).

109. Adolf Hilgenfeld, *Judentum und Judenchristentum: Eine Nachlese zu der Ketzergeschichte des Urchristentums* (Hildesheim: G. Olms, 1966).

110. Adolf Hilgenfeld, *Historisch-kritische Einleitung in das Neue Testament* (Leipzig: L. F. Fues, 1875).

tion" (rein literarhistorische Auffassung).[111] But in actuality, the shadow of Baur's tendency criticism is cast over the entire project. Hilgenfeld considers higher criticism to be "one of the most lively areas of theological research," and asserts that it "has entered into an ongoing battle with ecclesiastical tradition."[112] His introductory section traces the history of the science of introduction and attends to major figures like Michaelis and de Wette. Richard Simon is honored as the father of the genre, and Eichhorn is hailed as the first to apply higher criticism fully and consistently.

The bulk of the work is divided into three sections. The first deals with the history of the NT canon and the history of NT criticism. In regard to the canon, Hilgenfeld views the collection of NT books as an expression of the church's resolution of the conflict between Petrine and Pauline Christianity.

> With the explicit recognition of Paul alongside of Peter (and the other twelve apostles), we step onto the soil of the catholic church. Through the fact that Paul and the Pauline writings were joined to the recognition of the primitive apostle [Peter] and the primitive apostolic writings, one received a complete apostolic canon of Scripture, that is, the new Scripture canon of the catholic church, in which the original conflict between the primitive apostolic and Pauline Christianity ceased.[113]

Hilgenfeld rehearses the history of NT criticism from Origen to Ewald and claims that recent support of the priority of Mark is motivated by opposition to Baur's tendency criticism.

The second part of Hilgenfeld's *Introduction* considers the writings of the NT individually. Here he follows a historical rather than a canonical order. In the apostolic age, the scene is dominated by the life and letters of Paul. Hilgenfeld's presentation of the career of the apostle owes much to Acts: he seems to accept, for instance, the historicity of Paul's study with Gamaliel. Hilgenfeld is inclined to interpret the conversion psychologically as the experience of a persecutor who was shaken in his own convictions. In contrast to Baur, Hilgenfeld accepts 1 Thessalonians as authentic; it expresses the same eschatology as 1 Corinthians and expects the imminent end of history. He believes Galatians was written around 55 C.E., probably from Ephesus; it battles Judaizing opponents who advocate the Christianity of the Jerusalem apostles. Agreeing with Baur, Hilgenfeld holds that there were only two factions in Corinth: the Paul-Apollos group and the Cephas-Christ group. He interprets speaking in tongues as ecstatic speech that had been imported from Palestine by the Judaizers in an

---

111. Adolf Hilgenfeld, *Die Evangelien, nach ihrer Entstehung und geschichtliche Bedeutung* (Leipzig: S. Hirzel, 1854), iv.
112. Hilgenfeld, *Einleitung*, iii.
113. Ibid., 71.

effort to counter Paul's wisdom preaching. The "letter of tears," mentioned in 2 Cor. 2:4, represents a lost epistle written prior to 2 Corinthians. Second Corinthians is accepted as a unified document that reflects the increasing bitterness of the conflict with the opponents. Their claim to belong to Christ (2 Cor. 10:7) echoes their slogan of 1 Cor. 1:12 and supports the Jerusalem leaders' claim to superiority as disciples of Jesus. Against Baur, Hilgenfeld argues that Romans 9–11 does not constitute the heart of the epistle. It was written to reconcile the Jewish and gentile factions in the Roman church: the Jews are referred to as the "weak," the Gentiles as the "strong." Hilgenfeld accepts both Philemon (written from the Caesarean imprisonment) and Philippians (from the Roman imprisonment) as authentic. Hebrews, on the other hand, was written not by Paul but by an Alexandrian Paulinist, probably Apollos.

Still discussing the apostolic age, Hilgenfeld turns to other writings of apostles and apostolic persons. He thinks the Apocalypse, written after the death of Nero and before the destruction of Jerusalem (68–69), was actually authored by John the son of Zebedee. As Baur had argued, it expresses an anti-Pauline tendency. Hilgenfeld's analysis of the Gospel of Matthew detects two strata of material: (1) a primitive Hebrew gospel; and (2) additions that are incorporated into the Greek canonical Matthew.[114] The primitive gospel he thinks was written by Matthew himself, around 50–60. Although the canonical Gospel holds some universal sympathies, it is essentially Jewish and anti-Pauline. The Gospel of Mark is dependent on Matthew but independent of Luke.[115] According to Hilgenfeld, Mark presents a transition from the Jewish Matthew to the Pauline Luke—a position equally dependent on *Tendenzkritik*, although with results different from Baur's. Mark represents a period of harmony between the Jewish and gentile Christians in Rome, and was probably written during the reign of Domitian (81–96). The Epistle of James presents a Jewish Christianity similar to the religion of the Essenes. The author does not know the authentic Pauline letters, but he argues against the Paulinism of Hebrews. The author of the Lucan documents is not a pure devotee of Paul, but a compromising Paulinist.[116] He uses Matthew and Mark as sources and knows the letters of Paul. "He himself presents the new Gospel as the first attempt at a Pauline presentation of the gospel story."[117] The tendency of "Luke" is anti-Jewish and pro-Pauline. The "we-sections" of Acts represent a source used by the author who was not a travel companion of Paul. The

---

114. Hilgenfeld's analysis of Matthew is presented in full detail in his *Evangelien*, 43–120.
115. Ibid., 121–50.
116. Ibid., 151–226.
117. Hilgenfeld, *Einleitung*, 555.

Gospel of Luke was written after Mark and before Marcion, that is, about 100–110 C.E.

Turning to the literature of the post-apostolic age, Hilgenfeld discusses 1 Peter. He believes it was written from Rome at the time of Trajan's persecution. Although he writes in the name of Peter, the author uses the Pauline epistles and celebrates the triumph of Pauline Christianity. From about the same period is 2 Thessalonians, an apocalyptic document written by a Paulinist. Hilgenfeld believes Gnosticism arose from a Jewish anti-Paulinism but became increasing anti-Jewish and, eventually, supra-Pauline. Colossians, written in the time of Hadrian, addresses gnostic opponents. Ephesians, a reworking of Colossians by an Asian Paulinist, is designed "to present the transition from early Christianity to a catholicism of the Pauline variety."[118] According to Hilgenfeld, the author of the Fourth Gospel knew the Synoptic Gospels and used their material to present a distinctive, unified composition which is at the same time anti-Jewish and anti-Gnostic.[119] In relation to the book of Revelation, "The Johannine Gospel is the spiritualized Johannine apocalypse. The Johannine prophecy has become Gnosis; the Holy Spirit is no longer understood above all as the proclaimer of the future, but especially as the spirit of truth."[120] Although the Quartodecimanians of Asia Minor enlisted the support of the Johannine tradition for their position in the Easter controversy, the Gospel of John, with its presentation of Christ as the paschal lamb, actually represents the Pauline and Roman view.[121] This shows that John was not the author and hints that the Gospel stems from the early stages of the Easter controversy, that is, from 120–140. The Pastoral Epistles express a Paulinism in conflict with a developed Gnosticism like that of Marcion; they were written around 150 C.E. The third and final section of Hilgenfeld's *Introduction* discusses the materials and history of NT text criticism.

The Tübingen school had an immense but not wholly positive influence on the history of NT research. For some theologians, anything Baur and his friends endorsed had to be bad, so that the endeavors of the Tübingen school encouraged a reactionary conservatism. The fundamental fault, according to many critics, was the dependence on the philos-

---

118. Ibid., 680.
119. See Hilgenfeld, *Evangelien*, 227–349.
120. Hilgenfeld, *Einleitung*, 736.
121. The Johannine presentation of the last supper as a meal observed prior to the Passover (John 18:28) and the death of Jesus as occurring at the time of the sacrifice of the Passover lamb are in accord with Paul's position (1 Cor. 5:7). Hilgenfeld's argument is presented in greater detail in his *Der Paschastreit der alten Kirche nach seiner Bedeutung für die Kirchengeschichte und für die Evangelienforschung* (Halle: C.E.M. Pfeffer, 1860).

ophy of Hegel. For them, a scholar like Bruno Bauer (1809–82)[122] was the horrible example of what happened to theologians who associated with the likes of Strauss and Baur. Bruno Bauer had begun as a right-wing Hegelian who believed the virgin birth to be the historical expression of the unity of the divine and the human: the virgin represented human receptivity, and the Spirit acted as the creative father. However, in a series of books on the Gospels,[123] Bauer moved relentlessly to the left and finally came to the conclusion that Jesus was a creation of the imagination of the early Christians; the historical Jesus never really existed. Bauer, whose most famous pupil was Karl Marx,[124] eventually abandoned academic life to become a farmer (in German, a *Bauer!*); he died a confirmed skeptic, in the words of Albert Schweitzer, "a pure, modest and lofty character."[125]

In addition to the concern with the philosophical presuppositions, some critics concentrated on the results of Tübingen's research. The reconstruction of early Christian history, for instance, came increasingly under attack. Although twentieth-century critics consider Tübingen's hypothesis to be an oversimplification, many nineteenth-century opponents of the Tübingen school were inclined to minimize the conflicts. Some were also more concerned to confirm the reliability of the sources than to present a historical reconstruction that made sense out of the data. Although it was sometimes abused, tendency criticism—the recognition that documents reflected a religious or theological perspective—continued to be employed in NT research. The method was especially effective in the analysis of the Acts of the Apostles, and after Tübingen, the study of the Gospel of John would never be the same.

ALTERNATIVES TO TÜBINGEN:
HENGSTENBERG, THOLUCK, AND EWALD

The foes of the Tübingen school were legion. Three representative scholars present the main contours of criticism: E. W. Hengstenberg (the return

122. For a survey of Bauer's life and thought, see Martin Kegel, *Bruno Bauer und Seine Theorien über die Entstehung des Christenthums*, Abhandlungen zur Philosophie und ihrer Geschichte 6 (Leipzig: Quelle & Meyer, 1908); Bruno Bauer, *The Trumpet of the Last Judgement against Hegel the Atheist and AntiChrist: An Ultimatum*, trans. Lawrence Stepelevich, Studies in German Thought and History 5 (Lewiston, N.Y.: Edwin Mellen Press, 1989), 1–56.

123. Bruno Bauer, *Kritik der evangelischen Geschichte des Johannes* (Bremen: C. Schunemann, 1840); *Kritik evangelischen Geschichte der Synoptiker*, 3 vols. (Leipzig: O. Wigand, 1841–42).

124. See Kathleen L. Clarkson and David J. Hawkin, "Marx on Religion: The Influence of Bruno Bauer and Ludwig Feuerbach on His Thought and Its Implications for the Christian-Marxist Dialogue, *Scottish Journal of Theology* 31 (1978): 533–55.

125. Albert Schweitzer, *The Quest of the Historical Jesus: A Critical Study of Its Progress from Reimarus to Wrede*, trans. W. Montgomery (New York: Macmillan, 1957), 138.

to orthodoxy), August Tholuck (the revival of Pietism), and Heinrich Ewald (militant historical criticism).

Ernst Wilhelm Hengstenberg (1802–1869)

At first glance, Hengstenberg appears to be a theological Rip Van Winkle who had slept right through the eighteenth century, but in reality his return to orthodoxy was informed and intentional. Born in Fröndenberg, a village of Westphalia, Ernst Wilhelm Hengstenberg was the son of a Reformed pastor. Because of fragile health, he was not sent to the public schools but was taught by his father at home. Hengstenberg began his university studies at Bonn, where he specialized in Semitic languages and Greek philosophy. After serving as a tutor at Basel, he continued his studies at Berlin. Convinced of the fundamental truth of the Augsburg Confession, Hengstenberg converted to orthodox Lutheranism. He began his teaching at Berlin in 1826, the successor of the dismissed de Wette.[126] Although noted for reading his lectures in a monotone, he impressed his students with the power of his intellect. In 1827, Hengstenberg founded the influential conservative periodical, *Evangelische Kirchenzeitung.* At Berlin, he opposed the theology of Schleiermacher and was allied with the more conservative faculty: Neander, Tholuck, and Olshausen.[127] Hengstenberg embraced a "level" Bible—wholly inspired and infallible from Genesis to Revelation. In principle, he rejected historical criticism and argued that God could reveal as God chose, without regard for historical conditions.[128] Hengstenberg, who had married nobility and acquired influence in the higher circles of Prussia, advocated the unity of state and church, throne and altar.

Hengstenberg's main contribution to biblical scholarship was in the area of OT studies. He wrote commentaries and an introduction in which he defended the Mosaic authorship of the Pentateuch. His major work, however, had implications for the history of NT research: his massive *Christology of the Old Testament* (1829).[129] In essence, this book strives to discover predictions of Jesus throughout the Hebrew Scriptures and constitutes an attempt to resurrect the defunct proof from prophecy that

---

126. See p. 221, above.

127. For Olshausen, see pp. 363–65, below.

128. For Hengstenberg, historical criticism was an expression of fallen humanity's effort autonomously to attain knowledge of God. See Samuel H. Nafzger, "Struggle against Rationalism: A Study of Ernst Wilhelm Hengstenberg's Understanding of Criticism" (Th.D. diss., Harvard University, abstracted in *Harvard Theological Review* 74 [1981]: 402).

129. E. W. Hengstenberg, *Christologie des Alten Testaments und Commentar über die Messianischen Weissagungen der Propheten,* 4 vols. (Berlin: L. Oehmigke, 1829); Eng. trans.: *Christology of the Old Testament, and a Commentary on the Messianic Predictions,* trans. Theod. Meyer, 2d ed., 4 vols. (Edinburgh: T. & T. Clark, 1854–58).

the deists had buried a century before. In discussing the prophecies of the Pentateuch, Hengstenberg acknowledges that the earlier predictions are general and the later become more specific. In the famous Gen. 3:14-15, for instance, the seed of the woman refers not to the person of the redeemer but to all the descendants of the woman. However, in Deut. 18:15, where it is prophesied that "God will raise up for you a prophet like me," Moses is referring specifically to Jesus Christ. In Genesis 18 the three strange visitors of Abraham are none other than the Logos and two inferior angels.

Hengstenberg's passion to find predictions everywhere is confirmed by his exegesis of the Song of Solomon. Although he admits that this ancient love poem is not really a prophetic book, Hengstenberg is convinced that it is seriously concerned with the coming Messiah.

> An important link in the chain of the Messianic hopes is formed by the Song of Solomon. It is intimately associated with Ps. lxxii., which was written by Solomon, and represents the Messiah as the Prince of Peace, imperfectly prefigured by Solomon as His type. As in this Psalm, so also in the Song of Solomon, the coming of the Messiah forms the subject throughout, and He is introduced there under the name of Solomon the Peaceful One.[130]

Of course, Hengstenberg has a field day with Isaiah, a book he accepts as a unity, written in the eighth century, and predicting the future events of the Babylonian captivity and the return from exile under Cyrus. In regard to 7:14, Hengstenberg notes the distinction between *bethulah* (virgin) and *almah*, but he argues that *almah* always means "unmarried woman," so that the text (which uses *almah*) implies a virgin birth. Thus, "if the mother of the Saviour was to be an *unmarried* person, she could be a virgin only; and, in general, it is inconceivable that the Prophet should have brought forward a relation of impure love."[131]

Regarding the NT, Hengstenberg had a special interest in the Johannine literature. His commentary on the Fourth Gospel was published from 1861 to 1864.[132] Questions of historical-critical introduction are presented at the end of the commentary in a section entitled "Concluding Observations." Hengstenberg believes John's purpose was apologetic and polemic: "to the Christological image of mist, he [John] would oppose the historical Christ in His full historical truth. That was the weapon with which he

---

130. Hengstenberg, *Christology* 1.151.
131. Ibid. 2.45.
132. E. W. Hengstenberg, *Das Evangelium des heiligen Johannes*, 2d ed., 3 vols. (Berlin: G. Schlawitz, 1867); Eng. trans.: *Commentary on the Gospel of St. John*, 2 vols. (Edinburgh: T. & T. Clark, 1865).

warred. To this was necessary the strictest historical fidelity."[133] According to Hengstenberg, all the Johannine writings—the Gospel, the three epistles, and the Apocalypse—were written by the same author, John the apostle, the son of Zebedee. Given Hengstenberg's understanding of inspiration, the problem of sources is not a major concern. He believes that John knew the Synoptics and consciously wrote to supplement and complete their work.

> It has been shown in the Commentary, that John everywhere assumes the existence of the first Gospels, and especially connects his Gospel with that of Luke; that his relation to his predecessors, however, is not that of a corrector, but of a corroborating witness and supplementer; that his design is always and most manifestly to make his Gospel with the former one and whole.[134]

In Henstenberg's view, the Gospel of John was written from Ephesus after the destruction of Jerusalem in the time of Domitian. Although John has not reproduced the discourses of Jesus verbatim (after all, Jesus spoke Aramaic), he has presented them accurately: "In favour of his ability, and his actual retention of the entire discourses, we need only appeal to the high degree of John's receptivity, the aid of other Apostles, to whom he might have recourse at need, and the assistance of the Holy Spirit."[135] Hengstenberg concludes: "The most rigid criticism has failed to detect a single word which Jesus might not have spoken, and in which the later relations of John are reflected."[136]

Hengstenberg's exegetical results are predictable. The Logos of the prologue finds its background in the Hebrew Scriptures, not in the Hellenistic Judaism of Philo. At Cana, the mother of Jesus expected a miracle— evidence which confirms the historicity of the birth narratives. The lack of wine resulted from the unexpected attendance of Jesus and his disciples, and the quantity of the water changed to wine displays the magnitude of the miracle. Jesus, of course, could not have contributed to drunkenness. "We are not to conclude . . . that the guests were intoxicated in this case. Where Jesus, His mother, and His disciples were, in the house of God-fearing people who had invited them, such a thing certainly could not occur."[137] As to the cleansing of the temple, Hengstenberg harmonizes the discrepancy between John and the Synoptics by concluding that there

---

133. Hengstenberg, *Commentary on John* 2.510.
134. Ibid. 2.523.
135. Ibid. 2.538.
136. Ibid. 2.540.
137. Ibid. 1.121.

were two cleansings. Similarly, he concludes that the last supper was the Passover meal; the reference to eating in John 18:28 refers to other later meals of the continuing Passover celebration. In regard to the silence of the Synoptics concerning the raising of Lazarus, Hengstenberg finds some credibility in the arguments that the Synoptics are concerned with the Galilean ministry, and that a report of the raising written while Lazarus was still alive would have endangered him and his family. But the crucial argument is clear: the divine plan called for John to relate the story. "We can hardly imagine the history of Lazarus' resurrection told in the manner of the first three Evangelists. It belongs essentially to the 'spiritual gospel.'"[138]

Hengstenberg also wrote a commentary on the book of Revelation.[139] He believed this book had relevance for his own troubled times. The letters to the seven churches, for example, were written "for the benefit of the church in all ages."[140] The Apocalypse, although composed in the time of Domitian, is designed to predict the entire future of the world from the time of the author, the apostle John, to the end of history. Thus, the beast of Revelation 13 does not refer to a Roman emperor (as most historical critics conclude), nor does it symbolize the pope of Rome (as scholars like Bengel believe[141]). Actually, the beast represents not any individual but the force of evil functioning throughout history—"the whole of the ungodly power of the world."[142]

Although Hengstenberg knew and even used the historical-critical method, his approach was essentially a return to Protestant scholasticism. For Hengstenberg, exegesis was enlisted in the service of orthodox theology. His christological reading of the OT represents an unhistorical imposition of Christian doctrine upon the Hebrew Scriptures. At the same time, Hengstenberg, for all his hatred of Enlightenment interpretation, shared its inevitable outcome: the reduction of the narrative of the Bible to sheer history. To be sure, the historical residue left by Hengstenberg was much larger than that of the Enlightenment critics. Yet, in spite of Hengstenberg's allegiance to the Scriptures, the Bible, like Lazarus, came forth, bound hand and foot: the poetry of the OT turned into allegory, the symbols of the NT reduced to facts.

---

138. Ibid. 2.27.
139. E. W. Hengstenberg, *Die Offenbarung des heiligen Johannes für solche die in der Schrift forschen*, 2d ed., 2 vols. (Berlin: L. Oehmigke, 1861); Eng. trans.: *The Revelation of St. John, Expounded for Those Who Search the Scriptures*, trans. Patrick Fairbairn, 2 vols. (Edinburgh: T. & T. Clark, 1851–52).
140. Hengstenberg, *Revelation of John* 2.384.
141. See p. 79, above.
142. Hengstenberg, *Revelation of John* 2.55.

August Tholuck (1799–1877)

If Hengstenberg represents a return to seventeenth-century scholasticism, Tholuck echoes the Pietism of the eighteenth. Friedrich August Gottreu Tholuck was born in Breslau of humble parents and with delicate health. In his youth, Tholuck was plagued by skepticism and argued that Islam was superior to Christianity. At the University of Berlin, however, he came under the sway of Schleiermacher and Neander.

> Even in early boyhood infidelity had forced its way into my heart, and at the age of twelve I was wont to scoff at Christianity and its truth. Hard has been the struggle which I have come through, before attaining to the assurance of that faith in which I am now blessed. I prove, however, in myself, and acknowledge it with praise to the Almighty, that the longer I live, the more does serious study, combined with the experiences of life, help me to recognize in the Christian doctrine an inexhaustible fountain of true knowledge, and serve to strengthen the conviction that all the wisdom of this world is but folly when compared with the glorious gospel of Jesus Christ.[143]

Tholuck began teaching at Berlin, first as an instructor and later as associate professor. In 1826, he was appointed full professor at Halle. When he moved, his reputation as conservative in theology and pietistic in faith preceded him, so that a military guard was deployed to protect him from the rationalistic students. Except for a tour of duty as chaplain to the Prussian embassy in Rome (1827–29), Tholuck remained at Halle for the rest of his career. A brilliant linguist, Tholuck was noted for his eloquent preaching. In time, he won the hearts of his students, who were frequently invited to his home for dinner.

Dissatisfied with the skepticism of the Enlightenment, Tholuck became the leader of a nineteenth-century neo-pietism, a revival of the religion of deep, personal faith.[144] In theology, Tholuck was a moderate who embraced reason but renounced rationalism. His thought, christocentric and steeped in pietism, is disclosed in his novel *Guido and Julius*.[145] The subtitle, *The True Consecration of the Skeptic*, indicates that Tholuck intended to answer de Wette's *Theodore*.[146] In Tholuck's judgment, de Wette had failed to present the seriousness of sin and the necessity of atonement, with the result that Theodore remained too skeptical and not really con-

---

143. Fred. Aug. Gottreu Tholuck, *Exposition of St. Paul's Epistle to the Romans, with Extracts from the Exegetical Works of the Fathers and the Reformers*, trans. Robert Menzies (Philadelphia: Sorin & Ball, 1844), x.

144. See Karl Barth, *Protestant Theology in the Nineteenth Century: Its Background and History*, trans. John Bowden (London: SCM Press, 1972), 508–18.

145. Frederick Aug. G. Tholuck, *Guido and Julius; or Sin and the Propitiator, exhibited in the True Consecration of the Skeptic*, trans. J. E. Ryland (Boston: Gould & Lincoln, 1854).

146. See pp. 222–23, above.

verted. The bulk of Tholuck's work is an exchange of dull letters between two students, Guido and Julius, letters crammed with biblical and patristic quotations, longer and more erudite than many of the doctoral dissertations of the day. According to the transparent plot, Guido and Julius are friends, united in the search for peace. They go to separate universities, Guido to study theology, Julius to learn history and philology. In the course of their studies, Guido becomes a skeptic who abandons theology for philosophy, and Julius is converted to pietistic Christianity and turns to theology. In one of his long letters (over eighty pages), Julius extols the glory of the experience of the redeemer: "the same Jesus who once calmed the waves of the Galilean sea, has been with you and me, to hush into an eternal calm the storm within our breasts."[147] This kind of authentic religious experience, of course, has eluded the rationalistic theologians:

> They have culled for themselves out of God's word a theology, which they call natural; probably because it is the theology of the natural man, in which they include the doctrines of freedom, of immortality, of providence, of God's paternal love—beautiful, glorious doctrines, had they not torn them from the living body; they are now cold, dead limbs, a sun shorn of its beams.[148]

Under the weight of these letters, Guido is eventually moved to accept salvation—a gift of God, received by faith. The novel concludes with Guido's account of witnessing the death-bed scene of an aged, revered pietist who passes from this life into the next in peace and confidence.

Tholuck's work on the NT includes a commentary on Romans (written when he was only twenty-five),[149] a commentary on Hebrews, and an exposition of the Sermon on the Mount which is usually recognized as his most erudite exegetical accomplishment.[150] In terms of the developments of NT criticism, Tholuck's most important work is his apologetic, *The Reliability of the Gospel Story*.[151] Here Tholuck begins with a survey of the rise of rationalism and its culmination in the work of D. F. Strauss. A major objective of the book is to provide historical proof for the miracle stories of the Gospels. Tholuck argues that the issue is fundamentally historical.

---

147. Tholuck, *Guido*, 107.
148. Ibid., 132.
149. Friedrich August Gottreu Tholuck, *Auslegung des Briefes Pauli an die Römer nebst fortlaufenden Auszügen aus den exegetischen Schriften der Kirchenväter und Reformatoren* (Berlin: F. Dümmler, 1824); Eng. trans.: *Exposition of St. Paul's Epistle to the Romans* (see n. 143, above).
150. A. Tholuck, *Philologish-theologische Auslegung der Bergpredigt Christi nach Matthäus, zugleich ein Beitrag zur Begründung einer rein-biblischen Glaubens- und Sittenlehre* (Hamburg: F. Perthes, 1833).
151. A. Tholuck, *Die Glaubwürdigkeit der evangelischen Geschichte, zugleich eine Kritik des Lebens Jesu von Strauss, für theologische und nicht theologische Leser dargestellt*, 2d ed. (Hamburg: F. Perthes, 1838).

Strauss errs, therefore, in his philosophical presuppositions, that is, his narrow notion that miracles are inherently impossible. For Tholuck, proof requires the historical analysis of each miracle story. In the course of the argument, Tholuck makes a case for the reliability of the narratives of the Gospels, all four of which he accepts as authentic and written by the authors to whom they have been traditionally ascribed. Luke, for example, he says, set out to write accurate history. He had been a companion of Paul and had visited Jerusalem, where he had abundant opportunity to interrogate eyewitnesses. In Tholuck's view, Luke was usually more reliable than Josephus. Tholuck is not seriously concerned with the synoptic problem, although he considers Griesbach's hypothesis[152] (accepted by Strauss) to be laughable (*lächerlich*).[153] Rather than slavish dependence on Matthew and Luke, Mark made use of reliable tradition from Simon Peter. The Gospel of John is authentic and historically accurate; its variations from the Synoptics are explained by two different, but fully reliable, perspectives that are analogous to those apparent in the different accounts of Socrates by Xenophon and Plato.

The same approach to critical questions is seen in Tholuck's *Commentary on the Gospel of St. John*.[154] In the preface, Tholuck affirms a venerable hermeneutical principle: "I was particularly desirous of explaining still more fully the Scriptures by means of the Scriptures themselves."[155] The introduction presents an account of the life of John the Evangelist, the son of Zebedee, beloved apostle, who remained in Jerusalem to care for the mother of Jesus until her death. Around 65, he moved to Ephesus where, during the reign of Domitian, he wrote the Apocalypse. Once depicted as one of the sons of thunder, John displays a gentleness in his Gospel which reveals the transforming power of Christ. "It may, therefore, be well presumed," writes Tholuck, "that those sublime qualities of love, humility and mildness, by which the writings of the Evangelist are distinguished, were the result only of the transforming grace of God,—of the influence of the Spirit of Christ on the disciple, who had yielded himself to him."[156]

In regard to the language of John, Tholuck notes that the style of the Gospel is superior to that of Revelation. He wonders how John's Greek could have improved so much in the time between 95 (when the Apoca-

152. See pp. 143–48, above.
153. Tholuck, *Glaubwurdigkeit*, 257.
154. A. Tholuck, *Commentar zum Evangelio Johannis*, 5th rev. ed. (Hamburg: F. Perthes, 1837); Eng. trans.: *A Commentary on the Gospel of St. John*, trans. A. Kaufman (Boston: Perkins & Marvin, 1836).
155. Tholuck, *Commentary on John*, ix.
156. Ibid., 17.

lypse was composed) and 100 (when the Gospel was written)! John intended to write not a supplementary Gospel, but a Gospel which supplements the tradition. He knew the tradition so well that he omitted some items he assumed to be widely known. He did not rely on the other Gospels as sources but may have used notes he had made on the discourses of Jesus. Actually, John would have been able to narrate the Gospel by the sheer power of his memory: "Christ promised to his disciples an extraordinary internal assistance, by which their memory even should be strengthened, so that their minds should recall every thing which they had heard of him (John 14:26)."[157]

Tholuck's exegesis of John is reminiscent of Hengstenberg. The background of the Logos is Jewish, not Philonic or gnostic. Although the terminology of the Cana story implies that the guests were intoxicated, Tholuck believes there was no excessive drunkenness. After considerable wrestling with the issue, Tholuck concludes that there were two cleansings of the temple. Indeed, "it would be altogether in consonance with the office and character of Christ to suppose that he checked those disorders every time he entered the Temple."[158] Tholuck is amazed that Nicodemus so badly misunderstands the teaching of Jesus, but he fails to detect a pattern in the parallel misunderstanding of the Samaritan woman.

> The woman, living only in earthly things, and without culture, does not in the least apprehend the deep meaning of the remark; she understands it literally. What condescension in the divine Redeemer, to unite himself to such weak, neglected minds; to lay open the hidden spark that comes from God and which even they carry within themselves![159]

Tholuck has no difficulty in accepting the miracles. Jesus, for example, "walks on the sea by that same power with which he rules nature."[160] In regard to the last supper, Tholuck harmonizes John and the Synoptics: either Jesus kept the Passover early or, more likely, John 18:38 refers to a different meal. Only rarely does rationalism raise its ugly head: Mary Magdalene did not recognize the risen Christ because he may have been wearing the gardener's clothes—shades of Griesbach and Paulus.[161] When all is said and done, Tholuck's Pietism has added an element of vitality to his understanding of the NT, but, in the main, the spirit is captive to an apologetic biblicism.

157. Ibid., 36.
158. Ibid., 102.
159. Ibid., 125–26.
160. Ibid., 158.
161. See pp. 141, 202, above.

Heinrich Ewald (1803–1875)

Georg Heinrich August Ewald thrived on conflict. On the right flank, he battled the opponents of biblical criticism (like Hengstenberg), whom he called the "un-free"; on the left, he attacked Strauss and the Tübingen school, whom he dubbed the "evil-free." The son of a weaver, Ewald was born in Göttingen. In 1820, he entered the university, where his major professor was J. G. Eichhorn. At Göttingen, Ewald mastered the Semitic languages, and his academic brilliance led to his appointment as professor at the age of twenty-seven. In 1837, Ewald became embroiled in the notorious affair of the "Göttingen Seven." In that year, the new ruler of Hanover revoked the liberal constitution of 1833. Considering this act to be a threat to political and academic freedom, Ewald and six other members of the Göttingen faculty (including the Brothers Grimm) signed a stern protest and were promptly dismissed. Reflecting on his action, Ewald, the only theologian in the group, wrote, "It was the religion . . . of Christ and the Bible, nothing else, which drove me to take so forcefully this step."[162] After his banishment from Hanover, Ewald worked for some months in the libraries of England, where he was noted as a person who "after copying Hebrew MSS for twelve hours at the Bodleian with nothing but a sandwich to sustain him, complained of the short time to work."[163]

From England, Ewald was called to a professorship at Tübingen, where he tilted his lance toward F. C. Baur. Indeed, controversy with Baur encouraged Ewald, who was primarily an OT scholar, to undertake research in early Christianity and its documents. In 1848, the political climate had changed in Göttingen, and Ewald returned to teach there, this time in the philosophical faculty. However, when Prussia annexed Hanover in 1866, Ewald refused to pledge loyalty to the king and was again removed from his professorship. A tall, commanding figure, Ewald lectured with a squeaky voice, yet a British auditor observed that he had "a glow of hidden fire" and an "appearance and delivery that suggested an inspired prophet."[164] Ewald was seriously concerned about his students, frequently returning the fees the poor had paid to participate in his classes. Among his students was one of the greatest biblical scholars of the century, Julius Wellhausen.

Ewald's OT publications included studies on Hebrew poetry, a three-

---

162. Cited in Lothar Perlitt, "Heinrich Ewald, Der Gelehrte in der Politik," in *Theologie in Göttingen: Eine Vorlesungsreihe*, ed. Bernd Moeller (Göttingen: Vandenhoeck & Ruprecht, 1987), 169.
163. Cited in T. Witton Davies, *Heinrich Ewald: Orientalist and Theologian, 1803–1903, A Centenary Appreciation* (London: T. F. Unwin, 1903), 10.
164. Cited in ibid., 10.

volume work on the prophets, a four-volume theology of the Old and New Testaments,[165] and his massive *History of Israel* (seven volumes). Ewald's fundamental position is set forth in his work on the nature and record of divine revelation.[166] In the first part, he discusses the revelation of the word of God. Humans can receive revelation because of their inherent spiritual capacity. Revelation unfolds in progressive stages, first to individuals and then to prophets who speak the word to the community. Moses presents a new understanding of God as the one true spiritual deity. Christ represents a higher stage. Conscious of his Messiahship and totally without error, Jesus was called to found the spiritual kingdom.

> As the truth and love, and thereby the definite will of God to men, may become in a man most perfectly living and effective, so this truth and this love of God and His eternal will to men were now manifest in the most perfect clearness and certainty,—no longer as from an invisible distant Deity, or according to the demand and prescription of a law; and the Word of God which, comprehending in itself the whole mind of God, penetrates and orders and sustains the whole universe from the beginning, but before all the universe is addressed to and seeks to guide mankind,— this Word, as we may now briefly say upon a calm retrospect of the appearing of Christ, was embodied and made human in the life of this one man, and in His perishable mortal body itself, that it might be manifest to all humanity as it was first manifest in Him.[167]

According to Ewald, the revelation in Christ cannot be superseded, "since a higher and more conspicuous revelation has neither actually come in the ages succeeding Christ, nor upon close consideration is it even possible."[168] This full and final revelation will be consummated when it is universally received in the final age of history.

After a discussion of revelation in heathenism and in Israel, Ewald turns to revelation in the Bible. According to Ewald, "we have had for a long time no other historical means than the Bible by which to satisfy ourselves of the nature and content of true religion as it has been revealed."[169] The Bible records events and experiences in which revelation has occurred. The writing was accomplished by persons, but sometimes the writers speak for others, so that the appearance in the NT of pseudon-

---

165. Heinrich Ewald, *Die Lehre der Bibel von Gott, oder die Theologie des alten und neuen Bundes*, 4 vols. (1871–76); Eng. trans. of selections from vols. 2 and 3 of this work: *Old and New Testament Theology*, trans. Thomas Goadby (Edinburgh: T. & T. Clark, 1888).

166. Heinrich Ewald, *Revelation; Its Nature and Record*, trans. Thomas Goadby (Edinburgh: T. & T. Clark, 1884). This book is based on Ewald's *Die Lehre der Bibel von Gott, oder die Theologie des alten und neuen Bundes*, 4 vols. (1871–76). The translation includes most of the first volume, *Die Lehre vom Worte Gottes* (1871).

167. Ewald, *Revelation*, 118.

168. Ibid., 121.

169. Ibid., 301.

ymous documents is not disquieting. In the main, the biblical record is reliable, but discrepancies (e.g., imperfections in copying) occur. The holiness of Scripture consists not in the letter but in its power to speak the word of God which is effective for human salvation. Above all, the Bible is the witness to God's revelation in history. Although the Scriptures display diversity, they fundamentally constitute a unity. Nothing can replace the biblical revelation. Its importance is confirmed by Jesus' use of the Hebrew Scriptures. For all of its defects, the total force of biblical research is to confirm the reliability of the scriptural record.

> Nevertheless, when we have submitted this whole province to the most exact researches, a new universal certainty arises which is just as far removed from these hazy and dark innovations as from that old security which was not at all secure against the gradual entrance of grave errors, and whilst an incalculable number of old prejudices once so perniciously prevalent has been irrevocably destroyed, the historical trustworthiness of the Bible has come forth with new certainty out of the fires of the keenest investigation.[170]

These principles are applied in the two volumes of Ewald's *History of Israel* that present the life of Jesus and the history of the apostolic age. In his *Life and Times of Christ* (1858),[171] Ewald sees Judaism as preparation for the higher religion of Jesus. As the messianic idea evolves, the older Davidic concept is "celestialized." "There prevails, therefore, at this time involuntarily the feeling, that the coming of the Messiah and of his kingdom must be still more wonderful, that is, must be accompanied by still higher unforeseen Divine powers and works, than had been ever before expected."[172] The idea of the celestial Messiah is developed by Daniel and Enoch, who combine the imagery of the heavenly son of man and the divine son of God. Before discussing the life of Jesus, Ewald analyzes the sources, an analysis more fully presented in his work *The Three First Gospels*.[173] In regard to the Synoptic problem, Ewald offers the most elaborate hypothesis since Eichhorn[174] and Marsh.[175] The hypothesis proposes a progression of sources that identifies ten documents:

1. A primitive collection of narratives, written in Greek, used by Paul, possibly written by Philip (an *Urmarcus*).

---

170. Ibid., 412–13.
171. Heinrich Ewald, *The History of Israel, VI: The Life and Times of Christ*, trans. J. Frederick Smith (London: Longmans, Green, 1883).
172. Ibid., 110.
173. Heinrich Ewald, *Die drei ersten Evangelien und die Apostelgeschichte*, 2d ed., 2 vols. (Göttingen: Dieter, 1871).
174. See pp. 151–52, above.
175. See pp. 299–301, above.

2. A collection of sayings, written by one of the apostles (the *logia* of Matthew).

3. The Gospel of Mark, written by John Mark, incorporating tradition from Peter. A second edition of this Gospel included material from 1 (*Urmarcus*) and 2 (*logia*).

4. The "Book of Higher History," which expanded Mark and moved in a spiritual direction.

5. The Gospel of Matthew, written for Jews and Jewish Christians, using 3 (Mark) and 2 (the *logia*) as sources.

6., 7., 8. Three other gospels, one of which, for example, included the birth stories which Luke later used.

9. The Gospel of Luke, written for Gentiles by Luke, the travel companion of Paul, around 75.

10. A third edition of the Gospel of Mark.

Obviously, Ewald assumes an evolutionary development of sources, moving from short and simple to longer and more detailed gospels. Also, in terms of the larger debate about the relationship of the Gospels, he affirms the priority of Mark, and supports a complex version of the two-document (Mark and the *logia*) hypothesis. Regardless of the development of the sources, the documents are essentially reliable: "not the least untruth intentionally crept into any of these narratives, and not the smallest thing was fictitiously invented therein in the low sense of the word."[176]

Ewald's exposition of the life of Jesus is moderately conservative. He considers the history prior to Jesus' ministry to be of secondary importance. He accepts the historicity of Jesus' birth in Bethlehem but recognizes Joseph as the father. The baptism was a decisive event in the evolving development of the higher religion.

> This solemn moment thus became the true natal hour of Christianity; all that was highest in the past ages concentrated itself in this moment for the formation of something new which must become the Consummation itself, and this new thing developed itself from the same moment unalterably and irresistibly, in conformity with its own spirit, in such a way that all the future was involved in it.[177]

According to Ewald, Jesus preached a spiritual kingdom—the realization of the true religion, involving cooperation between people and God. The kingdom was already present for those who received it, but it would be

---

176. Ewald, *Life and Times of Christ*, 148.
177. Ibid., 194.

fully consummated only in the future. Ewald accepts the historicity of most of the miracles but acknowledges that the idea of demon possession reflected a primitive misunderstanding of disease. However, Jesus healed such diseases by his spiritual power. Ewald accepts the Cana miracle as historical, although with spiritual meaning.

> If we wished here to inquire in a gross sense how mere water could possibly in a moment become wine, we should sadly dilute for ourselves this wine, which from that time can still always flow for us also. Shall then, water, in the best sense of the word, not everywhere now also become wine where Christ's spirit is operative in all its power?[178]

The raising of Lazarus presents Ewald with no problem, for, in his words, "nothing can be more historical than this occurrence."[179]

According to Ewald, the messianic consciousness of Jesus continued to develop throughout his career. During his ministry, Jesus used the title "son of man."

> But when he designated himself as the Messiah precisely by this simple general name, *the Son of man*, that really involved the same indescribable self-renunciation, love, and condescension which was involved in all his labours, and men did not suppose they heard the King and the God, but simply the man and son of man; although, at least for the thoughtful hearer, there must have been conveyed by the name a reference to the Book of Daniel, and thereby to Messianic conceptions.[180]

Later in his ministry, his consciousness as Messiah led Jesus to resolve to take his message to Jerusalem. Ewald, in presenting the passion narrative, relies heavily on the Gospel of John, which he accepts as authentic.[181] He thinks that the Synoptic evangelists err in locating the cleansing of the temple in the Passion Week, and that John is correct in placing the event at the beginning of Jesus' ministry. John is correct, too, in noting that the last supper was not a Passover meal but was observed on the day before. "However, the discrepancy amongst the Gospels regarding the time of this supper is . . . of comparative insignificance."[182]

Ewald's work *The Apostolic Age*[183] relies heavily on his reading of the Acts of the Apostles, a document written around 80 from Rome by Luke, a

178. Ibid., 251.
179. Ibid., 369.
180. Ibid., 231–32.
181. For Ewald's view of the Johannine literature see his *Die Johanneischen Schriften: Übersezt und Erklärt*, 2 vols. (Göttingen: Dieter, 1861). Although Ewald accepts the apostolic authorship of the Fourth Gospel, he believes Revelation was written not by the same author but by another John, probably John the presbyter.
182. Ewald, *Life and Times of Christ*, 419.
183. Heinrich Ewald, *The History of Israel, VII: The Apostolic Age*, trans. J. Frederick Smith (London: Longmans, Green, 1885).

travel companion of Paul. Luke's purpose was to write history, not to present theological tendencies, as Baur and his friends suppose. According to that history, the new age dawns with the event of the resurrection of Jesus. Ewald believes the narratives of the resurrection undergo a development from the true spiritual to a more material conception. "If we compare the above oldest and simplest narrative with this [Luke's account], which really after all only presents essentially the same facts, we cannot fail to see that this recognition of the risen Christ, which was at first surely purely spiritual, gradually sought and found support in a physical seeing and kindred reflections."[184] Similarly, Paul's conversion was essentially inward, although with outward manifestations. Ewald accepts Luke's account of the Jerusalem conference, including Peter's leading role in the gentile mission and the historicity of the apostolic decrees. He accepts 2 Thessalonians as Pauline but written earlier than 1 Thessalonians. Ewald does not bat an eye at the report of Paul's miraculous deeds in Ephesus.

> The healing power of the man who was always speaking such holy words, and himself living such a holy life, was so much in request that even the handkerchiefs and the short aprons which he wore on his breast at his work, were asked for and laid upon the sick while they were still warm from his skin; and in the case of certain evils, demoniacal possession for instance, relief was thereby found.[185]

Ewald posits two imprisonments for Paul: a first, from which he was released and made a journey to Spain; and a second, which terminated with his decapitation, around the year 65.

Heinrich Ewald presents NT scholars of the nineteenth century with a viable alternative to the Tübingen approach. He demonstrates that it is possible to employ the historical-critical method and still reach relatively conservative conclusions. Ewald, with his recognition of pseudonymous documents within the canon and his acknowledgment of discrepancies in Scripture, is no biblicist. He is also attuned to the Enlightenment belief in progressive revelation and is sensitive to the idea of the spirit in contrast to exclusive preoccupation with the letter. Like the mediating theologians and the neologians, Ewald attempts to combine natural and supernatural. However, he tends to reduce biblical literature to historical record, even though his idea of revelation in history involves religious experience and the significance of the biblical message for human salvation. In terms of future developments in NT research, Ewald's most questionable critical judgment may be seen in his historicizing of the Gospel of John. Perhaps

184. Ibid., 68.
185. Ibid., 391.

this may be explained by Ewald's weakest but most interesting trait: his passion to use criticism as a weapon against his foes.

SUMMARY

With Strauss and Baur, NT research assumes new dimensions: it adopts a comprehensive view of reality—Hegel's metaphysics—which incorporates a philosophy of history as a crucial element. Thus, the theological idea of revelation in history can be understood in terms of a total philosophical outlook, and historical reconstruction can take place within the framework of a larger ontology. On the basis of this comprehensive hermeneutic, the major issues of NT research are addressed: the life and significance of Jesus, and the history and faith of the early church. Strauss's *Life of Jesus* rigorously rejects rationalist and supernatural exegesis in favor of a methodology of myth. By means of this method, Strauss subjects the sources for the life and teaching of Jesus to skeptical scrutiny, and although his analysis of the Synoptic Gospels is meager, his rejection of the Gospel of John as a historical source is forcefully articulated. As to theology, Strauss's work, in contrast to Schleiermacher's, created a chasm between the Jesus of history and the Christ of faith. According to Strauss, historical research cannot sustain the Christ in whom most Christians believe. In similar fashion, F. C. Baur subjects the sources for the history of the early church to skeptical scrutiny. Just as Strauss abandoned the Fourth Gospel as a historical source, so Baur is critical of the historical data provided by the Acts of the Apostles. Baur's method of tendency criticism, whereby documents are analyzed according to their theological bias, raises questions about the historical reliability of all the NT books. As a result of Baur's work, the idyllic portrait of the early church as a community of peace and harmony is abandoned in favor of a picture of the church torn by conflicting factions. The witness of the apostles upon which the tradition of Christianity is built turns out to be not solid rock but the shifting sands of theological controversy.

The impact of Strauss and Baur on NT research is difficult to overestimate. Their work calls into question virtually all of the traditional views of Scripture—canon, inspiration, biblical authority. In regard to critical questions, followers of Baur, for example, Zeller and Hilgenfeld, demonstrate that one can adopt the Tübingen approach without accepting all of Baur's radical results. Thus, the documents need not be dated in the second century in order to fit into the scheme of a dialectical relation between Jewish and gentile Christianity. Similarly, tendency criticism can be employed in the analysis of NT documents without accepting Baur's conclusions about authorship. As to the future of NT research, the bitterness engendered in the course of the controversy created by Strauss and the Tübingen school would continue to cloud the theological picture. Personal animosities (e.g., between Baur and Ewald) and academic and political rivalries (e.g., between Berlin and Tübingen) would belie the objectivity which had been the goal of Enlightenment research. With Baur, NT research moves from a concern with biblical scholarship (including the OT) to a preoccupation with early church history; and with Strauss and Hilgenfeld, biblical scholarship is less an ecclesiastical, and more an academic, endeavor.

Although many nineteenth-century scholars were negative in their assessment of the Tübingen school, those who first provided answers and alternatives were less than convincing. In the main, the critics offered only a return to the past: orthodoxy (Hengstenberg), Pietism (Tholuck), mediating theology or neology (Ewald). What these critics lacked was a comprehensive view of reality that could move beyond the limitations of the Enlightenment. Strauss and Baur had attempted this in adopting Hegelian idealism, and although the critics identified this as Tübingen's fatal error, they offered no viable alternative of their own. To be sure, the adoption of the philosophical foundation suggested that the whole superstructure would collapse if the foundation crumbled. In short, if Hegel fell, Baur would fall, too. Although this is true in part, some of the critical results, like broken columns in an ancient ruin, could survive the fall and be incorporated into a new building. The strength of the Tübingen scholars, however, is seen not in their definitive answers but in their ability to speak effectively to their own time—to articulate their understanding of the Bible in terms of the prevailing philosophy of the day.

9

Literary, Historical, and Textual Criticism alongside and in the Wake of Tübingen

New Testament research in the first two-thirds of the nineteenth century was extensive and varied. As the burgeoning factories of the Industrial Revolution were manufacturing a multitude of commodities, so the academic centers of Europe were producing a great quantity of biblical criticism. Some of this productivity was simply the legacy of the eighteenth century, that is, the research of scholars like Semler and Michaelis, continued and expanded. The Enlightenment methods were refined, new questions were raised, and novel answers, like new patches on an old garment, were offered to the timeworn questions. Much of the activity was generated in response to Strauss and the Tübingen school. The notions that the gospel stories were largely myth and that the narratives of Acts were fictitious encouraged zealous study of the Christian sources. Were Strauss and Baur correct in their conclusion that Matthew was the earliest Gospel? Was it true that the Gospel of John was a second-century christological construction rather than an authentic account of the life of Jesus? And what of new discoveries of ancient manuscripts. Did they confirm the reliability of the text? And could they be incorporated into a still more trustworthy critical edition?

RESEARCH ON THE SYNOPTIC PROBLEM: GIESELER, MARSH, WILKE, WEISSE, AND MEIJBOOM

Once the theory of verbal inspiration had been abandoned, a variety of hypotheses were proposed to explain the interrelationship of the first three Gospels. Almost all conceivable theories had been advanced by the end of the eighteenth century.[1] Early in the nineteenth century, the most popular were (1) the hypothesis that Mark used Matthew and Luke as sources (Griesbach); (2) the theory that all three Gospels were ultimately dependent on a primitive gospel, written in Aramaic (Eichhorn); and (3) the hypothesis that the evangelists made use of written fragments and collections of fragments of the gospel tradition (Schleiermacher). The Tübingen school, employing Baur's tendency criticism, arrived at a position similar to Griesbach's: Matthew (the early Jewish Gospel) and Luke (the gentile Gospel) were used by Mark (the mediating Gospel).[2] According to Hilgenfeld's variation, Mark provided the bridge of transition from the earlier Jewish Gospel of Matthew to the later Pauline Gospel of Luke.[3]

Johann Carl Ludwig Gieseler (1792–1854): Common Oral Tradition

The hypothesis that the Gospels depended on a common oral tradition was advanced by Johann Carl Ludwig Gieseler. Born in Petershagen, near Hanover, Gieseler was educated at the University of Halle. In 1813, he joined the Prussian army to fight for liberation from Napoleon's domination. After teaching at the gymnasium level, Gieseler was appointed professor at the University of Bonn. In 1831, he joined the faculty at Göttingen, where he held administrative as well as professorial posts. Gieseler was primarily a church historian, and his multivolume *Lehrbuch der Kirchengeschichte* (1824–57) was noted for its rigorous use of historical-critical method.[4]

Gieseler's contribution to the discussion of the synoptic problem is presented in his *Historical-Critical Experiment Concerning the Formation and Earliest Fate of the Written Gospels* (1818).[5] Gieseler begins with some general observations, noting, for instance, that agreement is greater within the Gospel pericopes than in their settings. In reviewing previous attempts to solve the problem, he assesses two major approaches: (1) the hypothesis that the Gospels are somehow interdependent; (2) the theory that the Gospels rest on a common written source. He finds the first hypothesis unsatisfactory because, in his judgment, it cannot adequately explain why subsequent evangelists would disagree and even contradict their predecessor(s). He rejects the second because, in his opinion, theories

---

1. See p. 144, above.
2. See p. 268, above.
3. See p. 276, above.
4. Eng. trans.: John C. L. Gieseler, *A Compendium of Ecclesiastical History*, trans. Samuel Davidson, 4th rev. ed., 5 vols. (Edinburgh: T. & T. Clark, 1854–55).
5. Johann Carl Ludwig Gieseler, *Historisch-kritischer Versuch über die Entstehung und die frühesten Schicksale der schriftlichen Evangelien* (Leipzig: W. Engelmann, 1818).

concerning the use of a common source (e.g., by Eichhorn) require procedures for using sources that are too complex to be expected of ancient
authors. Moreover, in the apostolic age, the gospel was not written, but
presented orally, and oral tradition was considered more important than
written. Besides, no trace of a common, primitive written gospel can be
detected, and an early Christian writer like Paul, for example, knows of no
such document.

Gieseler's own view is that the source of the Gospels is a common oral
tradition; as he says, "the evangelists used one identical oral source."[6]
According to Gieseler, a common oral source can account for the agreements among the Gospels, and the variations can be explained by individual usage of the common source by the different evangelists. The
general order of the gospel narrative, beginning with the baptism of Jesus
and ending with the passion story, was an established feature of early
preaching. The tradition was shaped and transmitted by uneducated persons who expressed themselves in simple ways and in similar idioms. The
tradition, according to Gieseler, developed in three stages.

The first stage is represented by the oral preaching of the apostles. The
words and deeds of Jesus had made a profound impression upon their
memories. Like the Jews who memorized their stories and taught orally,
the apostles belonged to a preliterary culture. In such a culture, memory
functions better than it does in literate cultures. The more the memorized
tradition was repeated, the more definite its shape became. "One needs
only to observe one's own experience," writes Gieseler, "in order to recognize how powerfully through the constant repetition of the same narrative
a person is moved to a fixed form of presentation."[7] Thus, when Paul
implies that the gospel he preaches is the same as the gospel preached by
the other apostles, he is referring to this common, oral gospel.

The second stage of the developing tradition is seen in the teaching of
the later disciples. In this period, the gospel was first spoken in Syro-
Chaldean (i.e., Aramaic), but as the preachers moved beyond Palestine,
the gospel was translated (orally) into Greek. The fact that these preachers
were limited in their comprehension of the Greek language contributed
to the simplicity and uniformity of the oral tradition. In the third stage,
the tradition was finally committed to writing. The more widely the message was disseminated, the more the need of writing increased. At first,
the writings were private—documents designed to aid the memory. In
time, gospels were written for a wider audience by authors like the "many"
mentioned in Luke 1:1. The canonical Gospels were composed relatively

6. Ibid., 83.
7. Ibid., 98.

late and were not written, in Gieseler's opinion, by eyewitnesses. They were composed independently, but in the traditional order: Matthew and Mark reflect a more Jewish reading of the tradition, while Luke shows later, universal tendencies.

Herbert Marsh (1758–1839):
A Common Written Gospel

Herbert Marsh develops the view that the Gospels rest on a common Aramaic document, but he does this in a way which in effect fostered the two-document hypothesis. Marsh was born at Faversham, Kent, and educated at King's School, Canterbury, and St. John's College, Cambridge. In 1785, he traveled to the continent and studied for a time at Leipzig. He was appointed Lady Margaret Professor of Divinity at Cambridge in 1807, where he lectured in English instead of Latin—an innovation. His lectures, attended by townspeople as well as students, were so popular that they had to be held in the university church. In 1816, Marsh was appointed Bishop of Llandaff, and in 1819, he was made Bishop of Peterborough where he remained for the rest of his career.

Usually identified with the orthodox or high church party,[8] Marsh published works in church history and biblical studies. His point of view is apparent in a series of lectures on divinity that treat questions of biblical authority, criticism, and interpretation.[9] The first two parts (lectures 1–12) deal with the criticism of the Bible and attend to matters of historical introduction and text criticism. Part 3 (lectures 13–18), "On the Interpretation of the Bible," presents rules of exegesis. Marsh maintains, for example, that biblical words have the meaning which they had for their original readers, and that the same rules used for interpreting other writings should be applied to the study of the Scriptures. In short, Marsh advocates historical exegesis. Part 4 (lectures 19–22) discusses the interpretation of prophecy, and part 5 (lectures 23–26), "On the Authenticity of the New Testament," asserts that the NT books were written by the authors to whom they have been traditionally ascribed. Part 6 (lectures 27–30), "On the Credibility of the New Testament," argues on the basis of the moral character of the biblical writers that their accounts are reliable. Marsh also accepts the miracle stories as historical and claims that the raising of

---

8. See Vernon F. Storr, *The Development of English Theology in the Nineteenth Century 1800–1860* (London: Longmans, Green, 1913), 82, 183–85.

9. Herbert Marsh, *A Course of Lectures, Containing a Description and Systematic Arrangement of the Several Branches of Divinity: Accompanied with an Account, Both of the Principle Authors, and of the Progress, Which Has Been Made at Different Periods, in Theological Learning* (Cambridge: J. Smith, 1810–23).

Lazarus, for example, was reported by an eyewitness and confirmed by the judicial scrutiny of the Jewish leaders.

Marsh's discussion of the synoptic problem is presented in his "Dissertation on the Origin and Composition of Our Three First Canonical Gospels." Originally published separately (1798), this lengthy essay is included in Marsh's translation of Michaelis's *Introduction*.[10] At the outset, Marsh states the question: How are we to explain the agreements and disagreements among the first three Gospels? Like Gieseler, he notes and evaluates two major hypotheses: (1) that the succeeding evangelists copied the preceding; and (2) that the three evangelists independently used a common source. In regard to the first, he finds the theory of Marcan priority highly unlikely. Marsh also discusses the Griesbach hypothesis at length but rejects it, because, in his opinion, it does not adequately explain why Mark would have omitted so much material that is in Matthew and Luke. In regard to the second hypothesis, Marsh presents an extensive discussion of Eichhorn's idea of a common Aramaic source, a theory he prefers to any variation of the first hypothesis. He does not fully embrace it, however, because he believes Eichhorn fails to explain the verbatim agreements of words and sentences in the Greek gospels.

Having dispensed with the alternatives, Marsh proceeds to offer his own solution to the synoptic problem. His method is to present the material in parallel columns and then to analyze the data. According to Marsh, the thesis that best explains the agreements and disagreements will provide the best solution to the problem. Marsh's own hypothesis is that the authors of all three Gospels used a Semitic *Urgospel* (designated by the Hebrew letter Aleph), but each evangelist utilized a different copy of that common source. Matthew wrote in Hebrew (Marsh means "Aramaic") and made use of the Semitic *Urgospel*. Mark and Luke used different copies of the *Urgospel* and also employed a Greek translation of it:

> Lastly, as the Gospels of St. Mark and St. Luke contain Greek translations of Hebrew materials, which were incorporated into St. Matthew's Hebrew Gospel, the person, who translated St. Matthew's Hebrew Gospel into Greek, frequently derived assistance, from the Gospel of St. Mark, where St. Mark had matter in common with St. Matthew: and in those places, but in those places only, where St. Mark had no matter in common with St. Matthew, he had frequently recourse to St. Luke's Gospel.[11]

---

10. Herbert Marsh, "A Dissertation on the Origin and Composition of Our Three First Canonical Gospels," in John David Michaelis, *Introduction to the New Testament*, trans. Herbert Marsh (London: Rivington, 1802), 3.161–409. See pp. 131–38, above.

11. Ibid. 3.361.

Marsh's complex reconstruction of the sources and their use in the Synoptic Gospels can be summarized in eight stages:

1. *Aleph*: the earliest gospel, which included a narrative of the activity of Jesus from his baptism to his death; written in Chaldee (that is, Aramaic).
2. A Greek translation of *Aleph.*
3. Copies of *Aleph* to which material had been added—the different copies used by Matthew, Mark, and Luke.
4. A supplemental Semitic document (designated by the Hebrew letter *Beth*), which contained teachings, parables, and discourses; used by Matthew and Luke but in different copies.
5. Matthew's Hebrew (Aramaic) Gospel which made use of Matthew's copy of *Aleph* + *Beth* + material of his own. (Matthew was an eyewitness.)
6. Luke's Gospel: used his copy of *Aleph* + *Beth* + material found by his own investigation. Luke translated his sources into Greek and used the Greek translation of *Aleph* (2).
7. Mark's Gospel: used his copy of *Aleph* + additions of his own. Mark translated his sources into Greek and used the Greek translation of *Aleph* (2).
8. The canonical Matthew: a Greek translation of the Hebrew Matthew (5), which made use of the Gospels of Mark and Luke.

Although the evangelists copied sources, Marsh insists that "they are not to be considered as transcribers, but as authors."[12] Finally, Marsh tests his hypothesis by attempting to demonstrate its capability to explain the agreements and disagreements among the Synoptic Gospels. This is accomplished with considerable success, a result not unpredictable in view of the complexity and flexibility of Marsh's proposal. For instance, he argues that verbal agreements in all three Gospels can be explained by his theory that Mark and Luke copied from the early Greek translation of *Aleph*, while the Greek translator of Matthew copied from Mark.

At first glance, Marsh appears to present a variation of Eichhorn's hypothesis that the Gospels are dependent on a Semitic *Urgospel.* However, Marsh's notion that the translator of canonical Matthew made use of Mark and Luke assumes, at the same time, the hypothesis that succeeding Gospels copied preceding. In developing his solution, Marsh actually gives tacit support to the two-document hypothesis which was to triumph at the

---

12. Ibid. 3.409.

end of the nineteenth and beginning of the twentieth centuries.[13] His theory that Matthew and Luke made use of *Aleph* (a primitive narrative source) and *Beth* (an early collection of teachings) is parallel to the two-document hypothesis's view that Mark and Q (German, *Quelle* = "source") were the basic sources of the Synoptic Gospels. Most striking, however, is Marsh's conviction that all three of the Gospels were authentic, that is, written by Matthew, Mark, and Luke. This means that Marsh's eight-stage development of the gospel tradition had to transpire within the limits of the apostolic age. One has to wonder, too, why an evangelist like Matthew, himself an eyewitness to the events, would have needed or wanted to copy sources like *Aleph* and *Beth* at all.

Christian Gottlob Wilke (1786–1854): The Priority of Mark

The hypothesis that the Gospel of Mark was the earliest and the primary source of the Synoptic Gospels was most extensively presented by Christian Gottlob Wilke. Wilke was born in a small town in Saxony. After service as a chaplain in the Saxon army, Wilke labored for some years as a pastor at Hermannsdorf in the Erz mountains. In 1837, he retired to Dresden as a freelance writer. In 1846, he converted to Catholicism and moved to Würzburg, where he spent the balance of his career. Noted for his competence in biblical philology, Wilke published a widely used lexicon of NT Greek[14] and also wrote a book on NT rhetoric.[15] In 1837, Wilke responded to Strauss's *Life of Jesus* with a work on tradition and myth.[16] He appreciated Strauss as an alternative to a rising conservatism, but preferred "rational mysticism" to Strauss's mythical idealism. In other words, Wilke rejected supernaturalism, while seeking a rationalism sensitive to religious feeling.

Besides his important contribution to the synoptic problem, Wilke also composed a two-volume study of NT hermeneutics.[17] This work is arranged in two parts: the first deals with hermeneutical principles, and the second with hermeneutical method. In the first part, Wilke notes that NT hermeneutics is merely a particular expression of general principles of interpre-

13. See William R. Farmer, *The Synoptic Problem: A Critical Analysis* (Dillsboro, N.C.: Western North Carolina Press, 1976), 11–15.

14. Christiano Gottlob Wilke, *Clavis Novi Testamenti philologica usibus scholarum et iuvenum theologiae studiosorum accomodata*, 2 vols. (Dresden and Leipzig: Arnold, 1841).

15. Christian Gottlob Wilke, *Die neutestamentliche Rhetorik, ein Seitenstück zur Grammatik des neutestamentlichen Sprachidioms* (Dresden and Leipzig: Arnold, 1843).

16. See Albert Schweitzer, *The Quest of the Historical Jesus: A Critical Study of Its Progress from Reimarus to Wrede*, trans. W. Montgomery (New York: Macmillan, 1957), 111–13.

17. Christian Gottlob Wilke, *Die Hermeneutik des Neuen Testaments systematisch dargestellt*, 2 vols. (Leipzig: F.C.W. Vogel, 1843).

tation that apply to all literature. These principles are discussed in relation to four major areas. First, Wilke considers what he calls the "interpretability" (*Auslegbarkeit*) of the text, that is, the conditions—linguistic, psychological, and logical—that make interpretation possible. Second, Wilke discusses the construction and content of NT language. Here Wilke insists that attention be given to the literary genres (*Gattungen*) in which the NT message is expressed—whether, for example, the document is an epistle or a prophetic composition. As to content, Wilke believes the NT material is either historical (as in the Acts of the Apostles) or ideal, that is, concerned with concepts that are frequently (e.g., in the Gospel of John) presented through symbolic expressions. In the third area, Wilke turns to principles of exegesis. The purpose of exegesis is to find the basic meaning of each individual writing. The use of scientific exegesis is necessary because of difficulties in interpretation. The goal of exegesis is to represent what the author originally said. Thus, Wilke calls for historical interpretation, although he observes that biblical ideas (e.g., Paul's teaching about forgiveness) cannot be reduced to bare history. In the fourth area, Wilke offers some regulations for interpretation. Basically, the interpreter must follow the rules of Greek syntax. The text also must be viewed in its historical setting, and attention must be given to the religious experience of each author. "Every writer of the New Testament," says Wilke, "should be interpreted out of his own writing, so that that meaning expressed in the individual sentences of his discourse, in which the linguistic and spiritual elements are absorbed into one another, can be recognized as his own."[18]

In the second part of his *Hermeneutik*, Wilke presents details of exegetical practice. His discussion of syntax attends to such matters as the use of prepositions with different cases. In regard to lexicography, Wilke notes how root meanings are modified by usage. He also points out the need to analyze types of argument and the use of paradox. Concerning the interpretation of parables, Wilke, like G. L. Bauer before him,[19] anticipated principles which were developed in the twentieth century.

> According to the manner in which these are given in the New Testament writings, namely the Gospels, the following principles ought to be recognized before the attempt at interpretation: (a) the point of comparison of the parable, as manifold as its content may be, is only one; (b) the parables are not to be treated universally in the same way; (c) the simplest explanation is indeed the usual, but it is not always the correct.[20]

18. Ibid. 1.321.
19. See p. 188, above.
20. Wilke, *Hermeneutik* 2.302.

Concerning doctrinal expression, the exegete must give careful attention to terms and phrases that express biblical teaching—like Jesus' idea of the kingdom of God. In a concluding section, Wilke offers practical advice concerning the selection and use of commentaries and lexicons: "Finally, a lexicon of the NT should indicate not simply in what dialect the New Testament authors write, but what concepts and ideas they understand to be connected with the words which belong to their instruction."[21]

Wilke's solution to the synoptic problem is presented in his monumental work, *Der Urevangelist*.[22] Written in a convoluted and sometimes opaque style, this book is one of the most extensive treatments (over 690 pages) of the problem ever published. The sheer bulk of the work (compare Griesbach's original essay, reprinted in less than thirty pages)[23] added weight to Wilke's argument, over which he had labored for more than ten years. Wilke's conclusion is that the Gospels rest on a primitive written source, but a source not to be identified with Eichhorn's Aramaic *Urgospel* or Marsh's "Hebrew" *Aleph*. The primitive gospel is none other than the Gospel of Mark.

> We have therefore in our investigation come to the point that we can express the result of our research: Mark is the *Urevangelist*. His work is that which lies at the base of the two other Gospels of Matthew and Luke.[24]

In developing his argument, Wilke insists that the question of the relationship of the first three Gospels is to be answered not by tradition or presuppositions but on the basis of thorough analysis of the texts. He begins, therefore, by printing the Greek texts in parallel columns, arranged in three tables: one which presents material common to all three Gospels; another which presents the common material of Matthew and Luke; a third which presents the unique material of each of the Gospels.[25] Much of Wilke's argument is designed to demonstrate that other hypotheses cannot adequately explain the agreements and disagreements disclosed in these tables. The hypothesis of an oral *Urgospel* (Gieseler) is refuted by the evidence that the agreements are of a character that can only be explained by a written source. The hypothesis of an Aramaic *Urgospel* (Eichhorn) is

---

21. Ibid. 2.383–84.
22. Christian Gottlob Wilke, *Der Urevangelist, oder exegetisch kritische Untersuchung über das Verwandtschaftsverhältniss der drei ersten Evangelien* (Dresden and Leipzig: G. Fleischer, 1838).
23. B. Orchard and T.R.W. Longstaff, eds., *J. J. Griesbach: Synoptic and Text-critical Studies, 1776–1976*, Society for New Testament Studies Monograph Series 34 (Cambridge: Cambridge University Press, 1978), 74–102.
24. Wilke, *Urevangelist*, 684.
25. Although Wilke purports to work inductively, his first table prints Marcan material in the left-hand column, thus giving the impression that Mark is the text the other two Gospels follow. See Hans-Herbert Stoldt, *History and Criticism of the Marcan Hypothesis*, trans. and ed. Donald L. Niewyk (Macon, Ga.: Mercer University Press, 1980), 31–32.

refuted by the evidence that the agreements require a document written in Greek. Arguments against the Griesbach hypothesis recur throughout Wilke's book, although the opponent explicitly named is often Paulus,[26] who had adopted the theory that Mark used Matthew and Luke.

Wilke's argument for Marcan priority moves from what he thinks are the more obvious to the less apparent deductions from the parallel texts. As the exposition unfolds, arguments that have since become commonplace emerge. The argument from order, assuming the priority of Mark, observes that Matthew and Luke generally follow the order of Mark, but when they diverge from Marcan order, they do not agree in order with each other. The argument from content asserts that most of the material from Mark is found in Matthew and Luke; where Mark has additional details not found in Matthew and Luke, the additional material is explained either as later interpolations in Mark or as eliminations of Marcan material by Matthew and Luke. Wilke also argues from the literary integrity of the Gospels, that is, from his belief that each evangelist displays a distinctive style of composition. According to this argument, the common material of agreement among all three Gospels is in harmony with the style of Mark as a whole, so that the common material has its source in Mark.[27]

Working from the hypothesis of the priority of Mark, Wilke proceeds to argue that the additions made by Matthew and Luke represent their own style and tendencies. This is seen, for example, in Matthew's unique use of the phrase "kingdom of heaven" where Mark and Luke have "kingdom of God." "Each narrator," says Wilke, "has a special basis for his additions."[28] In Wilke's opinion, the evidence indicates that Mark's text is the most original: "The clearer the traces of an original text lying at the ground of the relationships become, the more the text of Mark can be distinguished from the others."[29] Some of the additions made by Matthew and Luke do not appear to be integral to the original narrative. In Matt. 12:7, for example, a quotation from Hosea 6:6 is added that introduces a foreign idea into the original text. Convinced that his hypothesis can explain the

---

26. See pp. 201–8, above.

27. Wilke's literary argument was countered by the vocabulary research of Zeller, which found the greatest originality to be in Matthew. See Eduard Zeller, "Studien zur neutestamentlichen Theologie: 4. Vergleichende Uebersicht über den Wörtervorrath der sämmtlichen neutestamentlichen Schriftsteller," *Theologische Jahrbücher* 2 (1843): 443–53; David B. Peabody, "Chapters in the History of the Linguistic Argument for Solving the Synoptic Problem: The Nineteenth Century in Context," in *Jesus, the Gospels, and the Church: Essays in Honor of William R. Farmer*, ed. E. P. Sanders (Macon, Ga.: Mercer University Press, 1987), 61–65.

28. Wilke, *Urevangelist*, 318.

29. Ibid., 321.

composition of Matthew and Luke, Wilke believes that the alternative (Griesbach) hypothesis—that Mark used Matthew and Luke—cannot explain the composition of Mark. Why, he asks, would Mark both shorten and expand? If Griesbach's view were adopted, "Mark would not have been an abbreviator, nor an epitomiser, nor an excerptor,—but a castrator of the other texts—or what else should one call the mutilator of borrowed sentences, the mixer of the mutilated?"[30]

Wilke gives limited attention to the problem of the non-Marcan material found in Matthew and Luke. In analyzing the discourses where these Gospels agree, he finds little evidence to suggest an independent source. Thus, Wilke concludes that Matthew used Luke. The resulting portrait of Matthew is almost as unflattering as the picture of Mark which Wilke finds implied by the Griesbach hypothesis: Matthew is a mere compiler. Could such a compiler be identified as the apostle Matthew? "That," answers Wilke, "we can in no way believe, and so we abandon the authenticity of the first Gospel."[31] What is really at stake for Wilke, in any case, is the originality and priority of the Gospel of Mark. He is fully convinced that his hypothesis is true: "Whatever one may still present against this view so as to promote different opinions, we maintain for all eternity under sign and seal that our conclusion is correct."[32]

Christian Hermann Weisse (1801–1866): Two-Document Hypothesis

The two-document hypothesis for solving the synoptic problem is formulated by Christian Hermann Weisse.[33] Born in Leipzig, Weisse was educated at the university there. After working for a time as a jurist, he turned to philosophy. From 1828 to 1837, Weisse served as associate professor at Leipzig, but when denied a promotion, he devoted himself to private research, including study of the Gospels. He returned to the academic ranks in 1841 and was appointed professor of philosophy at Leipzig in 1845. An important representative of nineteenth-century idealism, Weisse presents his point of view in his three-volume *Philosophical Dogmatics*.[34] Weisse understands God as the Absolute which is actualized in personality—a personal reality comprising reason, feeling, and will. This self-realization of God took place prior to creation, so that God both transcends and participates in creation. God's continuing creative activity

---

30. Ibid., 443.
31. Ibid., 692.
32. Ibid., 684.
33. For a summary of Weisse's life and NT research, see J. C. O'Neill, *The Bible's Authority: A Portrait Gallery of Thinkers from Lessing to Bultmann* (Edinburgh: T. & T. Clark, 1991), 126–34.
34. C. H. Weisse, *Philosophische Dogmatik, oder Philosophie des Christenthums*, 3 vols. (Leipzig: S. Hirzel, 1855–62).

occurs in history; revelation is history. Human nature is constantly being transformed in a continuing process of incarnation. This process is fully realized in Jesus—the "Son-Humanity" (*Sohnmensch*) who is the highest revelation of God. In this revelation, an ethical miracle is actualized in a unique individual—Jesus, a religious genius. Consequently, the historical Jesus is of crucial importance for Weisse's theological program.[35]

Although primarily a philosophical theologian, Weisse contributed to NT research. In addition to his important work on the synoptic problem, he published *Contributions to the Criticism of the Pauline Epistles to the Galatians, Romans, Philippians and Colossians*.[36] This short monograph presents the Greek text of the epistles in the left column and Weisse's translation in the right. In presenting the text, Weisse, who believes the Pauline letters had been subjected to interpolations and rearrangements, attempts to reconstruct the original form of the epistles. To the end of Romans 8, for example, he joins Romans 12–15; the intervening material (Rom. 9:6—11:36) together with 16:1-20 is printed separately as a fragment of a letter, probably addressed originally to Ephesus.

Weisse published two important works on the Synoptic Gospels. The first, *The Gospel History Critically and Philosophically Investigated*,[37] appeared the same year (1838) as Wilke's *Urevangelist*. Because of Weisse's concern with the historical Jesus, he gives serious attention to the development of the gospel tradition. His major quarrel with Strauss is Strauss's notion that the Gospels are a very late product of an increasingly unreliable tradition. For his own part, Weisse accepts the ancient tradition that the Gospel of Mark preserves the reminiscences of Peter. Mark, indeed, provides the narrative source used by Matthew and Luke. The Gospel of Mark displays an untutored, Semitic style and bears the marks of an original composition. Evidence that Mark presents an earlier form of the tradition than that reported by Matthew and Luke can be seen, for example, in Mark's failure to report birth stories—stories which are obviously later. In 8:45, the Gospel of Luke adds the name of Peter (which is lacking in Mark) to the narrative, because the author of Luke, in Weisse's opinion, is acknowledging that Peter (via Mark) is the source of the tradition.

According to Weisse, Matthew and Luke used another source besides Mark: the document Papias described as the *logia* of Matthew. This source, largely a collection of Jesus' teachings, was more faithfully followed by Matthew than by Luke. "Not only Mark is the common source of both,"

35. See his discussion of "Der geschichtliche Christus," in ibid. 3.289–409.
36. C. H. Weisse, *Beiträge zur Kritik der Paulinischen Briefe an die Galater, Römer, Philipper und Kolosser*, ed. E. Sulze (Leipzig: S. Hirzel, 1867).
37. C. H. Weisse, *Die evangelische Geschichte kritisch und philosophisch bearbeitet*, 2 vols. (Leipzig: Breitkopf and Härtel, 1838).

writes Weisse, "but, according to our definite conviction, also the collection of sayings of Matthew."[38] In attempting to establish the priority of Mark and the *logia*, Weisse presents the familiar arguments of the advocates of the two-document hypothesis. Matthew and Luke follow the order of Mark; when they depart from that order, they do not agree with each other. Matthew and Luke have other material in which they agree in form and content but not order, indicating independent use of a common written source—the *logia* of Matthew. Although he is concerned with the fundamental historicity of the tradition about Jesus, Weisse acknowledges that Mark is not an eyewitness. Moreover, he does not believe that Mark's transmission of the Petrine tradition guarantees the accuracy of the details of the Marcan narrative. In interpreting the gospel material, Weisse displays a skepticism reminiscent of Strauss. The miracle stories arise out of the religious imagination of the early Christians and are expressed in myth and legend; the idea of the resurrection has its source in the disciples' experience of the presence of Christ. Nevertheless, Weisse believes his work has two significant results: (1) Mark is the earliest Gospel; (2) the Gospels rest on reliable historical tradition.

Weisse's second book on the Synoptics, *The Question of the Gospels in the Present Situation*,[39] sums up the position of gospel research in mid-nineteenth-century Germany. In this work, Weisse notes the effect of Strauss's *Life of Jesus*: the historical foundation of Christianity has been undermined. In response, a negative reaction has fostered an unfortunate biblical literalism and orthodoxy. Although he does not agree with Ewald,[40] Weisse believes Ewald's more conservative reading of the tradition provides a framework for handling the larger question of the historical Jesus. For Weisse, the crucial issue has to do with historical revelation. In dealing with the sources, Weisse turns first to the Johannine material. He rejects the opposing alternatives of Ewald (who advocated the authenticity of the Gospel of John) and the Tübingen school (which relegated John to mid-second century). According to Weisse, the Fourth Gospel was written shortly after the death of John the apostle by a friend. It does present tradition from John, but not accurate historical detail. Its primary purpose is to present Jesus as the Christ.

In regard to the study of the Synoptics, Weisse asserts that Strauss's *Life of Jesus* demonstrates the need for research on the gospel sources. Weisse also notes that Baur's tendency criticism determines the latter's explanation of the origin of the Gospels and, thus, Baur's support of the Gries-

38. Ibid. 1.83.
39. C. H. Weisse, *Die Evangelienfrage in ihrem gegenwärtigen Stadium* (Leipzig: Breitkopf & Härtel, 1856).
40. See pp. 287–93, above.

bach hypothesis.[41] Weisse also reports research (e.g., by Schleiermacher) which understands the *logia* described by Papias as a collection of teachings. Recent research accepting the tradition that Mark presents the reminiscences of Peter is noted, along with Lachmann's claim that Mark's order is closer to the original than is that of Matthew or Luke. Weisse finds Wilke's argument for the priority of Mark convincing, although Wilke's notion that Matthew used Luke has been discredited. This result, however, has opened the possibility that the *logia* may be seen as the common source of Matthew and Luke—the theory developed in Weisse's own earlier work.

In relation to his earlier position, Weisse acknowledges that he is now less confident about the contents of the *logia* than he was at the time of writing his *Gospel History*. He also confesses that he is leaning toward the theory that agreements of Matthew and Luke against Mark may imply their use of an *Urmarcus*, an earlier, lost edition of Mark. Finally, Weisse notes that theological biases influence critical judgments: Wilke's work was discredited when it was embraced by Bruno Bauer; scholars like Ewald oppose in principle the tendency criticism of the Tübingen school. In sum, Weisse has formulated an early version of the theory which came to be known as the "two-document hypothesis," the theory that the Synoptic Gospels rest on a primitive narrative source and an early collection of teachings. Taken up and refined by prominent critics like H. J. Holtzmann, this hypothesis dominated synoptic research at the end of the nineteenth and throughout the twentieth centuries.[42]

Hajo Uden Meijboom (1842–1933)

To conclude this discussion of the synoptic problem, mention can be made of an obscure Dutch theologian, Hajo Uden Meijboom. Meijboom is worth mentioning because he provides a view of gospel studies from the west side of the Rhine. At the age of twenty-four, Meijboom, who was later to become a respected patristics scholar, wrote a doctoral dissertation entitled *History and Critique of the Marcan Hypothesis*.[43] The first part of the dissertation surveys the history of research on the synoptic problem. Of special value is Meijboom's review of gospel studies in nineteenth-century

---

41. See p. 268, above.

42. Holtzmann's work on the synoptic problem, *Die synoptischen Evangelien*, was published in 1863. Since most of his works appear later, the discussion of Holtzmann's contribution to NT research will be presented in volume 2 of this study.

43. Hajo Uden Meijboom, *Geschiedenis en critiek der Marcushypothese* (Amsterdam: Kraay, 1866); Eng. trans.: *A History and Critique of the Origin of the Marcan Hypothesis*, trans. and ed. John J. Kiwiet (Macon, Ga.: Mercer University Press, 1992). See Bo Reicke, "From Strauss to Holtzmann and Meijboom: Synoptic Theories Advanced during the Consolidation of Germany, 1830–70," *Novum Testamentum* 29 (1987): 1–21.

France. There the key figure is Eduard Reuss of Strasbourg who favored Marcan priority but believed canonical Mark was preceded by an earlier edition of Mark—an *Urmarcus*. Reuss influenced other French scholars, like Albert Réville who referred to the earlier edition of Mark as "Proto-Mark." The preference for Marcan priority is seen finally in Ernst Renan, whose best-selling *Life of Jesus* presupposed a version of the two-document hypothesis.[44] Meijboom's reading of the history also argues that the triumph of the Marcan hypothesis resulted in large part from reaction against Strauss and the Tübingen school, who had adopted the Griesbach solution.

The second part of Meijboom's dissertation presents a critique of the Marcan hypothesis. The main value of the critique is Meijboom's identification of presuppositions that have plagued research on the synoptic problem from the beginning. He detects three main assumptions that have been adopted by advocates of Marcan priority. First, they have assumed that the shortest Gospel must be the earliest, that the developing gospel tradition would persistently tend to include more material. Actually, the length of a Gospel, in Meijboom's opinion, is determined by the particular purpose of the author, who might, for reasons of his own, have decided to compose a shorter Gospel. Second, advocates of Marcan priority have assumed that Mark's style is primitive and thus represents an early formulation of the gospel narrative. But assessment of the style of a document is subjective, and the character of the style tells little about the date of the document. Finally, advocates of the Marcan hypothesis are frequently forced to compromise their position by positing a document earlier than Mark—an *Urmarcus* or Proto-Mark. This maneuver, in Meijboom's judgment, is a transparent effort to resolve difficulties of the Marcan hypothesis (e.g., agreements of Matthew and Luke against Mark) by the creation of a hypothetical document.

In the third part, Meijboom presents his own conclusion, namely, that the Griesbach hypothesis is the best solution to the synoptic problem. To make this case, Meijboom argues that the two-document hypothesis would require of Matthew a method of following sources which would be out of character for an ancient author. Meijboom also analyzes the texts in detail and concludes that the evidence supports Mark's use of Matthew and Luke. The double expressions of Mark, for example, are not redundancies, but conflations of material from the first and third Gospels. Taking a cue from Tübingen, Meijboom offers a type of tendency criticism of his own. He thinks the Gospel of Mark displays a high Christology and, thus, represents a later stage in the development of the gospel tradition, a point

---

44. See p. 377, below.

which proves that Meijboom has not escaped the danger of theological presuppositions.

Conclusion

The synoptic problem involves complexities that defy easy evaluation of the various solutions. On the basis of the history rehearsed above, some observations may be offered. The theory of a common oral tradition (Gieseler) seems least convincing, although it has been revived in the twentieth century. The nature of agreements appear to indicate some sort of literary dependency, indeed, a dependency involving *Greek* texts. Ideally, research on the problem should attend primarily to literary analysis, but as Wilke's approach reveals, even the way one arranges the parallel columns influences the outcome. This indicates that the investigation begins of necessity with a working hypothesis which then must be thoroughly tested. The credibility of the hypothesis depends on its capability of explaining the data, that is, the agreements and disagreements among the Gospels.

Another lesson to be learned from this history is that research on the synoptic problem should be isolated from theories about authenticity. When Marsh (like Griesbach before him) assumes apostolic authorship of the first Gospel, hope of solving the synoptic problem is diminished. Moreover, overly complex hypotheses (e.g., Marsh) do not commend themselves, because they require of ancient authors methods of using sources which are improbable. External factors—historical, political, or theological[45]— should not be allowed to predetermine the results. Although recent historians of the synoptic problem are sharply divided as to the role that reaction to Strauss and the Tübingen school played in the decline of the Griesbach hypothesis,[46] there can be little doubt that historical and theological concerns contributed to the ascendency of the two-document hypothesis. Wilke's comprehensive analysis of the literary issues is largely untouched by these concerns, but Weisse's solution is designed to support the historicity of the gospel tradition. Interestingly, the ascending two-

45. The belief that national and academic politics, as well as theological controversies, contributed to the advance of the two-document hypothesis is expressed by Reicke, "From Strauss to Holtzmann and Meijboom," 2–8.

46. The thesis that reaction to Strauss and Tübingen contributed to the decline of the Griesbach hypothesis is argued by Stoldt (*History and Criticism of the Marcan Hypothesis*, 227–35); Farmer (*Synoptic Problem*, 54–58); Reicke, ("From Strauss to Holtzmann and Meijboom," 8–18). These arguments are countered by C. M. Tuckett, "The Griesbach Hypothesis in the 19th Century," *Journal for the Study of the New Testament* 3 (1979): 29–60. Tuckett shows, among other things, that Wilke's results were not affected by Strauss and Baur. His argument that Weisse's conclusions were untouched by Tübingen is less convincing, although his observation that Weisse's objection was not to Tübingen's adoption of Griesbach's source theory but to the conclusion that all the Gospels were late and unreliable is essentially correct.

document hypothesis is a combination of two major theories articulated in the first two-thirds of the nineteenth century: (1) the theory that subsequent Gospels use a preceding one (Mark); and (2) the theory that the Gospels depend on a lost primitive document (the *logia* or Q).

THE AUTHENTICITY OF THE
GOSPEL OF JOHN: BRETSCHNEIDER AND TAYLER

Like the controversy concerning the Synoptic Gospels, debate about the authenticity of the Fourth Gospel was crucial for the reconstruction of early Christianity. As early as the end of the second century, Clement of Alexandria had observed that John was a different sort of Gospel. Eichhorn had exploited this observation critically in his *Introduction*,[47] and investigators of the synoptic problem had noted that the text of John did not fit nicely into the parallel columns of a synopsis. Yet, hardheaded historians like Paulus had continued to use the Fourth Gospel as the chronological framework upon which they constructed the life of Jesus.[48] The problem took on larger theological proportions, however, with Schleiermacher, whose *Life of Jesus* used the Fourth Gospel as the primary source.[49] Although Schleiermacher has frequently been maligned for his preference for the Gospel of John because of its support for his own Christology, the best critical minds of the day—Lücke and de Wette—argued for the authenticity of the Fourth Gospel.[50]

For Schleiermacher, the Jesus of history, reconstructed from the Gospel of John, was one with the Christ of faith—the Christ of Schleiermacher's own christological formulation. This position was attacked by D. F. Strauss.[51] According to Strauss, Schleiermacher had based his biography of Jesus on the least historical and most mythical of the Gospels. Schleiermacher's Christology, like that of the Fourth Gospel, was a theological fabrication without historical foundation. For Strauss, a chasm existed between the Jesus of history and the Christ of faith. Although F. C. Baur did not share Strauss's christological conclusions, he supported Strauss's critical judgment about the Fourth Gospel: it was not written until midsecond century and was more a theological construct than a historical account.[52] In the shadow of this larger controversy, historical-critical work on the Gospel of John had been going on. The research of two scholars may serve as examples.

47. See pp. 150–51, above.
48. See pp. 203–4, above.
49. See pp. 217–20, above.
50. See pp. 221–35, above.
51. See pp. 249–50, above.
52. See pp. 267–68, above.

Karl Gottlieb Bretschneider (1776–1848)

Karl Gottlieb Bretschneider was born in Gersdorf, Saxony. After study at Leipzig, he served for a time as an instructor at Wittenberg. He then became a pastor and, eventually, an official of the Saxon church (1816). Bretschneider published works in various theological fields, especially Reformation history. His most important contribution to NT research was his *Probability Concerning the Character and Origin of the Gospel and Epistles of John, the Apostle, Modestly Submitted to the Judgment of the Erudite* (1820).[53] In his preface, Bretschneider, as a sensitive pastor, notes that questioning the authenticity of a book like the Gospel of John constitutes a threat to the piety of the people. Hence he writes in Latin, presenting his case exclusively to the educated readership.

In a fascinating first chapter, Bretschneider asserts, contrary to popular belief, that the Fourth Gospel is not more suitable for faith than are the first three Gospels. The author of John, to be sure, intended to produce a Gospel that would lead to faith, not one that would supplement the data of the others. Nevertheless, the first three Gospels, with their clear and simple message, spoke potently to the concerns of people, presenting Jesus as the human savior endowed with the power of God. The Fourth Gospel, on the other hand, was concerned to defend the dignity of Jesus, presenting him as the Logos of Alexandrian philosophy. According to Bretschneider the resulting portraits of Jesus are dramatically different: "Since only one representation of Jesus, either that of the prior or that of the fourth writer, can be true to history, the conclusion is that Matthew, Mark, and Luke in their accounts have presented the true representation rather than the author of the Fourth Gospel."[54]

Much of the data within the Gospel of John, continues Bretschneider, does not square with reality. When John the Baptist is presented as comprehending the doctrine of the Logos, he appears to be depicted in the guise of an Alexandrian philosopher rather than in the camel's hair garment of a Judean prophet. Although the Baptist commends Jesus to his followers as the Lamb of God—the one greater than he, to whom he is to bear witness—John incongruously continues to have disciples of his own. Similarly, Nicodemus's notion that being born again requires return to the mother's womb is simply incredible on the lips of a teacher of Israel who would have known that Jewish proselyte baptism symbolized a new birth. "In all these things," says Bretschneider, "we do not appear to have strayed from the truth when we have concluded that the discussion

---

53. Carolus Theoph. Bretschneider, *Probabilia de evangelii et epistolarum Joannis, apostoli, indole et origine eruditorum judiciis modeste subjecit* (Leipzig: A. Barth, 1820).
54. Ibid., 36–37.

between Jesus, the disciples, the Jews and the Baptist were not true, but fictions, and above all, that the author of the Gospel had not been a companion of Jesus nor heard him teach."[55]

Bretschneider continues this line of argument (chaps. 2–3) by asserting that the author of the Fourth Gospel was neither an eyewitness to the events he records, nor a Palestinian, nor even a Jew. Since he is not an eyewitness, the author—who in Bretschneider's opinion does not use the Synoptics—draws his material from tradition about Jesus. Bretschneider makes this case by investigating Johannine texts which indicate the author's dependence on and the development of Christian tradition. For example, Jesus' metaphorical word about not fasting while the bridegroom is present (expressed in an earlier written form in Matt. 9:15, Mark 2:19, and Luke 5:34) is put into the mouth of John the Baptist and applied to Jesus as the bridegroom (John 3:29). Evidence that the author was not a Palestinian is seen in his inadequate knowledge of the geography of Palestine, for example, in his erroneous reference to "Bethany across the Jordan" (1:28). The suspicion that he is not a Jew is confirmed by the author's ignorance of Jewish practices, for instance, his idea that Caiaphas was high priest "that year" (11:49), as if the office were an annual appointment.

In chapter 4, Bretschneider presents his own theory of the origin of the Fourth Gospel. He believes it arose in response to opposition Christianity faced in mid-second century. Consequently, the arguments of the author address problems of his own time, rather than the opposition that the historical Jesus actually confronted from the Pharisees. For example, in answer to pagan charges such as those of Celsus that faith in the resurrection rested on the fanciful report of a few women, the author of John observed that Mary Magdalene's witness was confirmed by Peter and John, and that the doubts of skeptical Thomas were overcome by a resurrection appearance. Exorcisms were omitted from the narrative, in Bretschneider's opinion, because second-century Greeks would have been unimpressed by such primitive miracles; they preferred stories about deities who could change water to wine. According to Bretschneider, the Fourth Gospel is not history, but apologetics.

Bretschneider goes on to ask (chap. 5) if the authenticity of the Fourth Gospel can be established by its relation to the Apocalypse and the Johannine epistles. In regard to the former, Bretschneider argues that the vocabulary, style, and doctrine of the two documents are totally different and indicate different authors. He refutes Eichhorn's claim that the Apocalypse and the Gospel use the same terms (e.g., λόγος, lamb, κόσμος) by contending that these terms, although the same, are differently under-

---

55. Ibid., 64.

stood. In regard to the Johannine epistles, Bretschneider agrees that the Gospel of John and 1 John are by the same author, but he denies that the author is the apostle John. Even more clearly than the Gospel, the First Epistle refutes a Gnosticism of the second century. Moreover, the author of 1 John designates himself as a presbyter, not an apostle.

In the next chapter, Bretschneider asserts that use of the Gospel of John is not attested until late in the second century. The apostolic fathers betray no knowledge of the Fourth Gospel; Clement of Rome, for instance, refers frequently to Matthew, Mark, and Luke, but never mentions John. Justin Martyr, although he embraces the doctrine of the Logos, learned it not from the Fourth Gospel but from some other source. Even Tatian is said not to have known the Gospel of John. Stretching his argument beyond the credibility of most subsequent scholars, Bretschneider argues that heretics like Valentinus and the Montanists were unfamiliar with the Fourth Gospel. The followers of Valentinus, however, did know this Gospel, which was first used by heretics in Egypt. This leads Bretschneider to conclude that John was written in Egypt, transported to Rome by the Valentinians, and, with the support of the Roman church, recognized as authentic.

Bretschneider concludes:

> This is known for certain, that neither the apostle John, nor a companion of Jesus, nor a Christian born and living in Palestine, nor a native Jew, but some other Christian, devoted to Alexandrian teaching, honored with the title of presbyter . . . wrote the Gospel; and in writing he made use of tradition. . . . It is most certain that he lived in Egypt, partly because he followed an opinion concerning the Passover other than that which the churches of Asia Minor held, but which was held by the church of Alexandria; partly because his doctrine agrees principally with Gnosticism, and the Gnostics in Egypt were the first to know his Gospel, which they commended vigorously, and transmitted to Rome, and thus, with the authority of the Roman church, it was made public and credible.[56]

In an attempt to calm the storm created by this conclusion, Bretschneider, a few years after he had written the book, claimed that he had merely offered a tentative hypothesis; if the evidence indicated that it was mistaken, then it rightly deserved to be refuted, a response all too modest in view of the force of his arguments.

John James Tayler (1797–1869)

Almost a half-century later, similar arguments were articulated in England by John James Tayler. British biblical scholarship through the first two-

---

56. Ibid., 224.

thirds of the nineteenth century had been largely conservative.[57] Tayler belongs to a small company of critics who worked in the tradition of scholars like Connop Thrilwall, who, in 1825, had translated Schleiermacher's book on Luke. This kind of criticism, of course, had been confirmed in 1860 by the writers of the controversial volume *Essays and Reviews*.[58] Tayler was born in Surrey, the son of a Unitarian divine who taught him Latin. In 1814, Tayler entered Manchester College, then located in York, but after two years he moved to Glasgow where he received the bachelor's degree in 1818. In 1834 and 1835 Tayler traveled on the continent, where he made the acquaintance of German theologians. He taught church history at Manchester College, which had moved from York to Manchester and been renamed Manchester New College. In 1852, he was appointed professor of theology, and when the college moved again— this time to London—Tayler was made principal (1853).

Tayler published sermons, addresses, and historical works on religious life in England. His important contribution to NT research was his *Attempt to Ascertain the Character of the Fourth Gospel*.[59] In the preface, Tayler confesses that he had persisted in the orthodox view—even though he had twice read Bretschneider—until he acquired the insight that the spiritual power of a book did not depend on the identity of its author. Although he admired the faith of conservative Christians, Tayler called for free investigation: "The chief value which I attach to critical studies arises from my belief, that they will ultimately procure a firmer standing point, a clearer vision, and a directer spiritual action for the preacher of the pure and everlasting Gospel of Christ."[60] He concludes, "One thing is certain, a true religion can never rest on false history. We must first test the foundations, before any system, however fair and well-proportioned, can be securely built on them."[61]

Tayler begins by stating the problem: the difference between the "synoptical gospels," as he calls them, and the Gospel of John. The former set the ministry of Jesus in Galilee, present his teaching in the form of parables, and show restraint in regard to affirmation of Jesus' Messiahship. The Fourth Gospel, on the other hand, includes an extensive Judean ministry, presents Jesus' teaching in complicated discourses, and openly affirms his divine character. The Gospel of John locates the cleansing of the temple at the beginning of Jesus' ministry, while the Synoptics put it at

57. See Storr, *English Theology in the Nineteenth Century*, 177–98.
58. See pp. 348, 353, 358, below.
59. John James Tayler, *An Attempt to Ascertain the Character of the Fourth Gospel; Especially in Its Relation to the Three First* (London and Edinburgh: Williams & Norgate, 1867).
60. Ibid., xi.
61. Ibid., xiii.

the end. Exorcism, a frequently occurring miracle of the first three Gospels, is not mentioned by the Fourth.

> If the First Three Gospels represent Christ's public ministry truly, the Fourth cannot be accepted as simple, reliable history. If we assume the truth of the Fourth, we must reject on some fundamental points the evidence of the Three First. The question is, which of these two narratives are we to take as our guide, and accept as authentic for the main facts of the life of Jesus? . . . The decision of this question will affect our whole conception of the person and doctrine of Christ.[62]

Following in the footsteps of Bretschneider, Tayler goes on to investigate the possibility that the Fourth Gospel and the Apocalypse were written by the same author. Noting the differences of grammar and style, he concludes that they were not. The early tradition about John the son of Zebedee, however, portrays him as the kind of person who could have produced the Apocalypse. He was a simple, unlettered man strongly moved by messianic expectation, the sort of author who could have written Revelation with its barbarous Greek and its strident apocalypticism, but could not have written the Fourth Gospel, with its felicitous style and dearth of millennialism. Moreover, external testimony as early as Papias and Justin confirmed the Johannine authorship of the Apocalypse. Arguments to the contrary, especially that of Dionysius of Alexandria in the third century, are based not on solid tradition but on opposition to Revelation's chiliasm.

Turning to the external witness concerning the Fourth Gospel, Tayler notes that support for apostolic authorship is relatively late. In his opinion, Justin's knowledge of the life and teaching of Jesus is drawn from the Synoptics, not from the Gospel of John. No certain citation of the Fourth Gospel can be confirmed prior to Tatian (ca. 175), and the first to quote the Gospel and identify its author as John is Theophilus of Antioch, an identification supported by Irenaeus and Tertullian. And why did this Gospel eventually attain the status of an apostolic document? Because of the effectiveness of its Logos doctrine for harmonizing Christianity with the learning of the Greeks. In Tayler's opinion, this kind of Christianity developed after the Bar Kochba revolt when the church emerged from Jewish domination. After two destructions of Jerusalem, eschatological expectation was in decline, and the author of John reflects an understanding of the Eucharist in accord with the ideas of Ignatius and Justin.

Taking up an argument noted by Bretschneider and refined by Hilgenfeld,[63] Tayler asserts that the ancient paschal controversy provides evi-

---

62. Ibid., 7–8.
63. See pp. 277, 314, above.

dence against the Johannine authorship of the Fourth Gospel. The original commemorating of the Passover (and Easter) was on the fourteenth
day of the month Nisan in accord with Jewish reckoning. The Synoptic
Gospels support this observance, according to Tayler, by correctly
identifying the last supper as a Passover meal. With the Fourth Gospel,
this is changed: the crucifixion of Jesus is made to coincide with the
slaughter of the Passover lamb, and the Passover meal is observed later, on
Nisan 15. Contrary to the Fourth Gospel, the Quartodecimanians of Asia
Minor, claiming the support of Johannine tradition, continue to follow
the original practice. As the controversy unfolds toward the end of the
second century, the Fourth Gospel is actually used against the practice of
Asia Minor and in support of the Roman position. According to Tayler,
"The author of the Fourth Gospel, by assigning the Passion to the 14th of
Nisan, and holding up Christ himself as the true Passover, evidently
intended to do away with the last pretext for retaining any semblance to a
Jewish rite, and to free Christianity from the swathing-bands of Hebrew
thought and Hebrew usage, which checked its healthy growth and still
kept it in spiritual childhood."[64]

Tayler concludes that in the developing tradition two types of Christianity became associated with John. "There is evidence, I think, of two successive religious movements, each associated with the name of the apostle
John, in the two works which have been the subject of comparison in the
present inquiry;—an earlier one, closely connected with the Jewish Christianity of Palestine, in the Apocalypse,—and a later, the fruit of more
advanced development, in the Fourth Gospel."[65] According to Tayler, the
earlier document, the Apocalypse, was written by the apostle John;
the later, the Fourth Gospel, was written by John the presbyter. "If this
John were the author of the Fourth Gospel, we can account for its being
so uniformly referred to Ephesus; and we can understand how, in process
of time, when early traditions were easily confounded, the Apostle should
be substituted for the Presbyter as the author of the gospel—especially
where there was so much readiness to claim an apostolic origin for every
work of high ecclesiastical authority and influence, and where the two
Johns appear each of them to have stood in such close connection with
the church at Ephesus."[66]

Displaying a practical concern typical of British theologians, Tayler ends
with a discussion of the implications of his results for the Christian faith.
Although questioning the authenticity of such an important book may

---

64. Tayler, *Character of the Fourth Gospel*, 123.
65. Ibid., 153–54.
66. Ibid., 156.

seem detrimental, the historical critic must attend to the evidence. "To evade the conclusion to which that evidence legitimately leads, from the apprehension of assumed consequences, is really to distrust God, and to interfere with the possible order of his Providence."[67] To the objection that declaring the Fourth Gospel anonymous destroys its power, Tayler replies, "It is, therefore, of less importance to be able to pronounce with certainty of such and such a book, that it came from such and such a particular hand, than to feel sure that it issued from the original circle of the apostolic faith and zeal, and that, whoever be its author, it brings with it a true expression of the Spirit of the Living God."[68] When all is said and done, Tayler is convinced that the results of criticism are salutary, "performing . . . a great reparatory and conservative work . . . sweeping away an accumulation of antiquated beliefs and gratuitous assumptions, which obstruct the access to the pure teachings of Jesus Christ, and crush with their needless weight the free working of the Spirit of God."[69]

Conclusion

Looking back over the research of Bretschneider and Tayler, the observer can conclude that they anticipate the rising tide of the future: the authenticity of the Fourth Gospel would increasingly come into question. To be sure, denial of Johannine authorship by Strauss and Baur served to create a countercurrent in support of authenticity (e.g., by Ewald[70]) and thereby to extend the traditional view. Tayler is of special interest, because he is one of a few English-speaking theologians to say a good word for Tübingen. In addition to his reliance on Hilgenfeld, Tayler, who had difficulty accepting the literal interpretation of the bodily resurrection, cites with approval Baur's stress on the resurrection faith: "I fully hold with the late F. C. Baur—one of the freest and most fearless of modern Scriptural critics—that the belief in a risen Christ is the corner-stone of the Christian dispensation; that apart from that belief, its origin and history are an inexplicable enigma."[71]

As to the details of the argument, Bretschneider and Tayler deserve a mixed review. They are correct in their judgment that John presents a different picture of Jesus from that of the Synoptics, and that any attempt to adopt both accounts as historically reliable results in a divided Jesus. The Synoptics, although not immune to theological concerns, are more reliable as historical records, while the Fourth Gospel, although not obliv-

---

67. Ibid., 157–58.
68. Ibid., 174.
69. Ibid., 188.
70. See p. 291, above.
71. Tayler, *Character of the Fourth Gospel*, 171.

ious to the gospel tradition, is more concerned with christological confession. Bretschneider and Tayler are probably correct, too, in their conclusion that the Fourth Gospel was not written by a Palestinian eyewitness or by the same author as the Apocalypse. But Tayler goes beyond the evidence when he concludes that John the apostle is the author of Revelation and John the presbyter of the Fourth Gospel, and Bretschneider may be mistaken in his notion that the author was not a Jew.

The argument from the paschal controversy, although it raises questions concerning the Johannine and Ephesian tradition of the Fourth Gospel, proves little about the date of the document, because the picture of Christ as paschal lamb had already been presented by Paul (1 Cor. 5:7). Similarly, arguments which claim that the Logos idea and gnostic opposition cannot arise until the second century are forced. Bretschneider and Tayler also tend to ignore evidence that indicates knowledge of the Fourth Gospel prior to the end of the second century. Implicit in their research are questions which they fail to explore: Why were the orthodox reluctant to use the Fourth Gospel? and Why was it first used extensively by the heretics? In any case, more recent research is inclined to date the Fourth Gospel earlier, sometime around the end of the first century.

TEXT CRITICISM:
LACHMANN AND TISCHENDORF

Text (or lower) criticism—that most objective of the biblical sciences—made notable progress in the nineteenth century. In this period, the critics were heirs of the legacy of scholars like John Mill,[72] J. A. Bengel,[73] J. H. Wettstein,[74] and J. J. Griesbach.[75] This venerable tradition was further enriched by the discovery of new manuscripts and the refining of techniques for evaluating textual variants.

Karl Lachmann (1793–1851)

A decisive step was taken by Karl Konrad Friedrich Wilhelm Lachmann, a renowned classical philologist. Born in Braunsweig, Lachmann studied at Leipzig and Göttingen. After serving as an instructor first at Göttingen (1815) and then at Berlin (1816), he was appointed professor at Königsberg (1818) and finally at Berlin (1825). Although noted for his editions of the classics and his study of Homer, Lachmann made important contributions to NT research. Indeed, his short essay on the order of the narra-

72. See pp. 25–28, above.
73. See pp. 72–74, above.
74. See pp. 103–7, above.
75. See pp. 141–43, above.

tives in the Synoptic Gospels[76] took on large dimensions in the debate about the relationship of the first three Gospels. In investigating the problem, Lachmann confines his concern to a single issue: the question of the order of the narratives. He begins with a preliminary observation: "The diversity of the order of the narratives of the Gospels is not so great as it appears to many; it is clearly greatest when one compares either all these writings with one another, or Luke with Matthew; it is least if Mark is compared with the other two separately."[77]

Lachmann begins his exposition of this observation by comparing the order of narratives in Matthew and Mark. He notes that Matthew usually follows the same order as Mark, but sometimes departs from it. He argues against Griesbach's theory that Matthew has the more original order which Mark has altered. Following Schleiermacher's idea that Matthew used the *logia* (a collection of sayings of Jesus), Lachmann concludes that Matthew inserts narrative material into this earlier source. Consequently, Matthew is thought to have changed the order of the narrative according to his own purposes. Similarly, Lachmann notes that Luke very seldom deviates from the order of narratives found in Mark, and that when he deviates, the deviations can be explained by his own intention. Thus, in Lachmann's opinion, Mark is closer to the original order of the gospel narratives than either Matthew or Luke. Lachmann's conclusion should be read with care: "If in accord with this extensive agreement, it is nevertheless evident that they [Matthew and Luke] did not have available the pattern of Mark which they might imitate, what remains to be said except that the prescribed order which all followed individually, written before they wrote, had been established and confirmed by an evangelical tradition and authority?"[78] This means that, in Lachmann's opinion, the order of gospel narratives had been formulated prior to the writing of any of the Synoptic Gospels. Although Mark's order was closer to that primitive tradition than Matthew or Luke, neither Matthew nor Luke, in Lachmann's opinion, used Mark as a source. Later advocates of the two-document hypothesis, however, misconstrued Lachmann's argument to imply that Mark's order was itself the original order and that Matthew and Luke

---

76. Carolus Lachmann, "De ordine narrationum in evangeliis synopticis," *Theologische Studien und Kritiken* 8 (1835): 570–90. An English translation of the main part of this essay is in N. H. Palmer, "Lachmann's Argument," *New Testament Studies* 13 (1967): 368–78, and is reprinted in *The Two-Source Hypothesis: A Critical Appraisal*, ed. Arthur J. Bellinzoni, Jr., J. B. Tyson, and W. O. Walker (Macon, Ga.: Mercer University Press, 1985), 119–31.

77. Lachmann, "De ordine narrationum," 574.

78. Ibid., 582.

followed the order of Mark. This shift in the argument has been described as the "Lachmann fallacy."[79]

More substantial is Lachmann's contribution to text criticism. There he took the decisive step of radical departure from the *textus receptus*, the Received Text which had become standard in the sixteenth and seventeenth centuries. Griesbach, of course, had published a text which did not totally reproduce the Received Text, but his departures were few.[80] Lachmann's intent was not to reconstruct the original text but to recover the text of the NT which was used by the Eastern church at the end of the fourth century. To accomplish this goal, he ignored the later minuscule manuscripts and used the early uncials together with the old Latin, the Vulgate, and patristic sources. After five years of labor, Lachmann produced the first edition of his text in 1831,[81] an accomplishment greeted by harsh criticism even from progressive scholars like de Wette. In this edition, Lachmann does not present the books of the NT in canonical order. After Acts, he prints the Catholic Epistles (James; 1 and 2 Peter; 1, 2, and 3 John; and Jude), then the Pauline Epistles (Hebrews after 2 Thessalonians, and then the Pastorals followed by Philemon), and finally Revelation.[82] The text (totaling 460 pages) has no critical apparatus or device to indicate the sources of the accepted and the variant readings. Variants which have extensive support are noted in brackets in the text or are listed at the bottom of the page. At the end of the text (pp. 461–503), Lachmann prints a long list of readings from the *textus receptus*, which he rejects. These include such disputed texts as Matt. 6:13 (the liturgical ending of the Lord's Prayer), John 7:53—8:11 (the story of the woman caught in adultery), and 1 John 5:7-8 (the notorious text about the three heavenly witnesses).

In 1842 a first volume and in 1850 a second volume of a larger critical edition were published.[83] Volume 1 (720 pages) includes Lachmann's pref-

---

79. See B. C. Butler, *The Originality of St Matthew: A Critique of the Two-Document Hypothesis* (Cambridge: Cambridge University Press, 1951), pp. 62–71; reprinted as "The Lachmann Fallacy," in Bellinzoni, et al., *The Two-Source Hypothesis*, 133–42. See also Stoldt, *Marcan Hypothesis*, 150–54; W. R. Farmer, "The Lachmann Fallacy," *New Testament Studies* 14 (1968): 441–43. As Butler points out, the lack of agreement in order between Matthew and Luke against Mark can be explained on other hypotheses (e.g., the order: Matthew–Mark–Luke) as well as the priority of Mark; see C. M. Tuckett, "Arguments from Order: Definition and Evaluation," in *Synoptic Studies: The Ampleforth Conferences of 1982 and 1983, Journal for the Study of the New Testament*, Supplement Series 7 (Sheffield: JSOT, 1984), 197–219.

80. See pp. 141–43, above.

81. The following discussion is based on a reprint of Lachmann's 1831 edition, *Novum Testamentum Graece, ex recensione Caroli Lachmanni* (Berlin: G. Reimer, 1837).

82. The order of the Catholic Epistles preceding the Pauline is found in a majority of ancient manuscripts.

83. K. Lachmann, *Novum Testamentum Graece et Latine, Carolus Lachmannus rescensuit, Philippus Buttmannus, Ph. F. Graecae lectionis auctoritates apposuit*, 2 vols. (Berlin: G. Reimer, 1842, 1850).

ace and the texts of the four Gospels. Volume 2 (701 pages) includes another preface and the texts of the rest of the NT, printed in the same order as the earlier edition. The prefaces defend Lachmann's departure from the Received Text and deal with such matters as the textual evidence and critical principles he employs. In presenting the text, Lachmann prints his own Greek text at the top of the page and a Latin text (the Vulgate, with some inserted notations) at the bottom. In the middle of the page is a critical apparatus prepared by Philipp Buttmann. The number of variants listed is extensive, although the manuscript evidence is limited to Lachmann's relatively small collection of witnesses. In regard to Matt. 6:13, for example, the apparatus lists only Cyprian in support of the addition of "amen," while the rest of the liturgical material is simply noted as appearing in the Elzevir edition of 1624.

Constantin von Tischendorf (1815–1874)

Lachmann's work was surpassed by Lobegott Friedrich Constantin von Tischendorf, perhaps the greatest text critic of all times. Born in Saxony, Tischendorf was the son of a physician. He studied at Leipzig (1834–38), where his teacher was the eminent Greek grammarian, Johann G. B. Winer. In recognition of his intellectual brilliance, Tischendorf was appointed instructor at Leipzig at age twenty-five. He was promoted to associate professor in 1845, and full professor in 1859, although his teaching was constantly interrupted by farflung travels in search of biblical manuscripts. Later in life, when Tischendorf had attained considerable fame, visitors to his Leipzig residence found him a genial host, willing to converse with them in their choice of any of five languages: Greek, Latin, Italian, French, or German.

A pious, conservative Christian, Tischendorf was distressed by recent trends in NT criticism. His approach to higher criticism is displayed in his popular monograph, *When Were Our Gospels Written?*[84] The burden of this little book is to defend the authenticity of the Gospels, especially the Gospel of John. Confining the argument largely to the external evidence, Tischendorf begins with data from the end of the second century (the testimony of Irenaeus and Tertullian) and moves backward. He finds evidence that the earlier heretics and the apostolic fathers knew and used the canonical Gospels. In his opinion, the composition of the NT canon was firm by the end of the first century. Tischendorf thinks radical critics

---

84. Constantin Tischendorf, *Wann wurden unsere Evangelien verfasst?* 4th rev. ed. (Leipzig: J. C. Hinrichs, 1880); Eng. trans.: *Origin of the Four Gospels*, trans. William L. Gage (Boston: American Tract Society, 1867). For a shorter, more accessible Eng. trans., see *When Were Our Gospels Written? An Argument by Constantine Tischendorf, with a Narrative of the Discovery of the Sinaitic Manuscript* (New York: American Tract Society, 1866).

like Strauss and Renan turned out to be sheep in wolves' clothing, because they encouraged a reaction that forced scholarship to probe the depths of gospel historicity and authenticity.

> We can only call it opportune, that, through the radical character of the two most famous modern biographers of Jesus, the Tübingen inventor of fantasy and the Parisian creator of caricature, the opposing positions of belief and unbelief in the Gospels and in the Lord have become everywhere apparent. . . . Never before has the educated world together with the theologians and the Christian church so urgently asked: How do things stand concerning the foundation of our evangelical faith in the Lord? Nothing is easier than to deceive those who are not in the position to probe this greatest question of Christendom scientifically, especially under the pretense of learned and sincere research.[85]

Tischendorf's own role in the restoration of faith in biblical authority was to reconstruct a Greek text of the NT as close to the original as possible. As he wrote to his fiancée, "I am confronted with a sacred task, the struggle to regain the original form of the New Testament."[86] This struggle involved two arduous endeavors: the search for NT manuscripts and the production of a critical edition of the Greek NT. The story of Tischendorf's life in quest of biblical texts reads like a romantic travelogue.[87] Early in his career, he traveled to Paris to study Codex Claramontanus and Codex Ephraemi, a palimpsest which he painstakingly deciphered. He also visited the libraries at Cambridge, Oxford, and London. In Rome, he was allowed only six hours to study the important uncial, Vaticanus, but on the same trip, he gained important textual information from other Italian libraries.

Tischendorf's first visit to Sinai took place in 1844. He traveled from Cairo to St. Catherine's monastery by camel, a twelve-day trek through the barren wilderness. According to Tischendorf's account, the discovery of Codex Sinaiticus was a moment of high drama:

> I perceived in the middle of the great hall a large and wide basket full of old parchments; and the librarian, who was a man of information, told me that two heaps of paper like these, mouldered by time, had been already commit-

---

85. Tischendorf, *Evangelien*, 131.

86. Cited in Bruce M. Metzger, *The Text of the New Testament: Its Transmission, Corruption, and Restoration*, 2d ed. (New York and Oxford: Oxford University Press, 1968), 126.

87. A recent account is presented by James Bentley, *Secrets of Mount Sinai: The Story of the Oldest Bible—Codex Sinaiticus* (New York: Doubleday, 1986). See also Matthew Black and Robert Davidson, *Constantin von Tischendorf and the Greek New Testament* (Glasgow: University of Glasgow Press, 1981); Ian A. Moir, "Tischendorf and the Codex Sinaiticus," *New Testament Studies* 23 (1976): 108–15. A popular account is presented by Tischendorf's son-in-law, Ludwig Schneller, *Search on Sinai: The Story of Tischendorf's Life and the Search for a Lost Manuscript*, trans. Dorothee Schröder (London: Epworth, 1939).

ted to the flames. What was my surprise to find among this heap of papers a considerable number of sheets of a copy of the Old Testament in Greek, which seemed to me to be one of the most ancient I had ever seen.[88]

Although this tale has been frequently repeated, Bentley, with considerable justification, thinks it ought to be taken with a large grain of salt.[89] Tischendorf, with his evangelical piety, had little appreciation for Eastern monasticism and considered the monks of St. Catherine's to be ignorant and indolent. Moreover, the parchments had been around for about one thousand years, and it seems unlikely that they would have been consigned to a bonfire at the very time of Tischendorf's visit. In any event, Tischendorf was able to take forty-three sheets of the manuscript out of the monastery and back to Leipzig, where he published them. The originals were presented to the King of Saxony who placed them in the Leipzig University library.

In 1852, Tischendorf made a second visit to Sinai but saw only a fragment of Sinaiticus. The trip, nevertheless, yielded manuscript discoveries in Cairo, Alexandria, Jerusalem, Constantinople, Mount Athos, and other Near Eastern locations. In 1859, Tischendorf again sailed to Egypt with the support of Tsar Alexander II of Russia. While visiting St. Catherine's, Tischendorf was shown a codex which comprised 346 leaves and included the remainder of the parchments he had seen in 1844. The manuscript, which probably had about 730 leaves in the original, included a large portion of the OT, the complete NT, plus the Epistle of Barnabas and the *Shepherd of Hermas*. The pious Tischendorf, who could be trusted with almost anything except a manuscript, eventually persuaded the abbot to allow him to take the codex to Cairo. There, with the help of two Germans, he hastily copied the entire manuscript in a period of two months. Tischendorf urged the monks of St. Catherine's to offer the codex to the tsar as a gift, and, when that failed, he convinced them to allow him to carry it to Russia on loan, after signing a receipt which guaranteed its return in good condition. The tsar financed the publication of a facsimile which Tischendorf labored to make as close to the original as possible—a task which consumed more than two years. The result was an elegant edition in four folio volumes that brought Tischendorf wide acclaim and honorary degrees from both Oxford and Cambridge. Efforts by the monks to have the codex returned to St. Catherine's failed, and eventually the abbot agreed to award it to the tsar, who donated a large sum of money to the monastery. The manuscript was placed in the imperial library at

88. Cited in Bentley, *Secrets of Mount Sinai*, 86.
89. Ibid., 87–88.

St. Petersburg, where it remained until its purchase by the British Museum in 1933.

In 1866, Tischendorf traveled to Rome, where Pope Pius IX refused him permission to copy the treasured Codex Vaticanus. But under the pretext of studying the manuscript, Tischendorf spent eight days copying the text before his actions were detected. He then persuaded the editor, who was working on a new Catholic edition of the text, to allow him an additional six days. Tischendorf, whose speed and accuracy in copying was phenomenal, was able to complete his copy of the entire manuscript and publish his own edition of the codex, a publication which scooped the Catholic edition of 1868.

Tischendorf's first edition of the Greek NT was published in 1841, a small volume that reflected the influence of Lachmann. Although Tischendorf supervised the publication of three editions in Paris in 1842, his most important early text was the second Leipzig edition of 1849. This edition presented the Greek text that Tischendorf was to use in thirteen of his editions. It was prefaced by a prolegomena that set forth Tischendorf's text-critical principles. These principles are quoted in C. R. Gregory's prolegomena, which was published as the third volume of Tischendorf's famous eighth edition.[90] "The text," says Tischendorf, "ought to be sought solely from the ancient witnesses, and indeed especially from the Greek codices, but without neglecting the testimonies of the versions and the fathers."[91] Making use of this material, the critical edition should be based on the evidence and not on the tradition of the Received Text. Tischendorf's ancient witnesses included texts as recent as the ninth century, but he gave greatest weight to the oldest manuscripts that were confirmed by the testimony of the early versions and the patristic writers. In evaluating variants, Tischendorf laid down five rules:

1. Readings are suspect that are entirely peculiar to one or another of the witnesses, as also are those that appear by their very nature to have their origin from a learned person.
2. Readings, although supported by many witnesses, should be rejected if it is manifest or very probable that they have their origin from the errors of copyists.

---

90. Constantin Tischendorf, *Novum Testamentum Graece ad antiquissimos testes denuo recensuit, apparatum criticum omni studio perfectum apposuit, commentationem isagogicam praetexuit Constantinus Tischendorf. Editio octava critica maior, Volumen III: Prolegomena scripsit Casparus Renatus Gregory, additis curis Ezrae Abbot* (Leipzig: J. C. Hinrichs, 1884).

91. Ibid., 47.

3. In parallel passages, whether of the Old or New Testament, and especially in the Synoptic Gospels, to which special care was taken by the ancient copyists to bring the texts into agreement, preference should be given to those readings that show disagreement, except where there is some other weighty reason.

4. More probable than others is that reading which has given the occasion for the others or which appears to contain in itself the elements of the others.

5. Those readings should be studiously maintained which are commended by the unique Greek style of the authors of the New Testament, and no less by the usage of each of the writers.[92]

As to the grouping of manuscripts into families, Tischendorf believed they could be classified according to two pairs of ancient recensions: Alexandrian and Latin; Asiatic and Byzantine. The first pair included the oldest and most reliable witnesses and served as the main source for Tischendorf's critical editions.

Tischendorf's eighth edition is a monumental achievement. In 1864, this edition, which was published in eleven parts, began to appear. Eventually, the text was presented in two weighty volumes: the first, in 1869, included the Gospels and extended to 968 pages; the second, in 1872, included the rest of the NT and totaled 1,044 pages.[93] A third volume, which incorporated and elaborated Tischendorf's earlier prolegomena, was added after his death by C. R. Gregory.[94] As in his other editions, Tischendorf relied heavily on his own collations and manuscript discoveries, especially Codex Sinaiticus. He also made use of the most recent critical work of his contemporaries. For example, Tischendorf was familiar with research of the most important British text critic of the day, Samuel Prideaux Tregelles (1813–75).[95] Tregelles, who emerged from the laboring class, supported himself by working in an iron foundry while he learned Greek, Hebrew, and Aramaic. Like Tischendorf, he traveled widely to study and collate manuscripts, including a trip to Rome to study Vaticanus. Tregelles wrote a comprehensive history of text criticism from the Complutensian edition of 1514 through Tischendorf's second Leipzig edi-

92. Ibid., 53–54.

93. Constantin Tischendorf, *Novum Testamentum Graece ad antiquissimos testes denuo recensuit, apparatum criticum omni studio perfectum apposuit, commentationem isagogicam praetexuit Constantinus Tischendorf, editio octava critica maior,* 2 vols. (Leipzig: Giesecke & Devrient, 1869–72).

94. See n. 90, above.

95. Tischendorf's arrogance toward Tregelles is noted in the latter's correspondence; see T.C.F. Stunt, "Some Unpublished Letters of S. P. Tregelles relating to the Codex Sinaiticus," *Evangelical Quarterly* 48 (1976): 15–26.

tion; the book also included a presentation of his own critical principles.[96] Tregelles's text appeared in six parts, published between 1854 and 1872; it displayed his basic principle of primary reliance on the oldest manuscripts and versions.

Tischendorf does not present the books of the NT in canonical order, but in his second volume follows the same order as Lachmann, in which the Catholic Epistles precede the Pauline.[97] His text is printed at the top of the page and the critical apparatus at the bottom. Usually this extensive apparatus, which presents the evidence for the text and the variants, occupies about two-thirds to three-fourths of the page. Although Tischendorf made use of only sixty-four uncial manuscripts and only a fragment of one papyrus, his collection of text-critical data is still the largest and most reliable available in a single, usable edition of the Greek NT.[98] A few examples can illustrate the scope and character of Tischendorf's work. In regard to the longer ending of Mark, Tischendorf says that these verses were not written by Mark. He summarizes the arguments against authenticity in a note in the apparatus which extends to three pages. Similarly, he says that the story of the woman caught in adultery (John 7:53—8:11) was not authored by John. The argument supporting this conclusion, together with the textual evidence, stretches to ten pages in the critical apparatus. In regard to the controversial 1 John 5:7-8, Tischendorf argues that the words about the witnesses ("in heaven, the Father, the Word and the Holy Spirit; and these three are one. And there are three that testify on earth") are not authentic, a conclusion supported by four pages of critical apparatus.

With Tischendorf, text criticism had become a fully modern discipline. In the future, a vast amount of textual material would be discovered, methods for evaluating variants would be refined, and new theories about the groupings of texts would be developed. Yet, forthcoming editions of the Greek NT would not vary greatly from Tischendorf's, and text critics would continue to rely on his unequalled critical apparatus. The result was a text that NT interpreters could use with confidence. In regard to larger

---

96. Samuel Prideaux Tregelles, *An Account of the Printed Text of the Greek New Testament; with Remarks on Its Revision upon Critical Principles* (London: S. Bagster, 1854).

97. Although this is the order of most ancient manuscripts, Sinaiticus, Tischendorf's favorite codex, follows the order: Pauline epistles, Acts, Catholic Epistles.

98. See Kurt Aland and Barbara Aland, *The Text of the New Testament: An Introduction to the Critical Editions and to the Theory and Practice of Modern Textual Criticism*, trans. Erroll F. Rhodes (Grand Rapids: Wm. B. Eerdmans, 1987), 22–37. The Alands note that the four-volume edition of H. F. von Soden (*Die Schriften des Neuen Testaments in ihrer ältesten erreichbaren Textgestalt hergestellt auf Grund ihrer Textgeschichte*, 1902–13) contains a more detailed collection of variants than Tischendorf but is less reliable and made virtually impossible to use because of von Soden's system of symbols.

questions about biblical authority, Tischendorf illustrates the paradoxical role that text criticism continues to play. On the one hand, criticism is progressive, breaking the bonds of the revered *textus receptus* and constantly in search of new materials. On the other hand, text criticism is often moved by a conservative concern: recreating the original, pristine text of the NT. Yet criticism itself attests to the irony of the quest, since autographs of the NT documents are not extant, and each new manuscript discovery only adds to the number of perplexing variants.

SUMMARY

The issues reviewed in this chapter are concerned with the details of criticism, although they have important implications for the larger questions of NT research. On the surface, they demonstrate how sophisticated—compared with the amateurish beginnings of the deists—the study of the Bible has become. The historical-critical method, pioneered by Turretin and Ernesti and advanced by Semler and Michaelis, has been refined into an effective scientific instrument. Although many historical and exegetical questions remain unanswered and debate continues concerning fundamental issues, a considerable amount of work has been accomplished.

In regard to the synoptic problem, the sheer recognition that an issue exists—that the Gospels bear some sort of inner literary relationship—represents a departure from the older view of infallible inspiration. Moreover, in the course of the discussion, some solutions began to appear less viable, in particular, the hypothesis of a single lost source, oral or written, upon which the whole gospel tradition was based. The view that subsequent gospels used preceding ones has become widely accepted, and the increasingly popular two-document hypothesis has been articulated. Out of the many possible options, the question of priority has come down to two: Matthew or Mark. Also in the course of the investigation, attention has been directed to presuppositions that have continued to impede the solution of the problem, for instance, theories about the development of gospel tradition and notions about the way ancient authors used sources. Most important, the synoptic problem—the problem of establishing the oldest and most reliable sources—is of crucial importance for the reconstruction of the life and teachings of Jesus. If revelation happened in history, and if the high point of that revelation occurred in Jesus, then the assessment of the sources is of vast theological significance.

Similar issues have emerged in the study of the Gospel of John. Here the traditional view of authenticity and historical reliability has had the support of the prominent scholars, and the departure from orthodoxy has been heralded by lesser known figures like Bretschneider and Tayler. These scholars have functioned primarily as historical (higher) critics, evaluating the internal and external evidence, although with sensitivity to the implications of their work for the faith of the laity. In the spirit of the Enlightenment, they (especially Tayler) have argued that truth takes precedence over tradition and that authority does not demand apostolic authorship. Most important, the question of authorship is seen to have christological implications. In the course of arguing that the author was not an eyewitness, these scholars have shown that the Jesus of the Fourth Gospel is different from the Jesus of the Synoptic Gospels. Thus, by historical-critical method, Strauss's chasm between the Jesus of history and the Christ of faith has been confirmed. Which Jesus is the proper object of faith: the Jesus of historical reconstruction or the Christ of early Christian belief? Moreover, since the Jesus of the Fourth Gospel has developed out of the ongoing tradition and is designed to address the issues of a later time and culture, the biblical Christ appears to have continuity with tradition and continuing relevance. Perhaps the NT gains its importance as witness to what is essential in that historical and faithful tradition.

In the area of text criticism, NT research has been most successful. The dominance of the old Received Text has been overcome, and freedom for new research has been established. Here is one place where scientific method and religious faith coalesce: the quest for the restoration of the original text. To be sure, this quest reflects the Enlightenment concern with literal facticity—the concern for a text where every preposition is in place and a reliable basis for history and doctrine can be found. Nevertheless, the resulting modern critical text, based on extensive evidence and evaluated by critical methods is a significant achievement. Such a text is essential to the whole task of NT research: exegesis, historical reconstruction, and theological synthesis.

10

Moderate and Mediating Criticism

While controversy was raging concerning the radical work of Strauss and the Tübingen school, other scholars carried on NT research in calmer, more mundane ways. Roman Catholic theologians, whose long and venerable tradition had survived centuries of change, were not easily loosed from their moorings by waves of modernity. Loyal to the church, they adopted the new methods cautiously, seeking to enlist them in support of the ancient and enduring faith. British theologians, protected from the storms of the continent by the English Channel, launched a mediating course. Influenced by their own version of the romantic movement, they maintained the conservatism typical of their character while becoming increasingly open to the newer critical approach.

ROMAN CATHOLIC SCHOLARSHIP:
J. L. HUG

As NT research progressed through the nineteenth century, most Roman Catholic scholars were left sitting on the sidelines. The promise apparent in the pioneering work of Richard Simon[1] was not fulfilled in the later scholarship of his own tradition. Actually, Roman Catholic theology, in its debate with Protestantism, might have exploited the Enlightenment's erosion of the principle of *sola scriptura*, a point already suggested by Simon. If the new criticism had demonstrated that the Scriptures were not verbally inspired or infallible, if the authenticity and authority of the NT were called into question, then Protestant reliance on the Bible would seem to have become increasingly problematic. Roman Catholic scholarship, however, remained conservative in face of the modern developments. This was

---

1. See pp. 17–25, above.

due in large part to its loyalty to tradition, and although tradition and Scripture were viewed as twin sources of revelation, tradition affirmed the authenticity and authority of Scripture. The new intellectual movements were not only anti-traditional, they reached results which seemed to erode the normative character of the early tradition.

Text Criticism and Response to Strauss

In spite of this persistent conservatism, some Roman Catholics did participate in the development of NT research. This participation was encouraged in theological faculties associated with universities, where Catholic theologians encountered devotees of the new learning. At Tübingen, for example, a virtual theological renaissance occurred under the leadership of critical and progressive thinkers like Johann Sebastian von Drey (1777–1853) and Johann Adam Möhler (1796–1838).[2] In any event, the contribution of Roman Catholic NT scholars, often ignored by the historians, deserves to be mentioned.

Johannes Martin Augustinus Scholz (1794–1852) did significant work in the area of text criticism.[3] Scholz, a student of J. L. Hug (who is discussed below), was dean of the Catholic faculty at the University of Bonn. Like other text critics of the time, he traveled widely in Europe and the Near East in search of manuscripts. His efforts yielded 616 witnesses previously unknown, and his work stressed the importance of the geographical provenance of the various manuscripts. Scholz's text appeared in two volumes: the first, including the Gospels, in 1830, the second, including the rest of the NT, in 1836. This text is closer to the *textus receptus* than even Griesbach's, although surprisingly, it varies significantly from the hallowed Vulgate. Scholz's apparent sympathy for the Received Text results from his text-critical theory. Early in his work, Scholz grouped the manuscript material into five ancient families: Alexandrian, Western, Asiatic, Byzantine, and Cyprian. Later he adopted Bengel's theory of two ancient recensions: Alexandrian and Constantinopolitan. Although the Alexandrian was attested by the oldest manuscripts, Scholz believed the Constantinopolitan text had been standardized very early and its purity maintained into later times. Thus, this hypothetical text, which was represented by later manu-

---

2. See James Tunstead Burtchaell, "Drey, Möhler and the Catholic School of Tübingen," in *Nineteenth Century Religious Thought in the West*, ed. N. Smart, J. Clayton, S. T. Katz, and P. Sherry, 3 vols. (Cambridge: Cambridge University Press, 1985), 2.111–39.

3. For surveys of Scholz's text-critical research, see Bruce M. Metzger, *The Text of the New Testament: Its Transmission, Corruption, and Restoration*, 2d ed. (New York and Oxford: Oxford University Press, 1968), 123–24; Samuel Prideaux Tragelles, *An Account of the Printed Text of the Greek New Testament; with Remarks on Its Revision upon Critical Principles* (London: S. Bagster, 1854), 92–97; Frederick Henry Scrivener, *A Plain Introduction to the Criticism of the New Testament: For the Use of Biblical Students*, 2d rev. ed. (Cambridge: Deighton, Bell, 1874), 418–22; Marvin R. Vincent, *A History of the Textual Criticism of the New Testament*, New Testament Handbooks (New York: Macmillan, 1903), 106–9.

scripts, became the basis for Scholz's own edition, a text similar to the *textus receptus* which similarly depended on late manuscripts. Scholz's work was also marred by his errors in collation. Some years after the publication of his text, Scholz retracted his Constantinopolitan hypothesis. He acknowledged that if he were to publish a new edition, he would make more use of the Alexandrian text.

In addition to concern with text criticism, Roman Catholic scholars also reacted to the radical procedures of D. F. Strauss,[4] a reaction which involved them in broader issues of NT research.[5] Most Catholics, of course, were adamant in their opposition to Strauss, but Joseph Sprissler—a pastor who was suspended from his post because of his liberalism—hailed Strauss as the prophet of a new theological era.[6] Sprissler applauded Strauss's attack on rationalism, agreed with his opposition to extreme supernaturalism, and supported the idea that mythological interpretation had some validity. Yet, Sprissler, like other Catholic scholars who accepted the methods of higher criticism, believed Strauss had dehistoricized Christian beginnings and created a chasm between the Jesus of history and the Christ of faith that undermined the foundations of Catholic theology.

Roman Catholic opponents of Strauss focused on three main issues.[7] First, they rejected his philosophical presuppositions. They believed Strauss's understanding of divine immanence produced a pantheism that excluded the possibility of God's action, a view seen in Strauss's predisposition against the possibility of miracles. Martin Joseph Mack, professor of exegesis at Tübingen, insisted on a worldview which allowed for divine causality and openness to the possibility of supernatural happenings.[8] Second, Catholic scholars objected to Strauss's understanding and use of historical method. In their opinion, he presupposed that history constituted a closed system that excluded the possibility of any sort of historical uniqueness. Strauss's method, therefore, could not really cope with an event like the resurrection. Johannes Kuhn, who had taught NT exegesis at Giessen and, later, dogmatics at Tübingen, accepted the historical-critical method and rejected the notion that the truth of Scripture had to be a presupposition of biblical interpretation.[9] He also maintained that the biblical authors enlisted history in the service of theology—that faith

---

4. See pp. 246–58, above.

5. See William Madges, "D. F. Strauss in Retrospect: His Reception among Roman Catholics," *Heythrop Journal* 30 (1989): 273–92.

6. See William Madges, *The Core of Christian Faith: D. F. Strauss and His Catholic Critics*, (New York, Bern, Frankfurt am Main, Paris: P. Lang, 1988), 166–68.

7. Madges, "D. F. Strauss in Retrospect," 274–80.

8. Madges, *The Core of Christian Faith*, 91–101.

9. Ibid., 44–90. See also Donald J. Dietrich, *The Goethezeit and the Metamorphosis of Catholic Theology in the Age of Idealism* (Bern, Frankfurt am Main, Las Vegas: P. Lang, 1979), 176–90; James Tunstead Burtchaell, *Catholic Theories of Biblical Inspiration since 1810: A Review and Critique* (Cambridge: Cambridge University Press, 1969), 25–32.

shaped the gospel narratives. Nevertheless, Kuhn insisted that the Scriptures recorded a real history in which the transcendent God had acted, a history that contained revelation and was basic to the Christian faith.

Finally, the Catholic scholars rejected Strauss's construing of the Gospels as totally mythological. Although exegetes like Kuhn acknowledged that the Gospels contained mythical and legendary elements, they supported the essential historicity of the gospel narrative. As Kuhn said, "The historical character of Christianity rests namely upon the historical truth of the gospel story, and Christianity itself is nothing without it."[10] For Kuhn, as for his Catholic colleagues, the historical Jesus is crucial to the Christian faith.

> New Testament faith, where it appears in a characteristic way, is essentially a faith in Jesus the messiah, the reconciler and also the only necessary mediator of the salvation of humanity. . . . Their [the NT authors] preaching and teaching is, in general and in its deepest roots, not abstract but historical: a simple reference to the gracious action and mighty deeds of God in the course of time.[11]

Johann Leonhard Hug (1765–1846) and Higher Criticism

The most important Catholic biblical scholar of the first two-thirds of the nineteenth century was Johann Leonhard Hug. Born in Constance, the son of a locksmith, Hug studied at the University of Freiburg, where a Catholic seminary had recently been established. After further schooling at the seminary in Meersburg, Hug was ordained in 1790. He served for a short time as a smalltown vicar but soon was appointed to the Freiburg faculty, where he taught Semitic languages, OT, and NT. His NT instruction focused on Matthew, John, Romans, and the Corinthian letters. In interpreting these biblical books, Hug attended to their historical setting, making use of studies in geography and archeology. Hug had the distinction of bringing Catholic scholarship into conversation with Protestant biblical research. Although his work was conservative, Hug was not immune to the spirit of the Enlightenment: he considered the ethical teachings of Jesus to be the highest achievement of the human religious quest and the heart of the Christian faith.

Late in life, Hug joined with other Catholic theologians in the struggle against Strauss.[12] Hug was not opposed to historical-critical method per se and had read with appreciation the works of Michaelis[13] and

---

10. Cited in Madges, *The Core of Christian Faith*, 54.
11. Cited in ibid., 67.
12. Ibid., 125–51.
13. See pp. 127–38, above.

Griesbach.[14] Strauss, however, had gone too far, a judgment Hug made in response to Strauss's most conservative (third) edition. In Hug's opinion, Strauss had not really been faithful to the historical method but had presupposed the mythological approach without adequate warrant. Strauss had also adopted criteria of historicity that excluded genuine historical understanding, evident, for instance, in his notion that miracles were a priori impossible. Hug, a moderate supernaturalist, believed that the miracle stories had to be evaluated in terms of the testimony of the witnesses. Basic to this evaluation was Hug's conviction that Jesus was unique and able to employ his supernatural power in the performance of miracles to demonstrate his divine authority. "The people, like the apostles," said Hug, "had to see facts, which no human power sufficed to accomplish, acts of God, which certified the authorization of the new law-giver."[15] In particular, Hug objected to Strauss's presuppositions which denied the historicity of the resurrection, an event that Hug held to be unique and essential to Christianity.

Hug also questioned Strauss's understanding of myth. Although he agreed that myths belonged to the fabric of older cultures, Hug claimed that the development of early Christianity occurred in a post-mythical era that was concerned with history. The apostolic age, he asserted, was a time of skepticism about the mythological—a time concerned with reliable reports. Hug also opposed Strauss's theory that the OT was the myth-making source, for instance, that the predictions of the prophets were used to fabricate the gospel narratives. According to Hug, Jesus was unique, a Messiah different from Jewish expectation. Thus, Jesus, not the OT, was the creative force in shaping the gospel story. The Gospels, including John, presented history, not myth. When all the mythological trappings are stripped away, the outcome of Strauss's program is obvious: the historical foundation of Christianity has been undermined. As Hug says:

> Our position, the supernaturalistic one . . . is at bottom the natural position. An enemy to artificial methods, it despises the travestied Christ and the Straussian-mythological absurdity altogether. It honors the Christ, as he is given, and only this [Christ] benefits the world.[16]

Hug's major contribution to NT research is his weighty *Introduction to the New Testament*, first published in 1808.[17] In Part 1, Hug investigates the

14. See pp. 138–48, above.
15. Cited in Madges, *The Core of Christian Faith*, 129.
16. Cited in ibid., 139.
17. Joh. Leonhard Hug, *Einleitung in die Schriften des Neuen Testaments*, 3d rev. ed., 2 vols. (Stuttgart and Tübingen: J. G. Gotta, 1826); Eng. trans.: *Hug's Introduction to the New Testament*, trans. David Fosdick, with notes by M. Stuart (Andover, Mass: Gould & Newman, 1836). See also an earlier Eng. trans. based on the 2d ed.: *An Introduction to the Writings of the New Testament*, trans. Daniel Guildford Wait, 2 vols. (London: C. & J. Rivington, 1827).

age, genuineness, and credibility of the NT books, together with an extensive discussion of text criticism. Hug understands Jesus to be the final goal in the historical development of religion. The books of the NT gain their importance as records of his life and ethical teachings. They record the testimony of eyewitnesses, and the quality of their historical and geographical references attest to their reliability. This reliability is also confirmed by external evidence, including the testimony of heretics. Yet, beyond all this, Jesus himself is the surest proof of the reliability of the Gospels and the historicity of the miracles. "When I consider the character of the man whose portrait is drawn in the Gospels," says Hug, "I find it to be too lofty and noble for any Jewish mind to have invented."[18]

In regard to the text of the NT, Hug notes that the writing was on papyrus, that the books were dictated and read aloud, and that none of the original autographs are extant. Although the first recorded canon is the list of an unknown author in Rome at the beginning of the third century (the so-called Muratorian canon), Hug believes the canon took definite shape much earlier. Hug, like conservatives before and after, is troubled by the fact that errors have crept into the text. "It is inconceivable, when we reflect upon the reverence with which these writings were received, and the reputation of sanctity which they possessed, that such a thing could have happened; and yet it did, and the heretics, to whom it would perhaps be attributed, had no share in it."[19] In spite of the variants, Hug believes a reliable text can be reconstructed by attending to a hypothetical text that became standard in the third century (to which Codex Claramontanus is close), and to the supposed recensions of Origen (in Palestine), Hesychius (in Egypt), and Lucian (in Antioch). In evaluating variants, Hug believes texts that exhibit Hebraisms, a less refined style, and exegetical difficulties are more original.

In Part 2, Hug turns to higher criticism—the historical introduction to the individual books of the NT. He classifies the material into three types: the historical books, the writings of Paul, and the Catholic Epistles. The historical books, including the Gospels and the Acts of the Apostles, are given major attention (almost 200 pages, compared with about 100 for the Pauline letters). In regard to the Gospels, Hug believes they were written in the order in which they appear in the canon and by the authors to whom they have traditionally been attributed. Matthew, which has a Palestinian provenance, was written first, but some time after the events it records. Hug thinks the "desolating sacrilege" (24:15) refers to the defilement of the temple area by the Zealots. Taking this event as a point of departure, Hug concludes that Matthew was written after the Roman con-

18. Hug, *Introduction* (Fosdick trans.), 64.
19. Ibid., 85.

quest of Galilee but prior to the destruction of Jerusalem, that is, around 68. Matthew's purpose is to present Jesus as the Messiah. He is concerned to protect Jewish Christians from apostasy and to encourage the conversion of Jews. Hug believes Matthew wrote his Gospel in Greek, a language well known at the time in Palestine.

The Gospel of Mark was written by John Mark in Rome after the deaths of Peter and Paul. It records the gospel reminiscences of Peter. In discussing the sources of the Synoptic Gospels, Hug rejects the hypothesis of an Aramaic original (Eichhorn) and the theory of a common oral gospel (Gieseler). Hug also answers the argument that differences among the Gospels prove that succeeding Gospels did not use preceding: the differences, Hug argues, depend on the way the individual authors use their sources. Hug concludes that Mark used Matthew who was an eyewitness of virtually everything he reports. When Mark deviates from the order of Matthew, he attempts to follow a chronological order; Matthew's order, on the other hand, is according to subjects.

> He [Mark] did not then copy Matthew's book, but made use of it as the basis of his own; conferred greater particularity on Matthew's narrative . . . and moulded his predecessor's sketches into the form of complete history. He is not, as some have repeated from Augustine, the epitomist, but the reviser of Matthew; and sometimes his revision is so rigid that he seems positively to contradict him.[20]

The Gospel of Luke was written by Luke, the physician and travel companion of Paul. According to Hug, Luke was a Jewish proselyte and native of Antioch who later moved to Palestine. He used Mark as the primary source for his Gospel, but in places where Mark provided no material, he followed Matthew. "This coincidence with Matthew, however, is found only in narratives omitted by Mark; in other cases Luke adheres more closely to the latter than the former."[21]

The Gospel of John was written to prove that Jesus was the Christ and son of God. The author, John the apostle and son of Zebedee, made this case in opposition to heresy like that of Cerinthus and the Nicolaitans. Because of his concern with the nature of Christ, John omits ethical teaching but includes discourses which illuminate the divine glory of Jesus. John highlights this picture by his presentation of spectacular miracles, but not many of these, since his readers know the various wonders recounted in the other Gospels. John, in Hug's opinion, makes use of all three of the Synoptics. His account of the anointing of Jesus (12:1-8), for example, combines material borrowed from Matt. 26:6-13, Mark 14:3-9,

20. Ibid., 381.
21. Ibid., 398.

and Luke 7:36-50. According to Hug, each subsequent Gospel knows the preceding Gospels, and John consciously writes to supplement the others. John, of course, was an eyewitness to most of the events he records. This is confirmed, in Hug's judgment, by the vividness of the narrative and the intrinsic historicity of the account: the extent of the Jerusalem ministry, for example, correctly explains the growing opposition to Jesus. As to the supposed differences between John and the Synoptics, Hug harmonizes. The last supper was indeed a Passover meal, as the synoptics state, but, according to Galilean custom, it was observed a day early, as John reports.

In discussing the writings of Paul, Hug presents the epistles in chronological order. Thus, 1 Thessalonians is described first, followed by 2 Thessalonians, which Hug takes to be authentic. The Epistle to Titus is discussed next, in accord with Hug's notion that Paul sailed to Crete after he left Corinth en route to Ephesus (Acts 18:18-19); Titus was written shortly after his arrival in Ephesus, prior to his departure for the East. Galatians was also written from Ephesus after Paul's return from the East, following his second visit to Galatia (Acts 18:23); his original mission is noted in Acts 16:6, so that the people addressed in the epistle are the north Galatians (the territorial hypothesis). First Corinthians was written somewhat later from Ephesus, and 2 Corinthians was written after Paul moved from Asia to Macedonia. First Timothy, in Hug's opinion, was written shortly after this departure from Ephesus and, thus, between the writing of 1 and 2 Corinthians. Romans was composed during his short stay in Corinth on the eve of his departure for Jerusalem (Acts 20:3); its purpose was to reconcile gentile Christians and Jewish Christians, addressing the situation created by the return to Rome of Jews who had earlier been banished by Claudius.

Hug believes all the imprisonment letters are authentic, all written from Rome. The earliest of these, Ephesians, was originally an encyclical epistle, and the letter to the Laodiceans (Col. 4:16) was actually a copy of this letter which was sent to the church at Laodicea. Second Timothy was also written from this first Roman imprisonment—after Ephesians and before Colossians. Philemon was composed at the same time as Colossians, and Philippians still later. The heresy addressed in Ephesians, Colossians, and Timothy is an Eastern magical philosophy which can be called Gnosticism, a heresy which developed into a complete system in the second century. Hebrews, which Hug thinks was originally written in Greek, is accepted as authentic. "There is nothing at all, then, against Paul; on the contrary, every thing is in his favor, and proves the Epistle to be his."[22] Written just prior to Paul's release from the first imprisonment

22. Ibid., 601.

(65 C.E.), Hebrews reflects Paul's response to the Judaism he had encountered on his final trip to Jerusalem.

Hug accepts all of the Catholic Epistles as authentic.[23] The Epistle of James, in his opinion, was written by James, the brother of Jesus who became leader of the Jerusalem church. Hug notes the relationship between the Epistle of Jude and 2 Peter. He believes that Peter had a copy of Jude before him when he wrote his second epistle. Jude is identified as the brother of James and Jesus. According to Hug, the Apocalypse was written by John the apostle, author of the Fourth Gospel and the Johannine epistles. The Apocalypse was written while John was in exile on Patmos during the reign of Domitian. His epistles and Gospel were composed later, after the end of Domitian's rule.

As this brief survey shows, Roman Catholic biblical scholars deserve more attention than they usually are given. A scholar like Kuhn, for example, displays a high degree of theological sophistication. At first glance, Hug appears to contribute little to the advance of higher criticism: he affirms the authenticity of every NT book, a position which was increasingly difficult to accept in the nineteenth century. A careful reading of Hug's *Introduction*, however, will prove that he has not reached his conclusions with ease. Hug knows the literature and skills of criticism, he faces the critical issues head on, and he presents about as convincing an argument as the data allows. Moreover, Hug has raised important questions about methodology, especially Strauss's hermeneutic of myth. To be sure, analysis of Hug's *Introduction* will also suggest that conservative premises have predetermined his results, but Hug is certainly not the only nineteenth-century critic to have presuppositions—as the Catholic response to Strauss has demonstrated.

ROMANTICISM AND
IMAGINATION IN ENGLAND:
COLERIDGE, T. ARNOLD, STANLEY, AND JOWETT

After the tumultuous times of the deists,[24] a liberal biblical critic was about as easy to find in England as the sun in a London fog.[25] In Britain, scholar-

---

23. Hug discusses the Johannine epistles (all of which are accepted as authentic) in his chapter on the historical books in connection with his discussion of the Gospel of John.

24. See pp. 31–57, above.

25. See Nigel M. de S. Cameron, *Biblical Higher Criticism and the Defense of Infallibilism in 19th Century Britain* (Lewiston, N.Y.: Edwin Mellen Press, 1987). The basic conservative tenor of British scholarship is also affirmed by Vernon F. Storr, *The Development of English Theology in the Nineteenth Century, 1800–1860* (London: Longmans, Green, 1913). Storr also notes the rare exceptions; see 92–114; 362–97.

ship was concentrated in the two great universities at Oxford and Cambridge. These schools were dominated by the church, and the church fostered a conservative view of tradition and Scripture. Nevertheless, a movement of creative biblical scholarship—modern, yet moderate—developed in Britain. Spawned by a romanticism that was expressed in, for example, the poetry of William Wordsworth, this movement was reminiscent of the biblical interpretation of Lessing and Herder.[26] Its creative spirit was Coleridge, poet and neighbor of Wordsworth, who inspired a succession of disciples: Thomas Arnold, who taught Arthur Stanley, who, in turn, was the friend of Benjamin Jowett.

Samuel Taylor Coleridge (1772–1834)

Samuel Taylor Coleridge was born in Devon, the son of a scholarly educator and clergyman. From 1791 to 1794, Coleridge studied at Jesus College, Cambridge, but did not take a degree. The next year introduced a period of poetic productivity that included such classics as "The Rime of the Ancient Mariner" and "Kubla Khan." In 1798 and 1799, Coleridge lived in Germany, primarily at Göttingen, where he became acquainted with Eichhorn's lectures on the NT. Suffering pain from ill health, Coleridge became addicted to opium. In 1804, he traveled to Malta, where he served as secretary to the governor. Upon his return to England in 1806, Coleridge experienced a period of personal difficulties. Later, from 1816 to 1834, he lived with Dr. James Gillman in London. These years were a time of considerable literary production, including his major theological works.

Coleridge's religious thought reflects no clear theological system.[27] Early in his career, he had contemplated entering the Unitarian ministry, and his theology at the time was rationalistic. His daughter Sara reflects on this period, "when the elements of Faith were for his mind in a sort of chaos that was yet to be shaped by Reason, divinely illumined, into a spiritual world," but notes that "from this time forth [he] was a defender of historical Christianity."[28] The key to Coleridge's mature thought is found in his concept of Imagination. Taking up Kant's idea that the highest truths cannot be grasped by ordinary thinking, Coleridge draws a distinction between imagination (or Reason) and understanding. Understanding provides that kind of knowledge that is acquired by the senses, that is, objec-

---

26. See pp. 165–83, above.

27. For summaries, see David Pym, *The Religious Thought of Samuel Taylor Coleridge* (New York: Barnes & Noble, 1979); J. Robert Barth, *Coleridge and Christian Doctrine* (Cambridge: Harvard University Press, 1969); Claude Welch, "Samuel Taylor Coleridge," in *Nineteenth Century Religious Thought*, ed. N. Smart, et al., 2.1–28.

28. Samuel Taylor Coleridge, *Confessions of an Inquiring Spirit* (Philadelphia: Fortress Press, 1988), 80.

tive, scientific knowledge—knowledge of the phenomenal world. Imagination, or Reason, provides knowledge of spiritual and universal truths— truths which are beyond sense perception. Reason is expressed in the Johannine concept of the Logos and can be described as the "Spiritual Mind."[29] Obviously, Coleridge had adopted an epistemology antithetical to the position of John Locke which had dominated English thought throughout the eighteenth century.[30]

On the basis of this idea of knowledge, Coleridge developed his religious concepts. He identified God with universal reason, and he understood God to be personal or, perhaps, superpersonal. Religion is communication between God and humans, and Christianity "is the Perfection of Human Intelligence."[31] It is not a set of doctrines to be proved, but a way of life to be lived.

> The Gospel is not a system of Theology, nor a *syntagma* of theoretical propositions and conclusions for the enlargement of speculative knowledge, ethical or metaphysical. But it is a history, a series of events related or announced.[32]

The crucial event of this history is the incarnation of the creative Logos of God in the person of Jesus Christ—the word of God which effects the spiritual transformation of humans. Faith in Christ and the Christian gospel is confirmed not by logic but by moral suasion and personal experience. For Coleridge, revelation is both objective and subjective—given in history and received in faith. In interpreting the biblical revelation, Coleridge was opposed to rigid orthodoxy, on the one hand, and rational skepticism, on the other. The notion that the Scriptures were the result of divine dictation he found demeaning, suggesting that God was like a ventriloquist and the writers like automatons. Coleridge, no stranger to poetic inspiration, preferred a view that recognized the creative communication between God and inspired persons. The Bible becomes the word of God as it is read in faith, an experience in which the believer shares in the inspiration of the writer.

Coleridge's understanding of Scripture is most clearly set forth in his *Confessions of an Inquiring Spirit*, published in 1840, six years after his death. Originally, Coleridge had planned to append to his *Aids to Reflection* (1825) an imaginary conversation between an aged passenger and a young clergyman on shipboard. In the *Confessions*, these thoughts are expressed in a series of seven letters to an imaginary friend, probably written around

---

29. Samuel Taylor Coleridge, *Aids to Reflection and the Confessions of an Inquiring Spirit* (London: G. Bell, 1913), 135.
30. See pp. 33–39, above.
31. Coleridge, *Aids to Reflection*, xvi.
32. Ibid., 136.

1826, with the title "Letters on the Inspiration of the Scriptures." Coleridge says that his purpose is to present his own opinion on two questions:

> I. Is it necessary, or expedient, to insist on the belief of the divine origin and authority of all, and every part of the Canonical Books as the condition, or first principle, of Christian Faith?
> II. Or, may not the due appreciation of the Scriptures collectively be more safely relied on as the result and consequence of the belief in Christ; the gradual increase—in respect of particular passages—of our spiritual discernment of their truth and authority supplying a test and measure of our own growth and progress as individual believers, without the servile fear that prevents or overclouds the free honour which cometh from love? I *John* iv. 18.[33]

The letters which follow explicate Coleridge's preference for the second alternative.

After affirming faith in the transcendent triune God who is the creator of heaven and earth and the source of the incarnate word that accomplishes human redemption, the first letter declares that this faith is open to all and that Christianity is both historical and spiritual. The Bible, which witnesses to this faith, must be interpreted by the same principles that are used for other books, even though the Bible is a special book.

> I take up this work with the purpose to read it for the first time as I should read any other work,—as far at least as I can or dare. For I neither can, nor dare, throw off a strong and awful prepossession in its favour—certain as I am that a large part of the light and life, in and by which I see, love, and embrace the truths and the strengths co-organised into a living body of faith and knowledge . . . has been directly or indirectly derived to me from this sacred volume.[34]

Yet, there is a light higher than the light of Scripture—"the Light, of which light itself is but the *shechinah* and cloudy tabernacle; the Word that is the light for every man, and life for as many as give heed to it."[35] Thus, reading the Bible like any other book does not mean analyzing it as a collection of historical and doctrinal data. For Coleridge, the biblical text is a work of art, expressing in symbol a reality which is beyond the senses, a reality perceived in the imaginative response of the reader.[36]

The following letters make a case against verbal inspiration and biblical infallibility. Although he is willing to accept the views of the writers con-

---

33. Coleridge, *Confessions of an Inquiring Spirit*, 22.
34. Ibid., 25.
35. Ibid., 26.
36. See Steve Gowler, "Coleridge as Hermeneut," *Anglican Theological Review* 66 (1984): 161–72.

cerning their authority, Coleridge asserts that they make no claims to infallibility. He concludes that the doctrine of a divinely dictated Bible should be rejected as "superstitious and unscriptural."[37] The argument of the orthodox that Jesus and the apostles accepted the authority of the canon does little for the Christian belief in the NT, because the Bible of the earliest Christians was the Hebrew Scriptures. Moreover, the doctrine of verbal inspiration "petrifies at once the whole body of Holy Writ"[38] and destroys the vitality of this "breathing organism."[39] The attempt to preserve an infallible Bible forces scholars into specious harmonization of trivial details at the expense of the weightier matters of Scripture. "What, I say, could have tempted grave and pious men thus to disturb the foundation of the Temple, in order to repair a petty break or rat-hole in the wall, or fasten a loose stone or two in the outer court, if not an assumed necessity arising out of the peculiar character of Bible history?"[40]

In Letter 4, Coleridge argues that although the Bible contains religion revealed by God, not all that is in the Bible constitutes divine revelation. The assumption that the Bible contains all truth has encouraged scholars to tear texts out of context and to fabricate unbiblical doctrines. "By this strange mosaic, Scripture texts have been worked up into passable likenesses of Purgatory, Popery, the Inquisition, and other monstrous abuses."[41] Valid interpretation, on the other hand, requires careful research, but at its best, exegesis is a fallible, human endeavor. Indeed, a major fault of the literalists is their mistaken notion that human language is adequate to express divine truth, "as if God's meaning could be so clearly or fitly expressed in man's as in God's own words!"[42] For those who read in faith, the Bible requires no external proofs: "The truth revealed through Christ has its evidence in itself, and the proof of its divine authority in its fitness to our nature and needs."[43]

The last three letters support Coleridge's conviction that the teaching of Christ is more important than Scripture, although the Bible can and should be recognized as the word of God. For the Christian, faith in Christ holds priority, and Scripture gains its importance as witness to Christ. Nevertheless, the Bible properly understood is God's revelation. "We assuredly believe," he concludes, "that the Bible contains all truth necessary to salvation, and that therein is preserved the undoubted Word of

37. Coleridge, *Confessions of an Inquiring Spirit*, 30.
38. Ibid., 35.
39. Ibid., 36.
40. Ibid., 40.
41. Ibid., 43.
42. Ibid., 47.
43. Ibid., 48.

God."[44] Finally, Coleridge asserts that what he has been contending against is "Bibliolatry," a term he may have learned from Lessing.[45] In any case, Coleridge's liberalism is largely confined to questions of inspiration and authority. On matters of higher criticism, he remained conservative. In commenting on the Gospel of John, he wrote:

> I have studied with an open and fearless spirit the attempts of sundry learned critics of the Continent, to invalidate the authenticity of this Gospel, before and since Eichhorn's Vindication. The result has been a clearer assurance and . . . a yet deeper conviction of the genuineness of all the writings, which the Church has attributed to this Apostle.[46]

Nevertheless, Coleridge argued that the Johannine discourses are misunderstood by those who accept them as authentic. John, he contends, was concerned not with literal water, and flesh, and bread but with spiritual matters which had to be spiritually discerned. For Coleridge, John is the least factual of all of the Gospels but the most authentic witness to the significance of Jesus.

Thomas Arnold (1795–1842)

Because of his importance as a literary figure, Coleridge had considerable impact on British religious thought. In theology, his most important disciple was F. D. Maurice, but for the future of NT research, Coleridge's influence on Thomas Arnold was decisive.[47] Born on the Isle of Wight, Arnold entered Corpus Christi College at Oxford at age sixteen. In 1814, he graduated in classics with honors and was awarded a fellowship to Oriel College, Oxford, where he received a Master of Arts. In 1828, Arnold was appointed headmaster of Rugby School, the omnipresent "Doctor" in the popular *Tom Brown's School Days*, immortalized in his son Matthew's poem, "Rugby Chapel."[48] In 1833, Arnold published a pamphlet entitled "Principles of Church Reform," which argued that the church ought to conform to the teaching and spirit of Christ. Arnold was ardently opposed to the Oxford Movement, led by the Tractarians, Keble, Newman, and Pusey,

---

44. Ibid., 58.
45. Lessing's use of the term is clear (see p. 166, above), but David Jasper, in his introduction to *Confessions of an Inquiring Spirit* (p. 12), claims that Coleridge found the term in the writings of John Byrom, who died in 1763.
46. Coleridge, *Aids to Reflection*, 259.
47. For a comprehensive account of Arnold's life and work, see Arthur Penrhyn Stanley, *The Life and Correspondence of Thomas Arnold, D.D.*, 2 vols. (New York: Scribner's, 1895).
48. Matthew Arnold's views on biblical inspiration and criticism are set forth in his *Literature and Dogma*; see John Drury, ed., *Critics of the Bible, 1724-1873* (Cambridge: Cambridge University Press, 1989). In the spirit of Coleridge and Thomas Arnold, Matthew Arnold opposes literalism and argues against miracle and fulfilled prophecy as proofs for faith.

which advocated ecclesiastical orthodoxy. Arnold rejected, among other things, their understanding of apostolic succession, and he wrote a caustic criticism of their views in an article published in the *Edinburgh Review* entitled "The Oxford Malignants." In 1841, Arnold was appointed Regius Professor of Modern History at Oxford—an honor for which he had hoped for years—only to die a short time after presenting his inaugural address at the age of forty-six.

Arnold's basic point of view owes much to Coleridge. In a letter to W. W. Hull, Arnold wrote:

> We have got Coleridge's Literary Remains, in which I do rejoice greatly. I think with all his faults old Sam was more of a great man than any one who has lived within the four seas in my memory. It is refreshing to see such a union of the highest philosophy and poetry, with so full a knowledge, on so many points at least, of particular facts.[49]

Like Coleridge, Arnold advocated a practical Christianity, centered in faith in Christ—the revelation of God and the guide for life. In a note on a sermon entitled "Christ Our Pattern," Arnold declared:

> For in the person of Jesus Christ, there was given us an image of God which we might and should represent to ourselves in our own minds. . . . The man, Christ Jesus, represents to us not the Godhead as it is in itself, but all that we can profitably conceive of it.[50]

Basic to belief in Christ was recognition of the reality of the resurrection. In a sermon on the "Certainty of Christ's Resurrection" Arnold distinguished the raising of Jesus from other miracles:

> For they might stand or fall with no consequence to our eternal hopes, so long as this single one remained sure; but if this one could fail us, all the rest would profit us nothing. If Christ be not risen, our faith is vain, we are yet in our sins; and they who have died in the faith of Christians, have ventured their souls upon nothing, and have died to rise again no more.[51]

In making his case, Arnold notes that Christ both predicted his resurrection and accomplished it. All the evidence shows that Christ was really dead and after the resurrection was fully alive.

Early in the 1830s Arnold expressed his intention to engage in NT research. In a letter to the Archbishop of Dublin (1832), Arnold wrote of the need for a practical, nonsectarian commentary:

> I know of nothing more urgent than to circulate such an edition of the Scriptures, as might labor, with God's help, to give their very express image without human addition or omission, striving to state clearly what is God's

---

49. Stanley, *Thomas Arnold* 2.61.
50. Thomas Arnold, *Sermons*, 2d ed., 3 vols. (London: B. Fellowes, 1834), 3.40.
51. Ibid. 3.143.

will with regard to us now; for this seems to me to be one great use of a commentary, to make people understand where God spoke to their fathers, where He speaks to them; or rather—since in all He speaks to them, though not after the same manner—to teach them to distinguish where they are to follow the letter, and where the spirit.[52]

Arnold decided to meet this need himself by producing a commentary on the Pauline letters. Because of his controversy with the Tractarians, he originally planned to begin with the Pastoral Epistles. He believed his opponents' understanding of early church order could be countered by a proper exegesis of these epistles. Somewhat optimistically, he wrote that "no man yet ever fell or could fall into that heresy by studying the Scriptures."[53] However, Arnold changed his plan and decided to treat the Thessalonian correspondence first. In a letter to W. W. Hull (1836), he wrote, "I have begun the Thessalonians, and like the work much; but I dread the difficulty of the second chapter of the Second Epistle."[54]

Although Arnold's work on a commentary never resulted in publication, his letters and sermons are permeated by a concern with Scripture. "But one good was done by the Reformation, for which we cannot be too thankful;" he declared, "that is, it has made us understand that the sole authority for our faith is to be found in the Scriptures, and it has put the Scriptures, to speak generally, within the reach of all of us."[55] In the introduction to the third volume of his sermons, Arnold comments on the duty of the theologian and minister:

> His business is twofold, the interpretation of the Scriptures and the application of them. The first is a matter of criticism and philology; and every work that increases our knowledge of the languages in which the Scriptures were written; that assists us to fix the age and circumstances of the authors of the several books; or that throws light on the state of their times, in all its various divisions, is the proper study of a theologian.[56]

Arnold's letters also contain some of his views on higher criticism. He believed much of Daniel belonged to the Maccabean period, but he entertained no doubts about the authenticity of John. Thus, in a letter to Sir Thomas Pasley (1840), Arnold wrote that "the self-same criticism which has established the authority of St John's Gospel against all questionings, does, I think, equally prove the non-authenticity of a great part of Daniel."[57]

Arnold's major contribution to NT research is his essay "On the Right

52. Stanley, *Thomas Arnold* 1.287.
53. Letter to W. C. Lake, in ibid. 2.64.
54. Stanley, *Thomas Arnold* 2.61.
55. Arnold, *Sermons* 3.26.
56. Ibid. 3.viii.
57. Stanley, *Thomas Arnold* 2.174.

Interpretation and Understanding of the Scriptures."[58] He begins by noting a fundamental problem: a young person wants to read the Bible for spiritual benefit but finds it difficult to understand. Arnold's response affirms two basic principles of interpretation. First, the interpreter must recognize the character and historical setting of any biblical injunction. Some commandments are given to only one person or a single generation, while others are general and universal; the latter, but not the former, are applicable to all people. The applicability of a command is assessed by the situation in which it is presented. Thus, a command can be accepted as essentially the same command if it is offered in the same situation; a command can be seen as analogous in application if the circumstances are analogous; and a command is not to be taken as binding if it is presented in a contrary situation.

Arnold's second basic principle is that revelation was given progressively. "The revelations of God to man," he writes, "are gradual, and adapted to his state at the several periods when they were successively made."[59] Since people, especially in earlier times, were limited in their capacity to receive revelation, God had to accommodate divine truth to the limitations of human beings.[60] "In any communication between a Being of infinite knowledge and one of finite, it is obvious that the former must speak sometimes according to the view of the latter, unless it be his pleasure to raise him almost to his own level."[61] Arnold, like Lessing and Herder, believed the human race developed in a way analogous to the development of the individual—from childhood, through adolescence, to maturity. Consequently, God's revelation to humans in the era of infancy had to take primitive form, thus, for example, the description of God in anthropomorphic terms.

Arnold proceeds to explicate his principles by illustrations from the Bible. For example, the second of the ten commandments—to make no graven image—Arnold takes as universal: nothing can substitute for God, and no one should attempt to present the invisible God in bodily form. The command to Abraham to sacrifice his son, on the other hand, is not universal. It had meaning in its own time, when child sacrifice was understood as a special act of devotion, but it cannot apply to us who know such an act would be against the will of God. We know this because we have a higher revelation than Abraham—the revelation in Christ. Nevertheless, on the basis of analogy, this limited command can be seen to point to a

58. Arnold, *Sermons* 2.421–80.
59. Ibid. 2.430
60. A similar idea of accommodation had been developed in the eighteenth century by Semler; see pp. 123–24, above.
61. Arnold, *Sermons* 2.431.

larger truth: God's demands may require us to sacrifice that which is most dear to us.

In regard to the actual process of interpreting, Arnold delineates three types of material. First, some texts are religious in character: they present theological doctrines. In interpreting these, the exegete should employ a christological hermeneutic. For example, the biblical doctrine of the wrath of God, seen from the perspective of the crucifixion, teaches that God both abhors sin and loves sinners. Second, some texts are mixed: they are partly concerned with religion, partly concerned with history. Arnold puts the miracle stories in this class. He rejects the idea that miracles are a priori impossible and argues that God's power and concern for persons assures the reality of some miracles. Nevertheless, miracle stories can be subjected to historical investigation, and if they prove to be unhistorical, the book that records them is not fully inspired. A book which is uninspired, however, can contain divine revelation. For Arnold, credibility and canonicity do not require infallible inspiration.

Finally, some texts are primarily historical. If historical criticism finds inaccuracies or errors in these texts, their message is not thereby discredited. Credibility, according to Arnold, requires only faithful recording of events, not infallibility. Similarly, the genuineness of a biblical book does not demand that it was written by the author to whom it has been traditionally ascribed. The orthodox, therefore, are mistaken in their notion that questioning the authorship of canonical books represents a denial of faith. Nevertheless, Arnold is suspicious of German rationalistic intellectualism. He says that "there is in the rationalists a coldness and irreverence of tone, and so apparent an absence of all feeling of their own personal relations to God, as men and as sinners, while they are discussing, like indifferent spectators, his dealings with mankind in the abstract, that their intellectual fault is greatly aggravated by these moral defects."[62] In the end, Arnold comments that his intention throughout the essay is to distinguish between the Christian faith and questions about the Bible that are historical, critical, and scientific. The Christian faith is secure and cannot be destroyed by historical and scientific research—a conclusion reminiscent of Lessing.[63]

Arthur Penrhyn Stanley (1815–1881)

Thomas Arnold's intention to write commentaries on the Pauline letters was realized by Arthur Stanley and Benjamin Jowett. Arthur Penrhyn Stanley was the son of the Bishop of Norwich. From 1829 to 1834, Stanley

62. Ibid. 2.476.
63. See p. 168, above.

attended Rugby, where he fell under the spell of Thomas Arnold. He entered Balliol College, Oxford, in 1834. During the controversy concerning the Oxford movement, Stanley supported Arnold, a stance which cost his election as a fellow at Balliol. However, in 1838, he was elected a fellow at Oxford's University College and in the same year was ordained. From 1843 to 1851, Stanley served as a tutor at Oxford, where his students hailed him as "a singularly attractive and inspiring teacher."[64] In 1845, Stanley was appointed select preacher at Oxford, but his sermons on the apostolic age (1846–47)[65] were judged unorthodox, and Stanley was deemed unfit for the chair of exegesis. Together with his friend Benjamin Jowett, Stanley planned a commentary series that would realize Arnold's dream.

From 1856 to 1864, Stanley served as professor of ecclesiastical history at Oxford, where he lectured on the history of the Eastern church and the history of Judaism. Stanley declined the invitation to contribute to the *Essays and Reviews*, and when the inflammatory book appeared in 1860, he wrote a critical review. "The illusion . . . and the panic . . . which this volume has excited, has, I consider, put back the progress of Biblical criticism and sound theology in this country probably for five years."[66] However, when the Anglican bishops wrote a letter condemning the *Essays* and their authors, Stanley spoke in support of the right of free expression. In 1864, Stanley was appointed Dean of Westminster's in London, where he made efforts to reconcile the low and high church parties of the established religion. Stanley was a friend of the royal family and wielded great influence on religious life in England, including support for biblical criticism. Commenting on Coleridge's "Letters on Inspiration," he wrote, "The general impression left on the mind is the exceeding value and beauty of the Bible, and the exceeding evil of Bibliolatry."[67]

Some of Stanley's work as a church historian has implications for NT research. For instance, the third volume of his *Lectures on the History of the Jewish Church*[68] recounts the history of Judaism from the Babylonian captivity to the Roman destruction of Jerusalem (70 C.E.). Directly related to the history of early Christianity is his *Sermons and Essays on the Apostolical Age.*[69] In the preface, Stanley says that he is concerned not with theology but

64. Cited in Rowland E. Prothero, *The Life and Correspondence of Arthur Penrhyn Stanley*, 2 vols. (New York: Scribner's, 1894), 1.356.

65. Arthur Penrhyn Stanley, *Sermons and Essays on the Apostolical Age* (Oxford: J. H. Parker, 1847).

66. Cited in Prothero, *Stanley* 2.34.

67. Ibid. 1.114.

68. Arthur Penrhyn Stanley, *Lectures on the History of the Jewish Church*, 3 vols. (New York: Charles Scribner's Sons, 1902).

69. See n. 65, above.

with the history of the period—a history of great importance for the understanding of the NT. Stanley also puts in a good word for scholars on the east side of the Rhine.

> Until we have equalled the writers of Germany in their indefatigable indus-
> try, their profound thought, their conscientious love of knowledge, we must
> still look to them for help; and, even if we were as much superior to them in
> all other points as we are certainly inferior to them in those just mentioned,
> I know not how we should be justified in rejecting with contempt the
> immense apparatus of learning and criticism which they have brought to
> bear on the Sacred Writings,—why we should refuse the aid of the workmen
> of Tyre in building up the Temple of God at Jerusalem.[70]

In Stanley's opinion, a combination of German research and English prac-
ticality would be ideal.

In his sermon "The Three Apostles," Stanley declares that the revelation of God is given in Christ and that this revelation is communicated
through the persons closest to him—Peter, Paul, and John. Stanley believes
it important to recognize that these apostles were historical figures and
that they expressed their faith in a variety of ways. The reader of their
works must carefully distinguish what is central and lasting from what is
local and temporary. The special character of the apostles is determined
by their experience of Jesus and, in particular, their witness to the resurrection. In an essay on "The Traditionary Knowledge of the Apostolic
Age," Stanley notes the inadequacy of the tradition for reconstructing
early Christian history. He mentions, for example, Irenaeus's notion that
the ministry of Jesus lasted twenty years, and he concludes that the NT
must be recognized as the primary source.

Stanley's sermon "The Apostolic Office" is important in the context of
his opposition to the Oxford Movement. Stanley argues that the term
"apostle," used as a title, refers only to the Twelve and Paul. The title was
conferred by Christ and represented moral and spiritual authority—not
an ecclesiastical office. Special powers, like the gifts of healing, were
not granted exclusively to the apostles. Moreover, the power by which the
apostles performed miracles was not passed on to church leaders who
succeeded them, because "all these gifts ceased with the cessation of the
immediate circumstances which had called them forth, thereby adding
one to the many marks which divide, as by an impassable bar, the apostolical age from all that succeed."[71] In short, Stanley finds the doctrine of
apostolic succession—so dear to the Tractarians—without scriptural
support.

---

70. Stanley, *Apostolical Age*, vi–vii.
71. Ibid., 60.

Important for his reconstruction of early Christianity is Stanley's essay on "The Judaizers of the Apostolic Age." According to Stanley, the church's struggle with Judaizers developed in three stages. First, in the period of Acts 15 and the six earliest epistles of Paul, the main issue is circumcision, and the Judaizers follow and disrupt the Pauline mission. Second, in the time of the later Pauline letters and the epistles of Peter and Jude, the opposition takes two different forms: asceticism or licentiousness. Finally, in the era of the Johannine literature, the opposition begins to move in the direction of Gnosticism. "So far as the principles opposed by St. John had assumed any outward and definite shape at all, it is still the same ancient enemy that we have traced throughout, it is still not Gnosticism but Judaism, or, if we will have the word, it is not yet the Gnostic pure, but the Gnostic grafted on a Jewish soil."[72]

Stanley's major contribution to NT research is his commentary on 1 and 2 Corinthians, which first appeared in 1855.[73] In the preface, Stanley asserts that his purpose is historical: to reconstruct the contents of the Pauline letters in their original setting. He notes that Paul's style is not literary, but oral, displaying Hebraisms and characterized by vitality. In the introduction, Stanley presents the setting and occasion for the letter. Late in his Ephesian ministry, Paul heard of conflicts in the Corinthian church that were provoked by a possible visit of Peter and the presence of Apollos. Stanley, with his typical eloquence, describes Paul's dictation of 1 Corinthians.

> There is Paul himself, now about sixty years of age, and bearing in the pallor and feebleness of his frame, traces of his constant and recent hardships; his eyes at times streaming with tears of grief and indignation; the scribe, catching the words from his lips and recording them on the scroll of parchment or papyrus which lay before him.[74]

In answering the letter which he has received from the Corinthians, Paul is "sometimes quoting their very words."[75]

As to the format of the commentary, the material is divided into main sections that are introduced by a description of the setting or circumstances and concluded by a summary of the results, sometimes in the form of a "dissertation" (i.e., an excursus). These larger sections are divided into subsections in which Stanley presents Lachmann's Greek text with a translation (a corrected Authorized Version) beneath the text, and dou-

---

72. Ibid., 234.
73. Arthur Penrhyn Stanley, *The Epistles of St. Paul to the Corinthians, with Critical Notes and Dissertations*, 2d ed. (London: J. Murray, 1858). The 2d edition corrected errors of the first.
74. Ibid., 18.
75. Ibid., 16.

ble-columned notes beneath the translation; after the notes, he offers a paraphrase of the text and, finally, his running commentary on the passage. Stanley's notes attend to textual variants and matters of vocabulary and grammar; they include frequent references to classical and patristic sources. A few examples of Stanley's exegesis can illustrate the character of his work.

In regard to the Corinthian factions, Stanley suggests that the issue of factionalism is more important than the identification of the factions: "The Apostle here denounces party spirit as a sin in itself, irrespectively of the right or wrong opinions connected with it."[76] In any event, the discussion of factionalism has diverted Paul into a consideration of the gospel. Stanley's note on 1 Cor. 2:4 observes that λόγος refers to the form of preaching, while κήρυγμα describes its substance. In discussing 1 Corinthians 5, Stanley concludes that the case of incest "forms the crisis of the whole Epistle."[77] Delivering the offender to Satan for the destruction of his flesh refers to illness or death resulting from excommunication: a result similar to the fate of Ananias and Saphira (Acts 5:1-11), although the purpose here is remedial, since the man will ultimately be saved. On 1 Corinthians 7, Stanley observes that the conflicts about marriage result from the different backgrounds of the Corinthian Christians. The Jews believed marriage was an obligation, while some of the Gentiles, citing the practice of Paul, advocated celibacy. In an excursus on "The Apostle's View of Celibacy," Stanley argues that Paul's advice against marriage results from his concern to reduce the troubles of Christians in the impending eschaton and from his mistaken notion of the nearness of the end. In 1 Tim. 5:14, which Paul wrote at a later time, he appears to advocate the opposite: that young widows should marry and bear children. But at that time, Paul was concerned with a different issue: the danger of asceticism. As Stanley's exegesis indicates, texts must be interpreted in context, and their application may be different in different settings.

In discussing worship and assemblies (1 Cor. 11:2—14:40), Stanley displays sensitivity to cultural and social issues. He believes Paul's advice about veils is conditioned by the apostle's concern to conform to contemporary customs. In the course of his argument, Paul does affirm the subordination of women and, in doing so, misuses the Hebrew Scriptures. "Taken strictly, the woman is as much the image of God as the man; and the words in Gen. i.26, are in the original addressed to male and female equally."[78] In Gal. 3:28, Paul does support equality, although he believes in

76. Ibid., 38.
77. Ibid., 82.
78. Ibid., 192.

gradual improvement, not revolution. The factions at the table of the Lord are interpreted as socioeconomic and are viewed in relation to Hellenistic practice. Thus, Stanley says that "the richer members following probably the example of the common Grecian clubs, seized upon the portion of food which they had brought, before the poorer members could get hold of it (see xi.21) alleging in their defence that they were hungry (xi.34), and could not wait."[79] Speaking in tongues is also interpreted against the background of Hellenistic religion:

> It was a trance or ecstasy, which in moments of great religious fervour, especially the moment of conversion, seized the early believers; and this fervour vented itself in expressions of thanksgiving, in fragments of psalmody or hymnody and prayer, which to the speaker himself conveyed an irresistible sense of communion with God, and to the bystander an impression of some extraordinary manifestation of power, but not necessarily any instruction or teaching, and sometimes even having the appearance of wild excitement, like that of madness or intoxication.[80]

In commenting on 1 Corinthians 15, Stanley argues that the deniers of the resurrection are not like those opposed in 2 Tim. 2:17-18 who suppose the resurrection has occurred already. Instead, they may be Sadducees, Epicurians, or Greek skeptics. Stanley's note on 15:8 observes that ἔκτρωμα (miscarriage) describes the abruptness and inferiority of an experience, and he notes that the Latin equivalent was applied to senators who were appointed irregularly. In an excursus, "First Creed, and First Evidence of Christianity," He argues that 1 Cor. 15:3-4 represents a creedal formula. The term σῶμα in 15:44 means "organization" or "framework," and the "spiritual body" describes "the organization animated by the Divine life breathed into it from the Spirit of God."[81] In an excursus on "The Apostle's View of a Future Life," Stanley contrasts Paul's understanding of resurrection with the Greek idea of immortality:

> All the Apostle directly asserts is that, whatever body there may be after death, will be wholly different from the present, and that the infinite variety of nature renders such an expectation not only possible, but probable. . . . the Christian idea of a future state is not fully expressed by a mere abstract belief in the immortality of the soul, but requires a redemption and restoration of the whole man.[82]

Turning to 2 Corinthians, Stanley notes that earlier problems have become acute, because the local Judaizers are now supported by the arrival

79. Ibid., 204.
80. Ibid., 257.
81. Ibid., 330.
82. Ibid., 340–41.

of new teachers who come with recommendations from Jerusalem, questioning Paul's authority. Paul's answer—the least systematic of all his letters—is full of personal outbursts, and in the latter part (chaps. 10–13) he abandons dictating and takes up the pen to write with his own hand. In discussing 2 Cor. 2:1-10, Stanley concludes that the sorrowful visit refers to Paul's original mission in Corinth and the tearful letter is to be identified with 1 Corinthians. Stanley notes that 2 Corinthians 8 and 9 display a certain independence, and that there is a sharp break at chapters 10–13, where Paul makes extensive use of the first-person singular. Nevertheless, Stanley concludes that 2 Corinthians is a unity.

In interpreting 2 Corinthians, Stanley makes some notable suggestions. He believes the shift from the metaphor of a tent to one of clothing (5:1-10) is suggested by Paul's own craft, wherein Cicilian haircloth was used for fabricating both tents and wearing apparel. An excursus on "The Reconciliation of the World by Christ's Death" adopts an unorthodox view of the atonement. In Stanley's opinion, atonement can be appropriately described as reconciliation. The reference to the death of Christ in this context underscores reconciliation as accomplished by God's love. Propitiation is not offered to God; it is given by God. A final excursus explores the question of the paucity of references to the gospel narrative in the Pauline letters. Stanley answers that Paul's oral preaching would have contained more references to the life and teachings of Jesus than his letters. Moreover, Paul is concerned with the spiritual—the significance of the experience of Christ—more than the Christ after the flesh. Nevertheless, the epistles include references to the major aspects of Jesus' life: nativity, miracles, last supper, crucifixion, resurrection, and ascension. "These are the main facts which are recorded from the Gospel History. . . . From them a story might be constructed, which would not be at variance,—which in all essential points would be in unison,—with the Gospel narrative."[83]

Benjamin Jowett (1817–1893)

Stanley's collaborator on the project of the Pauline commentaries was Benjamin Jowett, the renowned translator of Plato. Jowett was educated at St. Paul's School and Balliol College, Oxford. He entered Oxford in 1836 and spent most of his life there. Elected a fellow of Balliol in 1838, Jowett was appointed tutor in 1842 and was ordained three years later. In 1854, he was bitterly disappointed when he was not elected Master of Balliol, although, in the same year, he was appointed Regius Professor of Greek. When *Essays and Reviews* (1860) appeared, Jowett was verbally abused but

83. Ibid., 594.

was supported at Oxford by the noted classical philologist, H. G. Liddell. Jowett was finally elected Master of Balliol in 1870 and later served as vice-chancellor of Oxford. When he died in 1893, his funeral sermon was preached by Frederick Temple, Archbishop of Canterbury. In point of view, Jowett was eclectic; he offered no theological system.[84] His library and the record of his reading indicate an interest in German theological works. In particular, he was moved by Kant's concern for morality, Hegel's philosophy of history, and Schleiermacher's idea of God-consciousness. Three main themes characterize Jowett's own theology: God as the transcendent being who possesses personality; Christ as the ultimate disclosure of divine truth; and religion which takes account of history and science.[85] In regard to the third theme, Jowett preached a sermon on "Darwinism and Faith in God" in which he tended to accept the biological aspects of Darwin's theory but found the concept of the survival of the fittest to be problematic: it presumed a competitiveness antithetical to Christian morality.

Jowett's contribution to the commentary series consists of a two-volume treatment of the Thessalonian correspondence, Galatians, and Romans.[86] Like Stanley, Jowett is concerned with the practical and moral understanding of Scripture, although he displays more exegetical skill and theological imagination. Indeed, Jowett's "dissertations" (excursuses) were treasured by the Anglican liberals, and a collection of them was published in a separate volume.[87] Jowett, like Stanley, uses Lachmann's text, which he thinks is "the most perfect that has hitherto appeared."[88] As to format, the first volume includes 1 and 2 Thessalonians and Galatians, and the second, Romans. Jowett presents the Greek text at the top of the page, with an English translation (Authorized Version) on the facing page; the notes are in double columns below. Each book is prefaced with a historical-critical introduction, and each chapter is introduced by a summary of the argument which follows.

In his introduction to 1 Thessalonians, Jowett presents an overview of the Pauline letters. "There is no system," he says, "which is presupposed in them; nor can any be constructed out of them without marring their

---

84. For a summary of Jowett's thought, see Peter Hinchliff, *Benjamin Jowett and the Christian Religion* (Oxford: Clarendon, 1987), 121–51.

85. See Peter Hinchliff, "Ethics, Evolution and Biblical Criticism in the Thought of Benjamin Jowett and John William Colenso," *Journal of Ecclesiastical History* 37 (1986): 91–110.

86. Benjamin Jowett, *The Epistles of St. Paul to the Thessalonians, Galatians, Romans, with Critical Notes and Dissertations*, 2d ed., 2 vols. (London: J. Murray, 1859).

87. Benjamin Jowett, *Theological Essays of the Late Benjamin Jowett*, ed. Lewis Campbell (London: H. Frowde, 1906).

88. Jowett, *Epistles of St. Paul* 1.vii. Tischendorf's eighth edition had not appeared, although his second Leipzig edition (1849) had been published.

simplicity. They have almost wholly a practical aim, and are fragmentary and occasional."[89] The continuity of the letters is found not in doctrine but "in the person of Christ himself, who is the centre in every Epistle."[90] During the course of writing the letters, Paul's thought has developed and changed to fit changing situations. In 1 Thessalonians he is concerned with the imminent coming of the Lord, an event described in traditional Jewish terms; later, Paul tends to spiritualize the idea of the kingdom of God. Jowett, arguing against Baur, affirms the authenticity of both 1 and 2 Thessalonians. In his notes, Jowett gives attention to textual and grammatical details. The phrase λόγον θεοῦ (1 Thess. 2:13), for instance, employs a subjective, not an objective, genitive; it refers to "the Divine word: not the word which tells of God, but the word of which God is the author."[91]

The notes and excursuses on the Thessalonian correspondence give attention to Paul's eschatological ideas. In regard to 1 Thess. 4:13, Jowett observes that although "falling asleep" is a euphemism for death in classical sources, it implies the idea of awakening in Christian texts. In his note on 1 Thess. 5:3, he mentions the varying, sometimes contradictory, expressions of eschatology in the NT and concludes that the important thing is not the form of expression but the practical lesson to be learned: the ethical implications of eschatology. Jowett's excursus "On the Belief in the Coming of Christ in the Apostolic Age" argues that Paul expected the eschaton to come soon. Eighteen hundred years of history have proved him to have been mistaken, and, from this, Jowett concludes that theologians should learn not to advance hypotheses which cannot be reconciled with the facts, for example, the idea that Paul was infallible. "He never claims this infallibility; it is we ourselves who love to ascribe it to him."[92] In an excursus "On the Man of Sin" (2 Thess. 2:1-12), Jowett argues that this cryptic figure represents a symbolic personification of evil. Thus, efforts to identify the anti-Christ as Cromwell or Napoleon are hopelessly misplaced, because Paul expected the fulfillment of his prediction within twenty or thirty years at most.

Second Thess. 3:17 prompts Jowett to write one of his most imaginative "dissertations": "On the Probability that Many of St. Paul's Epistles Have Been Lost." Jowett believes that during his twenty-five year ministry Paul must have written many more letters than those which are extant. Suppose, Jowett speculates, that a total of some thirty Pauline letters were written and that justification by faith was mentioned in only two. Reflection on this possibility indicates that theologians have been inclined to

89. Ibid. 1.3.
90. Ibid. 1.4.
91. Ibid. 1.59.
92. Ibid. 1.120.

construct theological systems on a minimum of evidence, microscopically scrutinized. "The writings of the Apostle," says Jowett, "like the words of our Saviour, are but a fragment of his life. And they must be restored to their context before they can be truly understood."[93]

In regard to Galatians, Jowett believes the members of the Galatian churches are Gentiles who had become Jewish proselytes prior to their acceptance of the message of Paul. The epistle was written to churches of north Galatia after Paul's second visit to the area and prior to his final visit to Jerusalem—thus, from the same period as 1 Corinthians. Jowett is undecided as to whether the revelation mentioned in Gal. 1:12 is to be identified with Paul's conversion, his trance in the temple (Acts 22:17), or his translation into the third heaven (2 Cor. 12:4). In any case, "The revelation of which he is here speaking is of another kind, moral and spiritual, rather than historical,—a revelation of Christ in him, as the expression in this passage implies,—not external information brought to him."[94] In connection with Galatians, Jowett presents some important excursuses: "On the Chronology of St. Paul's Life and Writings," in which Jowett reviews the data from Acts and the epistles separately, and then harmonizes; "On the Character of St. Paul," in which Jowett sees Paul as a religious leader of a prophetic type; "On the Quotations from the Old Testament in the Writings of Paul," in which Jowett carefully analyzes Paul's use of the OT and notes that there is a lack of evidence that he used the Hebrew text; "St. Paul and the Twelve," in which Jowett acknowledges that there were tensions but not fundamental disagreement between Paul and the Jerusalem leaders; and "St. Paul and Philo," in which Jowett notes parallels, but also distinct differences. In this final excursus, Jowett concludes that "Alexandrianism was not the seed of the great tree which was to cover the earth, but the soil in which it grew up. It was not the body of which Christianity was the soul, but the vesture in which it folded itself— the old bottle into which the new wine was poured."[95]

Jowett's lengthy (632 page) commentary on Romans reflects his moderate approach. Not a doctrinal treatise, the epistle is addressed to the church of Rome, which is made up largely of Gentiles, but Gentiles who have been converted to Christianity by Jewish believers. Thus, the subject of the letter is the unity between Jew and Gentile within the Christian church. "It is union with Christ which breaks through all other ties of race and language, and knits men together into a new body which is His Church."[96] In regard to the crucial phrase δικαιοσύνη θεοῦ, Jowett refuses

93. Ibid. 1.201.
94. Ibid. 1.266.
95. Ibid. 1.513.
96. Ibid. 2.30–31.

to be forced into a precise definition. "And so the expression 'righteous-ness of God,' instead of being confined to one abstract point of view or meaning, seems to swell out into several: the attribute of God, embodied in Christ, manifested in the world, revealed in the Gospel, communicated to the individual soul; the righteousness not of law, but of faith."[97] In an excursus "On the Imputation of the Sin of Adam," Jowett argues that the idea that sin is inherited from Adam is not consistent with other Pauline texts. The Augustinian interpretation fails to see that Paul frequently uses figurative language in interpreting the OT. "The difficulty of supposing him to be allegorising the narrative of Genesis is slight, in comparison with the difficulty of supposing him to countenance a doctrine at variance with our first notions of the moral nature of God."[98] Jowett argues that Romans 9–11 is an integral part of the epistle, a section in which Paul "first prays for the restoration of Israel, and then reasons for their rejec-tion, and then finally shows that in a more extended view of the purposes of God their salvation is included."[99]

Jowett appends two important excursuses to the end of his Romans commentary. "On Atonement and Satisfaction" refutes the traditional doc-trine of sacrificial, substitutionary atonement. In Jowett's opinion, the orthodox view rests on traditional sand rather than scriptural rock. The prophets opposed sacrificial practice with moral ideas, and Jesus did not affirm the doctrine of sacrificial atonement. Paul uses sacrificial lan-guage symbolically, and the only sacrifice with which Christians are con-cerned is moral and spiritual. According to Jowett, "The death of Christ is the fulfilment and consummation of His life, the greatest moral act ever done in this world, the highest manifestation of perfect love, the centre in which the rays of love converge and meet, the extremest abnegation or annihilation of self."[100] When this "dissertation" appeared in the first edi-tion of the commentary, Jowett was summoned to the office of Oxford's vice-chancellor to reaffirm his commitment to the Thirty-nine Articles. The second excursus, "On Predestination and Free Will," contends that Paul understands the two concepts paradoxically. Both are true: a person is saved by the grace of God, and receiving grace requires a human response—a paradox explicitly stated in Phil. 2:12. In explicating the para-dox, Jowett draws a distinction between foreknowledge and predestina-tion, and he asserts that the former can be affirmed without denial of human freedom. This means that human freedom is not necessarily in

97. Ibid. 2.54.
98. Ibid. 2.186.
99. Ibid. 2.270.
100. Ibid. 2.591–92.

conflict with the will of God. The unity beneath the paradox is found in the idea that God's grace works through human freedom. "For the freedom of man in the higher sense is the grace of God; and in the lower sense (of mere choice) is not inconsistent with it."[101] Above all, the idea of predestination must not be viewed as some abstract principle imposed upon history, but from the perspective of the experience of a free response to the powerful grace of God.

In terms of biblical research, Jowett is best known for "On the Interpretation of Scripture,"[102] his contribution to *Essays and Reviews*. *Essays and Reviews* (1860) was a collection of essays written by seven liberal scholars, six of whom were Anglican clergymen. Reflecting the spirit of the Enlightenment, these writers exposed the orthodox ideas of inspiration and supernaturalism to the bright light of rational inquiry. Actually, the essayists merely fanned into flame the spark which had been ignited by Coleridge, but in the minds of the establishment, they threatened to consume the traditional foundation of Christianity. Jowett's essay is the longest and, for biblical criticism, the most important in the volume. In essence, he echoes the familiar critical axiom: the Bible is to be interpreted like any other book. Thus, "although the interpretation of Scripture requires 'a vision and faculty divine,' or at least a moral and religious interest which is not needed in the study of a Greek poet or philosopher, yet in what may be termed the externals of interpretation, that is to say, the meaning of words, the connexion of sentences, the settlement of the text, the evidence of facts, the same rules apply to the Old and New Testaments as to other books."[103] The goal of interpretation is to discern the original meaning of the author in the historical setting of the text.

> The office of the interpreter is not to add another, but to recover the original one; the meaning, that is, of the words as they first struck on the ears or flashed before the eyes of those who heard and read them. He has to transfer himself to another age; to imagine that he is a disciple of Christ or Paul; to disengage himself from all that follows.[104]

Jowett proceeds to present approaches that impede valid interpretation. First, he mentions the false understanding of inspiration—a dogmatic view that is not supported by the biblical writers themselves. Jowett advocates a progressive idea of revelation and argues that no view of inspira-

---

101. Ibid. 2.619.
102. Benjamin Jowett, "On the Interpretation of Scripture," in *Essays and Reviews* (London: J. W. Parker, 1860), 330–433.
103. Ibid., 337.
104. Ibid., 338.

tion is valid which contradicts the facts of history or science. Next, Jowett scores the effort to force texts into conformity with established doctrines or creeds. This approach results in an overemphasis on some texts and neglect of others.

> The truth is, that in seeking to prove our own opinions out of Scripture, we are constantly falling into the common fallacy of opening our eyes to one class of facts and closing them to another. The favorite verses shine like stars, while the rest of the page is thrown into the shade.[105]

Finally, biblical interpretation is impeded by the failure to recognize that the Bible was written in the language of the ancient East and cannot be fit easily into the idiom of Western thought. When frantic efforts are made to find a modern meaning, the temptation to allegorical or fanciful exegesis looms large.

> Where there is no critical interpretation of Scripture, there will be a mystical or rhetorical one. If words have more than one meaning, they may have any meaning. Instead of being a rule of faith, Scripture becomes the expression of the ever-changing aspect of religious opinions. The unchangeable word of God . . . is changed by each age and each generation in accordance with its passing fancy. The book in which we believe all religious truth to be contained, is the most uncertain of all books, because interpreted by arbitrary and uncertain methods.[106]

Jowett turns to the objection that criticism will disturb the faith of pious people. He answers that theologians have an obligation to seek the truth and that the attempt to avoid critical issues will prove counterproductive: "Doubt comes in at the window, when Inquiry is denied at the door."[107] Indeed, responsible criticism will enhance rather than destroy the value of Scripture.

> When interpreted like any other book . . . the Bible will still remain unlike any other book; its beauty will be freshly seen, as of a picture which is restored after many ages to its original state; it will create a new interest and make for itself a new kind of authority by the life which is in it. It will be a spirit and not a letter; as it was in the beginning, having an influence like that of the spoken word, or the book newly found.[108]

As for Coleridge, so also for Jowett, to read the Bible like any other book does not mean to reduce Scripture to a bare historical record, but to listen to the text as classic literature, to hear the deeper, authoritative mean-

---

105. Ibid., 366.
106. Ibid., 371–72.
107. Ibid., 373.
108. Ibid., 375.

ing.[109] Finally, Jowett draws a distinction between interpretation and application of Scripture. Texts which spoke to a particular historical time are
not necessarily applicable to Christians in other ages. Thus, theologians
concerned with Scripture's application must discern the general, universal
truths: "That portion of Scripture which more than any other is immediately and universally applicable to our own times is, doubtless, that which
is contained in the words of Christ Himself."[110]

For readers who have been feasting on the sumptuous fare of the German critics, British scholarship seems about as exciting as brussels sprouts
and boiled potatoes. How the *Essays and Reviews* could have created such
a stir that two of its contributors were tried for heresy appears to be a
mystery. After all, the conviction that the Bible ought to be read like any
other book had been voiced a century earlier by Turretin, Wettstein, and
Ernesti.[111] Moreover, British scholarship lacked the sort of critical precision that had become standard at Göttingen, Tübingen, and Berlin. Questions of historical criticism, like the authorship of the Pastoral Epistles,
had not been reviewed with rigorous scrutiny, and an important issue like
the synoptic problem had scarcely been considered since the days of Herbert Marsh.[112] Similarly, the theological implications of criticism had not
been probed to sufficient depth. The problem of the Jesus of history and
the Christ of faith, made crucial by Strauss's critique of Schleiermacher,[113]
had not been articulated with adequate clarity, and the harmonized Jesus
who emerged looked more and more like an Oxbridge advocate of Victorian morality.

SUMMARY

The Roman Catholic and British scholars surveyed in this chapter share a
common commitment: an allegiance to an ecclesiastical establishment that
honors theological tradition. Consequently, their conclusions on matters
of higher criticism tend to be conservative. Hug, along with the English
theologians, demonstrates that in the face of Enlightenment advances,
conservatives can continue to make a case. In spite of Tübingen, traditional views of canon and authenticity are still being maintained. What is
at stake, however, may be even larger questions: Has the integrity of Scrip-

---

109. See James Barr, "Jowett and the Reading of the Bible 'Like Any Other Book,'"
Horizons in Biblical Theology 4, no. 2 (1982): 1–44; James Barr, "Jowett and the 'Original
Meaning' of Scripture," *Religious Studies* 18 (1982): 433–37.
110. Jowett, "On the Interpretation of Scripture," 413.
111. See pp. 94, 106, 109, above.
112. See pp. 298–301, above.
113. See pp. 249–50, above.

ture and tradition been purchased at the price of a higher view of revelation? Is there some understanding of historical revelation that can claim authority without absolutizing its objective expressions, some perception of truth that maintains historicity without the sacrifice of transcendence? In any event, Roman Catholic scholarship has entered the arena of biblical criticism, and scholars like Hug have prepared the way for the more radical work of Alfred Loisy and the Catholic modernists.[114]

British scholarship of the first two-thirds of the nineteenth century had achieved a significant goal: historical criticism had been established as the appropriate method for NT research. The line of scholars running from Coleridge to Jowett had appeared like a succession of John the Baptists, preparing the way for the Cambridge giants of the next generation: B. F. Westcott, J. B. Lightfoot, and F.J.A. Hort. Most important, the British scholars had a wide influence in the larger spheres of church and society. Whereas a scholar like Strauss was a theological maverick who had abandoned organized religion, British scholars remained within the establishment and made their mark on preachers and politicians. Consequently, the Victorian era—noted for its religiosity—reflected the insights of the new theological approach.

As to substance, British biblical scholarship offered an alternative to dogmatic orthodoxy, on the one hand, and radical criticism, on the other. It made possible a modern faith which could accept the findings of history and science without rejecting the foundations of the Christian faith. From the British perspective, both alternatives appear to be unduly literalistic: the orthodox affirmed the facticity of the biblical record, while the radical critics denied it—both preoccupied with factual history. Coleridge and his followers, by way of contrast, took up the torch that had been lit by Lessing and Herder, a light that illuminated Scripture as vital literary expression. For them, the concern was not with the letter but with the spirit of the Bible. The more one read it like any other book, the more the Bible's special character was disclosed. The Bible was viewed as a book radiant with vitality, aglow with the story of religious experience. In effect, this approach was not a denial of the historical, but an affirmation of it—a sensitive effort to reflect and recreate the original faith to which the Bible bore witness.

114. See Bernard M. G. Reardon, "Roman Catholic Modernism," in *Nineteenth Century Religious Thought*, ed. N. Smart, et al., 2.141–77.

11

Synthesizing Accomplishments

While many were concerned with the technical details of historical criticism, some scholars continued to engage in the practical task of interpreting the Scriptures for the study and enlightenment of clergy and people. This endeavor sometimes took the form of producing commentaries, aids to the reading of the NT that shared a legacy going back to patristic times and were ennobled by such Enlightenment exegetes as Grotius[1] and Locke.[2] In nineteenth-century England, Thomas Arnold's dream of producing scholarly, practical commentaries had been partially realized in the work of Stanley and Jowett.[3] Writing a commentary was a challenging task, requiring a synthesis of all the critical disciplines. Perhaps even more demanding was the effort of some, still under the cloud of D. F. Strauss,[4] to compose a life of Jesus that could be at the same time critical and constructive. This effort, too, required the synthesis of textual, historical, and literary skills, all enlisted in a concern to resurrect the memory of that solitary individual whose career was the ground and center of the Christian faith.

COMMENTARY SERIES:
OLSHAUSEN, MEYER, LANGE, AND GODET

Some scholars are remembered primarily for their biblical commentaries, and, in a few instances, this endeavor took the form of a whole commentary series in which a single author was the major contributor.

1. See pp. 9–11, above.
2. See pp. 35–39, above.
3. See pp. 344–45, 347, 350–53, 354–58, above.
4. See pp. 250–55, above.

W.M.L. de Wette, whose work is discussed in chapter 7,[5] produced the *Kurzgefasstes exegetisches Handbuch zum Neuen Testament,* a series comprising the entire NT, begun in 1835, completed in 1848, and repeatedly revised and expanded. The work of a few other NT commentators is worthy of note.

Hermann Olshausen (1796–1839)

Hermann Olshausen was born near Hamburg and educated at Kiel and Berlin, where he studied with de Wette. Olshausen began his teaching as an instructor at Berlin (1820) and moved to Königsburg (1821), where he was promoted to full professor in 1827. From 1834 to 1839, he served on the faculty at the University of Erlangen. Olshausen's early publications include an apologetic work, *The Genuineness of the Four Canonical Gospels* (1823), and two books on hermeneutics: *Ein Wort über tieferen Schriftsinn* (1824) and *Die biblische Schriftauslegung* (1825). Olshausen's series, *Biblical Commentary on the New Testament,* was originally published in four volumes over a ten-year period (1830–40). The English translation appeared in a British edition in ten volumes (1847–60), and an American in six (1856–58).[6] The commentary on the NT books from Matthew through 1 and 2 Thessalonians was written by Olshausen himself. Sections of this work have been published separately in individual volumes, and the continuing popularity of Olshausen's work is evidenced by recent reprints of his commentaries on Romans and the Corinthian correspondence.[7] The first three volumes of the American edition deal with introductory matters and the Gospels. The latter part of volume 3 and volumes 4 and 5 include the commentary on Acts and the Pauline letters (through 2 Thessalonians). Olshausen's main concern is to provide doctrinal meaning for the common reader, rather than philological research for scholars. Nevertheless, he deals with linguistic details and attends to matters of text and grammar.

Olshausen's basic approach can be detected in an essay that prefaces the American edition: "Proof of the Genuineness of the Writings of the New Testament for Intelligent Readers of All Classes."[8] In the preface to this essay, Olshausen makes a case for the application of historical criticism to the study of the NT books: "Investigation must rather serve to

---

5. See pp. 221–29, above.
6. Hermann Olshausen, *Biblical Commentary on the New Testament,* 6 vols., trans. A. C. Kendrick (New York: Sheldon, Blakeman, 1858).
7. Hermann Olshausen, *Studies in the Epistle to the Romans* (Minneapolis: Klock & Klock, 1983); *A Commentary on Paul's First and Second Epistles to the Corinthians* (Minneapolis: Klock & Klock, 1984).
8. Olshausen, *Biblical Commentary* 1.xxi-cxxxiii. Originally published in 1832, the essay was translated by David Fosdick.

confirm and fully establish belief in their purity and genuineness."[9] In spite of considerable evidence to the contrary, Olshausen believes that "it is nevertheless now agreed among scholars generally, that all the writings of the New Testament are genuine productions of the apostles."[10] He proceeds through the canon to confirm this conclusion. In regard to the synoptic problem, Olshausen supports the Griesbach hypothesis: Mark used Matthew and Luke. He believes Matthew was written in Hebrew by Matthew (also called Levi), one of the Twelve, prior to the destruction of Jerusalem. Mark was written by John Mark, who wrote under the direction of Peter. Luke and Acts were written by Luke, the travel companion of Paul, at the end of Paul's first Roman imprisonment.

In regard to the epistles, Olshausen believes the Pauline letters were collected early, probably by Paul himself. Colossians, Ephesians, and Philippians were written from the first Roman imprisonment, and 1 Timothy and Titus after Paul's release, prior to the second imprisonment during which he wrote 2 Timothy. Ephesians, in Olshausen's view, was originally a circular letter. Hebrews was authored not by Paul but by one of his friends or associates, most likely Apollos. In regard to the Catholic Epistles, Olshausen thinks them all to be genuine. His theory about the Petrine letters is imaginative: Peter dictated 1 Peter in Hebrew, and Silvanus translated it into Greek, giving it a Pauline cast; 2 Peter was the work of a different translator, who made use of Jude in the process. According to Olshausen, pseudonymous writings represent bad morality: "If, therefore, the Apostle Peter was not the author of this letter [2 Peter], the man who not only presumed to take upon himself the name of an apostle, but designedly endeavoured to make his readers think that he was the Apostle Peter, must have been a downright shameless imposter."[11]

Finally, Olshausen concludes that Revelation was written by John the apostle, whose Greek had improved markedly by the time he wrote the Fourth Gospel some twenty years later. For Olshausen, the question of authenticity is of utmost importance for establishing the ground of faith. Why then, he asks, did God allow critical problems—like the presence of textual variants—to intrude into sacred Scripture? Answer: the presence of problems is according to God's design, because a Bible without problems would have increased the culpability of those who disbelieve it. Thus, "the guilt of many persons would have been augmented, since they now have at least plausible reasons for their opposition to the truth, but in the other case would have had no such extenuation, and still would have

9. Ibid. 1.xxx.
10. Ibid. 1.xxxiii.
11. Ibid. 1.xcvii.

retained their hostility to God's word."[12] Although the authenticity of Scripture can be confirmed by historical-critical research, the ultimate ground is provided by the witness of the Holy Spirit. "On this conviction the assurance of the genuineness and divinity of Scripture forever rests, and much more securely, than upon any external historical proofs; for it wholly takes away the possibility of an attack in any quarter on the part of human sophistry, and leaves assurance safe in the unassailable sanctuary of our interior life."[13]

In view of this understanding of Scripture, examples of Olshausen's exegesis are predictable. On Matt. 1:18-25, he argues that mythological interpretation is inadmissible. Jesus was a historical person, and to construe his supernatural origin as a myth would imply an impure birth, because Mary was unmarried at the time of his conception. According to Olshausen, the mythical birth stories of other religions serve to heighten the human aspiration for a supernatural birth that is truly historical. Moreover, Jesus' miraculous birth is essential to his power to redeem, "since it is impossible that any one who is himself descended from the fallen human race of man could have any power to heal the hurt which they suffer."[14] In regard to the raising of Lazarus, Olshausen says, "The precision that characterizes this narrative furnishes the highest conceivable degree of historical certainty."[15] Jesus' weeping and mourning (Olshausen's translation of ἐμβριμώμενος, John 11:38) is not in response to the particular case of Lazarus, but in reaction to death in general—the wages of sin—which the unfortunate Lazarus has to face twice. In effect, Olshausen's exegesis implies a double miracle: raising from the dead, and preservation from bodily decomposition, for "the body of Lazarus, just because it was to be reanimated, was in the providence of God preserved from corruption."[16]

Heinrich August Wilhelm Meyer (1800–1873)

The most notable NT commentator of the nineteenth century was Heinrich August Wilhelm Meyer, the founder of a distinguished commentary series that has continued until today. The son of a shoemaker, Meyer attended the gymnasium in his native Gotha, where his religion teacher was K. G. Bretschneider.[17] His university studies were pursued at Jena (1818–20), where his professors included J. P. Gabler.[18] Meyer spent his

12. Ibid. 1.cxxvii.
13. Ibid. 1.cxxxiii.
14. Ibid. 1.173.
15. Ibid. 2.502.
16. Ibid. 2.513.
17. See pp. 312–14, above.
18. See pp. 184–87, above.

career as an active church leader—first as pastor and later as an official of the church in Hanover. He never held an academic post, declining an invitation to the faculty at Giessen. According to his customary practice, Meyer arose at 4:00 a.m. in order to engage in his indefatigable labor on the massive commentary series. Meyer's original plan was to publish a comprehensive study of the NT that would have three main parts— (1) a presentation of the text and translation; (2) a commentary on the Gospels and Acts; and (3) a commentary on the rest of the books, together with a handbook on historical-critical matters, and a history of exegesis. The first part of this project appeared in 1829, and the second part became Meyer's monumental *Kritisch exegetischer Kommentar über das Neue Testament*. In the preface to the English edition, Meyer, writing a few months before his death, described the purpose of his commentaries:

> They aim at exactly ascertaining and establishing on due grounds the *purely historical sense of Scripture*. . . . For exegesis is a historical science, because the sense of Scripture, the investigation of which is its task, can only be regarded and treated as a historical fact; as positively given, it can only be known, proved, established and set forth so as to be clearly and surely understood, by the positive method of studying the grammar, the *usus loquendi*, and the connection in detail as well as in its wider and widest sense.[19]

The first volume appeared in 1832; it presented comments on Matthew, Mark, and Luke, and totaled 419 pages. By 1847, the series had swelled to eleven volumes and included all the NT books from Matthew to Philemon, although Meyer did not himself write the comments on the Thessalonian correspondence or the Pastoral Epistles. As the series evolved, the earlier sections were repeatedly revised and expanded. The fifth edition (1864), for example, devoted a single volume to Matthew (*Erste Abtheilung, erste Hälfte*) and totaled 623 pages. A British edition, comprising twenty volumes, was published in English from 1873 to 1885, and an American edition was begun in 1884. The depth of Meyer's devotion to his task is disclosed in his preface to the fifth edition of his commentary on John, written in 1868: "So long as God will maintain for me in my old age the necessary measure of strength, I shall continue my quiet participation, as unimportant as it is, in the service of biblical exegesis."[20] Meyer was convinced that historical-critical exegesis, freed from dogmatic presuppositions, could provide the solution to the theological crisis of his time. In format, Meyer's commentaries offer a critical introduction to each book,

---

19. Heinrich August Wilhelm Meyer, *Critical and Exegetical Handbook to the Epistle to the Romans*, trans. John C. Moore and Edwin Johnson, ed. William P. Dickson, 2 vols. (Edinburgh: T. & T. Clark, 1873).

20. Heinr. Aug. Wilh. Meyer, *Kritisch exegetisches Handbuch über das Evangelium des Johannes*, 5th rev. ed. (Göttingen: Vandenhoeck & Ruprecht, 1869), ix.

followed by comments organized by chapters and preceded by a discussion of text-critical issues. The comments are presented in paragraph form, usually about one paragraph to each NT verse. Attention is given to linguistic, grammatical, and historical details. At some points, remarks (short excursuses) are added. Extensive references to secondary sources punctuate the text, and additional references are included in the footnotes. A few examples can illustrate the character of Meyer's work.

In regard to the Gospel of Matthew, Meyer believes it to be a Greek translation of a Hebrew (i.e., Aramaic) gospel which was largely a collection of sayings (*logia*). This original gospel was written by Matthew (also called Levi) the tax collector who was one of the Twelve. To this gospel, the translator added some unhistorical details; he also made use of Mark which was the earliest of the canonical Gospels. Commenting on Matt. 1:18-25, Meyer notes that the doctrine of the virgin birth can be established exegetically out of Matthew and Luke, but he observes that the origin of Jesus is not explained this way in the rest of the NT. From this observation, he concludes that the divine sonship of Jesus does not depend on a particular understanding of his conception.

> Exegetically, therefore, the proposition of faith, that in Jesus the only-begotten Son of God entered as man into humanity, cannot be made to depend upon the conception, which is recorded only in Matthew and Luke, but must also, irrespective of the latter, remain fast and immutable in its full and real meaning of the incarnation of the divine Logos, which took place, and takes place, in no other; so that that belief cannot be made to depend on the manner in which Jesus was conceived, and in which the Spirit of God acted at the very commencement of His human existence.[21]

Meyer's comments on Matt. 16:18 were disappointing to some of his contemporary Protestants. He recognized the popular distinction between πέτρος and πέτρα, but believed the latter, as well as the former, was used to depict Peter's character. Meyer explicitly rejects the notion that the church was to be built on Peter's confession and acknowledges that the text affirms the primacy of Peter—"the foundation on which a building is to be raised."[22]

In regard to Mark and Luke,[23] Meyer supports the traditional authorship. Mark was written by John Mark, who heard Peter preach and made

---

21. Heinrich August Wilhelm Meyer, *Critical and Exegetical Handbook to the Gospel of Matthew*, trans. Peter Christie, ed. Frederick Crombie, 2 vols. (Edinburgh: T. & T. Clark, 1883), 1.67.

22. Ibid. 1.419

23. Heinrich August Wilhelm Meyer, *Critical and Exegetical Handbook to the Gospels of Mark and Luke*, trans. Robert E. Wallis, ed. William P. Dickson, 2 vols. (Edinburgh: T. & T. Clark, 1890).

notes which he used in writing his Gospel, a Gospel addressed to gentile Christians and written before the destruction of Jerusalem. According to Meyer, Mark 16:9-20 did not belong to the original, because it is not found in many ancient manuscripts and does not conform to Marcan style. The Gospel did not end with 16:8, however, and the original ending was either lost or never completed. The third Gospel was written by Luke, the physician and travel companion of Paul. As to sources, Luke used Mark, the *logia* of Matthew, canonical Matthew, and other written and oral sources. Meyer discusses the census of Luke 2:1-2 at length and concludes that the author is mistaken in his account of an empire-wide census under Quirinius as governor of Syria. Meyer concludes, however, that some sort of registration did occur at the time of the birth of Jesus. He rejects the theory that the census was a fabrication designed to locate the birth of Jesus in Bethlehem.

Meyer's commentary on John is staunchly conservative. On the question of authorship, he argues that vividness of narrative indicates that this Gospel was "not the work of some later forger, but of an immediate eyewitness and recipient."[24] Meyer also argues that differences with the Synoptics actually support authenticity, because a forger would have attempted to harmonize. Similarly, a forger would have made overt apostolic claims, rather than remain anonymous. In Meyer's opinion, only a person who knew Jesus intimately—John, the beloved disciple—could have reached the depth of understanding which the Fourth Gospel reveals. The purpose of this Gospel is to present Jesus as the incarnate Logos to non-Palestinian believers who have merged into a Jewish-gentile Christian union. Although John knew the Synoptic Gospels, his main source was his own memory in unity with the Spirit—"a unity which is the gradually ripened and perfected fruit of a long life of recollection, blending all particulars in one true and bright collective picture, under the guidance of the Divine Spirit as promised by Christ himself."[25]

On John 1:1, Meyer presents a lengthy discussion of the Logos which concludes that the form of expression is Alexandrian, but the source of the concept is the Hebrew Scriptures. This term expresses "the self-revelation of the divine essence, before all time immanent in God . . . but for the accomplishment of the act of creation proceeding hypostatically from Him, and ever after operating also in the spiritual world as a creating, quickening, and illuminating personal principle, equal to God Himself in nature and glory . . . which divine self-revelation appeared bodily in

24. Heinrich August Wilhelm Meyer, *Critical and Exegetical Handbook to the Gospel of John*, trans. William Urwick, ed. Frederick Crombie, 2d ed., 2 vols. (Edinburgh: T. & T. Clark, 1883), 1.27.
25. Ibid. 1.52.

the man Jesus and accomplished the work of the redemption of the world."[26] In the phrase "the Word was God," Meyer argues from the context that the subject is λόγος and the predicate θεός; the article is omitted before Θεός, he thinks, in order to indicate the unity of essence without expressing the identity of person.

Meyer has little difficulty in accepting the supernatural. He understands both the changing of water into wine and the raising of Lazarus as historical events related by an eyewitness. The Cana miracle shows that Jesus has power over nature, and the large quantity of wine demonstrates the abundance of Christ's blessing—"what was left over may have been intended by Jesus as a present to the married pair."[27] In regard to Lazarus, Meyer argues that the Synoptics omit the miracle in order to protect Lazarus and his family from the threat of the Jewish leaders, a danger that no longer exists at the time of the writing of the Fourth Gospel. Commenting on John 2:13-22, Meyer contends that Jesus cleansed the temple twice: at the beginning of his ministry (reported to John) and during the Passion Week (reported in the Synoptics). John, rather than the Synoptics, is correct in regard to the last supper: it was not a Passover meal, and all efforts to harmonize John with the other three Gospels are doomed to failure. The Synoptics represent a tradition in which the supper is transformed into the ideal Passover.

The introduction to Meyer's commentary on Romans includes a sketch of Paul's career. Although this account harmonizes data from Acts and the epistles, Meyer's reconstruction has some distinctive features. He argues, for instance, that Ephesians, Colossians, and Philemon were written from the Caesarean imprisonment, while Philippians was composed in Rome. Meyer questions the hypothesis of a release and second Roman imprisonment, and concludes that the Pastoral Epistles—whose authenticity presupposes these events—are probably not authentic. The Epistle to the Romans does not present a doctrinal system, but a summary of Paul's gospel: "Paul wishes to lay before the Romans in writing, for their Christian edification . . . his evangelic doctrine . . . viewed in its full, specific character as the superseding of Judaism, in such a way as the necessities and circumstances of the Church demanded, as he would have preached it among them, had he been present in person."[28]

On Rom. 3:25, Meyer rejects the interpretation of ἱλαστήριον as the cover on the ark of the covenant (the mercy seat); he translates the term as "expiatory sacrifice." According to Meyer, the atonement is accom-

---

26. Ibid. 1.66–67.
27. Ibid. 1.143.
28. Meyer, *Romans* 1.31.

plished "through this utmost, highest, and holiest sacrifice offered for the satisfaction of the divine justice—through the blood of Christ—that justice might be brought to light and demonstrated."[29] In 5:12, Meyer does not detect a rigid doctrine of original sin. The phrase ἐφ ᾧ should not be translated "in whom" (i.e., in Adam), but "on the ground that"[30] all sinned. Nevertheless, the sin of Adam had a drastic result: "the death of all has its ground in the sin of Adam and the causal connection of that sin with death."[31] Meyer resists efforts to limit "all Israel" (11:26) to the spiritual Israel or a selection of Israel: "*All* Israelites who up to that time shall be still unconverted, will then be converted to salvation, so that at that term *entire* Israel will obtain saving deliverance."[32]

Meyer's commentary on Ephesians[33] answers the objections to Pauline authorship: the difference of style from the other epistles is explained by the depth of the subject matter, and the difference of thought is a figment of modern imagination. Meyer rejects the hypothesis that Ephesians was originally a circular letter and argues that the omission of ἐν Ἐφέσῳ in Eph. 1:1 is the work of a copyist who erroneously supposed that the epistle, because of its content, was not addressed to Ephesus. The surprising lack of personal references may be due to something in Paul's situation in prison that discouraged expressions of this sort. Meyer prefers Caesarea to Rome as the place of composition, because a runaway slave from Colossae would more likely appear there (Philemon 10), and Paul would hardly request the preparation of a guest room (Philemon 22) from the Roman imprisonment.

Johann Peter Lange (1802–1884)

Johann Peter Lange was the son of a Prussian farmer. Educated at the University of Bonn (1822–25), Lange served for several years as a parish pastor. In 1841, he was called to Zurich to fill the chair that had been denied to D. F. Strauss.[34] In 1854, he moved to Bonn as professor of dogmatics. Lange was a prolific author who wrote a three-volume work on dogmatics, a two-volume history of the apostolic age, and a life of Jesus

---

29. Ibid. 1.175.

30. Ibid. 1.249.

31. Ibid.

32. Ibid. 2.234. Vol. 2, translated by John C. Moore and Edwin Johnson, was published in 1881.

33. Heinrich August Wilhelm Meyer, *Critical and Exegetical Handbook to the Epistle to the Ephesians and the Epistle to Philemon*, trans. Maurice J. Evans, ed. William P. Dickson (Edinburgh: T. & T. Clark, 1884).

34. See pp. 247–48, above.

that ran to six volumes in translation.[35] Speaking about Lange's massive commentary series, Philip Schaff wrote, "It is the greatest literary enterprise of the kind undertaken in the present century."[36] The series, which included both OT and NT, was an international effort, employing the talents of German, Swiss, and Dutch scholars. Lange himself wrote the commentaries on Genesis, Exodus, Numbers, Matthew, Mark, John, Romans, Revelation, and (with the collaboration of van Oosterzee) James. The distinctive feature of the series is the presentation of the material under three heads: exegetical and critical; doctrinal and ethical; and homiletical and practical.

Lange's basic approach is set forth in a "General Introduction to the Holy Scriptures," which prefaces his Matthew commentary.[37] In this introduction, Lange advocates a theology of salvation history. The Bible is the unfolding account of revelation that includes all history seen from the Christian perspective: "Viewed in this light, the whole history of the world itself is simply the history of the restoration and transformation of the world into the kingdom of God."[38] The Bible which records this redemptive history is "the one harmonious and complete Word of God."[39] Although the biblical authors were allowed to express the divine word in their own idiom, the "Spirit of God was indeed strong enough to preserve the sacred writers from essential mistakes or false testimonies and traditions."[40] For Lange, the biblical message must be proclaimed: "That which gives to the sermon its value, is the Word of the living God, which is laid down objectively in the Scriptures, and expressed and applied by the preacher in a subjective form."[41]

An example of Lange's threefold comments can be seen in his discussion of Matt. 1:18-25. Under "Exegetical and Critical," Lange deals with details of the text: for example, the reference to Jesus as the "first born" (found in manuscripts which Lange follows) does not mean that Mary had children subsequently. Under "Doctrinal and Ethical," Lange discusses the sinlessness of Jesus, and the doubts of Joseph—doubts which prefigure the

---

35. J. P. Lange, *The Life of the Lord Jesus Christ: A Complete Examination of the Origin, Contents, and Connection of the Gospels*, trans. Sophia Taylor, ed. Marcus Dods, 6 vols. (Edinburgh: T. & T. Clark, 1864).

36. John Peter Lange, *The Gospel according to Matthew, Together with a General Theological, and Homiletical Introduction to the New Testament*, trans. Philip Schaff (New York: C. Scribner, 1865), viii.

37. Ibid., 2–19.

38. Ibid., 2.

39. Ibid., 12.

40. Ibid.

41. Ibid., 30.

later rejection of Jesus. Under "Homiletical and Practical," Lange points to such sermonic themes as the transformation of doubt into belief and the importance of women. In general, Lange's comments are conservative. He has no doubt that Jesus had the power to walk on water and that this power, "awakened by the wonder-working word of the Lord,"[42] could also function in a human like Peter. Harmonizing John and the Synoptics, Lange concludes that the last supper was a Passover meal. He believes the Fourth Gospel and Revelation were both written by the apostle John, and he claims that "the Gospel of John has no special eschatology."[43] In regard to Paul,[44] Lange adopts the thesis of a release from Roman imprisonment, followed by additional travel and a second imprisonment in Rome. Ephesians, Colossians, Philemon, and Philippians were written from the first imprisonment (62–64); 1 Timothy and Titus during the interim; and 2 Timothy from the second Roman imprisonment (67).

Frédéric Louis Godet (1821–1900)

Frédéric Louis Godet was born in Neuchâtel and educated at Bonn and Berlin. After working for some years as a pastor, he served as a professor in the theological academy of the Free Church in Neuchâtel from 1873 to 1887. Godet published lectures in apologetics and a two-volume collection of OT and NT studies. His continuing popularity is attested by a recent reprint of his essays on the Pauline letters.[45] Late in his career, Godet published his two-volume *Introduction au Nouveau Testament* (1893–98), which was translated into English.[46] He is best remembered for his commentaries on the Gospels of John and Luke, although he also published commentaries on Romans[47] and 1 Corinthians.[48]

Godet's *Commentaire sur l'évangile de saint Jean* was published in two volumes in 1864 and 1865.[49] The purpose of criticism, according to Godet,

42. Ibid., 271.

43. John Peter Lange, *The Gospel according to John*, trans. E. D. Yeomans and E. Moore, ed. Philip Schaff (New York: C. Scribner, 1884), 30.

44. J. P. Lange, *The Epistle of Paul to the Romans*, trans. J. F. Hurst, ed. P. Schaff and M. B. Riddle (New York: C. Scribner, 1870).

45. Frederic L. Godet, *Studies in Paul's Epistles* (Grand Rapids: Kregel, 1984).

46. F. Godet, *Introduction to the New Testament I: The Epistles of St. Paul*, trans. William Affleck (Edinburgh: T. & T. Clark, 1894); idem, *Introduction to the New Testament: The Collection of the Four Gospels and the Gospel of St. Matthew*, trans. William Affleck (Edinburgh: T. & T. Clark, 1894).

47. Frédéric Godet, *Commentaire sur l'épître aux Romains* (Neuchâtel: J. Sandoz 1879–80); Eng. trans.: *Commentary on St. Paul's Epistle to the Romans*, trans. A. Cusin, 2 vols. (Edinburgh: T. & T. Clark, 1880).

48. F. Godet, *Commentary on St. Paul's First Epistle to the Corinthians*, trans. A. Cusin, 2 vols. (Edinburgh: T. & T. Clark, 1886–87).

49. Eng. trans.: F. Godet, *Commentary on the Gospel of St. John*, trans. Frances Crombie, M. D. Cusin, and S. Taylor, 3 vols. (Edinburgh: T. & T. Clark, 1881); I cite, below, a reprint of the Eng. trans., the 3d ed., 3 vols. in one (Grand Rapids: Kregel, 1978).

is to put the reader in the historical situation of the biblical writer. In Godet's opinion, the Fourth Gospel was written by John, an eyewitness, who presents an account that is more historically accurate than that of the Synoptics. The discourses of John are authentic and go beyond the simple teachings of the parables to more profound instruction. "The inventor of such discourses would be more than a genius of first rank; he would need to be himself a Son of God, a Jesus equal to the true one."[50] On the story of the woman caught in adultery (John 7:53—8:11), Godet points out that the text is not only lacking in the oldest manuscripts, it also displays a style and message different from that of the Gospel of John. Godet rejects the theory that Mary Magdalene failed to recognize the risen Jesus because he had put on the gardener's clothes, and he argues that the resurrection involved a transformation: "there was a change in His whole person by His passing into a new life."[51]

In his preface to the second edition of his commentary on Luke (1870), Godet affirms the practical importance of his kind of historical exegesis.

> The most advanced ideas of modern unbelief circulate at the present time in all our great centres of population. In the streets of our cities, workmen are heard talking about the conflict between St. Paul and the other apostles of Jesus Christ. We must therefore endeavour to place the results of a real and impartial Biblical science within the reach of all.[52]

Consequently, Godet's work has an apologetic purpose: to establish the basic historicity of the biblical record. In this regard, Luke is the most historically reliable of the Synoptics.

> From all those facts established by exegesis, it follows that, if Luke's account has not, like that of John, the fulness and precision belonging to the narrative of an eye-witness, it nevertheless reaches a degree of fidelity which may be attained by a historian who draws his materials from those sources which are at once the purest and the nearest to the facts.[53]

According to Godet, those sources do not include Matthew or Mark (the Synoptics depend independently on a common oral source), but a Jewish genealogical record, Judeo-Christian documents in Aramaic, oral tradition, and a narrative of the Lord's Supper.

Examples of Godet's exegesis confirm his concern with history. In regard to the census (Luke 2:1-2), he argues that Luke has not confused two censuses, because he mentions the later enrollment in Acts 5:37. Thus,

50. Godet, *Commentary on John*, 123.
51. Ibid., 977.
52. F. Godet, *A Commentary on the Gospel of St. Luke*, trans E. W. Shalders and M. D. Cusin, 2 vols. (Edinburgh: T. & T. Clark, 1875), 1.ix.
53. Ibid. 2.378–80.

the census that occurred at the time of the birth of Jesus was an earlier enrollment, taken when Quirinius had some authority in the east, prior to his appointment as governor of Syria. The miracles must not be eroded by rationalistic or psychological explanations, nor explained away as mythological creations. "But the simple, plain, historical character of our Gospel narratives, so free from all poetical adornment and bombast, defends them against this suspicion."[54] In commenting on Luke 24:13-33, Godet displays historical imagination. He thinks the unnamed Emmaus pilgrim may have been Luke himself. This leads him to suppose that each evangelist has carved in his narrative a small niche for himself: Matthew as the converted tax collector (Matt. 9:9); Mark as the young man who fled naked from Gethsemane (Mark 14:51-52); Luke as the Emmaus pilgrim (Luke 24:13); and John as the beloved disciple (John 13:23; 20:2).

For sheer tedium, no literary genre can outdo the biblical commentary! Nevertheless, commentaries have been widely read throughout the history of NT interpretation, and they reflect the popular mind better than some of the more exciting monographs. The commentators discussed here considered their work to be practical—written not primarily for scholars (Olshausen), addressed to preachers (Lange), directed toward the crises of the time (Meyer, Godet). The fact that these commentaries were translated early into English affirms their universal appeal and extensive use. At the same time, they attest to the triumph of the historical-critical method—all determined to reconstruct the historical meaning of the text. Olshausen's assertion that the inner witness of the Spirit is more important than historical proofs suggests sensitivity to the problem of subjecting divine authority to human verification, but Olshausen fails to incorporate this insight into his usual method of historical apologetics. As to the practice of historical exegesis, Meyer has probably performed most adequately, and Godet, slightly less effectively. These two scholars have mastered the tools of critical research and possess a comprehensive knowledge of the secondary sources. With Meyer, virtually no critical or exegetical issue is left untouched.

All of these commentaries are more or less conservative—more, in the case of Olshausen, less in the case of Meyer. In particular, Meyer should be credited with meeting his own criterion: to present a historical interpretation free from dogmatic prejudgments; at points (e.g., on Peter's confession) he offers an exegesis contrary to his own theological position. Godet, although he is anxious to support Luke's reliability, does not ignore historical problems (e.g., the census). Olshausen, on the other hand, is willing

54. Ibid. 1.253.

to compromise criticism at the price of orthodoxy (e.g., his notion that critical problems belong to the divine design), and Lange's idea of salvation history involves a presupposition that determines the results. In spite of their adoption of a common method, these commentators have not arrived at a consensus concerning the historical beginnings of Christianity. They do not agree on a solution to the synoptic problem, and their common preference for the Fourth Gospel only serves to cloud the historical picture. Their failure to bring into sharp focus the lines of distinction between the Johannine and the Synoptic portraits of Jesus displays not only theological deficiency but a lack of historical clarity.

LIVES OF JESUS:
RENAN AND KEIM

The ultimate challenge to the NT critic is the reconstruction of the life of Jesus. For Christians, Jesus is the ground of faith—the normative revelation of the reality of God in history. If this conviction is correct, what Jesus said and did is of utmost importance. The writing of a life of Jesus, however, is fraught with a host of difficulties: fragmentary sources, conflicting traditions, and philosophical and theological presuppositions. Little wonder that many have contended that a life of Jesus cannot be written. Yet the attempt has been repeatedly undertaken, no author being content with the work of his or her predecessors. Schleiermacher could not accept the Jesus of Reimarus or Paulus, and Strauss found the Jesus of Schleiermacher to be a flimsy construct of faith. For many people, Strauss's presentation of Jesus as the mythical fabrication of the early Christians was the least satisfactory of all. Like Mary Magdalene, they could complain, "They have taken the Lord out of the tomb, and we do not know where they have laid him" (John 20:2). Two subsequent attempts to find the historical Jesus make a significant contribution to the history of NT research.

Ernest Renan (1823–1892)

Without question, the most popular life of Jesus ever written is Joseph Ernest Renan's *Vie de Jésus*. Renan was born in humble circumstances in Brittany.[55] His father died when he was only five, and his upbringing was left to his mother and beloved sister, Henriette. Renan's academic promise was apparent early, and a scholarship was secured to educate him for

---

55. For surveys of Renan's life and work, see Richard M. Chadbourne, *Ernest Renan* (New York: Twayne, 1968); Lewis Freeman Mott, *Ernest Renan* (New York and London: Appleton, 1921); William Barry, *Ernest Renan*, Literary Lives (London: Hodder & Stoughton, 1905).

the priesthood. He attended the seminaries of St. Nicholas de Chardonnet, Issy, and St. Sulpice in Paris. But as the time of his ordination drew near, Renan, shaken by doubts, broke with the church. He continued university studies in Paris, distinguishing himself in Semitic studies. In 1862, Renan was appointed professor of Hebrew at the College of France, but he was suspended immediately after his inaugural address because of his religious liberalism. In 1860 and 1861, Renan had traveled to Syria and Palestine for archeological research under a grant from Napoleon III. His sister accompanied him and urged Renan to write a life of Jesus; unfortunately she died in Byblos from an illness contracted during the journey. Renan wrote the first draft while still in the Near East, and dedicated the book to her memory. During the Franco-Prussian war, the mutual admiration of Renan and Strauss turned to enmity that was expressed in an exchange of hostile letters.[56] Renan was reinstated to his professorship in 1871 and elected to the French academy in 1879. His writings were extensive, including works in philosophy, Semitic languages, and religious history. Late in his life, Renan wrote the five-volume *Histoire du peuple d'Israel* (1887–93)[57] which covered Hebrew history from the nomadic beginnings to the Roman period.

Renan's *Life of Jesus* was destined to became a classic of French literature. When it first appeared in 1863, the book created an immediate sensation. Some 66,000 copies were printed within the first six months, and the book was translated into a dozen languages by the end of 1864. Actually, the work was designed as the first volume of an erudite chronicle of early Christianity: *Histoire des origines du christianisme.* The series eventually stretched to seven volumes and traced the history of Christianity from its origin in Jesus to its development at the end of the ancient world. Renan's approach can be seen in a preface, written under the shadow of unfavorable criticism, which he added to the thirteenth edition. Most important, he reaffirms his intent to write scientific history in the face of every form of supernaturalism.

> If the miracle has any reality, this book is but a tissue of errors. . . . If, on the contrary, miracle is a thing inadmissible, then I am right in regarding the books which contain miraculous tales as history mixed with fiction, as legends full of inaccuracies, errors, and systematic shifts.[58]

56. For this correspondence and Renan's political views, which influenced his interpretation of the history of Israel, see Leivy Smolar, "Ernest Renan's Interpretation of Biblical History," in *Biblical and Related Studies Presented to Samuel Iwry*, ed. A. Kort and S. Morschauser (Winona Lake, Ind: Eisenbrauns, 1985), 237–57.

57. Eng. trans.: Ernest Renan, *History of the People of Israel*, 5 vols. (London: Chapman & Hall, 1888–91).

58. Ernest Renan, *Life of Jesus* (Boston: Little, Brown, 1924), 12–13.

Producing a scientific history of Jesus, however, is problematic: "If in writing the Life of Jesus one should confine himself to setting forth those matters only which are certain, he must limit himself to a few lines."[59] This means that the project requires historical imagination, a characteristic Ernest Renan possessed in abundance.

In the introduction to his *Life of Jesus*, Renan reviews the sources. Among the extrabiblical authors, Philo is useful, since he "is truly the elder brother of Jesus."[60] In regard to the Synoptic Gospels, Renan opts for a version of the two-document hypothesis: "In other words, the scheme of the *Life of Jesus*, in the synoptics, rests upon two original documents—first, the discourses of Jesus collected by Matthew; second, the collection of anecdotes and personal reminiscences which Mark wrote from the recollections of Peter."[61] Renan's view of these sources is expanded in his later work on the Gospels (1877).[62] There he calls the discourse source the "Hebrew Gospel"—a gospel written in Syriac, shorter than the canonical Matthew. Mark, the "Greek Gospel," was written from Rome about 68. In his preface to the thirteenth edition of the *Life of Jesus*, Renan says, "Mark seems to me more and more the primitive type of the synoptic narrative, and the most authentic text."[63] Pseudo-Matthew—that is, canonical Matthew—was based on Mark and the Hebrew gospel, probably written in Syria. The third Gospel was composed by Luke, the companion of Paul, who used Mark and a Greek translation of the Hebrew gospel; Luke, in Renan's opinion, was "the most literary of the Gospels,"[64] but "very unhistoric."[65]

Renan's view of the Gospel of John continued to evolve. At the time of the first edition of the *Life of Jesus*, he believed the substance of the Gospel was composed by the apostle John, although it had been revised by his disciples. When he prepared the preface to the thirteenth edition, however, Renan was convinced that the author was not John, but one of his followers who wrote around 100; the discourses were totally fictitious, but the narrative contained valuable tradition. The argument in support of this position is developed in the appendix, where Renan presents elements of the Johannine narrative (e.g., the call of the disciples) that he believes rest on historical tradition superior to that of the Synoptics. In the sixth volume of the series, *History of the Origins of Christianity* (1879), Renan concludes that the Fourth Gospel was not written until the reign of

---

59. Ibid., 21.
60. Ernest Renan, *The Life of Jesus* (New York: Modern Library, 1955), 29.
61. Ibid., 37.
62. Ernest Renan, *The Gospels* (London: Mathieson, n.d).
63. *Life of Jesus* (Little, Brown ed.), 19.
64. Renan, *Gospels*, 147.
65. Ibid., 146.

Hadrian and is, in fact, "a pious fraud."[66] He also observed that the author had been infected with the gnostic disease he had hoped to cure.

> It is quite certain, however, that the author is at the same time the father and the adversary of Gnosticism, the enemy of those who allowed the real human nature of Jesus to evaporate in a cloudy Docetism, and the accomplice of those who would make him a mere divine abstraction. Dogmatic minds are never more severe than they are toward those from whom they are divided by a mere shade of difference. That Anti-Christ whom the pseudo-John represents as already in existence, that monster who is the very negation of Jesus, and whom he cannot distinguish from the errors of Docetism, is almost he himself.[67]

In the actual composition of the *Life of Jesus*, Renan's method was to use Matthew as the primary source for the teaching material, and Mark, supplemented by John, for narrative.

For Renan, Jesus was a figure of utmost importance for the history of the world. The agent of a major religious revolution, Jesus was born in a time of confusion and expectation.

> This confused mixture of clear views and dreams, this alternation of deceptions and hopes, these ceaseless aspirations, driven back by an odious reality, found at last their interpretation in the incomparable man, to whom the universal conscience has decreed the title of Son of God, and that with justice, since he has advanced religion as no other has done, or probably ever will be able to do.[68]

Renan's presentation of this incomparable character appears at first glance to be a topological biography, a sort of pious travelogue. From this perspective, the life of Jesus is portrayed against two backgrounds: Galilee, where all is pastoral and beautiful; and Judea, where all is harsh and barren.

Jesus was born and raised in Nazareth in lovely Galilee. "The environs, moreover, are charming; and no place in the world was so well adapted for dreams of perfect happiness."[69] In these beautiful surroundings, Jesus learned from nature. He was taught to read and write by a local teacher. He was captivated by the dreams of the prophets, and "the Psalms were in marvellous accordance with his poetic soul."[70] As Jesus' religious consciousness developed, he increasingly stressed morality and the fatherhood of God.

---

66. Ernest Renan, *The Reigns of Hadrian and Antoninus Pius* (London: Mathieson, 1888).
67. Ibid., 29.
68. Renan, *Life of Jesus* (Modern Library ed.), 79–80.
69. Ibid., 86.
70. Ibid., 94.

Jesus never once gave utterance to the sacrilegious idea that he was God. He believed himself to be in direct communion with God; he believed himself to be the Son of God. The highest consciousness of God which has existed in the bosom of humanity was that of Jesus.[71]

In his teaching, Jesus advocated love of neighbor and enemy, direct and intimate worship of God—all the best of Judaism expressed in the vivid images of nature.

A cloud overshadowed this idyllic picture when Jesus traveled south to encounter John the Baptist. John preached an apocalyptic message and instilled in Jesus revolutionary ideas. Under the influence of John, Jesus began to see himself as the Messiah who would work for the coming of a new order. In Jesus' mind, however, this new kingdom would not be political but spiritual. Jesus took for himself the title son of man, which in Semitic meant simply "man" but, for Jesus, was a term of messianic meaning. Back in friendly Galilee, Jesus attracted a group of followers—simple, pious folk, mostly fishermen.

The beautiful climate of Galilee made the life of these honest fishermen a perpetual delight. They truly preluded the kingdom of God—simple, good, happy—rocked gently on their delightful little sea, or at night sleeping on its shores.[72]

To communicate with these humble people, Jesus used the colorful parable, a form of teaching attractive to the poor, to women, and to children.

How this charming young teacher could have aroused bitter opposition is difficult to fathom, but the answer is to be found in hostile Judea. The city of Jerusalem was dominated by the scribes and Pharisees.

The science of the Jewish doctor, of the *sofer* or scribe, was purely barbarous, unmitigatedly absurd, and denuded of all moral element. To crown the evil, it filled with ridiculous pride those who had wearied themselves in acquiring it.[73]

Along with the scribes, the priestly system, promoted by the Sadduccees, was hopelessly corrupt. Jesus, encountering this sort of opposition in Judea, became increasingly revolutionary. "From this time he appears no more as a Jewish reformer, but as a destroyer of Judaism."[74] More and more, Jesus proclaimed apocalyptic notions; more and more, he saw the son of man as a figure of supernatural might. Jesus demonstrated this power by performing exorcisms—psychological cures accomplished by the force of his personality.

71. Ibid., 122.
72. Ibid., 184.
73. Ibid., 214.
74. Ibid., 224.

When demons wish to proclaim him the Son of God, he forbids them to open their mouths; but they recognize him in spite of himself. These traits are especially characteristic in Mark, who is pre-eminently the evangelist of miracles and exorcisms.[75]

Renan does not fully resolve the tension between the gentle Jesus and the messianic revolutionary—nor does he try; history, he thinks, is a chronicle of all sorts of inconsistencies. Nevertheless, what dominates Renan's portrait is Jesus as the teacher of a universal, moral religion—a sort of ethical humanism. This becomes apparent in Jesus' conversation with the Samaritan woman in which he advocates worship in spirit and truth. "He founded the pure worship, of all ages, of all lands, that which all elevated souls will practice until the end of time."[76] In spite of its revolutionary and apocalyptic overtones, the main theme of the kingdom of God is ethical and spiritual: "This true kingdom of God, this kingdom of the spirit, which makes each one king and priest; this kingdom which, like the grain of mustard-seed, has become a tree which overshadows the world, and amidst whose branches the birds have their nests, was understood, wished for, and founded by Jesus."[77]

By Jesus' final visit to Jerusalem, the opposition had become homicidal. It was encouraged, too, by the pretended raising of Lazarus (who was not really dead), a hoax contrived by Jesus that required the collusion of Mary and Martha. For Renan, this fraudulent effort of Jesus to promote his Messiahship is not detrimental to his character, because all religious leaders employ an element of deception. At any rate, the opposition was headed by the Pharisees and supported by a conservative priestly faction led by Annas. The decision to destroy Jesus, however, turned out to be a tactical error of monumental proportions. "Left free," says Renan, "Jesus would have exhausted himself in a desperate struggle with the impossible. The unintelligent hate of his enemies decided the success of his work, and sealed his divinity."[78] Since the Jews had no right of capital punishment, Jesus was taken to Pilate and charged with sedition, a charge based on a misunderstanding of his idea of the kingdom. Renan, always sensitive to feminine concerns, is fascinated by the minor role of Pilate's wife.

> She may have seen the gentle Galilean from some window of the palace, overlooking the courts of the temple. Perhaps she had seen him again in her dreams; and the idea that the blood of this beautiful young man was about to be spilt, weighed on her mind.[79]

75. Ibid., 254–55.
76. Ibid., 234.
77. Ibid., 267.
78. Ibid., 328.
79. Ibid., 352.

Renan understands the death of Jesus as a triumph. In an exalted eulogy, he addresses the fallen hero.

> Rest now in thy glory, noble initiator. Thy work is completed; thy divinity is established. Fear no more to see the edifice of thy efforts crumble through a flaw. Henceforth, beyond the reach of frailty, thou shalt be present, from the height of thy divine peace, in the infinite consequences of thy acts. At the price of a few hours of suffering, which have not even touched thy great soul, thou hast purchased the most complete immortality. For thousands of years the world will extol thee. Banner of our contradictions, thou wilt be the sign around which will be fought the fiercest battles. A thousand times more living, a thousand times more loved since thy death than during the days of thy pilgrimage here below, thou wilt become to such a degree the corner-stone of humanity, that to tear thy name from this world would be to shake it to its foundations. Between thee and God, men will no longer distinguish. Complete conqueror of death, take possession of thy kingdom, whither, by the royal road thou has traced, ages of adorers will follow thee.[80]

After the death of Jesus, the power of his memory, aroused by the imaginative Mary Magdalene, led the disciples to believe he was alive. Renan, in his later book on the apostles,[81] presents a fuller account of the rise of the resurrection faith. "The little Christian society," he says, "worked the veritable miracle; they resuscitated Jesus in their hearts by the intense love which they bore toward him."[82] Although they had strong hearts, the disciples, in Renan's opinion, had weak heads, and they were easily swayed by a woman noted for her instability. "The glory of the resurrection belongs, then to Mary of Magdala. After Jesus, it is Mary who has done most for the foundation of Christianity."[83] Some of Jesus' disciples returned to Galilee, where they were overwhelmed by his memory.

> At every step they recollected His words, attached, as it were, to the thousand events of the way. See this tree, this flower, this seed, from which he took up his parable! here is the little hill on which he delivered his most touching discourses; here is the little ship in which he taught. It was all like a beautiful dream commenced anew, like an illusion which had vanished, and then reappeared.[84]

Renan concludes that although the resurrection was a mere figment of the disciples' imagination, the memory of Jesus has been alive for eighteen centuries.

> But whatever may be the unexpected phenomena of the future, Jesus will not be surpassed. His worship will constantly renew its youth, the tale of his

80. Ibid., 368–69.
81. Ernest Renan, *The Apostles* (New York: Carleton, 1886).
82. Ibid., 57.
83. Ibid., 61.
84. Ibid., 73.

life will cause ceaseless tears, his sufferings will soften the best hearts; all the ages will proclaim that, among the sons of men, there is none born who is greater than Jesus.[85]

In spite of the popularity of Renan's *Life of Jesus*, its publication provoked an avalanche of negative criticism. The opposition was predictable, for this book was not the work of a German critic, but of a French savant— not an exercise in esoteric theology, but a highly popular literary achievement. Renan reacted to the hostility with an irenic spirit.

> Let us enjoy the liberty of the sons of God; but let us also refrain from being accomplices in diminishing virtue in the world—a result which would necessarily arise, were Christianity to be weakened. . . . Our disagreement with those who believe in positive religions, is, after all, purely scientific; we are with them in heart.[86]

When the dust had settled, serious critics continued to denigrate Renan's achievement, charging that, at best, it was a historical novel. Albert Schweitzer found "a kind of insincerity in the book from beginning to end"[87] and asserted that "down to the present day Renan's work forms the greatest hindrance to any serious advance in French religious thought."[88] While this judgment is unduly harsh, Renan has hardly produced a convincing picture of the historical Jesus. Instead, he offers a blurred image, filtered through the lens of his own literary imagination. Renan's Jesus, like a double exposure, is a composite of religious genius and primitive naïveté,[89] and his picture of first-century Judaism is, at the same time, a deplorable caricature. Yet for all the historical distortion and rhetorical excess, readers will continue to be fascinated by Renan's inventive reconstruction.

Much of the negative criticism of Renan is in reaction to the first draft of the *Life of Jesus*, hurriedly written on the site and under the sway of a creative passion. Readers who ponder the footnotes and study the introduction and preface to the thirteenth edition will be more favorably impressed with Renan as a historian. Indeed, Renan's erudition becomes increasingly apparent as one investigates the later volumes in his monumental series, *History of the Origins of Christianity.* For example, his book on

85. Renan, *Life of Jesus* (Modern Library ed.), 393.

86. Ernest Renan, *The Apostles* (New York: Brentano's, n.d.), 40.

87. Albert Schweitzer, *The Quest of the Historical Jesus: A Critical Study of Its Progress from Reimarus to Wrede*, trans. W. Montgomery (New York: Macmillan, 1957), 191.

88. Ibid., 190. Schweitzer's criticism is refuted by Étienne Trocmé ("Exégèse scientifique et idéologie: de l'École de Tubingue aux historiens français des origines chrétiennes," *New Testament Studies* 24 [1978]: 447–62), who considers Renan's influence on French scholarship to have been positive.

89. This point is made, although overstated, by John T. Noonan, "Renan's Life of Jesus: A Re-Examination," *Catholic Biblical Quarterly* 11 (1949): 26–39.

Paul presents a careful analysis of the authenticity of the epistles.[90] Renan classifies the Pauline letters into five categories: (1) those which are uncontested (Galatians, 1 and 2 Corinthians, and Romans); (2) those which are questioned by some scholars (1 and 2 Thessalonians and Philippians); (3) those which are more seriously questioned (Colossians and Philemon); (4) those which are doubtful (Ephesians); and (5) those which are clearly unauthentic (the Pastoral Epistles). For his own part, Renan accepts as authentic the epistles in the first three categories, although he acknowledges problems in connection with Colossians. In a later volume,[91] Renan contends that this letter was written from the Roman imprisonment after Paul had undergone changes in both his style and his theology.

In a perceptive discussion of the integrity of Romans, Renan argues that 16:3-20 was originally addressed to Ephesus, and 16:21-24 to Macedonia; he concludes that Romans was originally an encyclical, written primarily to three churches (Corinth, Ephesus, and Thessalonica)—an epistle of which a copy was sent "as an exception"[92] to Rome. As to Paul's letters in general, Renan notes that they were occasional, and he describes the process by which they were dictated:

> Now brisk, crude, polite, snarlish, sarcastic, then suddenly, tender, delicate, almost roguish and coaxing; happily expressed and polished to the highest degree; skillful in sprinkling his language with reticences, reserves, infinite precautions, malignant allusions, and ironical dissimulations, he came to excel in a style which required above everything original impulses. The epistolary style of Paul is the most individual that we have ever had.[93]

In these letters, Paul has transformed the human Jesus into a metaphysical figure.

> To Paul, Jesus is not a man who has lived and taught; He is the Christ who has died for our sins, who saves us, who justifies us; He is an altogether Divine Being: we partake of Him; we communicate with Him in a wonderful manner; He is for man Wisdom and Righteousness, Sanctification and Redemption; He is the King of Glory, All Powerful in Heaven and Earth, which is soon to be delivered to Him; He is only inferior to God the Father.[94]

In regard to the reconstruction of early Christian history, Renan is fully cognizant of the work of Baur and the Tübingen school, which he rejects. According to Renan, the leader of the Judaizing faction in the church is James, while Peter, with his typical vacillation, is sympathetic to both sides.

---

90. Ernest Renan, *Saint Paul* (London: Mathieson, 1912).
91. Ernest Renan, *The Anti-Christ* (London: Mathieson, 1889).
92. Renan, *Saint Paul*, xxx.
93. Ibid., 137.
94. Ibid., 184.

The struggle is a matter not of theological niceties, but of larger questions—"whether Christianity was to be a petty sect or a universal religion."[95] The role of Paul in shaping the future was enormous.

> One man contributed more than any other to that rapid extension of Christianity. That man has torn up the swaddling clothes so narrow and so prodigiously dangerous by which he was surrounded from his birth; he has proclaimed that Christianity was not a simple reform of Judaism, but that it was a complete religion, existing by itself. . . . He had not seen Jesus, he had not heard His voice. . . . The Christ who personally revealed himself to him is his own ghost; he listens to himself, thinking that he hears Jesus.[96]

In Renan's opinion, true Christianity is not to be found in the epistles of Paul, but in the Gospels that witness to the religion of Jesus.

Theodor Keim (1825–1878)

Less popular, but more substantial is the massive biography of Jesus by Karl Theodor Keim. Keim was born in Stuttgart and educated at Tübingen (1843–47), where he came under the influence of F. C. Baur. Keim also studied at Bonn. He began his teaching career at Tübingen as an instructor (1851–55). After a short interim as a pastor in Württemberg (1856–59), Keim was called to the chair of historical theology at Zurich (1860–73). In 1873, he moved to the faculty at Giessen, where he spent the balance of his career. Keim was admired as an eloquent preacher and respected for his publications in church history. His major work is *Geschichte Jesu von Nazara*, a comprehensive account of the life of Jesus which filled three large volumes, six in English translation.[97] At the outset, Keim declares his intention to approach the task as a pure historian, devoid of dogmatic presuppositions. Thus, "the facts should be allowed to speak clearly, fully, and impartially as in any other branch of history."[98] The importance of facts about Jesus is self-evident, because Jesus is the founder of Christianity. In the past, research on his life had been impeded by the conflict between scientific historiography and the faith of the church. But now, in Keim's time, a coalescence of these forces has provided the possibility for a fruitful accomplishment: historians have come to recognize that the ideal can come into history, and the church has increasingly affirmed the humanity of Jesus. In other words, Keim believes

---

95. Ibid., 43.
96. Ibid., 161.
97. Theodor Keim, *Geschichte Jesu von Nazara, in ihrer Verkettung mit dem Gesammtleben seines Volkes frei untersucht und ausführlich erzählt*, 3 vols. (Zurich: Orell, Füssli, 1867–72). Eng. trans.: *The History of Jesus of Nazara, Freely Investigated in Its Connection with the National Life of Israel, and Related in Detail*, 6 vols. (London: Williams & Norgate, 1873–83).
98. Keim, *History of Jesus* 1.15.

German idealism and a progressive church can join hands in the quest for the historical Jesus.

In assessing the sources, Keim considers the epistles of Paul to be the earliest and most reliable; he also thinks they contain "a solid kernel of the life of Jesus."[99] In regard to the Gospels, Keim believes Matthew to have been the earliest. Written around 66—but not by Matthew or an eyewitness—this Gospel was addressed to Jews and Jewish Christians in order to prove that Jesus was the Messiah. The third Gospel was composed by Luke, travel companion of Paul, around the year 90. As sources, Luke used an Ebionite version of Matthew, an earlier form of canonical Matthew, and Samaritan and Pauline traditions. Although he intended to write history, Luke was less than successful. "He has however done violence to the actual history in many instances, irrespective of his sources."[100] Reflecting the influence of Baur, Keim believes Mark used Matthew and Luke as sources and played a synthesizing role beyond the Jewishness of Matthew and the Paulinism of Luke. The Fourth Gospel was written not by John but by a Jewish Christian of Asia Minor, during the reign of Trajan (ca. 110–115). Although the author knew the Synoptics, his purpose was not historical, but doctrinal—even philosophical. Consequently, the story of Jesus has been transformed "into a phantom, a dream and a folly."[101]

> The historical weakness of the fourth Gospel is every day more decidedly, and also more universally admitted. Yet minds are again so dazzled by the incontestable splendours of the Gospel, that men are zealous to snatch away the wonderful work of art from the scorching fire of criticism.[102]

After an extensive discussion of the historical backgrounds, Keim turns to the childhood and youth of Jesus. He observes two conflicting traditions about Jesus' birth: the idea of a supernatural conception and the concept of preexistence. Keim abandons both of these and opts for a human birth. This conclusion, however, does not deny the uniqueness of Jesus, for the divine can function through the human. Indeed, "the tireless wrestling of God after a representation of a perfect, yes, a godlike being, a beloved godlike image in earthly form, and the restless striving of mankind after apprehension of God in the hallowed precincts of their spiritual life, have been crowned with a success worthy of God and humanity, the perfect godlike Man, in the Person of Jesus himself."[103] As he grew up in the setting of the Jewish home and the synagogue school, Jesus

---

99. Ibid. 1.64.
100. Ibid. 1.114.
101. Ibid. 1.171.
102. Ibid. 1.179–80.
103. Ibid. 2.67.

developed a profound consciousness of God, marked by deep humility. Keim imagines that Jesus had an attractive appearance—"healthy, vigorous, of expressive countenance."[104]

Jesus was influenced by John the Baptist, a prophet whose message was primarily ethical. Jesus had heard of John and made the long trek from Galilee to Judea to make his acquaintance. After spending time with the Baptist, Jesus submitted to baptism. In Jesus' case, this ritual was not a washing away of sins —Jesus, in Keim's view, had scarcely any impurities— but an acceptance of a call to Messiahship. Although Jesus kept his vocation secret for a time, he soon began to use the title son of man. The account of his temptation is a symbolic presentation of Jesus' struggle with his messianic calling. Once the news of John's imprisonment reached him, Jesus was confirmed in his own mission and began his ministry in Galilee.

In reconstructing the ministry of Jesus, Keim discerns three chronological periods. The first is the time of happy beginnings in Galilee—what Keim calls "the Galilean Springtime." In this period, Jesus functioned as a teacher who resembles a philosopher of idealism. Although the Sermon on the Mount is a collection of teachings, it includes the kind of instruction Jesus gave to his disciples. His central theme was Repent, the kingdom is at hand. Matthew correctly describes this coming order as the "kingdom of heaven." It is not a political but a spiritual kingdom that gives expression to the unity of the divine and the human—the kingdom of righteousness.

> Righteousness . . . is to Jesus more than simply the conformity of the creature to the will of the obedience-claiming and exalted God; it, the implantation of God in human nature, is more than mere humanity, mere virtue in human form; it is the attainment of the divine nature and life, the harmony of the human life with the divine life, the penetration of humanity into the divine perfection and its saturation with that perfection.[105]

Already this kingdom of the Fatherhood of God and the sonship of humans is present in Jesus who calls himself the son of man, a title that affirms his humanity and heralds the nearness of the kingdom.

> The Son of Man as the Messiah who, though veiled, is yet fully conscious of himself, of his greatness, and of his vocation,—this title, this fact, is a fresh guarantee of the strength of Jesus' faith in the immediate nearness of the kingdom of heaven, and explains his confidence: the kingdom was *where he was*, or it was waiting only for him to unveil himself, for God to unveil him.[106]

104. Ibid. 2.193.
105. Ibid. 3.65.
106. Ibid. 3.92.

In discussing the works of Jesus, Keim attends to the miracles. He observes the tendency of the developing tradition to heighten the miraculous and argues that, in view of this trend, some of the miracles (e.g., those created out of OT parallels) should be discounted. Nevertheless, others ought to be considered historical, especially the healings. These cures which appear to be miraculous are effected by the touch of Jesus— the influence of Spirit upon spirit. In Keim's opinion, they can be understood according to the "psychologico-ethic view."[107] Similarly, the exorcisms represent psychic cures of psychological disorders. Keim rejects the notions that Jesus had advanced medical knowledge and that he accommodated his superior views to the understanding of his contemporaries. Jesus shared the intellectual limitations of his time. As to specific miracles, Keim rejects as literal events the walking on water and the feeding of the multitude. Commenting on the story of Jairus's daughter (who may not have been dead in the first place), he says, "There is elsewhere no reliable trace whatever of any case of raising the dead by Jesus."[108]

The second period of Jesus' ministry is the time of growing opposition—"the Galilean Storms." Keim, who has unwarranted confidence in his reconstruction of chronological details, believes the turning point took place in the summer of 34 C.E., about eight months before Easter. At that time, opposition to Jesus became acute. The main opposition was from the religious leaders—the Pharisees, who attacked Jesus' challenge of the tradition regarding the sabbath and religious ceremonies. In the latter part of this period, Jesus took flight from the centers of danger, a particular feature of Keim's reconstruction of Jesus' career. According to Keim, this flight was provoked by Jesus' human desire to escape danger; but, much more, it was designed to prepare for his assault upon Jerusalem, that is, his intent to take his message to the religious center and to die there as Messiah. The flight included trips beyond the Jordan and into the regions of Tyre and Sidon. The confession at Caesarea Philippi indicates that the disciples recognized Jesus as Messiah. Jesus, in response to the confession, predicted his passion. According to Keim, Jesus did not at this time predict his literal resurrection, although he did expect that at death he would be exalted to heaven so as to return as son of man.

The third and final period of Jesus' ministry includes the events that transpired in Jerusalem. The period begins when Jesus left Galilee in the company of a caravan which was on the way to celebrate the Passover in the Holy City, a departure which took place on the third of April in 35 C.E.

---

107. Ibid. 3.197.
108. Ibid. 4.172.

Recounting Jesus' itinerary from Jericho to Jerusalem provides the occasion for Keim's caustic assessment of the Johannine account of the Judean ministry, including the raising of Lazarus:

> It will be thought cruel and violent when we determinedly reject the whole of this extensive enrichment of the life of Jesus by the Johannine account. This enrichment is no history, but the destruction of history. These journeys, these deeds and miracles, these addresses, these murderous attacks, are unhistorical.[109]

In the course of his reconstruction of the passion narrative, Keim wrestles with the question, Why did Judas betray Jesus? He answers that either Judas was disappointed with Jesus' idea of Messiahship or he was attracted to the Judaism of Jerusalem. According to Keim, the last supper was a Passover meal. Jesus, in the course of the supper, saw his body and blood symbolized by bread and wine. He also interpreted his impending death as an atoning sacrifice, an idea Keim considers beneath Jesus' more lofty insights.

> He could not make the forgiveness of God dependent on blood . . . but upon the gracious disposition above, which lets even the sinner live, and upon reformation and righteousness upon earth. It was upon this foundation that Jesus based his preaching of grace, which made the paternal love of God infinite, and His forgiveness, even of loads of sin, without bounds. It was his greatest satisfaction to exhibit the goodness and the immensity of the heart of God, who, in mercy to the penitent that asked but offered nothing, freely remitted millions of sins.[110]

In regard to the resurrection, Keim acknowledges the complexity of the problem. "The resurrection of Jesus is one of the best attested incidents in the New Testament; the details, however, swarm with contradiction and myth, and are the worst attested of any—the stories of Jesus's childhood not excepted—in all the sources."[111] In an effort to rely on the facts, Keim calls attention to the earliest account of appearances as recorded in 1 Corinthians 15. The account of the empty tomb is unreliable—a later attempt at objectification. The stories about the women, Matthew's account of the guard, and Luke's story of the Emmaus pilgrims are all legendary. Efforts to explain the resurrection by the supposition that the body had been removed or by the notion that Jesus had not really died are unconvincing. Keim concludes that the fundamental fact of the resurrection is the reality of the appearances. These visions are not subjective or self-

---

109. Ibid. 5.76.
110. Ibid. 5.329.
111. Ibid. 6.277.

generated but are phenomena from outside human consciousness, insti-
gated by God.

> If the visions are not something humanly generated or self-generated, if they
> are not blossom and fruit of an illusion-producing over-excitement, if
> they are not something strange and mysterious, if they are directly accompa-
> nied by astonishingly clear perceptions and resolves, then there still remains
> one originating source, hitherto unmentioned, namely, God and the glori-
> fied Christ.[112]

Finally, Keim presents an assessment of the significance of Jesus for the
history of the world. Although limited by his times, Jesus made a unique
contribution in the realm of religion—an understanding and embodiment of the unity of the divine and the human that has never been
surpassed. When all is said and done, Jesus' testimony to himself epitomizes the truth Keim's research has discerned.

> As for himself, he boasts of no equality with God, not even of a divine origin;
> he never desires worship for himself, but always only for God; he places
> himself with men under the omnipotence, omniscience, wisdom, and good-
> ness of God, admitting in all these points the limitation of his own human
> capacity, and thus by anticipation putting to the blush the towering, deifying
> expressions of after centuries. Yet he knows himself to be, in his understand-
> ing, in his life, in his actions, a master exalted above all past, present, and
> future, the final messenger of God, and more than that, the well-beloved,
> the Son of God above all sons, in the knowledge and fellowship of whom the
> Father finds satisfaction, as he in the Father.[113]

Given the state of NT research at the end of the sixth decade of the
nineteenth century, Keim's history of Jesus is a remarkable achievement.
Sensitive to the dominant theology of the day, Keim had mastered all the
skills of biblical criticism, and no important secondary source had escaped
his purview. Keim had learned from Baur, the greatest NT scholar of the
century, but had avoided the extremes of Tübingen criticism. For Keim,
the persistent problem of the Johannine literature—so impeding to the
progress of historical research—had been cut like a Gordian knot. Moreover, Keim offered a reconstruction of Jesus and his mission that made
historical sense. According to Schweitzer, "Nothing deeper or more beautiful has since been written about the development of Jesus."[114] For the
nineteenth-century intellectual, Keim presented a Jesus who was unique
without being supernatural, a noble, ethical teacher who is free from the
embarrassment of the miraculous.

---

112. Ibid. 6.361.
113. Ibid. 6.389–90.
114. Schweitzer, *Quest of the Historical Jesus*, 214.

To be sure, the orthodox, who preferred Keim to Strauss and Renan, were not satisfied. For them, Keim's Jesus was not divine enough to be their redeemer, nor human enough to share their weakness. Of course, by anyone's estimate, Keim had hardly kept his promise to remain an objective historian. His philosophical and theological presuppositions are apparent on almost every page. But, most of all, the magnitude of Keim's accomplishment is the measure of its weakness. Here is a life of Jesus too complete, too accurate, too fulsome in detail—above all, too confident. The observer stands in wonder at how, by some legerdemain, Keim has transformed a small collection of fragmentary sources into six ponderous volumes of accurate biography. In a sense, Keim epitomizes the course of Enlightenment criticism: he had become skeptical of the narrative of the Gospels; he remained confident in the science of the historians.

SUMMARY

The writers of commentaries and the biographers of Jesus synthesize the methods of biblical interpretation that have evolved in the study of the NT since the beginning of the Enlightenment. In effect, they have employed historical-critical exegesis in the interpretation of the texts in order to reconstruct the life and teaching of Jesus. These scholars demonstrate that the scientific method of historiography has become the dominant approach to biblical interpretation. Their intent has been to discern the literal, historical meaning of the documents of the NT in their original setting. Their assumption is that the original meaning of the texts, isolated from later interpretive tradition, is the true meaning, the meaning on which the faith of Christians depends (so Meyer). For the more conservative (Olshausen, Lange, and Godet), historical method functions as an apologetic to establish the truth, that is, the historicity of the biblical record.

Although these scholars accept the same historical method, they reach different critical results. In regard to the synoptic problem, important for the reconstruction of the historical Jesus, they disagree: Godet favors a common oral source; Olshausen and Keim (strange bedfellows) adopt the Griesbach hypothesis; Meyer affirms the priority of Mark; and Renan supports the two-document hypothesis. As to the Pastoral Epistles, Olshausen and Lange affirm their authenticity, but Meyer and Renan deny Pauline authorship. The apostolic authorship of the Gospel of John is accepted by all of these commentators, while both of the biographers of Jesus reject it. All of this indicates that the historical-critical method is hardly a panacea for all the problems of biblical research. The confidence of the eighteenth-century critics that an open mind, equipped with reason and informed by empiricism, could reach the correct, final interpretation had become a delusion. In practice, the historical-critical method functioned imprecisely on the basis of a conflicting variety of philosophical presuppositions. The commentators, for example, accepted the miracles but did not articulate an ontology that could embrace both the supernatural and the empirical-historical. Renan affirmed a naturalistic rationalism, Keim a version of idealism, and Lange a history of salvation theology; and all enlisted a historical-critical method in the service of their conflicting ideologies.

Along with their theological assumptions, these scholars also presupposed a hermeneutic: the original historical meaning of the NT texts is the meaning the text should have for the nineteenth century, indeed, for all time. Olshausen, for example, thought the move from the historical reconstruction of the text to the expression of true doctrine required no translation—no bridge between the then of the text and the now of the interpreter. Consequently, a text that recorded the supernatural conception of Jesus was understood as an expression of the doctrine of the virgin birth, without consideration of the different biologies assumed by the first and the nineteenth centuries. Similarly, when Renan insisted that miracles are a priori impossible, he may have advanced the understanding of the history beneath the text, but he missed the meaning of the biblical writers who assumed the reality of the supernatural. This failure to address the hermeneutical problem is apparent in the lives of Jesus surveyed in this chapter. For Renan, Jesus is limited to his time, a captive of primitive apocalyptic views, yet he is also an unsurpassed religious genius who exemplifies a universal, eternal, spiritual religion. For Keim, Jesus is a fully human being, without benefit of a supernatural birth; yet, for all his humility, Jesus surpasses all other religious leaders before and after, the son of God beyond all sons. These portraits of Jesus lack integrity; they fail to present a historical Jesus who can sustain the Christ of the authors' faith. The Jesus of these reconstructions has no place to lay his head: he is neither the Jesus of first-century Palestine nor the Christ of nineteenth-century Europe.

Epilogue

On the basis of a cursory view of the preceding chronicle, the reader may conclude that little progress has been made, that the journey has been from the skepticism of the deists to the doubts of Tübingen. Yet, in the course of the trip, considerable ground has been traversed and a variety of scenery observed. Like a ride on a roller coaster, the passengers get off where they got on, but along the way they have experienced a lot of ups and downs. In the history of NT research, however, the destination is not really the same as the point of departure, and for the future of the discipline, there can be no return to the pre-critical era; the gap between deism and Tübingen is immense. Looking back over the course of research from the beginning of the Enlightenment through the first two-thirds of the nineteenth century, some major features come into focus. In the larger view, the scene has been dominated by two primary perceptions of reality, two philosophical perspectives, that have influenced NT research.

The first of these is the worldview of the Enlightenment—the view that the universe operates according to mechanical principles that can be understood by humans. The world functions in accord with natural law, and human beings, using empirical observation and reason, can understand the nature and course of the universe. Acceptance of this worldview raised a crucial question for people of faith: If ultimate truth can be found in nature and in reason, what is the need for special revelation, for Scripture? The deists answered that there was no need, that Christianity is a religion of natural law and reason. Attempting to hold onto the traditional faith while embracing the new worldview, mediating theologians tried to harmonize, that is, to argue that special revelation was not in conflict with natural theology. J. S. Semler attempted a more ambitious synthesis.

According to Semler, a distinction could be drawn between religion and theology, whereby religion had to do with the inward experience of faith and theology dealt with the external expression of religion. The new rational method, then, could inform the procedures of theology but leave the deeper experience of faith untouched. Hence, in dealing with theology and theological documents (Scripture and tradition) the scholar was free to use the new critical method.

The second major perception of reality that shaped NT research was the philosophy of German idealism. Following the lead of Kant, theologians could turn inward and deal with morality and religious consciousness. Thus, Schleiermacher and his followers, notably de Wette and Lücke, could concentrate on the human and the historical rather than the metaphysical and the cosmic. With Hegel, a broader perspective was provided—a metaphysical vision that encompassed all of reality. Hegel was concerned with the Absolute Spirit that was being realized in history. From this perspective, theologians could see God incarnate in Jesus, and the actions of God unfolding in the history of early Christianity. For Strauss, Jesus was but a symbol of the larger divine-human unity that was unfolding in all of humanity. For Baur, the history of the church was the story of the dialectical progress of the Divine Spirit in history.

Throughout the whole period and in accord with both perceptions of reality, the importance of human reason was universally recognized. Already, with precursors like Grotius, the argument was advanced that revelation could not contradict reason, and Enlightenment scholars like Turretin made the case that reason and revelation were in harmony. With the deists, that position was challenged. They argued that much of the content of the Bible, the record of special revelation, was not in accord with reason but was marred by contradiction, a point seen in Reimarus's argument that the accounts of the resurrection of Jesus were riddled with inconsistencies. By way of contrast, the power and persistence of rationalism can be detected in conservative scholars like Lardner, who attempted to use reason in defense of the doctrine of biblical inspiration—as if the Spirit of the transcendent God were subject to human inquiry. Other conservatives, notably Pietists like Francke and Bengel, argued that reason had its limits, or that human rationality had been damaged by the fall (so Wesley). This sentiment sometimes took the form of an anti-intellectualism, and, in Britain, an aversion to German rationalistic biblical scholarship.

In this time of the rule of reason, there was also a continuing concern with the supernatural. The very idea of special revelation presupposed a belief in divine intervention, and the Bible, which recorded this revelation, was a collection of countless miracles. For a rational empiricist like

Locke, miracles and prophecy were the proofs of the truth of the special revelation. The deists attacked both proofs on the basis of natural theology and human reason, and much of the history of NT research in the eighteenth and nineteenth centuries is an apologetic defense. According to some, an argument can be based on the idea of God: if God was the author of natural law, God could, now and then, suspend the laws for particular purposes. Later it was argued that philosophies of history that precluded the miraculous were unduly rigid, and that history, especially from idealism's perspective, had more flexibility. The issue became especially acute in relation to the resurrection of Jesus. The deists argued that the idea was against natural law and that the witnesses, whose testimonies were inconsistent, were impeachable. With Strauss, the whole idea of supernaturalism came under relentless attack.

In the face of the problem of the supernatural, an effort was made to abandon the miraculous and redeem the Scriptures—to jettison the cargo and save the ship. This salvage operation took the form of rationalizing the miracles. In an early form of this approach, scholars observed that the uninformed people of NT times believed diseases were caused by demon possession, an observation shared by interpreters as traditional as Wesley. According to this view, demon possession was similar to mental disorders, and cures could be effected by psychological influence. As rationalistic exegesis advanced, this approach to the miracles was broadened: Jesus was not walking *on* the water but *by* the water (G. L. Bauer); the Emmaus pilgrims failed to recognize Jesus because he was wearing the gardener's clothes (Griesbach). This procedure reached a high point with Paulus, who argued that the dead who were presumed to have been raised were not really dead but merely saved from premature burial and that Jesus was not resurrected from the dead but only revived from a coma. In adopting this approach, Paulus thought he was redeeming Scripture by removing the stumbling block of the miraculous. But, although he made the Bible palatable for the nineteenth-century intellectual, Paulus betrayed the message of the writers of Scripture who were immersed in the supernatural.

In an effort to better understand the message of the NT, scholars attended to the question of hermeneutics: what was the proper method for interpreting Scripture? Scholars who gave explicit attention to the question included Francke, Turretin, Ernesti, Semler, Griesbach, Schleiermacher, Lücke, Wilke, Arnold, and Jowett. For most of these, hermeneutics involved the rules of interpretation—linguistic, grammatical, rhetorical—methods which abetted the literal understanding of the text. With Schleiermacher, hermeneutics was perceived in depth, not as a mere collection of philological principles but as a philosophy of understanding that involved the personal participation of writer and reader. Among the principles that were advocated by most of the hermeneuts was the Reformation dictum of interpreting Scripture by Scripture, sometimes refined by the presumption of a hermeneutical key—the centrality of Christ (Francke, Semler, Arnold, Jowett) or the analogy of faith (Wesley, Turretin, Lessing).

The primary approach that developed and prevailed was the historical-critical method. Already anticipated by Simon, this method was continually expanded and refined. As one of its basic tenets, the historical method opposed the assumption of theological presuppositions. One needed to approach the Scriptures, as Turretin said, with an empty mind. This principle was not only directed against the orthodox who read their ideas into Scripture; it was also turned (e.g., by the Roman Catholics) against the liberals (like Strauss) who presupposed the impossibility of miracles. Historical criticism, which made use of all the philological and historical disciplines, tended to stress the search for the *one* meaning of Scripture, that is, the meaning the original author intended and the original reader understood. Consequently, scholars like Ernesti, Semler, and Jowett were opposed to the search for many meanings in Scripture and, in particular, to allegorical interpretation. By the end of the nineteenth century, the historical-critical method had come to dominate biblical scholarship—even the scholarship of the orthodox and the conservatives.

In the course of the development of hermeneutical theory and practice, qualifications were imposed upon the historical method. Pietists like Francke, Bengel, and Wesley adopted the critical method for establishing the history of the text but insisted that the deeper meaning of Scripture required the possession of the Spirit. Exegetes needed not only the intelligent mind but also the affections—the deep feelings believers share with the Divine Spirit. While scholars like Semler opposed this approach as subjective, Semler's own distinction between religion and theology encouraged a similar inward exegesis. Herder and Lessing insisted that the spirit, not the letter, was important—that the truth of Scripture could be perceived by an intuitive grasp of universal, moral truths. Another approach which was encouraged by this inward and emotional emphasis was the method of ridicule, a subjective way of criticizing Scripture used effectively by the deists and Strauss.

The historical-critical method also adopted refinements that addressed the limitations of the biblical writers. The earlier method of accommodation, developed by Semler, acknowledged that the expressions of Scripture had to conform to the limits of the biblical worldview. Although the people of first-century Palestine believed in demon possession, Jesus did not; but he accommodated his teaching to their limited perspective.

Indeed, the whole idea of revelation in history involved a divine condescension that perceptive apostles like Paul understood. Thus, the intellectual superiority of Jesus and the apostles—the witnesses to the essence
of the biblical message—was affirmed, while the secondary limitations of
Scripture were acknowledged. Similarly, the hermeneutic of myth, developed by Eichhorn, Gabler, G. L. Bauer, and Strauss, could explain the
limited, even mistaken, expressions of the Bible as appropriate and meaningful. This attention to the perspective of the biblical writers also eventuated in F. C. Baur's tendency criticism, the view that the message of the
authors of Scripture was shaped by their theological bias.

Although the trend of NT research throughout this period was toward
a narrow historicizing of the Bible, some scholars insisted on viewing
Scripture as literature. The scholars concerned with hermeneutic, mentioned above, noted the variety of literary genres—Gospels, letters,
Apocalypse—which appeared in the NT. However, with Lessing and
Herder, Scripture was seen as a literary expression of faith, as poetry
and symbol. This line of interpretation was followed by the British roman-
tics. Coleridge opposed the reduction of Scripture to historical data
and doctrine, and he called for viewing the Bible as the expression
of religious imagination. He also noted the inadequacies of human language as a vehicle for communicating divine truth. In all of this, Coleridge
was followed by Thomas Arnold, Arthur Stanley, and Benjamin Jowett.
These British theologians were also determined to apply the deeper religious truths of Scripture to the practical lives of Christians, a concern
advanced by the production of NT commentaries. On the continent,
although with narrower historical emphasis, the practical needs of
preachers and people were also met by commentary series (Olshausen,
Meyer, Lange, Godet).

The results of a century and two-thirds of NT research can be assessed
in terms of lower and higher criticism. The account of the history of text
(lower) criticism is largely a story of unqualified success. The long tradition
of scholars from Mill through Bengel, Wettstein, Griesbach, Lachmann,
and Scholz to the great Tischendorf involved the collection of manuscripts and the development of principles of evaluation. The result was a
reliable, critical text that had abandoned the limitations of the old *textus
receptus* and reproduced the text of the ancient church—a text close to the
original. In regard to higher criticism, a host of scholars had refined the
science of historical introduction: Michaelis, Eichhorn, Schleiermacher,
de Wette, Hilgenfeld, and Hug. These scholars did not agree on all the
issues, but trends had emerged: the non-Pauline authorship of Hebrews;
the unauthenticity of the Pastoral Epistles; the problematic authorship of
the Catholic Epistles, especially 2 Peter and Jude. Of special interest are

Tübingen's attack on the reliability of Acts and Baur's reduction of the authentic Pauline letters to four, a view not even supported by Hilgenfeld. Although the authenticity of the Apocalypse was increasingly questioned (e.g., by Michaelis and de Wette), both Baur and Hilgenfeld argued for Johannine, apostolic authorship. Discussions of the integrity of the NT documents were not extensive, although the view of Semler and Baur that the final chapters of Romans did not belong to the original were generally rejected.

Careful attention was given to the problem of the sources of the gospel tradition. At the beginning of the Enlightenment, most scholars believed the Gospels were all authentic and written in canonical order. Chubb noted that they were anonymous and called for historical investigation. The resulting research produced a variety of answers to the synoptic problem. The hypotheses of an original oral tradition (Gieseler), or a lost *Urgospel* (Eichhorn), or a collection of fragments (Schleiermacher) became less and less attractive. Griesbach's position that Mark used Matthew and Luke was adopted by Paulus and supported—perhaps with negative effect—by the Tübingen school. The two-document hypothesis, advanced by Wilke's extensive argument for the priority of Mark and Weisse's discussion of Mark and the *logia*, was adopted in principle by Ewald and Renan and became increasingly popular. In regard to the Gospel of John, the majority of scholars supported authenticity, a position ably defended by Lücke. However, with Bretschneider and Tayler the critical questions were articulated, and with Strauss and Tübingen, the role of the Fourth Gospel as a historical source was radically diminished.

The results of eighteenth- and early nineteenth-century research can also be seen in the emerging historical reconstructions, especially in regard to Jesus and the early church. Notable lives of Jesus were produced by Reimarus, Paulus, Schleiermacher, Neander, Strauss, Ewald, Renan, and Keim. Of this group, Paulus and Keim were sensitive to the problem of a biography, that is, whether a life of Jesus could actually be written. Perhaps the most obvious trend in this research is the affirmation of the humanity of Jesus and, although there are exceptions (e.g., Olshausen), the rejection of the idea of supernatural birth. Much attention is given to the self-consciousness of Jesus and, in particular, to his understanding of his messianic mission, seen in his use of the title son of man, which is usually taken as a term of humility. Jesus is presented as the ethical teacher of universal spiritual religion (Renan), and, for some (Herder and Lessing), the religion *of* Jesus, not the religion *about* Jesus, is the proper concern. For most of the scholars, Jesus is in some sense the basis for faith—the revelation of God in history or the apex of an evolutionary revelatory process. For some (e.g., Neander), Jesus is the supreme divine miracle that makes all other miracles possible. The underlying assumption is that the Jesus of history and the Christ of faith are one and the same, an assumption explicated by Schleiermacher and demolished by Strauss.

In regard to the history of early Christianity, considerable work has been accomplished. In the course of historical reconstruction, the study of first-century Judaism has tended to be biased. Scholars like Lightfoot and Hilgenfeld have attended to Jewish backgrounds, but the picture of Judaism in the NT period has been influenced by theories of progressive revelation where Christianity is the higher religion, or by efforts to highlight Jesus and the early Christians in contrast to an inferior Jewish backdrop. With Reimarus, on the other hand, Jesus is at home in Judaism, and early Christianity is the unfortunate creation of apostolic fraud. The role of the apostles, particularly Paul, in shaping the history of the church has been debated. As early as Annet, scholars had viewed Paul as the culprit who distorted the religion of Jesus, while scholars like Morgan and Baur saw Paul as the true interpreter of Jesus and the founder of a universal religion. The conflict between the Jewish and gentile factions of the early church was noted as early as Lightfoot and was developed into a principle of historical reconstruction by Semler, a view expanded into a comprehensive pattern of early Christian history by Baur.

In the course of the history of NT research, attention was directed to theological matters. Gabler's distinction between systematic and biblical theology was decisive. Complete NT theologies were written by G. L. Bauer, de Wette, and F. C. Baur; and G. L. Bauer also produced a pioneering work in NT ethics. In the main, these theologians adopted a historical approach: their concern was to reproduce the original theology of the biblical writers. The relevance of these reconstructed theologies required a perception of universal truths that transcended historical limitations and that in the hands of systematic theologians could be applied to modern times (so Gabler); or, the deeper message of the NT—essentially an expression of the divine-human unity—was seen to have a continuity with the philosophical truth of the nineteenth century (so Baur). As to the theological details, traditional doctrines were largely eroded: original sin (e.g., by Jowett), atonement (e.g., by G. L. Bauer), predestination (e.g., by Turretin). The doctrine of plenary verbal inspiration had largely been abandoned, and even conservative scholars were content to argue for historical reliability rather than absolute infallibility. Biblical authority—and even the authority of the NT, which was recognized as higher—had been severely damaged. In its place, scholars affirmed belief in revelation in history, especially in Jesus, to which the NT was the primary record. For some, the NT was witness to a lofty spiritual religion, a faith that transcended the historical limitations of the Bible.

Throughout the history of NT research, a major motif has been announced—the claim that the Bible should be read like any other book. Already articulated by Turretin, Wettstein, and Ernesti, this theme has been played with variations throughout the whole composition. To be sure, scholars like Griesbach, Eichhorn, and Coleridge argued that although the method of interpretation was the same, the NT was in some sense a special book; and Schleiermacher contended that Scripture deserved a particular hermeneutic. Similarly, Jowett claimed that the interpretation of the Bible called for a special sensitivity and believed that the more the NT was read like any other book, the more its uniqueness became apparent. All of these qualifications suggest a distinction between a universal method of interpretation and a particular understanding of the content and quality of the biblical message. However, the question remains as to whether the presumption of the uniqueness of the book compromises the pretended objectivity of the investigation. In any event, the idea of reading the NT like any other book may be more a matter of principle than of practice. When one surveys the enormous amount of energy which has been expended in the study of the Scriptures in the eighteenth and nineteenth centuries, one is forced to conclude that the Bible has been assigned a position of importance which has been ascribed to no other book in the history of Western civilization.

Perceptive readers of this chronicle will have noticed how twentieth-century ideas have been anticipated by these earlier scholars: the theory that parables have one major point of application (Turretin, G. L. Bauer, Wilke); the notion that Onesimus was freed, returned to Paul, and eventually became a bishop (Wesley, Calmet); the thesis that the famine visit (Acts 11:30) is a doublet on the offering visit of Acts 21 (Zeller); the hypothesis that Romans was originally addressed to churches in the East and only a copy was sent to Rome (Renan). Perhaps these examples will suffice to show how extensive NT criticism has been in the period under review: very few problems in lower and higher criticism and very few exegetical issues have been missed. To be sure, new materials, new methods, and new solutions will be proposed, but the major issues of NT research had been articulated by 1870. Unsolved problems, of course, loom large. The question of the sources for the life of Jesus—the problem of the gospel tradition, oral and written—has not been answered; nor has the larger question of the relation of the Jesus of history—the Jesus of historical reconstruction—to the Christ of the believer's faith. This, too, is only a crucial feature of the still larger question: the relation of faith and criticism. Answers to these questions are not readily forthcoming, and, indeed, the quest for final answers may be illusory. New Testament scholarship may have to abandon the hope of final solutions in favor of the more mundane task of interpreting the Scripture for each successive generation. In that effort, the scholars of the eighteenth and nineteenth centuries have left a large legacy of insight, erudition, and untiring devotion.

Bibliography

INTRODUCTION

General Works on the History of New Testament Interpretation

Beiträge zur Geschichte der neutestamentlichen Exegese. Edited by Oscar Cullmann, et al. 30 vols. Tübingen: J.C.B. Mohr, 1955–88.

The Cambridge History of the Bible. 3 vols. Cambridge: Cambridge University Press, 1963–70.

Dugmore, C. W., ed. *The Interpretation of the Bible.* Edward Alleyn Lectures, 1943. London: SPCK, 1944.

Duling, Dennis C. *Jesus Christ through History.* New York: Harcourt Brace Jovanovich, 1979.

Farrar, Frederic W. *The History of Interpretation.* Bampton Lectures, 1885. Grand Rapids: Baker, 1961.

Gilbert, George Holley. *Interpretation of the Bible: A Short History.* New York: Macmillan, 1908.

Grant, Robert, with David Tracy. *A Short History of the Interpretation of the Bible.* 2d rev. ed. Philadelphia: Fortress Press, 1984.

Kissinger, Warren S. *The Lives of Jesus: A History and Bibliography.* New York and London: Garland, 1985.

Meyer, Gottlob Wilhelm. *Geschichte der Schrifterklärung.* Geschichte der Künste und Wissenschaften 11. Theologie 4. Geschichte der Exegese. 5 vols. Göttingen: J. F. Römer, 1802–9.

Rogerson, John, Christopher Rowland, and Barnabas Lindars. *The Study and Use of the Bible.* The History of Christian Theology. Vol. 2. Grand Rapids: Wm. B. Eerdmans, 1988.

Steinmann, Jean. *Biblical Criticism.* Translated by J. R. Foster. Twentieth Century Encyclopedia of Catholicism 63. New York: Hawthorn, 1958.

Walvoord, John F. *Inspiration and Interpretation.* Evangelical Society Publications. Grand Rapids: Wm. B. Eerdmans, 1957.

Wood, James D. *The Interpretation of the Bible: A Historical Introduction.* London: Duckworth, 1958.

The Early Church

Chadwick, Henry. "The Bible and the Greek Fathers." In *The Church's Use of the Bible: Past and Present,* edited by D. E. Nineham, 25–39. London: SPCK, 1963.

Flesseman-van Leer, Ellen. *Tradition and Scripture in the Early Church.* Assen: Van Gorcum, 1953.

Froehlich, Karlfried, ed. *Biblical Interpretation in the Early Church.* Sources of Early Christian Thought. Philadelphia: Fortress Press, 1984.

Gögler, Rolf. *Zur Theologie des biblischen Wortes bei Origenes.* Düsseldorf: Patmos, 1963.

Gorday, Peter. *Principles of Patristic Exegesis: Romans 9–11 in Origen, John Chrysostom, and Augustine.* Studies in the Bible and Early Christianity 4. New York and Toronto: Edwin Mellen Press, 1983.

Hanson, R.P.C. *Allegory and Event: A Study of the Sources and Significance of Origen's Interpretation of Scripture.* Richmond, Va.: John Knox Press, 1959.

Kelly, J.N.D. "The Bible and the Latin Fathers." In *The Church's Use of the Bible: Past and Present,* edited by D. E. Nineham, 41–56. London: SPCK, 1963.

Kugel, James L., and Rowan A. Greer. *Early Biblical Interpretation.* Library of Early Christianity. Philadelphia: Westminster Press, 1986.

Smith, Harold. *Ante-Nicene Exegesis of the Gospels.* Translations of Christian Literature, Series 6. 6 vols. London: SPCK, 1925–29.

Strauss, Gerhard. *Schriftgebrauch, Schriftauslegung und Schriftbeweis bei Augustin.* Beiträge zur Geschichte der biblischen Hermeneutik 1. Tübingen: J.C.B. Mohr, 1959.

Trigg, Joseph W. *Biblical Interpretation.* Message of the Fathers of the Church 9. Wilmington, Del.: Michael Glazier, 1988.

Wiles, Maruice F. *The Divine Apostle: The Interpretation of St. Paul Epistles in the Early Church.* Cambridge: Cambridge University Press, 1967.

The Middle Ages

Evans, G. R. *The Language and Logic of the Bible: The Earlier Middle Ages.* Cambridge: Cambridge University Press, 1984.

Lubac, Henri de. *Exégèse médiévale: les quatre sens de l'écriture.* Théologie 41, 42, 59. 4 vols. Paris: Aubier, 1959–64.

McNally, Robert E. *The Bible in the Early Middle Ages.* Woodstock Papers: Occasional Essays for Theology 4. Westminster, Md.: Newman, 1959.

Smalley, Beryl. *The Study of the Bible in the Middle Ages.* New York: Philosophical Library, 1952.

———. "The Bible in the Middle Ages." In *The Church's Use of the Bible: Past and Present,* edited by D. E. Nineham, 57–71. London: SPCK, 1963.

Renaissance and Reformation

Baroni, Victor. *La contre-réforme devant la bible: la question biblique.* Lausanne: Concorde, 1943.

Bentley, Jerry H. *Humanists and Holy Writ: New Testament Scholarship in the Renaissance.* Princeton, N.J.: Princeton University Press, 1983.

Forstman, H. Jackson. *Word and Spirit: Calvin's Doctrine of Biblical Authority.* Stanford, Calif.: Stanford University Press, 1962.

Fullerton, Kemper. *Prophecy and Authority: A Study in the History of the Doctrine and Intepretation of Scripture.* New York: Macmillan, 1919.

Gerrish, B. A. "Biblical Authority and the Continental Reformation." *Scottish Journal of Theology* 10 (1957): 337–60.

Klug, Eugene F. A. *From Luther to Chemnitz: On Scripture and the Word.* Kampen, Netherlands: J. H. Kok, 1971.

Lehmann, Paul L. "The Reformers' Use of the Bible." *Theology Today* 3 (1947): 328-44.

Oswald, Hilton C., and George S. Robbert, eds. *Luther as Interpreter of Scripture: A Source Collection of Illustrative Samples from the Expository Works of the Reformer in* Luther's Works: *American Edition.* St. Louis: Concordia, 1982.

Parker, T.H.L. *Calvin's New Testament Commentaries.* London: SCM Press, 1971.

Pelikan, Jaroslav. *Luther the Expositor.* Luther's Works, Companion Volume. St. Louis: Concordia, 1959.

Rabil, Albert, Jr. *Erasmus and the New Testament: The Mind of a Christian Humanist.* Trinity University Monograph Series in Religion 1. San Antonio, Tex.: Trinity University Press, 1972.

Reu, J. M. *Luther and the Scriptures.* Columbus, Ohio: Wartburg Press, 1944.

Rummel, Erika. *Erasmus'* Annotations *on the New Testament: From Philologist to Theologian.* Erasmus Studies. Toronto: University of Toronto Press, 1986.

Rupp, E. G. "The Bible in the Age of the Reformation." In *The Church's Use of the Bible: Past and Present,* edited by D. E. Nineham, 73–87. London: SPCK, 1963.

The Modern Period

Brown, Colin. *Jesus in European Protestant Thought: 1778–1860.* Grand Rapids: Baker, 1988.

Drury, John, ed. *Critics of the Bible: 1724–1873.* Cambridge: Cambridge University Press, 1989.

Frei, Hans W. *The Eclipse of Biblical Narrative: A Study in Eighteenth and Nineteenth Century Hermeneutics.* New Haven and London: Yale University Press, 1974.

Genthe, H. J. *Kleine Geschichte der neutestamentlichen Wissenschaft.* Göttingen: Vandenhoeck & Ruprecht, 1977.

Hunter, A. M. *Interpreting the New Testament: 1900–1950.* London: SCM Press, 1951.

Kümmel, Werner Georg. *The New Testament: The History of the Investigation of Its Problems.* Translated by S. M. Gilmour and H. C. Kee. Nashville and New York: Abingdon Press, 1972.

Morgan, Robert, with John Barton. *Biblical Interpretation.* Oxford Bible Series. Oxford: Oxford University Press, 1988.

Neill, Stephen, and Tom Wright. *The Interpretation of the New Testament: 1861–1986.* 2d ed. Oxford and New York: Oxford University Press, 1988.

O'Neill, J. C. *The Bible's Authority: A Portrait Gallery of Thinkers from Lessing to Bultmann.* Edinburgh: T. & T. Clark, 1991.

Reventlow, Henning Graf. *The Authority of the Bible and the Rise of the Modern World.* Translated by John Bowden. Philadelphia: Fortress Press, 1984.

Schweitzer, Albert. *The Quest of the Historical Jesus: A Critical Study of Its Progress from Reimarus to Wrede.* Translated by W. Montgomery. New York: Macmillan, 1957.

I. BACKGROUNDS AND BEGINNINGS

Formative Factors

Becker, Carl. *The Heavenly City of the Eighteenth Century Philosophers.* New Haven: Yale University Press, 1942.

Butterfield, Herbert. *The Origins of Modern Science, 1300–1800.* New York: Macmillan, 1981.

Cassirer, Ernst. *The Philosophy of the Enlightenment.* Princeton: Princeton University Press, 1951.

Cragg, Gerald R. *The Church and the Age of Reason 1648–1789.* Pelican History of the Church 4. London: Penguin, 1967.

———. *Reason and Authority in the Eighteenth Century.* Cambridge: Cambridge University Press, 1964.

Durant, Will, and Ariel Durant. *The Age of Louis XIV: A History of European Civilization in the Period of Pascal, Molière, Cromwell, Milton, Peter the Great, Newton, and Spinoza: 1648–1715.* The Story of Civilization 8. New York: Simon & Schuster, 1963.

———. *The Age of Voltaire: A History of Civilization in Western Europe from 1715 to 1756, with Special Emphasis on the Conflict between Religion and Philosophy.* The Story of Civilization 9. New York: Simon & Schuster, 1965.

———. *Rousseau and Revolution: A History of Civilization in France, England, and Germany from 1756, and in the Remainder of Europe from 1715 to 1789.* The Story of Civilization 10. New York: Simon & Schuster, 1967.

Gay, Peter. *The Enlightenment: An Interpretation.* New York: Alfred A. Knopf, 1968.

Hampson, Norman. *The Enlightenment.* Pelican History of European Thought. New York: Viking Penguin, 1982.

Hazard, Paul. *European Thought in the Eighteenth Century.* New Haven: Yale University Press, 1954.

Held, Julius S., and Donald Posner. *Seventeenth and Eighteenth Century Art: Baroque Painting, Sculpture, Architecture.* New York: Harry N. Abrams, 1971.

Redwood, John. *Reason, Ridicule and Religion: The Age of Enlightenment in England 1660-1750.* Cambridge: Harvard University Press, 1976.

Rudé, George. *Europe in the Eighteenth Century: Aristocracy and the Bourgeois Challenge.* Cambridge: Harvard University Press, 1985.

Solomon, Robert C. *History and Human Nature: A Philosophical Review of European Philosophy and Culture, 1750–1850.* New York and London: Harcourt Brace Jovanovich, 1979.

White, R. J. *Europe in the Eighteenth Century.* New York: St. Martin's Press, 1965.

Precursors

General Surveys

Meyer, Gottlob Wilhelm. *Geschichte der Schrifterklärung.* Vol. 3. Geschichte der Künste und Wissenschaften 11. Theologie 4. Geschichte der Exegese. Göttingen: J. F. Römer, 1804.

Reedy, Gerard, S.J. *The Bible and Reason: Anglicans and Scripture in Late Seventeenth-Century England.* Philadelphia: University of Pennsylvania Press, 1985.

Reventlow, Henning Graf. *The Authority of the Bible and the Rise of the Modern World.* Translated by John Bowden. Philadelphia: Fortress Press, 1985.

Scholder, Klaus. *Ursprünge und Probleme der Bibelkritik im 17. Jahrhundert: Ein Beitrag zur Entstehung der historisch-kritischen Theologie.* Forschungen zur Geschichte und Lehre des Protestantismus. Series 10, vol. 23. Munich: Chr. Kaiser, 1966.

Spinoza, Baruch. *Tractatus theologico-politicus.* Translated by Samuel Shirley. Leiden: E. J. Brill, 1989.

Strauss, Leo. *Spinoza's Critique of Religion.* Translated by E. M. Sinclair. New York: Schocken Books, 1956.

Zac, Sylvain. *Spinoza et l'interprétation de l'écriture.* Bibliothéque de philosophie contemporaine. Paris: Presses Universitaires de France, 1965.

Grotius

Primary Sources

Grotius, Hugo. *Annotationes in Novum Testamentum.* 2d rev. ed. 9 vols., plus index volume. Gronigen: W. Zuidema, 1826.

———. *The Truth of the Christian Religion.* Translated by John Clarke. Cambridge: J. Hall, 1860.

Secondary Sources

Freiday, Dean. *The Bible: Its Criticism, Interpretation and Use in Sixteenth and Seventeenth Century England.* Catholic and Quaker Studies 4. Pittsburgh, 1979.

Knight, W.S.M. *The Life and Works of Hugo Grotius.* Grotius Society Publications 4. London: Sweet & Maxwell, 1925.

Lysen, A., ed. *Hugo Grotius: Essays on His Life and Works.* Leyden: A. W. Sythoff, 1925.

Sotirovich, Vasilije M. "Divine Law in the Main Works of Hugo Grotius: An Interpretation." M.A. thesis, University of Chicago, 1957.

Voeltzel, René. "La Méthode théologique de Hugo Grotius." *Revue d'histoire et de philosophie religieuses* 32 (1952): 126–33.

Lightfoot

Primary Sources

Lightfoot, John [Lightfoote, John]. *A Commentary upon the Acts of the Apostles: Chronicall and Criticall.* London: A. Crooke, 1645.

———. [Lightfoote, John]. *Harmony of the Foure Evangelists: Among Themselves, and with the Old Testament.* London: A. Crooke, 1644.

———. *Horae Hebraicae et Talmudicae: Hebrew and Talmudical Exercitations.* Edited by Robert Gandell. 4 vols. Oxford: Oxford University Press, 1859.

———. *The Temple Service as it stood in the dayes of our Saviour.* London: A. Crooke, 1644.

Secondary Sources

Dalman, Gustaf. "In the Footsteps of John Lightfoot." *Expository Times* 35 (1923–24): 71-73.

Simon

Major Bibliography

Auvray, Paul. *Richard Simon (1638–1712): Etude bio-bibliographique avec des textes inédits.* Le Mouvement des idées au XVII siècle 8. Paris: Presses Universitaires de France, 1974.

Primary Sources

Simon, Richard. *Critical Enquiries into the Various Editions of the Bible.* Translated by N.S. London: T. Braddyll, 1684.

————. *Histoire critique des principaux commentateurs du Nouveau Testament, depuis le commencement du christianisme jusqu'à; notre tems, avec une Dissertation critique sur lex principaux actes manuscrits qui ont été cités dans les trois parties de cet óuvrage. Par Richard Simon, prêtre.* Rotterdam: R. Leers, 1693.

————. *Histoire critique du texte du Nouveau Testament, où l'on établit la vérité des actes sur lesquels la Religion chrétienne est fondée, par Richard Simon, prêtre.* Rotterdam: R. Leers, 1689. English translation: *A Critical History of the Text of the New Testament.* London: R. Taylor, 1689.

————. *Histoire critique des versions du Nouveau Testament, où l'on fait connaître quel a été l'usage de la lecture des Livres sacrés dans les principales Églises du monde, par Richard Simon, prêtre.* Rotterdam: R. Leers, 1690. English translation: *The Critical History of the Versions of the New Testament.* London: Newborough & Bennet, 1692.

————. *The New Testament of Our Saviour Jesus Christ; According to the Latin Edition: With Critical Remarks upon the Literal Meaning in Difficult Places.* Translated by W. Webster. 2 vols. London: J. Pemberted and C. Rivington, 1730.

Secondary Sources

Beaude, Pierre-Marie. "L'Accomplissement des prophéties chez Richard Simon." *Revue des sciences philosophiques et théologiques* 60 (1976): 3–35.

de Certeau, Michel. "L'Idée de traduction de la Bible au xviième siècle: Sacy et Simon." *Recherches de science religieuse* 66 (1978): 73–92.

Denis, M. Jacques. *Critique et controverse ou Richard Simon et Bossuet.* Caen: F. Le Blanc-Hardel, 1870.

Freiday, Dean. *The Bible: Its Criticism, Interpretation and Use in Sixteenth and Seventeenth Century England.* Catholic and Quaker Studies 4. Pittsburgh, 1979.

Lambe, Patrick J. "Biblical Criticism and Censorship in Ancien Régime France: The Case of Richard Simon." *Harvard Theological Review* 17 (1985): 149–77.

Le Brun, Jacques. "Meaning and Scope of the Return to Origins in Richard Simon's Work." *Trinity Journal* 3 (1982): 57–70.

Margival, Henri. *Essai sur Richard Simon et la critique biblique au XVII siècle.* Geneva: Slatkine Reprints, 1970.

Reventlow, Henning Graf. "Richard Simon und seine Bedeutung für die kritische Erforschung der Bibel." In *Historische Kritik in der Theologie: Beiträge zu ihrer Geschichte,* edited by Georg Schwaiger, 11–36. Studien zur Theologie und Geistesgeschichte des Neunzehnten Jahrhunderts 32. Göttingen: Vandenhoeck & Ruprecht, 1980.

Steinmann, Jean. *Richard Simon et les origines de l'exégèse biblique.* Paris: Desclée de Brouwer, 1960.

Woodbridge, John D. "German Responses to the Biblical Critic Richard Simon: From Leibnitz to J. S. Semler." In *Historische Kritik und biblischer Kanon in der deutschen Aufklärung,* edited by H. G. Reventlow, W. Sparn, and J. Woodbridge, 65–87. Wiesbaden: Harrassowitz, 1988.

Text Criticism

General Surveys of the History of
Text Criticism

Metzger, Bruce M. *The Text of the New Testament: Its Transmission, Corruption, and Restoration.* 2d ed. Oxford and New York: Oxford University Press, 1968.

Scrivener, Frederick H. *A Plain Introduction to the Criticism of the New Testament.* 2d ed. Cambridge: Deighton, Bell, & Co., 1874.

Vincent, Marvin R. *A History of the Textual Criticism of the New Testament.* New Testament Handbooks. New York: Macmillan, 1899.

Mill and Bentley

Primary Sources

Mill, John. *Novum Testamentum. Cum lectionibus variantibus MSS. exemplarium, versionum, editionum, SS. Patrum et Scriptorum ecclesiasticorum; et in easdem notis.* Oxford: Sheldonian, 1707.

————. *Novum Testamentum.* Edited by Ludolph Küster. Rotterdam: C. Fritsch and M. Böhm, 1710.

Secondary Sources

Bristol, Lyle O. "New Testament Textual Criticism in the Eighteenth Century." *Journal of Biblical Literature* 69 (1950): 101–12.

Fox, Adam. *John Mill and Richard Bentley: A Study of the Textual Criticism of the New Testament 1675–1729.* Oxford: Basil Blackwell, 1954.

White, R. J. *Dr. Bentley: A Study in Academic Scarlet.* East Lansing: Michigan State University Press, 1968.

2. THE ATTACK ON REVEALED RELIGION:
THE ENGLISH DEISTS

General Works on Deism

Gay, Peter. *Deism: An Anthology.* Princeton, N.J.: Van Nostrand, 1968.

Leland, John. *A View of the Principal Deistical Writers that have Appeared in England in the last and present Century.* 3 vols. London: B. Dod, 1756.

Orr, John. *English Deism: Its Roots and Its Fruits.* Grand Rapids: Wm. B. Eerdmans, 1935.

Pike, E. Royston. *Slavers of Superstition: A Popular Account of Some of the Leading Personalities of the Deist Movement.* Port Washington, N.Y., and London: Kennikat, 1931.

Reventlow, Henning Graf. *The Authority of the Bible and the Rise of the Modern World.* Translated by John Bowden. Philadelphia: Fortress Press, 1984.

Stephen, Leslie. *History of English Thought in the Eighteenth Century.* 2 vols. Harbinger Book. New York: Harcourt, Brace & World, 1962.

Waring, E. Graham, ed. *Deism and Natural Religion: A Source Book.* Milestones of Thought. New York: F. Ungar, 1967.

Locke

Primary Sources

Locke, John. *The Reasonableness of Christianity.* Edited by I. T. Ramsey. Library of Modern Religious Thought. Stanford, Calif.: Stanford University Press, 1858.

————. *John Locke: A Paraphrase and Notes on the Epistles of St. Paul to the Galatians, 1 and 2 Corinthians, Romans, Ephesians.* Edited by Arthur W. Wainwright. 2 vols. Clarendon Edition of the Works of John Locke. Oxford: Clarendon Press, 1987.

Secondary Sources

Attig, John C. *The Works of John Locke: A Comprehensive Bibliography from the Seventeenth Century to the Present.* Bibliographies and Indexes in Philosophy 1. Westport, Conn., and London: Greenwood, 1985.

Biddle, John C. "John Locke's Essay on Infallibility: Introduction, Text, and Translation." *Journal of Church and State* 19 (1977): 301–27.

Cranston, Maurice. *John Locke: A Biography.* New York: Macmillan, 1957.

Hefelbower, S. G. *The Relation of John Locke to English Deism.* Chicago: University of Chicago Press, 1918.

Squadrito, Kathleen. *John Locke.* Twayne's English Authors 271. Boston: Twayne, 1979.

The Deists

Primary Sources

Annet, Peter. *The History and Character of St. Paul, examined: In a Letter to Theophilus, a Christian Friend.* London: F. Page, n.d.

————. *The Resurrection of Jesus Considered; in Answer to the Tryal of the Witnesses,* By a Moral Philosopher. London: Author, n.d.

Chubb, Thomas. *The Comparative Excellence and Obligation of Moral and Positive Duties, 1730.* New York and London: Garland, 1978.

————. *A Discourse Concerning Reason, 1731.* Reprint. New York and London: Garland, 1978.

————. *The True Gospel of Jesus Christ Asserted.* London: T. Cox, 1738.

Collins, Anthony. *A Discourse of the Grounds and Reasons of the Christian Religion.* British Philosophers of the Seventeenth and Eighteenth Centuries. 1724. Reprint. New York and London: Garland, 1976.

Morgan, Thomas. *The Moral Philosopher.* 3 vols. Edited by G. Gawlick. Stuttgart-Bad Cannstatt: F. Frommann, 1969.

Sherlock, Bishop. *The Trial of the Witnesses to the Resurrection of Christ: In Answer to the Objections of Mr. Woolston and Others.* New York: Lane & Scott, 1849.

Tindal, Matthew. *Christianity as Old as the Creation.* Edited by G. Gawlick. Stuttgart-Bad Cannstatt: F. Frommann, 1967.

Toland, John. *Christianity Not Mysterious.* Stuttgart-Bad Canstatt: F. Frommann, 1964.

Woolston, Thomas. *Six Discourses on the Miracles of Our Saviour and Defences of His Discourses, 1727–1730.* British Philosophers and Theologians of the Seventeenth and Eighteenth Centuries. New York and London: Garland, 1979.

Secondary Sources

Bushell, T. L. *The Sage of Salisbury: Thomas Chubb, 1679-1747.* New York: Philosophical Library, 1967.

Craig, William Lane. *The Historical Argument for the Resurrection of Jesus during the Deist Controversy.* Texts and Studies in Religion 23. Lewiston, N.Y.: Edwin Mellen Press, 1985.

Reedy, Gerard. "Socinians, John Toland, and the Anglican Rationalists." *Harvard Theological Review* 70 (1977): 285–304.

Sullivan, Robert E. *John Toland and the Deist Controversy: A Study in Adaptations.* Harvard Historical Studies. Cambridge, Mass., and London: Harvard University Press, 1982.

3. SENSITIVE TO THE SPIRIT: THE PIETISTS

Background on Protestant Orthodoxy

Preus, Robert D. *The Theology of Post-Reformation Lutheranism: A Study of Theological Prolegomena.* St. Louis: Concordia, 1970.

Rogers, Jack B., and Donald K. McKim. *The Authority and Interpretation of the Bible: An Historical Approach,* 147–99. San Francisco: Harper & Row, 1979.

General Works on Pietism

Aland, Kurt, ed. *Pietismus und Bibel.* Arbeiten zur Geschichte des Pietismus 9. Witten: Luther-Verlag, 1970.

Beyreuther, Erich. *Geschichte des Pietismus.* Stuttgart: J. F. Steinkopf, 1978.

Bornkamm, H., F. Heyer, and A. Schindler, eds. *Der Pietismus in Gestalten und Wirkungen: Martin Schmidt zum 65. Geburtstag.* Arbeiten zur Geschichte des Pietismus 14. Bielefeld: Luther-Verlag, 1975.

Brown, Dale W. *Understanding Pietism.* Grand Rapids: Wm. B. Eerdmans, 1978.

Erb, Peter C., ed. *Pietists: Selected Writings.* Classics of Western Spirituality. New York: Paulist Press, 1983.

Greschat, Martin, ed. *Orthodoxie und Pietismus.* Gestalten der Kirchengeschichte 7. Stuttgart: Kohlhammer, 1982.

———, ed. *Zur neueren Pietismusforschung.* Wege der Forschung 440. Darmstadt: Wissenschaftliche Buchgesellschaft, 1977.

Groth, Friedhelm. *Die "Wiederbringung aller Dinge" im württembergischen Pietismus: Theologiegeschichtliche Studien zum eschatologischen Heilsuniversalismus württembergischer Pietisten des 18. Jahrhunderts.* Arbeiten zur Geschichte des Pietismus 21. Göttingen: Vandenhoeck & Ruprecht, 1984.

Kantzenbach, Friedrich Wilhelm. *Orthodoxie und Pietismus.* Evangelische Enzyklopädie 11/12. Gütersloh: G. Mohn, 1966.

Leube, Hans. *Orthodoxie und Pietismus: Gesammelte Studien.* Arbeiten zur Geschichte des Pietismus 13. Bielefeld: Luther-Verlag, 1975.

Ritschl, Albrecht. *Geschichte des Pietismus.* 3 vols. Bonn: A. Marcus, 1884.

Schmidt, Martin. *Pietismus.* 2d ed. Stuttgart: Kohlhammer, 1978.

———. *Wiedergeburt und neuer Mensch: Gesammelte Studien zur Geschichte des Pietismus.* Arbeiten zur Geschichte des Pietismus 2. Witten: Luther-Verlag, 1969.

Stoeffler, F. Ernest. *German Pietism during the Eighteenth Century.* Studies in the History of Religions 24. Leiden: E. J. Brill, 1973.

———. *The Rise of Evangelical Pietism.* Studies in the History of Religions 9. Leiden: E. J. Brill, 1971.

Stroh, Hans. "Hermeneutik im Pietismus." *Zeitschrift für Theologie und Kirche* 77 (1977): 38–57.

Wallmann, Johannes. *Der Pietismus.* Die Kirche in ihrer Geschichte 4. Göttingen: Vandenhoeck & Ruprecht, 1990.

Beginnings of the Pietist Movement: Spener

Primary Sources

Spener, Philip Jacob. *Pia Desideria.* Translated by T. G. Tappert. Seminar Editions. Philadelphia: Fortress Press, 1964.

Secondary Sources

Wallmann, Johannes. *Philipp Jakob Spener und die Anfänge des Pietismus.* Beiträge zur historischen Theologie 42. Tübingen: J.C.B. Mohr, 1970.

Principles of Interpretation: Francke

Primary Sources

Francke, August Hermann. *A Guide to the Reading and Study of the Holy Scriptures.* Translated by William Jaques. Philadelphia: D. Hogan, 1823.

———. *Werke in Auswahl.* Edited by Erhard Peschke. Berlin: Evangelische Verlagsanstalt, 1969.

Secondary Sources

Beyreuther, Erich. *August Hermann Francke, 1663–1727: Zeuge des lebendigen Gottes.* Marburg: Francke-Buchhandlung, 1956.

Bunke, Ernst. *August Hermann Francke: Der Mann des Glaubens und der Liebe.* 2d ed. Zeugen des gegenwärtigen Gottes 144/145. Giessen and Basel: Brunnen, 1960.

Kurten, Petra. *Umkehr zum lebendigen Gott: Die Bekehrungstheologie August Hermann Franckes als Beitrag zur Erneuerung des Glaubens.* Paderborner Theologische Studien 15. Paderborn: F. Schöningh, 1985.

Peschke, Erhard. *Studien zur Theologie August Hermann Franckes.* 2 vols. Berlin: Evangelische Verlagsanstalt, 1964–66.

———. "Zur Hermeneutik A. H. Franckes." *Theologische Literaturzeitung* 89 (1964): 98–110.

Sattler, Gary R. *God's Glory, Neighbor's Good: A Brief Introduction to the Life and Writings of August Hermann Francke.* Chicago: Covenant, 1982.

Text Criticism and Exegesis: Bengel

Primary Sources

Bengel, Johann Albrecht. *Erklärte Offenbarung Johannis oder vielmehr JEsu Christi. Aus dem revidirten Grunde-Text übersetz durch die prophetische Zahlen aufgeschlossen und allen, die auf des Werk und Wort des Herrn achten, und dem, was vor der Thür ist, würdiglich entgegen zu kommen begehren, vor Augen gelegt durch Johann Albrecht Bengel*. Edited by Wilhelm Hoffmann. Stuttgart: Brodhag, 1834.

————. [Bengel, John Albert]. *Gnomon of the New Testament*. Translated by J. Bandinel and A. R. Fausset. Edited by A. R. Fausset. 5 vols. 6th ed. Edinburgh: T. & T. Clark, 1866.

————. Η ΚΑΙΝΗ ΔΙΑΘΗΚΗ *Novum Testamentum Graecum ita adornatum ut Textus probatarum editionum medullam. Margo variantium lectionum in suas classes distributarum locorumque parallelorum delectum. Apparatus subiunctus criseos sacrae Millianae praesertim compendium, limam, supplementum ac fructum exhibeat inserviente Io. Alberto Bengelio*. Tübingen: G. Cotta, 1734.

————. *Die Offenbarung des Johannes*. Edited by Berthold Burbacher. Metzingen/Württ.: E. Franz, 1975.

————. [Io. Alberti Bengeli]. *Ordo temporum a principio per periodos oeconomiae divinae historicas atque propheticas ad finem usque ita deductus ut tota a series et quarumvis partium analogia semperiternae virtutis ac sapientiae cultoribus ex scriptura V. et N.T. tanquam uno revera documento proponatur*. Stuttgart: C. Erhard, 1741.

————. *Richtige Harmonie der Vier Evangelisten da die Geschichten, Wercke und Reden JEsu Christi unsers HErrn, in ihrer geziemend natürlichen Ordnung zur Befestigung, der Warheit, wie auch zur Ubung und Erbauung in der Gottseeligkeit vorgestellet-werden*. Tübingen: C. H. Berger, 1736.

————. *Sechzig erbauliche Reden über die Offenbarung Johannis, oder vielmehr Jesu Christi*. 3d ed. Edited by J.C.F. Burk. Stuttgart: Brodhag, 1758.

Secondary Sources

Brecht, Martin. "Johann Albrecht Bengels Theologie der Schrift." *Zeitschrift für Theologie und Kirche* 64 (1967): 99–120.

Burk, John Christian Frederic. *A Memoir of the Life and Writings of John Albert Bengel*. Translated by R. F. Walker. London: W. Ball, 1837.

Fritsch, Charles T. "Bengel, the Student of Scripture." *Interpretation* 5 (1951): 203–15.

Hehl, Werner. *Johann Albrecht Bengel: Leben und Werk*. Stuttgart: Quell, 1987.

Ludwig, Ernst. *Schriftverständnis und Schriftauslegung bei Johann Albrecht Bengel*. Sonderheft der Blätter für württ. Kirchengeschichte. Stuttgart: C. Scheufele, 1952.

Mälzer, Gottfried. *Bengel und Zinzendorf: Zur Biographie und Theologie Johann Albrecht Bengels*. Arbeiten zur Geschichte des Pietismus 3. Witten: Luther-Verlag, 1968.

————. *Johann Albrecht Bengel: Leben und Werk*. Stuttgart: Calwer, 1970.

Sauter, Gerhard. "Die Zahl als Schlüssel zur Welt: Johann Albrecht Bengels prophetische Zeitrechnung' im Zusammenhang seiner Theologie." *Evangelische Theologie* 26 (1966): 1–36.

The Evangelical Movement and
New Testament Research in England: Wesley

Primary Sources

Burtner, Robert W., and Robert E. Chiles, eds. *A Compend of Wesley's Theology*. New York and Nashville: Abingdon Press, 1954.

Wesley, John. *Explanatory Notes upon the New Testament*. London: Epworth Press, 1976.

————. *The Works of John Wesley*. 14 vols. Grand Rapids: Zondervan, 1872.

————. *The Works of John Wesley: Sermons.* Edited by Albert C. Outler. 4 vols. Nashville: Abingdon Press, 1984.

Secondary Sources

Arnett, William M. "John Wesley and the Bible." *Wesleyan Theology Journal* 3 (1968): 3–9.

Baker, Frank. "John Wesley, Biblical Commentator." *Bulletin of the John Rylands University Library of Manchester* 71 (1989): 109–20.

Clapper, Gregory S. *John Wesley on Religious Affections: His View on Experience and Emotion and Their Role in the Christian Life and Theology.* Pietist and Wesleyan Studies 1. Metuchen, N.J., and London: Scarecrow, 1989.

Deschner, John. *Wesley's Christology: An Interpretation.* Dallas, Tex.: Southern Methodist University Press, 1960.

Garrison, R. Benjamin. "Vital Interaction: Scripture and Experience. John Wesley's Doctrine of Authority." *Religion in Life* 25 (1956): 563–73.

Lee, Umphrey. *John Wesley and Modern Religion.* Nashville: Cokesbury, 1936.

Mullen, Wilbur H. "John Wesley's Method of Biblical Interpretation." *Religion in Life* 47 (1978): 99–108.

Rowe, Kenneth E., ed. *The Place of Wesley in the Christian Tradition: Essays Delivered at Drew University in Celebration of the Commencement of the Publication of the Oxford Edition of the Works of John Wesley.* Metuchen, N.J.: Scarecrow, 1976.

Scroggs, Robin. "John Wesley as Bible Scholar." *Journal of Bible and Religion* 28 (1960): 415–22.

Shelton, Larry. "John Wesley's Approach to Scripture in Historical Perspective." *Wesleyan Theology Journal* 16 (1981): 23–50.

Smith, Timothy L. "John Wesley and the Wholeness of Scripture." *Interpretation* 39 (1985): 246–62.

Stokes, Mack B. *The Bible in the Wesleyan Heritage.* New York and Nashville: Abingdon Press, 1979.

Williams, Colin W. *John Wesley's Theology Today.* New York and Nashville: Abingdon Press, 1960.

Wynkoop, Mildred Bangs. *A Theology of Love: The Dynamic of Wesleyanism.* Kansas City, Mo.: Beacon Hill, 1972.

4. DEFINING HISTORICAL RESEARCH: METHODS OF INTERPRETATION

General Works

Aner, Karl. *Die Theologie der Lessingzeit.* Hildesheim: G. Olms, 1964.

Cotoni, Helene. *L'Exégèse du Nouveau Testament dans la philosophie française du dix-huitième siècle.* Studies on Voltaire and the Eighteenth Century 220. Oxford: Voltaire Foundation, 1984.

Frei, Hans W. *The Eclipse of Biblical Narrative: A Study in Eighteenth and Nineteenth Century Hermeneutics.* New Haven and London: Yale University Press, 1974.

Hurst, John F. *History of Rationalism.* 9th rev. ed. New York: Nelson & Phillips, 1865.

Moderate Rationalism in Switzerland

General Works

Good, James I. *History of the Swiss Reformed Church since the Reformation.* Philadelphia: Publication and Sunday School Board of the Reformed Church in the U.S., 1913.

Turretin

Primary Sources

Turretin, John Alphonse [Turretine, John Alphonso]. *Dissertations on Revealed Religion.* Translated by W. Crawford. Belfast: J. Magee, 1778.

———. [Turretino, Joh. Alphonso]. *Oratio de componendis protestantium dissidiis, dicta statis Academiae Genevensis, solemnibus idibus Jun. MDCCVII.* London: W. Tayler, 1709.

———. [Turrettini, Joh. Alphonsi]. *Opera omnia, theologica, philosophica et philologica.* 3 vols. Leovardiae et Franequerae: H. A. de Chalmot et D. Romar, 1775. Vol. 2.

Secondary Sources

Beardslee, John Walter. *Theological Development at Geneva under Francis and Jean-Alphonse Turretin (1648–1737).* Ph.D. diss., Yale University, 1956; Ann Arbor, Mich.: University Microfilms, 1965.

de Bude, E. *Vie de J.-A. Turrettini: Theologien Genevois, 1671–1737.* Lausanne: G. Bridel, 1880.

Geiger, Max. "Die Unionsbestrebungen der schweizerischen reformierten Theologie unter der Führung des helvetischen Triumvirates." *Theologische Zeitschrift* 9 (1953): 117–36.

Heyd, Michael. "Un rôle nouveau pour la science: Jean-Alphonse Turrettini et les débuts de la théologie naturelle à Genève." *Revue de théologie et de philosophie* 112 (1980): 25–42.

Merk, Otto. "Jean-Alphonse Turretini zu Johann Jakob Wettstein." In *Historische Kritik und biblischer Kanon in der deutschen Aufklärung,* edited by H. G. Reventlow, W. Sparn, and J. Woodbridge, 89–112. Wolfenbütteler Forschungen 41. Wiesbaden: Harrassowitz, 1988.

Wettstein

Primary Sources

Wettstein, Johann Jakob. ΚΑΙΝΗ ΔΙΑΘΗΚΗ. *Novum Testamentum Graecum edionis receptae cum lectionibus variantibus codicum MSS. Editionum aliarum. Versionum et Patrum nec non commentario plenoire. Ex Scriptoribus veteribus Hebraeis, Graecis et Latinus. Historiam et vim verborun illustrante opera et studio Joannis Jacobi Wettenii.* 2 vols. Amsterdam: Dommerian, 1751–52. Reprint, Graz, Austria: Akademische Druck-u. Verlagsanstalt, 1962.

———. *Prolegomena ad Novi Testamenti Graeci editionem accuratissimam. E. Vetustissimus Codd. MSS, denuo procurandam: in Quibus agitur De Codd., MSS. N. Testamenti, Scriptoribus Graecis, qui N. Testamento usi sunt. Versionibus veteribus. Editionibus prioribus & claris Interpretibus: & proponuntur Animadversiones & Cautiones ad*

Examen Variarum Lectionum N.T. necessariae. Amsterdam: R. & J. Wettstein and G. Smith, 1730.

Secondary Sources

Hulbert-Powell, C. L. *John James Wettstein, 1693–1754: An Account of His Life, Work, and Some of His Contemporaries.* London: SPCK, 1937.

Miller, J. I. "Wettstein or Wetstein." *Journal of Theological Studies* 28 (1977): 118–19.

Ernesti

Primary Sources

Ernesti, Johann August. *Anmerkungen über die Bücher des neuen Testaments.* Leipzig and Quedlinburg: C. A. Reussner, 1786.

———. [Ernesti, Ioannis Augusti]. *Institutio interpretis Novi Testamenti.* 4th ed. Edited by C. F. Ammon. Leipzig: Weidmann, 1792. English translation: J. A. Ernesti, *Principles of Biblical Interpretation.* 2 vols. Translated by Charles H. Terrot. Edinburgh: T. Clark, 1832. Abbreviated English version: J. A. Ernesti, *Elements of Interpretation.* Translated by Moses Stuart. Andover, Mass.: Flagg & Gould, 1822.

———. *Lectiones academicae in epistolam ad Hebraeos, ab ipso revisae cum eiusdem excursibus theologicus, edidit commentarium in quo multa ad recentissimorum inprimus interpretum sententias pertinentia uberius illustrantur.* Edited by Gottlib Immanuel Dindorf. Leipzig: C. Fritsch, 1795.

Secondary Sources

Minear, Paul. "J. S. Bach and J. A. Ernesti: A Case Study in Exegetical and Theological Conflict." In *Our Common History as Christians: Essays in Honor of Albert C. Outler,* edited by J. Deschner, L. T. Howe, and K. Penzel, 131–55. New York: Oxford University Press, 1975.

Stevenson, Robert. "Bach's Quarrel with the Rector of St. Thomas School." *Anglican Theological Review* 33 (1951): 219–30.

5. REFINING HISTORICAL RESEARCH

General Works

Aner, Karl. *Die Theologie der Lessingzeit.* Hildesheim: G. Olms, 1964.

Frei, Hans W. *The Eclipse of Biblical Narrative: A Study in Eighteenth and Nineteenth Century Hermeneutics.* New Haven and London: Yale University Press, 1974.

Semler

Primary Sources

Semler, Johann Salomo. *Christliche freye Untersuchung über die so gennante Offenbarung Johannis, aus nachgelassen Handschrift eines fränkische Gelehrten herausgegeben.* Annotated by J. S. Semler. Halle: J. C. Hendel, 1769.

———. *Abhandlung von freier Untersuchung des Canon.* 4 vols. Halle: C. H. Hemmerde, 1771–76.

———. *Abhandlung von freier Untersuchung des Canon.* Edited by Heinz Scheible. Texte zur Kirchen- und Theologiegeschichte 5. Gütersloh: G. Mohn, 1967.

———. *Antwort auf das Bahrdtische Glabensbekenntnis.* Halle: C. H. Hemmerde, 1779.

———. *Hermeneutische Vorbereitung.* 2 vols. Halle: C. H. Hemmerde, 1765–69.

————. [Semleri, Io. Sal]. *Paraphrasis II. Epistolae ad Corinthios. Accessit Latina vetus translatio et lectionum varietas.* Halle: C. H. Hemmerde, 1776.

————. [Semler, Joh. Salomo]. *Paraphrasis Epistolae ad Romanos, cum notis, translatione vetusta, et dissertatione de appendice Cap. XV, XVI.* Halle: C. H. Hemmerde, 1769.

————. [Semler, D. Johann Salomo]. *Versuch einer biblische Dämonologie, oder Untersuchung der Lehre der heil. Schrift vom Teufel und seiner Macht.* Halle: C. H. Hemmerde, 1776.

————. *Vorbereitung zur theologischen Hermeneutik.* 2 vols. Halle: C. H. Hemmerde, 1760–61.

Secondary Sources

Donner, Herbert. "Gesichtspunkte zur Auflösung des klassischen Kanonbegriffes bei Johann Salomo Semler." In *Fides et communicatio: Festschrift für Martin Doerne zum 70. Geburtstag,* edited by D. Roessler, G. Voigt, and F. Wintzer. Göttingen: Vandenhoeck & Ruprecht, 1970.

Gastrow, Paul. *Joh. Salomo Semler: In seiner Bedeutung für die Theologie mit besonderer Berücksichtigung seines Streites mit G. E. Lessing.* Giessen: A. Töpelmann, 1905.

Hess, Hans-Eberhard. *Theologie und Religion bein Johann Salomo Semler: Ein Beitrag zur Theologiegeschichte des 18. Jahrhunderts.* Augsburg: W. Blasaditsch, 1974.

Hornig, Gottfried. *Die Anfänge der historisch-kritischen Theologie: Johann Salomo Semlers Schriftverständnis und seine Stellung zu Luther.* Forschungen zur Systematischen Theologie und Religionsphilosophie 8. Göttingen: Vandenhoeck & Ruprecht, 1961.

————. "Die Freiheit der christlichen Privatreligion. Semlers Begründung des religiösen Individualismus in der protestantischen Aufklärungstheologie." *Neue Zeitschrift für systematische Theologie und Religionsphilosophie* 21 (1979): 198–211.

————. "Hermeneutik und Bibelkritik bei Johann Salomo Semler." In *Historische Kritik und biblischer Kanon in der deutschen Aufklärung,* edited by H. G. Reventlow, W. Sparn, and J. Woodbridge, 219–36. Wolfenbütteler Forschungen 41. Wiesbaden: Harrassowitz, 1988.

————. "Der Perfektibilitätsgedanke bei J. S. Semler." *Zeitschrift für Theologie und Kirche* 72 (1975): 381–97.

————. "Semlers Lehre von der Heilsordnung: Eine Studie zur Rezeption und Kritik des halleschen Pietismus." *Pietismus und Neuzeit: Ein Jahrbuch zur Geschichte des neueren Protestantismus* 10 (1984): 152–89.

Huber, Fritz. *Johann Salomo Semler: Seine Bedeutung für die Theologie, sein Streit mit Gotthold Ephraim Lessing.* Berlin: R. Trenkel, 1906.

Karo, Gottwalt. *Johann Salomo Semler: In seiner Bedeutung für Theologie mit besonderer Berucksichtigung seines Streites mit G. E. Lessing.* Berlin: C. A. Schwetschke, 1905.

Schulz, Hartmut H. R. *Johann Salomo Semlers Wesensbestimmung des Christentums: Ein Beitrag zur Erforschung der Theologie Semlers.* Würzburg: Königshausen & Neumann, 1988.

Strathmann, Hermann. "Die Krisis des Kanons der Kirche: Joh. Gerhards und Joh. Sal. Semlers Erbe." In *Das Neue Testament als Kanon: Dokumentation und kritische Analyse zur gegenwärtigen Diskussion,* edited by Ernst Käsemann. Göttingen: Vandenhoeck & Ruprecht, 1970.

Michaelis

Primary Sources

Michaelis, Johann David. *Anmerkungen für Ungelehrte, zu seiner Uebersetzung des Neuen Testaments.* 4 vols. Göttingen: Vandenhoek & Ruprecht, 1790–92.

————. [Michaelis, John David]. *The Burial and Resurrection of Jesus Christ: According to the Four Evangelists.* Translated by G. Duckett. London: H. Hatchard, 1827.

————. [Michaelis, John David]. *Commentaries on the Laws of Moses.* Translated by Alexander Smith. 4 vols. London: F. C. and J. Rivington, 1814.

————. *A Dissertation on the Influence of Opinions on Language, and of Language on Opinions.* Language, Man, and Society. New York: AMS Press, 1973.

————. *Dogmatik.* 2d rev. ed. Tübingen: C. G. Frank and W. Schramm, 1785.

————. *Einleitung in die göttlichen Schriften des Neuen Bundes.* 4th rev. ed. 2 vols. Göttingen: Vandenhoeck & Ruprecht, 1788. English translation: John David Michaelis, *Introduction to the New Testament.* Translated by Herbert Marsh. 2d ed. 4 vols. London: F. and C. Rivington, 1802.

————. *Erklärung des Briefes an die Hebräer.* 2d rev. ed. Frankfurt and Leipzig: J. G. Garbe, 1780.

————. *Gedanken über die Lehre der heiligen Schrift von Sünde und Genugthuung, als eine der Vernunft gemässen Lehre.* Rev. ed. Göttingen and Bremen: J. H. Cramer, 1779.

————. [Michaelis, John David]. *Introductory Lectures to the Sacred Books of the New Testament.* London: W. Dawson, 1780.

————. *Lebensbeschreibung von ihm selbst abgefasst, mit Anmerkungen von Hassencamp.* Leipzig: J. A. Barth, 1793.

————. *Paraphrasis und Anmerkungen über die Briefe Pauli an die Galater, Epheser, Philipper, Colasser, Thessalonicher, den Timotheus, Titus und Philemon.* 2d rev. ed. Bremen and Göttingen: G. L. Förster, 1769.

Secondary Sources

Eichhorn, J. G. "Eichhorns Bemerkungen über J. D. Michaelis Litterarischen Character." In Michaelis, *Lebensbeschreibung von ihm selbst abgefasst, mit Anmerkungen von Hassencamp,* 145–226.

Smend, Rudolf. *Festrede in Namen der Georg-Augusts-Universität zur Akademischen Preisvertheilung, Am VIII. Juni MDCCCXCVIII: Johann David Michaelis.* Göttingen: W. F. Kaestner, 1898.

————. "Johann David Michaelis und Johann Gottfried Eichhorn—zwei Orientalisten am Rande der Theologie." In *Theologie in Göttingen: Eine Vorlesungsreihe,* edited by Bernd Moeller, 58–81. Göttingen Universitätsschriften A, 1. Göttingen: Vandenhoeck & Ruprecht, 1987.

Griesbach

Primary Sources

Griesbach, Johann Jakob. *Io. Iac. Griesbachii Theol. D. et Prof Primar in academia Jenensi Commentatio qua Marci Evangelium totum e Matthaei et Lucae commentariis decerptum esse monstratur, scripta nomine Academiae Jenensis, (1789. 1790) jam recog-*

nita multisque augmentis locupletata. In *J. J. Griesbach: Synoptic and Text-Critical Studies, 1777–1976,* edited by B. Orchard and T.R.W. Longstaff, 74–102. Cambridge: Cambridge University Press, 1978. English translation: "A Demonstration that Mark Was Written after Matthew and Luke," pp. 103–35.

————. *Novum Testamentum Graece. Textum ad fidem codicum versionum et patrum recensuit et lectionis varietatem.* 2 vols. 2d ed. Vol. 1: London: P. Elmsly; and Halle: J.J.C. Haeredes, 1796. Vol. 2: London: Payne & Mackinlay; and Halle: J.J.C. Haeredes, 1806.

————. *Opuscula academica.* Edited by Io. Philippus Gabler. 2 vols. Jena: F. Frommann, 1824–25.

————. *Synopsis evangeliorum Matthaei Marci et Lucae una cum iis Joannis pericopis quae omnino cum caeterorum evangelistarum narrationibus conferendae sunt. Textum recesuit et selectam lectionis varietatem adjecit D. Jo. Jac. Griesbach.* Halle: L. Curtian, 1809.

————. *Vorlesungen über die Hermeneutik des Neues Testament.* Edited by J.C.S. Steiner. Nürnberg: Zeh, 1815.

Secondary Sources

Delling, Gerhard. "Johann Jakob Griesbach. Seine Zeit, sein Leben, sein Werk." *Theologische Zeitschrift* 33 (1977): 81–99.

Farmer, William R. *The Synoptic Problem: A Critical Analysis.* New York: Macmillan, 1964.

Orchard, Bernard, and Thomas R. W. Longstaff, eds. *J. J. Griesbach: Synoptic and Text-Critical Studies, 1776–1976.* Cambridge: Cambridge University Press, 1978.

Reicke, Bo. "Griesbach und die synoptische Frage." *Theologisches Zeitschrift* 32 (1976): 341–59.

Stoldt, Hans-Herbert. *Geschichte und Kritik der Markushypothese.* 2d ed. Theologische Verlagsgemeinschaft. Giessen and Basel: Brunnen, 1986.

————. *History and Criticism of the Marcan Hypothesis.* Translated and edited by Donald L. Niewyk. Macon, Ga.: Mercer University Press, 1980.

Eichhorn

Primary Sources

Eichhorn, Johann Gottfried [Eichhorn, Jo. Godofr]. *Commentarius in Apocalypsin Johannis.* 2 vols. Göttingen: J. C. Dieterich, 1791.

————. *Einleitung in die apokryphischen Schriften des Alten Testaments.* Leipzig: Weidmann, 1795.

————. *Einleitung in das Neue Testament.* 5 vols. 2d rev. ed. Leipzig: Weidmann, 1827.

————. *Geschichte der Litteratur von ihrem Anfang bis auf die neuesten Zeiten.* 6 vols. Göttingen: Vandenhoeck & Ruprecht, 1805–11.

————. "Urgeschichte: Ein Versuch." *Repertorium für Biblische und Morgenländische Litteratur* 4 (1779): 129–256. Later edition: *Johann Gottfried Eichhorns Urgeschichte.* With introduction and conclusion by Johann Philipp Gabler. 2 vols. Altdorf and Nürnburg: Monath & Kustler, 1792.

————. "Versuch über die Engels-Erscheinungen in der Apostelgeschichte." *Allgemeine Bibliothek der biblischen Litteratur* 3 (1790): 381–408.

Secondary Sources

Hartlich, Christian, and Walter Sachs. *Der Ursprung des Mythosbegriffes in der Modernen Bibelwissenschaft.* Schriftender Studiengemeinschaft der Evangelischen Akadeinen 2. Tübingen: J.C.B. Mohr, 1952.

Smend, Rudolf. "Johann David Michaelis und Johann Gottfried Eichhorn—zwei Orientalisten am Rande der Theologie." In *Theologie in Göttingen: Eine Vorlesungsreihe,* edited by Bernd Moeller, 58–81. Göttingen Universitätsschriften A, 1. Göttingen: Vandenhoeck & Ruprecht, 1987.

6. NEW TESTAMENT RESEARCH AND THEOLOGICAL MEANING

Conservative Alternatives

Calmet

Primary Sources

Calmet, Augustin. *Calmet's Dictionary of the Holy Bible; with the Biblical Fragments.* 9th ed. Edited by Charles Taylor. 5 vols. London: H. G. Bohn, 1847.

———. *Commentaire litteral sur tous les livres de l'Ancien et du Nouveau Testment.* 8 vols. Paris: Emery, Saugrain, P. Martin, 1724.

———. *La Sainte Bible en Latin et en François; avec des notes litterales, critiques et historiques, des prefaces et des dissertations tirées du Commentaire de Augustin Calmet, Abbé de Senones, de M. l'Abbé de Vence, & des Auteurs les plus célébres: pour faciliter l'intelligence de l'Ecriture Sainte.* 14 vols. Paris: G. Martin, et al., 1750.

Lardner

Primary Sources

Lardner, Nathaniel. *The Case of the Demoniacs Mentioned in the New Testament: Four Discourses upon Mark v.19.* London: C. Henderson, 1758.

———. *The Works of Nathaniel Lardner, D.D., with a Life by Dr. Kippis.* 10 vols. London: Holdsworth & Ball, 1831.

The New Testament as Literature

Lessing

Primary Sources

Lessing, Gotthold Ephraim. *Gesammelte Werke.* Edited by Paul Rilla. 10 vols. Berlin: Aufbau-Verlag, 1956.

———. *Lessing's Theological Writings: Selections in Translation with an Introductory Essay.* Edited by Henry Chadwick. Stanford, Calif.: Stanford University Press, 1957.

Secondary Sources

Allison, Henry E. *Lessing and the Enlightenment: His Philosophy of Religion and Its Relation to Eighteenth-Century Thought.* Ann Arbor: University of Michigan Press, 1966.

Heftrich, Eckhard. *Lessings Aufklärung: Zu den theologisch-philosophischen Spätschriften.* Frankfurt am Main: V. Klostermann, 1978.

Michalson, Gordon E., Jr. *Lessing's "Ugly Ditch": A Study of Theology and History*. University Park and London: Pennsylvania State University Press, 1985.

Reimarus

Primary Sources

Reimarus, Hermann Samuel. *Apologie oder Schutzschrift für die vernünftigen Verehrer Gottes*. Im Auftrag der Joachim-Jungius-Gesellschaft der Wissenschaften Hamburg. Edited by Gerhard Alexander. 2 vols. Frankfurt am Main: Insel, 1972.

———. *Reimarus: Fragments*. Edited by Charles H. Talbert. Translated by Ralph S. Fraser. Lives of Jesus. Philadelphia: Fortress Press, 1970.

———. *Die vornehmsten Wahrheiten der natürlichen Religion*. Edited by Günter Gawlick. 2 vols. Hermann Samuel Reimarus Gesammelte Schriften. 1766. Reprint. Göttingen: Vandenhoeck & Ruprecht, 1985.

Semler, Joh. Salomo. *Beantwortung der Fragemente eines Ungenanten, inbesondere vom Zweck Jesu und seiner Jünger*. Rev. ed. Halle: Erziehungsinstitut, 1780.

Secondary Sources

Brown, Colin. *Jesus in European Protestant Thought, 1778–1860*, 1–55. Grand Rapids: Baker, 1985.

Hermann Samuel Reimarus (1694–1768): ein "bekannter Unbekannter" der Aufklärung in Hamburg. Vorträge gehalten auf der Tagung der Joachim Jungius-Gesellschaft der Wissenschaften Hamburg am 12. und 13. Oktober 1972. Göttingen: Vandenhoeck & Ruprecht, 1973.

Schmidt-Biggemann, Wilhelm. "Die destruktive Potenz philosophischer Apologetik oder der Verlust des biblischen Kredits bei Hermann Samuel Reimarus." In *Historische Kritik und biblischer Kanon in der deutschen Aufklärung*, edited by H. G. Reventlow, W. Sparn, and J. Woodbridge, 193–204. Wolfenbütteler Forschungen 41. Wiesbaden: Harrassowitz, 1988.

———. *Hermann Samuel Reimarus: Handschriftenverzeichnis und Bibliographie*. Veröffentlichung der Joachim Jungius-Gesellschaft der Wissenschaften Hamburg 37. Göttingen: Vandenhoeck & Ruprecht, 1979.

Schweitzer, Albert. *The Quest of the Historical Jesus: A Critical Study of Its Progress from Reimarus to Wrede*. Translated by W. Montgomery. New York: Macmillan, 1957.

Stemmer, Peter. *Weissagung und Kritik: Eine Studie zur Hermeneutik bei Hermann Samuel Reimarus*. Göttingen: Vandenhoeck & Ruprecht, 1983.

Strauss, David Friedrich. *Hermann Samuel Reimarus und seine Schutzschrift für die vernünftigen Verehrer Gottes*. Leipzig: F. A. Brockhaus, 1862.

Herder

Primary Sources

Herder, Johann Gottfried. *God: Some Conversations*. Translated by Frederick H. Burkhardt. Liberal Arts Library. Indianapolis: Bobbs-Merrill, 1940.

———. *Outlines of a Philosophy of the History of Man*. Translated by T. Churchill. New York: Bergman, 1800.

———. *Reflections on the Philosophy of Mankind*. Edited by Frank E. Manuel. Classic European Historians. Chicago and London: University of Chicago Press, 1968.

———. *Sämmtliche Werke.* Edited by B. Suphan. 33 vols. Hildesheim: G. Olms, 1967.

Secondary Sources

Bunge, Marcia. "Johann Gottfried Herders Auslegung des Neuen Testaments." In *Historische Kritik und biblischer Kanon in der deutschen Aufklärung,* edited by H. G. Reventlow, W. Sparn, and J. Woodbridge, 249–62. Wolfenbütteler Forschungen 41. Wiesbaden: Harrassowitz, 1988.

———. "The Restless Reader: Johann Gottfried Herder's Interpretations of the New Testament." Ph.D. diss., University of Chicago, 1986.

Clark, Robert T., Jr. *Herder: His Life and Thought.* Berkeley and Los Angeles: University of California Press, 1955.

Gillies, A. *Herder.* Modern Language Studies. Oxford: Basil Blackwell, 1945.

Gutzen, Dieter. "Ästhetik und Kritik bei Johann Gottfried Herder." In *Historische Kritik und biblischer Kanon in der deutschen Aufklärung,* edited by H. G. Reventlow, W. Sparn, and J. Woodbridge, 263–84. Wolfenbütteler Forschungen 41. Wiesbaden: Harrassowitz, 1988.

Koepke, Wulf. *Johann Gottfried Herder.* Boston: Twayne, 1987.

Scholder, Klaus. "Herder und die Anfänge der historischen Theologie." *Evangelische Theologie* 22 (1962): 425–41.

Beginnings in New Testament Theology

Gabler

Primary Sources

Gabler, Johann Phillip. *Kleinere theologische Schriften.* Edited by T. A. Gabler and J. G. Gabler. 2 vols. Ulm: Stettinischen Buchhandlung, 1831.

———, ed. *Johann Gottfried Eichhorns Urgeschichte.* 2 vols. Altdorf and Nürnberg: Monath & Kussler, 1792.

Secondary Sources

Boers, Hendrikus. *What Is New Testament Theology? The Rise of Criticism and the Problem of a Theology of the New Testament.* Guides to Biblical Scholarship. Philadelphia: Fortress Press, 1979.

Hartlich, Christian, and Walter Sachs. *Der Ursprung des Mythosbegriffes in der Modernen Bibelwissenschaft.* Schriften der Studiengemeinschaft der Evangelischen Akademien 2. Tübingen: J.C.B. Mohr, 1952.

Merk, Otto. *Biblische Theologie des Neuen Testaments in ihrer Anfangszeit: Ihre methodischen Probleme bei Johann Philipp Gabler und Georg Lorenz Bauer und deren Nachwirkung.* Marburger Theologische Studien 9. Marburg: N. G. Elwert, 1972.

Bauer

Primary Sources

Bauer, Georg Lorenz. *Biblische Moral des Neuen Testaments.* 2 vols. Leipzig: Weygand, 1804–5.

———. *Biblische Theologie des Neuen Testaments.* 4 vols. Leipzig: Weygand, 1800–1802.

———. *Hebraische Mythologie des alten und neuen Testaments, mit Parallelen aus der Mythologie anderer Völker, vornemlich der Griechen und Römer.* 2 vols. Leipzig: Weygand, 1802.

———. *Sammlung und Erklärung der parabolischen Erzählungen unsers Herrn.* Leipzig: C. G. Hilscher, 1782.

Secondary Sources

Hartlich, Christian, and Walter Sachs. *Der Ursprung des Mythosbegriffes in der Modernen Bibelwissenschaft.* Schriften der Studiengemeinschaft der Evangelischen Akademien 2. Tübingen: J.C.B. Mohr, 1952.

Merk, Otto. *Biblische Theologie des Neuen Testaments in ihrer Anfangszeit: Ihre methodischen Probleme bei Johan Philipp Gabler und Georg Lorenz Bauer und deren Nachwirkung.* Marburger Theologische Studien 9. Marburg: N. G. Elwert, 1972.

7. THE RISE OF LIBERALISM

General Works on Nineteenth-Century Culture, History, and Theology

Barth, Karl. *Protestant Theology in the Nineteenth Century: Its Background and History.* Translated by John Bowden. London: SCM Press, 1972.

Bruun, Geoffrey. *Nineteenth Century European Civilization: 1815–1914.* New York: Oxford University Press, 1960.

Holborn, Hajo. *A History of Modern Germany: 1648–1840.* Princeton, N.J.: Princeton University Press, 1982.

———. *A History of Modern Germany: 1840–1945.* Princeton, N.J.: Princeton University Press, 1982.

Lichtenberger, F. *History of German Theology in the Nineteenth Century.* Translated by W. Hastie. Edinburgh: T. & T. Clark, 1889.

Livingston, James C. *Modern Christian Thought: From the Enlightenment to Vatican II.* New York: Macmillan, 1971.

Pfleiderer, Otto. *The Development of Theology in Germany since Kant and Its Progress in Great Britain since 1825.* Translated by J. Frederick Smith. Library of Philosophy. New York: Macmillan, 1923.

Reinhardt, Klaus. *Der Dogmatische Schriftgebrauch: In de Katholischen und Protestantischen Christologie von der Aufklärung zur Gegenwart.* Munich: G. Schöningh, 1970.

Schaff, Philip. *Germany: Its Universities, Theology, and Religion.* Philadelphia: Lindsay & Blakiston, 1857.

Smart, Ninian, et al., eds., *Nineteenth Century Religious Thought in the West.* Vol. 1. Cambridge: Cambridge University Press, 1988.

Vidler, Alec R. *The Church in an Age of Revolution: 1789 to the Present Day.* Pelican History of the Church 5. London: Penguin, 1988.

Welch, Claude. *Protestant Thought in the Nineteenth Century. Volume 1: 1799–1870.* New Haven and London: Yale University Press, 1972.

Paulus

Primary Sources

Paulus, Heinrich Eberhard Gottlob. *Die drey Lehrbriefe von Johannes: Wortgetreu mit erläuternden Zwischensätzen übersetzt, und nach philologisch-notiologischer Methode erklärt.* Heidelberg: C. F. Winter, 1829.

————. *Exegetisches Handbuch über die drei ersten Evangelien.* 3 vols. Heidelberg: C. F. Winter, 1830–33.

————. *Das Leben Jesu, als Grundlage einer reinen Geschichte des Urchristentums.* 4 vols. Heidelberg: C. F. Winter, 1828.

————. *Philologisch-kritischer und historischer Commentar über das neue Testament.* 2d ed. 3 vols. Lübeck: J. F. Bohn, 1804–5.

Schleiermacher

Bibliography

Tice, Terrence N. *Schleiermacher Bibliography: With Brief Introductions, Annotations, and Index.* Princeton Pamphlets 12. Princeton, N.J.: Princeton Theological Seminary, 1966.

Primary Sources

Schleiermacher, Friedrich. *Brief Outline of the Study of Theology, Drawn up to Serve as the Basis of Introductory Lectures.* Translated by William Farrer. Edinburgh: T. & T. Clark, 1850.

————. *The Christian Faith.* Edited by H. R. Mackintosh and J. S. Stewart. Philadelphia: Fortress Press, 1976.

————. *A Critical Essay on the Gospel of St. Luke.* Translated by Connop Thrilwall. London: J. Taylor, 1825.

————. *Friedrich Schleiermacher's sämmtliche Werke.* Erste Abtheilung: Zur Theologie. 8 vols. Berlin: G. Reimer, 1836.

————. *Hermeneutics: The Handwritten Manuscripts.* Edited by Heinz Kimmerle. Translated by J. Duke and J. Forstman. American Academy of Religion: Texts and Translations 1. Missoula, Mont.: Scholars Press, 1977.

————. *The Life of Jesus.* Edited by J. C. Verheyden. Translated by S. M. Gilmour. Lives of Jesus. Philadelphia: Fortress Press, 1975.

————. *The Life of Schleiermacher, as Unfolded in His Autobiography and Letters.* Translated by Frederica Rowan. 2 vols. (London: Smith, Elder, & Co., 1860).

————. *On Religion: Addresses in Response to Its Cultured Critics.* Translated by Terrence N. Tice. Research in Theology. Richmond, Va.: John Knox Press, 1969.

Secondary Sources

Clements, Keith. *Friedrich Schleiermacher: Pioneer of Modern Theology.* Making of Modern Theology: Nineteenth and Twentieth Century Theological Texts. London: Collins, 1987.

Moretto, Giovanni. "Angezogen und belehrt von Gott: Der Johannismus in Schleiermachers 'Reden über die Religion.'" *Theologische Zeitschrift* 37 (1981): 267–91.

Niebuhr, Richard R. *Schleiermacher on Christ and Religion: A New Introduction.* New York: Charles Scribner's Sons, 1964.

Redeker, Martin. *Schleiermacher: Life and Thought.* Translated by John Wallhausser. Philadelphia: Fortress Press, 1973.

De Wette

Primary Sources

de Wette, Wilhelm Martin Leberecht. *Biblische Dogmatik Alten und Neuen Testaments, oder kritische Darstellung der Religonslehre des Hebraismus, des Judenthums and Urchristenthums: Zum Gebrauch akademischer Vorlesungen.* 3d rev. ed. Berlin: G. Reimer, 1831.

———. *Kurzgefasstes exegetisches Handbuch zum Neuen Testament.* 4 vols. Leipzig: Weidmann, 1845–48.

———. *Lehrbuch der historisch-kritischen Einleitung in die Bibel Alten und Neuen Testamentes.* Vol. 1: *Lehrbuch der historisch-kritischen Einleitung in die kanonischen und apokryphischen Bücher des Alten Testamentes.* 7th rev. ed. Berlin: G. Reimer, 1852. Vol. 2: *Lehrbuch der historisch-kritischen Einleitung in die kanonischen Bücher des Neuen Testaments.* 5th rev. ed. Berlin: G. Reimer, 1848; English translation: *An Historico-Critical Introduction to the Canonical Books of the New Testament.* Translated from the 5th ed. by Frederick Frothingham. Boston: Crosby, Nichols, & Co., 1858.

———. [de Wette, Guilelmus Martinus Leberecht]. *De morte Jesu Christi expiatoria commentatio.* Berlin: Libraria scholae realis, 1813.

———. *Theodore; or, the Skeptic's Conversion: History of the Culture of a Protestant Clergyman.* Translated by James F. Clarke. 2 vols. Specimens of Foreign Standard Literature 11. Boston: Hilliard, Gray, & Co., 1841.

———. *Ueber die Religion, ihr Wesen, ihre Erscheinungsformen und ihren Einfluss auf das Leben: Vorlesungen.* Berlin: G. Reimer, 1827.

———. *Vorlesungen über die Sittenlehre.* 2 vols. Berlin: G. Reimer, 1823–24.

———. *Das Wesen des christlichen Glaubens vom Standpunkte des Glaubens dargestellt.* Basel: Scheighauser, 1846.

Secondary Sources

Hagenbach, K. R. *Wilhelm Martin Leberecht de Wette: Eine akademische Gedächtnisrede.* Leipzig: Weidmann, 1850.

Lücke, Friedrich. *D.W.M.L. de Wette: Zur freundschaftlichen Erinnerung.* Hamburg: R. Perthes, 1850.

Otto, Rudolf. *The Philosophy of Religion: Based on Kant and Fries.* Translated by E. B. Dicker. London: Williams & Norgate, 1931.

Smend, Rudolf. "De Wette und das Verhältnis zwischen historischer Bibelkritik und philosophischem System im 19. Jahrhundert." *Theologische Zeitschrift* 14 (1958): 107–19.

———. *Wilhelm Martin Leberecht de Wettes Arbeit am Alten und am Neuen Testament.* Basel: Helbing & Lichtenhahn,1958.

Staehelin, Ernst. *Dewettiana: Forschungen und Texte zu Wilhelm Martin Leberecht de Wettes Leben und Werk.* Studien zur Geschichte der Wissenschaften in Basel 2. Basel: Helbing & Lichtenhahn,1956.

Lücke

Primary Sources

Lücke, Friedrich. *Commentar über das Evangelium des Johannes.* 3d rev. ed. 2 vols. Bonn: E. Weber, 1840–43.

————. *A Commentary on the Epistles of St. John.* Translated by T. G. Repp. Biblical Cabinet; or Hermeneutical, Exegetical, and Philological Library 15. Edinburgh: T. Clark, 1837.

————. *Grundriss der neutestamentlichen Hermeneutik und ihrer Geschichte: Zum Gebrauch für akademische Vorlesungen.* Göttingen: Vandenhoeck & Ruprecht, 1816.

————. *Versuch einer vollständigen Einleitung in die Offenbarung des Johannes oder Allgemeine Untersuchungen über die apokalyptische Litteratur überhaupt und die Apokalypse des Johannes insbesondere.* 2d rev. ed. 2 vols. Bonn: E. Weber, 1852.

Secondary Sources

Lange, Dietz. "Der theologische Vermittler Friedrich Lücke." In *Theologie in Göttingen: Eine Vorlesungsreihe,* edited by Bernd Moeller. Göttingen Universitäts-schriften A, 1. Göttingen: Vandenhoeck & Ruprecht, 1987.

Neander

Primary Sources

Neander, Augustus. *The Epistle of Paul to the Philippians, Practically Explained.* Translated by H. C. Conant. New York: L. Colby, 1851.

————. *The First Epistle of John, Practically Explained.* Translated by H. C. Conant. New York: Sheldon, Blakeman & Co., 1856.

————. *General History of the Christian Religion and Church.* Translated by Joseph Torrey from the 2d German ed. 5th ed. 5 vols. Boston: Crocker & Brewster, 1852.

————. *Die Geschichte der Pflanzung und Leitung der christlichen Kirche durch die Apostel.* 2 vols. Hamburg: F. Perthes, 1832–33. English translation: *History of the Planting and Training of the Christian Church by the Apostles.* Translated by J. E. Ryland. Revised according to the 4th ed. by E. G. Robinson. New York: Sheldon, 1865.

————. *The Life of Jesus Christ: In Its Historical Connexion and Historical Developement.* Translated from the 4th German ed. by J. M'Clintock and C. E. Blumenthal. 3d ed. New York: Harper & Brothers, 1850.

8. THE INFLUENCE OF
PHILOSOPHICAL IDEALISM

Strauss

Primary Sources

Stepelevich, Lawrence S., ed. *The Young Hegelians: An Anthology.* Texts in German Philosophy. Cambridge: Cambridge University Press, 1983.

Strauss, David Friedrich. *Der alte und der neue Glaube: Ein Bekenntniss.* Leipzig: S. Hirzel, 1872. English translation: *The Old Faith and the New: A Confession.* Translated by Mathilde Blind. 2 vols. in 1. New York: Henry Holt & Co., 1874.

————. *Die christliche Glaubenslehre in ihrer geschichtlichen Entwicklung und im Kampfe mit der modernen Wissenschaft dargestellt.* 2 vols. in 1. Frankfurt am Main: Minerva, 1984.

————. *Der Christus des Glaubens und der Jesus der Geschichte: Eine Kritik des Schleiermacher'schen Lebens Jesu.* Edited by Hans-Jürgen Geischer. Texte zur Kirchen- und Theologiegeschichte 14. Gütersloh: G. Mohn, 1971. English translation: *The Christ of Faith and the Jesus of History: A Critique of Schleiermacher's* Life of Jesus. Translated and edited by Leander E. Keck. Lives of Jesus. Philadelphia: Fortress Press, 1977.

———. *Das Leben Jesu, kritisch bearbeitet.* 2 vols. Tübingen: C. F. Osiander, 1835. English translation: *The Life of Jesus Critically Examined.* Edited by Peter C. Hodgson. Translated from the 4th ed. by George Eliot. Lives of Jesus. Philadelphia: Fortress Press, 1972.

———. *The Life of Jesus for the People.* 2d ed. 2 vols. London: Williams & Norgate, 1879.

———. *Streitschriften zur Vertheidigung meiner Schrift über das Leben Jesu und zur Charakteristik der gegenwärtigen Theologie.* New ed. in 1 vol. Tübingen: C. F. Osiander, 1841. English translation: *In Defense of My* Life of Jesus *against the Hegelians.* Translated and edited by Marilyn Chapin Massey. Hamden, Conn.: Archon Books, 1983.

Secondary Sources

Cromwell, Richard S. *David Friedrich Strauss and His Place in Modern Thought.* Fair Lawn, N.J.: R. E. Burdick, 1974.

Fischer, Kuno. *Über David Friedrich Strauss: Gesammelte Aufsätze.* Philosophische Schriften 5. Heidelberg: C. Winter, 1908.

Harris, Horton. *David Friedrich Strauss and His Theology.* Monograph Supplements to the Scottish Journal of Theology. Cambridge: Cambridge University Press, 1973.

Hodgson, Peter C. "Hegel's Christology: Shifting Nuances in the Berlin Lectures." *Journal of the American Academy of Religion* 53 (1985): 23–40.

Lawler, Edwina G. *David Friedrich Strauss and His Critics: The Life of Jesus Debate in Early Nineteenth-Century German Journals.* American University Studies 7; Theology and Religion 16. New York, Berne, and Frankfurt am Main: P. Lang, 1986.

Levy, Albert. *David-Frédéric Strauss: la vie et l'oeuvre.* Paris: F. Alcan, 1910.

Massey, Marilyn Chapin. *Christ Unmasked: The Meaning of* The Life of Jesus *in German Politics.* Studies in Religion. Chapel Hill and London: University of North Carolina Press, 1983.

Müller, Gotthold. "Ferdinand Christian Baur und David Friedrich Strauss in Blaubeuren (1821–1825)." In *Glaube Geist Geschichte: Festschrift für Ernst Benz,* edited by G. Müller and W. Zeller. Leiden: E. J. Brill, 1967.

———. *Identität und Immanenz: Zur Genese der Theologie von David Friedrich Strauss.* Basler Studien zur Historischen und Systematischen Theologie 10. Zürich: EVZ, 1968.

Zeller, Eduard. *David Friedrich Strauss in seinem Leben und seinen Schriften.* Bonn: E. Strauss, 1874.

Baur

Primary Sources

Baur, Ferdinand Christian. *Ausgewählte Werke in Einzelausgaben.* Edited by Klaus Scholder. 5 vols. Stuttgart-Bad Cannstatt: F. Frommann, 1963–75.

———. *The Church History of the First Three Centuries.* Translated by Allan Menzies. 3d ed. 2 vols. Theological Translation Fund Library. London: Williams & Norgate, 1887.

———. *Die Epochen der kirchlichen Geschichtschreibung.* In *Ausgewählte Werke,* vol. 2.

English translation: *On the Writing of Church History.* Edited and translated by Peter C. Hodgson. Library of Protestant Thought. New York: Oxford University Press, 1968.

————. *Kritische Untersuchungen über die kanonischen Evangelien, ihr Verhältniss zu einander, ihren Charakter und Ursprung.* Tübingen: L. F. Fues, 1847.

————. *Das Markusevangelium nach seinem Ursprung und Charakter. Nebst einem Anhang über das Evangelium Marcion's.* Tübingen: L. F. Fues, 1851.

————. *Paulus, der Apostel Jesu Christi. Sein Leben und Wirken, seine Briefe und seine Lehre: Ein Beitrag zu einer kritischen Geschichte des Urchristenthums.* 2d ed. Edited by Eduard Zeller. Leipzig: L. F. Fues, 1866. English translation: *Paul the Apostle of Jesus Christ, His Life and Work, His Epistles and His Doctrine: A Contribution to a Critical History of Primitive Christianity.* Translated from 2d German ed. by A. Menzies. 2d ed. 2 vols. London: Williams & Norgate, 1875.

————. *Die sogenannten Pastoralbriefe des Apostels Paulus aufs neue kritisch untersucht.* Stuttgart and Tübingen: J. G. Cotta, 1835.

————. *Vorlesungen über neutestamentliche Theologie.* Edited by F. F. Baur. Leipzig: L. F. Fues, 1864.

Secondary Sources

Friedrich, Peter. *Ferdinand Christian Baur als Symboliker.* Studien zur Theologie und Geistesgeschichte des Neunzehnten Jahrhunderts 12. Göttingen: Vandenhoeck & Ruprecht, 1975.

Geiger, Wolfgang. *Spekulation und Kritik: Die Geschichtstheologie Ferdinand Christian Baurs.* Forschungen zur Geschichte und Lehre des Protestantismus. 10th series, vol. 28. Munich: Chr. Kaiser, 1964.

Harris, Horton. *The Tübingen School.* Oxford: Clarendon Press, 1975. Reprint: *The Tübingen School: A Historical and Theological Investigation of the School of F. C. Baur.* Grand Rapids: Baker, 1990.

Hodgson, Peter C. *The Formation of Historical Theology: A Study of Ferdinand Christian Baur.* New York: Harper & Row, 1966.

Morgan, Robert. "Biblical Classics: II. F. C. Baur: Paul." *Expository Times* 90 (1978): 4–10.

————. "F. C. Baur's Lectures on New Testament Theology." *Expository Times* 88 (1977): 202–6.

Zeller

Primary Sources

Zeller, Eduard. *Die Apostelgeschichte nach ihrem Inhalt und Ursprung kritisch untersucht.* Stuttgart: C. Mäcken, 1854. English translation: *The Contents and Origin of the Acts of the Apostles, Critically Investigated.* Translated by Joseph Dare. 2 vols. Theological Translation Fund. London: Williams & Norgate, 1875–76.

————. "Geschichte der christlichen Kirche," *Neue Enzyklopädie der Wissenschaften und Künste für die deutsche Nation* 7.1–159. 2d ed. Stuttgart: Franck, 1858.

Secondary Sources

Hall, G. Stanley. *Founders of Modern Psychology,* 3–61. New York and London: D. Appleton, 1912.

Hilgenfeld

Primary Sources

Hilgenfeld, Adolf. *Die Evangelien, nach ihrer Entstehung und geschichtliche Bedeutung.* Leipzig: S. Hirzel, 1854.

———. *Historisch-kritische Einleitung in das Neue Testament.* Leipzig: L. F. Fues, 1875.

———. *Judentum und Judenchristentum: Eine Nachlese zu der Ketzergeschichte des Urchristentums.* Hildesheim: G. Olms, 1966.

———. *Die jüdische Apokalyptic in ihrer geschichtlichen Entwickelung. Ein Beitrag zur Vorgeschichte des Christenthums.* Amsterdam: RODOPI, 1966.

———. *Der Kanon und die Kritik des Neuen Testaments in ihrer geschichtlichen Ausbildung und Gestaltung.* Halle: C.E.M. Pfeffer, 1863.

———. *Der Paschastreit der alten Kirche nach seiner Bedeutung für die Kirchengeschichte und für die Evangelienforschung.* Halle: C.E.M. Pfeffer, 1860.

Hengstenberg

Primary Sources

Hengstenberg, Ernst Wilhelm. *Christologie des Alten Testaments und Commentar über die Messianischen Weissagungen der Propheten.* 4 vols. Berlin: L. Oehmigke, 1829. English translation: *Christology of the Old Testament, and a Commentary on the Messianic Predictions.* Translated from the 2d ed. by Theodore Meyer. 2d ed. 4 vols. Clark's Foreign Theological Library, n.s. Edinburgh: T. & T. Clark, 1854–58.

———. *Das Evangelium des heiligen Johannes.* 2d ed. 3 vols. Berlin: G. Schlawitz, 1867. English translation: *Commentary on the Gospel of St John.* 2 vols. Clark's Foreign Theological Library, 4th series, no. 5. Edinburgh: T. & T. Clark, 1865.

———. *Die Offenbarung des heiligen Johannes für solche die in der Schrift forschen.* 2d ed. 2 vols. Berlin: L Oehmigke, 1862. English translation: *The Revelation of St. John, Expounded for Those Who Search the Scriptures.* Translated by Patrick Fairbairn. 2 vols. Clark's Foreign Theological Library 22. Edinburgh: T. & T. Clark, 1851.

Secondary Sources

Nafzger, Samuel H. "Struggle against Rationalism: A Study of Ernst Wilhelm Hengstenberg's Understanding of Criticism." Th.D. diss., Harvard University. Abstract: *Harvard Theological Review* 74 (1981): 402.

Tholuck

Primary Sources

Tholuck, Friedrich August Gottreu. *Auslegung des Briefes Pauli an die Römer nebst fortlaufenden Auszügen aus den exegetischen Schriften der Kirchenväter und Reformatoren.* Berlin: F. Dümmler, 1824. English translation: *Exposition of St. Paul's Epistle to the Romans, with Extracts from the Exegetical Works of the Fathers and Reformers.* Translated by Robert Menzies. Philadelphia: Sorin & Ball, 1844.

———. *Commentar zum Evangelio Johannis.* 5th rev. ed. Hamburg: F. Perthes, 1837. English translation: *A Commentary on the Gospel of St. John.* Translated by A. Kaufman. Boston: Perkins & Marvin, 1836.

———. *Die Glaubwürdigkeit der evangelischen Geschichte, zugleich eine Kritik des Lebens Jesu von Strauss, für theologische und nicht theologische Leser dargestellt.* 2d ed. Hamburg: F. Perthes, 1838.

————. *Guido and Julius: or, Sin and the Propitiator, exhibited in the True Consecration of the Skeptic.* Translated by J. E. Ryland. Boston: Gould & Lincoln, 1854.

————. *Philologisch-theologische Auslegung der Bergpredigt Christi nach Matthäus, zugleich ein Beitrag zur Begründung einer rein-biblischen Glaubens- und Sittenlehre.* Hamburg: F. Perthes, 1833.

Ewald

Primary Sources

Ewald, Heinrich. *Die drei ersten Evangelien und die Apostelgeschichte.* 2d ed. Die Bücher des Neuen Bundes 1. Göttingen: Dieter, 1871.

————. *Die Johanneische Schriften: Übersezt und Erklärt.* 2 vols. Die Bücher des Neuen Bundes 2. Göttingen: Dieter, 1861.

————. *The History of Israel, VI: The Life and Times of Christ.* Translated by J. Frederick Smith. London: Longmans, Green, 1883.

————. *The History of Israel, VII: The Apostolic Age.* Translated by J. Frederick Smith. London: Longmans, Green, 1885.

————. *Die Lehre der Bibel von Gott, oder die Theologie des alten und neuen Bundes.* 4 vols. (Leipzig: F.C.W. Vogel, 1871–76). Partial English translation: *Old and New Testament Theology.* Translated by Thomas Goadby. Clark's Foreign Theological Library, n.s. 33. Edinburgh: T. & T. Clark, 1888.

————. *Revelation; Its Nature and Record.* Translated by Thomas Goadby. Clark's Foreign Theological Library, n.s. 19. Edinburgh: T. & T. Clark, 1884.

Secondary Sources

Davies, T. Witton. *Heinrich Ewald: Orientalist and Theologian, 1803–1903, A Centenary Appreciation.* London: T. F. Unwin, 1903.

Perlitt, Lothar. "Heinrich Ewald, Der Gelehrte in der Politik." In *Theologie in Göttingen: Eine Vorlesungsreihe,* edited by Bernd Moeller, 157–212. Göttingen Universitätsschriften A, 1. Göttingen: Vandenhoeck & Ruprecht, 1987.

9. LITERARY, HISTORICAL, AND TEXTUAL CRITICISM ALONGSIDE AND IN THE WAKE OF TÜBINGEN

The Synoptic Problem

Primary Sources

Gieseler, Johann Carl Ludwig. *Historisch-kritischer Versuch über die Enstehung und die frühesten Schicksale der schriftlichen Evangelien.* Leipzig: W. Engelmann, 1818.

Marsh, Herbert. *A Course of Lectures, Containing a Description and Systematic Arrangement of the Several Branches of Divinity: Accompanied with an Account, Both of the Principle Authors, and of the Progress, Which Has Been Made at Different Periods, in Theological Learning.* Cambridge: J. Smith, 1810–23.

————. "A Dissertation on the Origin and Composition of Our Three First Canonical Gospels." In John David Michaelis, *Introduction to the New Testament,* Vol. 3, part 1, 161–409. London: Rivington, 1802.

Meijboom, Hajo Uden. *Geschiedenis en critiek der Marcushypothese.* Amsterdam: Kraay,

1866. English translation: *A History and Critique of the Origin of the Marcan Hypothesis, 1835–1866: A Contemporary Report Rediscovered*. Translated and edited by John J. Kiwiet. Macon, Ga.: Mercer University Press, 1992.

Weisse, Christian Hermann. *Beiträge zur Kritik der Paulinischen Briefe an die Galater, Römer, Philipper und Kolosser*. Edited by E. Sulze. Leipzig: S. Hirzel, 1867.

———. *Die Evangelienfrage in ihrem gegenwärtigen Stadium*. Leipzig: Breitkopf & Härtel, 1856.

———. *Die evangelische Geschichte kritisch und philosophisch bearbeitet*. 2 vols. Leipzig: Breitkopf & Härtel, 1838.

———. *Philosophische Dogmatik, oder Philosophie des Christenthums*. 3 vols. Leipzig: S. Hirzel, 1855–62.

Wilke, Christian Gottlob. *Die Hermeneutik des Neuen Testaments systematisch dargestellt*. 2 vols. Leipzig: F.C.W. Vogel, 1843.

———. *Die neutestamentliche Rhetorik, ein Seitenstück zur Grammatik des neutestamentlichen Sprachidioms*. Dresden and Leipzig: Arnold, 1843.

———. *Der Urevangelist, oder exegetisch kritische Untersuchung über das Verwandtschaftsverhältniss der drei ersten Evangelien*. Dresden and Leipzig: G. Fleischer, 1838.

Secondary Sources

Butler, B. C. *The Originality of St. Matthew: A Critique of the Two Document Hypothesis*. Cambridge: Cambridge University Press, 1951.

Farmer, William R. "The Lachmann Fallacy." *New Testament Studies* 14 (1968): 441–43.

———. *The Synoptic Problem: A Critical Analysis*. Dillsboro: Western North Carolina Press, 1976.

Lindsay, James. *Seven Theistic Philosophers: A Historico-Critical Study*. Edinburgh and London: W. Blackwood & Sons, 1920.

Peabody, David B. "Chapters in the History of the Linguistic Argument for Solving the Synoptic Problem: The Nineteenth Century in Context." In *Jesus, the Gospels, and the Church: Essays in Honor of William R. Farmer*, edited by E. P. Sanders, 47–68. Macon, Ga.: Mercer University Press, 1987.

Reicke, Bo. "From Strauss to Holtzmann and Meijboom: Synoptic Theories Advanced during the Consolidation of Germany, 1830–70." *Novum Testamentum* 29 (1987): 1–21.

Stoldt, Hans-Herbert. *History and Criticism of the Marcan Hypothesis*. Translated and edited by Donald L. Niewyk. Macon, Ga.: Mercer University Press, 1980.

Tuckett, C. M. "Arguments from Order: Definition and Evaluation." In *Synoptic Studies: The Ampleforth Conferences of 1982 and 1983*. Journal for the Study of the New Testament, Supplement Series 7, 197–219. Sheffield: JSOT, 1984.

———. "The Griesbach Hypothesis in the Nineteenth Century." *Journal for the Study of the New Testament* 3 (1979): 29–60.

The Authenticity of the Gospel of John

Primary Sources

Bretschneider, Carolus Theoph. *Probabilia de evangelii et epistolarum Joannis, apostoli, indole et origine eruditorum judiciis modeste subjecit*. Leipzig: A. Barth, 1820.

Tayler, John James. *An Attempt to Ascertain the Character of the Fourth Gospel; Especially in Its Relation to the Three First*. London and Edinburgh: Williams & Norgate, 1867.

Text Criticism

Primary Sources

Lachmann, Karl. "De ordine narrationum in evangeliis synopticis." *Theologische Studien und Kritiken* 8 (1835): 580–90. Partial English translation: N. H. Palmer, "Lachmann's Argument." *New Testament Studies* 13 (1967): 368–78; Reprint: "Lachmann's Argument." In *The Two-Source Hypothesis: A Critical Appraisal,* edited by Arthur J. Bellinzoni, Jr., J. B. Tyson, and W. O. Walker, 119–31. Macon, Ga.: Mercer University Press, 1985.

———. *Novum Testamentum Graece, ex recensione Caroli Lachmanni.* Berlin: G. Reimer, 1837.

———. *Novum Testamentum Graece et Latine, Carolus Lachmannus recensuit, Philippus Buttmannus Ph. F. Graecae lectionis auctoritates apposuit.* 2 vols. Berlin: G. Reimer, 1842–50.

Tischendorf, Lobegott Friedrich Constantin von. *Novum Testamentum Graece, ad antiquissimos testes denuo recensuit, apparatum criticum omni studio perfectum apposuit, commentationem isagogicam praetexuit Constantinus Tischendorf. Editio octava critica maior.* 2 vols. Leipzig: Giesecke & Devrient, 1869–72. *Volumen III: Prolegomena scripsit Casparus Renatus Gregory, additis curis Ezrae Abbot.* Leipzig: J. C. Hinrichs, 1884.

———. *Wann wurden unsere Evangelien verfasst?* 4th rev. ed. Leipzig: J. C. Hinrichs, 1880. English translation: *Origin of the Four Gospels.* Translated by William L. Gage. Boston: American Tract Society, 1867. Shorter, popular English translation: *When were our Gospels Written? An Argument by Constantine Tischendorf, with a Narrative of the Discovery of the Sinaitic Manuscript.* New York: American Tract Society, 1866.

Tregelles, Samuel Prideaux. *An Account of the Printed Text of the Greek New Testament; with Remarks on Its Revision upon Critical Principles.* London: S. Bagster, 1854.

Secondary Sources

Aland, Kurt, and Barbara Aland. *The Text of the New Testament: An Introduction to the Critical Editions and to the Theory and Practice of Modern Textual Criticism.* Translated by Erroll F. Rhodes. Grand Rapids: Wm. B. Eerdmans, 1987.

Bentley, James. *Secrets of Mount Sinai: The Story of the World's Oldest Bible—Codex Sinaiticus.* New York: Doubleday, 1986.

Black, Matthew, and Robert Davidson. *Constantin von Tischendorf and the Greek New Testament.* Glasgow: University of Glasgow Press, 1981.

Metzger, Bruce M. *The Text of the New Testament: Its Transmission, Corruption, and Restoration.* 2d ed. New York and Oxford: Oxford University Press, 1968.

Moir, Ian A. "Tischendorf and the Codex Sinaiticus." *New Testament Studies* 23 (1976): 108–15.

Schneller, Ludwig. *Search on Sinai: The Story of Tischendorf's Life and the Search for a Lost Manuscript.* Translated by Dorothee Schröder. London: Epworth, 1939.

Scrivener, Frederick H. *A Plain Introduction to the Criticism of the New Testament: For the Use of Biblical Students.* 2d ed. Cambridge: Deighton, Bell, 1874.

Stunt, T.C.F. "Some Unpublished Letters of S. P. Tregelles relating to the Codex Sinaiticus." *Evangelical Quarterly* 48 (1976): 15–26.

Vincent, Marvin R. *A History of the Textual Criticism of the New Testament.* New York: Macmillan, 1903.

10. MODERATE AND MEDIATING CRITICISM

Roman Catholic Scholarship

Primary Sources

Hug, Johann Leonhard. *Einleitung in die Schriften des Neuen Testaments.* 3d rev. ed. 2 vols. Stuttgart and Tübingen: J. G. Gotta, 1826. English translations: *Hug's Introduction to the New Testament.* Translated by David Fosdick from the 3d ed., with Notes by M. Stuart. Andover, Mass.: Gould & Newman, 1836. *An Introduction to the Writings of the New Testament.* Translated by Daniel Guildford Wait from the 2d ed. 2 vols. London: C. & J. Rivington, 1827.

Secondary Sources

Burtchaell, James Tunstead. *Catholic Theories of Biblical Inspiration since 1810: A Review and Critique.* Cambridge: Cambridge University Press, 1969.

———. "Drey, Möhler and the Catholic School of Tübingen." In *Nineteenth-Century Religious Thought in the West,* edited by N. Smart, J. Clayton, S. Katz, and P. Sherry, 2.111–39. Cambridge: Cambridge University Press, 1985.

Dietrich, Donald J. *The Goethezeit and the Metamorphosis of Catholic Theology in the Age of Idealism.* European University Studies, Series 23: Theology 128. Berne, Frankfurt am Main, Las Vegas: P. Lang, 1979.

Keller, Erwin. "Johann Leonhard Hug (1765–1846)." In *Katholische Theologen Deutschlands im 19. Jahrhundert,* edited by Heinrich Fries and Georg Schwaiger, 1.253–73. Munich: Kösel, 1975.

Madges, William. *The Core of Christian Faith: D. F. Strauss and His Catholic Critics.* American University Studies, Series 7: Theology and Religion 38. New York, Bern, Frankfurt am Main, Paris: P. Lang, 1988.

———. "D. F. Strauss in Retrospect: His Reception among Roman Catholics." *Heythrop Journal* 30 (1989): 273–92.

Romanticism and Imagination in England

Primary Sources

Arnold, Thomas. *Sermons.* 2d ed. 3 vols. London: B. Fellowes, 1834.

Coleridge, Samuel Taylor. *Aids to Reflection and the Confessions of an Inquiring Spirit.* London: G. Bell, 1913.

———. *Confessions of an Inquiring Spirit.* Fortress Texts in Modern Theology. Philadelphia: Fortress Press, 1988.

Jowett, Benjamin. *The Epistles of St. Paul to the Thessalonians, Galatians, Romans, with Critical Notes and Dissertations.* 2d ed. 2 vols. London: J. Murray, 1859.

———. "On the Interpretation of Scripture." In *Essays and Reviews,* 330–433. London: W. Parker, 1860.

———. *Theological Essays of the Late Benjamin Jowett.* Edited by Lewis Campbell. London: H. Frowde, 1906.

Stanley, Arthur Penrhyn. *The Epistles of St. Paul to the Corinthians, with Critical Notes and Dissertations.* 2d ed. London: J. Murray, 1858.

———. *Lectures on the History of the Jewish Church.* 3 vols. New York: Charles Scribner's, 1902.

———. *Sermons and Essays on the Apostolical Age.* Oxford: J. H. Parker, 1847.

Secondary Sources

Barr, James. "Jowett and the Reading of the Bible 'Like Any Other Book.'" *Horizons in Biblical Theology* 4, no. 2 (1983): 1–44.

――――. "Jowett and the 'Original Meaning' of Scripture." *Religious Studies* 18 (1982): 433–37.

Barth, J. Robert. *Coleridge and Christian Doctrine*. Cambridge: Harvard University Press, 1969.

Cameron, Nigel M. de S. *Biblical Higher Criticism and the Defense of Infallibilism in Nineteenth-Century Britain*. Texts and Studies in Religion 33. Lewiston, N.Y.: Edwin Mellen Press, 1987.

Drury, John, ed. *Critics of the Bible, 1724–1873*. Cambridge English Prose Texts. Cambridge: Cambridge University Press, 1989.

Gowler, Steve. "Coleridge as Hermeneut." *Anglican Theological Review* 66 (1984): 161–72.

Hinchliff, Peter. *Benjamin Jowett and the Christian Religion*. Oxford: Clarendon Press, 1987.

――――. "Ethics, Evolution and Biblical Criticism in the Thought of Benjamin Jowett and John William Colenso." *Journal of Ecclesiastical History* 37 (1986): 91–110.

Prothero, Rowland E. *The Life and Correspondence of Arthur Penrhyn Stanley*. 2 vols. New York: Scribner's, 1894.

Pym, David. *The Religious Thought of Samuel Taylor Coleridge*. New York: Barnes & Noble, 1979.

Stanley, Arthur Penrhyn. *The Life and Correspondence of Thomas Arnold, D.D.* 2 vols. New York: Charles Scribner's, 1895.

Storr, Vernon F. *The Development of English Theology in the Nineteenth Century, 1800–1860*. London: Longmans, Green, 1913.

Welch, Claude. "Samuel Taylor Coleridge." In *Nineteenth Century Religious Thought in the West,* edited by N. Smart, J. Clayton, S. T. Katz, and J. Sherry. 3 vols. Cambridge: Cambridge University Press, 1985. 2.1–28.

II. SYNTHESIZING ACCOMPLISHMENTS

Commentary Series

Primary Sources

Godet, Frédéric L. *A Commentary on the Gospel of St. Luke*. Translated by E. W. Shalders and M. D. Cusin. 2 vols. Clark's Foreign Theological Library. Edinburgh: T. & T. Clark, 1875.

――――. *Commentary on the Gospel of St. John*. Translated from the 2d ed. by Frances Crombie, M. D. Cusin, and S. Taylor. 3 vols. Clark's Foreign Theological Library. Edinburgh: T. & T. Clark, 1881. Reprint: Translation of the 3d ed. 3 vols. in one. Grand Rapids: Kregel, 1978.

――――. *Commentary on St. Paul's Epistle to the Romans*. Translated by A. Cusin. 2 vols. Clark's Foreign Theological Library. Edinburgh: T. & T. Clark, 1880.

――――. *Commentary on St. Paul's First Epistle to the Corinthians*. Translated by A. Cusin. 2 vols. Clark's Foreign Theological Library. Edinburgh: T. & T. Clark, 1886–87.

———. *Introduction to the New Testament.* Vol. 1: *The Collection of the Four Gospels and the Gospel of St. Matthew.* Translated by William Affleck. Edinburgh: T. & T. Clark, 1894.

———. *Introduction to the New Testament.* Vol 2: *The Epistles of St. Paul.* Translated by William Affleck. Edinburgh: T. & T. Clark, 1894.

———. *Studies in Paul's Epistles.* Grand Rapids: Kregel, 1984.

Lange, John Peter. *The Gospel according to Matthew, Together with a General Theological, and Homiletical Introduction to the New Testament.* Translated from the 3d ed. by Philip Schaff. A Commentary on the Holy Scriptures: Critical, Doctrinal, and Homiletical 1. New York: Charles Scribner, 1865.

———. *The Gospel according to John.* Translated by E. D. Yeomans and E. Moore. Edited by Philip Schaff. A Commentary on the Holy Scriptures: Critical, Doctrinal, and Homiletical 3. New York: Charles Scribner, 1884.

———. *The Epistle of Paul to the Romans.* Translated by J. F. Hurst. Edited by P. Schaff and M. B. Riddle. A Comentary on the Holy Scriptures: Critical, Doctrinal, and Homiletical 5. New York: Charles Scribner, 1870.

———. *The Life of the Lord Jesus Christ: A Complete Examination of the Origin, Contents, and Connection of the Gospels.* Translated by Sophia Taylor. Edited by Marcus Dods. 6 vols. Edinburgh: T. & T. Clark, 1864.

Meyer, Heinrich August Wilhelm. *Critical and Exegetical Handbook to the Gospel of Matthew.* Translated from the 6th ed. by Peter Christie. Edited by Frederick Crombie. 2 vols. Critical and Exegetical Commentary on the New Testament. Edinburgh: T. & T. Clark, 1883.

———. *Critical and Exegetical Handbook to the Gospels of Mark and Luke.* Translated from the 5th ed. by Robert E. Wallis. Edited by William P. Dickson. 2 vols. Critical and Exegetical Commentary on the New Testament. Edinburgh: T. & T. Clark, 1890.

———. *Kritisch exegetisches Handbuch über das Evangelium des Johannes.* 5th rev. ed. Kritisch Exegetischer Kommentar über das Neue Testament 2. Göttingen: Vandenhoeck & Ruprecht, 1869. English translation: *Critical and Exegetical Handbook to the Gospel of John.* Translated from the 5th ed. by William Urwick. Edited by Frederick Crombie. 2d ed. 2 vols. Critical and Exegetical Commentary on the New Testament. Edinburgh: T. & T. Clark, 1883.

———. *Critical and Exegetical Handbook to the Epistle to the Romans.* Translated from the 5th ed. by John C. Moore and Edwin Johnson. Edited by William P. Dickson. 2 vols. Critical and Exegetical Commentary on the New Testament. Edinburgh: T. & T. Clark, 1873–81.

———. *Critical and Exegetical Handbook to the Epistle to the Ephesians and the Epistle to Philemon.* Translated from the 4th ed. by Maurice J. Evans. Edited by William P. Dickson. Critical and Exegetical Commentary on the New Testament. Edinburgh: T. & T. Clark, 1884.

Olshausen, Hermann. *Biblical Commentary on the New Testament.* Translated from the 4th ed. by A. C. Kendrick. New York: Sheldon, Blakeman, 1858.

———. *A Commentary on Paul's First and Second Epistles to the Corinthians.* Minneapolis: Klock & Klock, 1984.

———. *Studies in the Epistle to the Romans.* Minneapolis: Klock & Klock, 1983.

Lives of Jesus

Primary Sources

Keim, Theodor. *Geschichte Jesu von Nazara, in ihrer Verkettung mit dem Gesammtleben seines Volkes frei untersucht und ausführlich erzählt.* 3 vols. Zurich: Orell, Füssli, 1867–72. English translation: *The History of Jesus of Nazara, Freely Investigated in Its Connection with the National Life of Israel, and Related in Detail.* 6 vols. Theological Translation Fund. London: Williams & Norgate, 1873–83. Volume 1 was published in a 2d edition with a revised translation by Arthur Ransom in 1876.

Renan, Ernest. The original volumes of Renan's History of the Origins of Christianity are published in *Oeuvres complétes de Ernest Renan.* Edited by Henriette Psichari. Vols. 4–5. Paris: Calmann-Levvy, 1947.

———. *The Anti-Christ.* Translated by J. H. Allen. History of the Origins of Christianity 4. London: Mathieson, 1889.

———. *The Apostles.* History of the Origins of Christianity 2. New York: Carleton, 1886. This work also appears in another English edition with different pagination: New York: Brentano's, n.d.

———. *The Gospels.* The History of the Origin of Christianity 5. London: Mathieson, n.d.

———. *History of the People of Israel.* 5 vols. London: Chapman & Hall, 1888–91.

———. *Life of Jesus.* Translated from the 23d ed. Boston: Little, Brown, 1924.

———. *The Life of Jesus.* New York: Modern Library, 1955.

———. *The Reigns of Hadrian and Antoninus Pius.* The History of the Origins of Christianity 6. London: Mathieson, 1888.

———. *Saint Paul.* The History of the Origins of Christianity 3. London: Mathieson, 1912.

Secondary Sources

Barry, William. *Ernest Renan.* Literary Lives. London: Hodder & Stoughton, 1905.

Chadbourne, Richard M. *Ernest Renan.* Twayne's World Authors Series 34. New York: Twayne, 1968.

Mott, Lewis Freeman. *Ernest Renan.* New York and London: Appleton, 1921.

Noonan, John T. "Renan's Life of Jesus: A Re-Examination." *Catholic Biblical Quarterly* 11 (1949): 26–39.

Schweitzer, Albert. *The Quest of the Historical Jesus: A Critical Study of Its Progress from Reimarus to Wrede.* Translated by W. Montgomery. New York: Macmillan, 1957.

Trocmé, Étienne. "Exégèse scientifique et idéologie: de l'École de Tubingue aux historiens française des origines chrétiennes." *New Testament Studies* 24 (1978): 447–62.

Index of Subjects

Abba, 16

Accommodation hermeneutic, 15, 43, 123–24, 139, 176–77, 186, 188, 192, 346, 387

Acts of the Apostles, 13, 14, 36, 51–52, 134, 142–43, 149, 159, 192, 213, 214, 225, 239–41, 263–67, 271–73, 275–76, 291–92, 364, 369

Adultery, woman caught in, 16, 21, 74, 143, 206, 321, 327, 373

Affections, 68–69, 75–76, 87

Allegory, xiv–xvi, 20, 22, 45, 48, 77, 87, 96–97, 110, 113, 359

Analogy of faith, 83–84, 99, 110, 131

Apocalypse. *See* Revelation, book of

Apocalyptic, 71, 79, 172, 231, 274, 277, 379–80. *See also* Eschatology

Apocrypha
  OT, 148, 192
  NT, 26, 169, 324

Apostles, 32, 34, 52, 56, 60, 171, 189, 241, 297, 344, 349–50

Aramaic, 16, 21, 132, 134, 136, 151, 281, 297–300, 373

Ascension, 21, 52, 77–78, 139, 203, 207, 219–20, 239, 250, 353

Atonement, 11, 36, 54, 56, 78, 93, 101, 179–80, 195, 245, 249, 283, 353, 357, 369–70, 388

Authenticity, 22, 29, 30, 33, 54, 55, 56, 111, 131–32, 146, 154, 213, 298, 311–18, 322–23, 347, 364

Authority, xv, 20, 42, 74, 89–90, 101, 116–17, 122–23, 129, 137–38, 152, 160, 165, 174, 185, 187, 289, 323. *See also* Canon

Authorship. *See* Authenticity

Baptism, 9, 15–16, 24, 38, 171, 232, 240, 266, 312
  for the dead, 24, 38, 77–78, 159
  of Jesus, 12, 181, 290, 297, 300, 386

Berlin, 60, 209, 221, 229, 235, 247, 273, 283, 363, 372

Cambridge, 5, 11, 29, 44, 45–46, 298, 324, 339

Cana miracle, 47, 106, 227, 234, 238, 281, 291, 313, 369

Canon, xiv, 22, 55, 117–27, 129, 174, 213, 275, 335. *See also* Authority

Catholic Epistles, 21, 86, 131, 136, 152, 163, 214, 226, 338, 350, 364
  James, 34, 42, 136, 152–53, 163, 182, 214–15, 236, 241, 266, 276, 338
  1 Peter, 152–53, 214, 226, 266–67, 277, 364
  2 Peter, 10, 21, 26, 33, 86, 126, 153, 172, 214, 226, 267, 338, 364
  1 John, 136, 214, 226, 231–32, 236–37, 314
  2 John, 10, 11, 214
  Jude, 10, 21, 26, 42, 86, 122, 136, 182, 214, 226, 338

Census (of Luke 2), 106, 113, 161, 203, 216, 373–74

Christology, 24, 35–36, 56, 64, 67, 74, 77, 94, 120, 169, 189–92, 215, 220, 223, 229, 245–46, 250, 254, 260, 279–80, 342–43, 344, 383, 385, 389. *See also* Logos

Chronology, 71, 79, 86, 213, 240, 356, 387

Commentaries, 13, 22–23, 32–33, 35–38, 67, 71, 74–79, 85–88, 99–101, 110–12, 157–59, 201–2, 226–27, 232–35,

Index of Names

(Italic type indicates pages on which the main discussion of a person is found.)

Aland, B., 327 n.98, 430
Aland, K., 327 n.98, 409, 430
Albertus Magnus, 22
Alexander II of Russia, 324
Alexander, G., 170 n.52, 419
Allison, H. E., 167 n.28, 418
Ammon, C. F., 109 n.42, 414
Andrew of St. Victor, xvi
Aner, K., 116 nn.1, 3; 117 n.4, 412, 414
Annet, P., *49–52*, 398, 408
Apollonius of Tyana, 9, 47
Aquinas, T., xvi, 22
Aristotle, 68
Arius, 87
Arndt, J., 60
Arnett, W. M., 82 n.77, 412
Arnold, M., 343, 343 n.48
Arnold, T., 339, *343–47*, 348, 362, 394, 395, 396, 431
Attig, J. C., 408
Augustine, xv, xvi, 18, 19, 21, 22, 76, 143, 402
Augustus Caesar, 161
Auvray, P., 17 n.33, 44 n.37, 405

Bach, J. S., 108, 108 n.39, 115, 414
Bacon, F., 4
Baker, F., 85 n.93, 412
Baroni, V., 402
Barr, J., 360 n.109, 432
Barry, W., 373 n.55, 434
Barth, J. R., 339 n.27, 432
Barth, K., 89, 89 n.102, 93 n.3, 222 n.84, 283 n.144, 421
Barton, J., 403

Bauer, B., xx, 246, *278*, 278 nn.122–24; 308
Bauer, G. L., 150, 183, 184 n.108, *187–94*, 195, 228, 251, 302, 394, 396, 398, 399, 420
Baumgarten, S. J., 25, 38, 93, 117, 118, 128
Baur, F. C., 15, 126, 147, 246, 246 n.3, 247, 247 n.5, 250, 250 n.18, 254, 255, 256, *258–69*, 270, 271, 271 n.98, 273, 274, 275, 276, 277, 278, 286, 292, 293, 294, 295, 296, 307, 310 n.46, 311, 318, 355, 383, 384, 385, 389, 393, 396, 397, 398, 425, 426
Baur, F. F., 261 n.75, 426
Bayle, P., 91, 93
Beardslee, J. W., 96 n.15, 413
Beaude, P.–M., 17 n.33, 406
Becker, C., 404
Belaval, Y., 127 n.41
Bellinzoni, A. J., 320 n.76, 321 n.79, 430
Bengel, J. A., xxi, 27, 27 n.66, *69–80*, 84, 85, 86, 88, 89, 90, 104, 105, 107, 111, 112, 131, 282, 331, 393, 395, 396, 410, 411
Bengel, M. E., 74 n.47
Bentley, James, 323 n.87, 324, 324 n.88, 430
Bentley, Jerry H., 4 n.2, 402
Bentley, R., 25, *29*, 42, 104, 407
Benz, E., 246 n.3, 425
Bernard, E., 26
Betz, H. D., 126 n.36
Beyreuther, E., 409, 410
Beza, T., 22, 27
Biddle, J. C., 36 n.15, 408
Black, M., 323 n.87, 430
Bleek, F., xx
Blount, C., 39

Scripture Index

OLD TESTAMENT

APOCRYPHA

NEW TESTAMENT